D0023241

Police Field Operations

THEORY MEETS PRACTICE

Michael L. Birzer

Wichita State University

Cliff Roberson

California State University, Fresno (Retired)

Emeritus, Washburn University

PEARSON

Boston ■ New York ■ San Francisco
Mexico City ■ Montreal ■ Toronto ■ London ■ Madrid ■ Munich ■ Paris
Hong Kong ■ Singapore ■ Tokyo ■ Cape Town ■ Sydney

Senior Acquisitions Editor: Dave Repetto
Editorial Assistant: Jack Cashman
Senior Marketing Manager: Kelly May
Production Supervisor: Roberta Sherman
Editorial Production Service: Progressive Publishing Alternatives
Composition Buyer: Linda Cox
Manufacturing Buyer: Debbie Rossi
Electronic Composition: Progressive Publishing Alternatives
Interior Design: Denise Hoffman
Photo Researcher: Annie Pickert
Cover Designer: Kristina Mose-Libon

For related titles and support materials, visit our online catalog at www.ablongman.com

Copyright © 2008 by Pearson Education, Inc.

All rights reserved. No part of the material protected by this copyright notice may be reproduced or utilized in any form or by any means, electronic or mechanical, including photocopying, recording, or by any information storage and retrieval system, without written permission from the copyright owner.

To obtain permission(s) to use material from this work, please submit a written request to Allyn & Bacon, Permissions Department, 75 Arlington Street, Boston, MA 02116 or fax your request to 617-848-7320.

Between the time website information is gathered and then published, it is not unusual for some sites to have closed. Also, the transcription of URLs can result in typographical errors. The publisher would appreciate notification where these errors occur so that they may be corrected in subsequent editions.

Library of Congress Cataloging-in-Publication Data

Birzer, Michael L.
    Police field operations : theory meets practice / Michael Birzer & Cliff Roberson.
        p. cm.
    ISBN-13: 978-0-205-50828-0 (hardcover)
    ISBN-10: 0-205-50828-6 (hardcover)
1. Police patrol—United States. 2. Community policing—United States. I. Roberson, Cliff, II. Title.

HV8080.P2B57 2008
363.2′30973—dc22

2007017170

Printed in the United States of America

10   9   8   7   6   5   4   3   2   1   HAM   11   10   09   08   07

Photo credits appear on page 610, which constitutes an extension of the copyright page.

To the two greatest joys in my life, my loving wife, Gwynne, and my precious son, Michael Jr.

—Michael L. Birzer

To my grandchildren—Geneva, Nikkita, Isaiah, Trevor, Amy, and Iain

—Cliff Roberson

Contents

Chapter 2

Police Field Procedures   52

Chapter 3

Police Operations in a Community Policing Environment   104

Chapter 4

The Crime Scene and Preliminary Investigation   154

Chapter 5

Interviewing and Interrogation   200

Chapter 6

Handling Calls for Service   242

Chapter 7

Forensics   282

Chapter 8

Legal Constraints That Impact Police Operations   322

Chapter 9

Police Reports and Other Correspondence   364

Chapter 10

Police Communications   392

Chapter 11

Gangs and Drugs   422

Chapter 12

Police Operations in Culturally Diverse Communities   468

Chapter 13

Crime Mapping and Analysis   504

Chapter 14

Handling Terrorism and Natural Disasters   530

Chapter 15

Ethics and Police Operations   560

Preface

The text, *Police Field Operations: Theory Meets Practice,* is designed as a comprehensive, yet readable text on police field operations. The material in the text describes police field operations and is designed to be used in a one semester course on police operations or patrol procedures. While the chapters are designed to be independent units, they also build upon each other to provide a complete picture of police operations, including patrolling.

The authors have worked on this text for many months and in the process of developing this text are reminded of the comments of Sir Winston Churchill: "If you have an important point to make, don't try to be subtle or clever. Use a pile driver. Hit the point once. Then come back and hit it again. Then hit it a third time—a tremendous whack." In developing a manuscript, the preface is the last item developed. In that regard, Churchill stated: "Writing a book is an adventure. To begin with, it is a toy and an amusement; then it becomes a mistress, and then it becomes a master, and then a tyrant. The last phase is that just as you are about to be reconciled to your servitude, you kill the monster, and fling him out to the public." Accordingly, we hereby present this text to you.

To bridge the gap between theory and practice, twenty-one present and former police officers were interviewed regarding their experiences on the police force. Excerpts of their interviews are included in the text under "Voices of Experience."

In the past, readers have been of invaluable assistance to help us improve on future editions of the text. Accordingly, your input regarding any problems or suggestions for improvement is welcomed. Please send comments to the authors via Cliff Roberson's email at cliff.roberson@washburn.edu.

The first chapter is designed to provide the students with an overview of patrol operations, followed by a chapter on field procedures, and then a chapter on policing in the community policing environment. Next, we examine crime scene investigation and then interviewing and interrogation, followed by handling of calls for service in Chapter 6. Chapter 7 discusses forensics, followed by legal constraints that impact police operations. Next are chapters on police reports and police communications. Chapter 11 discusses both gang and drug issues. In Chapter 12, police operations in culturally diverse communities are examined, followed by a chapter on crime mapping and analysis. The final two chapters are on terrorism and natural disasters and ethics.

While the text lists the two of us as authors, this text would not have been possible except for the contributions of many others, including our editor David E. Repetto and his assistant Jack Cashman. We are grateful to the reviewers, Richard Dewey, Indiana River Community College; Margaret G. Austin, Central Piedmont Community College; Scott Rudeen, Brown College and Kaplan University; Michael Pittaro, Lehigh Valley College; Jack D. Howell, Excelsior College; Denny C. Powers, Columbia Campus South University; and Thomas J. Mason, Remington College, who pointed out our errors and provided us with directions on how to improve the text. Other contributors include Jack Howell, who assisted in the preparation of the supplements. A special thanks to our production supervisor Roberta Sherman, at Allyn & Bacon and also to Jeff Houck, at Progressive Publishing Alternatives.

Finally, a word of thanks to our "Voices of Experience" contributors who have provided us with valuable information regarding the "real life" in the police force: Albert Bettiyon, John Boal, Robert Boyer, Michael R. Bresett, Gregg Etter, Sr., John Hill, Richard Hough, Richard Kuiters, Leon (Lee) Kutzke, William Lally, David LaRose, Tom Mahoney, Tom Mason, Jack Maxwell, Mark McCoy, John Padgett, Scott W. Phillips, David Thornton, Mike Turner, Jeff Tymony, and Ronald Wilson.

Chapter 1

Police Patrol:
The Backbone of Policing

" The basic mission for which the police exist is to prevent crime and disorder. "

—Sir Robert Peel (1829)

CHAPTER OUTLINE

After completion of this chapter, you will be able to do the following:

- Explain the differences between police operations during the three eras of policing
- Discuss the influence of the English policing system on U.S. policing
- Explain the purpose of police patrol
- Describe reactive, proactive, and coactive policing
- Explain how a police department is organized
- Identify the variety of police patrol methods
- Discuss factors that should be considered in the allocation of police patrol
- Describe the role of the police supervisor
- Describe the police selection process
- Identify the differences between academy training, field training, and in-service training

INTRODUCTION

Mrs. Smith, a 75-year-old widow, is awakened from a deep sleep one warm summer evening. Half asleep, she glances at the digital alarm clock sitting on the nightstand beside her bed. The large red digital display reads 2:00 A.M. Mrs. Smith hears a noise coming from her backyard. A few seconds later she hears the noise again. It sounds like someone breaking into the storage shed where she keeps her lawn mower and other lawn equipment, along with some of her late husband's tools, which are worth a lot of money. Mrs. Smith is terrified. She frantically reaches for the phone and dials 911. She is so shaken that it takes her two times to dial 911.

After two rings the dispatcher answers and asks for the nature of the emergency. Mrs. Smith whispers to the dispatcher that she thinks someone is breaking into the storage shed in her backyard. The dispatcher calmly asks Mrs. Smith pertinent questions, while at the same time assuring her that police officers have been dispatched to her home and should arrive shortly. After several minutes the dispatcher informs her that **police officers** have just arrived at her residence and will be checking the backyard shortly. Mrs. Smith peeks out of her bedroom window into the backyard and is relieved when she sees the illumination of flashlights and hears the crackling of police radios in the night. She sees two police officers shining their flashlights on the shed. A few moments later she is contacted by a police officer. The police officer informs her that it appears

police officer / A member of a police department who is sworn to make arrests and carries a firearm. A police officer performs general patrol and/or special law enforcement assignments in the protection of life and property; enforces city, county, and state laws and regulations; performs a variety of activities and operations associated with crime prevention, traffic enforcement, crime/accident investigation and reporting, and related law enforcement areas; and performs related duties and responsibilities as required.

A "storefront" subpolice station. This one is located near Times Square, New York, NY. Similar storefront substations are located in most major cities.

someone was trying to break into the shed, but that they must have been scared off before gaining entry. The officer informs Mrs. Smith that she shouldn't worry because the chances are minimal that the criminal will return to finish the theft. The officer then advises her that the police will step up patrols in her neighborhood through the rest of the night. The officer pulls out his field notebook and asks Mrs. Smith a number of questions for the official police report.

Police patrol officers respond to crimes in progress as well as a variety of many other nonemergencies on a daily basis in the United States. According to the Bureau of Justice Statistics, in the year 2000 approximately 25.4 million violent crime and property victimizations were reported to the police. Violent crime was reported to the police at a higher percentage than personal theft (pocket picking and purse snatching) and property crime.

The police are charged with the prevention and detection of crime and the apprehension of offenders. They are responsible for the protection of citizens and the preservation of civil order. Police are considered by many as the "thin blue line" between order and disorder, between good and evil; others have a less flattering description of the police. Perceptions of the police, in large part, are shaped from people's experiences with them. We demand a lot from our police.

This chapter provides a broad overview of police function and is a foundation for other chapters in the book. Most of the topics that are introduced in this chapter are covered to a greater extent throughout the book.

A SKETCH OF THE POLICE

Police officers have awesome responsibilities. They have the authority to arrest and take people's liberties from them. They have the authority to stop drivers and to issue traffic citations that may cost a great deal, in terms of money to pay the fine and the time to appear in court. Police officers have the authority to use reasonable force, if necessary, to protect life and property. The police are also authorized to use the ultimate force, deadly force, to defuse a life-threatening situation. Think about this for a moment: What other professions allow their employees to justifiably take a human life? The decision to use deadly force is often made in a split second. Police officers don't have the luxury of researching what is the best course of action in dealing with a potentially life-threatening situation. Quite the contrary, they have to act immediately, as their failure to do so can be disastrous.

We expect the police to settle our problems and settle them quickly. It has been said that we love to love them, and we love to hate them. When carrying out the police mandate of preserving and safeguarding life and property, the police are sometimes caught in the not-so-envious position of "damned if we do, and damned if we don't."

The largest and most visible component of any municipal law enforcement agency is the patrol section, which consists of officers working in uniform twenty-four hours a day, 365 days a year. Patrol officers handle service calls in motor vehicles, on horseback, or on foot. Patrol is the essence of the police mission. Police patrol is considered the backbone of the police department. Although all aspects of the police organization have the responsibility of meeting the organization's mission, patrol usually takes the lead in this effort due to its size and visibility. In most cases, a citizen's only contact with the police department is with the men and women performing the patrol function. A great deal of this contact will be for traffic-related matters, such as stopping a motorist for speeding, running a red signal light, having a brake light burned out, and so on.

In many organizations, the patrol section also accepts the responsibility for the functional supervision of other units of the department during nontraditional working hours. For example, supervision of the Communications Unit or Records Unit may be provided by patrol supervisors between midnight and 8:00 A.M. or during weekends and holidays when police management personnel are not on duty.

Sometimes it is helpful to use a business analogy to describe policing. A business delivers some product or services to the customer. For example, your automobile insurance agent delivers automobile insurance to you. He or she makes sure that you are satisfied with your insurance policy and addresses concerns you may have about a particular clause in your policy. If you are involved in a vehicle accident, your agent would complete the necessary paper work and secure the reimbursement to repair your car. If the agent does a poor job of delivering these services to you, you may shop around for another insurance company.

In much the same way a business delivers services to customers, police departments deliver services. Like the insurance agent who is on the front line for an insurance company, the men and women of the patrol force are on the front line and deliver services to the citizens. These services are very broad. Citizens can't hire another police department like they can hire another insurance company if they are dissatisfied with the service they have received. However, if a police department has a tendency to deliver poor services to the citizenry, then this may cost the police agency dearly in terms of public and political support. Public and political support is necessary, especially when the police are trying to make an effective argument for budget increases. If the citizens are satisfied with the police department this may result in more voluntary compliance with laws and ordinances.

Unlike other public agencies, the police are faced with many more challenges that center on public safety and welfare. The police respond to a wide variety of criminal-related calls, noncriminal-related calls, and service-related calls. The police department is one of the few governmental agencies that a citizen can call twenty-four hours a day, seven days a week, and almost always be assured of getting a human response in the form of a police officer in a matter of minutes.

Perhaps a better way to illustrate the wide variety of calls that the police handle is to take a brief look at the **Uniform Crime Report (UCR)**.

The UCR is a collective effort on the part of city, county, tribal, and federal law enforcement agencies to present a nationwide view of crime. At some point, you have probably heard a media account that goes something like this, "The FBI reports that violent crime is down 6 percent." Basically, this means that the UCR data shows that violent crime is down. The Department of Justice and, specifically, the Federal Bureau of Investigation (FBI), manages the UCR system. Law enforcement agencies in the United States that participate in the UCR program provide the FBI with summarized reports on eight Part I offenses known to law enforcement and reports on persons arrested. Also included in the UCR is information about law enforcement officers killed and assaulted, and information on hate crimes. The UCR also summarizes other offenses that fall outside of Part I offense categories. These twenty-one offenses are called Part II offenses. Both Part I and Part II offenses are listed to give you a better idea of the types of activities that the police officers respond to. Once again, keep in mind that Part I and Part II offenses only represent a small part of the situations that police are called to investigate. There are many noncriminal-related and service-related matters that the police investigate and handle every single day.

Uniform Crime Report / The Uniform Crime Reports are crime indexes, published annually by the Federal Bureau of Investigation, which summarize the incidence and rate of certain reported crimes within the United States.

Part I Offenses

1. Criminal Homicide
2. Forcible Rape
3. Robbery
4. Aggravated Assault
5. Burglary
6. Larceny-theft (except motor vehicle theft)
7. Motor Vehicle Theft
8. Arson

Part II Offenses

9. Other Assaults
10. Forgery and Counterfeiting
11. Fraud
12. Embezzlement
13. Stolen Property: Buying, Receiving, Processing
14. Vandalism
15. Weapons: Carrying, Possessing, etc.
16. Prostitution and Commercialized Vice
17. Sex Offenses
18. Drug Abuse Violations
19. Gambling

20. Offenses Against Family and Children
21. Driving Under the Influence
22. Liquor Laws
23. Drunkenness
24. Disorderly Conduct
25. Vagrancy
26. All other offenses
27. Suspicion
28. Curfew and Loitering Laws (persons under 18)
29. Runaways (persons under 18)

Police officers working in local police departments constitute the majority of the sworn police officer population in the United States. A sworn police officer is someone who has taken an oath, carries a badge and a gun, can arrest and use reasonable force to do so, and is employed by a governmental entity, for example, the City of Los Angeles or the City of Houston. Police departments range in size from 40,435 officers that serve in the New York City Police Department to one-officer departments in smaller cities. The Bureau of Justice Statistics (2003) estimates that approximately 440,920 full-time sworn officers work in city police departments in the United States. More than half of all police departments have ten or less sworn officers, and that nearly 1,000 departments have only one officer employed. Do you find this hard to believe? If so, maybe this will help: Take a moment and think about the state where you live. How many major police departments can you think of that employ hundreds of police officers? You may be able to identify a few; however, you can probably identify a great many more police departments that employ fewer police officers, maybe fifty or less, and probably many that only employ ten or less police officers.

In a typical police department, the law enforcement agency prevents crime, investigates crimes, apprehends criminals, maintains order, and provides other miscellaneous services. A great many of these services are handled by the patrol function. Thus, it stands to reason that a substantial amount of a police department's operating budget is expended on patrol operations. In addition, the majority of personnel within a police agency are assigned to police patrol. Local police departments cost about $80,600 per sworn officer and $179 per resident to operate for the year (Bureau of Justice Statistics, 2003). Local police departments employ 565,915 people full-time, including about 441,000 sworn personnel. Sheriffs' offices have about 293,823 full-time employees, including about 165,000 sworn personnel (Bureau of Justice Statistics, 2003).

The Police Officer's Job

The job of a police officer in the twenty-first century can be challenging. Police officers are expected to do extraordinary things in very chaotic and, at times, dangerous situations. Police officers may spend hours with little or no activity and then suddenly and without warning have to face an armed robbery in progress, a suspect with a gun, a death scene, a serious traffic accident, or an abused child call.

Officers are expected to be familiar with businesses, schools, and habits of individuals who work the busy sections on their patrol beats. In the late 1960s a university research team reported a list of essential behavioral requirements that a patrol officer must possess to be successful. This listing is as valid in the twenty-first century as it was in the 1960s. According to the university research team, a police officer must:

1. Endure long periods of monotony in routine patrol, yet react (almost instantaneously and) effectively to problem situations observed on the street or to orders issued by the radio dispatcher (in much the same way that a combat pilot must react to interception or a target opportunity).

2. Gain knowledge of his or her patrol area, not only of its physical characteristics, but also of its normal routine of events and the usual behavior patterns of its residents.

3. Exhibit initiative, problem-solving capacity, effective judgment, and imagination in coping with the numerous complex situations presented; for example, a family disturbance, a potential suicide, a robbery in progress, an accident, or a disaster. Police officers clearly recognize this requirement and refer to it as "showing street sense."

4. Make prompt and effective decisions, sometimes in life-and-death situations, and be able to size up a situation quickly and take appropriate action.

5. Demonstrate mature judgment, as in deciding whether an arrest is warranted by the circumstances or a warning is sufficient, or in facing a situation where the use of force may be needed.

6. Demonstrate critical awareness in discerning signs of out-of-ordinary conditions or circumstances which indicate trouble or a crime in progress.

7. Exhibit a number of complex psychomotor skills, such as driving a vehicle in normal and emergency situations; firing a weapon accurately under extremely varied conditions; maintaining agility, endurance, and strength; and showing facility in self-defense and apprehension, as in taking a person into custody with a minimum of force.

8. Adequately perform the communication and recordkeeping functions of the job, including oral reports, preparation of formal case reports, and completion of departmental and court forms.

9. Have the facility to act effectively in extreme divergent interpersonal situations. A police officer constantly confronts persons who are acting in violation of the law, ranging from curfew violators to felons, and is constantly confronted by people who are in trouble or who are victims of crimes. Besides dealing with criminals, the officer has contact with para-criminals, informers, and people on the border with criminal behavior so he or she must also be "alley-wise." At the same time, the officer must relate to the people on his or her beat—businessmen, residents, school officials, visitors, and so on. His interpersonal relations must range up and down a continuum defined by friendliness and persuasion on one end and by fairness and force at the other.

10. Endure verbal and physical abuse from citizens and offenders (as when placing a person under arrest or facing day-in and day-out racial prejudice) while using only necessary force.

11. Exhibit a professional, self-assured presence and a self-confident manner in conduct when dealing with offenders, the public, and the courts.

12. Be capable of restoring equilibrium to social groups; for example, restoring order in a family fight, in a disagreement between neighbors, or in a clash between rival youth groups.

13. Be skillful in questioning suspected offenders, victims, and witnesses of crimes.

14. Take charge of situations, such as a crime or accident scene, yet not unduly alienate participants or bystanders.

15. Be flexible enough to work under loose supervision in most of the day-to-day patrol activities (either alone or as part of a two-person team) and also under the direct supervision of supervisors in situations where large numbers of officers are required.

16. Tolerate stress in a multitude of forms, such as meeting the violent behavior of a mob, arousing people in a burning building, coping with the pressure of a high-speed chase or a weapon being fired at the officer, or dealing with a woman bearing a child.

17. Exhibit personal courage in the face of dangerous situations which may result in serious injury or death.

18. Maintain objectivity while dealing with a host of "special interest" groups, ranging from relatives of offenders to members of the press.

19. Maintain a balanced perspective in the face of constant exposure to the worst side of human nature.

20. Exhibit a high level of personal integrity and ethical conduct, refraining from accepting bribes or "favors" and providing impartial law enforcement (Saunders, 1970, pp. 19–21).

DEVELOPMENT OF POLICE PATROL

The English Influence

The U.S. system of policing has its roots in Great Britain. The word "patrol" in early English meant to "walk or paddle in muddy water." There are several versions of how the word became associated with law enforcement. One popular version is that the police are "walking in muddy water" when they patrol the community looking for the dirty (criminal) aspects of its citizens. Patrolling is the most visible part of police work, and many citizens' opinions of the quality of the local police department are based on their observations of and contacts with police patrol officers.

Police patrols in the United States have not always operated around the clock, twenty-four hours a day, seven days a week. In fact, early police patrols were operated by citizen volunteers. Of course, you can probably identify many problems with this type of system. For one, the citizens had no training in police patrol operations. The citizens who performed the voluntary patrol duties were sometimes called "the rattle watch." They patrolled the city's streets equipped with weapons, green lanterns which were used to identify them, and wooden rattler sticks (wooden rattlers). Wooden rattlers were used to make noise, to literally shake and rattle the stick at the first sign of trouble. The rattling procedure was used as a device for warning citizens of a potential threatening situation, at which time they would gather in certain parts of the city to deal with the problem.

Citizens would also use the rattle upon learning of a fire in the community, at which time bucket-brigades were formed. Bucket-brigades were volunteers who would form lines at the nearest water supply, fill buckets with water, and pass them down a line until they reached the actual fire scene. When citizens were not on night watch patrol they returned home and conspicuously hung the lantern on the front of their home to show everyone that a night watchman lived there.

The U.S. "wooden rattle" system was similar to the English tradition of the "watch and ward" with its emphasis on the "Hue and Cry." In fact, the most popular model on which U.S. police departments was measured was the London Metropolitan Police (Carte & Carte, 1975). As noted earlier in this chapter, the U.S. police actually adopted many features of the British system of policing for use in U.S. cities.

In the English tradition, when the "Hue and Cry" was raised (day or night) for any felony, a complaint about the crime was lodged immediately by men who were subjects of the king, until the person pursued was captured. In some cases there were fines issued by the Court if the subjects were not captured. Imagine for a moment if the mayor of a U.S. city fined the police department for every crime that is not solved. In contemporary society this is an absurd notion. The "Hue and Cry" was the act of an individual who would alert the neighborhood to the recent commission of a crime, and sometimes entailed raising public support for pursuit or arrest of the criminal.

Much of the policing reforms in England that took place around 1829 were started by the English Home Secretary Sir Robert Peel. Sir Robert Peel is considered to be the father of modern-day policing. When Peel was named Home Secretary in 1822, he recognized that the state of London policing was in dire need of reform. Peel jumped in with zest into his new position. Sir Robert Peel proposed a bill in the English Parliament titled "London Metropolitan Police Act" or, as it is sometimes referred to, "The Peelian Reform," which was subsequently passed and became law in 1829. The bill outlined a plan to reform the London Metropolitan Police.

As a result of Peel's reform, the new metropolitan police force became known as "Peelers" or "Bobbies," named after Sir Robert Peel. Peel's nine principles of policing are the foundation on which today's U.S. community policing movement is based. Sir Robert Peel's Nine Principles are:

1. The basic mission for which the police exist is to prevent crime and disorder.

2. The ability of the police to perform their duties is dependent upon public approval of police actions.

3. Police must secure the willing cooperation of the public in voluntary observance of the law to be able to secure and maintain the respect of the public.

4. The degree of cooperation of the public that can be secured diminishes proportionately to the necessity of the use of physical force.

5. Police seek and preserve public favor not by catering to public opinion, but by constantly demonstrating absolute impartial service to the law.

6. Police use physical force to the extent necessary to secure observance of the law or to restore order only when the exercise of persuasion, advice, and warning is found to be insufficient.

7. Police, at all times, should maintain a relationship with the public that gives reality to the historic tradition that the police are the public and the public are the police; the police being only members of the public who are paid to give full-time attention to duties which are incumbent on every citizen in the interests of community welfare and existence.

8. Police should always direct their action strictly toward their functions and never appear to usurp the powers of the judiciary.

9. The test of police efficiency is the absence of crime and disorder, not the visible evidence of police action of dealing with it.

Peel goes on to state in his principles that,

- Every police officer should be issued a badge number, to assure accountability for their actions.
- Whether the police are effective is not measured on the number of arrests, but on the lack of crime.
- The proper training of police is at the root of efficiency.

It is important to keep in mind that Robert Peel proposed the policing reforms in 1829. Many of his ideas were thought to be radical for the time. In many respects, U.S. policing is a product of its English heritage. The English fingerprint is on many other parts of the U.S. criminal justice system, too. When the British colonists brought their criminal justice system to the colonies, they included the English common law, the high value placed on individual rights, the court system, and law enforcement institutions. Many of Robert Peel's principles can be found in U.S. police protocol. For example, Peel proposed that all police officers should be issued a badge number to ensure accountability for their actions. The next time you see a police officer, take a close look at his or her badge—there is a good chance you will see the badge number. From an operational standpoint this makes sense, as in many situations a citizen may not be able to obtain an officer's name, but the conspicuous badge number will make the officer identifiable. Not only do police officers have a badge number, but most agencies assign officers an identification number which is used on official police reports and for personnel records.

Robert Peel also advocated that training was an important aspect for proper police efficiency. Training is the lifeblood of U.S. police departments and the number of hours of academy training has increased drastically over the years. In most departments, police officers are required to attend formal recruit academy training prior to assuming police duties. The Bureau of Justice Statistics (2003) reported that in the largest jurisdictions new local police recruits were required to complete an average of 1,500 hours of training and 800 hours in the smaller jurisdictions. The Los Angeles Police Department requires recruits to complete eight months of academy training.

On average, about three-quarters of training hours were state mandated, with the remainder an agency requirement. Likewise, most states require police officers to receive a certain number of in-service training hours each year to maintain their law enforcement certification (Bureau of Justice Statistics, 2003).

Although the history of U.S. policing is sketchy, due to the lack of records kept by many police departments, the development of the police patrol can best be framed on three major eras: (1) the Political Era, (2) the Reform Era, and (3) the Community Policing Era.

Sir Robert Peel (1788–1850)

Sir Robert Peel was born in Lancashire, the son of a middle-class manufacturer. In 1822, Robert Peel became Home Secretary of England. As Home Secretary, Peel created the Metropolitan London Police in 1829. Today, all police officers in Britain are commonly referred to as "Bobbies." Originally, they were known as "Peelers," as they were the creation of Sir Robert Peel. They were also referred to as "bobbies" after Robert. The first thousand of Peel's police, dressed in blue tailcoats and top hats, began to patrol the streets of London in September 1829. The Peelers were issued a wooden truncheon carried in a long pocket in the tail of their coat, a pair of handcuffs, and a wooden rattle to raise the alarm. By the 1880s, this rattle had been replaced by a whistle. In 1829, Robert Peel's Metropolitan Police Act was passed; this provided permanently appointed and paid police constables (the Peelers). Known as the father of modern policing, his Peelian principles defined the ethical requirements police officers must follow in order to be effective. His most memorable principle is: The police are the public, and the public are the police.

Sir Robert Peel created the London Metropolitan Police in 1829. Police officers in London are nicknamed "Bobby" after Peel.

The Political Era

Political Era / An era of American policing which spanned from the 1840s until around the 1930s. This era was the bedrock of early American policing. During the Political Era, policing was dominated by political control. During this era there were close ties between the police and politicians.

The **Political Era** of policing, which spanned from the 1840s until around the 1930s, was the bedrock of early U.S. policing. During this time, policing was dominated by political control. There were close ties between the police and politicians. Carte and Carte (1975), in their informative book on police reform in the United States, describe the Political Era as marked with graft, brutality, and incompetence. Police officers were haphazardly selected and trained, and under constant political

PRACTICE HINTS

The Political Era of American policing was an era marked with corruption and political influence. The general effectiveness of the police was poor. In 1929, President Herbert Hoover formed the National Commission on Law Observance and Enforcement as a result of the crime problem of the 1920s. Part of the commission's study undertook the first national assessment of policing in the United States. The commission, which is most often referred to as the Wickersham Commission, was named after its chairman, George W. Wickersham, former U.S. Attorney General. The commission's report was published in 1931 and criticized the police for their failure to effectively deal with crime in the United States. The report chastised police for their general failure to detect and apprehend violent criminals. Even more indicting was the commission's criticism that the police lacked restraint when dealing with criminal suspects. Many suspects were beaten as a matter of routine, or worse yet, tortured in order to solicit information. Specific tactics included protracted questioning, threats and methods of intimidation, physical brutality, illegal detention, and refusal to allow access of counsel to suspects. The report declared that "the third degree is a secret and illegal practice."

pressure to enforce the laws according to the interest of politicians. The chief requirement for appointment to police service appeared to be proper political connections (Fogelson, 1977). Police officers were basically given a night stick and a badge and told to go police the city with absolutely no formalized training or education (Walker, 1998). During the Political Era, police officers were severely underpaid.

The Reform Era

The 1930s brought about the spark for reform in U.S. policing. This era, which spanned from the 1930s until the 1970s, was appropriately named the **Reform Era**. Factors that sparked the Reform Era included political corruption, the general ineffectiveness of the police in dealing with crime, and recommendations made by the Wickersham Commission report.

In 1929, President Herbert Hoover formed the National Commission on Law Observance and Enforcement as a result of America's concern over crime and disorder, particularly criminal gangs and mobs. It was the first national study on the criminal justice system. The commission came to be known as the Wickersham Commission, named after its chair, former U.S. Attorney General George Wickersham. The Commission published its report in 1931. Volumes 2 and 14 were concerned primarily with the police. For example, in volume 14, *The Police*, sweeping changes were proposed that the police could use as a guide to create a professional police force. Among the many recommendations made by the commission was the need for improvements in police training and personnel selection, organization, and management.

The reform model of policing, or professional model (as it is sometimes referred to), emphasized an organization indoctrinated along traditional lines: highly centralized, bureaucratic, and designed on the premise of divisions of labor and unity of control (Kelling & Bratton, 1993). The reform model of organization was modified and refined by Progressive Era police chiefs, most notably August Vollmer and O. W. Wilson. This model represented a reaction to the rampant corruption and other inequities that had plagued U.S. policing since its early days (Birzer, 1996).

To reduce the contaminating effects of local ward politics on line officers, the reform model centralized authority in police headquarters. To alleviate favoritism and petty corruption in neighborhoods, the reform model established beats and revolving assignments for patrol officers. To ensure officers performed their assigned duties, the reform model instituted a military-style structure of authority and discipline. To encourage personnel to follow the rules established by headquarters, proponents of the reform model believed that line-level officers should adhere to a rigid chain of command and be supervised closely through massive amounts of written policy pronouncements.

During the Reform Era, the main objective of police operations became crime control. Social service related functions were emphasized less and were thought of by many police authorities as not real police work. This differed greatly from the Political Era, where social service related activities were deemed important and the police performed many social service functions. One of the goals of these reforms was that police officers would not become too close to the citizens for fear of the influence of corruption and graft (Walker, 1998). The characteristics of the reform model of policing were: rapid response, efficiency, paramilitary organizational style, crime control, professional crime fighting, and police resources which focused much energy on arrests.

The reform model of policing for the most part accomplished what it was supposed to accomplish. It was very effective in reducing the contaminating effects of politics and in increasing the professional status of the police. However, as you

Reform Era / An era of American policing that sought to correct the inherent problems created by the Political Era. The Reform Era emphasized an organization indoctrinated along traditional lines: highly centralized, bureaucratic, and designed on the premise of divisions of labor and unity of control.

might imagine, police agencies during the Reform Era became out of touch with the citizens. In fact, reform-minded police leaders became so intent on shielding their agencies from political influences that police departments grew into some of the most detached and self-reliant public organizations in government.

Because the reform model was driven by technology and new scientific processes (police patrol cruisers, two-way radios, etc.) it greatly improved the ability of law enforcement agencies to investigate crimes that had been committed (Birzer, 1996). However, for much the same reason, it reinforced the estrangement of police officers from the citizens they served.

To address the problems that the Reform Era created, and as a result of research on police practices during the 1970s, police agencies began to initiate the changes required for the third policing era, community-oriented policing.

Research at a Glance on Traditional Policing

1. Increasing the number of police officers does not lower the crime rate or increase the proportion of solved crimes.
2. Randomized motor patrol neither lowers crime nor increases the chances of catching suspects.
3. Two-person patrol cars are no more effective than one-person cars in lowering crime rates or catching criminals.
4. Saturation patrol does not reduce crime; instead, it displaces crime.
5. The kind of crime that terrifies Americans most (mugging, rape, robbery, burglary, and homicide) is rarely encountered by police on patrol.
6. Improving response time on calls has no effect on the likelihood of arresting criminals or even in satisfying involved citizens.
7. Crimes are not solved through criminal investigations conducted by police, they are solved because suspects are immediately apprehended or someone identifies them (name or license number).

Source: Skolnick, J., & Bayley, D. H. (1986). *The new blue line*. New York: The Free Press.

Community Policing Era

Community Policing Era /
A currently evolving era of policing that promotes and supports organizational strategies to address the causes and reduce the fear of crime and social disorder through problem-solving tactics and police–community partnerships.

Community-oriented policing represents a shift from more traditional law enforcement because it focuses on prevention of crime and the fear of crime on a local basis. The **Community Policing Era** put law enforcement professionals on the streets and assigned them a beat so they could build mutually beneficial relationships with the people they serve. By earning the trust of the members of their communities and making those individuals stakeholders in their own safety, community policing makes law enforcement safer and more efficient.

Community policing is a philosophy that promotes and supports organizational strategies to address the causes and reduce the fear of crime and social disorder through problem-solving tactics and police–community partnerships. The Office of Community Oriented Policing Services, a wing of the U.S. Department of Justice, has funded more than 118,768 community policing officers and deputies (Office of Community Oriented Policing Services, 2004).

Table 1.1   Components Used with Community Policing

Organizational Elements	Operational Elements	External Elements
Philosophy adopted organization-wide	Enforcement of laws	Public involvement in community partnerships
Decentralized decision making and accountability	Proactive, crime prevention oriented	Government and other agency partnerships
Fixed geographic accountability and generalist responsibilities	Problem solving	
Utilization of volunteer resources		
Enhancers		

Source: U.S. Department of Justice, Office of Community Oriented Policing. Retrieved 11-9-06 from www.cops.usdoj.gov.

Community policing focuses on crime and social disorder through the delivery of police services that include aspects of traditional law enforcement, as well as prevention, problem solving, community engagement, and partnerships. The community policing model balances reactive responses to calls for service with proactive problem solving centered on the causes of crime and disorder. In order for community policing strategies to work, police and citizens must join together in addressing public safety and disorder problems. The core components of community policing are summarized in Table 1.1.

Police officers operating under the axiom of community policing are expected to work with the community to solve problems at the root level. Let's suppose that police officer John Q. Smith, who has been working the same beat every day for the past four years, reports for work one afternoon. He listens attentively to the sergeant as he reads from the daily bulletin about several burglaries that occurred during the previous shift in the beat area where Officer Smith works. Officer Smith decides to take some extra initiative, having just attended community-oriented policing training, by doing some initial scanning and analysis of the burglary problem. As a result of his scanning and analysis he discovers that all of the burglaries were reported to have occurred between 9:00 A.M. and 3:00 P.M., or as police officers sometimes refer to them, "daytime burglaries." Officer Smith examines other calls that occurred on his beat during the previous watch and he can't help but notice that the local middle school called in a report about three students who have been truant from school several times in the past few weeks. He also notices on the day the burglaries occurred, the school called in and reported the three students as truant. Officer Smith asks himself: Could the truancies be related to the burglaries? This is exactly what police officers operating under the community policing philosophy are required to do. In essence, police officers are required to become street-level criminologists.

It is recognized that the police alone cannot solve all of the crime-related problems that exist in our society, and that citizens can help the police tremendously in the resolution of crime and disorder problems. Community policing requires new and innovative approaches in tackling crime. According to Professor

Lawrence Sherman (1996), a more sensible approach to policing violent crime would conform to the following model:

- Map out the nature of the problems, classifying them into different categories and subcategories according to their most important characteristics.

- Determine the possible causes of each subcategory of a violent crime problem, separating those causes that police can affect and those causes that are beyond police control.

- List all of the possible police tactics or strategies that could affect any of the causes of the specific crime problem and develop an overall strategy that focuses on what appear to be the most potent (yet tractable) causes.

- Conduct field experiments to test the strategy and measure its effect on the specific crime problem (Sherman, 1996, pp. 28–29).

The assumption of how the police should deal with crime has changed as community policing evolved. For example, during the Reform Era, citizens took a more

Voices of Experience

Patrol Officer

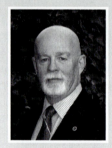

Excerpts from an interview between Cliff Roberson and retired police chief, Tom Mahoney. Professor Mahoney is currently the chair of administration of justice, Santa Barbara City College, Santa Barbara, California.

Q: *What does it take to be a good patrol officer?*
A: Patrol was always a challenge, but I learned it could be a lot of fun if you were an aggressive and curious police officer. And being a good patrol officer became an opportunity for me to promote later into other assignments such as investigations and undercover narcotics.

A good patrol officer has to be intensely curious. Now, being curious is different from being suspicious. "Curious" is looking at people and at their surroundings and asking yourself, "What's wrong with this picture?" Sometimes there's something wrong, sometimes not. "Suspicious" is looking at someone *knowing* they're doing something wrong and putting a good case together. While being "suspicious" is always needed to keep you alert and safe from the bad guys, the real key is curiosity. I always wanted to know why people behaved the way they did, why a person was at a certain location at a certain time, and what was it that made something seem out of place. Honestly, it was really the power of developing the subconscious mind. It's like walking into a room and immediately sensing that something is

out of place and, at first, not being able to put your finger on it. The subconscious tells you something is wrong; the conscious mind lets you solve the puzzle. A sense of curiosity and an active and well-trained subconscious mind helps make a good patrol officer.

Secondly, a good patrol officer must want to provide a service to the community. It is not just a paycheck. The officer must have the right attitude. You can be curious, and suspicious, but you must always be mindful of the rights of others. No officer is above the law, and no person, even a criminal, lacks the protections of the law.

A cop must also remember that, when he or she gets off-duty and goes home to the family, "The Job" is a separate part of his or her life and the family does not need to deal with any related problems and stress. It's not keeping secrets from your family, it's protecting them. The world of policing can be a nasty place. The job is best kept in the station house after you have hung your uniform in the locker and left. You don't stop being a police officer, but there's a life outside of policing. A good cop learns to enjoy that life. It's a challenge, but it can be done. ■

passive role in ensuring neighborhood safety and preventing crime. It was always left up to the police; they were the master crime fighters. Citizens basically stayed out of the way and the let the police do their jobs. Today's police officers are expected to work closely with citizens to solve crime problems. Police officers are expected to be resources, catalysts, and to utilize other resources within the community. These resources may be the health department, the fire department, clergy, school teachers and principals, citizens living in the affected area, and any other resources imaginable that may be useful in solving a neighborhood problem.

One of the authors (Birzer) was asked to assist a medium-sized sheriff's department located in the Midwest in the assessment of their community policing philosophy. There were several problems that were readily observed in the implementation phases of community policing in this department. One problem was that after deputies completed the initial community policing training there was no implementation policy for police operations beyond the training. In other words, nothing changed. After one training session, one of the police officers related the following: "This community policing stuff isn't really real police work." One other participant commented that, "the training was a waste of time because the brass will never let this stuff happen." They were right. In this case there was no commitment from the organization's command staff. There were absolutely no organizational transformation issues planned to support community policing, nor did the deputies and field supervisors have the authority to make needed decisions about problem solving in the field. This may not be an anomaly for this sheriff's department, and may indeed be the case in other law enforcement agencies. Community policing and problem-solving strategies will be discussed in greater detail in Chapter 3.

Voices of Experience

Part-Time Police Officer

Excerpts from an interview between Cliff Roberson and former police officer Robert Boyer. Professor Boyer is currently a professor of criminal justice at Luzerne County Community College, Nanticoke, Pennsylvania. Professor Boyer continues to work as a part-time police officer in Nanticoke, Pennsylvania.

Q: *Explain your duties and responsibilities as a part-time police officer.*

A: A part-time officer fills in when the full-time officers are on days off. I might work once a week or once a month. Generally, I work eight to forty hours a month, depending on the department's need. I am not the only part-time officer in the department. Working part-time and keeping current in policing helps me to be a better instructor.

The full-time police officers treat me no different from other officers. That may be because of my many years full-time experience as an officer before I started teaching. Sometimes, however, when the officers are involved in matters like contract negotiations, I am left out because the issues do not pertain to part-time personnel.

The part-time officers are compensated by the hour. The qualifications to be a part-time officer are exactly the same as the full-time officers. Every year we need to recertify with the state. Most part-time police officers in our area are new to the job. Many are waiting for full-time positions. ■

PRACTICE HINTS

Community policing has a positive impact on reducing neighborhood crime, reducing the fear of crime, and enhancing the quality of life in the community. It accomplishes these things by collaborative efforts of many resources, including the police, local government agencies, and community members. An important ingredient in community policing is problem solving. Problem solving identifies the concerns that community members feel are most threatening to their safety and well-being. These areas of concern then become priorities for collaborative police–community interventions.

THE PURPOSE OF POLICE PATROL

At this point in the chapter you should begin to realize that the majority of law enforcement functions are carried out by field patrol. Many years ago, O. W. Wilson, who was perhaps the leading architect of the professional model of policing, wrote that, "the basic purpose of police patrol is the elimination of the actual opportunity (or the belief that the opportunity exists) for successful misconduct" (Wilson & McLaren, 1977, p. 320). Wilson and McLaren described this activity as crime suppression and believed that the likelihood of arrest influenced the degree to which the potential offender is convinced that the opportunity for successful misconduct is absent. O. W. Wilson believed that opportunity reduction, which is best achieved by the impression of an "omni police presence" created by conspicuous police patrols, was the best prescription to suppress crime. There can be little argument today that the purpose of patrol is still in large part to eliminate the opportunity for crime and to suppress crime.

O. W. Wilson

Orlando Winfield (O. W.) Wilson is credited as being the lead architect of the professional police movement from the 1920s through the 1960s. Wilson served as chief of police in Fullerton, California and Wichita, Kansas, and superintendent of police in Chicago, Illinois. During Wilson's tenure as chief of police in Wichita, Kansas (1928–1939), he introduced many innovative approaches to law enforcement. These included techniques for the allocation and distribution of patrol manpower; new records and communications systems; a comprehensive planning program; advances in recruitment, selection, and training; and many other innovations. Also, while in Wichita he led the shift from foot patrol to automobile patrol, as well as conducting the first study of the effectiveness of one-officer squad cars.

Crime Control

Crime control is the obvious purpose of the police. The mere observation of the police taking an enforcement action illustrates crime control. Unfortunately, it is also a revelation that crime prevention efforts have failed. Crime control is most often associated with the patrol function. Patrol officers represent the front line of crime control efforts by responding to incidents of crime, as well as self-initiated arrests of offenders. You may be surprised to learn that crime is generally involved in a minority of the calls that police are assigned to handle and police spend far more time answering service-related calls (Whitaker, 1982). Professor David Bayley contends that policing is full of myths, and one long-standing myth is that the police are primarily crime fighters (Bayley, 1994).

So, why do so many citizens perceive that the police are in a daily battle responding to robbery call after robbery call? There are many reasons for this perception, and the entertainment media is one of the leading culprits. The television cop shows depict the glamorous crime-fighting role of the police and rarely give viewers a glimpse of the non-crime related and service functions of the police. Newspapers also find it less desirable to report the not-so-glamorous service-related functions of the police. These stories don't sell newspapers.

In one classic study, Webster (1970) analyzed the types of problems that police deal with on patrol in Baywood, California. Through the process of data reduction, the nearly 600,000 dispatched calls that he examined were reduced to 109 types of events. The 109 types of events were grouped into six categories labeled: crimes against persons, crimes against property, traffic, on-view, social services, and administration. He found that fewer than 17 percent of the dispatched calls for police involved crime.

Webster's study revealed that police work is generally tedious and wearisome, rather than exciting and dangerous. For example, drunk arrests constitute more than 40 percent of the total arrests, and 66 percent of the individuals arrested for being drunk had been arrested two or more times. In another study, Scott (1981) found that only 2 percent of police calls dealt with violent crime and 17 percent involved nonviolent crimes. Other studies have also found that the majority of police activities are indeed noncriminal and service related (Bittner, 1974; Haller, 1976).

Crime Prevention

Crime prevention is an important police operational component and involves many strategies. There is no substitute for the sound prevention of crime. Many police departments have crime prevention units that devote full attention to crime prevention activities. The authors have anecdotal accounts from police practitioners that one of the dangers inherent with crime prevention units is that they may give the impression that crime prevention is only the responsibility of an individual police unit. Individual crime prevention units may also give the impression that crime prevention endeavors to only cater to what is referred to in police circles as "dog and pony" shows, such as parades, car shows, and the like, and dressing a police officer in the "crime dog" suit in order to walk in the parade and wave at the citizens. This may do more for public relations than effective crime prevention.

crime prevention / Actions taken by the police and the community to reduce crime risks and build individual and community safety.

Crime prevention is the responsibility of every rank-and-file police officer within the department. The prevention of crime is an especially important function for the men and women serving in patrol functions. An organizational culture of crime prevention should be increasingly fostered within police agencies. Police patrol officers should increasingly become more involved in crime prevention activities. For example, when a police officer takes a report from a landlord regarding some rental problem, the police officer should counsel and educate the landlord on crime prevention techniques specific to landlords in order to avoid future victimizations. Some police agencies have started giving specialized crime prevention training to landlords.

Landlord Training

Landlord training programs are designed to promote positive and responsible partnerships between landlords, tenants, and the police. These partnerships are vital to effectively preventing drug dealing and other illegal activities at rental properties located within the communities and neighborhoods. By responsibly maintaining their property, landlords foster pride in the community and show respect for all residents of the community. It's also important to point out that these functions are being done not by a specialized crime prevention unit, but rather the men and women assigned to the police patrol function. Specifically, the training assists landlords in managing their properties by including information about:

- Preparing a rental property
- Screening applicants
- Rental agreements
- Active management
- Problem solving
- Recognizing illegal drug activity in the neighborhood

Neighborhood Watch

neighborhood watch / A citizens' organization devoted to crime prevention within their neighborhoods. Neighborhood watch members stay alert to unusual activity in their neighborhoods and contact the police.

You have probably seen it all too often. Perhaps you are driving through an area of the community where you live and all of a sudden there it is—a sign placed strategically in the neighborhood that reads, "NEIGHBORHOOD WATCH, WE CALL THE POLICE." **Neighborhood watch** programs are the largest and probably most known crime prevention programs in the United States. Neighborhood watch, or block watch, as it is sometimes called, is an effective way to get citizens more involved in the prevention of crime. Civic involvement, collaborative problem solving, and mutual commitment, which is advocated by neighborhood watch, has helped communities and neighborhoods reduce crime by significant numbers.

Whenever possible, neighborhood watch programs should be the responsibility of field patrol operations. Police officers working daily on the same beat should be aware of the identities and contact information for their neighborhood watch coordinators. It is also a good idea to communicate with these coordinators on a regular basis. Citizens who are involved in neighborhood watch programs can play a significant role in turning information over to the police, leading to the identification of a criminal. Think of it this way, wouldn't it be advantageous for a police officer working in a geographical area to have several hundred more eyes and ears than he or she may otherwise have without a neighborhood watch program?

Neighborhood watch is one of the most effective and least costly ways to prevent crime and reduce neighborhood fear. Members of neighborhood watch organizations learn how to make their homes more secure by working with the police department and utilizing crime prevention techniques. Members watch out for each other by reporting suspicious activities to the police. Neighborhood watch meetings are usually held at residents' homes and are facilitated by a police officer.

Neighborhood watch forges strong bonds among residents. Watch groups create a sense of community and pride by forming a unified group of citizens dedicated to improving their neighborhood. Partnering with law enforcement, citizens become their eyes and ears. These groups also serve as an empowering outlet for victims of crime by giving victims a greater sense of control, ensuring that what happened to them will be less likely to happen to others. A neighborhood watch program can also be a springboard for many other efforts to address the causes of crime, reduce crime, and improve neighborhood conditions, including youth recreation, childcare, economic development, senior citizen activities, and community beautification.

National Night Out

The National Association of Town Watch's annual National Night Out program, which is held on the first Tuesday in August, has been successful in promoting involvement in crime and drug prevention activities, strengthening police–community relations, and encouraging neighborhood camaraderie as part of the fight for safer streets. National Night Out has grown to involve over 34 million people from more than 10,000 communities. The program has grown to involve cities and law enforcement agencies from all fifty states, U.S. territories, Canada, and U.S. military bases around the world.

Along with the traditional porch-sitting and lights on, areas hold locally tailored events such as block parties, cookouts, parades, visits from law enforcement, rallies, and marches. National Night Out is a popular and effective strategy for heightening awareness, enhancing police–community relations, and bolstering volunteer morale. Police patrol operations should increasingly become involved in this annual event.

Neighborhood Nuisance Program

One other innovative crime prevention strategy that some police agencies are participating in is the Neighborhood Nuisance Program. The City of San Diego sponsors a program to help residents abate nuisances in their neighborhood (San Diego Police Department, 2006). Nuisances can include an unsightly property, excessive noise, gang activity, prostitution, drug activity, trespassing, and so on. The basis for the program is California law that makes property owners responsible for using their property in an ordinary and reasonable manner that is conducive to the peace and harmony of the neighborhood and does not interfere with the comfortable enjoyment of life and property by others. Property owners violate the law by allowing a nuisance to exist on their property whether they themselves live there or not. Once they become aware of the nuisance they become responsible for abating it.

Under the Neighborhood Nuisance Program, the affected residents work with a city representative who guides them through a process to abate the nuisance. The process involves the following steps: collection of evidence, documentation of the nuisance effects, notification and negotiation with the property owner, demand that the nuisance be stopped, and so on. If the owner fails to abate the nuisance, the residents can file a suit in small claims court where they can describe the nuisance and their efforts to resolve it. In addition to a court cost and service fees, the judge has the power to order the property owner to abate the nuisance and/or pay monetary damages to the residents.

Problem Solving

problem solving / A critical element of the community policing strategy. Problem solving is a tactic used to produce long-term solutions to problems of crime or decay in communities. Police, residents, and other agencies or organizations work together to identify and find the causes for neighborhood crime problems, then develop responses to the problems based on the problems' causes.

Problem solving is another purpose of police patrol. **Problem solving** is an important component of community policing. Recall that community policing is a collaborative effort between a police department and community that identifies problems of crime and disorder and involves all elements of the community in the search for solutions to identified problems.

Many of the problems that police encounter have only temporary solutions that are dictated by a standard operating procedure or by the law. One example of this is in the case of domestic violence where the victim has been assaulted. In a domestic violence case the police have little choice but to make an arrest as dictated by standard operating procedure and state law in most states.

Problem solving in community policing is an approach that produces long-term solutions to problems of crime or decay in communities. Police, residents, and other agencies work together to identify and find the causes of neighborhood crime problems, then develop responses to the problems based on the problems' causes.

Many times responses are not cookie-cutter, procedure-driven, or a one-response-fits-all. Responses may not be just police responses, but may be responses developed through joint police–community actions, which also involve participation by agencies such as the fire department, code enforcement, youth services, waste management, park and recreation, and others.

Traffic Responsibilities

Police patrol has an enormous responsibility to ensure the safe flow of traffic. This responsibility includes not only the enforcement of traffic laws, such as speeding, driving under the influence, and vehicle equipment laws, but also includes the investigation of vehicle accidents and directing traffic.

A police officer radios for additional officers to assist at the scene of a traffic accident. Part of the police function is the investigation of both non-injury and injury accidents.

The investigation of traffic accidents is an activity that most police officers are all too familiar with. Just within the City of New York in 2003 there were 84,949 traffic accidents, 54,438 of which were reported to the police. Of these, there were 344 deaths involving either the driver or a passenger (New York State, Department of Motor Vehicles, 2006).

According to the National Highway Traffic Safety Administration (2002), speeding is one of the leading contributing factors associated with automobile accidents, at an estimated economic cost of $40 billion each year. The detection of traffic violators is increasingly becoming high tech. For some time now the courts have accepted radar speed measuring devices as a reliable method for measuring vehicle speed. There are several methods of speed detection that police utilize.

Radar Speed Detection

At some time you have invariably overheard someone make a statement that police have a radar trap set up at a certain location. Radar is traditionally the primary method of speed enforcement in the United States. Radar guns aim an electromagnetic signal at a target vehicle and pick up the return signal reflected off the vehicle. The Doppler effect causes the frequency of the return signal to shift by an amount dependent on the relative speeds of the source of the original signal and the target. Speed radar devices measure the frequency of the reflected signal and compare it with the frequency of the original signal to determine the speed of the target vehicle.

Laser Speed Detection

During the 1980s, law enforcement agencies started to use laser and automated speed measuring devices. Laser devices, also known as LIDAR (light distance and ranging), use a time and distance calculation to measure speed. The devices aim a narrow band of light at the target vehicle and measure the time it takes to receive the reflected light. The advantage of laser speed measuring devices is that the laser light cannot be picked up by radar detectors. They are also beneficial because they can pinpoint a specific violator's vehicle in heavy traffic (Morrison & Jacob, 2000).

Photo Radar

You may have seen them on a highway or city street that you have driven on—video cameras that are placed at various locations. Have you ever wondered how they work and what they are used for? These devices are another tool that the police are using to enforce traffic laws. These video cameras are useful when a speeding vehicle emits a radar signal that triggers the cameras, which in turn photograph speeding vehicles as they pass a specified point. These devices use a low-powered Doppler radar speed sensor to detect speeding vehicles and trigger a motor-driven camera and flash unit to photograph vehicles traveling faster than a set speed.

Average Speed Calculator and Recorder

A vehicle average speed calculator and recorder uses a portable computer to accurately clock, calculate, and display speed based on the time a vehicle takes to travel a known length of road. These devices are mounted on the dash of the patrol car, which allows for easy access by the officer. They can be used in light or heavy traffic. The device gives an average speed output rather than instantaneous speed. One big advantage to speed averaging is that it prevents high measurements where a driver may inadvertently speed up for a few seconds and then return to the speed limit.

Aircraft Speed Surveillance

Officers in aircraft measure vehicle speeds based on the time it takes to travel between two or more pavement markings spaced a known distance apart. Information is transmitted to officers on the ground who then stop the violators and take appropriate enforcement action.

Roadside Electronic Signs

Imagine for a moment that you are driving on campus one autumn morning rather hurriedly because you are late for your police operations class. As you press down on the accelerator you notice a large electronic sign about fifty yards ahead sitting on the side of the road. As you drive closer to the sign you notice it reads in large red digital letters "YOUR SPEED IS 45 MPH." You hit the brakes and slow down immediately as you realize that you are speeding; the campus speed limit is 20 MPH. You frantically look in your rearview mirror in order to make sure that there are no campus police officers following.

Roadside electronic signs are an excellent tool to deter drivers who are compelled to speed. Electronic signs operate by measuring the speed of a vehicle and then reporting the speed on a large digital display sign. They can be used in areas where the police have had a large number of complaints about speeding vehicles or in those areas that have had a high incidence of accidents where speed was a contributing factor.

Objectives of the Police

- To prevent and control conduct widely recognized as threatening to life and property
- To aid individuals who are in danger of physical harm, such as the victims of violent attack
- To facilitate the movement of people and vehicles
- To assist those who cannot care for themselves, the intoxicated, the addicted, the mentally ill, the physically disabled, the old, and the young
- To resolve conflict, whether it be between individuals, groups of individuals, or individuals and their government
- To identify problems that have the potential of becoming more serious problems
- To create and maintain a feeling of security in communities

Source: Goldstein, H. (1977). *Policing a free society*. Cambridge, MA: Ballinger.

Police Patrol, Summing It All Up

The primary purpose of police patrol is to prevent and control crime. Police patrol officers accomplish this mandate by keeping order in their communities, making sure that people follow laws, and by protecting people and property. Officers patrol areas by walking or riding through them, and some by riding horses or bikes. While on patrol, officers watch for signs of criminal activity and talk to residents and businesspeople, trying to build relationships in their community. Officers are also called to respond to accidents, crimes in progress, fights, and other events. Officers evaluate the information they receive and determine the best way to respond.

Uniformed police officers make up the majority of the police patrol. Those who work in municipal police departments of various sizes, in small communities, and in rural areas have general law enforcement duties, including maintaining regular patrols and responding to calls for service. They may direct traffic at the scene of a fire, investigate a burglary, or give first aid to an accident victim. As will be discussed throughout this book, many urban police agencies are becoming more involved in community policing, a practice in which an officer builds relationships with the citizens of local neighborhoods and mobilizes the public to help fight crime.

The largest and most visible component of any municipal law enforcement agency is the patrol section. It consists of officers working in uniform twenty-four hours a day, 365 days a year. They handle calls for service from the public in motor vehicles, on horseback, or on foot. Patrol is the heart of the police mission and the backbone of the police department. Although all aspects of the police organization have the responsibility of meeting the organization's mission, patrol usually takes the lead in this effort due to its size and visibility.

DIFFERENTIAL RESPONSE

Some police agencies have abandoned the notion that every call for police service should be responded to as quickly as possible. Likewise, some agencies have attempted to manage the calls for service. **Differential response** to calls for service is a policy that abandons the traditional practice of responding to all calls for service. In differential response, responses to citizens' calls to 911 are matched to the importance or severity of the calls. For example, calls receive (1) an immediate response by police, (2) a delayed response by police, or (3) no police response, with reports taken over the telephone, by mail, or by having the person come to the police station in person (Walker, 1998). Conditions in which delayed or alternative responses are appropriate include:

differential response /
A system in which police calls are prioritized by the seriousness of the offense. For example, some calls for police services are time critical and some can be deferred. Some police responses must be made in person while others can be handled by a telephone report unit or other city departments.

1. Past burglaries, larcenies, or other thefts
2. Lost property
3. Crimes reported merely for insurance purposes
4. Past assaults without injuries

Research has concluded that differential response strategies have proven to show promise. Some departments that have implemented differential response strategies have diverted up to 50 percent of their calls to alternative responses without suffering any reduction in citizen satisfaction levels (Cahn & Tien, 1981).

Voices of Experience

Operations in a Small Department

Excerpts from an interview between Cliff Roberson and Michael Bresett, Chief of Police, Van Buren, Maine. Chief Bresett is also an adjunct professor at the University of Maine at Fort Kent.

Q: *Chief, describe to us how the Van Buren police department functions.*

A: The department has eight sworn officers. Four are full-time and four are part-time. The part-time are used primarily for shift coverage. One full-time officer, a sergeant, is used primarily for sex crimes investigations because he has training in that area. Two full-time officers work the night shift and two work the day shift. We have coverage from 8:00 A.M. in the morning until 3:30 A.M., so it is not quite twenty-four-hour coverage. After 3:30 A.M., we are on an on-call basis. The officers are required to live within twenty minutes of the station. For the most part, our officers patrol in one-person vehicle patrols.

Our jurisdiction is probably about 100 square miles with about 2,600 people. In cases of emergency we can call the state police for backup. There is also a U.S. Border Patrol stationed in the community and we can use them for backup. Van Buren is near the Canadian border. I can see the border from my house.

The pre-hire for full-time officers includes psychological testing, physical assessment, and poly-graph testing. If they have not attended a police academy, they are required to complete the academy within one year. All of our officers are certified by the state.

Q: *Does it work to be both the chief and a patrol officer?*

A: From my personal point of view, it is difficult to function as both the chief and a patrol officer. I am extremely busy, because most of the days I am on by myself. I am conducting traffic stops, investigations, handling crime scenes, and then testifying before budget and other committees and the city council. I also, as chief, have to deal with union problems, personnel issues, and other administrative duties.

Q: *Does your department handle homicide cases?*

A: In homicide cases, there are only a few police departments that are authorized to handle their own homicide investigations. The state police take over those cases because they have the equipment and expertise. Everything else we take care of, including bank robberies, child abuse, and so on. ∎

EFFECTIVENESS OF POLICE PATROL

Preventive patrolling is based on two assumptions: (1) patrolling improves police response time, and (2) improved response time will result in an increase in the number of crimes solved. A research study in Garden Grove, California indicated, however, that fast response time accounted for less than 5 percent of arrests for serious crimes and that the use of differential response (having different response standards for different situations) saved the department over $223,000 a year (Cahn & Tien, 1981).

For years, preventive police patrols were considered one of the best deterrents of criminal behavior. The visible presence of police was viewed as an effective crime prevention technique. However, a Kansas City patrol study seems to indicate that police patrols are not effective utilizations of the limited resources available. The Kansas City study divided the city into fifteen districts. Five of the districts retained normal police patrols, five districts greatly increased the number of police patrols, and the final five used the reactive approach and responded only when called by citizens. The researchers concluded that the variations in police patrol techniques appeared to have little effect on citizens' attitudes toward the police, their satisfaction with the police, or their fear of crime. The researchers concluded that patrolling:

1. Did not reduce crime.
2. Did not affect the rates of reporting crimes to the police.
3. Did not affect the effectiveness of the police.
4. Had no significant effect on the citizens' opinions of the effectiveness of the police.

(Kelling, Pate, Dieckman, & Brown, 1974)

While the study has been criticized because of its research design, it has greatly influenced the thinking of researchers on the effectiveness of police patrolling. Nevertheless, to date, the Kansas City study remains the most comprehensive study conducted to analyze the effectiveness of traditional preventive patrol.

REACTIVE, PROACTIVE, AND COACTIVE POLICING

Reactive Policing

The three main patrol functions within traditional reactive policing are routine patrol, immediate response to calls, and follow-up investigations (Cordner & Sheehan, 1999). **Reactive policing** is when the police respond to specific requests from individuals or groups in the community, which encompasses immediate response to calls and follow-up investigations. In other words, reactive policing is a police response after the crime has been committed. For example, when police respond to take a report of a bicycle that has been stolen from the backyard of a residence, the police are being reactive.

reactive policing / When police respond to crime calls after they have been committed.

Proactive Policing

Proactive policing involves the "police, acting on their own initiative, [to] develop information about crime and strategies for its suppression" (Crank, 1998, pp. 244–245). Preventing crime in a proactive manner sometimes involves using intelligence information. It is through credible intelligence that threats can be identified and appropriate countermeasures taken. Intelligence information does not always come from the general public; intelligence may be gathered from specialized policing units. For example, narcotics units, vice units, or gang units may gather intelligence information from surveillance and from informants who are sometimes involved in criminal activity.

proactive policing / When police work with the community to prevent crime. Community policing and neighborhood watch programs are two examples of proactive policing.

Specialized units often provide intelligence information to other police units who act on the information before a crime is committed, or the special unit may take action themselves and prevent a crime. Establishing neighborhood watch programs and setting a mock police car at a location where there have been complaints of speeding cars are also examples of proactive policing.

directed patrol / A strategy where police officers are assigned to patrol and give attention to specific problem areas that are identified through problem or crime analysis.

Directed patrol is largely a proactive police strategy. Directed patrol involves police officers being instructed to monitor specific areas that are identified through problem or crime analysis when they are not responding to dispatch calls (McKenna, 1998). Directed patrol units respond to "problem areas" that need specific police attention. For example, areas that are targeted by directed patrol may include problems such as illegal street racing, burglaries, and narcotics trafficking. Directed patrol tactics vary widely, however, the most rudimentary approach is to saturate an area temporarily with patrol officers (Sweeney, 2003). After directed patrol has been targeted in an area, it is then important for officers to examine underlying problems inherent within the specific area and to tailor solutions.

Coactive Policing

coactive policing / An approach where the police, the community, and other public and private resources work together to solve crime and crime-related problems.

Coactive policing is similar to proactive policing, however, in coactive policing the police utilize citizens and other community resources in an attempt to solve problems. For example, let's suppose that a police officer has been working the same beat area for four years. The officer prides himself on knowing most of the citizens living in the neighborhood he patrols. Within the past month, an escort service moved into a storefront in the middle of his beat. Subsequently, the officer has been bombarded with complaints from citizens. The citizens simply don't want the escort service in their neighborhood. What exacerbates the situation even more is the fact that there is an elementary school located a few hundred yards away from the escort service. The police officer learns through a confidential source that there are prostitution-related activities also going on at the escort service. The officer is beginning to get many complaints from citizens living in the area who are demanding that the officer do something soon. What would you do if you were a police officer faced with this dilemma? Specifically, how would you solve this problem by being coactive?

Recall that coactive policing involves not only the police solving community crime and disorder problems, but also other resources that may assist in solving problems (fire department, health department, neighborhood associations, department of public works, animal control, power company, the local telephone company, etc.). Returning to our fictional situation dealing with the escort service, which resources can you think of that may be beneficial in resolving the problem?

Let's assume that the escort service is advertising on a large marquee sign located in front of the building. The marquee sign has a fifty-foot electrical cord running across a public driveway and into the business, where it is plugged into an electrical socket. There is a violation of some sorts, but who would you call? What about the fire department? In most jurisdictions, the fire department has the legal authority to issue citations and temporarily close a business or establishment because of a fire hazard. Who would have ever thought that the fire department could play a role in solving the problem of an escort service opening in a neighborhood?

Take this one step further and assume that you have discovered that the escort service is serving food to their customers. Customers can come in after a hard day's work and grab a bite to eat while they wait their turn for the date of their choice. The problem here is that the escort service does not have a license to serve food. The health department could be contacted as a resource to help resolve this problem. The escort service could be written a citation for failure to have a food distribution license. The health department subsequently identifies several other health code violations in the building. Furthermore, the police officer, along with several other citizens, approaches the zoning department to investigate what would need to be done to change the zoning laws to prevent an escort service from opening in the neighborhood in the future. After several months, the owner of the escort service decides it would be cheaper to find another location in which to operate his business and voluntarily leaves the area.

The purpose of this hypothetical account is to get you thinking about coactive policing. In the hypothetical example it was the police department, along with citizens, the fire department, and the health department, that collaborated in a partnership to solve this problem. The elimination of the escort service from the neighborhood has a potential payoff in terms of citizen satisfaction many times greater than may ever be realized. To the citizens, the escort service moving into their neighborhood was call for concern. Police officers should remain mindful that citizen satisfaction often rests with the solution of minor order maintenance problems that don't take a great deal of time to effectively resolve.

Often, police officers think that the only concerns that citizens have are the serious crime-fighting tasks (e.g., robberies, burglaries, and drug dealing). There are many anecdotal accounts from citizens and police officers that disorder problems, such as the stop sign that has been missing at an intersection, the speeding cars near the local school, a burned out street light, the vacant house that has become a hang-out for idle juveniles, and litter in the local park, are also concerns. For example, a police officer was recently interviewed regarding the manner in which he managed his beat. This officer told the author that he recently made it a point to contact as many citizens as he could during a shift and ask them what their concerns were in the neighborhood. To his surprise, they were all primarily order main-

tenance problems. He spoke of an entire block of citizens that complained that a stop sign had been missing from an intersection nearby for weeks. The officer had the stop sign replaced the next day. Several citizens wrote letters to the chief of police commending the officer. The officer revealed during the interview that he was surprised at how he had satisfied so many citizens merely by having a stop sign replaced. Police officers should never think that the small disorder problems are not important concerns of the community.

PRACTICE HINTS

Coactive Policing

- Coactive policing is preventing crime and disorder.
- Coactive policing works to identify problems which affect quality of life in the community.
- Coactive policing is based on the police and other public and private resources working together to solve crime and disorder problems.
- The aim of coactive policing is to identify conditions that will need to be addressed to improve community safety.
- Coactive policing is a natural fit with community policing and problem-solving strategies.

ORGANIZATIONAL FEATURES

Police departments in the United States are not substantially different from the original British style of policing (Lagrange, 1993). There are certain organizational features common to almost all urban departments. Two such features are bureaucracy and the paramilitary model. The International City Manager's Association Municipal

Police Administration offers six general principles of organization for law enforcement agencies:

1. The work should be apportioned among the various individuals and units, according to some logical plan. (Homogeneity)

2. Lines of authority and responsibility should be made as definite and direct as possible. (Delineation of responsibility)

3. There is a limit to the number of subordinates who can be supervised effectively by one officer, and this limit seldom should be exceeded. (Span of control)

4. There should be "unity of command" throughout the organization. (Subordinates under the direct control of only one supervisor)

5. Responsibility cannot be placed without the delegation of commensurate authority, and authority should not be delegated to a person without holding him/her accountable for its use. (Delegation of responsibility)

6. The efforts of the organizational units and of their component members must be coordinated so that all will be directed harmoniously toward the accomplishment of the police purpose. The components thus coordinated will enable the organization to function as a well-integrated unit (Geller, 1991).

Police Department as Bureaucracy

bureaucracy / A concept referring to the way that the administrative execution and enforcement of legal rules is socially organized. Most police departments are highly bureaucratic. A bureaucratic organization is characterized by standard operating procedures (rule following), formal division of authority, hierarchy, and impersonal relationships.

Police departments are **bureaucracies**. A bureaucracy is a form of organizational structure that was developed by Max Weber, a German social scientist. Bureaucracy is defined as (1) government by bureaus, administrators, and petty officials, (2) the body of officials and administrators of a government or government departments, or (3) the concentration of power in administrators (Weber, 1947). Presently, bureaucracy is a term generally cast in an unfavorable light. We blame a lot of our problems and inactions on "bureaucracy" or "red tape."

Weber (1947) thought that a bureaucracy was the most rational system of organization available. According to Weber, managers who want to obtain efficiency and optimal organizational performance were forced to use a bureaucratic form of organization. The bureaucratic form of organization has a number of criticisms. One such criticism is that a bureaucracy dehumanizes employees in its use of standardized procedures for completing task assignments. Rather than defending the dehumanizing aspects of a bureaucratic form, Weber stated that bureaucracy was an irresistible organizational wave.

As noted earlier, bureaucracy is the basic organizational structure of police departments. According to Weber, bureaucracies have well-articulated policies which are impersonally and uniformly applied throughout the organization. Police departments uniformly have well-articulated policies which are impersonally and uniformly applied throughout the departments. Applying Weber's theory to a police agency, for it to be rational (i.e., a bureaucracy), the agency must contain the following elements:

1. **A specific division of labor**—Bureaucratic organizations have divided labor to an intensive degree of refinement. Tasks are broken down into the minutest particles of specialization so that even the newest unskilled employee can master a task with a minimum of skill and training. Most police departments have

divided their tasks and assigned officers to specialized tasks such as patrol, communications, traffic, and so on.

2. **Hierarchy of authority**—The progressive concentration of control over subordinate units in successively higher levels of authority in an organization's vertical command structure. Police departments are generally organized in successively higher levels of authority in a vertical command structure with the police chief at the apex.

3. **Expertise**—Employees are selected by comparing objective standards established for the organization for adequate performance of a job with the qualifications of the applicant. The chief criteria are how well the potential employee is suited by way of education, training, knowledge, and skill to perform the assigned function in the organization. This element is present in the average police department.

4. **Written records**—Bureaucratic organizations keep elaborate records for the purpose of achieving uniformity of action. Police departments are noted for keeping elaborate records and the establishment of standards or standing operating procedures (SOPs) to achieve uniformity of action.

Paramilitary and Chain of Command

Police departments not only tend to be bureaucratic, but are also modeled loosely after the military style of organization. A few of the characteristics borrowed from the military and present in police departments include:

- centralized command structure with a rigid chain of command
- clearly marked lines of communications
- strong discipline
- differentiation between ranks or positions
- authoritarian leadership
- distinguishing uniform

The operational units within a police department are also similarly classified to the military units of line, staff, and auxiliary units. Currently, there is discussion in U.S. police agencies to move away from the paramilitary system, especially as community-oriented policing strategies more fully blossom. The paramilitary structure may not be the most appropriate with contemporary policing. At one time, a rigid, centralized command structure represented the best prescription to deter corruption and misconduct. However, as policing evolves with community policing strategies, this centralized command and control structure with its emphasis on the paramilitary model will require redefinition.

In police departments there are sergeants that directly supervise police operations in the field. Lieutenants may also supervise police activities in the field or they may serve as watch commanders. The watch commander is usually the rank of a lieutenant or a captain and oversees all police operations during a specific shift. Naturally, the **chain of command** would dictate that a sergeant answers directly to a lieutenant, the lieutenant answers directly to the captain, the captain answers

chain of command / The line of authority and responsibility in a police agency along which orders are passed.

directly to a major, and so forth. A chain of command will vary from one department to the next and is dependent on such factors as size of the agency and shape of the organizational structure. A steep hierarchal organizational structure will generally have more levels in the chain of command, whereas a horizontal structure will tend to have fewer levels.

Most interagency communication in a police department operates on the chain of command principle. If a sergeant desires to communicate with the captain, he or she would first have to go through the lieutenant. If the lieutenant wishes to communicate with the chief of police, he or she would go through the chain of command (i.e., captain, major, deputy chief, and then the chief of police).

The chain of command principle is important in situations where large numbers of police officers are deployed. In these situations it is critical that each officer knows who they answer to. Suppose that numerous police officers are dispatched to a large gathering of persons who are protesting proposed immigration legislation. After the protesters see the police arriving at the scene they become unruly. Some of the protesters begin to yell epithets at the police. The situation is volatile and could erupt at any minute. The sergeant soon arrives at the scene and takes command. In other words, all police officers at the scene take orders from the sergeant. A few moments later a lieutenant arrives at the scene. The lieutenant assumes command at the scene. Every police officer at the scene, including the sergeant, now answers to the lieutenant. In situations such as these it is imperative that all police personnel know exactly who they answer to. This principle is called the *unity of command*.

Unity of command means that all organizational personnel operate under a single commander with the requisite authority to direct all personnel employed in pursuit of a common purpose. The unity of command principle also ensures that conflicting orders are not issued to the same police officers by several supervisors.

The Policing Enterprise

There are 17,784 state and local law enforcement agencies in the United States which employ 796,518 sworn personnel (Bureau of Justice Statistics, 2000). Sworn personnel are those public law enforcement officers that carry a weapon and have powers of arrest. Due to the fragmented nature of policing in the United States, there may be several law enforcement agencies operating within a single geographical county. For example, in Los Angeles County alone, there are over forty separate law enforcement agencies, and in those cities without a police department, law enforcement services are contracted by the Los Angeles County Sheriff's Department.

Not only is it likely that a county jurisdiction may have several police departments, in addition to a county sheriff's department, the highway patrol or state police may also patrol in the area. Furthermore, if there is a college or university located in the county, there is a good chance that it operates a university police department.

While there may be other law enforcement agencies in an area, such as sheriff's departments, state police, highway patrols, and campus police, city police still constitute the majority of the sworn police officers in the United States. Police departments range in size from the 40,435 in New York City to one officer departments in smaller cities. More than half of all police departments have ten or less sworn officers.

Almost all police departments, from the largest to the smallest, have similar goals. Most maintain jurisdiction over law enforcement matters within their city boundaries. There are a number of auxiliary police agencies that assist them. The most common auxiliary agencies are park police, airport police, transit police, and university police. The auxiliary police are created to handle special problems or special jurisdictional areas, like the airports and parks. The relationships between the city police and the auxiliary agencies differ in almost every city. In general, the auxiliary agencies have carved out a small portion of the city police's jurisdiction (normally geographic) over law enforcement. In most cases, in those limited geographic areas, like our airports, both the city police and the auxiliary police have concurrent jurisdiction. Police departments are headed by a police chief who is appointed by the mayor or city council.

PRACTICE HINTS

Police Organizational Terminology

- **Unity of Command:** All organizational personnel operate under a single commander with the requisite authority to direct personnel employed in pursuit of a common purpose.
- **Span of Control:** The number of persons that one person can effectively supervise.
- **Division of Labor:** Work specialization, the degree to which tasks in an organization are divided into separate jobs.
- **Department:** The primary organizational unit within a governmental structure.
- **Bureau:** Typically the largest unit within a police department.
- **Division:** A subdivision of a bureau.
- **Section:** A subdivision of a division.
- **Unit:** A subdivision of a section.
- **Watch or Shift:** A time division of the day for purposes of police assignment.
- **Beat:** A geographical area assigned to a police officer for patrol purposes whether on foot or motor vehicle.
- **Hierarchy of Authority:** The progressive concentration of control over subordinate units in successively higher levels of authority in an organization's vertical command structure. Police departments are generally organized in successively higher levels of authority in a vertical command structure with the police chief at the apex.

Multiple Jurisdictional Operations

Because of the fragmented nature of law enforcement agencies, a situation may arise where multi-agencies respond to an incident. So, who is in command of an incident where two, three, or even four police agencies are present at the scene? In multi-agency law enforcement operations, which may be necessary during times of mass public disorder or other large community events, unity of command may not be possible, but the requirement for unity of effort becomes paramount. It is wise for police administrators to enter into agreements with other law enforcement agencies within their geographical area that provide jurisdictional guidelines. Some jurisdictional authority may be specified by specific state statutes.

Consider the following scenario, which illustrates a multi-jurisdictional law enforcement response. Deputies from the local sheriff's department respond into the city limits to assist the police department with a large public gathering that has escalated into rock throwing and pushing and shoving. In this situation, the police department ideally should assume command of the scene, and the sheriff's department would serve to simply assist. Another example is the case where the sheriff's department initiates a high-speed pursuit which ends up in the city limits. There may be a previous agreement worked out by the police and sheriff's department that because the sheriff's department initiated the chase they retain command of the chase even though the chase continues into the city limits, where the primary law enforcement services are provided by the police department.

Figure 1.1 Police Department Chain of Command

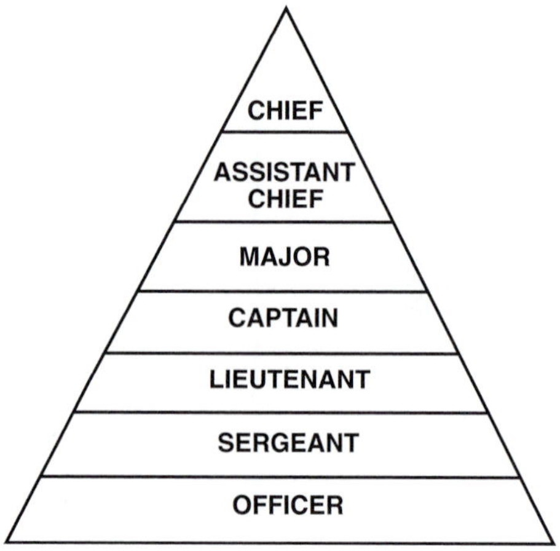

```
                    CHIEF
                  ASSISTANT
                    CHIEF
                    MAJOR
                   CAPTAIN
                  LIEUTENANT
                   SERGEANT
                   OFFICER
```

PRACTICE HINTS

At one time, a rigid, centralized command structure represented the best prescription to deter corruption and misconduct. As policing evolves into community policing strategies, the centralized command and control structure will require redefinition. Police operations must increasingly become decentralized through substations, neighborhood stations, satellite offices, or storefronts.

Decentralized Operations

Many police departments operate district, precinct, or division stations that are separate from headquarters. The advantages of decentralizing police operations is that it gives the community greater access to the police department. In some neighborhoods that have a disproportionately high crime rate, a police precinct or substation located in the neighborhood may reduce citizen fear of crime. About 3,000 such stations are operated by local police departments nationwide (Hickman & Reaves, 2003).

An estimated 12 percent of departments operate fixed neighborhood or community substations, including a majority of those serving a population of 50,000 or more. Two percent of departments operate mobile substations, including 27 percent of those serving 250,000 to 999,999 residents. Nationwide, local police departments operate an estimated 3,546 fixed substations, and 335 mobile substations (Hickman & Reaves, 2003).

Police Organizational Environment

Police departments are "open" systems as opposed to "closed" systems. A closed system is a system that is independent of external influences. An open system is one which is not independent of external influences. The police are influenced by the political, economical, and social pressures of the community in which the department is located. The external (environmental) influences on a police department require the department to be flexible to adapt to those pressures.

Organizational Clarification

To prevent internal conflict, members of an organization need to understand their duties and the duties and assignments of others. Two devices commonly used to demonstrate the structure of an organization, and inform members of the organization of their duties and assignments, are organizational charts and position descriptions.

Organizational charts are pictorial representations of the agency which map lines of authority for the entire organization. One major limitation of organizational charts is that they fail to delineate the informal structure that exists in every organization. Each position within a police department normally has a position description. The position description should include basic job functions and their relationship to others.

TYPES OF POLICE PATROL

There are many ways that the police provide patrol services to the community. The type of patrol may vary depending on the geographical layout and terrain of the community. The method of patrol used should always be based on the need to provide the most effective service to the community. Several other factors that may influence the type of police patrol at any given time are weather conditions and the general philosophy of the police department.

Foot Patrol

Foot patrol is the oldest patrol method and one that has received much attention through the years. Before the advent of the motor vehicle, foot patrol was the single most popular method of patrol. Subsequently, when automobiles became the most popular method of patrol for police departments, foot patrol increasingly lost it popularity. Foot patrol has recently been reintroduced to major population centers such as Newark, New Jersey and Houston, Texas.

Foot patrol is usually limited to smaller populated areas as a means to create higher officer visibility and as a venue to communicate with residents and business owners in the patrol area. Foot patrols are useful for special events such as parades, large community celebrations, dignitary protection, and public relations. Officers on foot can observe more than officers in vehicles. By being on the street an officer's sense of smell and sense of hearing are also improved. Research on foot patrols has resulted in a number of encouraging findings:

1. With the presence of foot patrol in neighborhoods, fear levels decrease significantly.
2. Alternatively, with the withdrawal of foot patrol, fear levels increase significantly.

A police officer keeps a watchful eye at the subway entrance.

3. Citizen satisfaction with the police increases with the presence of foot patrol in neighborhoods.

4. Police who patrol on foot have a greater appreciation for the values of the neighborhood residents than do police in automobiles.

5. Police who patrol on foot have greater job satisfaction, less fear, and higher morale than do officers who patrol in automobiles (Kelling, 1987).

Motorized Patrol

Motorized patrol has become the dominant form of police patrol in the United States. The evolution of the patrol car dates back to the 1930s when police reformer

---

PRACTICE HINTS

The Police Foundation found that introducing foot patrol in a mix of police strategies significantly enhances the citizens' perception of safety in the neighborhood. This is something no other police strategy had been able to do. Although introducing foot patrol seemed to have little effect on crime rates, it did have the following positive effects:

- Residents knew when officers were patrolling their neighborhoods on foot.
- Residents in areas patrolled by officers on foot thought that crime was less of a problem than did residents in areas with only motorized patrol.
- Residents in areas with foot patrol felt safer and less likely to be victimized.
- Residents living in areas with foot patrol took fewer steps to protect themselves against crime.
- Residents in areas with foot patrol were more satisfied with police services.

O. W. Wilson advocated replacing foot patrols with motor vehicle patrols. The obvious advantage to motorized patrol is that officers can carry more equipment, such as fire extinguishers, blankets, traffic cones, paperwork, extra tactical weapons, and so on. Motorized patrol also allows police officers protection from the elements, such as snow, rain, sleet, cold, and heat, while still patrolling their beats. The make and model of police vehicles varies by department. For example, in rural geographical areas that are usually patrolled by county sheriff's deputies the patrol vehicle may very well be a jeep or pick-up truck or some other type of sports utility vehicle equipped with four-wheel drive.

Single-Officer Units versus Two-Officer Units

Generally, a patrol vehicle occupied by one officer is more cost efficient than one occupied by two officers. In most cases, funding two officers in a vehicle is not economically practical. The debate between one-officer versus two-officer patrol techniques has always taken place within law enforcement agencies. Unions or associations, which represent the field officer, tend to support two-officer patrol vehicles. However, cost-conscious police administrators have generally favored the single-officer patrol vehicle concept. Research has found that one-officer units are just as efficient and safe as two-officer units (Boydstun, Sherry, & Moelter, 1977).

Bicycle Patrol

Bicycle patrol units provide an alternative method of patrol. Experience has shown that bike officers are an important tool in improving police–community relations because the officers are more accessible to citizens. Bike officers can provide a proactive, highly visible police service along with giving officers a "stealth" advantage when desired. Bicycles also allow officers access to areas not normally patrolled by motorized units.

Bicycle patrol is an effective method of patrol which is increasingly being utilized by a large number of police agencies.

Bicycles now come in a number of styles and models which can be used in a variety of geographical areas and a variety of terrain. A few uses for bicycle patrols include patrolling college campuses, community events, areas that are inaccessible by motor vehicle, parks, congested downtown areas, off-road terrain, and parking lots and garages located at large shopping and event centers. Furthermore, bicycle patrols are an excellent tool for use in community relations and also in crime prevention and detection.

Motorcycle Patrol

Motorcycle patrol has traditionally been used for traffic enforcement activities. Depending on weather conditions, motorcycle patrol may be used at any time of the year. Motorcycles are useful because they are agile and can be maneuvered through traffic and in areas where a vehicle could not travel. Motorcycle units can be used for special events, such as parades and escorts.

Motorcycle patrol is especially useful for traffic enforcement. For example, suppose a community has several large manufacturing plants which employ thousands of people. During shift changes, the main streets and throughways around the manufacturing plants have traffic tie ups, and there have been many incidents where motorists have disobeyed traffic laws, which has resulted in an increase in traffic accidents. Motorcycle units are ideal to enforce traffic laws in this situation due to their maneuverability. In the case where there is an automobile accident, it may take a police vehicle several minutes to maneuver through heavy traffic, while a motorcycle can maneuver and get to the scene much quicker in traffic-congested areas.

One of the chief disadvantages of motorcycle patrol is the risk imposed to the police officer. A motorcycle officer involved in one accident may result in a career-ending

Motorcycle patrol is useful in areas that are highly congested with traffic due to their maneuverability.

injury in which the officer would have to take a medical retirement. The motorcycle officer is also limited in the amount of equipment that can be carried on the motorcycle. In cases where a motorcycle officer makes an arrest, he or she would have to summon another officer with a motor vehicle to transport the offender to the booking facility. This may be problematic because it ties up two officers. One other disadvantage is that the officer is not protected from adverse weather conditions which can sometimes arise suddenly.

Aircraft Patrol

Aircraft units may be either an airplane (fixed wing or rotary wing) or a helicopter, depending on the needs of the agency. Aircraft patrol provides assistance to ground patrol units by observing areas that units on the ground cannot view. Aircraft can also be used for picking up and transporting prisoners over great distances. For example, if a suspect is picked up in New York and is wanted in Wichita, Kansas for homicide, a sheriff's department pilot would fly the department aircraft to New York and transport the suspect back to Kansas. One major drawback to aircraft patrol is that it is the most expensive form of patrol and requires highly trained personnel.

Water/Marine Patrol

Communities that are in close location to large bodies of water or beaches, shorelines, and inland waterways often use water/marine patrol to control crime. Water/marine patrols are also used to control water safety violations, search and rescue missions, and for a variety of traditional law enforcement functions. There are a number of crimes that can occur along our nation's coastlines. Crimes such as drug smuggling and other serious types of predatory crimes make marine patrol an ideal law enforcement tool. Marine patrol tends to be very expensive and requires special training on the part of police officers. The size and type of boat that a police department may use will depend on factors such as the size of the waterway or coast, and how often the boats will be used (i.e., just during the summer months or all year).

Mounted Horse Patrol

Horse patrol has a long history in policing and can be traced back to the last century. Many police departments cannot afford horses due to the special care that goes into stabling them and maintaining their diet and health. Mounted horse patrol is useful in areas that are difficult to reach or impractical with other patrol methods. They can be used in search and rescue missions, as well as traffic control. Mounted horse patrol is advantageous at events that attract a large number of persons, because it allows for mounted officers to maneuver through the crowd. They are also useful for public relations, such as parades and demonstrations. The horse is intimidating and may deter the crowd from engaging in disorderly conduct. The chief disadvantage is the maintenance cost; that is, it is expensive to care for a horse. Expenses include proper diet and nutrition, veterinarian care, housing, and the expense of training police officers.

Mounted police patrol officers patrol a local park.

ALLOCATION OF PATROL PERSONNEL

Traditional approaches to the allocation of police patrol have been haphazard and, in some cases, involved little more then dividing the total number of police patrol officers by three shifts and assigning them equally. This method of allocating is neither wise nor effective. On average, larger municipal police departments employ twenty-two full-time sworn personnel per 10,000 residents. County police departments and sheriffs' offices employ an average of ten or eleven officers per 10,000 residents, respectively. State law enforcement agencies employ an average of two officers per 10,000 residents (Reaves & Hickman, 2000). Allocation of patrol personnel involves determining the number of patrol units needed to be deployed during the time of day and day of the week. There are many factors that influence the allocation of police patrol.

Simply put, the allocation of police patrol should be driven by data. The primary consideration should be based on absolute need in order to provide the best possible service to the public. Allocation decisions in general are based on terrain, size, population, and the number of service and crime calls (workload). Workload assessments usually include evaluations of:

1. Number of incidents handled by patrol personnel during a specific time period.
2. Average time required to handle an incident at the patrol level (or measurement of a sampling of cases).
3. Calculation of the percentage of time, on average, that should be available to the patrol officer for handling incidents during a specific period (such as an eight-hour shift).
4. Time lost through vacation, holidays, and other leave, compared to the total time required for each patrol assignment (Commission on Accreditation, 2006).

Contemporary allocation methods have the luxury of being driven by sophisticated computer programs that have been customized for the specific purpose of patrol allocation. Computer software programs can calculate a variety of performance measures and recommend the effective allocation of police officers. Police authorities responsible for planning patrol allocation are encouraged to explore the various patrol allocation software programs available.

SPECIAL TACTICAL TEAMS

In some cases, patrol officers may require the assistance of the specialized tactical team to defuse a situation. SWAT (Special Weapons and Tactics Team) is a specialized unit found in many police departments. The SWAT team is generally activated to respond to tactical situations that are deemed high risk and/or require specialized training, expertise, and equipment. For example, sniper situations, barricaded suspects, hostage situations, dignitary protection, riots, search and arrest warrants, narcotics raids, and anti-terrorism operations may require the assistance of the SWAT team. It is important to point out that a nonviolent resolution is always the ultimate goal in any tactical deployment.

SWAT teams typically dress in military attire and are equipped with a variety of specialized weapons, including shotguns, tear gas, stun guns, and high-powered rifles for marksmen (snipers). They often use specialized equipment, including heavy body armor, entry tools, steel-reinforced boots, and night vision optics. Police officers assigned to the SWAT team are selected from applicants based on a range of criteria that may include: physical fitness, firearms proficiency, supervisory recommendation, and psychological assessment. SWAT team members are police officers who have received special training in a wide variety of tactics. These highly and specially trained officers spend a significant amount of time practicing for every conceivable situation where standard patrol response will not work.

The personnel makeup of a SWAT team usually consists of a negotiator, rifleman, and entry team member. The negotiator is used to talk out a suspect in order to avoid the necessity of making entry into a location or otherwise subjecting team members or a suspect to the violence of armed confrontation. The negotiator usually works from the SWAT command post. The rifleman is a sniper who usually works as a pair with another SWAT member. The rifleman is responsible for long-range reconnaissance of a target location and for protecting the team from hostile threat with long-range marksmanship skills. When negotiations with a suspect fail, the entry team is utilized. Members of the entry team are utilized for an emergency assault and/or entry. For example, the entry team may be used for an emergency assault on hostage-takers, they may be called to make a crisis entry in the case of a barricaded suspect, and they are increasingly used in high-risk search warrant entries.

Like many emergency calls that the police patrol responds to, such as hostage situations, barricaded persons with a gun, and the like, patrol officers play a critical role in the successful resolution. The initial actions of the first responding police officers are critical. When officers respond to a situation that will require a response from the SWAT team, the primary objective of the first responding police officers is

Los Angeles SWAT Team members issue a briefing to unidentified officials, at left in suits, while the Mexican Consulate was being secured after a hostage situation, Tuesday, Nov. 9, 2004. A man demanding media attention took a woman employee hostage at the Mexican consulate and was shot by LAPD officers. The woman was unharmed.

to contain and control the scene. Once the scene is contained, the SWAT team will have the primary responsibility to defuse the situation.

MANAGING AND SUPERVISING PATROL ACTIVITIES

Management and supervision are two distinctly different functions. Managing police operations refers to a broad variety of administrative tasks, such as organizing, planning, budgeting, coordinating, and controlling operations. On the other hand, supervision entails the actual hands-on supervision of police activities in the field.

The rank levels found at the management level and supervisory level will vary depending on the size and general structure of a police department. In small police departments, a sergeant may perform many of the duties that a lieutenant or captain performs in a large police department. In many medium and large police agencies it is not uncommon to find three layers of management: (1) upper-level management, (2) middle-level management, and (3) line-level supervision.

Upper-Level Management

Upper-level management usually consists of the chief of police, deputy chief of police (or assistant chief of police), and major. The top management team is usually involved in administration and rarely participates in field-level police functions, such as responding to calls or self-initiated police activities. Police management determines the mission for the organization and sets goals. Top management is accountable for the overall management of the organization.

Middle-Level Management

Middle managers ensure that the goals of the top management are carried out. In large police departments those in middle management usually hold the rank of captain or lieutenant. In smaller police departments the rank of sergeant may be included in middle management.

Those police personnel in middle-management positions usually have the responsibility of commanding bureaus or divisions. For example, in some police departments the captain may be a patrol division commander, while a lieutenant is the patrol watch commander. In this case, the lieutenant would be directly responsible for all field police activities during a specific time frame, for example third watch. If you have ever ridden as an observer with a police officer or simply been around police culture for any amount of time, you probably have heard the term watch commander.

The captain, on the other hand, is responsible for managing the entire patrol division. This would include developing goals and objectives for the division, budgeting, ensuring that the mission and directives passed down from the chief of police are carried out, and managing all activities within the patrol division.

Line-Level Supervision

Supervision, as part of the management process, refers to the act of overseeing people (Iannone & Iannone, 2001). Supervisors direct and control the work of employees in order to achieve the departmental goals. Supervisors directly oversee those police personnel who perform line functions. Line functions are those activities that work to accomplish the organizational objectives. Police patrol officers and detectives are examples of personnel who perform line functions.

Supervisors are the only level of management managing nonmanagers. Thus, most of the supervisor's time is allocated to the functions of directing and controlling. Sergeants are the frontline supervisors in most police organizations. The job of police sergeant differs from that of police officer. While performing essentially the same law enforcement duties, the police sergeant also has full supervisory responsibility for subordinates.

Police sergeants have the most day-to-day contact with police officers when compared to other ranks. The police sergeant holds one of the most important management positions in the department. Sergeants are crucial because they are concerned with the achievement of the police purpose. It is through the sergeant that orders and directives are given to those police officers at the bottom of the hierarchy. The sergeant plays an instrumental role in gaining the support of police officers to carry out the chief's programs, mission, and goals set for the department.

Police sergeants are responsible for preparing written performance evaluations on subordinates, recommending commendations and disciplinary action when appropriate to division commanders or the chief of police, responding to grievances at the first level, training new police officers, observing police officers' performance in the field, recording the performance of subordinates, demonstrating leadership and decision making in emergency situations, and providing other supervisory functions.

Duties of Police Sergeant

- Prepares patrol personnel roster and ensures that geographical beats are covered.
- Schedules vacation leave for police officers.
- Oversees scheduling of shift personnel.
- Make daily assignments based on needs.
- Ensures that the policies and procedures of the organization are followed.
- Conducts daily squad room briefing.
- Evaluates police officer performance.
- Conducts in-service training.
- Disciplines police officers when needed.
- Fields and investigates complaints from citizens.
- Disseminates and explains to police officers important department directives.
- Detects police officers' strengths and weaknesses.
- Provides leadership to subordinates.
- Personally responds to unusual occurrences.
- Personally responds to major crime scenes.
- Personally responds to serious traffic accidents.
- Gives on-the-scene media releases.
- Notifies and keeps chain of command informed of unusual occurrences or serious crimes committed during shift.
- Gives talks and speeches to community groups.
- Oversees problem-solving efforts on the part of police officers.
- Authorizes and approves arrests.
- Fields questions from police officers regarding operational procedures and state statutes.

BECOMING A POLICE PATROL OFFICER

In most police departments the field patrol division is where the majority of neophyte police officers will begin their careers. Thus, this section provides a brief sketch of the police officer applicant selection process. Police officers or administrators who desire additional information on recruitment and selection strategies should consult texts that focus full attention to police human resources strategies. This section is written in a manner to provide a general outline to the steps in selecting police officers.

Becoming a police patrol officer begins with the completion of the application for employment. Standards for becoming a police officer will vary from department to department, however, in many respects they are somewhat similar.

After a respective police applicant has been successfully recruited and has completed the requisite application for employment, the selection process begins. Selection is the screening of job applicants to ensure that the most qualified candidates are hired. The objective of the selection process is to predict those applicants who will be successful if hired for police work. It is of absolute necessity that the most qualified men and women are selected for the police service.

The selection of police officers is driven by a complex legal environment. Police administrators have a responsibility to ensure that all selection tests conform to the proper legal standards and that no part of the process is discriminatory. Any selection device used by a police organization, such as application forms, written tests, physical tests, interviews, and background investigations must be job-related.

In 1964, the U.S. Congress established the Equal Employment Opportunity Commission (EEOC). The EEOC is charged with the responsibility of administering the provisions of the Civil Rights Act. In 1972, the jurisdiction of the EEOC was expanded to include public sector employees. Title VII of the Civil Rights Act makes it illegal for public employers to discriminate against persons on the basis of race, sex, color, religion, or national origin. All criteria for hiring must be based on a "bona fide occupational qualification" (BFOQ). A BFOQ is any physical attribute and/or skill that an employer has proven is necessary for satisfactory performance of a particular job. According to the EEOC guidelines, the use of any selection procedure which has an adverse impact on the hiring, promotion, or other employment or membership opportunities of members of any race, sex, or ethnic group is considered to be discriminatory. Under EEOC guidelines, adverse impact is a substantially different rate of selection in hiring, promotion, or other employment decision which works to the disadvantage of members of a race, sex, or ethnic group.

PRACTICE HINTS

Police recruitment and selection are two distinct, but related activities. Police recruitment is the process of locating, identifying, and attracting capable applicants who have the minimum qualifications to be eligible for the selection process. The selection process, as discussed later in this chapter, is the process of subjecting police applicants to what amounts to a rigorous testing protocol.

Written Exam

Generally, most police selection processes begin with a job-related written police examination. Applicants are usually required to meet a minimum score in order to be considered further in the selection process. Some police departments hold year-round testing on a walk-in basis, while others hold testing at periodic times throughout the year. The written examination is an effective and cost-effective method of screening large numbers of police applicants. Written examinations for entry-level police positions are most likely to test areas such as basic arithmetic ability, reading comprehension, grammar, spelling, and writing skills. These areas have been shown to be job-related for police work.

Physical Ability Testing

Physical ability selection is the process of testing applicants for the strength and agility that are required to perform the job of a police officer. The purpose of physical agility testing is to simulate any number of job-related activities, such as jumping down from porches; climbing stairs; or walking along walls, rafters, pipes, or beams while in foot pursuit or while checking buildings for suspects. A period of running may be incorporated into each of the events to simulate the apprehension and control of a fleeting suspect. While these physical skills may appear to be skills that police use, there is a lack of agreement regarding the physical capabilities that should be tested and the standards that should be used to evaluate effective physical performance (Lonsway, 2003). Applicants generally have to obtain a passing score on the physical agility test in order to be considered further in the selection process.

Polygraph Testing

Pre-employment polygraph screening is used to verify information contained on a job application, and to learn if some relevant information has been omitted. Of particular concern is the applicant's past criminal activity, drug usage, morals, and job history.

Two specific advantages of using the polygraph as a pre-employment screening device are (1) some unqualified candidates will decide not to apply because they feel that the polygraph examination will reveal prior acts that will disqualify them from further consideration, and (2) it sends a message to the community that the department is expending every effort to hire only the most fit people as officers. The polygraph examination should be considered a separate phase from the background investigation, however, these two stages are mutually reinforcing when used correctly.

Oral Interview

The oral interview gives the interview board, made up of senior police officials, an opportunity to meet with and observe the communication skills of the candidate. During the interview the candidate is usually asked about background information he or she provided on the application form. The candidate may also be asked to respond to several hypothetical scenarios. Hypothetical scenarios are used to assess how the candidate would respond to stressful situations, as well as to assess problem-solving skills.

Psychological Assessment

conditional offer of employment / An employment offer extended to a police applicant contingent on the applicant successfully completing the latter stages of the selection process, such as psychological testing and medical and drug screening.

Psychological testing is usually conducted after a **conditional offer of employment** is made to the applicant. A conditional offer of employment is where the applicant is offered police employment contingent on passing the remaining selection tests. The specific psychological test used will vary from police agency to police agency.

Psychological tests are written, visual, or verbal evaluations administered to assess the cognitive and emotional functioning of police applicants. More specifically, psychological tests are used to assess a variety of mental abilities and attributes, including achievement and ability, personality, and neurological functioning. Psychological tests used in police officer selection may include the Minnesota Multiphasic Personality Inventory (MMPI), California Personality Inventory (CPI), Rorschach inkblots, figure drawings, and sentence completion tests.

Of the variety of psychological tests used by police departments, the MMPI remains popular. The MMPI is a written psychological test used to diagnose mental disorders. It is also used to screen for personality and psychosocial disorders, as well as being administered as part of a neuropsychological test battery to evaluate cognitive functioning. The MMPI should always be used in conjunction with other psychological tests. Furthermore, all psychological testing should be administered and interpreted by a trained psychologist or psychiatrist.

Background Investigation

The background investigation is literally an investigation into an applicant's background. The background investigation provides a wealth of insight into the candidate's personal and professional life and may provide some of the most important indicators of job success (Moriarty & Field, 1994).

Background checks of applicants are one of the most effective tools available to assist in making correct hiring decisions. A properly conducted background investigation may take several months to complete. It should naturally be carried out toward the end of the selection process. The background investigation usually focuses on talking with the applicant's former employers, teachers, friends, family members, and other acquaintances, and the examination of military records, court records, information about the use of illegal substances, and other crime-related information. The background investigator should keep in mind that the best information about a candidate is references developed by the applicant's listed references. The background investigator should make it a point to ask references listed by the applicant for the names of other persons who are acquainted with the applicant.

Medical and Drug Screening

Medical and drug screening is one of the last assessment procedures in the selection process. Medical and drug screening is usually administered after a conditional offer of employment is made to the applicant. During the medical screening, a designated physician performs a physical examination of the applicant. A physical examination is used to ensure that the applicant has no underlying medical condition that would prevent or limit him or her from performing the essential functions of the police job.

Drug testing is usually conducted as part of the medical screening. Pre-employment drug testing has become a very common selection device for police employment. The Bureau of Justice Statistics reports that about 88 percent of local police departments use drug testing as a pre-employment selection requirement. The courts have consistently upheld the use of drug testing as a police selection tool. The entire police hiring process is depicted as a flow chart in Figure 1.2.

Figure 1.2   Police Hiring Process at a Glance

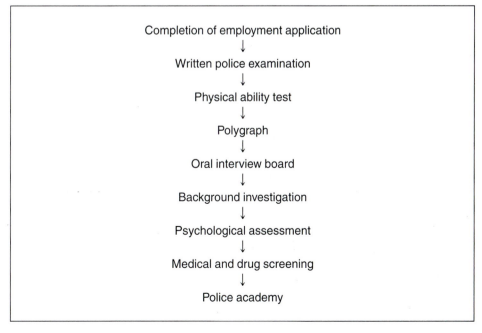

Note: The process is a multiple hurdle. Applicants are required to successfully complete one stage (hurdle) in order to proceed to the next stage.

TRAINING

After an applicant has successfully completed the selection process and is extended an offer of employment, he or she reports to the police academy for formal training. Next to the recruitment and selection of police officers, training is one of the most important functions of the police organization. It is through training that neophyte police officers learn the skills of policing. Training is also the process where veteran police officers learn new policing techniques and hone existing skills.

There are currently about 626 local and state police training academies operating in the United States (Hickman, 2004). Across all of these local and state academies, the median number of academy training hours required to become a certified law enforcement officer is 720 hours (Hickman, 2004). Police academy training across the United States is in no way uniform and varies in length and content. In some jurisdictions, police trainees attend the academy during the day and are allowed to go home in the evening, while in others the trainee may be required to physically stay at the academy for a number of weeks or months, similar to military basic training.

After a recruit graduates from the police academy most departments require that he or she successfully complete a field training program. Field training programs are designed to ease the transition of rookie police officers from the academy to the field. During the field training program, the officer is assigned to ride with a field training officer (FTO) for a specified period of time. One recent report indicated that the median number of hours for field training in U.S. police departments is 180 (Hickman, 2004). Field training officers are specially picked due to their exemplary performance and because of their willingness to work with new police officers. In most cases FTOs are required to complete specialized training.

Just because a recruit graduates from the academy and completes the FTO program doesn't mean his or her training is over. Many police agencies require a specified number of annual in-service training hours. In-service training is usually mandated by state law. The content of in-service training courses varies, but may include such courses as firearms refresher, use of force, defensive tactics, terrorism, hazardous materials, blood-borne pathogens, policy and procedure updates, community policing, problem-oriented policing, as well as any course which deals with new developments in the field.

SUMMARY

- Patrol operations are the backbone of a police department.
- The majority of a police department's personnel are assigned to the patrol function.
- Patrol in early English meant to walk or paddle in muddy water.
- Policing in the United States was heavily influenced by the London model of policing, which was the work of Sir Robert Peel. The police in London are called "Bobbies," named after their founder, Sir Robert Peel.
- "Hue and Cry" policing was the act of an individual who would alert the neighborhood to the recent commission of a crime, and sometimes entailed raising public support for pursuit or arrest of the criminal.
- In early U.S. history, policing was primarily done by volunteer citizens.
- The development of police patrol can best be framed on three major eras: (1) the Political Era, (2) the Reform Era, and (3) the Community Policing Era.

- The Political Era of policing was an era that was dominated by political control, or put another way, there were close ties between the police and politicians.

- The reform model of policing, or professional model as it is sometimes referred to, emphasized an organization indoctrinated along traditional lines—highly centralized, bureaucratic, and designed on the premise of divisions of labor and unity of control.

- The evolving community-oriented policing strategy represents a shift from more traditional law enforcement in that it focuses on prevention of crime and the fear of crime on a very local basis. Community policing also entails problem solving and organizational transformation.

- Patrol officers respond to a wide variety of crime and service-related calls on a daily basis. However, the vast majority of calls for police services are service related or noncriminal in nature.

- The primary purpose of police patrol is prevention and suppression of criminal activity.

- The police role in the prevention of crime involves many strategies. A few of these are neighborhood watch, National Night Out, proper training of landlords, and problem solving.

- The police patrol function ensures the safe flow and regulation of traffic. This responsibility includes not only the enforcement of traffic laws, such as speeding, directing traffic, enforcing driving under the influence laws, and vehicle equipment laws, but also includes the investigation of vehicle accidents.

- The police response to crime can best be divided into three distinct categories. The first is reactive policing, when a crime has been committed and the police respond and take a report. The second, proactive policing, is when the police attempt to prevent crime by being self-initiating or by establishing a crime prevention strategy. The third, coactive policing, involves the police working with other resources outside of the police departments to prevent and solve crime-related problems.

- Police departments are organized in a paramilitary fashion. There are usually three levels to a police department's management structure. The first is upper-level management, where typically you find the chief, assistant chief, and majors. The second level is middle management, which usually is made up of captains or lieutenants. The third level is line-level supervision, which consists of sergeants.

- The police operate under a chain of command with a clear unity of command. In other words, each police officer knows exactly who he or she answers to.

- In order to become a police officer one must go through a rigorous selection process. The selection process generally includes a written test, physical ability assessment, polygraph, oral interview, background investigation, psychological assessment, and medical and drug screening.

- Once a police applicant has successfully completed the selection process and is offered employment, he or she will report to the training academy where he or she will learn the craft of policing. Once formal academy training is completed, the new police officer is assigned to ride with a field training officer for a specified period of time.

- In-service training is post-recruit academy training that an officer receives throughout his or her career. Many states mandate that police officers receive a minimum number of hours of in-service training annually in order to retain their law enforcement certification.

Classroom Discussion Questions and Activities

1. Divide the class into three groups, one each to represent the Political Era, the Reform Era, and the Community Policing Era. Have each group discuss how police operations would have been conducted in their respective era.

2. Observe various television police episodes and have the students identify the circumstances where the police were being reactive, proactive, and coactive.

3. Identify an article in a newspaper where the police were engaging in some form of problem solving.

4. Identify a community problem and ask the students how they would solve the problem if they were a police officer.

Websites and Other Resources

Bureau of Justice Statistics Law Enforcement Statistics:
www.ojp.usdoj.gov/bjs/lawenf.htm

BJA Law Enforcement Training Database:
www.bjatraining.ncjrs.gov

Federal Law Enforcement Training Center:
www.fletc.gov

International Association of Chiefs of Police:
www.iacp.org

Police Executive Research Forum:
www.policeforum.org

National Sheriffs' Association:
www.sheriffs.org

National Neighborhood Watch Institute:
www.nnwi.org

National Night Out:
www.nationalnightout.org/nno

Offices of Community Oriented Policing Services:
www.cops.usdoj.gov

References

Bayley, D. H. (1994). *Police for the future*. New York: Oxford University Press.

Birzer, M. L. (1996). *Police supervision in the 21st Century. F.B.I. Law Enforcement Bulletin*. Washington, DC: U.S. Government Printing Office, 65, 5–11.

Bittner, E. (1974). Florence Nightingale in pursuit of Willie Sutton: A theory of the police. In H. Jacob (Ed.), *The potential for reform in criminal justice* (pp. 17–44). Beverly Hills, CA: Sage.

Boydstun, J. E., Sherry, M. E., & Moelter, N. P. (1977). *Patrol staffing in San Diego: One or two officer units*. Washington, DC: Police Foundation.

Bureau of Justice Statistics. (2003). *Local police departments 2003*. Retrieved June 7, 2006 from www.ojp.usdoj.gov/-bjs/pubalp2.htm#lpd.

Bureau of Justice Statistics, State and Local Law Enforcement Statistics. (2002). U.S. Department of Justice. Retrieved June 10, 2006 from www.oip.usdoj.gov.

Cahn, M. E., & Tien, J. M. (1981). *An alternative approach in police response: The Wilmington management of demand program*. Washington, DC: National Institute of Justice.

Carte, C. E., & Carte, E. H. (1975). *Police reform in the United States: An era of August Vollmer*. Berkeley, CA: University of California Press.

Commission on Accreditation for Law Enforcement Agencies. (2006). *Standards for law enforcement agencies* (5th ed.). Fairfax, VA: CALEA.

Cordner, G. W., & Sheehan, R. S. (1999). *Police administration* (4th ed.). Cincinnati, OH: Anderson Publishing.

Crank, J. P. (1998). *Understanding police culture*. Cincinnati, OH: Anderson Publishing.

Critchley, T. A. (1772). *A history of police in England and Wales* (*2nd ed.*). Montclair, NJ: Patterson Smith.

Fogelson, R. (1977). *Big city police*. Cambridge: Harvard University Press.

Geller, W. (1991). *Local government police management* (3rd ed.). Washington, DC: International City Managers Association, 275.

Goldstein, H. (1977). *Policing a free society*. Cambridge, MA: Ballinger.

Hale, C. D. (1982). *Patrol administration, local government police management*. Washington, DC: U.S. Government Printing Office, 115.

Haller, M. (1976). Historical roots of police behavior: Chicago 1890–1925. *Law and Society Review, 10*, 303–333.

Hickman, M. J. (2004). *State and local law enforcement training academies, 2002*. Washington, DC: Bureau of Justice Statistics.

Hickman, M. J., & Reaves, B. A. (2003*). State and local police departments, 2003*. Washington, DC: U.S. Department of Justice.

Iannone, N. F., & Iannone, M. P. (2001). *Supervision of police personnel* (6th ed.). Upper Saddle River, NJ: Prentice Hall.

Kelling, G. L. (1987). *Foot patrol*. Washington, DC: National Institute of Justice.

Kelling, G. L., & Bratton, W. J. (1993). *Implementing community policing: The administrative problem*. Washington, DC: National Institute of Justice.

Kelling, G. L., Pate, T., Dieckman, T., & Brown, C. E. (1974). *The Kansas City preventive patrol experiment: A summary report*. Washington, DC: Police Foundation.

Lagrange, R. L. (1993). *Policing American society*. Chicago: Nelson-Hall.

Lonsway, K. A. (2003). Tearing down the wall: Problems with consistency, validity, and adverse impact of physical agility testing in police selection. *Police Quarterly, 6*, 237–277.

McKenna, P. F. (1998). *Foundations of policing in Canada*. Scarborough, Ontario: Prentice Hall.

Morrison, K., & Jacob, B. (2000). Speed detection: From mounted to laser technology. *Police Chief, 67*, 42–46.

Moriarty, A. R., & Field, M. R. (1994). *Police officer selection.* Springfield, IL: Charles C. Thomas, Publisher.

National Highway Traffic Safety Administration. (2002). *Traffic safety facts: Speeding.* Retrieved June 12, 2006 from www.nhtsa.dot.gov.

New York State, Department of Motor Vehicles. (2006). *New York City accident data, 2003.* Retrieved June 12, 2006 from www.nydmv.state.ny.us/index.htm.

Office of Community Oriented Policing Services. (2004). *The cops mission.* Retrieved June 12, 2006 from www.cops.usdoj.gov.

Reaves, B. A., & Hickman, M. J. (2000). *Law enforcement management and administrative statistics, 2000: Data for individual state and local agencies with 100 or more officers.* Washington, DC: U.S. Department of Justice.

Reaves. B. A., & Hickman, M. J. (2002). *Bureau of justice statistics, Census of state and local law enforcement.* Washington, DC: U.S. Department of Justice.

Reith, C. (1952). *The blind eye of history.* London: Faber and Faber, p. 154.

San Diego Police Department. (2006). *Community resources and responsibilities: Neighborhood nuisance program.* The City of San Diego Police Departments. Retrieved June 11, 2006 from www.sandiego.gov/police/prevention.

Saunders, C. B. J. (1970). *Upgrading the American police.* Washington, DC: Brookings Institute.

Scott, E. J. (1981). *Calls for service: Citizen demand for initial police response.* Washington, DC: U.S. Government Printing Office, 28–30.

Sherman, L. W. (1996). Police in the laboratory of criminal justice. In G. W. Cordner, L. K. Gaines, & V. E. Kappeler (Eds.), *Police operations: Analysis and evaluation* (pp. 27–50). Cincinnati, OH: Anderson Publishing.

Skolnick, J., & Bayley, D. H. (1986). *The new blue line.* New York: The Free Press.

Sweeney, T. J. (2003). Patrol. In W. A. Geller & D. W. Stephens (Eds.), *Local government police management* (pp. 89–133). Washington, DC: International City Managers Association.

Walker, S. (1998). *The police in America: An introduction.* Boston: McGraw Hill.

Weber, M. (1947). *The theory of social and economic organization.* New York: Oxford University.

Webster, J. A. (1970). Police task and time study. *The Journal of Criminal Law and Criminology, 61*, 94–100. Retrieved June 8, 2006 from Sociological Abstracts database.

Whitaker, G. P. (1982). What is patrol work? *Police Studies, 4*, 13–22.

Wilson, O. W., & McLaren, R. C. (1977). *Police administration* (4th ed.). New York: McGraw Hill.

Chapter 2

Police Field Procedures

" They [the police] have the ability to take a person's freedom from them. In certain situations, they have the ability to take a person's reputation. And under certain circumstances, they have the authority to take a person's life. "

—Daryl Gates, Chief of Police, Retired, Los Angeles Police Department

CHAPTER OUTLINE

- ■ Introduction
- ■ Preparing for the Tour of Duty
- ■ Patrolling the Beat
- ■ Handling Offenders
- ■ Civil Unrest
- ■ High-Speed Pursuits
- ■ Weather and Natural Disasters
- ■ The Police Canine
- ■ Traffic Stops
- ■ Emergency Vehicle Operation
- ■ The Use of Force
- ■ Summary

OBJECTIVES

After completion of this chapter, you will be able to do the following:

- Describe what is involved in preparation for patrol.
- Understand the serious nature of police stress and burnout.
- Describe important factors that go into effective beat management.
- Identify officer safety factor issues when handling offenders.
- Define positional asphyxia and restraint asphyxia.
- Discuss the police response to social unrest.
- Discuss research conclusions centering on police pursuits.
- Provide a general overview of police pursuit procedures.
- Identify factors that need to be considered when responding to a weather or natural disaster.
- Identify the advantages of using trained police canines in police operations.
- Discuss police procedures when making a traffic stop.
- Discuss factors that go into police emergency response "code three" mode.
- Discuss the use of force continuum.

INTRODUCTION

Imagine for a moment that you are enrolled in a college course titled "Police Operations." To successfully complete the course, your professor requires that students do a ride along with a police officer for an eight-hour shift and then write a reflection paper on their experience. In order to meet this requirement you set up a ride along for second shift on a Friday evening. You purposely selected Friday evening because you think the chances are good that you will see some action.

It is 5:00 P.M. on Friday evening and you are about two hours into the eight-hour ride along. So far, it has been relatively quiet and you have only taken a few calls. One call involved a citizen who found a bicycle, and the other call was a burglary report. After these calls the officer spent thirty minutes completing paperwork and talking on the phone with the records section doing what he called "cutting the cases." The officer you are riding with asks you where you would like to eat dinner when suddenly you hear the voice of an excited officer over the police radio: "Number ninety-two, I am in pursuit of a vehicle traveling at a high rate of speed." The dispatcher's voice asks the officer for his location. The officer replies, "Ninety-two, we are south bound in the

4700 block of Broadway." You excitedly look at the officer you are riding with and are let down almost immediately. The officer explains that the pursuing officer is on the other side of the city, which means that you won't be in on the excitement, you will have to settle for listening to the pursuit on the police radio.

Suddenly you hear the supervisor's voice with a distinct sound of authority and control come across the police radio. The supervisor asks the pursuing officer, "What are the charges?" The pursuing officer responds, "Traffic." Then, the officer's voice comes across the radio: "Number ninety-two, he is not stopping. I am still in pursuit." The supervisor asks the dispatcher if the air section is available. The dispatcher's voice responds with "Negative." Another officer's voice comes over the radio: "Unit 292, I am in secondary pursuit position."

The supervisor's voice is heard over the radio again, as he asks the pursuing unit, "Can you identify the driver and do you have a good tag number?" The pursuing officer relays, "that's 10-4." After several seconds, the supervisor advises the dispatcher to call off the chase. Suddenly there is a loud tone emitted over the police radio and the dispatcher's voice loudly proclaims, "Attention all units—disregard the chase authority of Sergeant Harris." The dispatcher repeats the command: "Attention all units—disregard the chase authority of Sergeant Harris." This whole ordeal occurs in less than two minutes.

standard operating proce-dure / A written and codified manual of a police organization. The *Standard Operating Procedure Manual* is a roadmap that assists police officers in the field as a guide.

What did all this mean? Why did the supervisor ask if the air section was available? What did the officer mean when he said that he was the secondary pursuing officer? Why did the supervisor ask if the officer could identify the driver, and, more importantly, why did the supervisor call off the chase? Shouldn't the police pursue the violator with zeal? The short answer to these questions is that the officers and the supervisor were following **standard operating procedure**. Note that the concept

Voices of Experience

An Active Traffic Enforcement Program

Excerpts from an interview between Cliff Roberson and former police officer, Robert Boyer. Boyer is currently a professor of criminal justice at Luzerne County Community College, Nanticoke, Pennsylvania. Professor Boyer continues to work as a part-time police officer in Pennsylvania. In addition, he is the mayor of Wyoming, Pennsylvania.

Q: *What are the benefits of an active traffic enforcement program?*
A: It has a positive influence on crime concerns. Traffic enforcement programs are not designed to collect revenues. They are designed to prevent crime and save lives. They help intercept wanted individuals, detect stolen vehicles, prevent drug trafficking, and reduces accidents and protects lives. An active program includes monitoring traffic near schools during certain times and monitoring traffic on the heavily traveled highways. Just by monitoring traffic, we have discovered large quantities of drugs, etc. For example, once a red-light violation led us to the confiscation of an ice cooler full of cocaine in the back of a pick-up. We use directed patrols to decide where to monitor the traffic. This is done by charting the traffic problem areas and concentrating on those areas. ■

of standard operating procedure was taken from the Navy and originally was called *standing operating procedure*.

Standard operating procedures (SOPs) are prescribed procedures that police officers follow as a matter of routine. Put another way, standard operating procedures are established police procedures to be followed when carrying out a police operation. In almost every situation that the police are involved in while on patrol, there is a standard operating procedure to be followed. For every burglary in progress call, every armed robbery in progress, every suspicious character call, every shooting call, and every police pursuit, there is a standard operation procedure that directs and guides police officer reaction.

In addition to standard operating procedures, there were specific factors that the supervisor considered and weighed in making the decision to call off the chase. These factors included the time of day, which was about 5:00 P.M., which means heavy rush hour traffic; the fact that the charges were traffic; and the fact that the officer could identify the driver of the vehicle. We will discuss other related factors to be considered in pursuits later in the chapter.

This chapter presents an overview of basic police field procedures in specific situations. It would be virtually impossible to discuss every possible field procedure. What is accomplished in the following pages is an overview of a few of the more common situations encountered on patrol, as well as some of the more uncommon situations encountered. While it is recognized that some of the field procedures will vary depending on the police agency, generally the field procedures discussed in this chapter are standard police practice. The content of this chapter is broad to allow direction for a police agency that may be writing SOPs or simply updating existing SOPs. The material in this chapter will be informative to both police practitioners and students.

PREPARING FOR THE TOUR OF DUTY

Personal Preparation

Officer Smith is a five-year veteran of the police department. He has been assigned to third watch patrol for the entire five years, with the exception of a brief four-month assignment at the police academy to assist with a recruit class. Officer Smith is driving home at 8:00 A.M. from the police station after an eight-hour patrol shift because he works the graveyard shift, 11:00 P.M. to 7:00 A.M. His shift had been relatively uneventful other than several radio calls and a couple of traffic stops, one of which resulted in an arrest for driving under the influence. Officer Smith is so tired that he drags himself down the sidewalk to his apartment and opens the door only to hear the telephone ringing. He answers the telephone and is informed by the court liaison officer that a case is going to trial that he was involved in two years ago, and that he is needed to testify and should report to the courthouse as soon as possible.

Officer Smith arrives at the courtroom and is advised by the prosecutor that he will be called to testify within the next hour and to read over his police report. Officer Smith begins to read the report when he feels his eyes begin to get heavy; he thinks to himself, "I am so tired." One hour turns into two hours, and then three hours. The prosecutor finally makes contact with Officer Smith and informs him that another witness's testimony is taking longer than expected and that he should go and grab some lunch and be back by 1:30 P.M. Officer Smith leaves the courthouse and grabs some lunch. He reports back to the courtroom at 1:30 P.M. and is once again told that he will be called to testify shortly. Finally, at 2:15 P.M. he is called to testify. His testimony takes about forty minutes.

As Officer Smith is driving from the courthouse back to his apartment he fights to keep his eyes open. He finally arrives at his apartment at 3:30 P.M. It's been nearly twenty-three hours since he last slept. Officer Smith is only able to take a three-hour nap because he is scheduled to be at his part-time job as a store security officer at 7:00 P.M. He works at the part-time job until 10:00 P.M., at which time he leaves to head to the police station for the 10:45 P.M. squad meeting. By this time Officer Smith is surviving only on caffeine. He thinks to himself, "If I can make it through the patrol shift I can get a full day's sleep tomorrow."

This story is all too real. Police officers are challenged daily with how to work their normal patrol shift, make court appearances, spend quality time with their families, and work off-duty security jobs simply to make ends meet, and doing so while remaining both mentally and physically prepared for the worst event that could happen during a patrol shift. Simply put, police officers must be prepared for the unexpected at all times. The job of police officer is perplexing and stressful, but yet one of the most rewarding jobs. It is a job that from day-to-day may bring something different. At times the job can be boring, while other times it can be full of excitement. On one day it may be quiet with minimal radio calls, while the next day the officer may be so busy that he or she does not have time for a break.

It is crucial that police officers be mentally and physically prepared for patrol duty. The costs of not being prepared can be grave. The very nature of police work can mean that the officer can spend many mundane working hours, and then suddenly be faced with a crime in progress call, a serious automobile accident, or a high-speed pursuit. Thus, the officer has to always be prepared and ready to act on a second's notice. So, how does a police officer mentally and physically prepare for patrol duty?

If the officer feels that he or she is overly tired and not very alert, the officer may want to make an attempt to get a few minutes of brisk exercise before the shift. You are probably thinking, why exercise if you are overly tired? Exercise can actually recharge the officer for a few hours. The exercise does not have to be strenuous, just brisk. It may be that the officer can only get a ten- or twenty-minute walk in before the shift. If the police gymnasium is located at a close distance to the squad room, the officer can jump on the treadmill for a few minutes. Walking can actually decrease the risk of mental impairment and help prepare the officer for the patrol shift. The advantage to walking is that it is a simple exercise that can be done anywhere, at any time. During the shift, the officer can park the patrol car and get out and walk around for a few minutes several times throughout the shift. By participating in regular walking, the long-term health implications of stress may be offset. Research has linked stress to a host of physical ills, from back pain and stomach upset to high blood pressure and heart disease (Spilner, 2000). Sometimes the officer has to remind himself or herself that taking a walk will help in accomplishing more on the to-do list. A brief walk will make the officer feel better and be able to think more clearly, so he or she will become more productive.

It is important that an officer's personal appearance and hygiene be impeccable prior to reporting for duty, so time and attention should be given to ensure a

SWAT officer standing beside display table allows smiling teen boy to try on bulletproof vest at Police Neighborhood Festival, Hollywood, CA. The officer is attempting to build trust in the police as part of community policing tactics.

proper appearance. The officer should take a few moments to ensure that his or her uniform and equipment are in proper order and in compliance with departmental regulations. This includes checking to make sure that shoes are shined, the uniform is clean and pressed, handcuffs are working correctly, the field notebook is organized and in the pocket, extra ammunition is accounted for and affixed to the gun belt, the gun belt is clean and in good condition, and the firearm is ready for duty. Good appearance projects a positive image not only on the individual police officer, but also on the police department. An officer's appearance has the potential to leave a lasting impression on the citizenry. It has long been said that a good appearance commands respect.

Body armor is a vital piece of police equipment. If the officer has been issued body armor (bulletproof vest) it is imperative that he or she wear it. According to a report by the Bureau of Justice Statistics, 71 percent of local police departments, employing 74 percent of all officers, require field officers to wear protective body armor at least some of the time while on duty. Fifty-nine percent of departments, employing 59 percent of all officers, require field officers to wear body armor at all times while on duty. Twelve percent of departments, employing 15 percent of officers, require officers to wear body armor in certain high-risk circumstances, such as when serving warrants (Hickman & Reaves, 2003).

The police officer must ensure that all equipment is ready for duty. Think of it this way: An aircraft mechanic would never think of approaching his or her work without the best tools available, all in good operating order. The same should hold true for a police officer. Would you fly on an airplane across the country if you knew the aircraft mechanic that just serviced the aircraft did so with tools that were in poor condition? A police officer should never approach his or her work without his or her equipment being in nothing but the best operating order. The officer's safety, the safety of other officers, and the safety of the general public are dependent upon this.

The following headlines from the *New York Times* provide good reasons why police officers should wear body armor.

■ A Newark police officer was saved by his bulletproof vest last night when he was shot in the chest during a scuffle with two men in the city's South Ward. Officer William Conley, 34, suffered broken ribs in the shooting and was in good condition at University Hospital.

(*New York Times*, November 21, 1996, Late Edition, Section B, Page 8)

■ A plainclothes narcotics detective wearing a bulletproof vest survived being shot once in the chest and twice in the stomach at point-blank range yesterday morning and wrestled the gunman to the ground after a routine drug bust in the Bronx turned violent, the police said.

(*New York Times*, December 30, 1997, Late Edition, Section B, Page 1)

■ Scores of detectives and police officers went door to door through housing projects in Brooklyn yesterday in an intense manhunt for the sniper who shot a detective assigned to an anti-drug crackdown in Brownsville. The detective was saved by his bulletproof vest.

(*New York Times*, August 8, 1996, Late Edition, Section B, Page 4, Column 1)

■ A New York City police officer was shot twice in the chest at point-blank range yesterday evening but was saved by his bulletproof vest. The officer, Keith Schweers, 26, of the 113th Precinct in Jamaica, Queens, was on scooter patrol in Jamaica about 5:15 P.M. when he saw a man "acting suspiciously" on 110th Avenue and 157th Street, Commissioner William J. Bratton said.

(*New York Times*, October 31, 1995, Late Edition—Final, Section B, Page 3)

■ An undercover police officer was shot in the chest last night in Queens, but narrowly escaped serious injury because of his bulletproof vest, the police said. The officer, Richard Anderson, 26, was being treated last night for trauma at Elmhurst Hospital Center, the police said

(*New York Times*, August 9, 1995, Late Edition—Final, Section B, Page 3)

■ A 38-year-old police officer who was chasing a drug suspect in East New York, Brooklyn, was shot in the ribs yesterday, but the bullet was stopped by a protective shield sewn into the officer's denim jacket, the police said. The officer, Jacob Brown, a nine-year veteran of the force, was in good condition last night at Jamaica Hospital.

(*New York Times*, November 16, 1994, Late Edition—Final, Section B, Page 5)

---

cynicism / A modern cynic typically has a highly skeptical attitude toward social norms. In policing, officers may become cynical of the ritualistic purpose of police work and will tend to question the validity of a substantial proportion of beliefs, policies and procedures, and rules and regulations. Cynicism can affect the officer's productivity and impact the morale of other police officers.

An officer should try to project a positive attitude in everything he or she does while in uniform. Admittedly, this can be challenging in light of the fact that police officers see human beings at their worst, whether it is a criminal suspect or a victim of a brutal crime. Seeing human despair on a regular basis can affect an officer's attitudes and emotions. It is dangerous for an officer to allow his or her attitude to influence their actions. The majority of the citizenry that the police officer comes into contact with during a tour of patrol duty are law-abiding citizens who for the most part support the police.

Over time, police officers may begin to exhibit **cynicism**, especially those police officers who work in areas that have a disproportionate amount of crime. It is very easy when the officer sees so much crime on a daily basis to become cynical and develop an attitude problem. This problem is sometimes compounded with internal stressors within the police department. There are many anecdotal accounts from police officers relating that they are never really bothered from the stress of police duties in the field, it's the internal stressors within the department that become bothersome. Supervisors should be watchful for signs that an officer is developing a bad attitude toward the citizenry or other officers because this may lead to more serious problems. This may also be a sign that the officer is experiencing an excessive amount of stress and early intervention may be useful.

Excessive job stress and burnout can result from personal frustration and inadequate coping skills. **Burnout** is a psychological condition that is also referred to as *burnout stress syndrome*. Burnout has been found to be involved in a number of conditions, including physical, emotional, spiritual, intellectual, and interpersonal exhaustion (Iannone & Iannone, 2006). Police officers can minimize some of the results of stress by proper mental and physical preparation for police duties.

burnout / Job burnout is a form of stress that police officers may suffer to some degree at various times in their career. Burnout becomes critical when an officer is distressed and begins to feel fatigued and frustrated every day with no relief. In police culture, burnout is sometimes mistaken for an attitude problem.

PRACTICE HINTS

Police Stress and Burnout

1. Recognize burnout as a process that is ongoing. It does not happen overnight and you cannot always pinpoint its exact cause. Burnout happens over time and results from many factors.
2. Are there indicators of burnout that can be seen? Consider the physical, emotional, and social parts of life in respect to work burnout. Are any out of balance in your job? Is your body reacting to symptoms in these areas?
3. Get involved in physical activity. This can serve to be a healthy release for an overworked police officer. Regular walking is a good example. It allows your body to release tension through muscle activity.
4. Relaxation skills provide a sense of well-being. Sit in a comfortable chair. Think about relaxing muscles in your face, neck, and shoulders. Take a deep breath, hold it three seconds, then blow the breath out. Repeat several times. Relaxation techniques can give you renewed energy for the rest of the day.
5. Reconsider your work goals and life priorities. Did you set these goals when you were young and inexperienced? Have you updated them? Are they realistic goals? Have you pushed or stretched yourself too far? Have you set yourself up for failure? Changing goals is not always lowering standards—it's adjustment. Each day have goals that are reasonable. Share your goals with someone else.
6. Step back and try to look at your job from an outsider's point of view. Imagine how others might handle your responsibilities.

Source: Adapted from the American Institute for Preventive Medicine, 2001.

Other Preparation

In most police departments, preparation for duty begins with a squad meeting, or roll call, as it is sometimes called. The squad meeting is usually held fifteen to thirty minutes prior to the initiation of the patrol shift. Either the shift sergeant or the watch commander facilitates the squad meeting. While the actual content of the squad meeting may vary depending on the individual police agency, it is not uncommon that officers are debriefed regarding the most significant crime-related events and any unusual occurrences during the previous shift. Officers may also be informed of wanted persons that have been spotted in the district or community. In some departments this information is read from what is referred to as the "inner watch." The inner watch is a document that is prepared before each shift and details significant crime events that occurred over the last few shifts. In an effort to minimize paper, many police departments have begun to place the inner watch and other bulletins online so that the shift supervisor has electronic access to these announcements. In those departments that are technologically advanced, police officers themselves would have electronic access to the inner watch and other departmental-related information.

In some cases the shift sergeant may hold periodic inspections of police officers in order to ensure that their equipment is functioning properly and that grooming standards are within **departmental regulations**. An officer who has defective equipment may not be allowed to begin the patrol watch until the equipment has been repaired or replaced. Likewise, an officer with a uniform that looks in extreme disarray or is stained from last night's coffee may be asked by the supervisor to change into a clean and pressed uniform before beginning patrol duties.

departmental regulations / Police department regulations govern the conditions of police service, annual leave, overtime, promotion, and have an influence on almost all daily police activities. Departmental regulations are usually broader and cover internal matters, such as dress and grooming standards, when compared with standard operating procedures which focus more on field procedures.

Police officers should also communicate with the officer whom they are relieving on the previous shift. This provides police officers the opportunity to exchange information about any potential problems that the officer may experience during the forthcoming shift. For example, suppose that the second watch officer responded to the same loud party twice during his shift. The officer should communicate this information to the oncoming third-shift officer. If the third-shift officer receives a call of a loud party at this same location, he or she may take a different course of action. As opposed to giving a verbal warning to the party goers to keep the noise down, the officer, having knowledge that the second watch officer made two calls to the location, may be more inclined to issue a formal citation for the loud music or close the party down. It is also important to note that with sophisticated computer-aided dispatch technology the police officer has the ability to query the computer for calls at specific locations during previous shifts. In order to properly prepare for patrol duty, the officer should make an effort to know what has occurred on the beat during the previous shift.

Prior to beginning patrol duties it is important that the officer conduct an inspection of the police car. The officer should ensure that the emergency lights and siren are working properly. This may require that the officer briefly test them before leaving the police motor pool or the parking lot. Does the patrol car's engine seem to be running well? Is there any maintenance that is overdue that may be critical to the performance of the patrol car during the next shift? Are the tires on the patrol car properly inflated and does the tread look good?

All equipment carried in the patrol car should also be inspected. Such equipment may include, but not be limited to, a traffic accident investigation kit, traffic stop spikes, police report forms, traffic cones and flares, gas mask, protective riot helmet, bull horn, first aid kit, equipment used to investigate crime scenes, and any additional firearms and ammunition carried in the patrol unit. Finally, if the police car is dirty, it should be washed before it is put into service. Many police departments have a car wash which allows the officer to do a quick wash of the vehicle, while other departments contract with a car wash business in the community.

PATROLLING THE BEAT

After a police officer attends the squad meeting, he or she proceeds to the beat. As you will recall, a **beat** is the geographical area that a police officer is assigned for purposes of police patrol. The officer should be nonroutine when traveling to his or her beat. In other words, it is sound police practice to alternate the route that is traveled to the beat each day. This is important in the event that someone is trying to learn the police officer's habits.

beat / A geographical area of responsibility for a police patrol officer during a tour of duty. A beat is sometimes referred to as a response area or response zone.

Police patrol officers have an enormous amount of responsibly. Typically, Hollywood's portrayal of the officer on the beat is almost always glamorous crime-fighting

Voices of Experience

Patrol Officer

Excerpts from an interview between Cliff Roberson and retired police officer, John Hill, who is now an associate professor at Salt Lake Community College, Salt Lake City, Utah.

Q: *You have stated that you enjoyed your assignments as a patrol officer. Why?*

A: Even though there were quiet times, when you went to work each day, you never knew what action you were going to be involved in. Now, as a college faculty member, I know what I'm going to do each day. Patrolling was a challenge and was not routine. Most of our patrols were in our vehicles, but frequently we would park our vehicles and do a "park and walk" patrol, especially at malls and other public places.

As a patrol officer you were assigned a district and that district was yours. You handled everything that came in from that district. It gives you a sense of responsibility. Often you would need help from other officers, especially when there was a major crime in the district. You developed a sense of protection for that district. Often on the way home from the station I would go out of the way to drive through the district. You get to know the people and businesses in your district. Many people would think that would make your job harder to enforce the law in that district, but it actually made it easier and the citizens often assisted you in solving crimes once they got to trust you. In our department most of our patrols were single officer patrols. Sometimes there would be "manpower cars" that were available to assist the officer.

A typical day started before 8:00 A.M., 4:00 P.M., or 12 midnight; changing weekly when we would attend roll call to be briefed. If there were no pending calls, I would take a tour of the district. At roll call, you would be advised if something happened in your district since your last shift. The most aggravating situation would be when you came to work and the calls were backed up. You would make the calls and some people would be upset because they had been waiting for hours after their call. I would explain to them that I had just come on duty and that the prior shift was overloaded with calls. When there were calls stacked up often you would feel that the prior shift had been a little lazy and shifted the calls to you. It would be a better shift if you came out of roll call with no calls. Then you arrange your day to provide the best service to the district.

Most of our calls were dispatched by radio, later we had a computer in the vehicle and we received dispatches from it. While driving around on patrol I would normally be looking for anything out of the ordinary. You develop a sixth sense regarding what is not normal. You spend a lot of time talking to people. Someone riding with you may think you are wasting time, but I found that talking to people and building a sense of trust helped in the long run. ■

duties. The fact of the matter is that police officers perform a number of other vital responsibilities in addition to crime fighting. We review a few of these responsibilities in the following pages.

Knowledge of Persons

Police officers should be aware of persons who may pose potential criminal problems on their beats. The officer should always be aware of persons who have recently been released from prison, returned to the community, and are specifically residing on their beat. The Department of Corrections in most states notifies law enforcement agencies of upcoming prison releases that will be returning to the community. Police officers should make a point to keep track of parolees and others who have been recently released from prison and are living on the officer's beat. It is also a good idea to be conscious of registered sex offenders living on the beats. Police officers and the general public have access to registered sex offenders, usually through their state investigations agency's website and through the National Sex Offenders Data Base, which is maintained by the U.S. Department of Justice.

Police officers should get to know neighborhood watch coordinators, neighborhood association leaders, convenience store clerks, service station workers, the metropolitan local paper delivery persons, bar and club owners, local ministers or church leaders, the directors of youth clubs in the area, and school teachers and principals. All of these persons have the potential of making the police officer's job much easier by providing information on persons, places, or things. For example, you may ask why it is necessary for a police officer to establish a rapport with the metropolitan newspaper delivery person. Like the police officer, the newspaper delivery person delivers newspapers day after day in the same neighborhood. Thus, he or she gets to know things that are out of place. The newspaper delivery person typically delivers the newspaper at the earliest hours of the morning, when there is relatively minimal movement of traffic or people in neighborhoods. The newspaper delivery person may see a car leaving a neighborhood where a burglary or some other crime was just committed, or see a vehicle that looks out of place or suspicious. Many times the potential eyes and ears of the newspaper delivery person go untapped simply because the police officer doesn't make an effort to contact him or her and establish a rapport.

Police officers should be on the alert for suspicious acting persons on their beats, especially persons acting in a suspicious manner around businesses. It could be that a person's suspicious activity is for the purpose of casing a business or residence for a robbery or burglary. When an officer stops a suspicious person, he or she should check to ensure that the suspicious person does not have a **warrant** that has been issued for his or her arrest. The officer should complete a field interview card or enter the pertinent information on the suspicious character via the officer's laptop computer. Laptop computers are installed in many police vehicles. A recent Bureau of Justice Statistics study found that 83 percent of local police officers and 81 percent of sheriffs' officers worked for an agency that used in-field computers or terminals (Hickman & Reaves, 2003, p. 14).

Police officers should talk to as many people as possible during a shift. If possible, the police officer should try and contact as many potential offenders as possible during a patrol shift. The officer working the same area day after day should know

warrant / A writ or judicial order issued by a court of law directing a law enforcing officer to arrest or seize a specifically named person, or to search a specific known location for fruits or instrumentalities of a crime.

who is up to what, and who he or she must keep an eye on. If an officer stops a suspicious person and decides to do a brief **field interview**, legal guidelines and specific departmental policy should be followed. A field interview is a brief interview that a police officer conducts with a suspicious person. The field interview card or form which is completed usually captures such information as the name and physical description of the person, the time and date of the contact, and what explanation the person gave the officers for being in the area. If a number of burglaries or other crimes occur in the area, the investigators can query the field interviews that were conducted in the area and may potentially develop a suspect based on an observant officer who took a few extra minutes to complete the field interview card or form.

Because of the importance of protecting the safety of police officers during a field interview, the Court held in the *Terry v. Ohio* decision that when the police stop a person, they have the ability to conduct a quick surface search of the person's outer clothing for weapons. This is allowed if the officer has a reasonable suspicion that the person who has been stopped is armed and dangerous. This police action is commonly referred to as a "*Terry* stop." We discuss this in greater detail in Chapter 6.

Casual conversations with citizens are a critical law enforcement function. Actions such as knock and talk, conversing with persons in public, and other similar actions are encouraged but must end when the person indicates a desire to end the contact, and the officer has no reason to detain the person under applicable legal authority. Officers must recognize that perception can create community dissension as quickly as reality. Therefore, officers must take all reasonable steps to prevent giving a perception of stopping citizens without legal basis or in violation of their specific department policy. Likewise, creating an appearance that the person stopped is suspected of grievous conduct when no such reason exists is not a sound police practice. For example, an officer stops a person for a minor violation and more officers are present at the scene than necessary to safely complete the law enforcement business at hand. It must be remembered at all times that courtesy and respect toward all persons stopped and contacted by the police is critical to assure positive community impact and to minimize misperceptions about the purpose of the stop.

Inspection of Places

While it is important that police officers on patrol be aware of suspicious persons, it is equally important that they make a whole-hearted effort to inspect problem locations or potential problem locations. This may be as simple as inspecting a vacant house that could become a haven for idle youth. Likewise, abandoned buildings and other structures should be inspected on a periodic basis for vandalism and other illegal activities, and to ensure that homeless populations have not taken up refuge.

Adult entertainment establishments and bars located on the beat should also be inspected. Police officers will readily admit that some of these types of establishments are gathering spots for unsavory persons and for criminal activity involving prostitution and drugs. The periodic police presence in these establishments may deter certain criminal activities. Upon inspection of an adult entertainment establishment or bar, the officer should remain professional at all times. Patrons that look underage should be checked. The liquor license should be inspected to ensure that it is up-to-date and conspicuously hung, if this is the legal requirement. The police

field interview / A police practice of stopping a person and demanding an explanation of why that person is in a certain place at a particular time. This information is usually recorded on a field interview card and indexed for intelligence purposes.

should never give the impression that they are simply there to harass the club employees or patrons. Likewise, they should never accept any food, drinks, or other gratuities from any employee or owner of these establishments. This can backfire on the officer quickly, particularly if for some reason the officer upsets the club owner. For example, the club owner may take it upon himself to call internal affairs and report that the police officer has been taking free drinks and food from the club, and is getting very friendly with a few of the dancers.

There are many other locations that should be inspected by police patrol on a regular basis. These include, but are not limited to, buildings under construction, shipping docks, amusement parks, pool halls, pawnshops, and game arcades and parks that are known for mischievous activity. The surveillance of potential traffic hazards at major intersections should be done on a fairly routine basis. This may involve reporting a stop sign that is missing from an intersection or reporting a traffic signal light that is malfunctioning. Officers should make it a point to check businesses and other buildings after hours. Parking the patrol car and physically walking around the building checking windows and doors is a good way to do this, while at the same time getting a little exercise that will help the officer stay alert. This is especially important for those officers working third shift, or the midnight shift, as it is sometimes called.

The Beat Management Test

Police officers should ponder the following questions. Knowing the answers may significantly assist the officer in more effectively managing his or her beat.

1. What is the square mileage of your beat?
2. How many businesses (grocery stores, bars, adult entertainment establishments, game arcades, pool halls, etc.) are on your beat?
3. What's the name of one attendant who works at a gas station that is located on your beat?
4. What's the name of the newspaper carrier on your beat?
5. Where is the nearest fire station located?
6. Where is the nearest hospital located?
7. When does the neighborhood watch group(s) meet?
8. What's the name of the neighborhood watch coordinator(s) on your beat? Where do they live? How would you contact them?
9. How many burglaries occurred on your beat last month?
10. If there is a school located on your beat, what's the principal's name?
11. What is the median income level of residents living on your beat?
12. What are the racial characteristics of residents living on your beat?
13. What's the drive time from one side of your beat to the other during heavy traffic?
14. What's the name of one clerk working in a convenience store that is located on your beat?
15. If your beat has an active neighborhood association, who is the contact?
16. How many registered sex offenders live on your beat?
17. What are the most significant crime problems on your beat? Can you back this up with data?
18. Do you have any informants who you could turn to for information about criminal activity specifically occurring on your beat?
19. What are the most significant concerns of residents living on your beat?
20. When was the last time you parked the patrol car during down time and walked around a few neighborhoods talking with citizens?
21. If you have churches or places of worship located on your beat, do you know the name of one priest or minister serving the residents?

Answering Crime Calls

Obviously, a priority of the police is to answer crime calls. Crime calls can typically be divided into two categories: crimes in progress and crimes that have already occurred that the police respond to in order to take a report. One study found that the police spend about 29.1 percent of their time answering crime incidents (Mastrofski, 1983). This study found that of the 29.1 percent of crime incidents, only 3 percent involved violent crime; 15 percent involved nonviolent crime; 1.3 percent involved morals crimes, such as gambling, prostitution, obscene behavior, and pornography; and about 9.8 percent were suspicious circumstances, such as prowlers, gunshots, screams, suspicious persons, and the like.

Depending on the nature of the crime, the manner in which police respond may vary. For example, an armed robbery call almost always results in several officers being dispatched to respond. This is also the case for a burglary in progress or any other crime that is "in progress."

In some calls to crimes in progress, the agency's standard operating procedure provides guidance to the police response. For example, in a call to a robbery in progress, some agencies' standard operating procedures dictate that the officer whose beat the armed robbery originates on will use a weapon, such as the police riot shotgun or some other long rifle as the primary weapon, while other responding officers would use their side firearms as the primary weapon.

After receiving pertinent information from the dispatcher, police officers should respond to the crime in progress call immediately. Unless the call is such an emergency that the officer responds using red lights and siren, all officers should drive at a reasonable speed in order to get to the call quickly. Officers should obey all traffic laws when responding unless they are driving in the emergency mode using the red lights and siren. When an officer is dispatched to a crime in progress the first consideration is to "drive to arrive." The officer has an obligation to other police officers and the community to drive and arrive safely at the scene of the crime in progress. The first officer to arrive at the scene should quickly obtain as much information as possible and broadcast this information to other units responding to the call. Information that can later be vital to officers in the apprehension of a suspect(s) may include:

- The presence of suspects (i.e., how many).
- Possible routes of escape that could be used by the suspect.
- A description of the suspect(s) to include gender, race, approximate age, and any other distinguishing characteristics, such as a visible tattoo on the forearm, a full beard, a goatee, walking with a limp, etc.
- Description of suspect vehicle, including any unusual marks or distinguishing characteristics.
- The presence of any weapons, including description.
- If a weapon was seen, were there shots fired?

The first officer to arrive at the scene must make the determination to either request additional units or cancel any units already dispatched that will not be needed at the scene. Furthermore, he or she is responsible for requesting medical aid if needed. It is important for the first police unit that arrives on the scene to broadcast information to other units and to the dispatcher quickly. Units not involved in

emergency radio traffic /
Usually given to officers who
check out a potentially dangerous scene. This basically
means that officers should
keep minimal radio traffic
(stay off the radio) unless absolutely necessary or until
emergency traffic is released
by officers on the dangerous
scene.

the response should minimize their use of the police radio until the scene of the response is safe or the situation is declared under control. In many crimes in progress
calls the dispatcher will give the officers at the scene **emergency radio traffic**.
Emergency radio traffic basically alerts other police field units to limit their radio
traffic until the on-scene units advise the dispatcher to release emergency traffic. In
some departments, officers responding to a crime in progress call will switch to an alternate frequency, if such a frequency exists.

Responding police units should be alert to suspicious people or vehicles as they
approach the scene. The officer should avoid becoming so focused on getting to the
scene that fleeing suspect(s) or other persons related to the crime are missed. If suspects or vehicles are observed, the responding unit should broadcast identifying information so that other units can investigate. The primary responding officer should
always continue to respond to the scene and let other incoming police units investigate such observations. This is important in the case where a victim has been injured
and it is imperative to quickly provide medical aid. For crimes such as burglaries and
robberies in progress, police officers should attempt to arrive at the scene as quietly
as possible by:

- Turning off emergency lights and siren and slowing down for the final vehicular approach.
- Whenever possible, using parallel side streets for response routes.
- Parking the police vehicle in a position that is out of direct view of the scene, if
  practical.

Once in position, the first arriving unit should initially observe the crime scene
before taking any action. Find out as much information about the nature and seriousness of the call as possible before initiating action. If there is obvious and immediate danger to the life of another, or an obvious threat of serious property damage,
the police officer must take action initially to protect the victim and property.

Many police calls are crimes that have already occurred and the police are
called to investigate and make a report. For example, suppose one evening you are
out late. As you pull into the driveway to your home you immediately notice that
someone has thrown toilet tissue over your landscaping. As you walk closer to the
house you can't help but notice that someone has spray painted graffiti all over the
front of your garage door. Additionally, your garage window has been broken out
with a rock. Startled, you nervously pull the cell phone from your pocket and dial
911. The dispatcher asks for the nature of the emergency and you reply that someone has vandalized your home. The dispatcher asks several questions and then
informs you that an officer will be dispatched and should be there shortly.

After about forty-five minutes the officer arrives. He relates to you that it has
been a busy night and that's why it took so long to respond. The officer asks you
many questions, such as "When did you leave for the evening?" and "When did you
come home to find the vandalism?" You are also asked if you have any idea who
committed the vandalism. The officer pulls a camera from his patrol vehicle and
takes a few pictures of the broken window and of the graffiti, which according to the
officer appears to be gang graffiti. After about fifteen minutes the officer relates
to you that he will do a police report and that he will try to step up patrol in the
neighborhood.

The prior fictional scenario is an example of the police responding after a crime has occurred and taking a report. Police patrol officers engage in a significant amount of time taking reports on crimes that have already occurred. Think about this for a moment: How many times have you been the victim of a crime and called the police to make a report? Probably more times than you call the police and report that you are the victim of a crime in progress.

Community Policing Activities

With the evolving strategy of community policing, police officers are expected to incorporate this strategy into the way that they manage their beats. Community-oriented policing is the strategic process of establishing a community climate and an active partnership with the police. Community policing consists of three complementary core components: community partnerships, problem solving, and organizational transformation. The police patrol officer has responsibility for the first two: community partnerships and problem solving. Officers are more familiar with their beats than any other rank-and-file police officer. Police officers are exposed to the problems on their beats on a daily basis and are in the best position to react quickly to crime trends. Effective community policing has a positive impact on reducing neighborhood crime, helping to reduce fear of crime, and enhancing the quality of life in the community. It accomplishes these things by combining the efforts and resources of the police, local government, and community members.

The strategy of community policing requires that the police officers get in touch with the citizens living on their beats in order to learn what the citizens perceive to be problems in their neighborhood. One goal of community policing is to reduce crime and disorder by carefully examining the characteristics of problems in neighborhoods and then applying appropriate problem-solving remedies. As discussed previously, police patrol officers are in the best position to identify problems because they are exposed to the problems on their beats on a daily basis. It goes without saying that the police patrol officer is in the best position to tailor the best solutions to neighborhood problems.

Under the axiom of community policing, the police function includes the provision of services that in the recent past have been regarded as outside the scope of what the police normally do (Goldstein, 1990). These services include aiding accident and crime victims, arbitrating neighborhood and domestic disputes, and providing emergency medical and social services (Friedmann, 1992). Whenever possible the police officer should make regular contact with neighborhood watch coordinators and neighborhood association members, and attend neighborhood meetings. A discussion of the police officer's role in a community-policing environment is presented in greater detail in Chapter 3.

Administrative Tasks

The police officer's job on patrol entails a significant amount of administrative tasks. Every crime call that an officer responds to requires a **preliminary report**. Every traffic accident investigated and every traffic citation written requires that a report form or citation form be completed. The amount of paperwork that a patrol officer is responsible for completing can be time consuming.

preliminary report / A report that details a crime incidence completed by the first responding police patrol officer. The preliminary report is used by detectives in the subsequent follow-up investigation.

activity log / A log kept by police patrol officers during patrol shift. The log is a record of all activities performed by the officer during the patrol shift. For example, all dispatched calls, car stops, building checks, and other self-initiated activities are recorded. This includes the time the call or activity was initiated, the time the officer arrived at the scene, and the time the call was cleared.

Most police departments utilize a standard offense report form that can be used for all police reporting regardless of the crime. Other types of administrative tasks that the police officer on patrol will invariably have are maintaining an **activity log** and attending a neighborhood watch meeting or some other community meeting. The activity log is a form that the officer completes at the completion of any activity performed during the patrol shift. If the police officer leaves the police squad room and initiates a traffic stop while driving to his beat, this would be recorded on the activity log, along with the location and time of stop, the time cleared, and the action taken. If a traffic citation was issued, the citation number may be placed in the "activity taken" space.

Importance of Field Notes

One of the basic functions that a uniformed police patrol officer performs more than any other is writing reports. As the first officer on the scene, the uniformed officer conducts the preliminary investigation, and depending on departmental and/or jurisdictional policy, may be responsible for the entire investigation. The officer may conduct an outstanding investigation, but unless that officer can explain his actions and describe the particulars of the event clearly and accurately, no one will ever be aware of how well the investigation was done. An officer's field notes serve as notations concerning specific activities and events that an officer encounters in the performance of police duties. Field notes can serve as a general memory guide for an officer when writing the official report or when recalling key details at a later time. Field notes provide the foundation for the officer's report. Sketches included in the field notes can be useful later with crime scene reconstruction. Sketches made in the field notebook present the police officer with a graphic illustration of the crime scene that complements the written description. Field notes provide a better basis for documenting persons, places, times, dates, and events than an officer's memory. Police officers should consider their field notebooks to be essential parts of their equipment. The notebook should be one that the officer can easily carry in his or her pocket.

HANDLING OFFENDERS

Regardless of the nature of the crime, police officers should use the same uniform procedure when placing a suspect into custody. The police officer should never take anything for granted. It is a wise practice that there be at least two officers present when making an arrest; however, out of necessity, a great many arrests are made by one officer. An arrest must be based on **probable cause**. Probable Cause to Arrest is a set of facts and circumstances that would lead a reasonable and prudent person to believe that a crime has, is, or will be committed, and that the person in question committed the crime.

probable cause / Exists where the facts and circumstances within the officer's knowledge and of which he or she has reasonably trustworthy information is sufficient to warrant a person of reasonable caution to believe that an offense has been or is being committed.

When an officer makes an arrest it is always best if the offender voluntarily complies with the officer. However, in reality, it is impossible to predetermine a suspect's reaction to police arrest. The offender may submit peacefully or fight violently for their freedom. The offender may even fake sickness or resort to other trickery, in the hope that they might escape from police custody. This critical period, from the time prisoners are first placed under arrest until they are safely placed in the custody of the detention facility or lock up, requires increased vigilance on the part of every officer involved. This is the time when the prisoner has an opportunity to decide what action to pursue and may attempt to escape or violently attack the arresting officer or transporting officer. Some guidelines for the apprehension of the offender are:

- If possible, wait until you have a backup officer present before making the arrest.
- Remain alert at all times.
- Always expect the worst.
- Evaluate the suspect's demeanor and physical conditioning.
- Maintain a safe distance during the initial contact.
- After the suspect is handcuffed, advise him or her of the nature of the offense.
- When placing the suspect in custody do so quickly.
- Remove the subject to a safe but secure place as soon as possible to avoid bystander interference, if at all possible.

Handcuffing and Search

When handcuffing an offender, the officer should always expect the unexpected. For tactical reasons, it is best if the officer places the handcuffs on the offender prior to conducting a search for weapons. This reduces the chances that the offender may attempt to grab the officer's sidearm or resist the officer's commands. Offenders' hands should always be handcuffed behind their backs, except in the case of a serious handicap or conditions that would make handcuffing painful or impossible for the offender. Handcuffing an offender in the front increases the chances that a potential weapon could be retained by the offender, which could be used to inflict serious bodily harm. The quicker the offender is handcuffed the less likelihood of a physical confrontation between the offender and the officer. A handcuffed offender will have a more difficult time putting up a fight with their hands handcuffed behind their back. Once the handcuffs have been secured on the offender, advise him or her of the reason for the arrest and begin the search.

The search should be more than just a quick pat down. The quality of the search is of utmost importance, as "frisk" is not enough. A thorough search applies to all prisoners. Never assume that the prisoner was searched by another police officer; conduct your own search. At the time of the search, anything that can be used as a weapon should be taken away from the offender. Aside from the usual assortment of guns, knives, and other weapons, pencils, pens, heavy buckles, and similar items must be removed.

If possible, an officer of the same gender should be used to search offenders. A police officer may search a handbag or outer garment, such as an overcoat (after it has been removed). If the offender is wearing a wig, officers should carefully check under the wig. A female prisoner with a heavy handbag, a hat pin, or spiked heels can cause serious bodily harm to the officer or others if she is allowed to keep these items in her possession. If the officer feels some object through the clothing he or she should always ask the offender what is in their pocket before reaching into the pocket. This will prevent the officer from getting stuck with a syringe or from being cut with some sharp object in the offender's pocket. Some guidelines when handcuffing and searching offenders are:

- Handcuff first and search second.
- Keep a balanced position at all times.
- Keep the offender off balance.
- Watch the offender's head and shoulders for signs of movement.
- Keep verbal commands brief and clear (the offender has to understand what you want him or her to do).
- Keep a tight grip on the handcuffs during the entire handcuffing procedure.
- Don't simply pat down, grab and squeeze the clothing.
- Find out what is inside the pocket before reaching into it.
- Always expect the unexpected (be prepared for the worst).
- Check the snugness of the handcuffs to ensure that the prisoner cannot get his or her hands out of them.
- Police officers should never handcuff themselves to a prisoner. This is a good way to get seriously injured or killed.
- Double lock the handcuffs so they won't tighten up on the prisoner during transportation.
- Place the handcuffs on the prisoner snugly (not so tight that they cause pain to the prisoner or the prisoner's wrists are visibly traumatized).

positional asphyxia / Most simply defined as death that occurs because the position of a person's body interferes with respiration (breathing) and the person cannot get out of that position. Death occurs due to the person's inability to breathe anymore. Any body position that obstructs the airway or that interferes with the muscular or mechanical means of getting air into and out of the body will result in a positional asphyxia death if the person cannot get out of it.

restraint asphyxia / Restraining an offender in a manner to physically restrict the body's movement. The factor that distinguishes a restraint asphyxia death from a positional asphyxia death is that some form of restraint is the reason the victim could not escape the asphyxiating position.

Officers are responsible for the safety of prisoners in their custody and special care should always be used. Proper handcuffing procedure should be used to protect from positional or restraint asphyxia. **Positional asphyxia** occurs when the head and neck are turned or situated so as to obstruct the upper airway (interfering with the ability to breathe), and the reflex drive to right the head is dulled by alcohol, drugs, injury, or disease. This can result in death.

Restraint asphyxia occurs when one or more individuals restrain another, impairing the subject's ability to breathe. Mechanical impairment of respiration can occur in a prone (face down) restrained position, or in other positions, by restriction of chest and abdominal movements necessary for proper respiration. Restraints in such situations may include a combination of handcuffing hands and feet behind the back and with pressure applied to the torso, or laying the offender in a prone position for any length of time. These situations can interfere with respiratory movements and result in an asphyxia death. Exertion and drugs can be additive factors in such situations. Officers should use additional restraints as needed in the case of a combative offender.

Transporting Offenders

Prior to transporting a combative offender, additional restraining devices may be needed to secure a prisoner who violently resists arrest or who manifests mental disorders such that the prisoner poses a threat to himself or the public. Leg-restraining devices should be used on combative, kicking subjects at the discretion of the transporting officer. Hog-tying (hands and legs tied together behind the back) as a means to secure a combative prisoner *should never* be used. This method of securing a combative prisoner can lead to positional or restraint asphyxia. In all situations, if possible, the prisoner should be transported in an upright position to avoid the potential of restraint asphyxia. When transporting offenders, police officers should be conscientious of all traffic laws. The objective is to deliver the offender safely to the booking facility.

A large number of the prisoners transported by officers have been arrested for misdemeanor crimes and many of them may be under the influence of alcohol and/or drugs. Officers should be as cautious with this type of prisoner as they would be with the felony suspect. Be firm, but not abusive. No matter how agreeable a prisoner may seem to be, the officer should never be caught off guard. The "friendly drunk" may be wanted for a serious crime and is waiting for the officer to relax his or her alertness, so that the prisoner can attempt an escape.

When transporting female prisoners, officers should advise the dispatcher of the starting mileage and the destination when the transportation is initiated, and the ending mileage when the final destination is reached. This procedure is followed to avoid a later allegation of sexual misconduct. The ideal situation when transporting female offenders is that a female police officer rides along during the transport; however, this is not always possible.

The police vehicle must be thoroughly searched for weapons or evidence after the prisoner has been delivered to the booking facility. In some cases it is not that uncommon for weapons, narcotics, and other evidence to be found after a prisoner has been removed from the car. Officers should search assigned vehicles prior to the start of their shift or especially prior to transporting prisoners, especially if the officer intends to file charges on evidence found in the vehicle after transporting the prisoner. If a prisoner is sick or injured, he or she should be transported immediately to the nearest hospital for first aid before being taken to the booking facility. Common procedures for transporting an offender are:

- Always place a seat belt on the offender.
- Never handcuff an offender to any part of the police vehicle.
- Never make traffic stops or become involved in other police matters (unless life or death incidents) when transporting offenders. The offender's safety is your responsibility.
- Inspect the area where the prisoner will be seated before putting the prisoner there.
- Inspect the police vehicle after the offender is removed from the vehicle.
- Always search all prisoners before placing them in a vehicle.

Juvenile Offenders

Much of the same procedure should be followed when taking a juvenile offender into custody. When a male juvenile is taken into custody, he should be searched as thoroughly as an adult offender. Officers should make a preliminary search (purse, shoes, etc.) of female prisoners and maintain surveillance until a female officer or parental home authorities can make a more thorough search. It is permissible to handcuff juveniles using good judgment and depending upon circumstances involved. Two officers should always be present while transporting female juveniles. Juveniles should not be transported along with adult offenders. When dealing with juvenile offenders, police officers should be alert and firm. Juvenile offenders can be just as tricky as adult offenders.

PRACTICE HINTS

Summary Checklist for Prisoner Handling

1. Handcuff first; search second. Hands should be cuffed behind the back and the handcuffs should be double locked and checked for appropriate snugness.
2. Search a prisoner as many times as necessary until you are certain the prisoner possesses nothing with which to harm himself or someone else. Remove any and all items the prisoners could do damage with.
3. Keep your prisoner off balance and at a disadvantage while you search in detail from his or her rear. Do not overreach while searching and lose your own balance.
4. Do not allow friends or relatives of an arrestee to come in contact with the prisoner at the arrest site or in your vehicle once the prisoner is in your custody.
5. Do not try to control alone more prisoners than you can safely handle. Depending upon the circumstances, that limit may be one prisoner.
6. Watch your weapon retention practices around prisoners. Never allow an unsecured prisoner to get close to you.
7. Search every prisoner who comes into your custody. Never accept someone else's word that that "he's clean." Double check for yourself.
8. Remain constantly alert for threats during the prisoner transport process. More than a few prisoners have chosen this time period to attack.

9. Maintain a high level of alertness the entire time you are in the presence of any prisoner. Take nothing for granted based on the crime a prisoner is charged with. Realize that police officers have been murdered by every kind of prisoner.
10. You are responsible for your prisoner's welfare while he or she is in your custody. Question prisoners to see if they have medical problems requiring immediate treatment. Observe prisoners carefully for signs of injury or illness and seek medical help if in doubt.
11. Remember that prisoners who are extremely intoxicated, on drugs, or violently resistive may be in danger of respiratory arrest, particularly if required to lie restrained on their stomachs. Avoid hog-tying prisoners. Transport them in an upright position with an officer next to them for monitoring and control purposes.
12. Remain acutely aware of everyone and everything in your environment while you are handling a prisoner.

Source: From p. 94 in *Surviving the Street: Officer Safety and Survival Techniques* by Gerald W. Garner. Copyright © 2005. Courtesy of Charles C. Thomas Publisher, Ltd., Springfield, Illinois.

CIVIL UNREST

On April 29, 1992, four Los Angeles police officers were found not guilty of committing any crimes against Rodney King. Rodney King, an African-American, was pulled over for a traffic violation. According to the officers, King emerged from his automobile in an aggressive manner that suggested he might have been high on drugs. Before handcuffing King, the police delivered some fifty-six blows and kicks and a number of shocks from a Taser stungun to King, while almost twenty other officers stood by and watched. A man named George Holliday, standing on the balcony of a nearby building, videotaped the incident. The next day, he gave his eighty-one-second tape to Los Angeles TV Channel 5. By the end of the day, the video was being broadcast by TV stations around the world. After the announcement of the verdict, the Los Angeles police were caught fleeing the area where large-scale riots had erupted. The National Guard was then called in. The riots ended six days after they began and resulted in the deaths of forty-two people, the burning of 700 structures, the arrest of nearly 5,000 people, and almost $1 billion in property damage.

The police have historically had to deal with civil unrest, whether it is a small handful of demonstrators who have become rowdy or large-scale riots like the one described previously in Los Angeles. Facing a large and hostile crowd can be very scary for a police officer. It is easy for police officers during large demonstrations or civil unrest to become overwhelmed and overreact, especially if they have been inadequately trained or the agency has haphazard procedures to deal with such situations, or worse yet, none at all. It must always be remembered that a demonstration has the potential, if not properly controlled and contained, to escalate into a large-scale disturbance or riot.

Often the police are in a position to prepare for the possibility of civil unrest as a result of intelligence information that has been gathered by other police units. Likewise, many cities require groups wishing to protest to obtain a permit to hold a protest or demonstration. Permits usually require the group to furnish the date and times of their demonstration. This, of course, allows police authorities to prepare for the worst-case scenario, especially in cases where the demonstrators may be unpopular in a community.

A few examples of these types of unpopular groups include many fringe groups, such as the Ku Klux Klan, Arian Nation, the National Socialist Movement, and others, such as the Westborough Baptist Church, which operates out of Topeka, Kansas. You may recall the recent news reports regarding members of the Westborough Baptist Church, which is led by the Reverend Fred Phelps. Phelps and members of his church are known for their protests at the funerals of U.S. military personnel killed in Iraq. The pastor claims that U.S. soldiers are being killed in Iraq because they are fighting for a country that protects homosexuals. When the Phelps group conducts demonstrations they often attract counter-demonstrations and hecklers, and in some cases there have been near clashes between the two groups of demonstrators. It is imperative that police authorities properly prepare for such demonstrations.

Police officers should be cognizant at all times not to intervene or interfere with the lawful conduct of persons in the exercise of their constitutional rights, regardless of how the police officers themselves feel about the demonstrators. The police agency must recognize its obligation to protect the free exercise of constitutional rights, and the reasonable measures to do so while striving to maintain public order. Police intervention should only occur when violations of the law and threats to public safety require law enforcement response. The police are caught in a position where they have to protect the constitutional rights of demonstrators while doing so in a manner that will minimize the possibility of social unrest.

Planning

Planning is the key to the effective handling of demonstrations. Proper planning will also allow the police to develop a written action plan. The ideal situation, of course, is when the police can meet with the leaders or organizers of the demonstration, labor picketing, or mass protest in advance. The purpose of the meeting is to:

1. Inform organizers of the police agency's policies that are followed in such circumstances.
2. Provide organizers with information on laws and statutes that may apply.
3. Address any concerns of the organizers or sponsors.
4. Attempt to obtain a commitment for voluntary compliance with the law and reasonable public safety measures.
5. Identify contact persons for further consultation, if needed.

Remember, the police must safeguard the right of the group to protest while preventing civil unrest.

The following are important questions and should be carefully considered during the planning stages:

1. How many people are expected to be involved in the demonstration?
2. What specific boundaries will be maintained for the demonstrators, counter-demonstrators, and curious on-lookers?
3. Who is the leader(s) of the demonstration?
4. What other protests has the group conducted?
5. What time will the protest start and when will it end?
6. What type of counter-protest, if any, can be anticipated?
7. How many and how fast can police personnel be deployed to the scene if needed?
8. Where will the police command center be located?
9. Who will be in command in the event of a multi-jurisdictional response?
10. Are there large enough facilities to handle massive arrests if needed?
11. Will there be paramedics at the scene to treat minor injuries and heat-related problems if the demonstration is held during warm weather?
12. Where are the nearest medical facilities, in the event of injuries?

Written plans should be disseminated to all police personnel assigned to the demonstration. Likewise, police personnel should be debriefed prior to the demonstration. In some instances, it may be desirable for police officers to go through refresher training on such topics as riot control, dispersion of chemical agents, dealing with passive resisters, use of the baton, and other use of force issues.

Controlling the Crowd

There are several types of crowd classifications that police may encounter. The *casual crowd* is loosely organized and may lack any type of sound leadership structure. It is relatively easy for the police to disperse this type of a crowd. The *cohesive crowd* assembles for a common purpose, but without leadership. Spectators at a sporting event or concertgoers would be considered a cohesive crowd. For example the crowd at a sporting event would have a common purpose, but would think and act as individuals. The *expressive crowd* has a leader or leaders and assembles for some common purpose, usually expressing an attitude about a person, policy, or group. A crowd that has gathered at a political rally or event is an expressive crowd. The *aggressive crowd* has a leader or leadership structure and assembles for some common reason. This type of crowd is usually determined to accomplish a specific goal and more actively move toward their goal when compared with the expressive crowd. The aggressive crowd exhibits highly emotional tensions. This type of crowd creates a problem for the police because of its potential to become disorderly and escalate into a more serious situation.

During a demonstration or other event that attracts a large crowd, written plans and the agency's standard operating procedure should be closely followed. The primary objective of the police during a demonstration is to control the activities of the crowd. This includes being on the constant lookout for unusually disorderly persons or persons who appear to be inciting mob violence. These persons should be dealt with and removed as quickly as possible. The police should be as discrete as possible in removing these individuals so as to not attract attention from others in the crowd. It is possible that the removal of a person may attract scrutiny from other demonstrators, thus the police should exercise diligence. If the situation warrants, surveillance should be established to provide intelligence information about the disorder, such as crowd estimates or public safety hazards. Such surveillance may include the use of undercover personnel and photography.

It is ideal for the on-scene police commanders to be able to contact key leaders of the demonstration during the demonstration. Leaders of the demonstration may be willing to cooperate with the police to defuse a potentially disastrous situation. In the case that protesters are exhibiting conduct that is bordering on disorderly and illegal, police commanders should make contact with the leaders of the demonstration and ask for their cooperation in defusing the disorderly conduct of the demonstrators. There are always certain identifiable indicators leading up to a civil disturbance that police officers should be aware of. In order, they are: (1) irritable stage, (2) growth of crowd, (3) milling, (4) precipitating event, (5) hysterical and uncontrolled violence, and (6) spread of violence (Whisenand & Cline, 1971).

It is important for police officers at all times to remain professional and not lose their cool during a protest. This may be difficult and require much discipline on the part of the individual police officer, especially in cases where the officer personally disagrees with the purpose of the demonstration, such as a demonstration by a white supremacy group. The simple overreaction on the part of one police officer can aggravate the crowd. The 1965 Watts riot is an example of this. Watts is a neighborhood located in Los Angeles. The Watts riot erupted from a routine arrest of a drunk driver. A Los Angeles police officer stopped a motorist, whom he suspected of being intoxicated. When a crowd of primarily African-American on-lookers began to taunt the police officer, a second officer was called in. According to eyewitness accounts, the second officer struck crowd members with his baton, and news of the act of police brutality soon spread throughout the neighborhood. The incident, combined with escalating racial tensions, overcrowding in the neighborhood, and a summer heat wave, sparked violence on a massive scale.

Riots

In the event that the demonstration gets out of control and erupts into a **riot**, the police must act quickly. In a riot the primary objective of the police is to protect life

riot / A public disturbance by three or more persons acting in an unruly and disorderly manner, and resulting in the potential risk of injury to persons, damage to property, and disruption of the public peace.

Crowds watch fire at Picfair Theater at Pico & Fairfax during LA riots, April 1992. The riots were incited by the Rodney King incident involving misconduct by the LAPD.

and property while bringing an end to the unrest. If a command post has not been established it should be as soon as possible. The command post should be selected based on the security and safety of the area, the proximity to the areas of operations, and the access to transportation and communications facilities. A perimeter should be established as soon as possible to limit access to the area of the riot. The police should make use of the loud speaker or a bull horn and issue commands to the rioters and others who may be caught in the middle of the riot. It is important for the police to communicate to the rioters to disperse and leave the area. The police should establish an exit point(s) for the crowd, while ensuring that the rioters are contained and do not affect other parts of the surrounding neighborhoods.

Dispersion Techniques

There are many techniques that can be used in crowd dispersal. A brief sketch of the fundamentals of crowd dispersion is offered in this section. Police officers are encouraged to consult with the policies and procedures of their agency for specific dispersion techniques.

A field force should be assembled and may be employed for the dispersal and/or arrest operations. It will operate under the control of the on-scene commander. Teams should be formed of at least six to eight officers for dispersal. The size of the teams should be based on the size of the group being contained and officer safety.

Announcement by bull horns or loud speakers advising persons to disperse or leave the affected area should be made, thereby setting the stage for arrests for those who remain. Uninvolved civilians should be requested to leave the area. It is important for the police to communicate to the crowd exactly what they want them to do. If the police desire the crowd to disperse using a certain exit or area, this should be communicated. The on-scene commander should ensure that an avenue of escape is available so nonviolators can leave the affected area. The on-scene commander may also order the use of less lethal force, such as chemical agents, if other efforts fail to disperse the crowd. At no time should police officers engage in verbal confrontation with the crowd. Likewise, when dealing with a large crowd or mob, it may be best to ignore minor infractions. The enforcement of minor infractions may incite the rioters into more escalated violence.

In riot situations, verbal commands may not be effective and it may be necessary for the police to form a skirmish line and advance through the crowd with the objective to disperse the crowd. However, it is important to point out that whenever possible sufficient police personnel should be gathered before any enforcement action is taken.

One technique that may be used is to assemble an adequate number of officers and approach the mob as a unified group. The unified group of police officers is presented as an inverted "V" into the group, whereby the crowd can be moved to either side as police officers advance. If arrests are made, those arrested are placed inside the "V" and handed off to waiting officers. Once the officers begin to advance in formation through the crowd, the crowd is able to move away to either side of the line, much like a snow grader on a snow-packed street.

As pointed out previously, when approaching rioters, it is important to allow its members an escape route. If the rioters are not allowed an escape route, this may perpetuate further violence and resistance. Persons who are given a chance to leave but refuse to do so should then be arrested. Only the minimal amount of force necessary to make the arrest should be used. It only takes one officer using excessive force to aggravate the crowd further. The police should continually issue clear and understandable commands to the crowd; likewise the police should under no circumstances issue an order that the police officers are not able to carry out.

PRACTICE HINTS

- **Civil Disturbance**—An unlawful assembly that constitutes a breach of peace, or any assembly of persons where there is imminent danger of collective violence, destruction of property, or other unlawful events.
- **Mass Arrest**—A mass arrest situation exists when the number of persons to be arrested exceeds the agency's ability to perform normal arrest and reporting procedures.
- **Arrest Teams**—These teams may be formed in instances of civil unrest. Police officers are divided into teams of two to four to make the physical arrests of perpetrators involved in an incident.
- **Processing Teams**—Teams of officers who will process persons who are arrested.
- **Processing Site**—A location identified that can adequately facilitate the processing and handling of large groups.

HIGH-SPEED PURSUITS

The January 15, 2006 issue of the *Los Angeles Times* reported the somber news, "Three Anaheim co-workers were dead Saturday and two others badly injured after a van, driven by a man who allegedly had stolen two bottles of liquor from a bar and was fleeing from police, struck their car." Also, consider this headline, which appeared in the November 19, 2005 issue of the *Seattle Post-Intelligencer*, "Women Killed in Crash after Chase Identified." According to the Seattle police, a thirty-three-year-old woman died after the car she was riding in flipped over and crashed into a building. Seattle police began to chase the car after it went through a stop sign. During the chase, someone in the car tossed out a cup filled with narcotics, according to police, although officers thought it could be a gun.

In another case, a deputy sheriff working in a Midwestern community was sitting in the parking lot of a convenience store one evening about 10:30 P.M. doing paperwork. He looked up and saw a vehicle leaving the parking lot with no headlights on and traveling at a high rate of speed. The deputy became suspicious that the convenience store may have just been robbed, so he began to pursue the vehicle as he radioed for the dispatcher to call the convenience store and check to see if they had been robbed. The deputy eased up closer to the rear of the vehicle and activated the emergency red lights and siren. The vehicle failed to stop and continued traveling at a high rate of speed. The suspect vehicle entered into a busy intersection, ignoring the red traffic signal, and broadsided another vehicle traveling through the intersection. The driver of the broadsided vehicle was killed immediately and the driver and passenger in the suspect vehicle were seriously injured. Why did they leave the parking lot in such a hurry without their headlights on? The answer is for seven dollars worth of gasoline. That's right; they put seven dollars worth of gasoline in their tank without paying for it and took off. The pursuit lasted two minutes, and at the conclusion of the two minutes there was a serious accident that resulted in the death of one innocent citizen, and serious injury to the driver and passenger of the suspect vehicle.

police pursuit / A police pursuit is an active attempt by an officer operating a police vehicle to apprehend the driver or occupants of a motor vehicle when the driver is aware of those attempts and is resisting apprehension by fleeing in the motor vehicle.

Police pursuits are dangerous not only for the police and the suspect, but also the general public. In spite of the safety and liability issues that center on police pursuits, the number of pursuits in the United States continues to increase (Hill, 2002). The irony is that research tends to indicate that police pursuits turn dangerous rather quickly. So, for the most part they are not long and drawn-out chases like the glamorized pursuits depicted in the Hollywood cop shows, where the police pursue the suspect across the city before the suspect is apprehended or before the suspect crashes. One study found that 50 percent of all police pursuit collisions occur in the first two minutes of the pursuit, and more than 70 percent of all collisions occur before the sixth minute of the pursuit (Alpert, 1998).

Police authorities are faced with a not-so-envious decision on whether the risk of pursuing a fleeing suspect outweighs the risk of endangering police officers, the public, and the suspect in a chase. Police pursuits can result in great liability for the police agency, and lawsuits arising from police pursuits are just behind those involving the use of force (Barker, 1998). Most police departments have some form of written chase policy and many of these agencies restrict vehicle pursuits according to specific criteria, such as speed or offense (Hickman & Reaves, 2003). Barker (1998) comprehensively reviewed the research on police pursuits and concluded the following:

1. Emergency vehicle operation, particularly high-speed pursuit, is probably the most dangerous of all police activities.
2. There are more police vehicle chases each year than police shootings.
3. The police kill and injure more people each year during police chases than they do with their firearms.
4. The highest percentage of accidents occurring during pursuits are reported in small agencies and the lowest percentage are reported in very large agencies.
5. Pursuits at any speed and for any length of time are dangerous; approximately 30–40 percent involve traffic accidents.

6. A significant number of the accidents that occur during pursuits result in injuries and deaths and many of the victims are innocent civilians not connected to the pursuits.

7. The overwhelming number of pursuits are initiated for minor traffic violations.

8. The fleeing driver is seldom a fleeing felon.

9. The majority of pursuits are initiated between 2000–0400 hours.

10. Pursuits are most likely to occur on Friday, Saturday, or Sunday.

11. The majority of pursuits are of relatively short duration; that is, ten minutes or less. However, it should be understood that ten minutes or less at speeds in excess of 80 miles per hour covers a long distance.

12. The majority of injuries and deaths can be reduced by the adoption and implementation of a sound emergency operation policy.

Liability Issues

Police pursuits can be costly to the local government in terms of legal settlements. Police supervisors and officers should be keenly aware of the potential liability issues centering on police pursuits. Because of the critical nature of police pursuit situations, police executives must establish appropriate policy governing the actions of their officers during such incidents. Police executives must first consider the constraints and allowances set forth by state and federal statutes and court decisions applicable within their jurisdiction, and they must create a policy that balances the need to apprehend offenders in the interests of justice with the need to protect citizens from the risks associated with police pursuits (Pipes & Papes, 2001). Barker (1998) found a number of factors that determine the extent of pursuit liability:

1. **Purpose of Pursuit:** What is the need or reason for the pursuit? Does the reason warrant the risks involved? Has the violator only committed a traffic violation? Could the violator be apprehended at a later time?

2. **Driving Conditions:** This involves a general assessment of equipment, weather, and roadway and traffic conditions.

3. **Use of Warning Devices:** Warning devices on emergency equipment are a statutory requirement in most states during emergency vehicle operation. Nevertheless, the overreliance on warning devices, which leads to reckless actions, can create a liability risk.

4. **Excessive Speed:** Speed, especially speed when crossing an intersection against the light or a sign, is a critical consideration.

5. **Use of Force:** Force, such as firearms, ramming, boxing, bumping, or spike strips should be used when authorized by law and departmental policy. Whether or not the officers have been trained in their use will also become a liability issue.

6. **Continuation of the Pursuit:** A pursuit that is continued when the level of danger of the pursuit outweighs the benefits to be gained will increase the level of liability. Would a reasonable, trained police officer have continued the pursuit under the circumstances?

State troopers arresting suspect. Note the position of the backup officer.

Pursuit Procedure

Police departments should engage in motor vehicle pursuits subject to the limitations and guidelines intended to maximize public safety and minimize the likelihood that the suspects will elude arrest. Generally, officers should not engage in or continue pursuits when the apparent risk created by the pursuit outweighs the necessity for immediate apprehension. Before a pursuit is initiated, officers must have a reasonable suspicion that the driver or occupants are involved in criminal activity or have committed a law violation, and must have emergency equipment activated, which includes the siren warning device and emergency lights, which should be visible on the patrol car. Upon initiating a pursuit, the officer should immediately notify the dispatcher and provide the location, speed, and direction of travel, reason for initiating the pursuit, and the description of the vehicle and occupants.

As soon as it is evident that the driver of the pursued vehicle is fleeing, officers should activate their emergency lights, siren, and headlights, and leave these on at all times during the pursuit. Most states' legal statutes provide that emergency vehicles are exempt from certain traffic regulations, however, it is important to point out that officers are not relieved from the responsibility to drive with due regard for the safety of all persons. Reckless disregard for the safety of others is unacceptable.

Ordinarily, only vehicles equipped with both overhead emergency lights and warning sirens should enter into pursuits. Only in rare circumstances should an unmarked police vehicle be involved in a pursuit. When a fleeing vehicle constitutes an immediate threat, unmarked emergency vehicles may pursue initially, until a marked unit can undertake the pursuit. Motorcycle and bicycle officers should never become involved in a chase due to lack of safety and protection of the officers. Pursuits are dangerous enough for officers in patrol cars let alone officers on bicycles or motorcycles.

State of California Statute—Authorized Emergency Vehicles

California Vehicle Code § 21806. Authorized emergency vehicles

Upon the immediate approach of an authorized emergency vehicle which is sounding a siren and which has at least one lighted lamp exhibiting red light that is visible, under normal atmospheric conditions, from a distance of 1,000 feet to the front of the vehicle, the surrounding traffic shall, except as otherwise directed by a traffic officer, do the following:

(a) (1) Except as required under paragraph (2), the driver of every other vehicle shall yield the right-of-way and shall immediately drive to the right-hand edge or curb of the highway, clear of any intersection, and thereupon shall stop and remain stopped until the authorized emergency vehicle has passed. (2) A person driving a vehicle in an exclusive or preferential use lane shall exit that lane immediately upon determining that the exit can be accomplished with reasonable safety.

(b) The operator of every street car shall immediately stop the street car, clear of any intersection, and remain stopped until the authorized emergency vehicle has passed.

(c) All pedestrians upon the highway shall proceed to the nearest curb or place of safety and remain there until the authorized emergency vehicle has passed.

Generally, no more than two law enforcement vehicles should engage in the direct pursuit of a motor vehicle unless otherwise approved by the on-duty supervisor. The primary chase unit will be the initiating vehicle until another unit is assigned to perform the task. The secondary unit is responsible for assisting the primary unit in safely apprehending the suspects and assisting with communications when necessary. In other words, in some pursuits the primary pursuing officer is trying to watch the road and drive effectively while pursuing the suspect vehicle. In this case, the secondary unit would be the pursuit caller, keeping the dispatcher and other officers informed of the direction of the pursuit. Other units should be alert to the progress of the pursuit, but should not engage in direct pursuit or follow the primary or secondary pursuit vehicles without authorization.

In a pursuit, police officers should be diligent about the safety of others. Officers approaching an intersection should visually check for cross traffic and proceed only when the intersection is clear to pass, and only at a speed reasonable and prudent for existing conditions.

Officers should not duplicate extremely high speeds or driving maneuvers made by the fleeing vehicle. Likewise, it is an unwise practice to pursue suspects the

PRACTICE HINTS

Authorized Emergency Vehicle—A vehicle using an audible signal device, such as a siren and emergency lights.

Emergency Response also known as "code three"—The operation of an authorized emergency vehicle when responding to an emergency situation.

Emergency—Any event where the information known to the officer at the time leads the officer to a reasonable conclusion that an immediate police presence is necessary to protect person(s) from death or bodily injury or to render aid to a person believed to be injured or ill.

wrong way on the interstate or controlled access highways unless authorized by the duty supervisor. Officers should avoid driving on the wrong side of divided roadways or the wrong way on one-way roadways and only do so when absolutely necessary. In some situations officers may be tempted to ram or strike the fleeing vehicle; however, this should be avoided unless deadly force is justified.

In determining whether to initiate or continue a pursuit there are a number of factors that should be considered:

1. **Nature of Offense:** In the case of a serious crime, especially involving violence or the potential for danger if apprehension is delayed, a pursuit may be justified. A minor offense may not justify a pursuit.
2. **Time of Day:** May influence risk created by the pursuit due to the level of activity occurring on or near the roadway, as well as lighting conditions and visibility. For example, a pursuit during 5:00 P.M. rush hour traffic would pose a serious risk to the general public.
3. **Traffic Volume:** The presence and amount of vehicular and pedestrian traffic affects the level of risk to innocent persons.
4. **Location of Pursuit:** The proximity to businesses, residences, schools, and other congested areas may increase the risk.
5. **Weather Conditions:** Pursuits are more dangerous during inclement weather such as rain, snow, or fog.
6. **Road Conditions:** Road surface, sight distance, roadway width, and roadside hazards, must be taken into account.
7. **Availability of Assistance:** Pursuits are more dangerous when other units are not in the vicinity to control traffic and assist in the apprehension.
8. **Traffic Violations:** The driving behavior of the fleeing driver may create unacceptable risks; for example, excessively high speeds, violating stop signs or traffic signals at high speeds, or other frequent hazardous violations.

Aspects of a Police Pursuit That Should Always Be Scrutinized

1. The potential harm present during the pursuit.
2. The reason that police officers pursue a traffic offender. (Even though some traffic offenses, such as speeding, may at first appear to warrant police intervention to stop the danger presented to others, police intervention can increase rather than lessen the danger.)
3. The availability of other means either to apprehend individuals or to stop the need for pursuits.

Source: Urboyna, K. R. (1991). The constitutionality of high-speed pursuits under the fourth amendment. *Saint Louis University Law Journal, 35*, 35–205.

Helicopter Support

A National Institute of Justice study found that helicopters can provide a valuable service to law enforcement in pursuit situations (Alpert, 1998). In a pursuit, the police helicopter becomes the primary pursuit unit when the air crew has a visual on the fleeing vehicle. Once the helicopter has a visual on the suspect vehicle, all police vehicles should terminate the pursuit and reduce speed to give the appearance that they are not still attempting to apprehend the violator. Ground units should still proceed in the direction of the suspect vehicle as noted by the police helicopter unit. The police helicopter is also useful in assisting in directing other pursuit units into position to assist in stopping the pursued vehicle, and also as a platform for illuminating the area during pursuits that appear after dark.

Manual for Police of New York State

Section 11B4: Pursuit Driving

    (a) Understand that pursuit driving at high speeds is inherently dangerous to you, to occupants of the pursued vehicle, and others. It can result in a serious accident causing deaths, injuries, and the destruction of patrol vehicles. A reckless disregard for the safety of others may subject you, as the pursuit driver, to criminal charges or a civil damage lawsuit.

    (b) In deciding whether to pursue a vehicle, use good judgment and carefully consider the following factors in evaluating whether the risks of the pursuit are warranted:

        (1) Availability of alternate means to stop the vehicle or apprehend the suspect.

        (2) The safety of other motorists and pedestrians.

        (3) The nature of the offense.

        (4) The road and weather conditions.

        (5) The traffic conditions.

        (6) The time of day or night.

        (7) The kind of vehicle involved.

        (8) Your knowledge of the area.

        (9) The population density of the area.

    (c) Except in extreme emergency, do not pursue a vehicle when you are transporting prisoners or passengers.

Tire Deflation Devices

The police should try to end a vehicle pursuit safely and quickly. If it has been determined that the suspect is a threat to the general public and has committed a violent crime, the pursuit must continue. The objective in this case is to defuse the chase in the best interest of police, the public, and the suspect. For this reason, many police agencies have begun to use tire deflation devices or spike sticks, as they are sometimes called, as a means to disable a fleeing suspect's vehicle. Tire deflation devices allow the police to quickly and safely end high-speed pursuits. The spike system tire deflation device only takes one officer to deploy. Replaceable spikes stay in the tire when they are run over, releasing all the air from the tire through the hollow spikes. Thus, spike sticks slowly deflate the tires of speeding cars and bring them to a controlled stop, which is the ideal outcome.

    Police officers may deploy tire deflation devices to terminate the pursuit according to their specific department procedure. In some cases where use of a tire deflation device would pose serious risk to the officer, suspect, or the general public, a supervisor may order it not to be used. Officers should be trained on the deployment of tire deflation devices before using them. Tire deflation devices should not be used in locations where geographic configurations increase the risk of injury to the suspect, such as on roadways bounded by steep descending embankments or curves. At all times known traffic conditions should be considered. Tire deflation devices should not be used to stop vehicles with less than four wheels (motorcycles, mopeds, etc.). The officer deploying a tire deflation device should always make an announcement on the radio just prior to deployment of devices: "STOP STICK IS DEPLOYED AT (location), STOP STICK IS DEPLOYED AT (location)." This is to prevent police vehicles from traveling across an area where the stop stick has been placed.

The Bureau of Justice Statistics reports that tire deflation spikes are regularly used by U.S. police departments, including a majority of the departments serving a population of 25,000 or more (Hickman & Reaves, 2003). The following caveats are offered to police officers who may have the occasion to use a tire deflation device, such as spike sticks, in the field:

- Police officers should receive the proper training. Only specially trained police officers should deploy road spikes, and they must be in a safe place to do so.
- "Spike Stick" deployment zones must be developed taking into account the safety of the public, police, and offender; the risk of property damage; whether there is sufficient time to safely establish a zone; traffic conditions; whether it is the most appropriate resolution strategy; and whether or not it is more appropriate to terminate the pursuit.
- Police officers should follow strict safety procedures for removing spikes from the road.

PRACTICE HINTS

"Road spikes" or "spike sticks" are devices used by law enforcement in an attempt to stop vehicles that are fleeing and fail to stop. Police departments around the nation have for years used portable tire spikes to bring car chases to a halt, but the problem has been that the spikes stop every car that crosses them, including police cars and the vehicles of innocent bystanders. Fortunately, the new remote-controlled tire spikes can target just one vehicle, puncturing its tires in about two seconds, before quickly reverting to a nondeployed position.

WEATHER AND NATURAL DISASTERS

Weather and natural disasters often occur suddenly and without warning. If you are a police officer working in a southeastern coastal community, hurricanes are a concern. If you are a police officer working in other parts of the country, then tornadoes may represent the seasonal threat. Disasters such as these create special problems for the police because looters prey on others' misfortunes. Another concern is the location and identification of the victims, both alive and deceased, of such disasters.

You may recall the media images from Hurricane Katrina, the seemingly callous looters carrying away as much property as they could hold from stores and businesses in New Orleans. Who can forget the images of looters carrying boxes of sneakers, cases of liquor, television sets, and other electronic items that they had just looted? To the casual observer, the Hurricane Katrina disaster represented lawlessness at its worst. Many questioned how some could blatantly loot stores and businesses while human corpses floated nearby in the flood waters. As a result of the large-scale looting, New Orleans

Mayor Ray Nagin ordered 1,500 police officers to leave their search and rescue assignments and return to the streets to stop looting that had become extremely hostile.

There are seven factors that need to be considered when responding to a weather or natural disaster.

1. **Identify the scope of the problem.** The initial officers checking out the scene should conduct an initial assessment of the problem. What areas of the community have been impacted? In the event of a hurricane or tornado, an initial assessment on property damage should be conducted, and if possible, an assessment of the severity of injuries. It is also important to assess power or electrical problems. It is not uncommon in weather or natural disasters for live electrical lines to be down across roadways, which creates a potentially lethal situation for motorists or curious citizens. If it is possible, an initial assessment of power outages in the area should be performed.

2. **Notify the dispatcher.** Once the preliminary assessment has been completed, the officers should relay this information as quickly as possible to the dispatcher. During the first hours after the disaster new information will be uncovered and relayed to the dispatcher. Generally, the dispatcher will begin to notify the police supervisors and the command structure so that an adequate number of police officers will be deployed into the area.

3. **Establish a command post.** The command post is a critical link between police commanders and units in the field. Many police departments have vehicles that have been converted to mobile field command posts (e.g., a bus or a recreational vehicle) and can literally be driven to the scene of the disaster. Command posts are usually equipped with necessary items that may include barricades, barrier tape, signs for the scene, communications equipment (including portable police radios and mobile cellular phones), a public address system, first aid material, and maps.

   The initial police officers or supervisors on the scene should establish the location of the command post. This location should naturally be established away from any potential hazards, but close enough to establish a command presence. The general approachability to the command post should also be considered. For example, are there open and accessible streets that can be traveled to get to and from the command post? The command post should be established in a large enough geographical area to accommodate parking for numerous police vehicles and the debriefing of a large number of police officers. Once the command post has been established, personnel at the command post should notify concerned departmental members about developments. The command post will also make on-scene command decisions that will be communicated to the officers in the field.

4. **Render aid to victims.** A priority of police officers at the scene of a disaster is to render aid to victims. In some cases this may simply be to summon first aid personnel or paramedics to the location of a victim. In other situations it may involve assisting rescue and fire personnel in clearing an area in order to get to an injured victim or it may involve the officer administering first aid until the paramedics arrive on the scene.

5. **Contain the scene.** The scene should be contained. In other words, all throughways that lead into the area of a natural disaster should be strictly

controlled. It's not that uncommon for looters to travel to the scene of a natural disaster with the intent to profit, or for curious sightseers to travel to the scene. Only persons with a need to be there should be allowed on the scene. It is generally a good practice to establish a specific area for the news media. Furthermore, the media should be given specific guidelines as to how close they may get to the damaged areas. A primary objective here, of course, is to safeguard the general safety of the media personnel.

6. **Control looting and other ancillary criminal behavior.** It is of utmost importance for the police to control looting and other criminal behavior at the scene of a disaster. Field police officers should be assigned geographical quadrants to patrol. On-scene command should issue a verbal directive to police field units on how to handle looters. In some situations, looters may simply be told to leave the scene, while in others they may need to be aggressively arrested. This decision is dependent on a number of factors, including the number of field units deployed on the scene, the ability to deploy back-up units as needed to assist an officer who has detected a number of looters, and the ability to transport offenders to the booking facility.

7. **Locate and identify deceased victims.** One of the sad realities of a natural disaster is the loss of life. Police officers may be asked to assist fire and rescue personnel in the location and identification of deceased victims. The location and identification of deceased victims usually involves the search, recovery, and removal of bodies, body parts, and personal effects.

The recovery usually begins after the search efforts have been completed. Generally, police officers who are assigned to a recovery team mark the location where a body has been recovered with a flag, stake, spray paint, or some other method, then record pertinent information pertaining to the recovery, photograph the body, and then move on until all the bodies have been recovered. The recovery of the disaster's victims should be viewed as a priority due to the unpleasant nature of decomposing corpses.

All human remains, including personal effects and other items, are considered evidence when they are recovered, regardless of the type of incident, mainly because they might be very useful later in the identification of the remains. Even in cases of a natural disaster, personal effects might be very critical in leading to identification of the deceased. An accurate system of identifying human remains should begin at the scene of a natural disaster. The first thing that a police officer should do is assign a unique reference number to a discovered fatality victim. This reference number should include the time, date, and location where the victim was found. Care should be used to not duplicate the reference number. Second, write the reference number information on a card and secure it on the body of the victim. Many police departments make use of body tags similar to the ones used in military warfare. Third, photograph the victim. Photographs should include such things as the reference number, an overview photograph of the location where the body was discovered, full-length body photograph, facial photograph, photographs of any distinguishing mark(s) found on the body, and photographs of all clothing and personal effects. Police officers should also take note that a natural disaster can result in an ancillary crime scene due to a breakdown in social order and laws, as was the case in New Orleans in 2005 after Hurricane Katrina.

A designated notification team should notify the victim's family once identification has been made. Because of the psychological burdens placed on a victim's family, the official notification should be made as soon as possible. In cases where there are many deceased victims, it is wise for the police to debrief family members at a specific location several times throughout the day. In such a case, there may be a church or community building nearby that may be used as temporary housing facilities for victim's families.

THE POLICE CANINE

The **police canine** is a dog that has been trained to assist police officers in the performance of police duties. Dogs and canine handlers are invaluable in assisting law enforcement in tracking, scouting, searching for suspects or missing persons,

police canine / A dog that is trained specifically to assist police officers and similar law-enforcement personnel with their work. They are also known as police K-9s.

Voices of Experience

K-9 Unit

Excerpts from an interview between Cliff Roberson and retired police officer, Mike Turner. Turner also teaches for ITT and Maric College in Vista, California.

Q: *Would you relate to us your experiences in a K-9 unit?*
A: Once I was selected for the K-9 unit, I had to take 230 hours of training before I could take the dog on the street. In addition, I had to pass departmental certification.

My dog was dual-qualified, which meant that he could act to catch the bad guys on the street and also could be used as a drug search dog. In our K-9 unit, we worked evenings from 8:00 P.M. until about 3:00 A.M. in the morning because that was when the dogs were needed the most. The K-9 unit officers would respond to normal radio calls until there was a need to use a K-9 and then we responded to that call. We were also attached to SWAT in a tactical K-9 role. In the SWAT situations, we would normally maintain the perimeter in case the individual ran.

The dog lived with my family. The department would pay for a kennel to keep him in, provided dog food, and paid for the health care of the dog. The dog became a member of our family. With a dog, you need to be willing to do continuous training with him and in your off-time you still were required to care for the dog. It is pretty much an around-the-clock job.

During the normal tour of duty, we would handle routine patrols and would keep alert for the "hot calls." If I made an arrest, I could not transport the person with the dog, so I was required to call for another officer to transport the arrested person. We were regular officers with an additional tool, the dog, which other officers did not have.

My dog was a German shepherd. He was from Germany. Most K-9s come from overseas. When we needed a new dog, our trainer took a trip overseas and selected the dog. Because my dog was from Germany, I had to learn German commands. Another officer had a dog from Czechoslovakia and he had to learn Czech commands. Before I received the dog he had basic obedience and initial apprehension training of how to bite and release. We had to fine tune the training. We also had to develop a working rapport with our dogs.

The K-9 unit had a friendly rivalry with SWAT. Once we responded to a shooting call at a house. One suspect trying to escape was located and captured by the dog in a ditch. SWAT cleared the house and stated that the second offender was not in the house and had escaped. To take advantage of every training opportunity, after a house was cleared, we usually hid someone in the house for the dog to find. This allows the call to end in a positive experience for the dog. A fellow officer hid in the house and I took the dog in as a training exercise. The dog found the other suspect hiding in the house. I made sure that the SWAT officers realized that they had overlooked the suspect. ∎

building searches, and crowd control. Certain police canines are also trained in detection of narcotics and explosives. Some canines are trained for the recovery of bodies. This type of canine is referred to as a cadaver dog. Cadaver dogs are specially trained in detecting the odor of decomposing bodies. The use of canines increases officer safety by allowing canines to perform functions officers would otherwise have to perform.

The breed of the dog used in police work is usually the preference of the handler. However, when it comes to the general purpose patrol dog, the popular rule of thumb is that longer muzzled dogs have greater senses of smell. Consequently, most patrol dogs are long-snouted animals, like the German shepherd and a Belgian breed called the Malinois (Scoville, 2005). The Labrador retriever has been found by some to be an ideal bomb dog because of its single-mindedness, while blood hounds have had remarkable success detecting scents on ejected shells (Scoville, 2005). Regardless of breed, police dogs should be selected based on their temperament, physical fitness level, inquisitive nature, intelligence, boldness, agility, and ability to interact with people.

The advantages of using trained police dogs as part of police operations include the psychological, deterrent, and intimidating effects that the dog has on potential offenders; aiding police officers in the apprehension of an offender; crowd control; searching hard-to-reach locations, such as densely wooded areas; and the protection of police officers. Prior to a police dog being used for police duties, both the dog and its handler undergo an extensive amount of training. The dog and the handler work and train as a team. In essence, the police dog and the handler form a bond. The primary purpose of a police dog is not as a primary attack dog, but rather a dog that gets along with other officers and the public when it is not given the command to attack (Hamilton, 2003).

Police canines are used in numerous capacities, including apprehension of suspects, tracking operations, drug detectors, explosives, accelerants (arson investigation), guards and deterrents, and as patrol partners.

There is a general hesitancy among police management in using dogs because of the potential liability. However, as long as there are strict procedures for using the canine, the liability problems seem to be largely unfounded. If a dog and its handler have been given the proper training, the training has been documented, good recordkeeping procedures are in place, the department has a standard operating procedure pertaining to the use of the police dog, and the handler uses good judgment in the deployment of the dog, the chances of any litigation resulting in a payout is minimal (Hamilton, 2003).

There are some important guidelines that should be considered when developing a police canine unit for use in police operations:

1. The budget should be secured to fully meet the needs of the K-9. This includes kennel expenses that the handler incurs, proper veterinarian care, and a proper vehicle for the handler and K-9 to patrol in.
2. Dogs and their handlers should be carefully selected.
3. Proper training should be secured and documented for the K-9 and its handler.
4. Dogs should only be assigned to the handler that has trained with the dog.
5. The dog should be kenneled at the handler's home.
6. Standard operating procedures should be written and reviewed by the department's legal staff.
7. Administration of the K-9 unit should be diligent, including carefully kept records which detail the dog's performance. This is especially important in the case of drug sniffing dogs. In court this is often a criteria in establishing the reliability of a K-9 (i.e., how many times has the dog alerted the handler to drugs and drugs have been discovered).

There are several duties that an officer who has requested canine assistance should carry out:

- Secure the scene until the canine arrives. This includes sealing the area and avenues of escape as much as possible.
- Avoid contaminating the area in any way (physical presence, chemical or other contaminating substance).
- Keep the area clear of foot traffic. The canine may pick up a trail on the freshest scent.
- Police vehicles should not be parked with the engine running in the immediate area. This can be a distraction for the canine. Other distractions, such as lights, noise, and radio, should be kept to a minimum.
- If tracking a person who has fled from a vehicle, do not enter the vehicle.
- If clothing or an article the party touched can be located, it should not be disturbed, but pointed out to the canine handler.
- Officers providing perimeter coverage should minimize contamination of the area.
- Brief the canine handler with all known facts and circumstances of the case.

■ Do not assist the canine team unless requested to do so by the canine handler. The canine team has been trained to work specifically as a team, and unwanted assistance could impact the team's effectiveness.

If the field officer has been asked to assist the canine team, he or she should always attempt to stay some distance behind the canine team while tracking, unless otherwise instructed by the canine handler. Usually, staying about 50 feet behind the canine team will suffice. Likewise, the assisting officer should remain behind the handler and dog at all times and keep out of unsearched areas. The assisting officer should also keep conversation and police radio traffic to a minimum.

TRAFFIC STOPS

In most cases, the traffic stop is the only contact that citizens will have with a police officer. The main reason police officers conduct traffic stops is to enforce the law and to encourage voluntary compliance with these laws. The goal is to reduce injuries and deaths on our roadways. During a traffic stop, the police officer must remain courteous and professional, while at the same time being alert for officer safety issues. Every traffic stop has the potential for danger. Many officers are killed each year and thousands more are injured in traffic-related incidences. For example, the U.S. Department of Justice reports that from 1995 to 2004, there were fifty-six officers who gave the ultimate sacrifice and were killed while conducting a car stop for a traffic violation (U.S. Department of Justice, 2005, table 29).

A police officer should never approach a traffic stop as a "routine traffic stop." There is no such thing as a routine traffic stop. Often during traffic stops police officers encounter uninsured drivers, suspended driver's licenses, persons who are under the influence of alcohol or drugs, drug traffickers, illegal firearms, and persons who are wanted fugitives.

An important role of the police is to promote traffic safety through both education and enforcement.

POLICE IN ACTION: Traffic Stops

"There is no more misunderstood law enforcement duty than traffic enforcement."
—Dean Scoville, 2006

Traffic enforcement may at times seem tedious and futile. Alert traffic stops, however, have helped end the careers of some of America's most prolific murderers.

David Berkowitz, the New York "Son of Sam" killer who killed six people, was caught because he received a parking ticket near the location of one of his murders.

Ted Bundy, who murdered more than two dozen young women, caught the attention of a Utah Highway Patrol Officer because he was driving with his lights off. After he escaped from Colorado, he was caught for driving in Pensacola, Florida with stolen plates on his vehicle. The officer was alerted to his vehicle because of his driving tactics.

Joel Rifkin, a former gardener and prolific murderer, was caught in New York State because he was driving a vehicle without a license plate.

Randy Craft, who was convicted of sixteen murders, was stopped by California Highway Patrol officers for erratic driving and submitted to a field sobriety test. Later, the officers found a shrouded body in his car.

William Lester Suff, who was convicted of murdering prostitutes in the Riverside, California area, was caught when he made an illegal U-turn.

Timothy McVeigh, the Oklahoma City federal building bomber, was collared by an Oklahoma highway patrol officer on Interstate I-35 for driving without a license plate.

Wayne Williams, who was considered the murderer in the Atlanta Child Murders, was cited for stopping on a bridge. Later the body of one of the victims was discovered in the river below the bridge.

James E. Swann Jr., the Shotgun Stalker in the Washington, DC area, was stopped for running a red light and the officer found a recently fired shotgun in the vehicle.

Larry Eyler, a conflicted homosexual who killed gay men, parked his pick-up on a highway. An officer stopped to investigate and noticed him moving along a tree line with a potential victim who was tied up.

Source: Scoville, D. (2006). Killer stops. *Police: The Law Enforcement Magazine, 30 (6),* 42–44.

Preparing for the Traffic Stop

When a police officer decides to stop a vehicle for a traffic violation, he or she should not rush the stop, but rather initiate the stop when and where the officer feels comfortable. Officer safety should be a primary consideration. The officer should obtain as much detail as possible before stopping the vehicle. There are many anecdotal accounts from police officers relating how they prefer to run the tag displayed on the vehicle they are planning to stop prior to stopping the vehicle. This practice allows the officer to discern if the tag belongs on the vehicle and if the tag or vehicle has been reported stolen.

The officer should conduct an assessment of how many occupants are in the vehicle, and, if possible, how they are acting. Do they appear to be looking nervously back at the officer? Are they reaching under the seat? Are they reaching across the seat? Are they moving around erratically? Are they throwing items out of the vehicle? These are important questions that should be answered, prior to initiating the stop. A police officer reported that as he was preparing to stop a vehicle for lane straddling one evening by following the vehicle and checking the tag, the driver and the passenger switched seats while the car was in full motion. Upon stopping and initiating an investigation it was discovered that the driver who had switched seats with the passenger was driving under the influence. It was discovered that the passenger who had switched seats and was, operating the vehicle when it was stopped was also over the legal alcohol limit, and he too was arrested for driving under the influence. It's not often that police officers make two arrests for driving under the influence from the same vehicle at the same time.

The location of the stop is an important consideration for the officer. It cannot be overemphasized that the officer should stop the violator where he or she feels comfortable. If the stop will take place during the night shift, the officer may wish to follow the violator's vehicle to a well-lighted area before the stop is initiated. This can improve the officer's visibility of the occupant(s) of the vehicle. Likewise, if the officer feels suspicious about something he or she has observed, the officer may wish to follow the vehicle until a backup unit is close and then stop the violator.

The Stop and Making Contact

Once the officer feels comfortable, the stop should be initiated by activating the emergency lights on the patrol car. If the violator fails to stop, the officer should then activate a few blasts of the siren or air horn and this will usually get the violator's attention. The emergency overhead lights should always stay activated during the car stop to provide safety for the officer. If the officer has not done so already, he or she should notify the dispatcher of the location of the stop, the tag number, and the vehicle description. Vehicle stops should always be called in to the dispatcher. In some jurisdictions, standard operating procedures not only require that police officers furnish this information to the dispatcher, but also the number of occupants of the vehicle. If for some reason the officer is not required to notify the dispatcher of the stop, at the very least the officer should write the tag number and a vehicle description on the activity sheet or clipboard.

The patrol vehicle should be positioned behind the violator's vehicle about 10–15 feet and just slightly (a few feet) to the left. This will provide protection for the officer from traffic and allow the officer to have a full visual of the driver's side door. Turning the wheels of the patrol car sharply to the left can offer the police officer some protection from gunshot rounds to the lower leg extremities. Turning the wheels sharply to the left also positions the engine block of the patrol car between the officer and the violator's vehicle. This offers some protection from gunshot rounds too, and if need be the officer can take cover behind the upper portion of the vehicle. If the stop is made after nightfall, the patrol car's spotlight or alley lights can be used to illuminate the interior of the violator's vehicle.

Upon walking up to the vehicle to make contact with the violator, it is a good idea for the officer to pull up on the trunk of the violator's vehicle to ensure that it is secured and that no one is hiding in the trunk. As the officer continues walking to the driver's side window he or she should do a cursory peek into the backseat through the rear window while keeping an eye on the driver's actions. In the event that the officer is stopping a van that does not have side rear windows, obviously it is impossible to view inside the rear of the van. In this case, the officer should listen for any unusual movement noises coming from inside the van.

The officer should be alert for the driver or passenger who reaches under the seat during the officer's approach. It could be that they are attempting to stash something under the seat, or worse yet, grab a weapon from under the seat. If the officer observes a sudden movement such as this, he or she must become more suspicious, call for a backup unit, and investigate further.

The officer should stand just to the rear of the driver's window to the point where the driver has to physically turn his or her head back to see the officer. This puts the officer in the best position to take action if need be. The officer should never stand in front of the driver's door. If the driver desires to harm the officer then all she or he has to do is open the door in an aggressive manner and knock the officer to the ground. Once the approach is made, the officer should request to see the violator's driver's license and registration. After the violator has produced the driver's license and registration, the officer should inform the violator what he or she is being stopped for. By asking for the driver's license and registration first, the officer avoids a situation in which the violator wants to argue with the officer about the purpose of the stop. In some cases the officer may also request to see current proof of insurance. While talking with the driver the officer should look for any contraband that may be in plain view inside of the vehicle. As many police officers will tell you, they are never surprised to find drugs or weapons in plain view.

Once the initial contact is made, the officer may wish to write the traffic ticket or warning while standing at the driver's door. Some officers prefer to go back to their patrol vehicle and write the ticket. If the officer does return to the patrol vehicle, while walking back to the patrol unit he or she should carefully keep an eye on the driver and occupant(s). It is not advisable that the officer sit in the patrol unit while writing the ticket. The best position is standing outside of the unit, preferably to the rear of the patrol unit on the passenger side. The driver and occupant(s) of the violator's vehicle should remain seated in their vehicle at all times. If the driver or occupant begins to exit their vehicle, the officer should explain to the driver or occupant that for their own safety they should remain in the vehicle. While writing the ticket, the officer should keep a watchful eye on what is going on in the violator's vehicle.

The officer should return to issue the traffic ticket taking the same route as when initiating the stop. When recontacting the violator, the officer should explain the ticket thoroughly to the driver. Always avoid lecturing the driver when issuing the citation. Oftentimes a lecture by the officer may aggravate the driver and lead to an argument. Arguing with a traffic violator is not the officer's job. Neither is debating the traffic ticket with the violator. The officer should advise violators who want to argue about the citation that they have the right to appear in court and contest the ticket if they feel it was unjustly issued.

Once the contact has concluded, the officer should thank the violator for his or her cooperation. The officer should never say things such as "have a nice day" to a violator. This is inappropriate and may make the violator angry. The officer should end the contact with: "please slow down and drive carefully." The officer should remain at the scene of the stop with emergency lights activated until the violator has had a chance to pull safely back into the flow of traffic.

emergency operations mode / When a police car is traveling with red lights and siren in operation. This is sometimes referred to as "code three" driving.

EMERGENCY VEHICLE OPERATION

There are a number of situations in which officers operate in an **emergency operations mode**. The emergency vehicle operation mode, or "code three" as it is sometimes called, is when the officer drives with red lights and siren activated in order to respond quickly to a police call.

Previously in this chapter we discussed the high-speed pursuit as one such situation when the police respond code three; however, there are many other emergency situations that the police may need to respond to in a code three mode. When an officer is allowed to run code three to a call will vary from agency to agency. In some police agencies officers are authorized to drive code three when responding to injury accidents, while in others they are not. There are some calls that always result in a code three response. An officer in trouble will almost always result in a code three response from other police units, usually numerous other police units. Police officers reading this text are advised to consult their agency's standard operating procedure for the specific emergency vehicle operations guidelines of their agency. While most agencies' standard operating procedure will dictate response modes to a given call, officers should always weigh the following information:

- The nature of the call and the information received from the dispatcher.
- The immediate presence of an officer needed at the scene.
- Whether other emergency service providers are at, or responding to the scene.
- Whether there are other units closer to the call.
- Other relevant information available to the officer at the time.
- The risk created by the emergency response.
- The prevailing conditions, such as weather, lighting, roadway conditions, visibility, and traffic volume.
- The reaction that the approach of a vehicle with emergency lights and siren might cause at the scene of the incident.

Like many other police activities, driving code three is dangerous and carries with it a significant amount of potential liability. Generally, most state statutes define code three driving as a police vehicle operating with red lights illuminated and siren in operation. Furthermore, most state statutes allow police officers while operating in a code three mode to disregard traffic laws. For example, the State of

Texas Vehicle Code—Emergency Vehicle Operations

546.001. PERMISSIBLE CONDUCT. In operating an authorized emergency vehicle the operator may:

1. park or stand, irrespective of another provision of this subtitle;
2. proceed past a red or stop signal or stop sign, after slowing as necessary for safe operation;
3. exceed a maximum speed limit, except as provided by an ordinance adopted under Section 545.365, as long as the operator does not endanger life or property; and
4. disregard a regulation governing the direction of movement or turning in specified directions.

Texas statute pertaining to emergency vehicle operations allows officers to disregard traffic laws.

Driving Code Three

Responding code three to a call requires a police officer to be especially cautious and to drive in a defensive manner. Simply put, driving in a defensive manner means not only taking responsibility for yourself and your actions, but also keeping an eye on the other guy.

The police vehicle has often been touted as the most dangerous weapon in a police officer's arsenal. A moving vehicle develops thousands of foot-pounds of energy. The police officer as a driver has the responsibility not to use that energy to injure or kill others, or damage their property. Paying attention makes it possible to see, recognize, and avoid the hazards lurking on the road; these are the three basic elements of defensive driving. The primary attribute necessary for safe defensive driving when operating code three is alertness, and paying attention is the most important driving task because it helps create the time you need to recognize hazards and avoid a collision. As a general rule, officers should not respond in a code three mode when the response creates a risk greater than the emergency at the scene of the incident.

When driving code three, police officers should always drive with both hands on the steering wheel. An officer should never pass another vehicle on the right. Passing should only be done on the left side of traffic. Think about it for a moment, what is generally the legal requirement for motorists when they see an approaching emergency vehicle? They pull over to the right and stop. Obviously, an officer that is passing traffic on the right can cause an accident. When approaching an intersection with a red signal light or stop sign, it is recommended that officers come to a complete stop and then proceed with caution. This is in light of the fact that many state statutes, like the Texas statute, only require that police officers slow at red signal lights and then proceed with due caution. Individual police agencies' standard operating procedures are usually more restrictive on emergency vehicle operations than most state statutes.

A few problems that police officers should be aware of when operating code three are tunnel vision, hydroplaning, and skidding. Each of these problems has the potential to result in an accident.

Tunnel vision is the central vision with loss of or a lack of attention to peripheral vision. Tunnel vision occurs when police officers driving code three get so focused on what's going on directly in front of them that they ignore or may not be aware of cross vehicle or pedestrian traffic. In other words, the officer's inability to recognize things outside of the tunnel area is particularly dangerous and may result in an accident.

If an officer finds himself or herself running code three on a wet roadway, *hydroplaning* could be a potentially serious problem. Hydroplaning occurs when the tread on your tires cannot channel all the rainwater out from under the tires or from under each patch of tire that is supposed to be resting on the road and providing the police vehicle with traction. The first indication that the police vehicle is hydroplaning will be when the vehicle pulls suddenly in deeper water and begins to slide out of control, or the officer may be approaching a curve and discover that the vehicle doesn't respond to the steering input. If the police vehicle begins to hydroplane, do not touch the brakes, because this may cause the vehicle to go further out of control. The officer should simply slow down by smoothly lifting his or her foot from the accelerator and letting the vehicle coast down to the point where the hydroplaning stops.

Skidding can also be problematic when driving code three. A type of skid that is common in code three driving is the oversteer, or "fishtailing" as it is sometimes called. Fishtailing occurs when the front wheels of the patrol vehicle are taking a shorter path than desired and the rear end breaks loose and fishtails. If an officer finds himself or herself in an oversteer skid, the first thing to do is let off the accelerator pedal, stay off the brake, or smoothly release brake pressure if already applied. The officer should then as quickly as possible turn the steering wheel in the direction that he or she wants the front of the car to go. This means aligning the tires of the police vehicle with the direction of the intended travel.

The risks of driving code three are many. The only sure thing that an officer can do is drive in the most prudent manner, and to drive defensively. An officer who violates state law or departmental standard operating procedures while driving code three brings a great deal of liability on himself or herself, and the police agency. When driving code three officers should always remember to:

1. Never assume that emergency equipment has actually made other drivers aware of their presence.

2. Never approach any intersection at a speed faster than would permit a safe stop should a hazard suddenly appear.

3. Always be prepared for the unexpected, "stupid" driving maneuver on the part of others in the traffic environment.

4. Never assume that they have the right away, regardless of the intersection being approached. (Autin, 1989, p. 210)

THE USE OF FORCE

Law enforcement officers are confronted daily with situations requiring the use of force to successfully make an arrest or ensure public safety. Law enforcement officers are legally justified in using force to make an arrest, and they do not have to retreat from an arrest when the suspect is resisting. The degree of force used depends on what the officer perceives as reasonable and necessary under the circumstances at the time the decision to use force is made.

The absolute guideline in the use of force is that only the minimal amount of force necessary to make an arrest or defuse a situation should be used. Imagine for a moment that a police officer is investigating a disturbance at a neighborhood bar involving a rowdy drunk. Let's suppose that the rowdy drunk assaulted the owner of the bar after the owner refused to serve the drunk any additional alcoholic drinks. Subsequently, and without incident, the drunk is placed under arrest and handcuffed by the investigating officer. While the officer is walking the drunk to the police car the handcuffed and belligerent drunk attempts to run from the officer, but falls to the ground after about ten yards. The officer then delivers several blows with his PR-24 baton to the suspect as he lays handcuffed on the ground. Is this force reasonable? Is this the minimal amount of force necessary? The short answer is "no". In this case the officer went too far by striking the handcuffed drunk with the baton. The drunk was in custody and handcuffed. In this case it would be very difficult for the officer to justify that the use of force was necessary.

How do police officers know what force to use in which situations? This is a perplexing dilemma that police officers face every day. When the use of force is reasonable and necessary, officers should, to the extent possible, use an escalating scale of options and not employ more forceful means unless it is determined that a lower level of force would not be, or has not been, adequate. Most police agencies have adopted a use of force continuum. Typically, the use of force continuum consists of six levels: (1) physical appearance, (2) verbalization, (3) weaponless strategies, (4) CAP-STUN, (5) impact weapons, and (6) lethal force. The use of force continuum provides a guide for police officers as to how much force they should use in a given situation.

The use of force continuum represents an escalation in force from the preceding level when a situation warrants such escalation. Each situation that a police officer encounters is unique. Good judgment and the circumstances of each situation will dictate the level on the continuum of force at which an officer will start. Depending on the circumstances, officers may find it necessary to escalate or de-escalate the use of force by progressing up or down the force continuum.

The police officer does not have to enter at the lowest option on the use of force continuum. The officer can enter at the level that is reasonable to defuse the situation. If a suspect approaches an officer with a deadly weapon, let's say a knife, the officer should meet this force by drawing his or her weapon and ordering the suspect to drop the knife. If the suspect fails to drop the knife and makes an aggressive move toward the officer, the officer is justified in using lethal force. It is important to point out that the objective of the officer should be to approach each

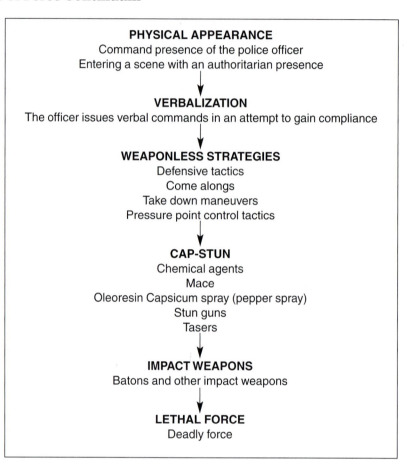

PRACTICE HINTS

Use of Force Continuum

PHYSICAL APPEARANCE
Command presence of the police officer
Entering a scene with an authoritarian presence

VERBALIZATION
The officer issues verbal commands in an attempt to gain compliance

WEAPONLESS STRATEGIES
Defensive tactics
Come alongs
Take down maneuvers
Pressure point control tactics

CAP-STUN
Chemical agents
Mace
Oleoresin Capsicum spray (pepper spray)
Stun guns
Tasers

IMPACT WEAPONS
Batons and other impact weapons

LETHAL FORCE
Deadly force

situation on the lowest level of the continuum as possible, in order to achieve the best resolution to the problem. We discuss police use of force, including legal consideration, in greater detail in Chapter 6.

Tasers

There has been some debate on whether electric Tasers should be placed in the use of force continuum. One argument is that Tasers should not be placed before weaponless strategies on the continuum because officers may get into the habit of using them on every suspect who resists regardless of severity of the resisting actions of the suspect. In other words, there is some argument that Tasers should not be used as a compliance tool, such as using a Taser on a suspect who is running away or would not follow commands to raise their hands, turn around, or to simply lie on the ground. However, there is some thought that as a matter of officer safety, the Taser should be placed directly after verbalization on the continuum. The logic of this view is that this would prevent the officer from having to physically engage the suspect until he or she is in complete compliance. The Taser weapons are touted by many law enforcement authorities as a safe, nonlethal alternative to using a gun in a violent confrontation.

Electric Taser guns are a relatively new defensive weapon in the police arsenal. The biggest selling point for using the Taser is that it has the potential to reduce the number of police shootings. Many law enforcement agencies authorize their officers to use the Taser as a less than lethal force option. One problem with the Taser is that there is not much objective empirical data on the potential harm that the Taser could cause a suspect. Most of the evaluations that have been completed on the Taser are from Taser manufacturers themselves. Of course, these evaluations should be viewed with caution. Police commanders should make informed and cautious decisions when equipping their officers with Tasers.

Some have described being hit with a Taser as a very painful experience. A sheriff's deputy serving with a Midwestern sheriff's department volunteered to get shot with a Taser gun during a training session put on by his agency. The deputy equated being hit with the Taser to getting shocked by an electrical socket in your home, and being hit in the funny bone. Listen to what he said: "If you have ever accidentally shocked yourself in a wall socket in your home, that's what it feels like, but only multiplied several times. You are completely helpless. I could see what was going on around me, but I could not move. I was paralyzed. Another way I would describe it is like being hit in the funny bone. Imagine being hit in

---

PRACTICE HINTS

Electric Taser Gun at a Glance

The electric Taser is a handgun-sized weapon that can deliver 50,000 volts to an unruly suspect from distances up to 18–30 feet away. Tasers fire small dart-like electrodes that stick to the suspect. The electrical voltage can then be administered by the officers. Newer versions of the Taser allow for neuromuscular disruption without needing metal prongs penetrating the skin. Use of the device allows police to deal with unruly suspects from a relatively safe distance without having to resort to deadly force. There has been some concern over allegations of the effect that Taser guns may have on people with heart problems, as well as their potential use as torture devices and their effect on people under the influence of drugs. These concerns, along with a lack of independent studies on the dangers of the Taser gun, have led many agencies to allow it to be used only by special units or by supervisors.

your funny bone, but magnify it 100 times. If I wasn't being held up by two other deputies, I would have fallen to the ground. It was very painful. Once it was over I felt fine, but when I was being shocked, it definitely incapacitated me."

SUMMARY

- Police officers often face stressful events in their lives. Many police officers work one or two part-time jobs to simply make ends meet. They struggle to find time to spend with their families, only to be called in for court testimony during their off-duty hours. They may report for patrol duty with minimal sleep, which results in their alertness being diminished.

- Regardless of the stress that police officers are burdened with, they have to mentally and physically prepare for patrol duties. The proper preparation could mean the difference of risking serous injury to themselves, citizens, or other officers. Proper patrol preparation is being alert. If an officer feels himself or herself becoming sleepy, a short, brisk walk could go a long way in rejuvenating the officer.

- An officer's appearance should be impeccable prior to initiating a tour of duty. Equipment checks should be made and improperly operating equipment should be replaced.

- Prior to a tour of duty, police officers attend a squad meeting or squad debriefing. The meeting is usually held about fifteen to thirty minutes prior to assuming patrol duties. The meeting is conducted by a supervisor or watch commander, and police officers are debriefed about significant crime events occurring during the prior shifts.

- The officer should also make it a point to check the patrol vehicle out thoroughly. This includes the red lights, siren, air horn, police radio, equipment, tires, and other important items or equipment.

- Any police equipment that is not functioning correctly should be reported immediately. An officer should never take a patrol vehicle on the streets that is not running properly or one where the red lights or sirens are malfunctioning.

- It is good practice for the officer to meet briefly with the officer he or she is relieving. This is an ideal venue to exchange information about persons, places, or events occurring on the beat.

- During a tour of duty the officer should always be on the lookout for potential hazards on the beat. This may include frequent contacts with law-abiding citizens and persons who are known to the officer to be delinquent or criminal. Establishments such as bars and adult entertainment clubs should be inspected on a periodic basis. Many of these establishments are known hang-outs for shady individuals.

- If an officer has the occasion to make an arrest, he or she should always view officer safety as a priority.

- Once an arrest has been made, the suspect should be handcuffed first and then searched. A handcuffed suspect is much less likely to attempt to resist the officer.

- Departmental standard operating procedures should be followed when handcuffing and transporting a suspect to the booking facility.

- When dealing with offenders, the officer should always expect the worse. In other words, he or she should anticipate problems before they occur. An unprepared officer is a potential liability to himself and others.

- Police officers usually respond to crimes that have already occurred and crimes in progress while patrolling their beat. The type of crime in progress will dictate the police response. For example, some calls will require the police to run with red lights and siren, while other crimes in progress may require a more stealthy response.

- Unfortunately, the police are often called to deal with civil unrest. Whether it is a small gathering of demonstrators or a crowd that is out of control, the police must respond quickly and effectively.

- If the police have knowledge of a demonstration or other large event, they should plan as much as possible. Ideally, this would involve the leaders of the demonstration or protest meeting with the police. The police would then have the opportunity to inform the group about what police action will be taken and relevant state laws.

■ If a demonstration gets out of control and results in a riot, the primary objective of the police is to safeguard life and property while ending the civil unrest as quickly as possible.

■ High-speed pursuits pose a serious liability for the police. The police should always weigh the risk associated with continuing the pursuit with the risk of serious injury to persons or property. There are several factors that should be considered in the decision to continue a pursuit, including time of day, weather, charges, whether the officer has the driver identified, and availability of the air section, to name a few.

■ Weather and natural disasters can be overwhelming for the police agency in terms of ensuring adequate police resources are available to respond to a disaster. This not only includes police personnel, but also equipment.

■ The first objective of the first officer who has checked out the scene of a disaster is to assess the scope of the problem and communicate this back to the dispatcher.

■ Police concerns at the scene of a natural disaster include containing the scene, collecting evidence that may have been spread out over a great distance, controlling for looters, removing curious citizens who have traveled to see the disaster scene, the location and recovery of the injured, and the recovery and identification of deceased victims.

■ The police canine is a valuable asset for police operations. The canine can be used for tracking missing persons or suspects, crowd control, bomb detection, narcotics detection, officer protection, and to aid in the recovery of bodies. It is important that the police dog be trained with the canine handler and that the department has the proper budget to maintain the dog.

■ For liability purposes it is imperative that the police agency keep the proper records on the canine's training and performance. Standard operating procedures should also be developed for canine operations and closely followed.

■ Most citizens' only contact with the police will be through traffic stops.

■ The police officer must always expect the worst on a traffic stop. There is no such thing as a routine traffic stop.

■ The officer should initiate the traffic stop when and where he or she feels comfortable. As much information should be obtained prior to initiating the stop.

■ An officer should practice good officer safety techniques during a traffic stop.

■ Like pursuit driving, responding to emergency calls in a code three mode (red lights and siren) is dangerous and can pose great liability for the police agency if the officer running code three was driving negligently and was involved in an accident.

■ Officers should always weigh the risks associated with code three driving. Factors that may influence the decision to run code three are weather conditions, the nature of the emergency, as well as the location of other emergency responders.

■ Police officers can use force to make an arrest or defuse a situation.

■ Police officers should always use the least amount of force necessary to defuse a situation.

■ Police officers use a "force continuum," a spectrum of force alternatives, to moderate the level of response used in a given situation.

■ The use of force continuum provides a general guideline for the police to follow in a situation where force will be used. The lowest level of force is the mere command presence of the officer, and flows to the highest level on the continuum, which is deadly force.

■ Each situation is unique. Good judgment and the circumstances of each situation will dictate the level on the continuum of force at which an officer will start. Depending on the circumstances, officers may find it necessary to escalate or de-escalate the use of force by progressing up or down the force continuum.

■ Police agencies should develop use of force policies that address a wide spectrum of force issues. This includes the use of firearms and other weapons, and particular use of force issues such as firing at moving vehicles, verbal warnings, positional asphyxia, bar arm restraints, the use of chemical agents, and the use of electric Taser guns.

Classroom Discussion Questions and Activities

1. Ride as an observer with a police officer and observe situations where you believe the officer is following standard operating procedures.

2. Interview two police officers from two different law enforcement agencies about their emergency vehicle operating procedures. How are they different or similar?

3. Form groups and discuss the pros and cons to the police driving in an emergency red lights and siren mode.

4. What is the use of force continuum?

5. Describe a few of the issues centering on the use of Taser guns.

6. Describe the factors that should be taken into consideration in the decision to continue a police pursuit.

7. Describe how a police canine can assist in police operations.

Websites and Other Resources

Police Pursuit Website:
www.policedriving.com

Missouri Police Canine Association:
www.mopolicek9.com

National Police Canine Association:
www.npca.net

Los Angeles County Canine Association:
www.lacpca.com

Uniform Crime Report:
www.fbi.gov/ucr/ucr.htm

Bureau of Justice Statistics, Use of Force by Police:
www.ojp.usdoj.gov/bjs/abstract/ufbponld.htm

Bureau of Justice Statistics, Police Use of Force: Collection of National Data:
www.ojp.usdoj.gov/bjs/abstract/puof.htm

Solving Crime Problems in Residential Neighborhoods:
www.ncjrs.org/txtfiles/164488.txt

References

Alpert, G. P. (1997). *Police pursuit: Policies and training.* Washington, DC: U.S. Department of Justice.

Alpert, G. P. (1998). Helicopters in pursuit operations. *National institute of justice: Research in action.* Washington, DC: U.S. Department of Justice.

American Institute for Preventive Medicine. (2001). *Ten tips for preventing burnout.* Retrieved June 21, 2006 from infotech@wellnesscheckpoint.com.

Autin, J. H. (1989). *Law enforcement driving.* Springfield, IL: Charles C. Thomas Publisher.

Barker, T. (1998). *Emergency vehicle operations: Emergency calls for pursuit driving.* Springfield, IL: Charles C. Thomas Publisher.

Becker, H. S. (1973). *Outsiders: Studies in the sociology of deviance.* New York: Free Press.

Federal Bureau of Investigation. (2004). *Officers killed and assaulted 2004.* Retrieved from www.fbi.gov/research.htm.

FBI, U.S. Dept. of Justice (2005). "Law Enforcement Officers Killed in 2004," Washington, DC. G.P.O.

Friedmann, R. R. (1992). *Community policing: Perspectives and prospects.* New York: St. Martin's Press.

Garner, G. W. (2005). *Surviving the street: Officer safety and survival techniques.* Springfield, IL: Charles C. Thomas Publisher.

Goldstein, H. (1990). *Problem oriented policing.* New York: McGraw Hill.

Hamilton, M. (2003). How to start a K-9 unit: Four legged cops can help you catch more criminals and cut your department's costs. *Police: The Law Enforcement Magazine, 27,* 18–20.

Hickman, M. J., & Reaves, B. A. (2003). *Local police departments 2003*. Bureau of Justice Statistics. Retrieved from www.ojp.usdoj.gov/bjs/abstract/lpd03.htm.

Hill, J. (2002). High speed police pursuits: Dangers, dynamics, and risk reduction. *FBI Law Enforcement Bulletin, 71*, 14–18.

Iannone, N. F., & Iannone, M. P. (2006). *Supervision of police personnel* (6th ed.). Upper Saddle River, NJ: Prentice Hall.

Mastrofski, S. (1983). The police and non-crime services. In G. Whitaker and C. Phillips (Eds.), *Evaluating the performance of criminal justice agencies* (p. 40). Beverly Hills, CA: Sage.

Merton, R. K. (1968). *Social theory and social structure*. New York: Free Press.

Pipes, C., & Papes, D. (2001). Police pursuits and civil liability. *FBI Law Enforcement Bulletin, 70*, 16–21.

Rivara, F. P., & Mack, C. D. (2004). Motor vehicle crash deaths related to police pursuits in the United States. *Injury Prevention, 10*, 93–95.

Scoville, D. (2005). Working with dogs: What K-9 handlers want you to know about their four-legged creatures. *Police: The Law Enforcement Magazine, 29*, 44–46.

Scoville, D. (2006). Killer stops. *Police: The Law Enforcement Magazine, 30*(6), 42–44.

Spilner, M. (2000). *Prevention's complete book of walking: Everything you need to know to walk yourself to better health*. Emmaus, PA: Rodale.

Urboyna, K. R. (1991). The constitutionality of high-speed pursuits under the fourth amendment. *Saint Louis University Law Journal, 35*, 35–205.

Whisenand, P. M., & Cline, J. L. (1971). *Patrol operations*. Englewood Cliffs, NJ: Prentice Hall.

Chapter 3

Police Operations in a Community Policing Environment

" The police at all times should maintain a relationship with the public that gives reality to the historic tradition that the police are the public and that the public are the police; the police are the only members of the public who are paid to give full-time attention to duties which are incumbent on every citizen in the interest of community welfare. "

—Sir Robert Peel
Founder, London Metropolitan Police, 1829

CHAPTER OUTLINE

OBJECTIVES

OBJECTIVES

After completion of this chapter, you will be able to do the following:

- Define the community policing strategy.
- Identify and discuss the core components of community policing.
- Identify the components of the SARA model of problem solving.
- Describe the differences in traditional policing, versus community policing.
- Discuss evaluations of community policing.
- Describe the role of community in terrorism prevention and detection.

INTRODUCTION

Officer Harris, an eight-year veteran of the police department, works the second watch patrol in a mid-sized U.S. city. One evening while on patrol, Officer Harris receives a radio call to report to a local park and investigate a group of rowdy juveniles. Officer Harris thinks to himself that it won't take long to clear the juveniles out of the park. This is the fourth time in the past month that Officer Harris has responded to this same call. It's always the same handful of juveniles that congregate. He always handles the situation the same way by ordering the juveniles to leave the park. He arrives at the park a few moments later and observes a group of about ten juveniles standing around listening to loud music and bouncing a basketball back and forth.

Officer Harris, still sitting in his patrol vehicle, picks up the microphone of the public address system and loudly orders the juveniles to leave the park at once, telling them if they return again this evening they will be issued citations. He watches as the juveniles slowly walk out of the park. After a few minutes, Officer Harris checks back in service with the dispatcher and drives to his favorite restaurant to grab a bite to eat. While eating his dinner, he thinks to himself that he did not even have to leave his vehicle to take care of the call.

Now, imagine another version of the same account. Officer Smith, a three-year veteran of the police department, works the second watch patrol in a mid-sized U.S. city. One evening while on patrol she receives a radio call to investigate a group of rowdy juveniles in the local park. Officer Smith thinks to herself that she has responded to this same call several times during the past month. She arrives at the park and observes a group of about ten juveniles bouncing a basketball and listening to loud music. She gets out of the patrol car and initiates conversation with the group of juveniles.

After several minutes, Officer Smith learns that the juveniles live a few blocks from the park and that they usually gather in the park a few nights a week to play pick-up basketball games, but about one month ago the rim broke off of the backboard. The juveniles inform Officer Smith that because they can't play basketball they meet, hang out, and listen to music because there is nothing else to do. Officer Smith has learned that this gives the impression to the citizens living near the park that the juveniles are idle and looking for trouble.

The next day Officer Smith calls the parks and recreation department and reports the broken basketball rim. Within a few days the rim is replaced. Several weeks pass and Officer Smith checks the log for any police calls at the park. She notices that there have been no additional police calls at the park. While she is patrolling around the park one evening she observes the group of juveniles playing basketball. One of the juveniles flags her over and thanks her for getting the basketball rim fixed. The juvenile then proceeds to inform her about a vehicle that has been driving around the park and selling drugs. The juvenile supplies Officer Smith with a tag number and description of the driver. Officer Smith asks the juvenile, "Why are you giving me this information?" The juvenile replies, "You helped us out and we owe you one. Besides, we don't want someone selling drugs in our neighborhood; I've got a little brother and sister that play in this park, too."

The first account involving Officer Harris represents a fairly common and traditional approach to patrol, which goes something like this: get to the call, deal with the problem quickly, and then get back in service. However, the second account involving Officer Smith represents a community policing approach that utilizes problem solving. The first approach does little to solve the underlying problem, which in this case was the broken basketball rim. Because the basketball rim was broken the juveniles could not play basketball. They passed the time by hanging out and listening to loud music. Citizens living in the neighborhood interpreted this as a group of idle juveniles looking for trouble.

Notice in the second approach to the problem that Officer Smith discovered that the underlying problem was the broken basketball rim. Once the broken basketball rim was replaced, the police calls (incidents) in the park resolved. It only took Officer Smith a few minutes to make a telephone call to the parks and recreation department and report that the basketball rim was broken. However, the first response to the problem by Officer Harris would likely result in additional calls to the park. Officer Harris offered a temporary solution to the problem by ordering the juveniles to leave. Chances are that he will be dealing with the same problem the next weekend. Which approach do you think is the most effective?

The hypothetical scenario presented represents the nature of many calls for police services in the United States. Police routinely respond to minor order maintenance problems that don't take a significant amount of police time or resources to solve. The resolution of small order maintenance problems can sometimes result in payoffs in terms of citizen satisfaction that can never be fully realized. Citizens who are satisfied with the police department are more likely to cooperate with the police and voluntarily comply with laws and ordinances. This chapter introduces the reader to community-oriented policing with its emphasis on problem solving. The chapter also discusses how police officers can utilize this strategy on the job and provides several examples.

THE EMERGENCE OF COMMUNITY POLICING

Since the 1994 Crime Act set community policing in motion, two-thirds of U.S. police departments and 62 percent of sheriff's offices have full-time personnel performing **community policing** (National Institute of Justice, 2004). Community policing has been presented in the literature as constituting a viable way to prevent crime, as well as being applied to the goals of organizational change. Community policing involves fundamental and strategic change in almost all areas of policing (Palmiotto, Birzer, & Unnithan, 2000). It is a relatively new approach to law enforcement designed to reduce and prevent crime by increasing interaction and cooperation between local law enforcement agencies and the people and neighborhoods they serve. It represents a new era of police services where the government asks the public to help in resolving crime-related problems (Thurman & Reisig, 1996).

community policing / A strategy of policing that focuses on the police working with the public to prevent and solve crime-related problems. Community policing is a strategy that entails organizational reengineering, problem solving, and partnerships.

Community-oriented policing is not a program, it is a philosophy or strategy, a way each department member from the top to bottom, sworn to nonsworn, views their job. This philosophy must permeate the entire organization, local government, and community, not just the "community policing officers" or the patrol division (Mastrofski & Ritti, 2000).

Community policing is a philosophy based on the concept that the police and citizens working together in creative ways can solve contemporary community problems related to crime, fear of crime, social and physical disorder, and general neighborhood conditions. The philosophy is founded on the belief that achieving these goals requires the police to develop a new relationship with citizens, allowing them the power to set local police priorities and involving them in efforts to improve the overall quality of life in their community. Community policing shifts the focus of police work from just handling random crime calls to addressing community concerns. It has grown from a few small foot patrol projects to the preeminent reform agenda of modern policing.

Voices of Experience

Community Policing

Excerpts from an interview between Cliff Roberson and former police officer Robert Boyer. Professor Boyer is currently a professor of criminal justice at Luzerne County Community College, Nanticoke, Pennsylvania. Professor Boyer also continues to work as a part-time police officer in Pennsylvania. In addition, he is the mayor of Wyoming, Pennsylvania.

Q: *How do police officers feel about community policing?*
A: At first, a lot of police officers viewed community policing as social work. But as officers began to understand what it was and how it made their job easier down the road, they accepted it. Most officers now look at community policing as a partnership idea, with the police and the community working together to solve community problems. For example, drugs are not just a police problem, but also a community problem. When you have the police and the community working together to target a problem, the officer's job will be easier. ■

Community policing has evolved from strategies such as police–community relations, team policing, crime prevention, and foot patrol. However, a major thrust for community policing was initiated with the research findings of the 1970s. Many of these findings shattered a few of the traditional assumptions about police patrol strategies. Two such studies were the Kansas City Preventive Patrol Experiment and the Newark Foot Patrol Study.

The Kansas City Preventive Patrol Experiment

For years, preventive police patrol was considered one of the best deterrents of criminal behavior. Preventive patrol is based on the premise that in between calls for service, officers are expected to randomly cruise neighborhoods, seeking out and deterring crime. Preventive patrol, or random patrol, as it is called in some localities, creates the illusion of a significant police presence. It is believed that preventive patrol decreases citizens' fear and deters would-be offenders. However, **The Kansas City Preventive Patrol Experiment** seems to indicate that preventive patrol may not be as effective as previously thought.

In 1972, with funding and technical assistance from the Police Foundation, the Kansas City, Missouri Police Department launched a comprehensive, scientifically rigorous experiment to test the effects of police patrol on crime. The experiment began on October 1, 1972 and continued through September 30, 1973; it was administered by the Kansas City Police Department and evaluated by the Police Foundation.

The study divided Kansas City into fifteen districts. Five of the districts retained normal police patrols, five districts greatly increased the number of police patrols, and the final five used the reactive approach and responded only when called by citizens. The researchers asked the following questions:

1. Would citizens notice changes in the level of police patrol?
2. Would different levels of visible police patrol affect recorded crime or the outcome of victim surveys?
3. Would citizen fear of crime and attendant behavior change as a result of differing patrol levels?
4. Would the citizens' degree of satisfaction with the police change?

Information was gathered from victimization surveys, reported crime rates, arrest data, a survey of local businesses, attitudinal surveys, and trained observers who monitored police–citizen interaction. The researchers concluded that the variations in police patrol techniques appeared to have little effect on citizens' attitudes toward the police, their satisfaction with the police, or their fear of crime (Keeling, Pate, Diekman, & Brown, 1974).

While the study has been criticized because of its research design, it has greatly influenced the thinking of researchers on the effectiveness of police patrol. Nevertheless, the Kansas City study remains the most comprehensive study conducted to analyze the effectiveness of traditional preventive patrol.

Newark Foot Patrol Study

Until relatively recently there were minimal evaluations on the effectiveness of **foot patrol** activities. One of the more referenced studies on foot patrol is the Newark Foot

Kansas City preventive patrol experiment / This seminal experiment found that traditional routine patrol strategies in marked police cars do not appear to affect the level of crime, nor does it affect the public's feeling of security. The experiment demonstrated that urban police departments can successfully test patrol deployment strategies and that they can manipulate patrol resources without jeopardizing public safety.

foot patrol / A method where police officers patrol their assigned beat on foot. The objective is that police officers will become better acquainted with citizens and thus more knowledgeable about community concerns. Many police agencies have brought foot patrol back into their operations as a result of evolving community policing strategies.

Patrol Experiment, which was conducted in 1978. In 1973, the New Jersey state legislature passed the Safe and Clean Neighborhoods Act. Unique in the nation and aptly named, this legislation sought to create safe and clean neighborhoods. Foot patrol was specifically mandated as part of an effort to expand the presence and visibility of police protection.

At the invitation of the governor of New Jersey, the Police Foundation evaluated foot patrol in twenty-eight New Jersey cities (Police Foundation, 1981). Newark was selected as the primary evaluation site. The evaluation began in February 1978 and ended in January 1979. The Police Foundation evaluation posed the following questions:

1. Does foot patrol improve police–citizen relationships?

2. Do citizens feel safer when officers patrol on foot?

3. Does foot patrol reduce crime?

4. Will citizens report more crime when they have closer contact with the police?

5. Will more arrests be made in foot-patrolled areas?

6. Will foot patrol officers be more satisfied with their jobs and have more positive attitudes about citizens?

7. Will citizens' fear of victimization be lessened?

PRACTICE HINTS

Traditional Policing Is Based on Three Primary Assumptions:

1. **Preventive patrol:** Based on the premise that in between calls for service, officers are expected to randomly cruise neighborhoods, seeking out and deterring crime. Preventive patrol, or random patrol, as it is called in some localities, creates the illusion of significant police presence. Many police reformers, most notably O. W. Wilson, believed that preventive patrol decreases citizens' fear and deters would-be offenders.

2. **Rapid response:** Common wisdom suggests that responding quickly to the scene of an incident increases the police's ability to catch the offender. In addition, a quick response aids in victim assistance. As a result, calls for police services are dispatched swiftly and new technology is continuously sought to improve response time.

3. **Follow-up criminal investigation:** When offenders are not caught initially, law enforcement agencies rely on follow-up investigations. Evidence is gathered and leads in the case are pursued for the purpose of closing and clearing cases.

Eight foot patrol beats in Newark were matched demographically. Foot patrol was continued in four randomly selected beats, and discontinued in four others. Foot patrol was also initiated in four beats where it had not previously been used. Researchers then began comparing reported crime, arrest and victimization rates, citizen fear and satisfaction with police services, as well as the attitude of foot patrol officers and officers on motorized patrol.

The Police Foundation contends that introducing foot patrol along with a variety of other police strategies significantly enhances the citizens' perception of safety in the neighborhood. This is something no other police strategy had been able to do. Although introducing foot patrol seemed to have little effect on crime rates, it did have the following positive effects:

1. Residents knew when officers were patrolling their neighborhoods on foot.

2. Residents in areas patrolled by officers on foot thought that crime was less of a problem than did residents in areas with only motorized patrol.

3. Residents in areas with foot patrol felt safer and less likely to be victimized.

4. Residents living in areas with foot patrol took fewer steps to protect themselves against crime.

5. Residents in areas with foot patrol were more satisfied with police services.

Residents in areas where foot patrol was introduced clearly changed their attitudes about crime and how they felt about the safety and livability of their neighborhoods. They were also more satisfied with police services. While foot patrol had no effect on recorded crime rates, it should be noted that citizens feel threatened by noncriminal (disorderly) behavior as well, and that this threat of victimization may dramatically alter their lives. In response to a perceived threat, they may nail their windows shut, carry lethal weapons, or avoid walking in their own neighborhood. Thus, fear can undermine the viability of major cities and erode the quality of urban dwellers.

PRACTICE HINTS

Significant Policing Research of the 1980s

1. The Birmingham, Alabama Police Department conducted a study on the use of differential police response strategies. These strategies included call prioritization, call stacking, delayed response, supervisory override of dispatch authority, and the use of teleserve units. These strategies were designed to reduce the call load so patrol officers would have more uncommitted time to address crime problems in their areas.

2. The Newark, New Jersey Police Department Foot Patrol Study showed that the police could develop positive attitudes about citizens and promote positive attitudes toward the police if they spent time on foot in their communities. The assumption was that positive attitudes would result in the exchange of information about crime and disorder problems.

3. Herman Goldstein developed the concept of problem-oriented policing. Goldstein maintained that the police should move away from a reactive, incident orientation and move toward identifying and addressing the crime and disorder problems that continued to drain police resources. The concept was tested at the Newport News, Virginia Police Department and was found to be effective. An implication from this study was the need to develop formal call-screening procedures to accurately discriminate between emergency and non-emergency calls for service. It was further suggested that call-

stacking procedures be developed so calls could be prioritized with varying delays, thereby ensuring that the most urgent calls received the quickest response. If call dispatching could be managed more efficiently, patrol officers would have more uncommitted time.

4. The Kansas City Directed Patrol Study demonstrated that officers could make better use of their time by using various tactical responses to deter specific crimes. These efforts were guided by crime analysis and supported through citizen reporting strategies, such as teleserve and walk-in reporting.

5. The San Diego Police Department instituted a community-oriented policing project in the early 1970s. The concept of "beat profiling" was first used by patrol officers to learn about the topographic, demographic, and call histories on their beats. The officers also had the discretion to develop "tailored patrol strategies" to address crime and citizen concerns. In actuality, these studies suggest that police managers begin rethinking how to more effectively allocate and use their resources, especially their most precious resource, the patrol officer. These studies also indicate that the police need to enlist citizens' support and participation.

Source: Community Policing Consortium: www. communitypolicing .org. Accessed online November 13, 2006.

Voices of Experience

Failure to Arrest

Excerpts from an interview between Cliff Roberson and former police officer,
Scott W. Phillips, currently a professor at Buffalo State College, Buffalo,
New York.

Q: *Tell us about a time you failed to arrest a law violator.*
A: Once when I was a rookie, my training partner and I answered this call regarding a disturbance of peace. It was about 11:00 A.M. and the individual involved was a drunk. The training officer, my partner, just tells him to beat it. I think to myself: "This individual is drunk, it is a public place, and he is disturbing the peace—why didn't we arrest him?" A short while later we received another disturbance call. When we responded, we discovered that it was the same drunk. This time he was lying on someone's front porch. Again, the training officer just told the drunk to go home and stop bothering people. My thought was: "Why aren't we arresting this guy?" It was only after I had been with the department for a time did I realize that because of resources, time constraints, the severity of the crime, and other issues that I learned that officers cannot arrest every single person who violates the law. If they did, they would not be available for emergency calls, traffic enforcement, and other needed situations. The officer has to weigh those factors in determining whether to take official actions. ■

Implementation

Evaluations have found there are many variations in how community policing strategies among police agencies are implemented (Taylor-Green, 1993). There are some police departments that implemented community policing as a specialized approach. These departments may have a community policing unit comprised of a select number of officers. Other police departments have implemented community policing as a holistic operational strategy. In other words, all rank-and-file police personnel practice community policing. Regardless of how community policing is implemented, the core elements of problem solving and community partnerships are especially important and will be expanded on later in the chapter. There are also many programs that have emerged as part of community policing operational strategies. A few of these programs include:

- Neighborhood watch associations
- Specialized problem-solving units
- Community action units
- Foot and horse patrols
- Permanent patrol assignments (assigning an officer to the same beat for a long period of time)
- Neighborhood town meetings
- Community newsletters
- Storefront stations
- Citizen police academies

- Citizen volunteers
- Chief's advisory boards
- Victim recontact programs
- Auxiliary volunteer programs

Traditional Policing versus Community Policing

Community policing differs from traditional law enforcement strategies because it allows police officers the freedom to expand the scope of their jobs. Police officers in this sense are challenged to become community problem solvers and encouraged to use their time creatively. Likewise, the police officer will be required to discern vast amounts of information and recognize available resources to apply to problem solving. The differences between traditional policing and community policing are detailed in Table 3.1. Notice how the focus of the traditional policing strategy is largely based on efficiency and the focus of the community policing strategy is effectiveness.

In the traditional model of policing, the police devote a significant amount of their resources responding to calls from citizens. While this is an important police mandate, too small a percentage of their time is spent acting on their own initiative to prevent or reduce community problems. Likewise, traditional policing strategies have created a few other problems for police agencies. Moore and Stephens (1991, pp. 112–113) describe these problems as follows:

- The police are having a very tough time dealing with crime by themselves.
- Effective crime control depends on an effective working partnership between the police and the citizens in the communities they serve.
- The public police are losing market share in the safety and security business.
- The public police contribute to the quality of life in their communities in many ways other than by controlling crime.
- The administrative instruments now being used to ensure accountability and control of police officers cannot reliably do so.
- The police are routinely held accountable for the fairness and economy with which they use force, authority, and money.
- Rather than seek insulation from political interference, it is more appropriate for police agencies to make themselves more accountable to political institutions and citizens alike.

CORE COMPONENTS OF COMMUNITY POLICING

The foundation of community policing rests on close and mutual ties between the police and community (Community Policing Consortium, 2006). Community policing does not imply that police are no longer in authority or that the primary duty of preserving law and order is subordinated. However, tapping into the expertise and resources that exist within communities will relieve police of some of their burdens. In

Table 3.1 Comparison of Traditional and Community Policing Strategies.

Question	Traditional Policing	Community Policing
Who are the police?	A government agency principally responsible for law enforcement	Police are the public, the public are the police; the police officers are those who are paid to give full-time attention to the duties of every citizen
What is the relationship of the police force to other public-service departments?	Priorities often conflict	The police are one department among many responsible for improving the quality of life
What is the role of the police?	Focus on solving crimes	A broader problem-solving approach
How is police efficiency measured?	By detection and arrest rates	By the absence of crime and disorder
What are the highest priorities?	Crimes that are high value (e.g., bank robberies) and those involving violence	Whatever problems disturb the community the most
What, specifically, do police deal with?	Incidents	Citizens' problems and concerns
What determines the effectiveness of police?	Response times	Public cooperation
What view do police take of service calls?	Deal with them only if there is no police work to do	Vital function and great opportunity
What is police professionalism?	Swift, effective response to serious crime	Keeping close to the community
What kind of intelligence is most important?	Crime intelligence (study of particular crimes or series of crimes)	Criminal intelligence (information about the activities of individuals or groups)
What is the essential nature of police accountability?	Highly centralized; governed by rules, regulations, and policy directives; accountability to the law	Emphasis on local accountability to community needs
What is the role of headquarters?	To provide necessary rules and policy directives	To preach organizational values
What is the role of the liaison department?	To keep the "heat" off operational officers so they can get on with the job	To coordinate an essential channel of communication with the community
How do the police regard prosecutions?	As an important goal	As one tool among many

Source: Sparrow, M. K. (1988). *Implementing community policing.* Washington, DC: U.S. Department of Justice, National Institute of Justice, pp. 8–9.

fact, every definition of community policing shares the idea that the police and the community must work together to define and develop solutions to problems (Sadd & Grine, 1994). The goal of community policing is the prevention and reduction of crime and disorder problems in neighborhoods by examining problems and applying problem-solving techniques (Green, 1996; Hope, 1994). In order for community policing to be effective there are three complementary core elements: (1) community partnerships, (2) problem solving, and (3) organizational change.

Community Partnerships

community partnerships / A strategy that entails the police and the public working together in partnerships to solve problems in the community.

Community partnerships involve the police and the community, the government body, other service agencies, and the criminal justice system working together as a team to solve community problems (Peak & Glensor, 1999). Partnerships go beyond the standard law enforcement emphasis. Effective partnerships recognize the value of activities that contribute to the orderliness and well-being of a neighborhood. These activities may include helping accident or crime victims, helping resolve domestic and neighborhood conflicts (e.g., family violence, landlord–tenant disputes, or racial harassment), working with residents and local businesses to improve neighborhood conditions, controlling automobile and pedestrian traffic, providing emergency social services and referrals to those at risk (e.g., adolescent runaways, the homeless, the intoxicated, and the mentally ill), protecting the exercise of constitutional rights (e.g., guaranteeing a person's right to speak, protecting lawful assemblies from disruption), and providing a model of citizenship (helpfulness, respect for others, honesty, and fairness).

Community partnerships connect citizens back to the policing process. In essence, police officers and citizens work together to make the neighborhood safer. It is a good beat management practice that police officers should always be aware of the resources they have on their beats that may assist in solving a problem or preventing a crime. Is there a role for the local school to play, the gas station attendant, the newspaper carrier, neighborhood watch group, the convenience store clerk, the faith-based community, the fire department, and the like? Often, police officers may not recognize the opportunity they have to develop partnerships with citizens living on their beats that may bring welcome resources to the table. It is important that all elements of the community work together in order to effectively deal with crime.

There is much speculation on the importance of police officers working in partnership with citizens and other private and public organizations in order to solve problems and improve the quality of life in neighborhoods. For example, Professor Robert Trojanowicz (1990) observed that community policing requires a department-wide philosophical commitment to involve average citizens as partners in the process of reducing and controlling the contemporary problems of crime, drugs, fear of crime, and neighborhood decay, and in efforts to improve overall quality of life in the community.

Problem Solving

problem solving / The systematic identification of the actual and potential causes of crime and conflict within the community that can be analyzed with the results guiding development of measures that address the problems in the short, medium, and long-term. Problem solving also involves conflict resolution and other creative methods to address service delivery and police–community relations problems.

Problem solving is an important component of community policing. It is designed to address both large and small problems within a community. The goal of problem solving is to eliminate the root causes of problems that potentially could become serious police-related problems if not taken care of early. Problem solving is designed to identify and remove the causes of recurring crime and disorder problems that harm communities (Palmiotto, 2000).

One of the first steps involved in problem solving is the identification of specific concerns that community members feel are most threatening to their safety and well-being. These concerns then become priorities for joint police–community interventions. How do you think that a police officer would go about discovering citizen concerns? The easiest way is to simply ask the citizens. This may include the police officer putting together a survey and administering it to a specific neighborhood. It may involve the police officer, during down time on patrol, getting out of the patrol car and going door-to-door talking with citizens. You would be surprised by the information that can be revealed just by knocking on a few doors. Many officers may find that most of the problems that citizens experience and report are small order maintenance problems that don't take much time for the officer to resolve. Often, what the police officer thinks is important may differ from what the citizens think is important. Police officers tend to think in terms of serious crimes, while citizens often think in terms of the juveniles congregating around the street corner, or the stop sign that has been missing for weeks, or the vacant house that has attracted graffiti, or the vacant lot with the grass and weeds that are 3 feet high. Nevertheless, the police officer has to tap into the citizens as to what they think are the problems and issues that face the neighborhood.

A survey or the simple knock on the door can give the impression that the police officer genuinely cares about the community. Police officers should get out of

Voices of Experience

An Encounter with a Juvenile

Excerpts from an interview between Cliff Roberson and former police officer, Ronald Wilson, currently Chair, Criminal Justice Department, Colorado Northwestern Community College.

Q: *Assume you are a patrol officer and you encounter a juvenile who has violated the law. What actions do you take?*

A: When the officer encounters a juvenile who has violated the law, the officer has to make a decision as to what should be done with this child. The officer has a lot of discretion. The officer can give the child a warning and turn him or her loose on the street, the officer can take the child and turn him or her over to the parents, or the officer can bring the child into the station and refer the matter to the youth bureau for investigation or some type of in-house community program.

Q: *What does the officer consider in making the above disposition decision?*

A: There are two primary factors. First, what type of offense is it? If it is a major felony, the officer is generally required to bring the juvenile to the station. If it is a minor offense, then the officer has more discretion. The second factor is the juvenile's attitude. If the juvenile has a good attitude and is willing to admit his or her mistake, the chances are that he or she will not be taken to the station unless it is a major felony. The presence of a complaining witness also factors into the officer's decision, because we essentially work for these people, the citizens. If the citizens demand that we take action, we probably will. ◼

their patrol cars and meet citizens whenever possible. This is especially important in neighborhoods that are disproportionably affected by crime and disorder. There are anecdotal accounts from a few police departments relating that they require their officers to get out of the patrol cars and make contacts with citizens a specific number of hours per week.

Professor Herman Goldstein is considered by many to be the pioneer of problem-oriented policing. Goldstein started something big. During the 1980s, a number of law enforcement agencies throughout the United States and in other countries began a wide variety of problem-solving policing initiatives as part of their community policing strategies.

SARA / A problem-solving model that stands for (S) scanning, (A) analysis, (R), response, (A) assessment.

There are a number of problem-solving techniques that can be utilized by police officers. Many of the techniques may be specific to the agency; however, there is one generic problem-solving model that is used by many agencies. It is one of the most popular models and is known by the acronym **SARA**.

Scanning (S) identifies a problem through a variety of sources of information, such as calls for service and citizen surveys. Citizens must consider the problem as important for this phase to succeed.

Analysis (A) requires the examination of the nature of the problem. Input from police and residents pertaining to the problem is important, as well as the collection of data the department may have about the frequency, location, and other significant characteristics of the problem.

Response (R) fashions one or more preferred solutions to the problem. This step, as well as the preceding analysis step, benefits from creative deliberation, or "thinking outside the box." Input clearly should come from police personnel, but also from residents, experts, and other individuals who can address the problem thoughtfully.

Assessment (A) evaluates the effectiveness of the expected solution. Agencies must evaluate the solution as objectively as possible because this step speaks to end products, the key theme in problem-solving initiatives.

According to Goldstein (1990), the key elements of problem-oriented policing entail a number of important assumptions:

- A problem is the basic unit of police work rather than a crime, a case, calls, or incidents.

- A problem is something that concerns or causes harm to citizens, not just the police. Things that concern only police officers are important, but they are not problems in this sense of the term.

- Addressing problems means more than quick fixes; it means dealing with conditions that create problems.

- Police officers must routinely and systematically analyze problems before trying to solve them, just as they routinely and systematically investigate crimes before making an arrest. Individual officers and the department as a whole must develop routines and systems for analyzing problems.

- The analysis of problems must be thorough, even though it may not need to be complicated. This principle is as true for problem analysis as it is for criminal investigation.

- Problems must be described precisely and accurately and broken down into specific aspects of the problem. Problems often aren't what they first appear to be.

SARA Problem-Solving Model

Scanning:

- Identifying recurring problems of concern to the public and the police.
- Identifying the consequences of the problems for the community and the police.
- Prioritizing those problems.
- Developing broad goals.
- Confirming that the problems exist.
- Determining how frequently the problems occur and how long they have been taking place.
- Selecting problems for closer examination.

Analysis:

- Identifying and understanding the events and conditions that precede and accompany the problems.
- Identifying relevant data to be collected.
- Researching what is known about the types of problems.
- Taking inventory of how the problems are currently addressed and the strengths and limitations of the current responses.
- Narrowing the scope of the problems as specifically as possible.
- Identifying a variety of resources that may be of assistance in developing a deeper understanding of the problems.

- Developing a working hypothesis about why the problems are occurring.

Response:

- Brainstorming for new interventions.
- Searching for what other communities with similar problems have done.
- Choosing among the alternative interventions.
- Outlining a response plan and identifying responsible parties.
- Stating the specific objectives for the response plan.
- Carrying out the planned activities.

Assessment:

- Determining whether the plan was implemented (a process evaluation).
- Collecting pre- and post-response qualitative and quantitative data.
- Determining whether broad goals and specific objectives were attained.
- Identifying any new strategies needed to augment the original plan.
- Conducting ongoing assessment to ensure continued effectiveness.

Source: From *Problem-Oriented Policing* by Herman Goldstein. Copyright © 1990. Reprinted by permission of the McGraw-Hill Companies.

- Problems must be understood in terms of the various interests at stake. Individuals and groups of people are affected in different ways by a problem and have different ideas about what should be done about the problem.

- The way the problem is currently being handled must be understood and the limits of effectiveness must be openly acknowledged in order to come up with a better response.

- Initially, any and all possible responses to a problem should be considered so as not to cut short potentially effective responses. Suggested responses should follow from what is learned during the analysis. They should not be limited to, nor rule out, the use of arrest.

- The police must proactively try to solve problems rather than just react to the harmful consequences of problems.

- The police department must increase police officers' freedom to make or participate in important decisions. At the same time, officers must be accountable for their decision making.

Goldstein's contribution to the idea of police problem solving is primarily a response to several concerns. First, police departments tend to overemphasize operational effectiveness outside the department. Second, police departments devote too little time to developing measures for reducing and preventing crime and, instead, tend to concentrate almost exclusively on reactive policing. Third, police departments largely ignore the wealth of community resources that are available to solve problems that eventually become matters of the police. Similarly, they tend to make poor use of a second important resource, their rank-and-file police officers, whose time and talent have not been used effectively (Goldstein, 1990). Harris (2005, p. 58) writes that "problem-oriented policing, with its focus on taking a holistic view of troubled situations, is central to preventive policing." It's clear that Harris is arguing that problem-solving approaches applied to troubled situations are a central underpinning of community policing.

Organizational Change

organizational change / Sometimes referred to as organizational reengineering. A process of reviewing and changing an organizational culture. Organizational change may include changes in policy and procedures, organizational values, organizational structure, management, and leadership. Organizational change is necessary for the successful implementation of community policing strategies.

Organizational change involves substantial administrative issues that are beyond the scope of this book and are covered briefly here. For police officers or students who desire additional information on organizational change dynamics, consult the numerous management and administration textbooks that address this important area.

Typically, the concept of organizational change is in regard to organization-wide change, as opposed to smaller changes, such as adding new officers, modifying a program, and so on. Examples of organization-wide change might include a change in mission; restructuring operations; new technologies; mergers; major collaborations; "rightsizing"; and new programs, such as community policing reengineering, and so on. Some experts refer to this as *organizational transformation*. The term designates a fundamental and radical reorientation in the way the organization operates. Usually, organizational change is provoked by some major outside driving force, such as substantial cuts in funding, policing research, and the like. Transition to a new chief of police can provoke organization-wide change when his or her new and unique personality and style pervades the entire organization. There have been many police chiefs who were hired as change agents or community policing change agents. It's not that uncommon to see advertisements for a chief of police that state: "knowledge of community policing a must."

Organizations must undertake organization-wide change to evolve to a different level in their lifecycle. Going from a highly reactive model of policing to a more proactive model, such as community policing, is an example of this. In order to have community policing change within a law enforcement agency, the nature of the organization itself must change. Thus, how effectively change is implemented will in large part determine whether that organization sustains community policing as a new policing model or retrenches to a more traditional style of policing.

Organizational change requires a clear recognition that forging community policing partnerships and implementing problem-solving activities will necessitate changes in the organizational structure of policing. The police organizational structure is typically pyramidal in design and has many bureaucratic layers that separate the top command and administration from line-level personnel. This is sometimes referred to as the line organization or the military type organization. In the straight line organization, the channels of authority and responsibility extend in a direct line from top to bottom within the structure. There is a move with community policing to flatten the existing police structure. Flat organizations will have shorter lines of communication between top and bottom levels of the organization (Johnson, 1994). Accordingly, the communications are likely to be faster and have less chances of distortion.

Properly managed change involves recognition of the need for change, the communication of a clear vision that change is possible, the identification of the concrete steps needed for positive change to occur, developing an understanding of the benefits of change, as well as the creation of an organization-wide commitment to change.

Typically, there is strong resistance to change because people are afraid of the unknown. Many police officers think things are just fine and

PRACTICE HINTS

Benefits of Flattening the Organizational Structure

1. Communication enhancement (fewer layers of the chain of command to send information through).
2. Empowerment of employees at the bottom of the organization to make more decisions.
3. Increased participation in the problem-solving process of those employees closest to the problems.
4. Improved service delivery: the police officers at the bottom of the pyramid are closest to the customer (citizen) and are in an advantageous position to identify methods to improve service delivery.
5. Enhanced bottom-up input on policy development.
6. Improved coordination of services internally within the police department.
7. Reduced bureaucracy, red tape, and time delays.

don't understand the need for change. Many are inherently cynical about change. The most effective approach to address resistance is through increased and sustained communications and education. For example, the police command staff or the police chief should meet with all rank-and-file officers for the purpose of explaining the reason for the change, how it generally will be carried out, and where others can go for additional information. Ideally, the chief of police should do this. Communicating change is very important and even in large police agencies this is possible. The chief can hold several large assemblies of officers for this purpose. More ideally, the chief can simply visit all squad meetings over the course of a few weeks. The practice of having the chief of police visit squad meetings may send the impression to the officers that the chief is committed to the change process.

The buy-in from the rank-and-file is important when implementing community policing. If the chief can hold debriefing sessions, it will assuredly go a long way in demonstrating to the rank-and-file that the chief is a supporter of the new community policing philosophy. The chief's personal appearance at the squad room or station house can go a long way in getting a buy-in from the officers, supervisors, and middle-level management. During these meetings the chief should explain to the rank-and-file officers where community policing will take the department, what it means for police operations, and where the department wishes to be in the short term (one to three years) and in the long term (five to ten years).

A plan should be developed and communicated to the rank-and-file police officers. Plans do change, that's fine, but communicate that the plan has changed and why. Forums should be held for organization members to express their ideas for the plan. They should be able to express their concerns and frustrations as well. This is very important because with community policing participatory management techniques are practiced when possible. Under the traditional model of policing, input from the police officer in the field was limited. This is in large part due to the military chain of command, the bureaucracy, and the general rank structure. Successful organizational change must involve top management, including the command staff and chief of police. Change is usually best carried out as a team-wide effort.

WHAT COMMUNITY POLICING IS NOT

We have discussed to a great extent what community policing is. However, it is also important to have some idea of what community policing is not. Or, put another way, to debunk some of the myths that go along with community policing. Police officers reading this book know all too well that when a new strategy is introduced in policing it is often met with a fair amount of resistance. Let's face it, the police just don't like change.

The police tend to get comfortable and set in their ways, and any change causes discomfort. Community policing is no different. Community policing is a tough sell to rank-and-file police officers. During a community policing training session a few years ago, one of the officers present made a rather boisterous comment to the effect of "policing is going to hell in a hand basket with all of this social work crap you're pushing down our throats, they just don't want us to be cops anymore." This sentiment is probably exhibited, or at least felt, by a great many rank-and-file police officers.

Much of the cynicism toward community policing is simply because the police officers don't know any better. They have been battling crime the way they were trained, under many of the assumptions of the traditional policing model. Police officers wholeheartedly feel that they are being effective at what they do. In the following few sections we will bring to light some of the common criticisms toward community policing.

Community policing is soft on crime. This is not true. Community policing does not abandon the traditional law enforcement strategy, it simply supplements it by making traditional approaches much more effective. With the community policing strategy, if a suspect has violated the law, chances are he or she is still going to get arrested. The criminal justice system is still considered a viable solution. However, community policing goes beyond the arrest, which in many cases is only a short-term solution, and the officer experiences the same problem when the suspect gets out of jail. The goal of community policing is to identify and resolve underlying problems that resulted in the arrest in the first place. Recall that one of the elements of community policing is problem solving. If, for example, the problem happens to be a drug house operating in the neighborhood, then the drug house will be targeted for not only potential enforcement action, but also action taken to evict the occupants of the drug house if they happen to be renting the property.

Community policing is just another specialized program. This is not true. In reality, the most effective community policing approach is when it is implemented as a holistic operating strategy within the police department. The rank-and-file police officers within the police agency practice community policing. Community policing may start as a pilot program, but it should have a specific date when implementation will begin within the rest of the police agency. Departments that only assign a handful of police officers to community policing duties will find it more difficult to get a buy-in from rank-and-file police officers. In many cases the officers assigned to the specialized community policing function are seen as having special privileges, such as working flex hours, not having to respond to police calls, and having take-home police vehicles. Of course, this can result in much resentment on the part of police officers.

Community policing is best practiced as an organization-wide strategy. A recently televised interview of a chief of police from a medium-sized police agency in the Midwest reveals a significant problem. The topic of the interview was community policing. The chief referred to community policing as a *program* on five different occasions. The chief then told the news reporter that his department has made cuts in its community policing program for other departmental priorities. The moral of this story is that programs come and go, and strategies live on.

Community policing is a philosophy and a strategy intended to improve the quality of life through proactive law enforcement, clientele involvement in decision making and in finding solutions, with the officer serving as the catalyst for obtaining needed community services. It does not offer a quick fix. It requires a long-term commitment by police to work with community members to reach mutually agreed-upon goals. Forming lasting partnerships to eradicate the underlying causes of crime will take effort, time, and patience on the parts of all involved.

Community policing will require more officers on the street. This is not necessarily true. If community policing is implemented correctly, each and every police officer in the field should practice community policing. Keep in mind that the actual implementation strategy falls under the auspice of organizational change, which is an important component of community policing. In fact, many community policing experts argue that the organizational change should be done before the community policing is implemented in the field.

Community policing is foot patrol strategies of the past. This is not true. Foot patrol can be utilized as part of the community policing strategy. However, community policing is not just foot patrol.

Community policing is not a top-down approach. Community policing involves participation and relies on input from all levels of the department, and from average citizens, their constituents, and not just police executives and community leaders. Doesn't it make sense that police executives solicit the input of the police officers in the field who are exposed to the community's problems on a daily basis and perhaps are in the best position to have input on policy pronouncements that will directly impact the way they go about their jobs?

INCORPORATING COMMUNITY POLICING ON THE JOB

By now, you have a general working knowledge of community policing. However, definitions and descriptions of community policing that are written in textbooks can be a little confusing. The conceptual definitions of community policing are somewhat broad (Oliver, 2004). Definitions of community policing often sound good in theory, but lack discussion of how the strategy actually works in the field. In other words, how can police officers practice community policing on the job? This is what most officers desire, the hands-on information about how community policing works. In the following sections a discussion is provided on how community policing strategies can be incorporated on the job, along with a few examples. The role of the police officer in community policing is discussed first.

PRACTICE HINTS

Ten Principles of Community Policing

1. Community policing is a community-based philosophy. The direction for law enforcement efforts comes more from listening to the citizens of the community about what concerns them than from law enforcement assumptions about what the community wants.

2. Community policing focuses on creative problem solving. All persons involved are encouraged to look at the bigger picture to solve pattern or chronic problems.

3. Community policing promotes the development of trust. It emphasizes a direct working relationship between citizens and the police to develop the ownership of problems.

4. Community policing establishes a broader role for each law enforcement member. Each member serves as a liaison with the community and assists its citizens in solving community problems.

5. Community policing stresses community involvement and emphasizes citizen participation in the problem-solving process. This means that the community must accept its responsibility to actively participate in problem solving. Community policing acknowledges that the police cannot be successful without citizen assistance.

6. Community policing is proactive, not reactive. Community policing anticipates problems and prevents them from occurring or continuing.

7. Community policing emphasizes providing help where it is needed most. Community policing especially provides for closer contact with juveniles and the elderly as a means of better understanding their needs.

8. Community policing enhances traditional policing through interaction with the community. Law enforcement will continue to respond to emergencies and perform in traditional capacities. They will also explore a wide range of responses to community problems and ask for citizen assistance as part of the problem-solving process.

9. Community policing involves everyone within a law enforcement agency. Successful community policing is not limited to the patrol section; it is a change in the policing philosophy of the entire agency.

10. Community policing personalizes law enforcement service. Law enforcement members work directly with the citizens they serve to identify and prioritize problems, and to devise and implement problem-solving strategies.

Source: From *Community policing*, 2nd ed., by R. Trojanowicz and B. Bucqueroux. Copyright © 1998 by Matthew Bender & Company, Inc. Reprinted by, permission of Matthew Bender & Company, Inc., a member of the LexisNexis Group. All rights reserved.

Community Policing and the Role of the Police Officer

The role of the police officer under the axiom of community policing will be much more challenging because police officers will have to go beyond the traditional police response in many calls that they handle. Community policing is smart policing. It entails police officers solving substantial crime and disorder-related problems in neighborhoods. In some instances this may call for an arrest, while in other situations it may entail soliciting other recourses that can more appropriately deal with the problem at hand. Nevertheless, police officers become street-level criminologists. Officers operating in a community policing environment will be required to think creatively and independently. This includes the ability to create a vision and develop appropriate steps for solving problems (Ortmeier, 2002).

Police officers must recognize that they are interdependent with the community. Forming partnerships with the community is a critical role of the police officer. An active outreach to the community provides the officer with a better flow of information and a more accurate understanding of the problems and expectations in the neighborhood. Continual interaction between officers and the citizens living on their beats can serve as a catalyst in mobilizing the citizens to protect themselves (Sweeny, 2003). Police and citizen interaction can also result in the identification of resources that can assist in problem-solving endeavors.

Domestic Violence

Domestic violence is a pattern of abusive behavior in any relationship that is used by one partner to gain or maintain power and control over another intimate partner. Domestic violence incidents can be perplexing for police officers. The actual amount of domestic violence in our society is not well known. Violence between intimates is difficult to measure; it often occurs in private, and victims are often reluctant to report incidents to anyone because of shame or fear of reprisal. Consequently, the police officer responds to the report of a domestic violence with minimal background history about the problems that the parties are experiencing.

domestic violence /
Violence that occurs within a family or an intimate relationship, including spouse beating and child abuse. Domestic violence is one of the most common forms of gender-based violence and is often characterized by long-term patterns of abusive behavior and control.

Domestic violence can be physical, sexual, emotional, economic, or psychological actions or threats of actions that influence another person. This includes any behaviors that intimidate, manipulate, humiliate, isolate, frighten, terrorize, coerce, threaten, blame, hurt, injure, or wound someone.

- **Physical Abuse:** Hitting, slapping, shoving, grabbing, pinching, biting, hairpulling, biting, and so forth. Physical abuse also includes denying a partner medical care or forcing alcohol and/or drug use.

- **Sexual Abuse:** Coercing or attempting to coerce any sexual contact or behavior without consent. Sexual abuse includes, but is certainly not limited to, marital rape, attacks on sexual parts of the body, forcing sex after physical violence has occurred, or treating someone in a sexually demeaning manner.

- **Emotional Abuse:** Undermining an individual's sense of self-worth and/or self-esteem. This may include, but is not limited to, constant criticism, diminishing one's abilities, name-calling, or damaging one's relationship with his or her children.

- **Economic Abuse:** Making or attempting to make an individual financially dependent by maintaining total control over financial resources, withholding one's access to money, or forbidding one's attendance at school or employment.

- **Psychological Abuse:** Causing fear by intimidation; threatening physical harm to self, partner, children, or partner's family or friends; destruction of pets and property; and forcing isolation from family, friends, or school and/or work.

The traditional police response for dealing with domestic violence was to talk one of the parties into leaving for the evening. The officers might also advise the parties that if the police return to the residence for the same problem that evening, someone was going to jail. Archaic approaches such as this are neither effective nor an appropriate police procedure. Furthermore, traditional approaches did little to attempt to solve the underlying problem.

In order to think about the police response to domestic violence, let's imagine a medical analogy. Suppose that the patient is feeling under the weather and schedules an appointment to see a doctor. During the visit to the doctor's office the patient will most likely first see the nurse who spends a few moments asking some questions and preparing the patient for the visit with the doctor. The nurse will ask the patient about medications he or she is currently taking, specific symptoms the patient is experiencing, as well as taking blood pressure measurements, the patient's weight, and perhaps temperature.

After the nurse completes the initial consultation, the patient sees the doctor. The doctor will ask the patient to describe exactly how they are feeling. The patient may be asked to describe the pain and where it originates from. The doctor carefully listens and reviews the patient's history. The doctor may poke and prod the patient and listen to the patient's cardiovascular system with a stethoscope. Based on the symptoms that the patient describes and the doctor's physical examination, a diagnosis is made. In some cases the doctor may hold off on making a diagnosis until further medical testing is done. Nevertheless, in medicine, the doctor studies the patient's symptoms and medical tests in order to make a diagnosis and to treat the underlying pathology.

This same strategy may be beneficial for the police officer when investigating a domestic violence situation. For example, when investigating a domestic violence call the police officer should ask questions of both parties, such as: How long has the violence been going on? Who struck whom? Are there any injuries? Has this occurred in the past? Have the parties been through mediation or sought help in the past? The officer should take a history, similar to a history that is taken in a medical facility. The police officer should attempt to gain enough information in order to make a diagnosis and treat the underlying problem.

Consider that the diagnosis may be that one of the parties involved in the domestic violence had been drinking all day and while in an intoxicated stupor assaulted his wife, which resulted in visible injury. The police officer initially treats the problem (the assault) by arresting the husband for battering his wife. However, the arrest alone may do little to resolve the underlying problem. In fact, there may be years of history that the police are not aware of when they investigate the report of domestic violence. It may be that the batterer has a history of alcohol or drug abuse. The alcohol and drug abuse may be the underlying cause of the problem. The objective here would be to convince the person to get alcohol or drug treatment for his problem. The officer might do this by furnishing contact information for alcohol and drug rehabilitation, or making a referral.

Police officers may find the following suggestions helpful when investigating domestic violence:

- Make an arrest if there is evidence of injury (many states require this under the mandatory domestic violence arrest laws).
- Gain as much history as possible in order to tailor a potential solution.

- Refer both parties to mediation services or other resources available in the community that may be offered free or on a sliding scale. Provide parties with phone numbers and contacts for these services.

- The police officer should physically follow up and make contact with the victim the next day after the initial incident. Follow-up contact accomplishes several objectives. First, it presents the opportunity for the officer to advise the victim and the offender of any additional resources and provides an opportunity for the victim to ask additional questions not thought of the day of the incident. Second, it sends a message to the offender that domestic violence will not be tolerated and if it happens again the offender will be arrested again.

- In neighborhoods that have a high incidence of domestic violence calls, the police officer may find it beneficial to coordinate a community violence program that features speakers from the crisis centers, battered women's shelters, and other resources that are available in the community to assist victims of domestic violence. Many victims of domestic violence may not be aware of resources available, and if made aware, may take the first step to emancipate themselves.

- Police officers should make every effort to reach out to a family where domestic violence is present. Many times the police officer that offers to listen and acknowledges what is going on helps chip away at the walls that surround and isolate families living with abuse.

Notice how these approaches deviate from the traditional police responses to domestic violence, which often involved having one party leave for the evening until things cooled off. Domestic violence must be approached proactively by police officers.

State Domestic Violence Resources

ALABAMA	Alabama Coalition Against Domestic Violence Post Office Box 4762 Montgomery, AL 36101 Phone: 334-832-4842 Fax: 334-832-4803 Hotline: 1-800-650-6522 Website: www.acadv.org Email: info@acadv.org
ALASKA	Alaska Network on Domestic Violence and Sexual Assault 130 Seward Street, Room 209 Juneau, AK 99801 Phone: 907-586-3650 Fax: 907-463-4493 Website: www.andvsa.org
AMERICAN SAMOA	American Samoa Coalition Against Domestic and Sexual Violence Flo Ainuu American Samoa Coalition Post Office Box 7285 Pago Pago, American Samoa 96799-7285

Phone: 684-258-2892
Email: ascadsv@yahoo.com

ARIZONA   Arizona Coalition Against Domestic Violence
               301 East Bethany Home Road, Suite C194
               Phoenix, AZ 85012
               Phone: 602-279-2900
               Toll-Free: 1-800-782-6400
               Fax: 602-279-2980
               Website: www.azcadv.org
               Email: acadv@azcadv.org

ARKANSAS   Arkansas Coalition Against Domestic Violence
               1401 West Capitol Avenue, Suite 170
               Little Rock, AR 72201
               Phone: 501-907-5612
               Toll-Free: 1-800-269-4668
               Fax: 501-907-5618
               Website: www.domesticpeace.com

CALIFORNIA   California Partnership to End Domestic Violence
               Post Office Box 1798
               Sacramento, CA 95812
               Phone: 916-444-7163
               Toll-Free: 1-800-524-4765
               Fax: 916-444-7165
               Website: www.cpedv.org
               Email: info@cpedv.org

COLORADO   Colorado Coalition Against Domestic Violence
               1120 Lincoln Street, Suite 900
               Denver, CO 80203
               Phone: 303-831-9632
               Toll-Free: 1-888-788-7091
               Fax: 303-832-7067
               Website: www.ccadv.org

CONNECTICUT   Connecticut Coalition Against Domestic Violence
               90 Pitkin Street
               East Hartford, CT 06108
               Phone: 860-282-7899
               Fax: 860-282-7892
               Hotline: 1-888-774-2900
               Website: www.ctcadv.org
               Email: info@ctcadv.org

DELAWARE   Delaware Coalition Against Domestic Violence
               100 West 10th Street, #703
               Wilmington, DE 19801
               Phone: 302-658-2958
               Toll-Free: 1-800-701-0456
               Fax: 302-658-5049
               Website: www.dcadv.org
               Email: dcadv@dcadv.org

DISTRICT OF COLUMBIA	District of Columbia Coalition Against Domestic Violence 5 Thomas Circle, N.W. Washington, DC 20005 Phone: 202-299-1181 Fax: 202-299-1193 Website: www.dccadv.org Email: info@dccadv.org
FLORIDA	Florida Coalition Against Domestic Violence 425 Office Plaza Tallahassee, FL 32301 Phone: 850-425-2749 Toll-Free: 1-800-500-1119 Fax: 850-425-3091 Website: www.fcadv.org
GEORGIA	Georgia Coalition Against Domestic Violence 114 New Street, Suite B Decatur, GA 30030 Phone: 404-209-0280 Fax: 404-766-3800 Website: www.gcadv.org
HAWAII	Hawaii State Coalition Against Domestic Violence 716 Umi Street, Suite 210 Honolulu, HI 96819 Phone: 808-832-9316 Fax: 808-841-6028 Website: www.hscadv.org
IDAHO	Idaho Coalition Against Sexual and Domestic Violence 815 Park Boulevard, #140 Boise, ID 83712 Phone: 208-384-0419 Toll-Free: 1-888-293-6118 Fax: 208-331-0687 Website: www.idvsa.org Email: jmatsushita@idvsa.org
ILLINOIS	Illinois Coalition Against Domestic Violence 801 South 11th Street Springfield, IL 62703 Phone: 217-789-2830 Fax: 217-789-1939 Website: www.ilcadv.org Email: ilcadv@ilcadv.org
INDIANA	Indiana Coalition Against Domestic Violence 1915 West 18th Street Indianapolis, IN 46202 Phone: 317-917-3685 Toll-Free: 1-800-538-3393 Hotline: 1-800-332-7385 Fax: 317-917-3695

	Website: www.violenceresource.org
	Email: icadv@violenceresource.org
IOWA	Iowa Coalition Against Domestic Violence
	515 28th Street
	Des Moines, IA 50312
	Phone: 515-244-8028
	Hotline: 1-800-942-0333
	Fax: 515-244-7417
	Website: www.icadv.org
	Email: icadv@aol.com
KANSAS	Kansas Coalition Against Sexual and Domestic Violence
	634 SW Harrison Street
	Topeka, KS 66603
	Phone: 785-232-9784
	Fax: 785-266-1874
	Website: www.kcsdv.org
	Email: coalition@kcsdv.org
KENTUCKY	Kentucky Domestic Violence Association
	Post Office Box 356
	Frankfort, KY 40602
	Phone: 502-209-5382
	Fax: 502-226-5382
	Website: www.kdva.org
LOUISIANA	Louisiana Coalition Against Domestic Violence
	Post Office Box 77308
	Baton Rouge, LA 70879
	Phone: 225-752-1296
	Fax: 225-751-8927
	Website: www.lcadv.org
	Email: leighlcadv@aol.com
MAINE	Maine Coalition to End Domestic Violence
	170 Park Street
	Bangor, ME 04401
	Phone: 207-941-1194
	Fax: 207-941-2327
	Website: www.mcedv.org
	Email: info@mcedv.org
MARYLAND	Maryland Network Against Domestic Violence
	6911 Laurel-Bowie Road, Suite 309
	Bowie, MD 20715
	Phone: 301-352-4574
	Toll-Free: 1-800-634-3577
	Fax: 301-809-0422
	Website: www.mnadv.org
	Email: info@mndadv.org
MASSACHUSETTS	Jane Doe, Inc./ Massachusetts Coalition Against Sexual Assault and Domestic Violence
	14 Beacon Street, Suite 507

	Boston, MA 02108
	Phone: 617-248-0922
	Fax: 617-248-0902
	Website: www.janedoe.org
	Email: info@janedoe.org
MICHIGAN	Michigan Coalition Against Domestic and Sexual Violence
	3893 Okemos Road, Suite B-2
	Okemos, MI 48864
	Phone: 517-347-7000
	Fax: 517-347-1377
	Website: www.mcadsv.org
	Email: general@mcadsv.org
MINNESOTA	Minnesota Coalition for Battered Women
	590 Park Street, Suite 410
	St. Paul, MN 55103
	Phone: 651-646-6177
	Crisis Line: 651-646-0994
	Toll-Free: 1-800-289-6177
	Fax: 651-646-1527
	Website: www.mcbw.org
	Email: mcbw@mcbw.org
MISSISSIPPI	Mississippi Coalition Against Domestic Violence
	Post Office Box 4703
	Jackson, MS 39296
	Phone: 601-981-9196
	Toll-Free: 1-800-898-3234
	Fax: 601-981-2501
	Website: www.mcadv.org
MISSOURI	Missouri Coalition Against Domestic Violence
	718 East Capitol Avenue
	Jefferson City, MO 65101
	Phone: 573-634-4161
	Fax: 573-636-3728
	Website: www.mocadv.org
MONTANA	Montana Coalition Against Domestic and Sexual Violence
	Post Office Box 818
	Helena, MT 59624
	Phone: 406-443-7794
	Toll-Free: 1-888-404-7794
	Fax: 406-443-7818
	Website: www.mcadsv.com
	Email: mcadsv@mt.net
NEBRASKA	Nebraska Domestic Violence and Sexual Assault Coalition
	825 M Street, Suite 404
	Lincoln, NE 68508
	Phone: 402-476-6256

	Fax: 402-476-6806
	Website: www.ndvsac.org
	Email: help@ndvsac.org
NEVADA	Nevada Network Against Domestic Violence
	220 South Rock Boulevard, Suite 7
	Reno, NV 89502
	Phone: 775-828-1115
	Hotline: 1-800-500-1556
	Fax: 775-828-9911
	Website: www.nnadv.org
	Email: administrator@nnadv.org
NEW HAMPSHIRE	New Hampshire Coalition Against Domestic and Sexual Violence
	Post Office Box 353
	Concord, NH 03302
	Phone: 603-224-8893
	Domestic Violence Hotline: 1-866-644-3574
	Sexual Assault Hotline: 1-800-277-5570
	Fax: 603-228-6096
	Website: www.nhcadsv.org
NEW JERSEY	New Jersey Coalition for Battered Women
	1670 Whitehorse Hamilton Square
	Trenton, NJ 08690
	Phone: 609-584-8107
	Fax: 609-584-9750
	Website: www.njcbw.org
	Email: info@njcbw.org
NEW MEXICO	New Mexico Coalition Against Domestic Violence
	201 Coal Avenue Southwest
	Albuquerque, NM 87102
	Phone: 505-246-9240
	Toll-Free: 1-800-773-3645
	Fax: 505-246-9434
	Website: www.nmcadv.org
NEW YORK	New York State Coalition Against Domestic Violence
	350 New Scotland Avenue
	Albany, NY 12208
	Phone: 518-482-5464
	Toll-Free English: 1-800-942-6906
	Toll-Free Spanish: 1-800-942-6908
	Fax: 518-482-3807
	Website: www.nyscadv.org
	Email: nyscadv@nyscadv.org
NORTH CAROLINA	North Carolina Coalition Against Domestic Violence
	123 West Main Street, Suite 700
	Durham, NC 27701
	Phone: 919-956-9124
	Toll-Free: 1-888-232-9124

	Fax: 919-682-1449
	Website: www.nccadv.org
NORTH DAKOTA	North Dakota Council on Abused Women's Services
	418 East Rosser Avenue, #320
	Bismark, ND 58501
	Phone: 701-255-6240
	Toll-Free: 1-888-255-6240
	Fax: 701-255-1904
	Website: www.ndcaws.org
OHIO	Action Ohio Coalition for Battered Women
	36 West Gay Street, Suite 311
	Columbus, OH 43215
	Phone: 614-221-1255
	Toll-Free: 1-888-622-9315
	Fax: 614-221-6357
	Website: www.actionohio.org
	Email: actionoh@ee.net
	Ohio Domestic Violence Network
	4807 Evanswood Drive, Suite 201
	Columbus, OH 43229
	Phone: 614-781-9651
	Hotline: 1-800-934-9840
	Fax: 614-781-9652
	Website: www.odvn.org
	Email: info@odvn.org
OKLAHOMA	Oklahoma Coalition Against Domestic Violence and Sexual Assault
	3815 North Sante Fe Avenue, Suite 124
	Oklahoma City, OK 73118
	Phone: 405-524-0700
	Fax: 405-524-0711
	Website: www.ocadvsa.org
OREGON	Oregon Coalition Against Domestic and Sexual Violence
	380 Southeast Spokane Street, Suite 100
	Portland, OR 97202
	Phone: 503-230-1951
	Fax: 503-230-1973
	Website: www.ocadsv.com
PENNSYLVANIA	Pennsylvania Coalition Against Domestic Violence
	6400 Flank Drive, #1300
	Harrisburg, PA 17112
	Phone: 717-545-6400
	Toll-Free: 1-800-932-4632
	Fax: 717-545-9456
	Website: www.pcadv.org
PUERTO RICO	Puerto Rico Coalition Against Domestic Violence and Sexual Assault
	Coordinadora Paz Para La Mujer

	Post Office Box 193008
	San Juan, PR 00919
	Phone: 787-281-7579
	Email: pazmujer@prtc.net
	Puerto Rico Office of the Women's Advocate
	Fernandez Juancus Station
	Box 11382
	Santurce, PR 00910
	Phone: 787-721-7676
	Fax: 787-725-9248
RHODE ISLAND	Rhode Island Coalition Against Domestic Violence
	422 Post Road
	Warwick, RI 02888
	Phone: 401-467-9940
	Hotline: 1-800-494-8100
	Fax: 401-467-9943
	Website: www.ricadv.org
	Email: ricadv@ricadv.org
SOUTH CAROLINA	South Carolina Coalition Against Domestic Violence
	and Sexual Assault
	Post Office Box 7776
	Columbia, SC 29202
	Phone: 803-256-2900
	Toll-Free: 1-800-260-9293
	Fax: 803-256-1030
	Website: www.sccadvasa.org
SOUTH DAKOTA	South Dakota Coalition Against Domestic Violence
	and Sexual Assault–Pierre Office
	Post Office Box 141
	Pierre, SD 57501
	Phone: 605-945-0869
	Toll-Free: 1-800-572-9196
	Fax: 605-945-0870
	Website: www.southdakotacoalition.org
	Email: chris@sdcadvsa.org
	South Dakota Coalition Against Domestic Violence and
	Sexual Assault – Sioux Falls Office
	Post Office Box 1402
	Sioux Falls, SD 57101
	Phone: 605-271-3171
	Toll-Free: 1-877-317-3096
	Fax: 605-271-3172
	Website: www.southdakotacoalition.org
	Email: siouxfalls@sdcadvsa.org
TENNESSEE	Tennessee Coalition Against Domestic and Sexual
	Violence
	Post Office Box 120972
	Nashville, TN 37212
	Phone: 615-386-9406

	Toll-Free: 1-800-289-9018
	Fax: 615-383-2967
	Website: www.tcadsv.org
	Email: tcadsv@tcadsv.org
TEXAS	Texas Council on Family Violence
	Post Office Box 161810
	Austin, TX 78716
	Phone: 512-794-1133
	Toll-Free: 1-800-525-1978
	Fax: 512-794-1199
	Website: www.tcfv.org
UTAH	Utah Domestic Violence Council
	320 West 200 South, Suite 270-B
	Salt Lake City, UT 84403
	Phone: 801-521-5544
	Fax: 801-521-5548
	Website: www.udvac.org
VERMONT	Vermont Network Against Domestic Violence and Sexual Assault
	Post Office Box 405
	Montpelier, VT 05601
	Phone: 802-223-1302
	Domestic Violence Hotline: 1-800-228-7395
	Sexual Assault Hotline: 1-800-489-7273
	Fax: 802-223-6943
	Website: www.vtnetwork.org
	Email: vtnetwork@vtnetwork.org
VIRGIN ISLANDS	Virgin Islands Domestic Violence and Sexual Assault Council
	Women's Coalition of St. Croix
	Post Office Box 222734
	Christiansted, VI 00822-2734
	Phone: 340-773-9272
	Fax: 340-773-9062
	Website: www.wcstx.com
	Email: wcscstx@attglobal.net
VIRGINIA	Virginia Sexual and Domestic Violence Action Alliance – Charlottesville Office
	508 Dale Avenue
	Charlottesville, VA 22903-4547
	Phone: 434-979-9002
	Hotline: 1-800-838-8238
	Fax: 434-979-9003
	Website: www.vsdvalliance.org
	Email: info@vsdvalliance.org
	Virginia Sexual and Domestic Violence Action Alliance – Richmond Office
	1010 North Thompson Street, Suite 202
	Richmond, VA 23230

	Phone: 804-377-0335
	Hotline: 1-800-838-8238
	Fax: 804-377-0339
	Website: www.vsdvalliance.org
	Email: info@vsdvalliance.org
	Virginia Sexual and Domestic Violence Action Alliance – Toano Office
	102 Industrial Boulevard
	Toano, VA 23168
	Phone: 757-566-4602
	Hotline: 1-800-838-8238
	Fax: 757-566-4670
	Website: www.vsdvalliance.org
	Email: info@vsdvalliance.org
WASHINGTON	Washington State Coalition Against Domestic Violence–Olympia Office
	101 North Capitol Way, Suite 302
	Olympia, WA 98501
	Phone: 360-586-1022
	Hotline: 1-800-562-6025
	Fax: 360-586-1024
	Website: www.wscadv.org
	Email: wscadv@wscadv.org
	Washington State Coalition Against Domestic Violence–Seattle Office
	1402 - 3rd Avenue, Suite 406
	Seattle, WA 98101
	Phone: 206-389-2515
	Hotline: 1-800-562-6025
	Fax: 206-389-2520
	Website: www.wscadv.org
	Email: wscadv@wscadv.org
WEST VIRGINIA	West Virginia Coalition Against Domestic Violence
	4710 Chimney Drive, Suite A
	Charleston, WV 25302
	Phone: 304-965-3552
	Fax: 304-965-3572
	Website: www.wvcadv.org
WISCONSIN	Wisconsin Coalition Against Domestic Violence
	307 South Paterson Street, #1
	Madison, WI 53703
	Phone: 608-255-0539
	Fax: 608-255-3560
	Website: www.wcadv.org
	Email: wcadv@wcadv.org
WYOMING	Wyoming Coalition Against Domestic Violence and Sexual Assault
	Post Office Box 236
	409 South Fourth Street

Laramie, WY 82073
Phone: 307-755-5481
Hotline: 1-800-990-3877
Fax: 307-755-5482
Website: www.wyomingdvsa.org

Source: U.S. Department of Justice, Domestic Violence Resources, www.usdoj.gov/ovw/domestic
violenceresources.htm

Burglaries

Burglary, also called breaking and entering or house breaking, is a crime related to theft. It typically involves someone breaking into a house with the intent to commit a crime. Burglary represents one of the most common threats to our property. The FBI reports that in the United States there is one burglary committed every 14.7 seconds. Burglary also represents one of our greatest fears—the fear that someone broke into our residence, took our property, and invaded our privacy. If you have been the victim of a burglary you know this feeling all too well. Most burglary calls involve a fairly standard response by the police. The response usually includes the officer gathering information on the stolen property, such as the physical description, unusual markings or engraving, and serial numbers. If appropriate, the officer may also call for the crime lab to process the scene.

In addition to the standard police response to a burglary, there are some things that police officers can do to possibly encourage the prevention of burglary. Police officers should counsel burglary victims on preventive techniques. It doesn't do any good if the victims of burglary do not change their behavior (e.g., locking the garage door at night, closing the shed door at night, leaving a light on, dead bolting doors). The most logical advice that a police officer can offer to citizens who have been victimized by burglary is target hardening, or making their home more difficult to enter.

The officer should also pay close attention to crime data on his or her beat that may indicate an increase in burglaries in the area. If this is the case, the officer should investigate further in an attempt to discern if the method of operation is the same. This is the process of looking for similar or recurring themes. The SARA model of problem solving is a good model to use when examining a number of burglaries occurring in an area. Other crime increases or other calls for police services that may be correlated with the burglaries should be identified, for example, an increase in drug-related activity in the area, or juveniles who have been reported truant from school. If the burglaries have been occurring during the day, it would be wise for the officer to follow up on truancy reports from local schools. It may be that the truant juveniles are responsible for committing the burglaries. The idea is to scan all relevant patterns or incidents that may be related.

The officer should also examine the area where burglaries have occurred for environmental factors that may present the opportunity for a burglar to commit the crime. It may be that a neighborhood is poorly lit at night, which is contributing to the burglaries. If this is the case, the police officer could initiate a door-to-door campaign or disseminate a letter to citizens living in the affected neighborhood to turn

burglary / The unlawful entry into a structure to commit a felony or theft. For reporting purposes this definition includes: unlawful entry with intent to commit a larceny or felony, breaking and entering with intent to commit a larceny, housebreaking, safecracking, and all attempts to commit any of the aforementioned.

their porch lights on after nightfall. It is well-established that good lighting is one of the most effective crime deterrents. When used properly, light discourages criminal activity, enhances natural surveillance opportunities, and reduces fear. Remember, with community policing the police officer increasingly becomes more involved in the prevention of crime as opposed to just responding, taking a report, and informing the victims that a detective will contact them in the near future.

Police officers should be knowledgeable of **Crime Prevention Through Environmental Design** techniques or CPTED (pronounced sep-ted). Crime Prevention Through Environmental Design and community policing can be viewed as part of a comprehensive crime prevention strategy. CPTED emphasizes a problem-solving approach to crime prevention, as well as close cooperation between police and residents in reducing both crime and fear of crime (Fleissner & Heinzelmann, 1996). CPTED involves strategies that focus on changing environmental factors that would otherwise make it easy for criminal behavior to occur. Put another way, CPTED is the proper design, alteration, and effective use of the built environment, which may lead to a reduction in the fear and incidence of crime, and an improvement in the quality of life (Crowe, 2000).

Crime Prevention Through Environmental Design goes beyond simply recommending a deadbolt lock on doors and windows as a way to prevent burglaries. The four basic tenets of CEPTD are (1) natural access control, (2) natural surveillance, (3) territorial reinforcement, and (4) target hardening. Whenever possible, police officers should examine homes and businesses for the possibility of applying CPTED principles.

Crime Prevention Through Environmental Design (CPTED) / A multidisciplinary approach to deterring criminal behavior. CPTED strategies rely upon the ability to influence offender decisions that precede criminal acts. Most recent implementations of CPTED occur solely within the built environment.

Natural Access Control
- Walkways and landscaping that direct visitors to the proper entrance and away from private areas.

Natural Surveillance
- All doorways that open to the outside should be well lit.
- The front door should be at least partially visible from the street.
- Windows on all sides of the house provide full visibility of property.
- Sidewalks and all areas of the yard should be well lit.
- The driveway should be visible from either the front or back door and at least one window.
- The front door should be clearly visible from the driveway.
- Properly maintained landscaping provides maximum viewing to and from the house.

Territorial Reinforcement
- Front porches or stoops create a transitional area between the street and the home.
- Property lines and private areas should be defined with plantings, pavement treatments, or fences.
- The street address should be clearly visible from the street with numbers a minimum of 5 inches high that are made of nonreflective material.

Target Hardening

- Interior doors that connect a garage to a building should have a single cylinder deadbolt lock.

- Door locks should be located a minimum of 40 inches from adjacent windows.

- New houses should not have jalousie, casement, or awning style windows.

- Exterior doors should be hinged on the inside and should have a single cylinder deadbolt lock with a minimum 1-inch throw.

- All windows should have locks.

- Sliding glass doors should have one permanent door on the outside; the inside moving door should have a locking device and a pin.

Drug Activity

Many neighborhoods across the United States have experienced a significant amount of drug activity. Some neighborhoods are literally held hostage by drug dealers. In the past, the investigation of drug dealers at the neighborhood level has often been left up to a specialized narcotics unit. However, there are things that police officers can do to address drug dealing at the neighborhood level using community police strategies. The problems caused by drug dealing in a neighborhood can be so severe that it can destroy the quality of life for the entire neighborhood. Neighborhood drug dealing is more than just a police problem, it is a problem that may indicate serious neighborhood dysfunction.

At the first report of drug activity in a neighborhood the police officer has several courses of action. First, the officer may wish to do some preliminary investigation work, by gathering some basic information, such as the identity of the occupants of the residence, and inquiring to see if the residence in question is a rental or if the occupants are buying the home, or if the drug dealing originates from an apartment complex. The presence of drug dealing in an apartment complex sometimes attracts other criminals as tenants, because drug dealing can mask their activities or provide them with a ready market for their activities. The officer should enlist the property owners' help in closing a drug market. If the occupants are renting the home, the landlord can be contacted and informed about the suspected drug activity. In some cases, the landlord can evict the tenants.

A check of citizens living in the area would also be beneficial so that the officer may learn traffic patterns; that is, when traffic is heaviest at the residence. The officer may elect to conduct a "knock and talk" and approach the occupants of the residence

---

PRACTICE HINTS

Strategies of Crime Prevention Through Environmental Design (CPTED)

1. **Natural Access Control**—A design concept directed primarily at decreasing crime opportunity by denying access to crime targets and creating in offenders a perception of risk. Gained by designing streets, sidewalks, building entrances, and neighborhood gateways to clearly indicate public routes and discouraging access to private areas with structural elements.

2. **Natural Surveillance**—A design concept directed primarily at keeping intruders easily observable. Promoted by features that maximize visibility of people, parking areas, and building entrances; doors and windows that look out onto streets and parking areas; pedestrian-friendly sidewalks and streets; front porches; adequate nighttime lighting.

3. **Territorial Reinforcement**—Physical design can create or extend a sphere of influence. Users then develop a sense of territorial control while potential offenders, perceiving this control, are discouraged. Promoted by features that define property lines and distinguish private spaces from public spaces using landscape plantings, pavement designs, gateway treatments, and CPTED fences.

4. **Target Hardening**—Accomplished by features that prohibit entry or access: window locks, dead bolts for doors, interior door hinges.

and inform them of the complaints and suspicions. The objective here is that the drug dealers will leave the neighborhood voluntarily if they know the police are on to them. However, one disadvantage to this approach is that it is a temporary solution and may displace the problem to another neighborhood.

One other approach that the officer may find beneficial is to solicit the assistance of citizens living in the neighborhood. The officer could contact residents living near the suspected drug house and request that they jot down a few notes when they see traffic coming and going at the residence, and, ask if they can jot down tag numbers. Police officers may be surprised at the willingness of citizens to assist if only asked. Under traditional policing strategies citizens weren't often asked to assist the police because drug dealers were viewed as solely a police problem. Recall that with community policing, the police will increasingly form partnerships with the citizens and other resources to tackle crime and disorder problems that impact communities.

In one community, police officers who were investigating drug activities in a neighborhood loaned a pair of binoculars and an audio tape recorder to a citizen living across the street from the suspected drug house. The citizen was happy to assist the officers with recording tag numbers into the audio recorder. As one of the officers reported, "He was happy to help us out, he is retired and rarely leaves his house, he is a wealth of intelligence information, he sees everything that goes on in the neighborhood, and he gave us volumes of tag numbers and descriptions of vehicles and persons."

Public awareness of the drug house may be enough to encourage the drug dealers to move along, but suppose that months of investigation of the drug house have not been remarkable. Mobilizing citizens may be the next crucial step. Organizing neighborhood meetings and block parties has the potential of getting the drug dealers' undivided attention and demonstrates a strong united front. Placing banners and signs in conspicuous areas may also show drug dealers that the community is aware of, and will not tolerate, their activities. Most drug dealers are somewhat paranoid of detection, so the presence of an anti-drug campaign may force drug dealers to move out of the area.

Enlisting the aid of the city public works department to clean up the streets, placing brighter lights in street lights, or simply cleaning up litter may go a long way in giving the impression that the community is taking a stake in the area. Planting flowers and trees in areas that have seen urban decay will also improve the appearance of the area. You may ask what the correlation is between planting flowers and ridding the neighborhood of a drug dealer. This may seem like a radical strategy, but it can work. The appearance of the neighborhood may go a long way in preventing and deterring drug dealers and other criminal elements from taking up business in the neighborhood.

Professors James Q. Wilson and George L. Keeling (1982) presented the **broken windows theory** to explain the signaling function of a neighborhood that may nurture criminal activity. The *broken windows theory* suggests that there is a sequence of events that can be expected in deteriorating neighborhoods. Evidence of decay (e.g., accumulated trash, broken windows, deteriorated building exteriors, abandoned cars) that remains in a neighborhood for a reasonably long period of time is part of the sequence of events that can be expected in deteriorating neighborhoods. Many neighborhoods where drug dealing is prevalent indeed show evidence of these sequencing of events. Likewise, citizens who live and work in the area feel more vulnerable and begin to withdraw. They become less willing to intervene to maintain public order or to address physical signs of deterioration. The *broken windows theory* suggests that neighborhood order strategies, such as the ones listed here, may help to deter and reduce neighborhood-related crime:

broken windows theory /
Based on an article titled "Broken Windows" by James Q. Wilson and George L. Kelling, which appeared in the March 1982 edition of *The Atlantic Monthly*. This theory uses the analogy that if a few broken windows on a vacant residence are left unrepaired, the tendency is for vandals to break more windows. Eventually, they may even break into the building, and if it's unoccupied, take up residence in the building or light fires inside. Broken windows and other neighborhood decay give the impression that no one cares about the neighborhood, which then becomes breeding grounds for criminal activity. The idea is that small disorder problems should be promptly addressed by the police and the community or they may lead to more serious crime problems.

Sign printed in English, Spanish, Chinese, and Arabic on wall with graffiti identifies immigration center, NYC. The varieties of languages indicate that the police need to understand how to handle individuals whose basic language is not English.

- Replacement of broken windows on vacant homes or buildings.
- Quickly removing abandoned vehicles from the street.
- Promptly cleaning up illegally dumped items, litter, and spilled garbage.
- Quick paint-out of graffiti.
- Finding (or building) better places for teens to gather than street corners.
- Applying fresh paint on buildings.
- Cleaning up sidewalks and street gutters.
- Keeping grass and weeds cut in vacant lots.

There are certain characteristics that may be evident with suspected illegal drug activity in neighborhoods. Police officers will find it helpful to inform citizens of the following when initiating a neighborhood drug enforcement campaign:

- Be aware of an unusually large amount of traffic coming to the building—in cars, taxis, or walking—often at strange hours. This traffic is usually quick, with people staying only a short time. Sometimes they don't go in at all; instead, someone comes out to meet them.
- Report to the neighborhood police officer if drugs or drug paraphernalia (syringes, pipes, packaging baggies, etc.) are found in the area.
- Report and take note of repeated, observable exchanges of items, especially where money is visible.
- Report anyone that offers to sell you drugs, or conversations about drugs that you overhear.
- Report noxious odors from or around the building, such as chemical smells.
- Report a building where no owner or primary renter is apparent, and no home activities, yard work, painting, or maintenance, seem to be going on.

It is truly the spirit of community policing when neighborhood police officers partner with citizens to combat drug activity in the community. Neighborhood involvement is imperative. Cleaning up drug-infested neighborhoods requires a toolkit full of tools to get rid of the problems. Police presence, civil action, code enforcement, neighborhood clean-ups, and altering the appearance of a neighborhood are all actions that will allow for improvement in the quality of life for citizens. While partnerships are an important component in community policing, police officers should also ensure that citizens don't try and take the law into their own hands or that they are not placed in a position that would jeopardize their safety and welfare. Drug dealers have the potential to use violence to protect their drugs and to protect themselves from other drug dealers.

Combating Drug Dealing in Privately Owned Apartment Complexes

1. Enlist property owners' help in closing a drug market.
2. Enforce laws and agreements violated by drug dealing in privately owned apartment complexes by researching what specific laws or agreements are being violated (e.g., local laws, state laws, federal laws, apartment lease agreements).
3. Take intensive police enforcement action.
4. Increase place guardianship. Research suggests that improved place management can block opportunities for certain crimes, such as drug dealing. Ways to increase place guardianship include: (1) showing the owner the financial costs of having a drug market on the property, (2) engaging the mortgage bank that holds the loan on the property, (3) outlining the physical risks to the owner, (4) providing training for the landlord, and (5) engaging tenants or neighbors in information gathering and market disruption.
5. Make physical changes at the property, such as limiting access to the property, limiting escape routes, and increasing lighting.
6. Send notification letters to and meet with property owners concerning drug dealers.
7. Apply civil remedies, including abatement procedures.
8. Evict drug dealers.

Source: Adapted from U.S. Department of Justice. (2002). *Drug dealing in privately owned apartment complexes*, Problem-Oriented Guides for Police Service, Number 4. www.cops.usdoj.gov.

Traffic Accidents

More people are killed or injured in traffic-related accidents than any other type of accident. The annual economic cost of traffic accidents is astronomical. An important part of the police function is ensuring the safe movement of traffic. Invariably, police officers will be called to investigate traffic accidents. Some traffic accidents can be prevented, while many others cannot. While traffic accidents will inevitably occur, police officers on patrol should be cognizant of accidents that seem to happen again and again at the same location. Recurring accidents at one location may indicate a problem that if solved will reduce or even resolve the number of accidents at the location. Education, enforcement, and engineering should be used in order to resolve or reduce recurring traffic accidents.

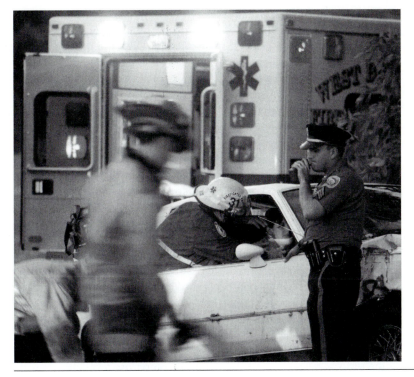

Durham, NC. A police evidence technician examines the wreckage of a vehicle involved in a three-car accident on the Durham Freeway Thursday, March 28, 2002, where a car crossed the median cutting one car in half and severely damaging another. Southbound traffic was diverted for several hours before the scene was cleared near noon.

Some roadways are notorious for being accident prone. The specific reasons may be subtle and not immediately obvious. In order to discover the cause of accidents that seem to occur often at a certain location involves engineering factors such as alignment, visibility, camber and surface conditions, and road markings. Locations that are accident prone should be carefully inspected for these causative factors. The location should be inspected for a missing or obstructed stop sign, a malfunctioning traffic signal, or other factors that may perpetuate the incidence of traffic accidents. Police officers should review the data on accidents that occur repeatedly at a specific location, as this may reveal the obvious causative factors.

Factors that should be noted may include specific patterns, such as a particular day or time that accidents seem to be most prevalent. In industrial areas it may be that the traffic patterns are inconsistent with other times of the day, which may be contributing to accidents. Accidents may tend to occur during shift change at a large manufacturing plant as workers try to rush out of the parking lot. If this is determined to be a causative factor, the officer should work with management to stagger shift change times a few minutes in order to avoid a large volume of traffic leaving the plant at the same time. If traffic accidents are occurring after dark in a specific area, perhaps it may be a lighting problem in the area. If after reviewing available data it is determined that traffic violations are the contributing factors, then tailored enforcement should be initiated at the location. Officers should also pay particular attention to hazard visibility factors, including intersections, merging lanes, bends, crests, school zones, and pedestrian crossings. Temporary hazards may include road construction, parked or disabled vehicles, accidents, traffic jams, and wild animals (especially deer).

Traffic laws and ordinances are often haphazardly enforced. Police officers may enforce traffic laws with little justification of why they are concentrating on a specific location. Delattre and Cornelius (2003, p. 601) make this point when they ask, "Where should the police set up speed checkpoints? In locations most convenient to the police—locations where police can most easily catch the largest number of speeders and write the most tickets? Or in locations where there have been accidents or complaints from the public and where speeding is clearly hazardous? If police operate from the premise that the purpose of traffic laws is to foster safety and efficiency in travel, in other words, if the purpose of traffic laws is to serve the public interest, the answer becomes clear."

With community policing, officers should increasingly rely on both word of mouth from citizens and official accident data when making enforcement decisions. If an area has a high incidence of traffic accidents in which speed is a contributing factor, then specific enforcement activities should be tailored to that area. Likewise, a conspicuous police presence may be required at an accident-prone location for a short period of time.

The educational component is also important in the prevention of accidents. Police officers managing their beats should make it a point to educate the citizens on traffic-causing behaviors. If there is a location that has demonstrated a high incidence of traffic accidents, the officer should approach community groups, such as neighborhood watch associations or home owners' associations, communicate information regarding the increase in traffic accidents, and inform them of preventive techniques. Some officers have gone to the extent of preparing a brochure for dissemination in the community. The purpose of the brochure is to inform the citizens of increases in traffic accidents at a particular area and to suggest prevention techniques.

In those cases where it is determined that repeated accidents are the result of driver behavior, behavioral control factors are recommended. Behavioral control factors may include built-in obstacles that limit the ability of a vehicle to travel at high speeds or in a certain direction and may include crash barrels, speed bumps, pedestrian islands, raised medians, high curbing, guard rails, and concrete barriers.

Graffiti

graffiti / Illegal or unauthorized defacing of a building, wall, or other structure or object by painting, drawing, or otherwise marking it with words, pictures, or symbols. Graffiti is often painted on property by gang members who use it as a means to mark their territory and communicate with rival gang members.

In recent years, **graffiti** has become an increasing problem. Chances are that in some areas of your community you have observed this trend. Many neighborhoods are plagued by graffiti, which can devalue property and make citizens feel unsafe in their neighborhoods. Graffiti may be the result of idle juveniles out for a night of fun, who decide to spray paint graffiti on the side of the building or the result of gangs who leave their mark on a neighborhood and provoke rival sets into a violent confrontation. Graffiti is how gangs identify and claim their "turf."

Gangs typically leave their mark in the form of graffiti on fences, buildings, sidewalks, and at times, even homes. Graffiti may spell out a gang name, the gang's geographic area, or a numeric identifier. It can sometimes show an entire list of gang nicknames, called a "roll call" or "roster." Gang graffiti serves several purposes, all of which are understood by other "gang bangers," even members of rival sets. Graffiti has been called the "newspaper of the streets" and communicates many messages, including violent challenges, warnings, as well as bragging about crimes that have been committed. Graffiti can also be used to show disrespect for a rival gang. For

Entrance to Thomas Edison HS with graffiti covering the doors, Philadelphia, PA.

example, Blood sets may refer to Crip sets as "Crabs" and Crip sets may use "Slobs" in their graffiti as an insult to Blood sets.

Graffiti presents a rather perplexing problem for police officers, as the officer must discern whether the graffiti represents street gang graffiti or tagger graffiti. Tagger graffiti differs from street gang graffiti in that it is generally more intricate and more "artistic" than street gang graffiti (Gomez, 1993). Taggers see graffiti as an art form. The lettering may be entwined and turned upside down or sideways to the point of looking more like a maze than letters. The graffiti that taggers paint on walls usually is done in several colors and might include caricatures of animals or humans. On the other hand, street gang members put up graffiti to increase their visibility, threaten rivals, and to intimidate residents in the area. It is usually much more primitive and sometimes more easily read than graffiti done by taggers. If it is determined that the graffiti is gang related, the officer should attempt to interpret the meaning of the graffiti. In some cases gang graffiti is the first sign of a future act of gang violence, such as one gang invading the other's territory. Gang graffiti should be removed as soon as possible.

Gang graffiti that includes "187" indicates a threat to kill. "187" is the California penal code for homicide, and when used in street graffiti tells rival gangs that those who painted the graffiti intend to kill them. Hispanic gangs often use the number "13." The "13" may be represented as "XIII," "X3," "13," or with the word "trece." Hispanic gangs tend to use the number "13" because the thirteenth letter of the alphabet is "M." This is significant because the "M" refers to the Mexican Mafia. It may also be used to designate Mexico, the homeland.

In some cases the officer may actually catch the suspect in the act of vandalizing the property. Let's suppose that an officer on patrol drives up on a vandalism. The officer catches a juvenile spray painting graffiti on the back of a school building. Normal police procedure dictates that the officer handle it one of two ways. First, the officer may take the juvenile into custody, make an official police report, release the juvenile to his or her parents, and forward the case to the investigations division. Second, the officer may take the juvenile into custody and book him or her into the juvenile detention facility. These two approaches represent a fairly standard police response.

Let's consider a community policing response to the hypothetical vandalism-in-progress case. Recall that the police officer has taken the juvenile into custody for spray painting graffiti on a school building. Let's suppose that the officer is familiar with the juvenile and sees him around the neighborhood frequently. The officer recognizes that the juvenile is not known to be troublemaker and the officer is satisfied that the juvenile is not a member of a gang. The officer makes the decision to take the juvenile home to his parents.

After explaining to the juvenile's parents about the vandalism, the officer asks the parents if they would agree to an informal resolution. The officer relates to the parents that he has a good relationship with the principal of the school and that he (the officer) would like to handle this incident informally. In other words, the officer wants to take a chance on the juvenile. The officer explains to the parents that the next day after school dismisses, their son will be required to clean the spray painted graffiti off the side of the building. The parents agree to this resolution. After all, it's a much better outcome than having to pick their son up from the juvenile detention facility. The officer telephones the principal of the school and explains the situation. The principal informs the officer to do what he thinks is best.

In this case, the officer handles the incident informally using a nontraditional police response to the problem. It should be pointed out that an informal response may not be effective or appropriate in every situation; however, with community policing officers are empowered to make these types of field decisions that are in the best interest of the community. Police patrol officers are in the best position to make such decisions because they are exposed to neighborhood problems on a daily basis. It only makes sense that officers are allowed the discretion to fully perform their jobs in consort with the community policing strategy.

Paying attention to the small quality-of-life issues, such as graffiti, pays big dividends that can prevent the downward slide of neighborhoods. The Minneapolis Police Department suggests some things that citizens can do to help prevent the proliferation of graffiti in neighborhoods. These suggestions were accessed via their website at www.ci.minneapolis.mn.us/graffiti/. Police officers should keep these guidelines close at hand for educating the community.

Protect Your Property:
- Keep your property well maintained. Remove graffiti immediately after receiving confirmation from the police.
- Plant clinging vegetation, like ivy, to protect walls and other large flat surfaces.
- Plant thorny or thick bushes and fences in front of large walls.
- Eliminate anything that could encourage loitering after hours (benches, pay phones, etc.).
- Limit access to roofs—move commercial dumpsters away from walls and cover drainpipes to prevent vandals from scaling them.
- When painting your property, consider darker colors that are less attractive to graffiti vandals.
- Increase lighting around your property; use motion detectors to draw attention to movement.

- Textured walls are a deterrent to graffiti writers. Consider texturing outside walls if you are a regular victim of graffiti.

- Consider applying a protective coating that provides a barrier between your property's surface and the graffiti. Several different brands and prices are available. Check the Yellow Pages under "Graffiti Removal & Protection."

- Organize: There are many advantages when block clubs, neighborhood organizations, and other groups band together to protect their environment.

- Form a neighborhood graffiti removal crew and help those who are not able to do so themselves.

- Get neighborhood businesses to sponsor clean-up and prevention efforts.

- Create a watch force for areas frequently vandalized.

- Involve community youth in removing graffiti.

- Help identify and apprehend graffiti writers involved in graffiti.

- Participate in the city's public property adoption (adopt-a-litter container, adopt-a-block, and adopt-a-street) programs.

Police in Action

Tagger Language

Battle: A contest between crews
Bomb: Multicolored tag in large bubble letters
Buff: To remove graffiti
Crew: Group of individuals that tag together
Caps: (Fat/skinny) Spray can nozzles used to vary the style and width of paint
Fade: To blend colors
Fresh: Really good graffiti
Get Up: To put up a large amount of graffiti tags
Graf: Graffiti
Heavens: Hard to reach high areas, such as freeway signs and the tops/upper floors of buildings
Hit/Hit Up: To tag
Landmarks: A prime location where graffiti won't quickly be erased
Mob: A whole crew doing graffiti on a wall at the same time
Piece Book: A tagger's sketch book
Rack: To steal from off the store rack
Streak: Short for mean streak, solid paint stick that looks like chalk and is used on dark surfaces
Tag Banging: To use violence to defend a tag
Toy: A new, inexperienced writer
Throw Up: One layer of spray paint filling in bubble letters that are outlined in another color
Wild Style: A complicated piece constructed with interlocking letters
Yard/Train Yard: Gathering place
Zine: Short for magazines

Robbery

robbery / The crime of seizing property through the use of force or the threat of the use of force. Because violence is an ingredient of most robberies, this sometimes results in the serious injury or murder of the victims.

Robbery is the act of unlawfully taking the property from another, with the threat of force or the actual use of force such as, "give me your money or else." There are several types of robberies. The first is *business establishment robbery* (e.g., when the suspect enters into the business and demands money from the employee). According to the Uniform Crime Report, robberies of business establishments make up about 25 percent of all robberies. Business establishment robberies can include a convenience store, gas station, restaurant, clothing store, and the like.

Another type of robbery is the *individual robbery,* which is the most common. An example of this would be walking to the subway one evening when you are approached by a robber who demands your wallet. A *strong-armed robbery* occurs when you are approached by a robber who demands your money and begins to deliver blows to your head while at the same time ripping your wallet from your pocket. Extreme force is used in a strong-armed robbery. A *home invasion* is another type of robbery that occurs when the robber knocks at the door and crashes through it when the person answers, demanding money or other property.

carjacking / A crime of motor vehicle theft from a person who is present. In many cases the carjacker is armed, and the driver of the car is forced out of the car at gunpoint.

Another type of robbery is **carjacking**. Imagine one evening that you are driving home from a long day at work. While waiting at an intersection for the signal light to change, your door is suddenly ripped open and the person pulls you onto the street, jumps into your car, and drives off. You have just been the victim of a carjacking. Carjacking is a type of robbery that has received much attention in recent years. Carjacking is an attempted or completed robbery of a motor vehicle by a stranger that includes the use or threat of use of force. Because cars are becoming more difficult to steal, many criminals are finding it easier to steal a car with the owner in the vehicle and the key in the ignition.

The common misconception about carjacking is that it only occurs in high crime areas. Carjacking can occur anywhere at any time. Some of the windows of opportunity that carjackers typically look for are intersections controlled by stop signs or lights, garages and parking lots for mass transit, shopping malls, grocery stores, self-serve gas stations and car washes, automated teller machines, residential driveways and streets as people get into and out of their vehicles, highway exit ramps, or any place that drivers slow down or stop. Police officers should educate citizens that if they are the victim of a carjacking not to argue with the suspect, especially if they are threatened with a gun or other weapon.

Police officers at some point in their careers may have the occasion to investigate or assist in the investigation of a robbery. In many cases, robbers preselect their targets. A business that has been robbed several times during a short period of time should alert the officer that it may be something specific about the business that is making it an ideal target for robbery.

Research has shown that robbers typically have a risk/reward criterion, but usually consider two main factors when choosing a location to rob. The first factor is the amount of available cash on hand; the more cash the better for the robber. Second is the ability to escape from the scene without getting caught. The risk criteria that might deter them from committing the robbery are the number of employees on duty, high customer traffic, video surveillance cameras, silent alarm systems, bad escape routes, and the presence of security or the police. The balancing factor is the perception of available cash versus the risk of getting caught. In essence, the greater the score the more risk the robber will undertake.

Tips to Citizens to Prevent Carjacking

- Before entering your car, be alert to any activity near your Pay attention to your surroundings.
- Have your keys in hand when approaching your vehicle.
- If someone is loitering around your unoccupied car as you approach, keep walking. Do not attempt to get into your car until they are gone.
- Keep your windows closed and doors locked while driving.
- When stopped at a traffic signal or sign, stay far enough away from the vehicle in front of you so you can see the rear wheels. This will allow you to have enough room to leave quickly, if needed.
- If your vehicle is bumped from behind, do not get out. Drive to a well-lighted, safe area first, and then get out of your vehicle. This is a common tactic used by carjackers to steal cars.
- Be suspicious of strangers asking for directions, change, or handing out flyers. If you feel uncomfortable, pull out carefully and leave the area, even if it means running a red light or stop sign.
- If you suspect you are being followed, never drive home—change directions, go to a safe area, and call the police.
- Be alert when using drive-up ATM machines.

Police officers should use the investigation of a robbery not only as an attempt to identify the assailant, but also as an opportunity to educate the owner on prevention techniques. This is especially important in cases where the crimes are committed repeatedly against the same business. There are factors that make a business more susceptible to robbery, which necessitates conducting an inspection of the premises and advising management of preventive measures that can be taken that may prevent a future robbery. There are some specific robbery tips that the officer may consider as part of the robbery prevention education:

- Install a robbery alarm. If a silent alarm is installed ensure that it can be reached inconspicuously by the employee.
- Install a video recorder and ensure that it faces the front counter.
- Take greater precautions during opening and closing, when businesses are more vulnerable.
- Do not make cash handling or bank deposits part of a routine.
- Keep a low volume of cash on hand.
- Do not open the business before or after regular business hours.
- Greet all customers. This reduces their anonymity and lets potential robbers know you are paying attention.
- Watch for suspicious customers. Robbers often shop until all other customers are gone.
- Some stores may keep the door locked at all times and have an electronic buzzer to open the door for customers.
- Make sure the store is well-lighted, especially the entrances and cash register.

- From the cash register, you should be able to see all areas of the store, as well as outside to the parking lot or street. This allows surveillance of customers and potential robbers.
- Placing the cash register on a raised platform increases visibility.
- If there are blind spots in the store, use mirrors to increase visibility.
- The view through the front windows should not be obstructed with advertisements and posters so that motorists or a passing police car can readily see inside of the business.

COMMUNITY POLICING AND TERRORISM

terrorism / The unlawful use of force or violence against persons or property to intimidate or coerce a government, the civilian population, or any segment thereof, in furtherance of political or social objectives.

Since the September 11, 2001 attacks on the World Trade Center and the Pentagon, **terrorism** has become one of the most pressing issues facing federal, state, and local law enforcement agencies. There is some speculation that because of the increasing threat of terrorism and homeland security that community policing will become less of a priority of police agencies. To de-stress community policing strategies because of increased terrorism threats is neither wise nor in the best interest of the community. Community policing is a strategy that goes hand-in-hand with proactive approaches aimed at preventing terrorism. In fact, expanded community policing strategies would seem to be the natural response to terrorism.

The community policing strategy is important for the police in preparing for possible terrorist acts and in responding to the fear they may create (Scheider & Chapman, 2003). Through partnerships and ongoing communication with citizens, police officers can reduce the fear of terrorism. For example, in response to community concerns about anthrax as a weapon of bioterrorism, police officers can fill an important role by providing accurate information about the threat (Carter & Holden, 2003). By opening themselves up to citizen input, police officers will become knowledgeable about, and responsive to, the varying concerns of different communities (Skogan, 1994). As Carter and Holden (2003, p. 299) point out, "What if the flight instructors who trained the September 11 operatives had been aware of terrorism concerns and had good ties with the police? Might the instructors have given an important lead to police and prevented the attacks?"

Community policing offers viable opportunities for the police to learn about potential terrorists working in concert with the community. If citizens recognize something that doesn't look right in their neighborhood, and if they have an open relationship with their neighborhood police officers, they are more likely to report this information. Thus, community policing holds promise as a valuable means of strengthening communications and investigations (Carter & Holden, 2003).

The problem-solving component of community policing appears to be well-suited in the identification and investigation of possible terrorist activity. Scheider and Chapman (2003) argue that police departments can use many existing data sources ahead of time to develop detailed risk management and crisis plans. Identifying potential terrorist targets in local jurisdictions is an important first step. Police can determine what in their jurisdictions (dams, electric grids, chemical warehouses, large-scale public gatherings) are potential terrorist targets. Community policing strategies encourage agencies to conduct complex analyses of the possible threats and of their relative likelihood of occurring. Agencies in conjunction with other

Firefighters working to put out fire caused by the World Trade Center attack. One of the lessons learned as the result of this attack is the need for the law enforcement, fire departments, and other service agencies to work together in a coordinated response.

government, social, and community entities can develop detailed crisis prevention and response plans. Finally, the community policing model encourages continual refinement of these plans to suit changing conditions and threat levels.

DOES COMMUNITY POLICING WORK?

Mary Ann Wycoff and Jeffrey Skogan investigated the implementation and impact of community policing in Madison, Wisconsin and found very positive results. They found that it was possible for a traditional police department to change and that the community and officers both benefited from improved attitudes. Attitudes of police toward the organization and their work improved. Accompanying these changes was a reduction in citizens' perceptions that crime was a problem in their neighborhood, and increased beliefs that police were working on problems of importance to people in the neighborhood (Wycoff & Skogan, 2001).

An evaluation of the Community Patrol Officer Program in New York City found many reasons for satisfaction and optimism for the future. The study evaluated New York City's Community Patrol Officer Program (CPOP), which attempts to put community policing into practice at the beat level. Beginning as a pilot project in 1984, and expanding to all seventy-five precincts in 1989, the program gives the individual community patrol officer (CPO) responsibility for addressing crime and order-maintenance problems in a sixteen by sixty block beat, which is usually patrolled on foot. Data were collected in 1986–1988 from interviews with CPOs and their supervisors, and from observation and records of fifty-four CPOP beats. The most important function of the CPO is to carry out problem solving in the beat area. Community patrol officers were most effective in attacking street-level drug problems, least effective with parking and traffic problems. Community leaders reported that CPOP units contributed significantly to improved relations between the police and the community. The core of CPOP is the application of the problem-solving process in the context of a local community.

Researchers David Weisburd and John Eck found evidence to support continued investment in police innovations that call for greater focus and tailoring of police efforts, combined with an expansion of the tool box of policing beyond simple law enforcement. The strongest evidence of police effectiveness in reducing crime and disorder is found in the case of geographically focused police practices, such as hot-spots policing. Community policing practices are found to reduce fear of crime, but the researchers do not find consistent evidence that community policing (when it is implemented without models of problem-oriented policing) affects either crime or disorder. A developing body of evidence points to the effectiveness of problem-oriented policing in reducing crime, disorder, and fear (Weisburd & Eck, 2004).

The Chicago Police Department formed teams of officers who were dedicated to tackling problems in their own small beats. Evaluations found changes in the visibility of policing, new optimism about the quality of police service, and evidence that crime, social disorder, and physical decay decreased in the community policing districts. Every district registered some successes, and those who benefited included home owners, renters, whites, and African-Americans (Skogan & Hartnett, 1997).

The Wichita, Kansas Police Department initiated community policing by assigning seventeen specially trained community police officers to four high-crime target neighborhoods. They were asked to work with the community to accomplish something that many officers felt was impossible. Three goals were identified: (1) reduce prostitution and crime, (2) improve police–community cooperation through partnerships, and (3) improve the appearance of the neighborhood. The neighborhood created a steering committee to guide the neighborhood initiative. The Wichita Police Department reported most impressive results. During a twenty-week evaluation period, prostitution decreased 41 percent and prostitution-related crimes decreased 47 percent. In addition, 911 calls to the neighborhood decreased 16 percent (Cole, 2001).

SUMMARY

- Community policing is the evolving strategy of policing in the United States.
- The core components of community policing include partnerships, problem solving, and organizational transformation.
- Community-oriented policing represents a shift from more traditional law enforcement in that it focuses on prevention of crime and the fear of crime on a very local basis.
- In part, community policing evolved from strategies such as police–community relations, team policing, crime prevention, and foot patrol. However, the initial spark of finding better ways to police communities and the movement toward community policing

strategies was initiated with the research findings of the 1970s that shattered a few of the traditional assumptions about police patrol strategies.

- Research studies increasingly challenged police to change their way of thinking, as well as their strategies in battling crime and disorder problems, and a growing fear of crime among the general citizenry. Community policing strategies are a direct carry-over from past police practices, such as team policing, and police–community relations programs.
- Community-oriented policing is not a program, it is a philosophy or strategy, a way each department member from the top to bottom, sworn to non-sworn, view their jobs.

■ Community policing differs from traditional law enforcement because it allows police the freedom to expand the scope of their jobs. Police in this sense are challenged to become community problem solvers and encouraged to use their time creatively.

■ In problem solving, police officers, citizens, and other public and private entities work together to address the underlying problems that contribute to crime and disorder by identifying and analyzing problems, developing suitable responses, and assessing the effectiveness of these responses. The police may rely less heavily on enforcement and may look at a wide variety of other options suitable in solving a problem.

■ Professor Herman Goldstein is considered by many to be the pioneer of problem-oriented policing. Problem solving is an important component of community policing. As a result, during the 1980s, a number of law enforcement agencies throughout the United States and in other countries began a wide variety of problem-oriented policing initiatives as part of their community policing strategy.

■ One of the most popular problem-solving models is known by the acronym SARA. This acronym stands for Scanning, Analysis, Response, and Assessment. The SARA model presents a systematic way in which a police officer can investigate problems.

■ Community policing is a strategy that is designed to be intertwined with all police activities. Under the axiom of community policing, individual line officers are given the authority to solve problems and make operational decisions suitable to their roles, both individually and collectively.

■ Under community policing, police officers focus not only on enforcement, but also on crime prevention and proactively addressing the root causes of crime and disorder. Likewise, citizens actively engage in collaborating on prevention and problem-solving activities with a goal of reducing victimization and fear of crime.

■ Community policing is a strategy that goes hand-in-hand with proactive approaches aimed at preventing terrorism. Expanded community policing strategies would seem like the natural response to terrorism. Problem-solving models seem to be well-suited to preventing and responding to terrorist activity.

■ Evaluations of community policing are still somewhat lacking in the sense that there has not been an overall evaluation of community policing. However, many of the evaluations that have been completed show that community policing holds much promise as a policing strategy. The one common theme among community policing evaluation is that the strategy appears to make citizens feel safer about their neighborhoods.

Classroom Discussion Questions and Activities

1. Compare and contrast community policing and traditional policing strategies.

2. Discuss how police research contributed to the movement to community policing.

3. Have students identify and discuss community policing activities in their community.

4. Identify a community problem and have students utilize the SARA problem-solving model as a guide to solving the problem.

5. Conduct a crime prevention study applying the Crime Prevention Through Environmental Design (CPTED) techniques to a location close to campus.

6. Discuss ways that community policing can assist police with terrorism prevention.

Websites and Other Resources

Community Policing Consortium
  www.communitypolicing.org/

Michigan State University Regional Community
  Policing Institute
  www.cj.msu.edu/~outreach/rcpi/default.htm

National Center for Community Policing Publications
  www.cj.msu.edu/~people/cp/webpubs.html

Center for Problem Oriented Policing
  www. popcenter.org/

References

Carter, D. L., & Holden, R. N. (2003). Terrorism and community concern. In W. A. Geller and D. W. Stephens (Eds.), *Local government police management* (pp. 291–311). Washington, DC: International City Manager's Association.

Cole, S. (2001). South Central prostitution project. In Q. Thurman, Z. Zhao, & A. L. Giacomazzi, *Community policing in a community era* (pp. 242–245). Los Angeles, CA: Roxbury Publishing.

Community policing consortium: A framework for community policing. (n.d.). Retrieved July 26, 2006 from www.communitypolicing. org/ mod1. html.

Community Policing Consortium. (1997). *Module two: Mobilizing the community for collaborative partnerships.* Washington, DC: Community Policing Consortium.

Cordner, G. W. (1999). Elements of community policing. In L. Gaines and G. Cordner (Eds.), *Policing perspectives: An anthology* (pp. 137–149). Los Angeles, CA: Roxbury Publishing.

Crowe, T. D. (2000). *Crime prevention through environmental design* (2nd ed.). Woburn, MA: Butterworth-Heinemann.

Delattre, E. J., & Cornelius, B. J. (2003). Practical ideals for managing in the new millennium. In W. A. Geller and D. W. Stephens (Eds.), *Local government police management* (pp. 599–614). Washington, DC: International City Manager's Association.

Fleissner, D., & Heinzelmann, F. (1996). *Crime prevention through environmental design and community policing.* Washington, DC: National Institute of Justice.

Goldstein, H. (1990). *Problem-oriented policing.* Boston: McGraw Hill.

Gomez, M. (1993). The writing on our walls: Finding solutions from distinguishing graffiti art from graffiti vandalism. *University of Michigan Journal of Law Reform, 26*, 633–708.

Green, L. (1996). *Policing places with drug problems.* Thousand Oaks, CA: Sage.

Harris, D. A. (2005). *Good cops.* New York: New Press.

Hope, T. (1994). Problem oriented policing and the drug market locations: Three case studies. In R.V. Clark (Ed.), *Crime prevention studies,* Vol. 21, Monsey, NY: Criminal Justice Press.

Johnson, R. A. (1994). Police organizational design and structure. *FBI Law Enforcement Bulletin, 63*, 5–7.

Keeling, G., Pate, T., Diekman, D., & Brown, C. E. (1974). *Kansas City preventive patrol experiment.* Washington, DC: Police Foundation.

Mastrofski, S. D., & Ritti, R. R. (2000). Making sense of community policing: A theory based analysis. *Police Practice and Research: An International Journal, 1*, 183–210.

McElroy, J. E., Cosgrove, C. A., & Sadd, S. (1998). *CPOP: The research–An evaluative study of the New York City community patrol officer program.* New York: Vera Institute of Justice.

Moore, M., & Stephens, D. A. (1991). *Beyond command and control: The strategic management of police departments.* Washington, DC: Police Executive Research Forum.

National Institute of Justice. (2004, November). *Community policing beyond the big cities.* Washington, DC: U.S. Department of Justice.

Oliver, W. M. (2004). *Community oriented policing: A systematic approach to policing.* Upper Saddle River, NJ: Prentice Hall.

Ortmeier, P. J. (2002). *Policing the community.* Upper Saddle River, NJ: Prentice Hall.

Palmiotto, M. J. (2000). *Community policing: A policing strategy for the 21st century.* Gaithersburg, MD: Aspen Publishers.

Palmiotto, M. J., Birzer, M. L., & Unnithan, N. P. (2000). Training in community policing: A suggested curriculum. *Policing: An International Journal of Police Strategies and Management, 23*, 8–21.

Peak, K. J., & Glensor, R. W. (1999). *Community policing and problem solving: Strategies and practices* (2nd ed). Upper Saddle River, NJ: Prentice Hall.

Police Foundation. (1981). *The Newark foot patrol experiment.* Washington, DC: Police Foundation.

Sadd, S., & Grine, R. (1994). Innovative neighborhood oriented policing: An evaluation of community policing in eight cities. In Dennis P. Rosenbaum (Ed.), *The challenge of community policing* (pp. 13–26). Toronto: Canadian Scholars Press.

Scheider, M. C., & Chapman, R. (2003). Community policing and terrorism. *Homeland Security Journal,* retrieved August 10, 2006 from www. homelandsecurity. org/journal/articles/Scheider-Chapman.html

Skogan, W. G. (1994, November). *Community participation and community policing.* Paper presented at the Workshop on Evaluating Police Service Delivery, University of Montreal and Solicitor General Canada.

Skogan, W. G., & Hartnett, S. M. (1997). *Community policing, Chicago style.* New York: Oxford University Press.

Sparrow, M. K. (1988). *Implementing community policing.* Washington, DC: U.S. Department of Justice, National Institute of Justice, pp. 8–9.

Sweeny, T. J. (2003). Patrol. In W. A. Geller and D. W. Stephens (eds.), *Local government police management* (pp. 89–133). Washington, DC: International City Manager's Association.

Taylor-Green, H. H. (1993). Community policing in Florida. *American Journal of Police, 12*, 141–155.

Thurman, Q. C., & Reisig, M. D. (1996). Community-oriented research in an era of community-oriented policing. *American Behavioral Scientist, 39*, 570–586.

Thurman, Q. C., & Zhao, J. (2003). *Contemporary policing: Controversies, challenges, solutions.* Los Angeles: CA: Roxbury Publishing.

Thurman, Q. C., Zhao, J., & Giacomazzi, A. L. (2001). *Community policing in a community era*. Los Angeles, CA: Roxbury Publishing.

Trojanowicz, R. C. (1990). Community policing is not police-community relations. *FBI Law Enforcement Bulletin, 59*, 10–12.

Trojanowicz, R., & Bucqueroux, B. (1998). *Community policing: How to get started* (2nd ed.). Cincinnati, OH: Anderson Publishing, p. 8.

U.S. Department of Justice. (2003). Uniform Crime Report. The data was obtained from the Federal Bureau of Investigation website at www. fbi. gov/ucr/ucr.htm [accessed online August 9, 2006].

Weisburd, D., & Eck, J. E. (2004). What can police do to reduce crime, disorder, and fear? *The Annuals of the American Academy of Political and Social Science, 593*, 42–65.

Wilson, J. Q., & Keeling, G. L. (1982, March). Broken windows: The police and neighborhood safety. *Atlantic Monthly*.

Wycoff, M. A., & Skogan, W. K. (2001). *Community policing in Madison: Quality from the inside out. An Evaluation of implementation and impact*. Washington, DC: U.S. National Institute of Justice.

Chapter 4

The Crime Scene and Preliminary Investigation

" My name is Sherlock Holmes. It is my business to know what other people don't know. "

—Fictional Detective Sherlock Holmes
The Final Problem

CHAPTER OUTLINE

- Introduction
- The Role of Patrol in the Preliminary Investigation
- Initial Steps in the Investigation
- Photographing the Scene
- Crime Scene Search
- The Nature of Evidence
- Types of Evidence
- Cybercrime
- Summary

After completion of this chapter, you will be able to do the following:

- Describe the role of the first responder to a crime scene.
- Discuss the preliminary crime scene assessment.
- Describe techniques used to document the crime scene.
- Identify the different types of fingerprints that may be left at a crime scene.
- Discuss techniques used in photographing the crime scene.
- Discuss the crime scene search techniques.
- Discuss proper evidence documentation and packaging.
- Identify the various classifications of evidence.
- Discuss the general nature of cybercrime.
- Discuss the investigative considerations of cybercrime.

INTRODUCTION

Dennis L. Rader was arrested on February 25, 2005, after a thirty-one year investigation and hunt for the serial killer. He has been sentenced to 175 years to life for ten murders that were committed in the Wichita, Kansas area from 1974 to 1991. He was married with two grown children, was a Cub Scout leader, and president of his Lutheran church. No one suspected Rader to be the notorious BTK serial killer. To the casual observer, he was an ideal citizen and neighbor.

Rader, the self-named "BTK strangler," which stands for "Bind them," "Torture them," and "Kill them," gave an apt description of his **modus operandi (MO)**. [*Modus operandi* (often used in the abbreviated form MO) is a Latin phrase, meaning "mode of operation." It is used in police work to describe a criminal's characteristic patterns and style of work.] Rader developed a pattern or "MO" for his murders. He would drive around the city until he found a potential victim. At that point, he would stalk the person until he knew the pattern of their lives and when would be the best time to strike. Rader would often stalk multiple victims at a time, so he could continue the hunt if one victim didn't work out. When Rader murdered, he would break into the house, cut the phone lines, and hide until his victim came home.

Rader calmed his victims by pretending to be a rapist who needed to work out his sexual fantasies on them. This caused many of his victims to be more cooperative and even help him, thinking that once the rape was over, he would leave them alone. Instead, Rader would kill them in brutal and

modus operandi / Often abbreviated as "MO," this is a Latin phrase, translated as "mode of operation." It is used in police work to describe a criminal's characteristic patterns and style of work.

grotesque fashion, strangling the victims until they were near death, bringing them back to consciousness, and then strangling them again. The sight of the victim's struggle sexually aroused Rader. In many of the crimes, Radar masturbated over the victim until he ejaculated, leaving semen on the corpse.

After his arrest, Rader seemed to enjoy telling investigators about his crimes. Using personal jargon for his killing equipment, Rader casually described his victims as his "projects" and at one point likened the murders of his victims to killing animals by saying he "put them down." Rader created what he called a "hit kit," a briefcase or bowling bag containing the items he would use during murders. The hit kit contained guns, tape, rope, and handcuffs. He also packed what he called "hit clothes" that he would wear for the crimes and then dispose of. Rader told investigators that he was possessed by a demon from an early age and could not contain himself.

What was even more chilling, after each murder the elusive BTK strangler taunted authorities with clues, puzzles, and obscene letters that boasted of the crimes and knowledge of details of the crimes. Then suddenly, in 1988, the BTK strangler seemingly vanished, the letters stopped, and the murders remained a cold case for years.

The letters resumed in 2004, after some twenty-five years of silence. A few years before the BTK strangler ended his silence, the cold case became hot. Two Wichita Police Department detectives were assigned to work on the unsolved 1986 killing of twenty-eight-year-old Vicki Wegerle, a wife and mother found bound and strangled in her Wichita home. Police found a man's DNA under her fingernails. The profile was entered into a newly developed national database of criminals, but there was no match. However, DNA tests showed that the same killer had been in the homes where BTK strangled a family of four in 1974, and another victim in 1977. This evidence, in part, was used to apprehend Dennis Rader as the BTK strangler.

The BTK strangler case illustrates the importance of thoughtful and thorough crime scene investigations. The detectives investigating the BTK murders in the 1970s had the foresight to collect semen and other evidence left at the scene by the killer even though scientific analysis techniques at that time were somewhat limited, and DNA analysis for use in crime scene investigations was unheard of. It was this very evidence some thirty years later that assisted in identifying Rader as the BTK strangler.

The investigation of crime is an important mandate of the police. Even the smallest police organization is not exempt from this mandate. In most medium and large police departments there are usually personnel assigned to a specialized unit who have the responsibility for the follow-up investigation of crime. In many small police departments the investigation of crime at all stages is handled by the patrol force. Regardless of whom within the police organization conducts the follow-up criminal investigation, the patrol force plays an important role in the crime scene investigation process. The actions taken at the outset of an investigation at a crime scene can play a critical role in the successful resolution of a case. The treatment and preservation of the crime scene is vital to the identification and ultimate prosecution of the perpetrators. A crime scene that is handled in a haphazard manner can be detrimental for the successful resolution of the case, not to mention the police department's reputation.

Serial killer Dennis Rader, the self-named "BTK Strangler" which stands for Bind them, Torture them, Kill them, is seen in a Sedgwick County courtroom in Wichita, Kansas during the first day of testimony in a sentencing hearing following a previous hearing where he pled guilty to ten counts of first-degree murder. Rader a 60-year-old former church congregation president and Boy Scout leader, haunted Wichita with killings for over three decades.

The diligent investigation of the crime scene is both necessary and critical. This chapter is designed to provide you with the basics involved in the crime scene and preliminary investigation. Our focus in this chapter will be broad, as we don't break down the investigation of specific crimes, but rather provide an overview of preliminary considerations that should be taken at the crime scene. These considerations are appropriate and necessary regardless of the type of crime. Strictly speaking, there is a logical protocol that is required of the police at the crime scene, whether it is a burglary, robbery, or homicide investigation. However, there are no normative criteria for judging the success or failure of an investigation. Just because a crime remains unsolved does not indicate a deficiency in the investigation; nor does a conviction of the accused necessarily mean that the investigation was conducted in an intelligent manner (O'Hara & O'Hara, 2003). As O'Hara and O'Hara (2003, p. 6) report: "An investigation can be considered a success if all the available information relevant and material to the issues or allegations of the case are uncovered." Many cases simply will go unsolved because of a lack of evidence.

The case of the BTK strangler discussed previously is a good example. This was a case involving ten murders that went unsolved for over thirty years, not because the police were ineffective, or that they conducted a poor investigation. Quite to the contrary, they utilized some of the best and emergent technology when it became available, which included a satellite tracking device borrowed from the Department of Defense. Scores of psychiatrists and psychologists, FBI agents, and profilers attempted to furnish information that would assist in solving the cases. The BTK strangler case simply paralyzed the largest city in Kansas with fear for many years. Citizens coming home from work would make it a point before they entered their homes to check the phone line to ensure that it had not been cut, and then to check the windows around the house to ensure that they were not broken. During the BTK killing spree, many citizens purchased guns and chemical mace products for self-protection.

THE ROLE OF PATROL IN THE PRELIMINARY INVESTIGATION

The Initial Patrol Response

preliminary investigation / The investigation of the crime scene usually performed by first responding police officers immediately after the crime has been detected and reported.

evidence / Anything that assists in proving or disproving a fact. Any object that can establish that a crime has been committed, or any object that can link a suspect to a crime, or provide a link between the victim and a crime. The weapon used in a homicide is considered evidence that can assist in proving the crime of murder.

proof beyond a reasonable doubt / The level of certainty a juror must have to find a defendant guilty of a crime. Proof beyond a reasonable doubt is proof of such a convincing character that you would be willing to rely and act upon it without hesitation. The burden of proof in a criminal trial before an individual may be found guilty.

crime scene / A location where a criminal offense occurred and where evidence of the crime may be located. It is not necessarily the only location where the crime took place. Indeed, there are primary, secondary, and often tertiary crime scenes.

The **preliminary investigation** is the primary responsibility of the patrol force that is responsible for the initial documentation of the scene. Documentation of the crime scene may include photographs, diagrams and/or written reports.

Internal and external photographs are taken if the crime was committed in a residence, building, or other structure. External and aerial photographs are taken if the crime was committed in a field or some other rural area. If there are human remains on the scene and a weapon, the location and appearance are both important to document. **Evidence**, which is subsequently documented, collected, and placed in proper containers, may require special handling, especially if it is large or present on a wall, floor area, side of a building, or a door (which may have been impacted with gunshot, for example).

In the investigation of any crime, the investigator must interview witnesses and any other persons who may have knowledge of the crime. The investigator must then search for and collect evidence with the hope that the offender will be identified. Innocence is always assumed for every suspect no matter what the suspect has allegedly done or regardless of your feelings toward the suspect. The guilt of the suspect must be probed later in a court of law. The burden of this guilt is called **proof beyond a reasonable doubt**. This cannot be accomplished by haphazard investigative techniques.

When a crime has been committed, all efforts are directed into recording the facts of the crime, identification of the perpetrator(s), and their apprehension and arrest. The responsibility of the first responding officer on the scene is to report the incident and secure the area until relief arrives, or the laboratory or official scene investigators take over the scene. Initial responding police officers may also be needed after the scene has been secured to relay findings to other officers or investigators who are investigating clues and collecting preliminary statements from witnesses, neighbors, or members of the family of the victim(s).

The investigation of a crime typically begins when patrol officers arrive at the **crime scene**. The crime scene is the site or location where the crime took place. There may be more than one crime scene involved in a specific crime. For example, there may be secondary or even tertiary crime scenes. Suppose that the victim of a sexual assault is kidnapped from her residence and forced to drive to a field located in a rural area, where she is then sexually assaulted. The suspect then drives the victim to a hotel room and sexually assaults her again. In this case, there are three separate crime scenes: the victim's residence where she was abducted, the field where the first assault took place, and the hotel room where the second assault took place. Another example is a crime where a victim of a homicide was killed at one location and then driven by the suspect to another location, where the victim's body was subsequently disposed of. In this case, where the victim was killed is one crime scene, and where the victim's body was disposed of is the second crime scene. Crime scene processing occurs at locations where a crime has been committed.

The preliminary investigation of the crime scene includes care of injured persons, apprehension of the offenders if still present at the scene, and the securing and protection of the crime scene pending a search for physical evidence; this also includes keeping on-lookers and media personnel away from the scene. This is important

Voices of Experience

Law Enforcement in the Military

Excerpts from an interview between Cliff Roberson and former police officer, Thomas J. Mason. Professor Mason is currently Chair, Criminal Justice Department, Remington College, Tempe, Arizona.

Q: *Can you tell us about your experiences as a police officer in the military?*

A: I served in the U.S. Air Force as a law enforcement specialist. I joined at the age of seventeen and served for twenty-five years.

A military policeman serves in different jurisdictions and is required to assimilate the law of the different jurisdictions. I was in the security police, which is similar to the army's military police. After basic training and prior to being assigned to the security police, an airman is sent to a technical school where the individual learns the duties, techniques, and concepts of being a security police person. After that, the individual may be sent to an advanced course. Myself, I went to a ten-week course on working with K-9s.

After you are assigned to your first operational unit, you are required to undergo extensive on-the-job training. There is a laundry list of information that you need to learn as a security officer. For instance, in traffic enforcement we are required to take training in the certification requirements of each state or jurisdiction that we are assigned to. If there is a local certification school, then the officer will also attend it. Whatever breath mechanism is being used in that jurisdiction or state we were required to use and receive training on that mechanism. The need for complying with local requirements is based on the fact that the security police also enforce traffic regulations on civilians who enter the base. Every couple of years when an officer is transferred to a new location, the officer must learn the laws of the new state or jurisdiction.

The crimes that a security police officer investigates are very similar to that of any city police department and range from homicide to traffic regulations. In foreign countries, the security officer is required to coordinate with the foreign police departments. For example, in Italy we had to coordinate with the Italian National Police. They were more liberal in allowing people to drink and drive and in the use of breathalyzer test limits than we are in the United States. If we stopped an Italian civilian, we were required to immediately contact the Italian National Police. If we stopped an American civilian who worked on the base for a minor offense, then we had jurisdiction to handle the case without referring it to the Italian police. In cases with American civilians involving serious crimes, we were required to call the Italian police. The rules and practices are similar in other countries. The United States has status of forces agreements with the foreign countries that provide guidelines for dealing with these problems.

When dealing with foreign nationals on the base, we had the authority to detain them and then we had to contact the Italian police. It was important that the security officers learn basic commands in the foreign language, because the foreign national may not understand English. Beyond the basic commands, the base security police have available interpreters to handle communications with foreign nationals. ■

because it ensures that evidence will not be tampered with or walked on by persons who should not be within the perimeter of the crime scene. Wilson and McLaren (1977, p. 348) in their classic text, *Police Administration* (4th ed.), summarized both the direct and investigative duties in a Chicago Police Department training bulletin. These duties have changed very little today and can still serve as a guide for police.

P   Proceed to the scene with safety and dispatch

R   Render assistance to the injured

E   Effect arrest of perpetrator

L   Locate and identify witnesses

I   Interview complainant and witnesses

M   Maintain scene and protect evidence

N   Note all conditions, events, and remarks

A   Arrange for collection of evidence

R   Report incident fully and accurately

Y   Yield responsibility to detectives

One of the most important responsibilities of the first responding officers at the crime scene, next to aiding the injured and apprehending perpetrators that may still be on the scene, is protecting the scene until relieved by a supervisor or the assigned investigating officer or unit. While en route to the crime scene officers should constantly be alert for potential suspects, witnesses, and/or vehicles leaving the scene. The responding officer(s) should conduct an initial preliminary investigation to a point where a lapse in the investigation would not hamper or jeopardize the outcome of the case. Patrol officers should cease the preliminary investigation when the investigation demands special skills and the attention of the investigators. The actions of first responding police officer(s) at the crime scene are often the foundation for the successful resolution of the crime (Lee, Palmbach, & Miller, 2001).

Once patrol receives the call to report to a crime scene, their initial response should be expedient, but done so in a safe and prudent manner. Upon arrival, the officers should immediately assess the scene and treat the incident as a crime scene until it is determined otherwise. One of the most important aspects of securing the crime scene is the preservation of the scene in order to ensure minimal disturbance to the physical evidence.

Generally, the investigations unit should be called on all serious or major crimes, such as homicide, life-threatening assaults and batteries, rapes involving crime scene processing, scenes where there is a large amount of evidence to process, robberies involving life-threatening injuries, major burglary scenes, fatality accidents, or when it is determined that the need exists to process the crime scene. Of course, this will vary somewhat depending on the standard operating procedure of the police agency. In some police agencies investigators will not respond to relatively minor crime scenes, while in others they may. Likewise, in some smaller police agencies the patrol officer performs many of the investigative duties that an investigator may perform in a larger police agency. Officers working in smaller police departments are sometimes called "generalists" because of their versatility in the police function.

Regardless of the nature of the crime, officers should always evaluate the crime scene closely to determine the need to contact the investigations unit. Specific conditions that may necessitate the need to call the investigations unit may include whether there is a likelihood the collection of fingerprints will entail special techniques, if photographs other than general crime scene photos are needed, or if there is need to collect evidence that is beyond the expertise of the patrol officer.

Self-Protection

Controlling individuals at the crime scene is an important function of the first responding officers. Policing is a hazardous profession. Officers put themselves into potentially dangerous situations in order to protect and serve the communities in which they live. Consequently, they must constantly educate themselves about the

Voices of Experience

Oklahoma City Bombing Investigation

Excerpts from an interview between Cliff Roberson and former police officer, Mark R. McCoy, currently a professor at the University of Central Oklahoma. Professor McCoy also served as an investigator for the Oklahoma State Bureau of Investigation (OSBI) where he specialized in computer-related investigations.

Q: *It is my understanding that you were involved in the investigation of the Oklahoma City bombing. Tell us about the investigation.*

A: At the time I was a resident agent in Stillwater, Oklahoma, which is about sixty miles north of Oklahoma City. When the bombing occurred, about half the agents in the Oklahoma State Bureau of Investigation were assigned to help with the investigation. We assisted the FBI in running leads and coordinating the investigation. The FBI brought hundreds of agents into Oklahoma and many were not familiar with the local area. Our agents assisted in evidence recovery. It was amazing how large the investigation was. We had thousands of leads that were coming in twenty-four hours a day. The leads had to be assigned to agents and investigated. It was estimated that several hundred investigators were present at the scene. In addition, leads were forwarded to investigators all over the country. At the command center, there were ten to fifteen agents just answering the telephones as the leads were coming in. One of the biggest problems was identifying the victims. Our fingerprint people had to go to the homes of the children and dust their toys for latent fingerprints in order to identify the child victims. ■

dangers they might face and how to minimize those risks. Responding to the crime scene is no exception, and officer safety is a primary concern.

While the officers will receive pertinent information about the crime from emergency communication dispatchers, the first responding patrol officers should avoid the practice of relying on this information exclusively. It is always a possibility that the crime is still in progress and that the dispatchers did not have this information. The responding officers must be prepared to deal with a potentially dangerous situation, as well as being prepared to defend themselves and the public from a suspect who still may be present at the scene. In cases where there is a likelihood that the suspect is still on the scene, the officers should request a backup if one has not already been assigned. Likewise, the responding officers should anticipate potential threats while en route to the crime scene. Will the suspect be on the scene? Will the victim's relatives turn in anger on the emergency responders? What kind of hazards can the officer expect? What is the extent of the crowd that may have gathered? These and other questions must be considered and hasty contingencies developed that may allow the officer to overcome any potential threat that presents itself (Gardner, 2005).

The responding officers must first ensure that no personal harm can result from a hidden suspect. If it is determined that the suspect is still present at the scene, the officers should detain and remove the suspect as soon as possible. The search and arrest of the suspect must be done in a manner so as not to destruct physical evidence that may link the suspect to the crime scene. If the suspect is apprehended in the area near the crime scene, never return the suspect to the crime scene. This practice will prevent potentially contaminating the scene, or an altercation between the victim, victim's family, or others who may still be present at the crime scene. In cases where the victim needs to identify the suspect, it should be done in a more controlled environment. It is

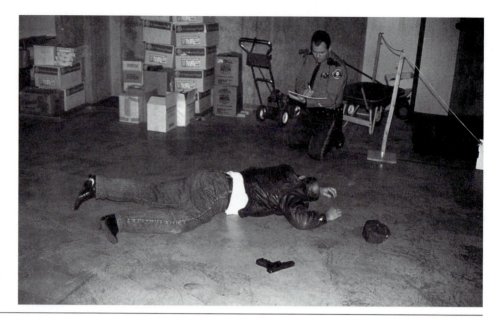

Policeman writing notes examines man lying on ground next to handgun inside. The officer will also be required to make sketches of the area and provide a detailed record of the event that led to the shooting.

PRACTICE HINTS

The Basics of Taking Suspects into Custody

1. Check for weapons—if present, remember to be aware of safety and that they are evidence. Firearms will need to be recorded and unloaded (don't handle or dry fire them!)
2. Remove from the scene and isolate suspect. If necessary, stay with the suspect while the suspect uses any restroom facilities.
3. Do not let the suspect return to the scene.
4. Document the condition of the suspect (describe, photograph, etc.).
5. Document the behavior of the suspect and record any spontaneous statements made by the suspect.
6. Document any injuries of the suspect and record the condition of the suspect's clothing.

Source: Lee, H. C. (2001). *Henry Lee's crime scene handbook*. New York: Academic Press, p. 53.

dying declaration / A statement by a person who is conscious and reasonably believes that death is imminent concerning what he or she believes to be the cause or circumstances of death that can be introduced into evidence during a trial in certain cases.

extremely important that the officers at the crime scene not allow any suspect to contaminate the crime scene in any manner.

Care for the Injured

After controlling any dangerous situations or persons, medical attention should be provided to injured persons while minimizing the contamination of the scene. Officers should either provide direct emergency first aid to injured persons or allow paramedic first responders to aid the injured persons. In some jurisdictions it is common that emergency paramedics arrive at the scene of a crime before the police. If this is the case, the officer should obtain the name, unit, and location of the medical facility where the victim is to be taken. Medical personnel should be instructed not to clean up the crime scene and to avoid removal or alteration of items originating from the scene. The names of all paramedic personnel should also be recorded by the officer.

If there is a chance that the victim may die, an attempt should be made to obtain a **dying declaration**. A dying declaration is a statement made by a person who reasonably believes he or she is about to die, concerning the cause or circumstance surrounding his or her impending death. The victim of a life-threatening assault may make a dying declaration implicating her neighbor, John Smith, as the person who attacked her. A dying declaration is considered credible and trustworthy evidence based upon the general belief that most people who know that they are about to die do not lie. As a result, it is an exception to the hearsay rule, which prohibits the use of a statement made by someone other than the person who repeats it while testifying during a trial, because of its inherent untrustworthiness.

Changes or alterations made to the crime scene by paramedics should be carefully documented. Consideration must be given to the eventual reconstruction of the condition of the injured party prior to administering first aid. Officers should point out potential physical evidence to paramedics and ask them to minimize contact with such evidence. It is also critical that officers stop needless destruction of evidence by relatives or friends of the victim who may be on the scene, otherwise a tremendous amount of evidence may be lost to the case. Assisting and guiding paramedics during the care and removal of injured persons will minimize the risk of contamination and loss of evidence. If the victim or suspect is transported to a medical facility, a police officer should be sent with the victim or suspect in order to document any comments made by the victim and to preserve evidence.

Securing the Crime Scene

Police patrol officers are typically the first to arrive at the scene of a crime. As discussed previously, they have the responsibility to arrest the perpetrator if he or she is still on the scene, and call for an ambulance if necessary. It is paramount that the scene is secured so that evidence is not destroyed. Once the officer has ensured that the suspect is no longer on the scene and there is not an immediate need to administer first aid, the crime scene is then defined and secured. The first responding officers are responsible for scene protection until relieved by a supervisor or the assigned investigating officer.

The proximity of the crime scene boundaries should be determined as soon as possible. Defining and controlling the crime scene boundaries provides a means for protecting and securing the crime scene. The number of crime scenes and their boundaries are determined by their location(s) and the type of crime. It is recommended that boundaries be established beyond the initial scope of the crime scene(s). Boundaries can always be reduced in size if necessary, but they cannot be expanded as easily once the investigation has been initiated. Boundaries of the scene(s) should be started at the specific focal point and extended outward to include where the crime occurred, potential points and paths of entry and exit, and places where the victim and evidence may have been moved. Be aware of trace and impression evidence while assessing the scene.

Persons present within the crime scene boundaries should not smoke; chew tobacco; use the bathroom; eat or drink; move any items, including weapons (unless necessary for the safety and well-being of persons at the scene); adjust the thermostat; or open windows or doors. The crime scene should be maintained as it was found. Any item(s) at the crime scene should not be touched unnecessarily. If the officer does move or reposition an item or touch something, it should be documented.

An attempt should be made to determine the extent to which the crime scene was protected prior to the officer's arrival. Barricade tape should be put up around the crime scene and a **crime scene log** should be started. Barricade tape is used for a variety of reasons and is designed to protect and identify above-ground hazardous areas or elements such as construction sites, work areas, crime scenes, crowd control, and any potentially dangerous areas. Barricade tape used in police work is usually reflective bright yellow and plastic with a large black visible legend printed continuously across the tape that reads, "POLICE LINE — DO NOT CROSS."

crime scene log / A log that is kept at the crime scene, that documents persons present at the crime, what time they arrived, what time they left, and what action they took. This includes not only police personnel, but also medical and fire personnel. Provides permanent documentation of those present at the crime scene.

A crime scene log is a report that documents all personnel and their actions at the scene of the crime, including the time of their arrival and the location of their presence at the scene. As discussed previously, first responders should remove, secure, and debrief all persons found within the crime scene. This includes obtaining their names, addresses, place of employment, and phone numbers. If an eyewitness is present, the first responding officer should check with the crime scene investigators to see if they want to interview the person at that time. Arriving personnel should not be allowed to enter the secured crime scene unless necessary for investigation. The first responding officer should not allow anything to be removed from the crime scene. Challenge any person attempting to enter. Even other officers who arrive at the crime scene just to take a look should be reminded of the possibility of contaminating the crime scene.

PRACTICE HINTS

Crime Scene Log

SCENE LOG

Date:	
Location:	
Case Number:	

Name	Time In	Time Out

As most police officers know, at the scene of a major crime there is always the tendency of some police officers to want to get a quick look at the scene or the victim. This practice should be discouraged. Only officers that are involved in the investigation should be permitted to physically enter the crime scene. The first responding officer should ascertain why a person is entering the crime scene and make the appropriate notation on the crime scene log. Actions should be taken to restrict unauthorized personnel from entering the crime scene.

A command post should be established as soon as possible at the scene of a major crime. It is never acceptable to establish the command post within the perimeter of the crime scene. For example, it would be disastrous to establish the command post at the kitchen table inside the residence where a homicide has occurred. It may be necessary to establish a unified command with the fire department incident commander in crime scenes that involve a fire death. A command post established outside the perimeter may also assist in keeping unauthorized persons from entering the crime scene.

All officers present on the scene should complete a written report of what they did at the scene. It is a wise practice to photograph personnel who attempt to enter the scene without authorization. This is advantageous so that their identities can be revealed at a later time, if needed. The first responding officers should report extreme violations of the crime scene protection protocol to a supervisor, who should take immediate action.

Note taking for appropriate narrative reports and/or offense reports should be in progress by this step. First responding officers should concentrate on the immediate area of the crime. If this stage of action is undocumented and poorly organized then all subsequent events in the crime scene search may lack direction. Pertinent information may include:

- Time of arrival
- Weather conditions
- Approximate time of offense
- Time offense was discovered
- Identity of other officers present, medical personnel, first responders, and others
- Identify of relief officer(s)
- Interview results
- Any physical evidence information and how it was collected

Information should be obtained from other persons regarding the original conditions of the crime scene, such as persons that discovered the crime, paramedics, fire department personnel, and other personnel that may have arrived at the scene prior to the police. In the case where officers are relieved by an officer of a different shift, all pertinent information about the crime should be passed along to the relief officer in writing, whenever possible. The need for scene protection will vary according to location, lapse of time since the offense, prior contamination of the scene, and similar factors, including adjusting the perimeters of the crime scene as needed. Generally, it is the investigation unit's responsibility to conduct a crime scene search at major crime scenes. In any crime scene investigation, it is

PRACTICE HINTS

First Responding Police Officer(s) Duties at a Glance

- Take control of the crime scene immediately.
- Arrest suspect still at the crime scene.
- Administer first aid as needed.
- Remove all persons from the crime scene.
- Determine the extent to which the scene has been protected. Obtain information from personnel who have knowledge of the original condition.
- Establish a perimeter to protect the scene.
- Continue to take extensive notes.
- Keep out unauthorized personnel (when personnel who have no bona fide need to be on the scene insist on entering, record their names and the times they were on the scene, for court purposes).
- Record all persons who enter and leave the crime scene.
- Maintain control of the scene until relieved by designated personnel. When another officer arrives to assume control of the scene, verbally confirm this as a fact and record the time and the officer's name and rank.

important that the following two crime scene considerations be observed: (1) you cannot overdocument physical evidence, and (2) there is only one chance to perform the job properly.

News Media

The news media represents a potential problem for officers who are charged with securing the crime scene. Oftentimes the media arrives at the crime scene shortly after the first responding officers. Officers should keep in mind that most members of the media simply want to get a story as soon as possible. Furthermore, the media can play an insurmountable role in assisting the police in the identification of victims, suspects, and in ultimately solving the crime. The police should as a matter of policy release as much information to the public through the media without jeopardizing the outcome of the case.

How far can the media go in photographing and reporting information about the crime scene? The media may report and photograph anything they observe while legally at a crime scene. The media should be allowed to be close enough to the scene to be able to obtain film footage for their newscasts. Sometimes, media personnel will try to get too close to the crime scene or even enter the scene in order to get better photographs. The first responders have a responsibility to control the media and restrict them from entering the actual crime scene. Additional officers should be called to assist if needed.

The first responding officers should not release information to the media and should refer media questions to the on-scene commander. Once the crime scene has been secured, there should be a location established for the media to gather. This will make it convenient for police commanders or the public information officer to locate media personnel for the purpose of providing updates on the case. Police authorities should remain in periodic contact with the media for the purpose of updating them on the investigation.

The Neighborhood

Regardless of the seriousness of the crime, a neighborhood check should be conducted. In other words, officers should walk the neighborhood and inquire from citizens if they saw or heard anything unusual prior to or during the approximate time of the crime. Many police officers have solved burglaries and other crimes by simply doing a neighborhood check. In one case, an officer was conducting a neighborhood check regarding a burglary, and found that one of the neighbors living a few houses from the victim's house had observed two juveniles breaking the window in order to gain entry. The witness was able to identify the juveniles. It is difficult to estimate the number of crimes that could be solved if officers got into the habit of walking the neighborhood and talking with citizens during the investigation of a crime. In many cases the citizens may be reluctant to get involved or approach the police with information, so the police should make an effort to approach citizens.

Turn Over Control of the Scene

Once investigators arrive at the scene and assume control, the first responding police officer's job is still not over. The first responding officer should provide a detailed crime scene briefing to the investigator in charge of the scene. The scene briefing is the only opportunity for the next in command to obtain initial aspects of the crime scene prior to the subsequent investigation. Police officers may then be assigned to secure and control certain locations at the scene, or they may be assigned to assist in interviewing witnesses and searching the crime scene.

Procedure for Turning Over Control of the Crime Scene

The initial responding officer should:

1. Brief the investigator(s) taking charge of the crime scene.
2. Assist in controlling the crime scene.
3. Turn over responsibility for the documentation of entry or exit.
4. Remain at the scene until relieved of duty.

INITIAL STEPS IN THE INVESTIGATION

The Initial Assessment

It would be impossible to propose a step-by-step procedure that offers guidance to every situation that a police officer may encounter; however, there are basic principles that should be adhered to in every case. As a rule of thumb, first responding officers and investigators should approach the crime scene investigation as if it will be their only opportunity to preserve and recover these physical clues.

Investigators should consider all case information or statements from witnesses or suspects carefully in their objective assessment of the scene. It is not uncommon for investigations to change course a number of times during such an inquiry and physical clues, initially thought irrelevant, may become crucial to a successful resolution of the case (Osterburg & Ward, 2004).

Search Warrant

An important first step in the crime scene investigation is to evaluate search and seizure issues to determine the necessity of obtaining **consent to search** or a **search warrant**. [Consent to search is given by a person who has legal care, custody, and control of the property or location.] If consent to search is obtained, it should be in writing. Most police agencies have a "consent to search form" as part of their written forms. Consent searches are a legitimate means of obtaining evidence, but it is always best to obtain a search warrant. The gold standard is: when in doubt, obtain a search warrant.

The controlling principles governing search warrants are generally provided by the U.S. Constitution's Fourth Amendment. The Fourth Amendment of the U.S. Constitution, which is part of the Bill of Rights, guards against unreasonable searches and seizures. The procedure for obtaining a search warrant involves the presentation of an affidavit to a judge or magistrate by a law enforcement officer requesting that the magistrate issue the search warrant based on the probability of criminal activity.

consent to search / Authorization given to the police to search someone's home or other location by the person who has care, custody, and control of such place.

search warrant / An official order signed by a judge or magistrate authorizing a search of someone's home or other location. The controlling principles governing search warrants are generally provided by the U.S. Constitution's Fourth Amendment.

Voices of Experience

Crime Scene Investigations

Excerpts from an interview between Cliff Roberson and police officer, David A. Thornton, Arvada, Colorado. Officer Thornton is also an adjunct instructor for Westwood College and the University of Phoenix.

Q: *Would you explain to us how you do a crime scene investigation?*

A: The crime scene investigation starts with the 911 call. The actions of the first responder are often the most critical aspect of a successful investigation. If the investigation begins with evidence overlooked or ignored, it is difficult or impossible to make up for lost ground. Officer safety is one of the first priorities that should be considered at the crime scene and therefore it is essential that the scene is tactically secure. The first responder also observes, evaluates, secures the scene, and perhaps most significant to the ongoing investigation, he or she protects the evidence. In any crime scene, the first responder secures the area and makes critical observations, such as the condition of the point of entry and lighting and items moved overlooked, or placed or dropped by the offender. First responders must remember that as they are searching the house, they must touch only those things that are necessary. They must try not to disturb the scene and not to move an item unless necessary, in order keep the scene pristine— as close to the way the criminal had left the scene as possible. If a door is opened during the initial response, the trained first responder must remember which door was opened and how the door appeared prior to it being altered. Before any item is moved at a crime scene, the item must be documented and photographed. While safety must be the first priority in any investigation, dangerous items, such as guns, are the first thing that most of us grab. The trained first responder will be certain that this is only done when there is an immediate safety risk. Proper training teaches us that it is easier and better for the investigation to keep people away from a gun rather than move the gun unnecessarily.

After securing the scene, the officer should begin focusing on taking steps to apprehend the suspect. The second officer is generally assigned to set up a perimeter system around the scene. Also during this time, there may be victims that need medical care. A crime scene may be hectic and therefore the crime scene needs to be managed. Police officers are self-sufficient and motivated. If they are not properly trained or communicated with, they may start doing things on their own, and even with the best intentions, this could still result in the loss of evidence.

Q: *Are there special problems when dealing with crime scenes where an "officer involved" shooting has occurred?*
A: They are difficult on many levels. When an officer is shot, not only do officers have to do their job, but they are also personally attached to the injured or dead officer. The emotions can be crippling and might produce obstacles in managing the crime scene. Officers should try to detach from the trauma and the reality of the situation and conduct the investigation with professionalism. ■

PRACTICE HINTS

Crime Scene Investigative Factors

1. Initial discovery and security.
2. Report of finding and call for support by other law enforcement authorities, if necessary.
3. Processing by laboratory.
4. Processing by medico-legal investigations.
5. Review by special investigations arson, explosives, blood splatter.
6. Review of scene by prosecuting attorneys.

Source: Eckert, W. G. (1986). *Homicide investigation.* Wichita, KS: The Milton Helpern International Center of Forensic Sciences at the Wichita State University, p. 11.

Mock Consent to Search Form

CONSENT FORM

I, _____, the _____
      (Person giving consent)   (Owner, tenant, manager, etc.)

Of the _____ located in _____
        (Residence, business, vehicle, etc.)   (City)

At _____ do and voluntarily give my consent to _____
                                                                     (Name of official)

Of the _____and any other investigator or law enforcement
        (Name of agency)

officer participating in the investigation of the police incident, to search the
property described above and the surrounding areas of the premises, including
any structures or vehicle situated on or adjacent to the property, to examine
and remove any evidence to the crime which occurred on or about

_____
      (Date and Time of Crime)

This written permission is being given by me to the above named personnel. I further authorize these persons to inspect and remove any item of evidence, which
may be related, directly or indirectly.

                                                    _____
                                                    Signature

WITNESSES

_____
_____   DATE _____ TIME _____

The Walk-Through

A preliminary walk-through of the crime scene should be completed by the crime
scene investigators. Generally, the walk-through should be conducted with individuals who will be responsible for processing the scene. The crime scene walk-through
provides an overview of the entire scene, identifies any threats to scene integrity,
and ensures protection of physical evidence. Prior to the walk-through, a narrative
technique should be selected such as written notes, audio record of the events, or
video recording. Written and photographic documentation provides a permanent
record. At this stage, it is important during the scene walk-through that the investigators avoid contaminating the crime scene. Due care should be given where the investigators and police officers step within the scene. The preliminary documentation of the scene should be noted as it is observed.

Crime scene photographs, video recordings, diagrams/sketches, and drawings
are good ways to document the crime scene. The sketch or diagram of the crime
scene establishes a permanent record of items, conditions, and distance/size relationships. For example, the sketch may depict the location of a weapon to the victim, or the location of droplets of blood to the victim. Sketches and diagrams offer
an ideal supplement to photographs. A rough sketch drawn at the scene is normally

not drawn to scale and is used as a model for a finished sketch. In general, the following should be included on the rough sketch:

- Specific location
- Date
- Time
- Case identifier
- Preparer
- Weather conditions
- Lighting conditions
- Scale or scale disclaimer
- Compass orientation
- Evidence
- Measurements
- Key or legend

In some cases, number designations on the sketch can be coordinated with the same number designations depicted on the evidence log. The general progression of the crime scene sketch should lay out basic perimeter, depict the location of fixed objects such as furniture, record the position of evidence, record appropriate measurements, and set forth a key or legend and compass orientation.

During the initial walk-through, it is important to delineate which areas will be searched, paying special attention to potential problem areas. Transient physical evidence should be identified and protected. A determination should be made about personnel and equipment needs. Furthermore, specific assignments should be made

PRACTICE HINTS

Initial Assessment of Crime Scene

- Evaluate safety issues that may affect all personnel entering the scene(s) (e.g., blood-borne pathogens, hazards).
- Evaluate search and seizure issues to determine the necessity of obtaining consent to search and/or a search warrant.
- Evaluate and establish a path of entry/exit to the scene to be utilized by authorized personnel.
- Evaluate initial scene boundaries.
- Determine the number/size of scene(s) and prioritize.
- Establish a secure area within close proximity to the scene(s) for the purpose of consultation and equipment staging.
- If multiple scenes exist, establish and maintain communication with personnel at those locations.
- Establish a secure area for temporary evidence storage in accordance with rules of evidence/chain of custody.

- Determine and request additional investigative resources as required (e.g., personnel/specialized units, legal consultation/prosecutors, equipment).
- Ensure continued scene integrity (e.g., document entry/exit of authorized personnel, prevent unauthorized access to the scene).
- Ensure that witnesses to the incident are identified and separated (e.g., obtain valid ID).
- Ensure the surrounding area is canvassed and the results are documented.
- Ensure preliminary documentation/photography of the scene, injured persons, and vehicles.

Source: National Institute of Justice. (2000). *Crime scene investigation: A guide for law enforcement.* Washington, DC: U.S. Department of Justice, p. 3–4.

of police personnel. It cannot be overemphasized the importance of taking extensive notes to document the scene, physical and environmental conditions, and personnel movements.

PHOTOGRAPHING THE SCENE

The aim of photographing the crime scene is to capture the most useful amount of detail possible. When photographing evidence, or for that matter any part of the crime scene, there are generally three types of crime scene photos: overall or long-range photographs, mid-range photographs, and close-up photographs. This protocol of photographs enables the viewer to gain a clear concept of where each object or area interrelates to another.

The perpetrator's point of entry and the point of exit should be photographed in the same manner (i.e., overall, mid-range, close-up). Likewise, the point of entry and exit should be shown in such a manner that the marks of force will be shown clearly. A scale may also be used and depicted in the photograph. Overall photos of a residence should depict the house numbers.

This same procedure should be followed in both property and person's crimes. For example, if photographs of an assault victim are taken, an overall photo should be taken, a mid-range photograph of the injury or trauma, and then a close-up photograph should be taken of the same. In some cases, aerial photographs of a crime scene may be helpful, especially if the scene is located in a rural area. In crimes such as a rape–homicide, infrared ultraviolet photography of the body may detect latent bite marks, since hemorrhaging can occur in tissue under the skin. The location of foreign hairs and fibers, biological fluids, and stains can also be depicted.

Overall Photographs

Overall (long-range) photographs taken with a wide-angle lens (28–35 mm range) capture the scene as it is. This type of image provides anyone who has not been present at the scene a good overall layout. Overall photographs should be taken from all angles or directions of the crime scene; this is very important in order to show what is surrounding the residence. Overall photos consist of overall photo shots of the scene, including overall room shots if the crime was committed inside a residence or other structure. At a burglary scene, long-range photo shots can assist in answering several questions, such as whether the residence is secluded in a rural area or in a residential area, and whether there are fences or gates on the property where the crime occurred, along with other landmarks.

Mid-Range Photographs

Mid-range photographs are usually taken with a normal lens (45–55 mm range). The purpose of the mid-range photographs is to give greater detail than given in the overall shots. In the case of a bloodletting scene, the mid-range image could capture a single bloodstain pattern. The key concept to mid-range photos is to tie together all evidence in the crime scene. This range of photograph is also useful to show tools used in the burglary in relation to the item(s) they were used on, to depict windows that were broken, and to show the pattern of broken glass that was left by the suspect(s).

Close-Up Photographs

Close-up images taken with a macro lens give the greatest amount of detail. When photographing bloodstains, a medium velocity impact pattern can contain thousands of individual stains that require individual images. Close-up photography allows you to establish the magnification rate and size of items at the crime scene, and shows the specific details of the evidence at the scene. This can assist the investigator in writing a more accurate report, and will assist in remembering the case at some future time.

PRACTICE HINTS

Photographing the Crime Scene

- Photograph the crime scene as soon as possible.
- Prepare a photographic log that records all photographs and a description and location of evidence.
- Establish a progression of overall, medium, and close-up views of the crime scene.
- Photograph from eye level to represent the normal view.
- Photograph the most fragile areas of the crime scene first.
- Photograph all stages of the crime scene investigation, including discoveries.
- Photograph the condition of evidence before recovery.
- Photograph the evidence in detail and include a scale, the photographer's name, and the date.
- Take all photographs intended for examination purposes with a scale. When a scale is used, first take a photograph without the scale.

- Photograph the interior crime scene in an overlapping series using a normal lens, if possible. Overall photographs may be taken using a wide-angle lens.
- Photograph the exterior crime scene, establishing the location of the scene by a series of overall photographs including a landmark.
- Photograph entrances and exits from the inside and the outside.
- Photograph important evidence twice.
- A medium-distance photograph that shows the evidence and its position to other evidence should be taken.
- A close-up photograph that includes a scale and fills the frame should be taken.

CRIME SCENE SEARCH

The purpose of the crime scene search is to obtain physical evidence that is useful in establishing that an offense has been committed, identifying the method of operation employed by the perpetrator, reducing the number of suspects, identifying the number of suspects, and identifying the perpetrator (Swanson, Chamelin, & Territo, 1996, p. 55). *Physical evidence* is any object that can establish that a crime has been committed, or any object that can link a suspect to a crime, or can provide a link between the victim and a crime. In a trial, evidence in the form of all or part of a physical object is intended to prove a fact. Suppose that the victim is shot with a semiautomatic handgun that is later recovered. The handgun is physical evidence. Physical evidence can also be classified as imprints or compressions, such as footwear patterns, tire tracks, tool marks, scratches, and bite marks. Physical evidence may also be in the form of trace material, such as paints and other deposits, hair and other fibers, pollens, glass, and polymers.

Crime scene commanders should discuss the search with involved police personnel before initiating the crime scene search. In major or complicated searches, it may be necessary to establish a command post for communication and decision making. Personnel involved in the search should be aware of the types of evidence usually encountered and the proper handling of the evidence. If possible, preliminary personnel assignments should be made before arriving at the scene. Officers assigned to the crime scene search should not be tasked with an assignment that is beyond their aptitude, training, and experience.

There are several types of crime scene search patterns that may be used and will vary depending on the nature of the crime scene and type of terrain. The method used to search a crime scene where the victim was murdered inside of a house will differ significantly than if the victim was taken to a rural area and murdered in a field. It is always best to define the limits of the search in very broad terms.

Strip Method

The *strip method* search pattern requires that the area be blocked out in the form of a rectangle. Search team members then proceed at the same pace along paths parallel to one side of the rectangle. When evidence is discovered, the person who discovers the evidence announces the discovery and the search is halted until the evidence is collected. Prior to collecting the evidence, a photograph may be taken of the discovery and an investigator who has been assigned to collect the evidence may be called to collect the evidence. After the evidence is collected the search is continued. Once the searchers reach the end of the rectangle they turn around and begin to walk back along new lanes or paths.

Grid Method

The *grid method* search pattern is a modification of the strip method. A grid search is simply two parallel searches, offset by 90 degrees, performed one after the other. The

Figure 4.1   Diagram of a Strip Search of a Crime Scene

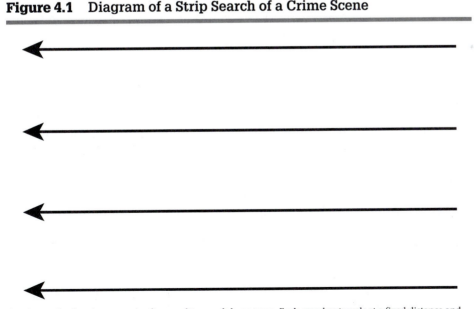

A strip search of a crime scene is often used to search large areas. Each searcher travels at a fixed distance and all travel in the same direction.

Figure 4.2   Diagram of a Grid Search of a Crime Scene

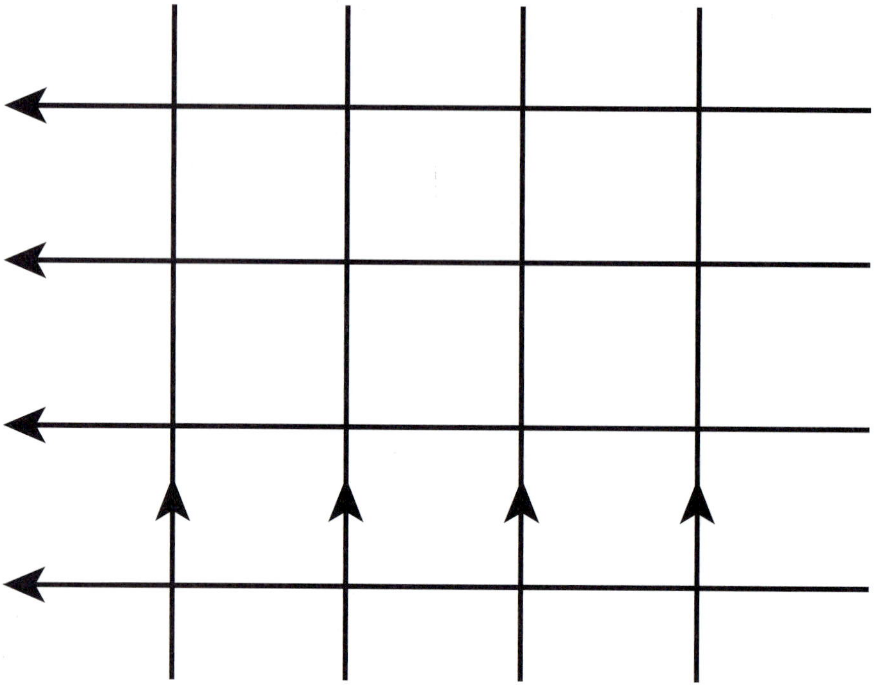

A grid search of a crime scene is similar to a strip search, but after completing the search in one direction, the area is then re-searched at a 90 degree angle.

grid search method requires that the area be searched along horizontal and vertical lines of a grid.

Zone Method

The *zone method* search pattern requires the crime scene be divided into zones or quadrants for individual searching. Depending on the size of the area, zone quadrants may be cut into another set of zone quadrants. The zone search method is ideal to use in an indoor crime scene because these scenes typically comprise readily definable zones.

Spiral Method

The *spiral method* search pattern is where the collection of evidence is carried out in a circular pattern working toward a fixed point at the center. There are two methods used in conducting the spiral method, the outward search and the inward search. In the outward spiral method, investigators follow each other in the path of a spiral, beginning on the outside and spiraling in toward the center. In the inward spiral method, the investigators start in the center of the search area and proceed in circling around in an outward motion. The spiral method is generally used for special conditions of the search. There is always the possibility that when using the inward

Figure 4.3   Diagram of a Zone Search of a Crime Scene

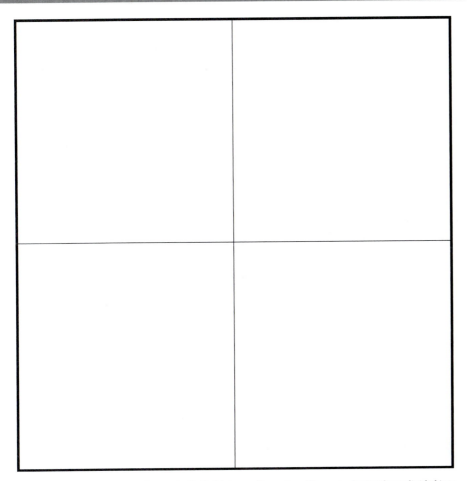

In a zone search of a crime scene the area is divided into smaller sectors. The scene depicted was divided into four quadrants, but if necessary could be subdivided into sixteen areas.

spiral method evidence could be destroyed as investigators walk toward the center to begin the search.

Wheel Method

The *wheel method* search pattern is similar to the spiral method. In the wheel method, the search area is considered to be essentially circular. The search team gathers at the center of the circle and proceeds outward along the radii. This search method may have to be repeated several times depending on the size of the circle. The wheel search method does have a few limitations. One limitation is the large increase of relative area to be observed as the investigator departs from the center (O'Hara & O'Hara, 2003). The wheel method is also difficult when searching larger areas, and is usually used for smaller crime scenes.

Figure 4.4   Diagram of a Spiral Search of a Crime Scene

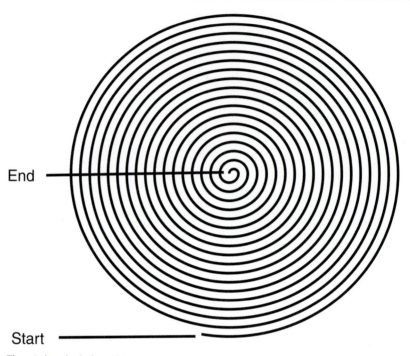

The spiral method of searching a crime scene usually involves a single searcher who walks in a slightly decreasing, less-than-concentric circle from the outermost boundary toward the center of the search area.

THE NATURE OF EVIDENCE

All physical evidence must be examined and closely evaluated for information that may assist in the identification of the suspect. The proper collection of physical evidence is required to confirm or disprove reasonable lines of inquiry in order to determine the causes of incidents. Physical evidence can prove a fact in issue based on its demonstrable physical characteristics, and it can conceivably include all or part of any object. In a murder case, the physical evidence includes the body itself, the weapon used to commit the crime, pieces of carpet spattered with blood, and casts of footprints or tire prints found at the scene of the crime. The police have to satisfy legal standards pertaining to the collection and preservation of crime scene physical evidence. According to Fox and Cunningham (1985, p. 14), in order to satisfy legal requirements, the investigator(s) must be able to:

1. Identify each piece of evidence, even years after it was collected.
2. Describe the location and condition of the item at the time it was collected.
3. Assist in establishing that, from the time of its collection until presentation in court, the evidence was continuously in proper custody.
4. Assist in describing any changes that may have occurred in the evidence between the time of collection and the subsequent introduction as evidence in court.

Prior to the search for evidence being initiated, the investigators should ensure that:

1. The crime scene has been properly secured and contained.
2. An on-duty prosecutor has been called and briefed (if it is a major crime scene).
3. A search warrant (if applicable) has been obtained for the premise (crime scene to be searched).
4. Search personnel have been briefed about the crime scene and the nature of evidence that is likely to be discovered. Search personnel should also be briefed as to the type of search technique that will be used. In cases where bodily fluids or other biological evidence may be collected, search personnel should wear proper protective clothing.
5. An initial walk-through, video recording, and sketch have been made of the entire crime scene.
6. Sufficient evidence packaging material is on hand.
7. Specific personnel have been designated evidence collectors. When search members find some evidence, they should summon the designated evidence collector, at which time the evidence will be photographed, documented, and collected. Having a specific person designated as evidence collector reduces the **chain of custody** of the evidence. The chain of custody is a concept in jurisprudence that applies to the handling of evidence and its integrity. In other words, it is a process that tracks the movement of evidence through its collection, safeguarding, and analysis lifecycle, by documenting each person who handled the evidence, the date and time it was collected or transferred, and the purpose for the transfer.

chain of custody / A chronological record of those individuals who have had custody of the evidence from its initial acquisition until its final disposition.

In the following sections, techniques for collecting some of the more common evidence that police officers encounter at a variety of crime scenes are discussed. When in doubt about how to properly collect a piece of evidence, call someone who knows, and don't attempt to guess at how to collect the evidence. One wrong guess could destroy or contaminate a crucial piece of evidence that is needed to successfully connect a suspect to the crime.

TYPES OF EVIDENCE

The proper collection, preservation, and storage of evidence is imperative if the evidence is to be useful when it is tested and presented in court. The property and evidence unit within the police agency has the responsibility to safely store all items that are properly packaged and marked. The responsibility to properly package and mark the evidence falls completely on the officer that collects the evidence.

Evidence is a piece of information that supports a conclusion. As noted previously, it can consist of an object, such as a gun used to commit the crime, or it can be someone's observations (what they heard or saw). In the following section we place most of our emphasis on evidence as a physical object—something you can see and touch. Perhaps the analogy of a jigsaw puzzle is appropriate to describe crime scene evidence. Like a jigsaw puzzle, the crime scene contains pieces of evidence that help to piece together the crime. Every piece of evidence is an important piece of the puzzle, no matter how small.

Voices of Experience

The Capture and Prosecution of Serial Killer and Rapist Joseph Patrick Washington

Excerpts from an interview between Cliff Roberson and former police officer, John L. Padgett, presently a lead faculty at the Institution of Justice, Westwood College, Colorado.

Q: *How did the identification and capture of serial killer Joseph Patrick Washington occur?*

A: We had been looking for the individual for over two years. At the time the police thought they had two different serial offenders in the Augusta, Georgia area, a serial killer and a serial rapist, because of the different MOs. The serial killer's victims were female drug users who came from the southern tip of the city. The victims were all found dead along a remote road. The victims' bodies were nude with multiple cuts and abrasions. More often than not, there would be two gunshot wounds, one to an appendage and one to the head. The only evidence that would link a subject to the victims was a vehicle with a broken taillight with a round symbol near the center of the taillight.

The police knew that the serial rapist was targeting prostitutes near the center of town. The rapist would entice the girls into his car, take them to a remote location, rape them, and then throw them out of the car. He would then stand above the victims and shoot them with a small caliber handgun. The only description the police had of his vehicle was that it had no knob on the gear shift lever and a broken cell phone antenna on the rear window.

At the time, we were working a "power shift," which means that the oncoming detail would start work an hour before the other shift went off duty. During that hour the oncoming detail would target highly visible troubled areas within the city. My partner and I would review the case and determine what we wanted to focus on during that power shift. We were assigned to the midnight shift. I had my officers set up roadblocks within two miles of the crime scenes looking for a vehicle with a broken taillight and a round center emblem.

After several weeks of negative results, I decided to go back to the basics. I obtained from the city manager a detailed map of the city and plotted the last known areas that each of the victims had been seen in before their deaths. I then went to the neighborhood one night and parked. I noticed a female walking alone down the street. I stopped her and identified myself. I asked her what she knew about the man who was hurting all the girls from the neighborhood. She looked down and hesitated and then stated that she had been with him last night—that they had gone to a local motel. When they entered the room she became afraid of him and ran away. She provided the name he used when he registered at the motel and his car tags. She described the vehicle as having no knob on the gear shift lever, a broken cell phone antenna, and a broken taillight with a round center emblem. It was later discovered that he used the same motel for each of his crimes. He would trade drugs for sex, and then force the victims to go to the remote location, strip them nude, and then chase and kill them.

With the information from the young girl and the motel operator, the police arrested Washington at his home. Washington's car had a broken taillight with a center emblem, missing gear shift knob, and a broken cell phone antenna. Washington was convicted of five of the crimes and received a combined prison sentence in excess of 700 years. ∎

Note: Washington died in prison after serving less than three years. According to court records, Washington forced the women into his car at gunpoint, drove to a remote location, shot them, and then raped them, prosecutors said at his 1995 trial. One witness testified that Washington had said he wanted to infect as many women as he could because his former girlfriend had given him HIV.

Class and Individual Characteristics

Evidence is typically considered to have class characteristics or individual characteristics. **Class characteristics** are traits or characteristics of evidence that cannot be traced back to a particular individual. [Class characteristics are those characteristics that are common to a group of similar objects.] For example, suppose you purchase a pair of New Balance model 767 running shoes. All New Balance model 767 running shoes have the same shape and same tread design. These are considered class characteristics. Other examples of evidence with class characteristics may include size, color, manufacturing patterns, or taxonomic classification (Gardner, 2005). Glass fragments that are too small to be matched to broken edges and tool marks are also examples of class characteristics (Swanson, Chamelin, & Territo, 1996).

[**Individual characteristics** are those characteristics that are unique to a given object and set it apart from similar objects.] **Individual characteristics** allow for the comparison of the evidence to a specific person. Put another way, evidence with individual characteristics can be identified as originating from a particular person. For example, suppose for the past four months you complete your daily three-mile run wearing your New Balance model 767 running shoes. Over the four months your shoes begin to show wear. The treads begin to wear down and they begin to develop pits, marks, and gouges. These pits, marks, and gouges are individual to your shoes, since no one has walked over the exact same surfaces in the exact same way as you have in your New Balance running shoes. Other examples of individual characteristics may include, but are not limited to, fingerprints, palm prints, and footprints. No two fingerprints, palm prints, or footprints are the same.

class characteristics / Evidence that has characteristics that are common to a group of similar objects. Examples of evidence with class characteristics include soil, glass, and paint.

individual characteristics / Evidence that has characteristics that are unique to a given object and set it apart from similar objects. Examples of evidence with individual characteristics include fingerprints, palm prints, and footprints.

Associative Evidence

Associative evidence is any evidence that can direct a suspect to a crime (Horswell & Fowler, 2004). For example, hair is associative evidence. Because hairs can be transferred during physical contact, their presence can associate a suspect to a victim or a suspect/victim to a crime scene. The types of hair recovered and the condition and number of hairs found all impact on their value as evidence in a criminal investigation. Comparison of the microscopic characteristics of questioned hairs to known hair samples helps determine whether a transfer may have occurred.

associative evidence / Any evidence that can link a suspect to a crime.

Tracing Evidence

Every person physically involved in a crime leaves some trace of his or her presence behind at the crime scene. Recall in the BTK strangler example discussed previously that the killer was known to leave semen at the scene of the crime. This is called **tracing evidence**. No matter how much the suspect tries to clean up a crime scene, something is generally left behind. It may not always be detected, but it's difficult to take any kind of violent action without shedding something. Trace evidence, though often insufficient on its own to make a case, may corroborate other evidence or even prompt a confession.

tracing evidence / Evidence that results from the transfer of small quantities of materials. Tracing evidence is usually in the form of small particles and includes such items as hair, paint, glass, and fibers.

Testimonial Evidence

Testimonial evidence is evidence obtained from individuals who are generally witnesses, survivors, or any other person at the scene who has knowledge of the

testimonial evidence / Evidence that may be presented by witnesses at a trial or other type of hearing. Generally, testimonial evidence is given by a witness to the crime or by an expert.

crime. For example, a witness related to a police officer that the suspect of a crime was observed wearing a red shirt with vertical blue stripes. The description of the suspect's clothing is testimonial evidence.

Fingerprint Evidence

fingerprint evidence /
Fingerprints collected at a crime scene or on items of evidence from a crime scene. Fingerprint evidence can assist in identifying the perpetrator of a crime.

Fingerprint evidence is one of the most common types of evidence that the investigator will collect from the crime scene. Fingerprints collected at a crime scene, or on items of evidence from a crime scene, can be used in forensic science to identify suspects, victims, and other persons who touched a surface. However, the usefulness of fingerprints before any suspect is identified depends on two things: (1) the likelihood that the offender has prints on file (i.e., the likelihood of prior arrest in the jurisdiction), and (2) the investigator's ability to search the files rapidly (Williams, 2003).

Fingerprints provide an extremely reliable means of identification. The system is based on the fact that no two individuals have the same fingerprints. Fingerprints are covered by minute ridges frequently interrupted by endings or forks that are known as characteristics. Each person has a uniquely different distribution of characteristics that develop in the womb and persist throughout life. They even remain unchanged some time after death, making the recognition of corpses possible. Fingerprint evidence found at a crime scene constitutes latent, plastic, or visible fingerprints.

Latent fingerprints are impressions produced by the friction ridge skin on human fingers, palms, and soles of the feet. Latent fingerprints are caused by natural oils and perspiration between your fingerprint ridges being transferred to the surfaces that are touched, leaving invisible fingerprints. Latent literally means "invisible". Thus, latent fingerprints are the hardest to find because they cannot be seen by the naked eye.

In order to see latent fingerprints, they have to be made visible by exposing them, and depending on the surface, different methods will be used. The most common method for latent fingerprint processing is using fingerprint powder and a soft brush. Fingerprint powder is an effective technique that has a long history of use in crime scene investigation. It comes in dark or light colors so that, depending on the color of the surface, the powder gives the best contrast. In some cases, fluorescent powders can be used so that the print can be viewed under ultraviolet light. Once developed, the fingerprints can be photographed and lifted with tape. Hard, nonporous and glass-like surfaces offer the possibility to lift an identifiable set of latent fingerprints (Saferstein, 1995).

Plastic fingerprints are produced when the friction ridge on the finger, palm, or sole comes into contact with a softer surface and makes a three-dimensional impression into the receiving surface. Imagine pressing your finger against a bar of soap or a piece of wax; this results in a plastic fingerprint. Plastic fingerprints are visible to the naked eye.

Visible prints generally result when friction ridges are coated with material that is transferred to another surface, leaving the outline or impression of the friction ridge visible. For example, a burglar cuts his hand while breaking into a house and subsequently leaves a bloody fingerprint on the back door of the residence. Visual prints usually do not need to be dusted and may only need to be enhanced. Visible prints should be photographed, and the object with the visible print should be packaged and collected. If the object cannot be collected, then the photograph will become the evidence (Lee, Palmbach, & Miller, 2001).

PRACTICE HINTS

Conditions Affecting the Quality of Latent Fingerprints

1. **The surface on which the print is deposited.** Plastic prints can last for years if undisturbed. Latent prints on smooth surfaces, such as porcelain and glass, can be developed after a similar period; while those left on porous material, like paper, vary more in how long they can survive. Latent prints on documents can fade or deteriorate beyond the point of being useful under conditions of high humidity or if they become wet. Otherwise, latent prints on paper are fairly stable and can be developed even years after they were made.

2. **The nature of the material contaminating the fingerprint.** Latent fingerprints resulting from contamination by soot, safe insulation, and face powder can quickly be destroyed, while those made with blood, ink, or oil can last longer periods of time under favorable conditions.

3. **Any physical or occupational defects of the person making the print.**

4. **How the object on which the prints appear was handled.** The distance between friction ridges is very small, and if the finger moves even slightly, that ridge detail can be lost.

5. **When the finger leaving the print is very contaminated.** When both the ridge surfaces and their valleys get filled up, this results in a smeared appearance with little value as evidence.

Source: From *Criminal Investigation*, 6th., by C.R. Swanson, N.C. Chamelin, and L. Territo. Copyright © 1996. Reprinted by permission of the McGraw-Hill Companies.

Most fingerprints submitted will be on paper, glass, metal, or other smooth-surfaced objects. When the investigator finds it necessary to pick up articles containing latent prints, he or she should touch as little as possible, and then only the areas least likely to contain identifiable latent prints, such as rough surfaces. While gloves or handkerchiefs may be used to pick up such exhibits, any unnecessary contact should be avoided. Although using a cloth to pick up exhibits prevents leaving additional prints on the articles, the cloth may wipe off or smear any prints originally present, unless great care is taken.

Large articles containing latent fingerprints, such as glass, metal, and firearms, should be placed on wood or heavy cardboard and fastened down with string to prevent shifting and contact with other objects in transit. Bottles and glasses that have been collected as evidence may be placed vertically on a board and placed in the bottom of a box. The base of the bottle or glass can be surrounded with nails to hold it in place, and the top can be either inserted through a hole in a piece of cardboard or held in position with a wooden board nailed to the container's lid.

Papers and documents containing latent fingerprints should be placed individually in cellophane or a manila envelope. Such a container can be sandwiched between two sheets of stiff cardboard, wrapped, and placed in a box for mailing. All such evidence should be marked in some distinctive manner, as is the case with any other

PRACTICE HINTS

Handling Fingerprint Evidence

- Evidence should be submitted for latent print examination as soon as possible after its discovery.
- The primary concern in all cases is the prevention of adding prints to evidence, or of destroying those already present.
- All pieces of evidence submitted should be packaged in such a way as to eliminate or minimize the surfaces of the article from contacting the packaging material.
- Protect latent print evidence from careless and improper handling and packaging that may damage any latent prints that may be present and render them useless.

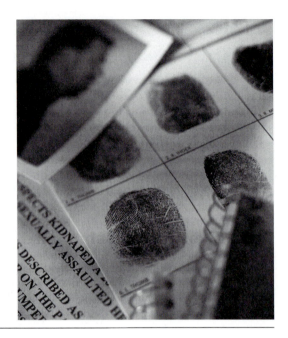

Properly collected fingerprint evidence can result in the identification and prosecution of a crime assailant.

type of physical evidence. Precautions should be taken when marking evidence not to damage or destroy potential latent fingerprints. Lifted, developed latent prints should also be marked or sealed in marked envelopes.

Soft and porous surfaces such as paper can't be dusted for fingerprints, so the most common method used is iodine fuming. This is a procedure where the surface of the paper is placed in an enclosed space with iodine crystals, which are then heated up. The vapor from the crystals sticks to the oily fingerprints and allows them to become visible.

There are several other types of fingerprint lifting procedures that are beyond the purpose of this book, including ninhydrin spray, tetramethylbenzidine, and cyanoacrylate (super glue) techniques.

Bloodstains

When handling blood or other biological evidence, the investigator should wear latex gloves and clothing that protects against infectious deceases. Police officers investigating crime scenes where there is blood and/or other bodily fluids present must be aware of the risk of exposure to blood-borne pathogens, including Hepatitis B, Hepatitis C, and HIV/AIDS. Wearing gloves and protective clothing will prevent against the contamination of evidence from fingerprint oil or other biological residue that may be present on the human hand.

Blood that is in liquid pools should be picked up on a gauze pad or other clean sterile cotton cloth and allowed to air dry thoroughly at room temperature before packaging. It should be refrigerated or frozen and taken to the laboratory as quickly as possible. Delays beyond forty-eight hours may make the samples useless. If close to the laboratory, deliver the stained object immediately. Again, if unable to deliver to the laboratory, or if the object must be mailed, allow the stain to air dry completely before packaging.

It is important that bloodstained evidence not be heated or placed in bright sunlight to dry. Hang clothing and similar articles in a room where there is adequate ventilation. If not completely dry, label and roll in paper or place in a brown paper bag or box and seal and label the container. Place only one item in each container. The container should not be plastic.

For dried bloodstain evidence on clothing, if possible, these items should be wrapped in clean paper and placed in a brown paper bag or box then sealed, labeled, and placed in a packaging container. For small solid objects, send the whole stained object to the laboratory, after labeling and packaging. For large solid objects, cover the stained area with clean paper and seal the edges down with tape to prevent loss or contamination. If material containing wet bloodstains is tightly packaged, the blood will undergo serious and foul-smelling decomposition. In some cases it may be impractical to deliver the whole object to the laboratory. If this is the case, scrape the stain onto a clean piece of paper, which can be folded and placed in an envelope. It is important not to scrape directly into the evidence envelope. Scrape blood from objects using a freshly washed and dried knife or similar tool. Wash and dry the tool before each stain is scraped off. Seal and mark the envelope. Never attempt to wipe dried stains from an object using a moistened cloth or paper because this will diminish the value of the evidence. The officer should document the exact procedure used in packaging bloodstained evidence because this assuredly will be a focus of defense attorneys if the case reaches trial.

Saliva, Seminal Stains, and Sexual Assault Evidence

Saliva evidence is not found that often at the scene of a crime. If it is found, however, saliva should be collected on a sterile gauze pad or swabs, and allowed to air dry before being packaged. It should then be packaged in paper (plastic containers should not be used) and sent to the lab.

A crime scene which indicates a substance on a window that may be blood. The crime scene individuals who process the scene will take samples of the substance as well as pictures of the scene. This scene appears to show that a wounded individual left the scene by the window.

Seminal stains are often, but not always, found on clothing, blankets, and sheets. Allow these stains to air dry, and then wrap in paper and package in paper bags. Do not use plastic bags for packaging seminal evidence. For sex offense cases, the victim should always be examined by a physician. A sexual assault evidence collection kit should be used to collect evidence from the victim. Medical personnel will perform the sexual assault examination at the hospital or medical facility. The rape kit will be turned over to police after the exam. The rape kit usually includes such items as the rape exam report, clothing, pubic combings, head hair combings, swabs of oral specimen, swabs of vaginal specimen, swabs of rectal specimen, fingernail scrapings, and blood samples.

It is very important that the instructions on the kit be followed with care in order to gain the greatest benefit from the collected evidence. All garments such as under shorts, panties, or other items should be labeled and packaged separately. If a shirt and panties are collected as evidence from the victim, they should be marked and packaged each as a separate piece of evidence. If these items are damp or wet from seminal stains, they should be air dried completely prior to packaging.

Hair Evidence

An examination of human hair can occasionally reveal the race of the individual from whom it came and the part of the body from which it originated. Human hair can be compared to determine whether or not two samples could have a common origin. The value of the laboratory examinations of such specimens will depend upon the amount of hair recovered and the characteristics found in the examinations.

All hair present at a crime scene should be recovered. If possible, use tweezers or forceps to pick up hair, placing the hair in paper bindles or coin envelopes, which should then be folded and sealed in larger envelopes. The outer sealed envelope should be properly labeled. If hair is attached, such as in dry blood, or caught in metal or a crack of glass, the officer should not attempt to remove it, but rather leave hair intact on the object. If the object is small, mark it, wrap it, and seal it in an envelope. If the object is large, wrap the area containing the hair in paper to prevent loss of hairs during shipment.

As discussed previously, in rape cases, the victim's pubic region should be combed prior to collecting known standards. Collecting standards entails obtaining known hair samples from the victim, suspect, or any other possible sources for comparison with unknown specimens. The recommended method for collecting head hairs is to start by having the person from whom they are being collected bend over a large sheet of clean paper. The person should then rub or massage the head so that loose hair will fall out on the paper. More should then be gathered by plucking them from representative areas all over the head. A total of fifty to one hundred hairs are desired. It is important not to cut the hair. This same method may be used to collect hairs from other parts of the body. Thirty to sixty pubic hairs are required. When the person is a suspect, hair should be gathered from all parts of the body even though there may only be an interest in hair from the head at that particular time.

Glass

Windows are frequently broken in burglaries, headlights are broken in hit-and-run cases, and bottles or other objects may break or leave fragments on personal belongings of suspects involved in various crimes. In cases where a suspect has been apprehended shortly after the crime was committed, and where broken glass may be contained on the suspect, the suspect's shoes and clothing or other objects contaminated with glass should be wrapped in paper and submitted to the laboratory for examination.

Glass found at hit-and-run scenes should be recovered. The search should not be limited to the point of impact, because headlight glass may be dropped off at some distance away as the vehicle leaves the crime scene. Glass from different locations should be kept in different containers. All glass should be collected because more than one type may be present. In addition, if just a few representative samples are saved, individual pieces that could be physically matched with glass remaining in the headlight shell of the suspected vehicle may be overlooked.

Small glass fragments should be placed in paper bindles, then placed in coin envelopes, pill boxes, or film cans that can be marked and completely sealed. Large glass fragments should be placed in boxes. Separate individual pieces of glass with cotton or tissue to prevent breakage and damaged edges during shipment. Seal and mark the box containing them.

Paint

Paint evidence is frequently encountered in a variety of crime scenes, including hit-and-run cases, on tools used by burglars, and occasionally in other types of cases. In the case of a hit-and-run, paint may be transferred to the clothing of the victim. In this case, it is important that a careful examination be conducted on all areas of clothing, with particular attention being paid to areas showing pressure glaze, tears, or other contact. If paint is located, do not remove the paint, but mark the garment, carefully wrap it by rolling it in paper, and send it to the laboratory.

Paint evidence can identify the color of the suspect's vehicle in a hit-and-run case; however, it must be remembered that many modern cars have more than one color and the paint transferred only represents the color of the particular area on the car that made contact with the victim. Rarely will an examination of paint transfer on clothing indicate the make and model of the vehicle involved, because only portions of the top oxidized layer on the cars are usually transferred. In addition, many vehicles are repainted using colors and types of paint that may be different from those specified by the automobile manufacturer. The color and type of paint selected by the car owner for repainting the vehicle may also be the same as that used by a different automobile manufacturer, which could cause confusion in the search for the responsible car.

Sometimes whole chips of paint will be transferred to the clothing. If these chips contain several layers, and in particular if they come from a repainted car, such evidence may have great value when the responsible vehicle is located. Chips of paint may also be found on the ground near the point of impact in some cases.

Samples for comparison should be collected from all areas showing fresh damage on suspected vehicles. This is very important because the paint may be different in type or composition in different areas, even if the color is the same. If the paint can be flaked off by bending the metal slightly, remove it in this manner. If not, scrape or chip the paint off, using a clean knife blade. Carefully wipe the blade before collecting each sample. Collect all layers down to the metal. Place each sample in a separate container.

Cross transfers of paint commonly occur in hit-and-run cases of two or more vehicles. If loose paint chips are found, attempt to remove and place them in a paper bindle. If the transfers are smeared on the surfaces, flake off chips or scrape paint from the vehicle, including the transferred paint, as well as the top layer of paint originally on the car. Transfers recovered from different areas should be kept in separate containers. Do not place samples directly into envelopes—place them into paper bindles. When cross transfers occur, always collect contaminated samples from each vehicle from areas immediately adjacent to each transfer collected. This is of great importance, because such specimens permit the laboratory to distinguish between the transferred paint and the paint originally present on the vehicle.

Paint evidence can also be present on burglary tools that are used to gain entry into buildings, safes, or other places. Tools often contain traces of paint, as well as other substances, such as plastic. Due care must be taken that such traces are not lost. If such transfers may be present, wrap the end of the tool containing the material in clean paper and seal with tape to prevent loss. No attempt should be made to set the tool into marks or impressions found. If this is done, transfers of paint or material can occur and any traces found later will have no significance as evidence.

Specimens of all paint should be collected from all that which the tools may have come in contact with at the crime scene. These samples should include all layers present. It is important not to destroy the tool mark when collecting the paint. If possible, cut out around the mark, and send it to the laboratory. The tool itself may contain paint or other coatings, tracings of which may be left at the crime scene. A careful search should be made for such matters, particularly in each tool mark.

In order to prevent contamination of paint evidence, it is best to keep all samples collected in separate containers. Small paper bindles can be used to collect and hold many paint samples. A satisfactory method is to tape one side of the bindle to the side of the vehicle, building, or safe just under the area where the sample is to be collected. By holding the bindle open with one hand, and using a clean knife blade, paint can be scraped loose and into the bindle. With the sample in the bindle, scotch tape can be removed and the open end of the bindle folded several times. It can be placed in a coin or mailing envelope, which can be marked and sealed. Scotch tape may be used to seal the bindle, but such containers should never be stapled.

PRACTICE HINTS

Packaging and Storage of Trace Evidence

- Paper bindles are commonly used for storage of trace evidence such as hair, fibers, paint chips, or other minute particles.
- Paper bindles are preferred over plastic containers for trace items that may be moist, carry an electrostatic charge, or require DNA analysis.
- Paper bindles are preferred over envelopes for trace items because they lack manufactured folds, corners, and openings where evidence can be lost.
- Seal a bindle with evidence tape. Never staple the bindle.
- A sealed bindle should be placed inside an envelope or other suitable container.

Firearm Evidence

Common sense along with sound police policy dictates that a loaded gun should never be submitted into evidence. Forensic laboratory personnel tend to get upset if a loaded gun ends up in the lab for examination. In some cases it is acceptable to leave unfired cartridges in the magazine of a weapon, provided the magazine is removed from the gun. It is sound policy that a firearm with the cartridge in the chamber should never be shipped by any method, even if the weapon is not cocked or is on safety. The bore or chamber should not be tampered with or cleaned in any manner. Likewise, never attempt to fire the gun before it is examined in the laboratory.

If an officer has to leave a weapon loaded when it is submitted into evidence the officer who collects the weapon should mark it with several red tags that read: "LOADED WEAPON." This will alert forensic lab personnel that a loaded weapon has been submitted for processing.

You may have seen Hollywood TV cops picking up a weapon used in a crime by inserting a pencil into the barrel. While this may be entertaining for viewers, Hollywood's method is wrong and should be avoided. Under no circumstance should an officer pick up a weapon by placing a pencil or other object in the end of the barrel. This method could destroy evidence. The weapon should be fully identified. Record serial number, make, model, and caliber of the weapon, and mark it in some manner that does not detract from its value before sending it to the laboratory. Marking firearms is important because duplicate serial numbers are sometimes found on different guns of the same make and general type. Do not confuse model numbers or patent numbers with serial numbers.

Weapons should ideally be placed in a strong cardboard or wooden box and well packed, to prevent shifting during transit. Rifles or shotguns should not be taken apart. If blood or other material, which may pertain to an investigation, is present on the gun, place a clean paper around the gun and seal it with tape to prevent movement of the gun and loss of the sample during shipment.

Bullets and Ammunition

Bullets that have been recovered from a crime scene should not be marked. Wrap recovered bullets in paper and seal in separate labeled pill boxes or envelopes.

Submit all bullets recovered to the laboratory. A conclusive identification may be possible on only one of several bullets recovered even when they all appear to be in good condition. Do not attempt to clean recovered bullets before sending them to the laboratory. Bullets recovered from a body should be air dried and wrapped in paper. Never wash any ammunition that has been collected as evidence. Washing may destroy trace evidence.

Cartridge Cases

Recovered cartridge cases should be wrapped and sealed in separate labeled pill boxes or envelopes. Fired shotgun shells should be marked either on the inside or outside of the paper or plastic portion of the shell. If an examination is required to determine if a shotgun shell or cartridge case was fired by a specific weapon, submit the weapon and all recovered unfired ammunition. All evidence cartridge cases or shotgun shells recovered should be submitted to the laboratory. Some cartridge cases may contain more identifying detail than others. These identifying details will be of particular importance in the investigation. It is important to wrap each cartridge in paper to prevent damaging the breech clock, firing pin, or other markings. Pill boxes or envelopes make excellent containers in which to place wrapped cartridge cases. All containers should be labeled and sealed.

Always attempt to recover unused ammunition for comparison purposes when firearms are obtained as evidence. If not in the weapon itself, subjects often have additional ammunition in their cars, clothing, houses, or other locations. It may be important for test purposes to duplicate exactly the make, type, and age of the ammunition used in the crime. Other ammunition in the suspect's possession may be identical to that fired during the crime.

Unfired ammunition should not be marked individually. The box with the ammunition may be marked without marking every round in the box. In the case of gunpowder stains, submit clothing or other material showing evidence of gunpowder residue or shot holes to the laboratory. The clothing should be carefully wrapped in clean paper and folded as little as possible to prevent dislodging powder particles. Photographs of the pattern will not suffice, as in most instances microscopic examination and chemical tests must be conducted on the exhibits themselves. Each item should be packaged separately.

For gunpowder or shot pattern tests to have significance, it is essential to obtain ammunition identical in make, type, and age to that used at the crime scene. This duplicate ammunition is necessary for firing in the weapon in question to determine the distance of the muzzle of the weapon from the victim or other object at the time the questioned bullet was fired.

Gunshot residue presents a potential problem when collecting this type of evidence. Gunshot residue is extremely fragile evidence and should be collected as soon as possible (preferably within three hours of the discharge of the firearm). Use laboratory-supplied kits if they have been made available. If laboratory kits are disseminated, officers should be diligent and carefully follow the directions. In the case of live subjects, if more than six hours have passed or if the subject has washed his hands, it is unlikely that meaningful results will be obtained. If gunshot residue is present on the victim of a homicide, whenever possible gunshot residue collection should be performed prior to moving the body. If this is not possible, protect the hands by placing paper bags over them.

Tool Marks

Tool marks are encountered most frequently in burglary cases, but can also be found at other types of crime scenes, too. The evidence consists of striations or impressions left by tools on objects at the crime scene and various types of tools found in the possession of suspects. In other cases, it is possible by means of physical and other comparisons to prove that parts of tools left at crime scenes were broken from damaged tools found in the possession of suspects. In many cases, it is possible to identify the specific tool that made the questioned marks by means of a laboratory comparison of tools and marked objects. In some instances, it is also possible to prove that marks of various types on tools were produced by objects they came into contact with at the crime scene.

All areas on recovered tools that contain transferred paint, building material, or other contamination should be wrapped in paper and packaged to prevent the prying blades or cutting edges contacting any other surface or object. Attempts should never be made to fit tools into questioned marks or to make test marks prior to laboratory examination. If done, the questioned mark or tool may be altered and this may make any laboratory examination valueless. In addition, traces of transferred paint or other stains on the tool may be lost, or additional material may be transferred to the tool.

It is always best to submit the whole object containing tool marks to the laboratory instead of just removing the area containing the mark. If this is not possible, carefully photograph and sketch the area containing the mark. Although this photograph will not be sufficient to allow the laboratory to perform a tool mark comparison with the tool, it will assist the laboratory to determine how the mark was made so that test marks can be more easily made.

Casts of tool marks can be made by person(s) who have considerable experience in this work. Poor casts are useless for comparison purposes and some marks will be damaged if improper methods are used. Package the object containing tool marks in a manner so that no alteration or damage will occur during shipment. Small objects should be wrapped with clean paper and placed in envelopes or boxes, while important areas on larger objects can be protected with paper. Whole, large objects should be packed in cartons or crates, if not delivered in person.

Controlled Substances

The laboratory handles the analysis of marijuana, medicinal prepared drugs, and other drugs that may be involved in a criminal case or found in the possession of subjects involved in various crimes. Medicinal prepared drugs are drugs that have therapeutic value. For example, the drug methamphetamine has no medicinal value, while other drugs, like sleep medications, do have medicinal purposes.

Each sample of material recovered should be placed in a paper container, which can be sealed and marked. It is important to properly seal loose material, particularly in the case of marijuana. Some drugs, like phencyclidine (PCP), should be packaged in heat-sealed bags.

Medicinal preparations found in prescription boxes or bottles should be left in these containers, which can be sealed and marked. The information on the prescription label may be of assistance to the laboratory. By means of chemical tests, most controlled substances and common drugs can be identified.

Many pills, tablets, and other medicinal preparations are very difficult to analyze and identify unless either large quantities are available for testing, or some clues are present as to the general type of material they contain. In all cases where prescriptions are involved and the drug store and prescription numbers are known, a check of possible container content should be made at the drug store named on the label. With this information, the laboratory will often be able to determine whether or not the contents of the containers are the same as the material described.

While controlled substances can be identified in routine cases, some laboratories may not normally attempt to identify all medicinal preparations that may be encountered in criminal investigations. Unless specific instructions to the contrary are received, such materials are usually tested only for common preparations and their possession may violate the law. All evidence of this nature should be brought to the laboratory in a sealed package.

Narcotics Field Testing

Police officers increasingly have access to narcotics field testing kits. Narcotics field testing kits allow police officers in the field to do a quick test or a presumptive test of suspected illicit drugs seized from a suspect. Narcotics field kits use reagents and can give clues about the identity of drugs. Field testing kits are easy to use and have evolved over the past few years.

The chemical reagents used to test the suspected illicit drugs are housed inside glass ampoules that are located in clear, hard plastic packets. There are usually one or two glass ampoules inside each of the tubes. To perform the test, the officer places a small sample of the drug inside the tube, ensuring that the drug falls to the bottom of the packet. The first ampoule should be broken and then the tube should be shaken to mix it with the drug. The officer then watches for color changes. If there is

Substances that appear to be methamphetamines. The substances will be collected and forwarded to a crime lab for analysis.

PRACTICE HINTS

Submission of Drug Evidence to the Lab at a Glance

- The request for analysis should indicate which specimen was in the possession of a specific individual.
- If one bag is used to hold numerous specimens that are the same, the bag should not be given a separate item number.
- Different bags containing a number of specimens found in the same place or on the same person should have the same item number with sequential subnumbers (e.g., item 1-A, 2-B, 3-C, 4-D, 5-E).
- Submit separate drugs by type. Do not mix specimens with other unlike drugs.
- List what you suspect the drug evidence is (e.g., marijuana, cocaine, methamphetamines).
- List the names of additional suspects involved in the case.
- The officer should keep in mind that for single defendant cases, only one sample from one specimen is usually analyzed.
- For multiple defendant cases, only one sample from one specimen per defendant is usually analyzed.
- **Note:** If needed for trial, additional samples selected at random and consisting of a representative sampling can be analyzed upon written request.
- If syringes are submitted to the laboratory, they should be conspicuously marked as being a "SYRINGE." The lab in some cases may require that the officer call the lab personally before submitting a syringe. A syringe makes a considerable risk for both the officer that collected it and the laboratory personnel who will analyze it.

a second ampoule, follow the directions for the individual test as to the timing of the breakage of the second ampoule. Once the second ampoule is broken, shake the tube again and observe for any color changes. The specific color change will depend on the drug being tested for. A positive color indicator is located on the packet to assist in interpreting the reaction.

Many field tests now come in the spray form, where the officer simply sprays the reagent on the suspected narcotic and waits a few seconds for a color change. For example, Cannabispray is an aerosol-based drug field test kit for the detection and identification of marijuana, hashish, and other related drugs. In a case where the officer believes a substance to be marijuana, the officer simply sprays a small sample of the marijuana with the spray. If the sample turns a reddish purplish color, this would indicate a positive presence of marijuana. Field tests are available for a wide variety of drugs that police officers may come into contact with. It should be remembered that a field test is not a substitute for a test performed in the laboratory by a qualified chemist.

PRACTICE HINTS

How to Package and Submit Selected Drug Evidence at a Glance

Powders
- sealed clear plastic bags
- druggist folds
- sealed pill boxes
- vials
- glassine or foil envelopes

Tablets and Capsules
- sealed clear plastic bags or original containers
- do not write on tablets or capsules
- separate by suspect to include type of drug, appearance, and different locations and package them individually

Liquids
- leak-proof containers
- refrigerate beverages or any liquids that may spoil

Vegetation
- sealed, clear plastic or paper bag
- must be air dried prior to placing in sealed bags
- submit used bowls only from pipes and package separately

Plants
- if identification of the actual plant is needed, submit up to four intact plants, otherwise submit dried leaves from plants—use sealed paper bags or cardboard boxes, no plastic should be used.
- all plants should be air dried
- in some cases, plants may be submitted with stripped leaves if root is missing
- intact plant(s), including roots and stems
- photograph or video the plants at the scene
- remove all loose dirt from roots

Packaging of Money

It is not uncommon for police officers to come across money that will be collected as evidence. In drug investigations police commonly seize money, or in the case of a robbery some of the stolen cash may be recovered. The evidence custody receipt used by the agency should clearly indicate if the actual money is to be retained on the property or elsewhere. Some agencies may transfer money to the accounting unit if the money is to be held for a long period of time. As a general guide, the following steps should be completed and verified by two officers when dealing with money:

1. **Currency:** Indicate the number of specific bills and then the total dollar amount of these specific bills.
2. **Coin:** Indicate the number of specific coins and then the total dollar amount of these specific coins.
3. **Subtotal:** Indicate the subtotal of the bills and coins.
4. **Total Amount:** Indicate the total dollar amount of the money placed into the currency envelope.
5. **Entered and Sealed By:** Record the name of the officer who completed the counting of the currency.
6. **Identification Number:** Record the identification number of the officer who completed the counting of the currency.
7. **Date:** Indicate the date that the currency was counted.

8. **Time:** Indicate the time that the currency was counted.

9. **Seal:** All manufacturer seams and openings must be sealed by tamper-resistant evidence tape.

Handling Contaminated Money

Money contaminated with drug residue, blood, urine, or any other body fluid must be carefully handled. A biohazard bag should be used to package contaminated money. The following steps are recommended when packaging contaminated money:

1. Complete a money inventory sheet. This will vary depending on the agency and police officers should refer to their agency's standard operating procedure.

2. Include the type of contaminant and the denomination of the contaminated bills and/or coins.

3. Place the contaminated money in a biohazard bag.

4. Seal the bag and fold it to fit into a currency envelope.

5. Ensure that the amounts on the currency envelope match the amounts on the money inventory sheet.

6. Place a biohazard sticker on the outside of the currency envelope.

Questioned Documents

All questioned documents involved in a particular investigation should be submitted to the laboratory for examination. This is important because questioned documents are identified by a comparison of similarities, plus an absence of divergences or dissimilarities. In order to make an identification, sufficient handwriting, typewriting, or other evidence must be available on which to base an opinion. This means that all questioned material is needed, as well as sufficient exemplars or known specimens.

It is very important to have sufficient handwriting examples for comparison with the questioned document. One or two signatures on a suspect's driver's license or a draft card, in many cases, do not contain sufficient individual characteristics on which to base a conclusion. In some instances, such an examination may substantiate a suspicion and this should be considered as an investigational lead. However, it is necessary to obtain and examine additional standards to support this suspicion.

Collected specimens that were made in business transactions, such as receipts, promissory notes, credit and employment applications, letters, and fingerprint card signatures are writings that, in most cases, represent the individual's most normal writing. It is significant in many cases that these writings be of the same date as the questioned document. Specimens should be requested from a suspect at the first interview because the suspect may be uncooperative at a later date.

The conditions surrounding the preparation of the questioned document should be duplicated as nearly as possible when the requested exemplars are obtained. If yellow-lined paper and blue ink were used to produce the questioned document, the same or similar color and type of paper and instrument should be used. If the suspect document is a threatening letter and the note is either handwritten or block lettered, the same style should be requested from the writer. Have subjects write their names and addresses several times and brief personal histories. This should be removed and another sheet of paper furnished. Dictate the exact words and numbers that appear on the questioned document. In the case of a check case, the specimens should be taken on blank checks or slips of paper of the appropriate size. It is not possible to determine the number of specimens necessary for identification in any specific case; therefore, about twelve specimens or more should be obtained for each questioned document.

PRACTICE HINTS

Evidence Collection Steps at a Glance

- Where is the evidence located? Is it located at one crime scene or more than one?
- Establish what is likely to be relevant and admissible. When in doubt, err on the side of collecting too much rather than not enough.
- Question what else may be evidence as you work through the collection steps.
- Document each step of the process.
- Document all persons involved. Make notes of who was there and what they were doing, what they observed, and how they reacted.

Other Evidence Tips

The nature of the package or container used to secure evidence once it has been collected is governed by the nature of the intended contents. A clean Styrofoam cup may make an excellent temporary container for water-based liquid, however, it would not be advisable to use a Styrofoam cup to store gasoline or some other hazardous liquid materials.

Paper and plastic envelopes, glass and plastic bottles and vials, cardboard pill boxes, and small metal ointment tins may be used to package a very wide variety of evidence. In many cases, the package, in addition to providing protection to the item, must serve as the means of identifying the contents. Thus, it should be properly marked so that there can be no later question of what it contains.

The officer collecting evidence should mark the evidence container with name, identification number, date, and time of collection. Because of the divergent types of physical evidence that may be found at a crime scene, it is difficult to give general rules about the means that should be used to identify them. However, one reasonable rule is that any item that is likely to be presented in court, which can be permanently marked without damaging its intrinsic or evidential value, should be marked. Most departmental standard operating procedures specify proper procedures for marking evidence. Police officers reading this book are encouraged to check their agency's policy and procedure manual for specific evidence packaging guidelines. While most evidence packaging procedures are fairly uniform, there may be some slight variation between individual police agencies.

CYBERCRIME

As technology advances in society, so too will the technology that is used to facilitate the commission of crimes. The Internet, computer networks, and automated data systems present an enormous new opportunity for committing criminal activity. Computers and other electronic devices are being used increasingly to commit, enable, or support crimes perpetrated against persons, organizations, or property.

cybercrime / Criminal offenses carried out with the use of the computer. Child pornography, theft of a password or user identification, and releasing viruses are examples of cybercrime.

Computer crime, also known as **cybercrime**, e-crime, or electronic crime is committed when a computer is the target of a crime, or the means adopted to commit a crime. Many of the crimes are not new, just the tool (computer) used to commit the crime. There is much evidence that suggests that computer crime is increasing rapidly. Because of the increasing use of computers and other forms of technology in the commission of crimes, law enforcement will increasingly come into contact with electronic evidence. Electronic evidence can be in the form of computers, telephones, digital cameras, pagers, printers, and the like. This section's primary focus is on computer crimes.

Computer crimes often include the unauthorized use of a computer, which might involve stealing a username and/or password, and creating or releasing a malicious computer program. Releasing computer viruses and computer worms can be disastrous and costly to literally thousands of computer users who might innocently open an email contaminated with the virus or worm. There are many other crimes committed with the use of the computer. These crimes may include using a computer printer and graphics software for forgery or even counterfeiting.

Electronic evidence is information and data of investigative value that is stored on or transmitted by an electronic device. As such, electronic evidence is latent evidence or evidence that cannot be readily seen by the naked eye. In the case of a computer, the inside of the computer that holds the physical evidence cannot be seen.

Law enforcement treatment of electronic evidence is just as critical as when collecting and documenting other types of evidence. It is not uncommon for officers to encounter electronic devices during their day-to-day duties. In some cases, investigators may wish to direct the collection of electronic evidence, or they may perform the collection themselves. Handling electronic evidence at the crime scene normally consists of the following steps:

- Recognition and identification of the evidence
- Documentation of the crime scene
- Collection and preservation of the evidence
- Packaging and transportation of the evidence (National Institute of Justice, 2001)

First responders should use due caution when seizing electronic devices. The improper access of data stored in electronic devices may violate provisions of certain federal laws, including the Electronic Communications Privacy Act. Additional legal processes may be necessary. Investigators should consult with their local prosecutor before accessing stored data on a device. Because of the fragile nature of electronic evidence, examination should be done by appropriate personnel. It is recommended that police agencies identify local computer experts before they are needed. These experts should be "on call" for situations that are beyond the technical expertise of the first responding police officer or investigator.

Cyberstalking

While a relatively new phenomenon, cyberstalking has become an increasing problem for law enforcement authorities. There are currently not many laws on the books to help the victims of cyberstalking. Furthermore, many police departments lack the expertise to investigate crimes of cyberstalking. The U.S. Department of Justice estimates that there may be tens or even hundreds of thousands of cyberstalking victims in the United States (U.S. Department of Justice, 1999a). Cyberstalking takes place as part of a continuum of other crimes of sexual violence or interpersonal violence. Cyberstalking is simply an extension of the physical form of stalking, but the perpetrator uses the computer, email, or other electronic means to stalk the victim.

Especially perplexing for law enforcement in the investigation of cyberstalking are the jurisdictional limitations. In many cases, the suspect may be located in a different city, state, or country than the victim. This makes it difficult or even impossible for local law enforcement to investigate the incident. Even if a law enforcement agency is willing to pursue a case in another state, it may be problematic to obtain assistance from out-of-state agencies when the conduct is limited to harassing email messages and no actual violence has occurred. A number of cyberstalking cases have been referred to the Federal Bureau of Investigation or the U.S. Attorney's Office because the victim and suspect were located in different states and the local agency was not able to pursue the investigation.

Research has found that the ability of an online stalker to instill fear and gain control over a victim reflects the same method of operation that an offline stalker uses (D'Ovidio & Doyle, 2003; Spitzberg & Hoobler, 2002). Although the prevalence and incidence of cyberstalking remain unknown, anecdotal reports suggest that cyberstalking appears to be expanding at a rapid pace, especially among the nation's youth. The following is advice that police officers can offer to cyberstalking victims:

- Make it clear to a person who is making unwanted contact that you don't want to be contacted again.
- Save (print) all communications for evidence. Do not edit or alter them in any way. Also, keep a record of contacts with Internet system administrators or law enforcement officials.
- Consider blocking or filtering messages from the harasser. Many email programs have a filter feature, and software can be easily obtained that will automatically delete e-mails from a particular email address or that contain offensive words.
- If harassment continues after you have asked the person to stop, contact the Internet Service Provider (ISP). Most ISPs have clear policies prohibiting the use of their services to abuse another person. Often an ISP can try to stop the conduct by direct contact with the stalker or by closing the stalker's account.
- Contact your local law enforcement agency and inform them of the situation in as much detail as possible. In appropriate cases, they may refer the matter to state or federal authorities (Flanders et al., 2002).

Assessing Cybercrime Evidence

The assessment of cybercrime evidence can seem like a deviation when compared to the way police officers and investigators approach other crime scenes; however,

Tips to Prevent Cyberstalking

- Always select a gender-neutral username for your email address or for chat. Don't pick something cute, such as "miskitty@someisp.com" or use your first name if it is obviously female. Because the majority of online victims are female, this is what harassers look for.
- Keep your primary email address only for people you know and trust.
- Get a free email account and use that for all your other online activity.
- Don't fill out profiles! When you sign up for your email account, whether it's through your ISP (such as AOL or CompuServe), or a free one (such as Yahoo!), fill out as little information about yourself as possible.
- Do block or ignore unwanted users. Whether you are in a chat room or using Instant Message (IM), you should always check out what options/preferences are available to you. Take advantage of the "Block all users except those on my buddy list" or add unwanted usernames to an Ignore list in chat. If anyone bothers you and won't go away, put them on block or ignore!
- Don't defend yourself. Most people naturally want to defend themselves, but a reaction from you is just what the harasser wants. They are "fishing" for someone to latch onto and harass.
- Lurk (i.e., read messages and don't respond or post any) on newsgroups, message boards, mailing lists, or chat rooms before "speaking" or posting messages.
- Ego surf. Put your first name and last name in quotes in a search engine such as Yahoo!, Google, or Dogpile and see if there are any results regarding you. Better yet, use TracerLock to do it for you on a regular basis. The service is free.
- Never give your password to anyone, especially if someone sends you an IM. Your ISP will never ask you for your password while you are online or via email.
- Don't provide your credit card number or other identifying information as proof of age to access or subscribe to a website run by a company you are not familiar with.
- Instruct children to never, ever give out personal information online (e.g., real name, address, or phone number) without your permission.
- Be very cautious about putting any pictures of yourself or your children online, or allowing anyone else (relatives, schools, dance academies, sports associations) to publish any photos. Some stalkers become obsessed with an image. A random email address or screen name is simply much less attractive to most obsessive personalities than a photograph.

Source: The Florida Department of Law Enforcement. Accessed online November 18, 2006 at www. fdle. state. fl. us/ Fc3/.

investigators should keep in mind that they are essentially performing the same function—the difference is that in cybercrime the evidence that is desired is contained inside the computer. Nevertheless, a thorough assessment of all potential evidence contained in the hardware and software is critical to the effective investigation of cybercrimes.

Investigators should discuss whether other forensic processes need to be performed on computer evidence (e.g., DNA analyis, fingerprint, tool marks, trace, and questioned documents). The investigation may necessitate the need for pursuing other investigative avenues to obtain additional digital evidence. This may include sending a preservation order to an Internet Service Provider (ISP) for the purpose of identifying remote storage locations and obtaining email. Consideration should also be given to the relevance of peripheral components to the investigation. In forgery or fraud cases, noncomputer equipment such as laminators, credit card blanks, check paper, scanners, and printers should be considered. Other potential evidence that should be considered includes spreadsheets, documents, databases, and financial records. Information should also be determined such as email accounts, email addresses, Internet Service Provider used, names, network configuration and users, system logs, passwords, and usernames. This information may be obtained through interviews with the system administrator and users (U.S. Department of Justice, 1999b).

SUMMARY

- The first responding patrol officers play a critical role in the crime scene investigation. A careful and thoughtful response to the crime scene can prevent the destruction and/or contamination of evidence. The investigation of a crime typically begins when patrol officers arrive at the crime scene.

- The patrol officer who is the first to arrive at the scene of a crime must determine what sort of crime has been committed, how serious it is, what evidence is likely to be at the scene, and decide on whether the crime scene warrants calling the investigations unit.

- The first responding patrol officers have the responsibility to apprehend the suspect if still present at the scene, provide first aid to the injured, and to secure the crime scene.

- Once the crime scene has been turned over to the investigations unit, the first consideration is to obtain a search warrant for the crime scene, if necessary. A search warrant is a written warrant issued by a judge or magistrate which authorizes the police to conduct a search of a person or location for evidence of a crime and seize the evidence.

- The search of the crime scene should be thoughtful and thorough. The search of the crime scene can be described as the search for the truth, as far as it can be determined in an after-the-fact investigation.

- The specific search technique at the crime scene is largely dependent on the geographic location of the crime scene. A crime scene that is confined inside of a residence will differ from a crime scene in a rural area. Various crime scene search techniques include strip, wheel, zone, or spiral.

- The duties of the criminal investigator are complex in nature. The investigator must determine that a crime has been committed. Once it is determined what type of crime has been committed, the investigator must discern enough about the circumstances of the crime to be able to identify and arrest those responsible. In order to accomplish this, the investigator gathers evidence. Likewise, the investigator may talk to persons and interview suspects.

- Evidence can be in the form of associative, trace, fingerprint, and testimonial. Hair evidence is a type of associative evidence because it can establish an association between a suspect and the crime. Tracing evidence is any evidence left behind by the suspect at the crime scene. Fingerprint evidence can be in the form of latent fingerprints or visible fingerprints.

- Latent fingerprints are those that cannot be seen by the naked eye; visible fingerprints can be seen. Most fingerprints discovered at a crime scene will be on paper, glass, metal, or other smooth-surfaced objects.

- Testimonial evidence is obtained from witnesses, survivors, or any other person at the crime scene that has knowledge of the crime.

- *Corpus delicti* evidence is a term used to refer to the actual victim's body in a murder case.

- Before evidence is handled, its nature and position must be recorded and should be photographed. A rough sketch showing the location of the evidence should also be used. In any case, regardless of who finds real or possible evidence, only one person, the leader of the search or the designated evidence custodian, should handle it from that point on, until delivered to the examining laboratory. Once the evidence has been picked up it should be marked, tagged, or otherwise identified so that there will be no doubt in court that it is the item it is represented to be.

- Many evidentiary items will require packaging and/or preservation. The nature of the evidence will have a major influence on the techniques to be employed. For example, a sample of blood should be placed in an airtight, impervious container (such as glass) no larger than necessary, and tightly sealed and refrigerated. On the other hand, items that have been bloodstained should be treated somewhat differently. They must not be placed in an airtight container. Allow a bloodstained shirt to thoroughly air dry, then package it in paper.

- Narcotics field testing kits allow for the identification of suspected illicit narcotics. Police officers can literally obtain instant reaction when field testing suspected illicit narcotics. Narcotics field kits use reagents that can give clues about the identity of drugs.

- Many criminals are facilitating their crimes with the use of the computer. Computer crime is committed when a computer is the target of a crime, or the means adopted to commit a crime. Most of the crimes are not new except for the tool used to commit the crime, the computer.

- Cyberstalking is the threatening behavior or unwanted advances directed at another person using the Internet and other forms of computer communications. The investigation of cyberstalking is a perplexing problem for law enforcement due to the jurisdictional problems. The suspect may be in another city, state, or country. Because of the jurisdictional problems, many cyberstalking cases have been turned over to the Federal Bureau of Investigation.

Classroom Discussion Questions and Activities

1. Have the class discuss what they would do if they were a first responding police officer at the scene of a crime.

2. Discuss what the first responding officer(s) should do when arriving at the scene of a crime.

3. Discuss the different types of crime scene search techniques.

4. Discuss the most common way of lifting latent fingerprints.

5. Set up a mock crime scene and have groups of students play the role of first responding officer(s) and investigators.

6. Hide some mock evidence in a field and have students demonstrate a search technique in locating the evidence.

7. Make a list of evidence that has individual characteristics and a list of evidence that has class characteristics.

Websites and Other Resources

Reporting Computer-Related Crimes:
www.justice.gov/criminal/cybercrime/reporting.htm

FBI Computer Squad:
www.emergency.com/fbi-nccs.htm

New York State Police—Bureau of Investigation:
www.troopers.state.ny.us/Criminal_Investigation/

State of Wyoming—Division of Criminal Investigation:
www.attorneygeneral.state.wy.us/dci/

B.T.K.—Birth of a Serial Killer:
www.crimelibrary.com/serial_killers/unsolved/btk/index_1.html

References

D'Ovidio, R., & Doyle, J. (2003). A study on cyberstalking: Understanding investigative hurdles. *FBI Law Enforcement Bulletin, 72(3),* 10–17.

Eckert, W. G. (1986). *Homicide investigation.* Wichita, KS: The Milton Helpern International Center of Forensic Sciences at the Wichita State University.

Flanders, D. L., Goldman, L., Ortley, L., Sargent, D. M., & Thomas, D. R. (2002). Investigation of stalking cases: A model protocol for Maryland law enforcement officers. Accessed online at www.marcpi.jhu.edu.

Fox, R. H., & Cunningham, C. L. (1985). *Crime scene search and physical evidence handbook*. Washington, DC: U.S. Government Printing Office.

Gardner, R. M. (2005). *Practical crime scene processing and investigation*. New York: CRC Press.

Horswell, J., & Fowler, C. (2004). Associative evidence: The locard exchange principle. In J. Horswell (Ed.), *The practice of crime scene investigation* (pp. 45–55). London: CRC Press.

Lee, H. C., Palmbach, T., & Miller, M. T. (2001). *Henry Lee's crime scene handbook*. New York: Academic Press.

National Institute of Justice. (2000). *Crime scene investigation: A guide for law enforcement*. Washington, DC: U.S. Department of Justice, pp. 3–4.

National Institute of Justice (2001). *Electronic crime scene investigations: A guide for first responders*. Accessed online at www.ncjrs.gov/pdffiles1/nij/187736.pdf.

O'Hara, C. E., & O'Hara, G. L. (2003). *Fundamentals of criminal investigation* (7th ed.). Springfield, IL: Charles C. Thomas Publishers.

Osterburg, J., & Ward, R. (2004). *Criminal investigation* (4th ed.), Cincinnati, OH: Anderson.

Saferstein, R. (1995). *Criminalistics: An introduction to forensic science*. NJ: Prentice Hall.

Spitzberg, B. H., & Hoobler, G. (2002). Cyberstalking and the technologies of interpersonal terrorism. *New Media & Society, 4,* 71–92.

Swanson, C. R., Chamelin, N. C., & Territo, L. (1996). *Criminal investigation* (6th ed.). New York: McGraw Hill.

U.S. Department of Justice. (1999a). *Cyberstalking: A new challenge for law enforcement and industry: A report from the Attorney General to the Vice President*. Washington, DC: U.S. Department of Justice, pp. 2–6.

U.S. Department of Justice. (1999b). Forensic examination of digital evidence: A guide for law enforcement. Accessed online at www.ncjrs.gov/pdffiles1/nij/199408.pdf.

Williams, G. L. (2003). Criminal investigations. In W. A. Geller & D. W. Stephens (Eds.), *Local government police management* (4th ed., pp. 169–205). Washington, DC: International City Manager's Association.

Wilson, O. W., & McLaren, R. C. (1977). *Police Administration* (4th ed.). New York: McGraw Hill.

Chapter 5

Interviewing and Interrogation

> " I keep six honest serving men
> They taught me all I knew
> Their names are **What** and **Why** and **When**
> And **How** and **Where** and **Who**. "
>
> —Rudyard Kipling, *The Elephant's Child* (1902)

CHAPTER OUTLINE

OBJECTIVES

After completion of this chapter, you will be able to do the following:

- Explain the difference between an interview and an interrogation.
- Describe the objectives of both the interview and the interrogation.
- List and discuss the various approaches to interviewing.
- Describe the advantages and disadvantages to nondirective and directive interviewing.
- List the recommended structure of an interview.
- Describe and explain the basic principles of interrogations.
- Discuss the use of polygraph examinations during a criminal investigation.
- Explain the concepts involved in detecting deception.
- Explain the law of interviewing and interrogation.

INTRODUCTION

Often, the terms *interviewing* and *interrogation* are treated as if they are interchangeable. In addition, whether the label *interview* or *interrogation* is used frequently depends upon the point of view of the user. A police officer may testify in court that the defendant was *interviewed* over a period of three hours, and the defense counsel in cross-examination questions the officer regarding the three-hour *interrogation*.

There is a distinct difference between the two terms. An **interview** is a nonaccusatory questioning of an individual for the purposes of obtaining information (Inbau et al., 2004, p. 5). Interviews are normally conducted during the early phase of an investigation and tend to be free flowing and relatively unstructured.

An interrogation is accusatory questioning of a suspect (Inbau et al., 2004, p. 7). The purpose of an interrogation is to learn the truth. Unlike interviews, an interrogation involves active persuasion, which is when the interrogator uses tactics that will dominate the questioning and are directed toward persuading the suspect to tell the truth. Interrogations are conducted only after the investigator has concluded that the individual being questioned is guilty of the crime.

The *Manual for Police of New York State* (2005, pp. 2, 5, 25) explains that while questioning is the basis of both an interview and an interrogation, they have distinctly different focuses. The purpose of an **information gathering interview** is to get information by questioning a person about knowledge of an event or its circumstances, whereas the focus of an interrogation is to obtain information by questioning a suspect about participation in an offense, to seek

interview / A nonaccusatory questioning of an individual for the purposes of obtaining information.

information gathering interview / An interview generally conducted during the preliminary investigation of a crime with the purpose of gathering information.

201

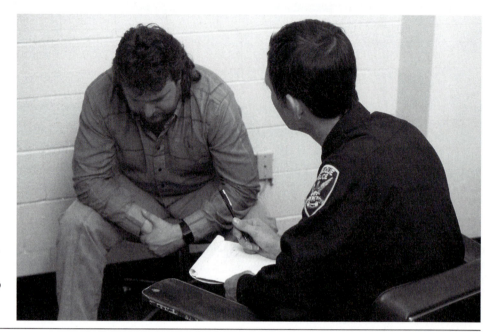

Police detective interviews witness at police station, Dubuque, IA. Note the police officer is using a relaxed approach in an attempt to get information from the witness.

an oral admission, and, if possible, to get those admissions documented in a written confession.

Basic objectives in both interviews and interrogations for law enforcement purposes include:

- Secure accurate information
- Distinguish fact from falsehood
- Identify and convict the criminal or criminals
- Assist the victim and the recovery, if appropriate, of the victim's property

PRINCIPLES OF INTERVIEWING

Art of Interviewing

Felix Lopez, a personnel specialist, contends that: "Interviewing is very much like piano playing, a fair degree of skill can be acquired with the necessity of formal instruction, but there is a world of difference in craftsmanship, in technique, and in finesse between the amateur who plays 'by ear' and the accomplished concert pianist" (Lopez, 1975, p. 1).

Stewart and Cash (1988, p. 3) define interviewing as, "A process of dyadic, relational communication with a predetermined and serious purpose designed to interchange behavior and involving the asking and answering of questions." To them the word *process* denotes a dynamic, ever-changing interaction, with many variables operating with and acting upon one another, and a degree of system without being fixed. They see *dyadic* as denoting that an interview is a person-to-person interaction between two parties or units. The interaction between *units* indicates that the interview

Voices of Experience

Interrogation Technique

Excerpts from an interview between Cliff Roberson and former police officer,
John L. Padgett, presently a lead faculty at the Institution of Justice,
Westwood College, Colorado.

Q: *When you interrogated suspects did you have any special techniques?*
A: When I interrogated suspects in my office, I always had available what I referred to as the "three sins:" strong black caffeinated coffee, chocolate candy, and menthol cigarettes. When the individual did not want to talk, I would take my time and give them cigarettes, coffee, and candy. After a while, they would sit there and become relaxed. Often they would start talking, waive their rights, and provide a complete statement as to what happened. I don't know why it worked, but more often than not it did. ■

may be between more than two people, but never more than two units (an interviewer party and an interviewee party), such as two members of the police department jointly interviewing a husband and wife. The word *relational* suggests an interpersonal connection between the two parties. According to Stewart and Cash, at least one party to the interview comes to the interview with a goal and has planned the interview to focus on specific subject matter. To them, the asking and answering of questions is crucial to the interviewing process. Questions are tools that are used by the interviewer. Few interviews are successful unless purposeful questions are used throughout the process and are asked at the appropriate time (Stewart and Cash, 1988, p. 5).

While interviewing takes talent, it is talent that is learned from experience and training. To be a successful interviewer, you need a background in human behavior, psychology, and communications. An officer learns the art of interviewing just like learning to fire a weapon. In learning interviewing expertise, like weapons training, some officers seem to have a natural ability and others need to work at it.

PRACTICE HINTS

The word *interview* implies cooperative consent to provide information. The fact that eyewitness accounts of an event differ does not mean that one of them is lying, nor is it impossible for several witnesses to tell the same story. How each witness perceives an event is often very different. People also tend to exaggerate, fabricate, and prevaricate.

Truth is the ultimate goal of every interview you conduct or incident that you investigate.

Types of Interviews

For crime investigations, there are five basic types of interviews: information gathering, selection interviews, dealing with problems of the interviewee's behavior, problem solving, and persuasive interviews. The information gathering interview is generally conducted during the preliminary investigation of the crime. The purpose of this interview is to determine what happened and why. The **selection type interview** is used in law enforcement to screen out or weed out individuals. Some interviews are designed to deal with certain behavior problems, such as two neighbors who are involved in a heated argument and the purpose of the interview is to reduce the tension between them. **Problem solving interviews** in law enforcement are

selection type interview /
An interview that is used in law enforcement to screen out or weed out individuals.

problem solving interview /
An interview that is directed to determine who committed the crime.

typically directed to determine **who** committed the crime. Interviews are also conducted in an attempt to persuade the interviewee to provide information regarding someone else's criminal behavior.

Approaches to Interviewing

directive approach / Where the interviewer establishes the purpose of the interview and controls its pacing.

nondirective approach / Where the interviewer allows the interviewee to determine the approach and scope of the interview.

Regardless of the type of interview or its purpose, there are two basic approaches to interviewing: directive and nondirective. Each has its distinct advantages that are discussed in this section. In the **directive approach**, the interviewer establishes the purpose of the interview and controls its pacing. The **nondirective approach** is where the interviewer allows the interviewee to determine the approach and scope of the interview. The nondirective approach is used quite frequently in counseling, performance appraisals, and problem solving. The directive approach is used frequently in criminal investigations.

Example of a directed interview:

Interviewer: What is your name?

Interviewer: Did you see what happened?

Interviewer: What happened?

Interviewer: Where were you when it happened?

Interviewer: Who else was involved?

Advantages of the directed approach include:

- Easier to teach to a new interviewer.
- More efficient because it takes less time.
- It can be supplemented by other methods of data collection.
- It can be replicated by controlling the variables such as voice, facial expressions, and appearance.

Ernesto Miranda with his attorney John J. Flynn, at his second trial in Phoenix, Arizona on February 24, 1967. By a jury, he was found guilty of rape and kidnapping. His first trial was reversed in the now famous *Miranda v. Arizona* case in which the U.S. Supreme Court placed the requirement that prior to in-custody interrogation, the police must advise an accused of his or her rights.

Disadvantages of the directed approach include:

- It is inflexible.
- The approach is limited in variety and depth of subject matter.
- It limits the interviewer's range of techniques.
- There are more effective and efficient means of data collection.
- The validity of the information obtained may be questionable.

Example of a nondirective interview:

Interviewer: Tell me, what should I be looking for?

Interviewee: (provides a response)

Interviewer: Why is that important?

Interviewee: (explains)

Interviewer: What is your responsibility in the incident?

Advantages of the nondirective approach include:

- Allows the interviewer to probe deeply into the matter.
- Provides a pattern of the subjective thinking of the interviewee.
- May provide information or a direction that the interviewer was unaware of.
- Gives the interviewer greater flexibility.
- Tends to generate more information.
- Gives the interviewee freedom to provide lengthy answers and to volunteer information.
- It does not lead the interviewee as to what information you are seeking.

Disadvantages of the nondirective approach include:

- It requires a more experienced interviewer than the directed interview.
- Interviewer must possess some psychological insight and sensitivity.
- It often generates excessive and nonrelevant information.
- The requirement of adaptation to each interviewee reduces the opportunity to replicate the interview.
- It is time consuming.

Sympathetic or Logical Approach

"Just the facts, ma'am."
    —Joe Friday, from the TV series: *Dragnet*

The interview may be approached from either a sympathetic or a logical approach. With the sympathetic approach, you attempt to sympathize with the interviewee or the accused and gain his or her confidence. This approach is often successful when interviewing involves a victim or

PRACTICE HINTS

Interviewee's Questions

Experienced interviewers will never walk away from an interview with the feeling that they gave more information than they received. Your objective in an interview is to get information, not give it. Under most circumstances, it is unwise to share information that you obtained from other interviewees with the subject of your present interview. As a general practice, you should not answer the interviewee's questions.

possible suspect in a crime of passion. The logical approach involves establishing a superior psychological position with the interviewee by conducting a "no nonsense" interview and creating the atmosphere that you have the evidence and are just providing the interviewee with an opportunity to explain his or her actions. This approach works with sociopaths whose crimes involve intelligence and cunning rather than emotion. It also works with career criminals.

Timing and Setting of the Interview

Interviews during a criminal investigation should be conducted as soon after the event as reasonably possible; whereas interrogations of suspects should be postponed until after the victim and other witnesses have been questioned.

The proper setting of the interview will make the questioning easier. The initial interview may be at the crime scene where there will be circumstances laden with confusion or distraction. Generally, the initial interview will obtain only the gist of the information that a person has. A more thorough interview, if appropriate, should be conducted at a later time in a more favorable setting. The follow-up interview should be conducted in private and without interruptions, if possible.

The *Manual for Police of New York State* (2005, pp. 2–7) recommends that prior to the follow-up interview, the interviewer should:

- review all available information
- make a list of the points that are needed to be explored
- consider whether the interview should be recorded
- remove, if possible, any physical barriers that may hinder the interview
- if interviewing a juvenile, determine if state law requires the presence of his or her guardian

Structure of the Interview

The first few minutes of an interview probably determine the amount of information that will be received from the interview. The attitudes formed in those initial moments may have a lot to do with the success of your interview and the amount of cooperation that you receive from the interviewee. The *Manual for Police of New York State* (2005, pp. 2, 5, 26) recommends the following actions:

- Greet the interviewee in a cordial and sincere manner.
- Identify yourself by name, rank, or position title and organization.
- Show your credentials.
- Put the interviewee at ease by introducing a topic that both of you can discuss without strain or awkwardness.
- Create a favorable atmosphere by
  - controlling your personal feelings
  - not visibly reacting to the answers received from the interviewee
  - displaying a sincere interest in the interviewee
  - maintaining eye contact
- Do not be overly familiar.

- When the interviewee is at ease and you have established a good rapport, direct the interview toward the desired topic.
- Avoid the use of police jargon or legal sounding words, such as:
  - prosecution
  - confession
  - criminal
  - perpetrator
  - patrol unit
- Take notes, unless the note taking hampers the interview.
- Allow the interviewee to give a complete answer or account of the story without interruption.
- Avoid or limit questions that may be answered by "yes" or "no."
- Listen and evaluate the information you are receiving from the interviewee.
- Be alert to what is said and what is not said.
- Observe the body language of the interviewee when providing an answer to a question.
- Once the interviewee has finished the story, ask direct questions to clarify and expand on the information already provided.
- An abrupt closure to the interview may cause the loss of valuable information. It may be helpful to summarize what has been covered and ask the interviewee if anything was omitted or should be added.
- If possible, get a written statement from the interviewee.

Obtaining Written Statements

There are certain commonly accepted procedures that should be followed in taking written statements from witnesses. One fact that should always be remembered is that often a person starts out as a witness and ends up as a suspect. **Note:** Any written statements provided by a witness must be shared with the defense counsel prior to trial.

The written statement may be handwritten, typewritten, or computer generated. If the statement is handwritten, it should be in ink and made by the witness, unless the witness for some reason is unable to reduce the statement to writing. Typewritten or computer-generated statements are preferable to handwritten statements and should be the only types of written statements prepared by an officer for the witness. When taking a written statement from an individual who may later be a suspect, if possible, have another officer present as a witness.

The first part of the statement should contain the identity of the person giving the statement. The identity should include at least: full name, place of residence, date of birth, marital status, employment, and contact information. In most cases, the goal is to obtain as much information as possible in the statement. Under most circumstances, do not try to shorten the statement. Always allow witnesses to give the details in their own language. After the statement is finished, read it and if necessary ask the witness to amplify with additional paragraphs events that need clarification. After the statement is finished, have the witness reread the statement and ask if the statement is true and correct. Have the witness sign and date the last page and initial the other pages. If any other person is present, including another

PRACTICE HINTS

A successful tactic used by many interviewers is to gain an unspoken psychological advantage over the interviewee. This may be through the location of the interview or by the arrangement of the furniture in the interview room. The idea is to make the interview subject feel slightly uneasy without knowing why.

officer, ask the person to sign the statement as a witness.

If the witness refuses to sign the statement, try to determine why the individual does not wish to sign it. Often it is advisable to suggest to the unwilling witness that maybe the refusal to sign the statement is because the statement contains false information. Frequently, this will cause a change of mind and the statement will be signed. Never order the person to sign the statement. If the individual insists on not signing the statement, make detailed notes as to the conversation and attach your notes to the unsigned statement. If another officer is present, have the other officer sign as a witness to the statement.

Levels of Interactions

According to Stewart and Cash (1988, p. 22) there are three levels of interactions in interviews. Level 1 interactions deal with relatively safe, nonthreatening areas of inquiry. Most interviews will start at level 1. For example, the officer will introduce himself or herself and ask the interviewee's name. Level 2 interactions deal with more intimate, threatening, or controversial areas of inquiry. The majority of a law enforcement interview will probably be conducted at level 2. Level 3 interactions deal with highly controversial or intimate areas of inquiry. At this point, the interview will most likely change from being an interview to being an interrogation. Stewart and Cash see the levels of interaction as similar to a door. The door is merely ajar in level 1 interactions, half open in level 2 interactions, and wide open in level 3 interactions.

FIELD INTERVIEWS/INVESTIGATIVE STOPS

It is a normal police practice to stop suspicious persons in public places for the purposes of questioning them or conducting an investigation. Until the *Terry v. Ohio*, 392 U.S. 1 (1968) case, there was a question as to whether this procedure constituted a violation of the Fourth Amendment, because the officers generally do not have probable cause to detain and question the individuals.

In *Terry v. Ohio*, an officer observed Terry and two other men walking back and forth in front of a store. The officer decided that the men were casing the store for a possible robbery. When he approached them and asked for identification, he received only mumbled replies. He then grabbed Terry, turned him around, and patted him down. The officer found a pistol in Terry's pocket. Terry, an ex-con, was arrested for carrying a concealed weapon. The Court upheld the search and found no Fourth Amendment violation.

The Court held that a police officer may temporarily detain a person for questioning if the officer has a reasonable suspicion that criminal activity may be involved. The officer may pat down for weapons only if the officer has the additional reasonable suspicion that the pat down is necessary for safety reasons. *Temporary detention* and *reasonable suspicion* are discussed in Chapter 6 in the section on searches and seizures.

A **field interview** is similar to an investigative stop, except there is an absence of suspicious circumstances. In the **investigative stop**, there is the possibility that

field interview / The stopping and interviewing of a person by a police officer when there is an absence of suspicious circumstances.

investigative stop / The stopping and interviewing of a person where there is the possibility that criminal activity may be occurring or has occurred.

Ohio State Highway Patrol Officers conducting a traffic checkpoint for drivers' licenses in 1949.

criminal activity may be occurring. In the field interview, the officer is seeking information. It is frequently stated that a good police officer is a curious person and when something seems different or unusual, the officer asks questions.

When conducting the interview or stop, the officer generally must conduct the questioning on the spot and does not have the opportunity to select the optimal setting. If possible, for safety reasons, the interview or stop should be conducted in a well-lighted area and in private. As a general rule, the first questions asked should appear to be satisfying your curiosity, rather than investigating criminal behavior. Some examples are: "Do you live around here?" and "Where is your car?" Try not to alert the individual that you are concerned about possible criminal activity.

> ### PRACTICE HINTS
>
> A written record should be made of every investigative stop or field interview. Many departments require their officers to fill out a form in either a notebook or on a card that contains information as to why the officer was suspicious, any statement given by the person contacted, and any identification provided. Always assume, but do not indicate in any manner, that any person you stop and question is a danger to your safety.

PRINCIPLES OF INTERROGATION

Art of Interrogating

"The defendant's own confession is probably the most probative and damaging evidence that can be admitted against him."
    —Former Supreme Court Justice Byron White, *Bruton v. United States* (1968)

Devallis Rutledge, former chief deputy prosecutor for Los Angeles County, defines **interrogation** as a "controlled questioning calculated to discover and confirm the truth from the responses of an individual, in spite of his or her intentions and efforts

interrogation / Controlled questioning calculated to discover and confirm the truth from the responses of an individual, in spite of his or her intentions and efforts to conceal the truth.

Miranda Myths / The concept that there are numerous misconceptions about what the *Miranda v. Arizona* decision means. Two of the most popular misconceptions are: (1) anything gained in violation of Miranda is inadmissible, and (2) the warning must be given on traffic stops.

to conceal the truth" (Rutledge, 2001, p. 1). Rutledge claims that interrogation is one of the most important tools in law enforcement. He contends that **Miranda Myths** have prevented law enforcement officers from using the tools of interrogation to the fullest extent possible. To combat the "Miranda Myths," Rutledge (2001, p. 5) states:

- There are legally permissible ways to question a suspect without giving the suspect a Miranda warning.

- There are times when it is legally permissible to use tricks and deceit to get a confession.

- It is sometimes permissible to re-interview a suspect without giving a new Miranda warning. **Note:** *People v. Brueseke*, 25 Cal. 3rd 691 (1972) holds that it is not necessary to re-warn the suspect unless a substantial time has passed (e.g., more than twenty-four hours).

- There are psychological ploys that may be used by law enforcement officers that will usually remove a suspect's defenses to telling the truth and allow you to get a confession.

PRACTICE HINTS

The Difference Between a Confession and an Admission

confession / A direct acknowledgment of guilt on the part of the individual providing the statement.

admission / A statement provided by an accused of a fact or facts pertinent to the issue that helps establish the accused's guilt, but does not admit actual guilt.

A **confession** is a direct acknowledgment of guilt on the part of the individual providing the statement. A confession acknowledges guilt either by statement of the details of the crime or an admission of an ultimate fact. An **admission** is a statement provided by an accused of a fact or facts pertinent to the issue that helps establish the accused's guilt, but does not admit actual guilt. The statement, "I murdered her" is a confession, whereas the statement, "I shot her in self-defense" is an admission because the latter statement does not admit guilt and in and of itself will not establish guilt.

Steps of Interrogation

The late John E. Reid, former professor of law at Northwestern University Law School, developed the technique known as "Reid's Nine Steps of Interrogation." The interrogation techniques developed by Reid are probably used by more law enforcement agencies than all the other interrogation techniques combined. ABC News in its *20/20* program on June 18, 1999 stated that the Reid techniques were so psychologically sophisticated that they could induce an innocent person to confess. Cliff Roberson, who attended one of Professor Reid's early workshops, concluded that ABC News may have overstated its claim, but not by much. Reid's organization, now known as John E. Reid and Associates, annually conducts workshops on interrogation. The workshops are very intense and productive.

Reid's nine steps are briefly described here (Inbau et al., 2004, pp. 214–219):

- Step 1: Involves a direct and positive confrontation of the suspect with the information that the suspect is considered as the person who committed the offense.

- Step 2: The investigator expresses a theory to the suspect as to why the suspect committed the offense. In this step, the investigator generally attempts to affix moral blame for the crime on someone else or on the circumstances.

- Step 3: Involves the actions to be taken by the investigator for handling the suspect's initial denial of guilt.

- Step 4: Involves the overcoming of the suspect's reasons as to why the suspect would not or could not commit the crime.

- Step 5: Involves keeping the suspect's attention and the displaying of sincerity by the investigator.

- Step 6: Involves recognizing and using the suspect's passive mood to the advantage of the investigator and telling the suspect the benefits of telling the truth.

- Step 7: Is the utilization of an alternative question, a suggestion of a choice to be made by the suspect concerning some aspect of the crime, for example, "Was this the first time?"

- Step 8: Involves having the suspect orally relate the details of the crime.

- Step 9: Involves the recommended procedures for converting an oral confession into a written one.

USE OF THE POLYGRAPH AND CVSA

The **polygraph (lie detector)** is an instrument that records physiological reactions of the person being examined to specific questions in an effort to detect deception. The word *polygraph* literally means "many writings." The records of a polygraph examination are interpreted by an expert (polygraphist) who will normally give an opinion as to whether there was an indication that the person being examined was deceptive to certain questions. Generally, the results or even the fact that a polygraph examination was given are not admissible in court.

Any statement made by the person being examined, however, may be admissible in evidence as an admission. Prior to admitting the statement, the prosecution

polygraph (lie detector) / An instrument that records physiological reactions of the person being examined to specific questions in an effort to detect deception.

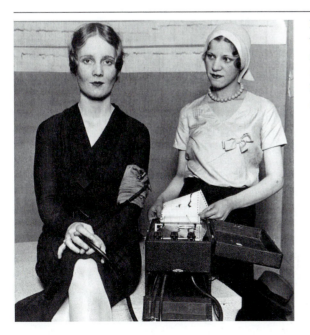

Early lie detector being used by the Chicago Police Department in 1930. Ruth Hillman, left, is shown with the lie detector band on her arm. Ruth Richman right, is looking at it.

must establish that the statement was not caused by any force, threats, or promises of leniency. In some states, the courts consider the use of a polygraph inherently coercive and thus the statements are inadmissible. In *State v. Johnson*, 193 Wis 2d 382 (1995), the Wisconsin State Supreme Court held:

> Although polygraph test results are inadmissible in criminal proceedings, statements made in post-polygraph interviews may be admissible. If the post-polygraph interview is so closely related to the mechanical portion of the polygraph examination that it is considered one event, the post-polygraph statements are inadmissible. On the other hand, post-polygraph interviews may be found to be distinct both as to time and content from the examination which precedes them, and the statements made therein admissible. This determination is made after consideration of the totality of circumstances of the individual case.
>
> The . . . "one event" touchstone is a mosaic of many fragments, and among other factors to be considered are: the time between the end of the polygraph examination and the interview during which the defendant said something that he or she seeks to suppress; whether the defendant was still attached to the polygraph machine when he or she made the incriminating statements; whether the post-polygraph interview was in the examination room or some other place; whether the defendant was told that the polygraph examination is over; and whether . . . the polygraph examiner interrogates the defendant making frequent use of and references to the charts and tracing he had just obtained.

Computer Voice Stress Analyzer (CVSA) / An instrument that tries to detect deception by analyzing the level of stress in a person's voice.

The **Computer Voice Stress Analyzer (CVSA)** tries to detect deception by analyzing the level of stress in a person's voice. Questions asked during a polygraph are limited generally to "yes" or "no" responses, whereas the CVSA can analyze any spoken word. Both the polygraph and the CVSA should be used only as tools of an investigator, never as a substitute for an investigation.

HUMAN LIE DETECTOR

Comedian Groucho Marx once stated: "There is one way to determine if a man is honest—ask him" (Wallace & Roberson, 2004, p. 145). An experienced questioner can sense when a person is being untruthful. David J. Lieberman (1999), a board-certified hypnotherapist, notes that people lie for many different reasons and often their lying does not benefit anyone. Lieberman notes that it takes two individuals for a lie to be effective—one to make the lie and one to believe it. Lieberman stated in one of his workshops for law enforcement officers that Abraham Lincoln is said to have posed the following question: "How many legs would a sheep have if you called its tail a leg?" "Four," explained Lincoln. "Because calling its tail a leg doesn't make it one" (Lieberman, 1999, p. 2).

Lieberman has identified forty-six clues to deception. He divides the clues into the following seven sections:

- Body language
- Emotional states
- Interpersonal interactions
- Verbal content

- How something is said
- Psychological profile
- General indications of deceit

Lieberman notes that certain variables such as gender, ethnicity, and cultural background can influence how we interpret various clues. For example, the use of gestures and personal space vary by cultural background. He, however, concludes that for the most part, these factors are negligible and can be ignored. Lieberman recommends that once you conclude that the individual is lying to you, generally it is better not to confront the individual immediately with an accusation of deceit until after you have received all the information you can; then determine how you can best use this insight to your advantage.

Body Language

Many of Lieberman's clues involve the fundamentals of body language, others use more advanced techniques and processes. He notes that many clues are so subtle that they can easily be missed unless you are trained to detect them. Some of the basic clues are:

- **Eye contact.** Little or no direct eye contact is a classic sign of deception. (**Note:** All research reports and books that the authors reviewed in this area emphasized the importance of eye contact in detecting deception.)
- **Arms and hands animation.** According to Lieberman, when a person is lying or keeping something in, the person tends to be less expressive with the hands or arms.
- **Artificial movements.** If the person's arm movements and gestures are stiff and almost mechanical; that is, the movements are contrived and not natural— the person is being deceptive.
- **Keeping legs and arms in.** When a person sits with the legs and arms close to the body, perhaps legs crossed but not outstretched, the person is keeping something in.
- **Cover-up.** If the individual's hand goes straight to the face while the individual is responding to a question or when making a statement, this often is an indication of deceit.
- **Partial shrug.** The shrugging of one's shoulders is usually a gesture that indicates ignorance or indifference, but if the gesture is fleeting and you only catch a glimpse of it—it's a sign that the movement is not a true emotion and the individual is trying to deceive you.

Tami Hoag, Prior Bad Acts

Following is an excerpt of a dialogue between Detective Kovac and Anka from Tami Hoag's *Prior Bad Acts*, p. 145.

"Do you have something going on with Mr. Moore?"
"Mr. Moore is my employer."
"He's not more than that to you?"
"No, of course not."

The answer was a beat too slow, and she didn't quite meet his eyes.

"You're not sleeping with him?"
"No! I'm going upstairs now. I have nothing more to say to you."
   Indignation, outrage.

But she still didn't quite meet his eyes.

Emotional States

Inconsistencies between gestures, words, and emotions are great indicators of deception. Examples include:

- **Timing.** If a person's head begins to shake in a confirming direction before or as the words come out, that is generally an indication that the individual is being truthful. If, however, the timing is off and the shake comes after the statement, it is not based on emotion—instead it is based on deception.
- **Contradiction and Consistency.** Not only should timing be observed, but the interviewer needs to pay attention to the type of gestures, for example, a person who is lying or hiding something will rarely point a finger at the interviewer or others. Also, look for a smile that doesn't seem to be a happy smile.

Interpersonal Interactions

Be aware of a person's posture in and of itself and in relation to the surroundings. Contrary to popular opinion, a person who is wrongly accused of something does not become defensive. A guilty individual becomes defensive.

Lieberman contends that a person who is lying will rarely have physical contact with the person to whom the deception is directed. This is an unconscious reduction of the level of intimacy to help alleviate the person's guilt for deceiving the interviewer. When a person feels confident about a situation and conversation, the person tends to be erect or sits up straight—a sign that the individual feels good about himself or herself. Insecure individuals often stand or sit hunched over and frequently have their hands in their pockets.

Verbal Content

The words that are chosen to convey a message are very reflective of the person's true feelings. Lieberman claims that if a person uses the language "It wasn't me" instead of "It was not me," the person is more likely to be telling the truth. A deceptive person wants to emphasis the "not" and therefore tends not to use the contraction of "was not." He also contends that persons telling the truth are not concerned about whether you understand them—they are willing to clarify. Dishonest persons want to be sure that you understand their point immediately so that they can change the subject. For example, compare the statement: "I'm pretty sure I have never cheated on a test" with the statement: "No, I would never cheat on a test." The proponent of the second statement wants to make sure you understand the answer and move on; a sign of deception.

An implied answer is often given when the individual does not want to answer the question asked. If the question asked is: "Did you like Mary?" An answer similar to: "I rarely saw her" indicates that the interviewee does not want to answer the question. Lieberman also contends that guilty persons tell their story in dribs and drabs until they get a verbal confirmation to stop. They speak to fill the gap left by silence.

How Something Is Said

One rule of thumb concerns the speed at which an individual answers a question. A guilty person takes more time and tries to come up with the "right" answer, which takes more time than merely giving an honest answer. Pacing is also important. A rapid response to a question with a one-word answer and then being slow to add additional content is a sign of deception. The individual was quick in the denial, but needed time to make up the follow-up information. The tone of the voice is also an excellent indicator of truth. A deceitful statement is frequently delivered in a flat voice devoid of any real emotion.

LAW OF INTERVIEWING AND INTERROGATION

In this section, we will examine the suspect's right to counsel when being interrogated. There are two separate constitutional amendments that must be considered in any questioning of a suspect by law enforcement. The Fifth Amendment provides that an individual may not be compelled to provide an incriminating statement against himself or herself. The Sixth Amendment right to counsel attaches when the investigation is no longer a general inquiry, but focuses in on the individual. For ease of understanding the basic legal principles, we will examine the accused's rights under the Sixth Amendment first.

Sixth Amendment's Right to Counsel During Interrogation

"In all criminal prosecutions, the accused shall . . . have the right to the assistance of counsel for his defense."

—from the Sixth Amendment

As the reader will note, the Sixth Amendment guarantees many rights to defendants. It has even been called "the defendant's amendment." Included in those rights is the right to assistance of counsel. The U.S. Supreme Court noted, " . . . of all the rights that an accused person has, the right to be represented by counsel is by far the most pervasive, for it affects his ability to assert any other rights he may have" (*Powell v. Alabama*).

In early England, an accused person had no right to a counsel. A neutral judge would look after both the accused person's rights and the rights of the King or Queen. Originally, the right to counsel under the Sixth Amendment was interpreted to mean that the accused has only a right to have counsel present during a criminal trial (Monk, 2000, p. 134). As will be noted, the Sixth Amendment is now considered to provide the defendant with the right to effective representation of counsel.

The leading U.S. Supreme Court case on when the right to counsel attaches is *Escobedo v. Illinois*, 378 U.S. 478 (1964). Danny Escobedo's brother-in-law, Manuel Escobedo, a Chicago convict, was shot on the night of January 19, 1960, and without a warrant Danny Escobedo was arrested the next day, at 2:30 in the morning. He was released at 5:00 P.M. that afternoon, after Warren Wolfson, his lawyer, obtained a writ of *habeas corpus*. During that period, he made no statement to the police. On January 30, Benedict DiGerlando, a man in police custody, told the police that Danny Escobedo had killed Manuel. The police re-arrested Escobedo between 8:00 and 9:00 P.M. that day. He was then taken to the police headquarters and questioned without letting him speak to or even see his lawyer.

Danny Escobedo was arrested for murder and interrogated for several hours at a Chicago police station. The police refused his counsel's request to consult with him because he had not been charged with a crime. The U.S. Supreme Court in *Escobedo v. Illinois* held that an individual had a right to counsel as soon as the investigation focused on him or her.

The Escobedo's lawyer described the ensuing events in the following terms:

On that day I received a phone call (from "the mother of another defendant") and pursuant to that phone call I went to the Detective Bureau at 11th and State. The first person I talked to was the sergeant on duty at the Bureau Desk, Sergeant Pidgeon. I asked Sergeant Pidgeon for permission to speak to my client, Danny Escobedo. . . . Sergeant Pidgeon made a call to the Bureau lockup and informed me that the boy had been taken from the lockup to the Homicide Bureau. This was between 9:30 and 10:00 in the evening. Before I went anywhere, he called the Homicide Bureau and told them there was an attorney waiting to see Escobedo. He told me I could not see him. Then I went upstairs to the Homicide Bureau. There were several Homicide Detectives around and I talked to them. I identified myself as Escobedo's attorney and asked permission to see him. They said I could not. . . . The police officer told me to see Chief Flynn who was on duty. I identified myself to Chief Flynn and asked permission to see my client. He said I could not. . . . I think it was approximately 11:00. He said I couldn't see him because they hadn't completed questioning. . . . For a second or two I spotted Escobedo in an office in the Homicide Bureau. The door was open and I could see through the office.

I waved to him and he waved back and then the door was closed by one of the officers at Homicide. There were four or five officers milling around the Homicide Detail that night. As to whether I talked to Captain Flynn any later that day, I waited around for another hour or two and went back again and renewed my request to see my client. He again told me I could not. . . . I filed an official complaint with Commissioner Phelan of the Chicago Police Department. I had a conversation with every police officer I could find. I was told at Homicide that I couldn't see him and I would have to get a writ of *habeas corpus*. I left the Homicide Bureau and from the Detective Bureau at 11th and State at approximately 1:00 A.M. [Sunday morning]. I had no opportunity to talk to my client that night. I quoted to Captain Flynn the Section of the Illinois Criminal Code which allows an attorney the right to see his client.

During his questioning, Escobedo was tricked into saying he knew that DiGerlando had killed Manuel, making him an accomplice. He was then found guilty of first degree murder and was sentenced to prison for twenty years, with his "confession" which he later recanted.

His attorney petitioned to the Illinois Supreme Court, where the conviction was affirmed and then to the U.S. Supreme Court. The Court, in an opinion by Justice Arthur Goldberg, ruled 5-to-4 in favor of Escobedo, overturning his previous conviction on the grounds that his confession was not admissible in a court of law. Justice Goldberg, in the majority opinion, spoke for the first time of "an absolute right to remain silent." Escobedo had not been adequately informed of his constitutional right to remain silent rather than be forced to incriminate himself. Justice Goldberg wrote:

> No system worth preserving should have to fear that if an accused is permitted to consult with a lawyer, he will become aware of, and exercise his rights. If the exercise of constitutional rights will thwart the effectiveness of a system of law enforcement, then there is something very wrong with that system.

The Escobedo case stands for the proposition that when a police investigation is no longer a general inquiry into an unsolved crime, but has begun to focus on a particular suspect, the accused has a constitutional right to keep silent and to consult with an attorney. If the accused is denied the assistance of counsel in violation of the Sixth Amendment, no statement extracted by the police during the interrogation may be used against him at a trial. Escobedo was decided before Miranda v. Arizona, which emphasizes whether the appropriate warnings have been given and given correctly, and whether the right to remain silent has been waived.

In *Michigan v. Jackson*, 475 U.S. 625 (1986), the U.S. Supreme Court held that once this right to counsel has attached and has been invoked, any subsequent waiver during a police-initiated custodial interview is ineffective. The Sixth Amendment right to counsel after criminal proceeding has commenced is, however, offense specific. It cannot be invoked once for all future prosecutions and it does not attach until a prosecution is commenced—that is, at or after the initiation of adversary judicial criminal proceedings—whether by way of formal charge, preliminary hearing, indictment, information, or arraignment [*United States v. Gouveia*, 467 U.S. 180 (1984)].

If you read both Escobedo and Alvarado, there seems to be a disagreement as to when the right to counsel attaches. Escobedo states that the right to counsel attaches when the investigation begins to focus on a particular individual, while Alvarado discusses whether or not criminal charges have been initiated against the accused. There is an important distinction between the two cases. In Escobedo, the defendant had not been charged, but had requested an attorney. In this case, because the investigation had focused on him as being involved in the murder, his request to see his attorney should have been honored. A different problem existed in the Alvarado

CASE STUDY: *United States v. Alvarado*
2006 U.S. App. LEXIS 6055 (4th Cir. Va. 2006)

The case touches upon the sovereign authority of the state and federal governments to create and enforce criminal laws. The Commonwealth of Virginia charged the defendant with state drug offenses, provided him with counsel, and subsequently dismissed the charges against him. After filing a federal criminal complaint, federal investigators gave the defendant appropriate Miranda warnings and then questioned him outside the presence of his state-appointed lawyer about his involvement in federal drug crimes. The defendant contends that the incriminating statements he made during this interrogation should have been suppressed at his federal trial because they were taken in violation of his Sixth Amendment right to counsel.

Facts: On the evening of October 1, 2003, state and federal law enforcement officers were conducting surveillance of an Econo Lodge Motel in Dumfries, Virginia. The officers had received a tip from a confidential source that cocaine would be delivered to the motel. They observed Francisco Lara-Hernandez and another suspected drug trafficker enter the motel, and state law enforcement officers subsequently arrested them.

Special Agent Jordi Clop of the Federal Bureau of Alcohol, Tobacco, and Firearms participated in this surveillance and interrogated Lara-Hernandez after he was placed under arrest. Lara-Hernandez stated that he had recently returned to the hotel from North Carolina with approximately 500 grams of cocaine. He indicated to Clop that the cocaine was now across the street in Room 333 of the Days Inn Hotel. He also disclosed that three individuals, one wearing a red t-shirt, were in the room and that two vehicles, including a white truck, were associated with the drug ring. Law enforcement officers observed defendant Samuel Constanza Alvarado (Alvarado), clad in a red t-shirt, exit Room 333 and climb into a white truck. State police officers arrested the defendant upon his entering the truck.

The defendant did not speak English, but Agent Clop was fluent in Spanish. Agent Clop gave the defendant his Miranda warnings, and the defendant agreed to talk with Clop. From this conversation, Agent Clop determined that the defendant was staying in Room 338 of the Days Inn, and received the defendant's permission to search the room. Law enforcement officers

eventually recovered 250 grams of cocaine from Room 333 and a suitcase full of marijuana and a handgun from Room 338. In the early morning hours of October 2, 2003, the defendant was transported to a police station in Prince William County, Virginia. Agent Clop interrogated him at the police station after the defendant was again read his Miranda rights.

On October 2, the Commonwealth of Virginia issued arrest warrants for Alvarado. The Commonwealth charged him with both possession with intent to manufacture, sell, give, or distribute cocaine and conspiracy to manufacture, sell, give, or distribute cocaine. According to the warrants, these charges concerned only the events on or about October 2, 2003. The defendant requested counsel, and the Commonwealth appointed him a lawyer. Virginia retained custody of the defendant until December 5, 2003, when he had his preliminary hearing. At this hearing, the Commonwealth dismissed its charges against him. (Apparently, the federal agents had requested that the Commonwealth decline prosecution of the case and allow the defendant to be prosecuted in federal court.)

On December 4, 2003, the day prior to Alvarado's preliminary hearing in state court, federal agents had filed a federal criminal complaint against the defendant, and requested a warrant for his arrest. This warrant was issued. Agent Clop was present at the Prince William County courthouse when the defendant's state charges were dismissed, and immediately took him into federal custody. The defendant was subsequently transported to a Prince William County police station.

At the station, Alvarado told Agent Clop that he was glad to see him and wanted to give him his side of the story. Agent Clop interrupted the defendant to give him Miranda warnings. In this conversation, the defendant provided incriminating statements about his involvement in the drug conspiracy. Specifically, he described in detail the events of October 1–2, 2003. He also mentioned that he had gone on a previous trip to obtain cocaine from a source in North Carolina, and that he had been involved with other co-conspirators in drug distribution since at least August 2003. After about forty-five minutes of questioning, Agent Clop took the defendant before a judge to make his initial appearance.

On February 5, 2004, a grand jury indicted Alvarado on two counts. First, it charged him with conspiring to distribute 500 grams or more of cocaine, in violation of 21 U.S.C. §§ 841(a)(1), 846 (2000). According to the indictment, the defendant conspired with at least three different individuals between August 2003 and October 2003. Second, the grand jury charged Alvarado with distributing cocaine on or about September 27, 2003, in violation of 21 U.S.C. § 841(a)(1) and 18 U.S.C. § 2 (2000). Prior to trial, the defendant moved to suppress all the incriminating statements made over the course of his conversations with Agent Clop. The defendant alleged that these statements were taken in violation of his Fifth and Sixth Amendment rights to counsel. The district court denied his motion and found that Agent Clop properly read the defendant his Miranda rights.

Alvarado was tried in front of a jury between April 28 and May 4, 2004. At the trial, Agent Clop testified about the incriminating remarks that the defendant made to him on December 5, 2003. The jury convicted the defendant on both counts. Based on the Presentence Investigation Report, the district court enhanced the defendant's sentence on a number of grounds, including possession of a dangerous weapon and obstruction of justice. It ultimately sentenced him to 121 months on each count, with the sentences to run concurrently. The defendant appealed his convictions and sentence.

Alvarado alleges that his inculpatory statements of December 5, 2003 should have been suppressed at his trial, because they were taken in violation of his Sixth Amendment right to counsel. He contended that commencement of formal proceedings on his state charges caused the Sixth Amendment right to counsel to attach to his federal charges as well, because the state and federal charges were the "same offense."

Court's Holding: The Court disagreed. The Court stated that since the charges were from separate sovereigns, state and federal offenses are not the same for purposes of the Sixth Amendment right to counsel. Different sovereigns often define and prosecute similar crimes in different ways. For even applying the traditional test to determine whether two conspiracies are the same, the state and federal offenses in this case are distinct.

The Sixth Amendment provides that "in all criminal prosecutions, the accused shall enjoy the right . . . to have the Assistance of Counsel for his defense." The right attaches only after the commencement of formal charges against a defendant. The right is also "offense specific," and "cannot be invoked once for all future prosecutions." Even though an accused has a Sixth Amendment right to counsel for the Commonwealth offense—because formal charges had been brought— the right does not automatically attach to federal offenses with which he has not been charged.

The Court has continually held that federal and state crimes are not the same offense, no matter how identical the conduct they proscribe. An act denounced as a crime by both national and state sovereignties is an offense against the peace and dignity of both and may be punished by each [*United States v. Lanza*, 260 U.S. 377, 382 (1922)].

Both the state and federal governments, for example, must respect the Sixth Amendment right to counsel once each brings its own formal charges, and the Fifth Amendment right to counsel applies broadly to all law enforcement custodial interrogation, state or federal.

The defendant was formally charged with state offenses, and Virginia, following the dictates of the Sixth Amendment, provided him counsel. The defendant was later placed in federal custody, and the district court found that Agent Clop properly read him his Miranda rights. In fact, Agent Clop testified that Alvarado was eager to speak on December 5, and Clop had to interrupt him in order to provide the required warnings. While federal and state law enforcement authorities did engage in joint investigation, such collaborative efforts can hardly be dispositive of government misconduct. The record squarely shows that each sovereign properly accorded the defendant the safeguards the Constitution requires in their separate prosecutions.

case. In Alvarado, the defendant never asked for an attorney prior to giving his statement to the federal agent. If an individual has been charged in a criminal case and has been appointed or has retained counsel, the government may not question the individual without the individual's attorney present. To question a defendant who has been charged without the defendant's attorney present is a violation of the Sixth

Amendment. If the individual has not been charged, the individual has a right to counsel before being questioned, but must request the attorney.

Sixth Amendment Rights Involved in Law Enforcement Questioning

- If the defendant has been formally charged with a crime and has an attorney, the government may NOT question the defendant without the defendant's counsel being present.
- If the investigation is in the general stages and has not focused on a person or persons, the individuals being questioned may refuse to answer any questions that may incriminate them. They, however, do not under the Sixth Amendment have a right to counsel.
- If the investigation has focused upon a particular person or persons, the suspect or suspects have a right to counsel. Under the Sixth Amendment, they may be questioned without the presence of an attorney as long as no request for an attorney has been made.
- The issue as to whether individuals must be advised of their right to counsel prior to questioning is a Fifth Amendment issue, not a Sixth Amendment question. To answer this issue, Miranda and the cases that explained and interpreted Miranda must be examined.

Fifth Amendment Restrictions on Questioning

"No person . . . shall be compelled in any criminal case, to be a witness against himself . . ."

—from the Fifth Amendment

The preceding clause from the Fifth Amendment prohibits forcing defendants to testify against themselves. This right was applied to state criminal prosecutions in 1964 by the U.S. Supreme Court case, *Malloy v. Hogan*, 378 U.S. 1 (1964). The right against self-incrimination was a part of English common law in the sixteenth and seventeenth centuries. In 1637, John Lilburne, a Puritan printer, was accused of treason for distributing pamphlets critical of the King. A special royal court, the Star Chamber, heard the case. The Star Chamber used a system of inquisition or questioning the accused under oath. If the individual answered the questions and admitted his guilt, he was found guilty of the crime. If the individual denied that he committed the offense, his soul was in jeopardy for lying under the oath of God. Lilburne refused to take the oath required by the Star Chamber. His assertion of the right against self-incrimination led Parliament to abolish the Star Chamber and to forbid any oath requiring a person to "confess or to accuse himself or herself of any crime." An English legal commentator noted that, "it is far pleasanter to sit comfortably in the shade rubbing red pepper into a poor devil's eyes than to go about in the sun hunting evidence" (Monk, 2000, p. 128).

In 1776, the right against self-incrimination was included in the Virginia Declaration of Rights for the Commonwealth of Virginia. At least three other states recognized this right and advocated that it be a part of the federal constitution. The right became a part of the Fifth Amendment to the U.S. Constitution.

In *Ashcraft v. Tennessee*, 322 U.S. 143 (1944), Justice Black stated:

Our conclusion is that if Ashcraft made a confession it was not voluntary but compelled. We reach this conclusion from facts which are not in dispute at all. Ashcraft, a citizen of excellent reputation, was taken into custody by police officers. Ten days' examination of the Ashcrafts' maid, and of several others, in jail where they were held, had revealed nothing whatever against Ashcraft. Inquiries among his neighbors and business associates likewise had failed to unearth one single tangible clue pointing to his guilt. For thirty-six hours after Ashcraft's seizure, during which period he was held incommunicado, without sleep or rest, relays of officers, experienced investigators, and highly trained lawyers questioned him without respite. From the beginning of the questioning at 7 o'clock on Saturday evening until 6 o'clock on Monday morning Ashcraft denied that he had anything to do with the murder of his wife. And at a hearing before a magistrate about 8:30 Monday morning Ashcraft pleaded not guilty to the charge of murder, which the officers had sought to make him confess during the previous thirty-six hours.

We think a situation such as that here shown by uncontradicted evidence is so inherently coercive that its very existence is irreconcilable with the possession of mental freedom by a lone suspect against whom its full coercive force is brought to bear. It is inconceivable that any court of justice in the land, conducted as our courts are, open to the public, would permit prosecutors serving in relays to keep a defendant witness under continuous cross-examination for thirty-six hours without rest or sleep in an effort to extract a "voluntary" confession. Nor can we, consistently with constitutional due process of law, hold voluntary a confession where prosecutors do the same thing away from the restraining influences of a public trial in an open court room.

The Constitution of the United States stands as a bar against the conviction of any individual in an American court by means of a coerced confession. There have been, and are now, certain foreign nations with governments dedicated to an opposite policy: governments which convict individuals with testimony obtained by police organizations possessed of an unrestrained power to seize persons suspected of crimes against the state, hold them in secret custody, and wring from them confessions by physical or mental torture. So long as the Constitution remains the basic law of our Republic, America will not have that kind of government.

In *Brown v. Mississippi*, 297 U.S. 278 (1936), Brown, a black man, was accused of murdering a white man. When he denied the accusation, a group of men seized him, and with the participation of the deputy, they hanged him by a rope to the limb of a tree. They let him down, hanged him again, and when he was let down the second time, he still protested his innocence. He was then tied to a tree and whipped, and still declining to accede to the demands that he confess, he was finally released and returned with some difficulty to his home, suffering intense pain and agony. The record of the testimony shows that the signs of the rope on his neck were plainly visible during the so-called trial. A day or two thereafter the said deputy, accompanied by another, returned to the home of the said defendant, arrested him, and departed with the prisoner toward the jail in an adjoining county, but went by a route which led into the State of Alabama. While on the way, in that state, the deputy stopped and again severely whipped the defendant, declaring that he would continue the whipping until he confessed. The defendant then agreed to confess to such a statement as the deputy would dictate, and he did so, after which he was delivered to jail. The Court reversed the conviction.

Probably few of us would approve the tactics used by prosecutors in the Ashcraft and Brown cases. What if the police do not actually use force or threaten the accused? What if the police merely fail to advise an accused of the right to remain silent? This issue was the focal point of *Miranda v. Arizona*, 384 U.S. 436 (1966). Chief Justice Earl Warren wrote that, "even without employing brutality. . .the very fact of custodial interrogation exacts a heavy toll on individual liberty and trades on the weaknesses of individuals." Justice Warren noted that custodial interrogation is inherently coercive.

In the Miranda decision, the Court established the Miranda warning rule. Under the rule, individuals in custody must be advised of their rights before they are interrogated. Failure to adhere to the rule will make any statement given by the individuals inadmissible as evidence. The exceptions to this rule will be discussed later. The requirement appears at first glance to be a very clear rule, but when is an individual in custody and what constitutes interrogation or questioning?

The Infamous Life of Ernesto Miranda

On March 13, 1963, eight dollars in cash was stolen from a Phoenix, Arizona bank worker. Police suspected and arrested Ernesto Miranda for committing the theft. During two hours of questioning [interrogation?], Mr. Miranda, who was never offered a lawyer, confessed not only to the eight dollar theft, but also to kidnapping and raping an eighteen-year-old woman eleven days earlier. Based largely on his confession, Miranda was convicted and sentenced to twenty years in prison.

Miranda's attorneys appealed. First, they appealed unsuccessfully to the Arizona Supreme Court, and then to the U.S. Supreme Court. On June 13, 1966, the Court, in deciding the case of *Miranda v. Arizona*, 384 U.S. 436 (1966), reversed the Arizona Court's decision, granted Miranda a new trial, at which his confession could not be admitted as evidence, and established the Miranda rights of persons accused of crimes.

Ernesto Miranda was given a second trial at which his confession was not presented. Based on the evidence, Miranda was again convicted of kidnapping and rape. He was paroled from prison in 1972, having served eleven years. In 1976, Ernesto Miranda, age thirty-four, was stabbed to death in a fight. Police arrested a suspect who, after choosing to exercise his Miranda rights of silence, was released (Longley, 2006).

The *Manual for Police of New York State* (2005, pp. 2, 5, 26) advises that after informing the suspect of his or her rights, the officer should ask the following questions or take the following actions:

- "Do you understand each of the rights that I have explained to you?"
- If the suspect does not answer "yes," then re-inform the suspect of those rights.
- The suspect's silence cannot be considered as a waiver of the Miranda rights.

Mechanics of the Miranda Warning

Miranda Advisement

- You have the right to remain silent.
- Anything you say can be used against you in court.
- You have the right to an attorney and to have the attorney present while you are being questioned.
- If you cannot afford an attorney, one will be appointed for you before any questioning begins.

Note: In *California v. Prysock*, 453 U.S. 355 (1981), the U.S. Supreme Court stated that it "never indicated that the rigidity of Miranda extends to the precise formation of the warning given a criminal defendant." Accordingly, it appears that the precise wording of the advisement is not required as long as the essential elements of the warning are conveyed.

- The prosecution has the duty to establish that the defendant knowingly, voluntarily, and explicitly waived the rights. Therefore, the officer should take detailed notes concerning the advisement and the suspect's reactions to the advisement.

Interrogation or Its Functional Equivalent

Miranda warnings are required when an in-custody suspect is interrogated. The courts have broadened the meaning of interrogation to include the "functional equivalent" of interrogation. For example, interrogation includes any words or actions by the police that the police should know are reasonably likely to elicit an incriminating response from the suspect [*Brewer v. Williams*, 430 U.S. 387 (1977)].

In *Rhode Island v. Innis*, 446 U.S. 291 (1980), the U.S. Supreme Court held that the focus in determining if interrogation has occurred is on the suspect. The subjective intentions of the officer to elicit incriminating responses are not the key. The test is whether the officer should have known that the words or actions were likely to elicit an incriminating response from the suspect. Under this test, any peculiar susceptibilities of the suspect known to the police are relevant in determining what the officer should have foreseen as likely responses. In the Brewer case, the police knew that the suspect was deeply religious and that the officer's "Christian burial speech" would elicit an incriminating response from the suspect. In that case, a small child was missing and the suspect was being transported by the police. Brewer had contacted an attorney and had invoked his Miranda rights. The officer made the comment that it would be nice to locate the body so that a good Christian burial would be conducted. The suspect told the police where the body could be found, and incriminating evidence was found there. The Court held that the comments of the officer were functionally equivalent to an interrogation, because they were designed to obtain information from the suspect.

In Custody

Under the Miranda definition, a person is in custody when the individual is otherwise deprived of freedom of action in any significant way. In *Berkemer v. McCarty*,

468 U.S. 420 (1984), the U.S. Supreme Court established an objective test to determine whether the suspect was in custody. The Court stated that an officer's unarticulated plan to arrest the suspect has no bearing on the question of custody. The only relevant inquiry, according to the Court, is how a reasonable person in the suspect's situation would have understood the situation.

The Court has made a distinction between *seizure* and *custody*. To constitute custody under Miranda, the loss of freedom must be significant. Stopping a motorist on a public road to issue a traffic citation may constitute a temporary seizure, but not custody for the purposes of Miranda requirements. In determining the custody question, the nature and seriousness of the crime in question is immaterial. Even a person arrested on a minor offense should be given the Miranda warnings prior to custodial interrogation. The location of the interrogation may have a bearing on the "in custody" issue, but it is not the key factor. In *Orozco v. Texas*, 394 U.S. 324 (1969), the defendant was determined to be in custody when he was interrogated in his bedroom, whereas in *Oregon v. Mathiason*, 429 U.S. 492 (1977), the accused was not considered in custody even though the questioning took place at the police station. In the latter case, the police had informed the suspect before the interrogation began that he was not in custody, and he was allowed to leave after the questioning was completed. In the Orozco case, the officers entered the accused's home at 4:00 A.M. It was a forcible entry, and a reasonable person would have believed that the defendant was under arrest.

After the Individual Invokes Miranda

If individuals indicate that they do not want to talk or want to see an attorney, questioning must immediately stop. In *Edwards v. Arizona*, 451 U.S. 477 (1981), the U.S. Supreme Court held that when an accused has invoked the right to have counsel present during a custodial interrogation, a valid waiver of that right cannot be established by showing only that a response was given to further police-initiated custodial interrogation, even if the individual has been advised of his or her rights. An accused, having expressed the desire to deal with the police only through counsel, is not subject to further interrogation by the authorities until counsel has been made available, unless the accused initiates further communication, exchanges, or conversations with the police. The Court stated that, "this rule is designed to prevent police from badgering a defendant into waiving his previously asserted Miranda rights."

In *Fare v. Michael C.*, 442 U.S. 707 (1979), the Court referred to Miranda's "rigid rule that an accused's request for an attorney is *per se* an invocation of his Fifth Amendment rights, requiring that all interrogation cease." And, in a case where a suspect in custody had invoked his Miranda right to counsel, the Court again referred to the "undisputed right" under Miranda to remain silent and to be free of interrogation "until he had consulted with a lawyer."

The Court has held that after initially being advised of Miranda rights, the accused may validly waive the rights and respond to interrogation. In *North Carolina v. Butler*, 441 U.S. 369, 374-375 (1979), the Court indicated that additional safeguards were necessary when the accused asks for counsel. The Court held that when an accused has invoked the right to have counsel present during custodial interrogation, a valid waiver of that right cannot be established by merely showing that the accused responded to further police-initiated custodial interrogation, even if the individual has been advised of his or her rights. The Court noted in Edwards that once an accused has expressed the desire to deal with the police only through counsel, the individual is not subject to further interrogation by the authorities until counsel has been made available, unless the accused initiates further communication, exchanges, or conversations with the police.

Language Problems

If there is a question as to whether the suspect understands the English language, the officer should delay questioning until the suspect may be advised of the rights in his or her native language. As the U.S. District Court in Kansas noted in *United States v. Castorena-Jaime*, 117 F. Supp. 2d 1161 (2000), language barriers are a factor to consider, because they may impair a suspect's ability to act knowingly and intelligently. Language is not a stumbling block when the suspect is also advised of the rights in a language that is ostensibly understood. It becomes a more difficult problem when the Miranda rights are given in English only. In these instances, the courts consider what effort the officer made to communicate, whether the defendant responded that the rights were understood or ever indicated that they were not understood, and what the defendant displayed in English language skills.

The U.S. Court of Appeals for the Sixth Circuit found an English-only Miranda warning insufficient where the defendant was a West German national who had resided in the United States only three months, could not drive, had no friends in the United States other than her husband, and spoke only broken English [*United States v. Short*, 790 F.2d 464, 469 6th Cir. (1986)]. The Court looked to several other factors in reaching this conclusion. The defendant was not familiar with the American criminal justice system. A social services officer present during the interrogation testified that she questioned whether the defendant understood the implications of the answers and that she thought the defendant appeared ignorant and evidenced judgment limitations. The magistrate judge appointed an interpreter for her at trial. The defendant's written statement contained language that obviously was not hers, and the statement appeared, at best, to be the agent's interpretation of her halting English.

Fruit of the Poisonous Tree

"Despite what lower courts might sometimes incorrectly rule, failing to Mirandize a suspect does not violate the Fourth Amendment."
—Devallis Rutledge (2004, pp. 82–84)

The **Fruit of the Poison Tree Doctrine** holds that evidence obtained by exploiting an unreasonable search or seizure is subject to suppression at trial. According to Rutledge, what judges and lawyers refer to as the *derivative evidence exclusionary rule* basically makes any evidence inadmissible if it was derived from an earlier violation of the defendant's constitutional rights. Devallis Rutledge is a former police officer and chief prosecutor for the Los Angeles County District Attorney's Office.

Rutledge questions whether the same consequence follows from the failure to follow the Miranda procedures. According to Rutledge, if you learn the whereabouts of contraband or evidence from a statement that doesn't comply with Miranda, the contraband or evidence is not required to be suppressed as "poisonous fruit" of the inadmissible statement.

"Fruit of the Poison Tree" Doctrine / A rule of evidence that holds that evidence obtained by exploiting an unreasonable search or seizure is subject to suppression at trial.

When Has a Suspect Invoked Miranda Rights?

Some examples of how the courts have interpreted whether the defendant invoked rights under Miranda:

- "I guess I need a lawyer." [*People v. Zolnay*, 15 Cal. 3d 729 (1975)]
- "Is there an attorney here, present, close?" [*People v. Duran*, 132 Cal. 3d 156 (1982)]
- "Well, maybe I should talk to my attorney, Mr. Corbin." [*People v. Munoz*, 83 Cal. App. 3d 993 (1978)]
- "I don't know if I should have a lawyer here or what ...." [*People v. Russo*, 148 Cal. App. 3d 1172 (1983)]
- "Does an accused's request for counsel at an initial appearance on a charged offense constitute an invocation of his Fifth Amendment right to counsel that precludes police-initiated interrogation on unrelated, uncharged offenses?" The U.S. Supreme Court said no in *McNeil v. Wisconsin*, 501 U.S. 171 (1991).

Compare the preceding decisions with the following court decision, which held that the defendant's statement did not invoke his Miranda rights:

- "Um-hmm yeah. If I want an attorney, I got to wait all day . . . ." and "I need one, but you can go ahead and ask me questions." [*People v. Smith*, 187 Cal. App. 3d 666 (1982)]

Rutledge claims that the Miranda rule is an admissibility rule for criminal trial judges. All Miranda ever said was that courts could not admit as evidence of guilt a statement obtained by custodial interrogation, unless the defendant had first been told of the rights and had agreed to waive them and talk: "Miranda conditioned the admissibility at trial of any custodial confession, on warning a suspect of his rights." To support his contentions, he cites two cases: *Missouri v. Seibert*, 159 L. Ed. 2d 643 (2004) and *United States v. Patrone*, 948 F.2d 813 1st Cir. (1991).

Rutledge points out that a number of previous court decisions, grasping the distinction between Miranda and the Constitution, had already rejected a *fruit of the poison tree* extension of Miranda, allowing limited uses of statements and their derivative evidence. Examples of these limited uses include:

- Locating witnesses to the crime. [*Michigan v. Tucker*, 417 U.S. 433 (1974)]
- Impeaching the defendant's trial testimony. [*Harris v. New York*, 401 U.S. 222, (1971) and *Oregon v. Hass*, 420 U.S. 714 (1975)]
- Probable cause for arrest. [*United States v. Morales*, 834 F.2d 35, 38 2d Cir. (1987)]
- Probable cause for a search warrant. [*United States v. Patterson*, 812 F.2d 1188 9th Cir. (1987)]
- Recovery of physical evidence. [*United States v. Villalba-Alvarado*, 345 F.3d 1007 8th Cir. (2003)]

Rutledge warns that actual coercion, such as mistreatment or the use of threats or overbearing promises of leniency, may make a statement and its derivative fruits completely inadmissible for any purpose, and may cause civil liability if found to be so egregious as to "shock the conscience."

Exceptions to Miranda

These are the major exceptions to using admissions obtained in violation of the Miranda requirements:

- The use of voluntary statements taken without complying with the Miranda requirements for purposes of impeaching the defendant's testimony at trial—"Miranda does not give the defendant the right to lie on the stand."
- Public safety exception—when necessary to obtain information immediately.
- Where the suspect is being interrogated by an undercover agent and the suspect does not know that the agent is a law enforcement officer.

In *Harris v. New York* 401 U.S. 222 (1971), the defendant took the witness stand and denied being involved in drugs. When arrested, he had given a statement to the police regarding his drug involvement, but the defendant had not been warned as required by the Miranda case. During cross-examination at his trial, the defendant was questioned by the prosecutor regarding specific statements he had made to the police immediately following his arrest. The statements contradicted the defendant's direct testimony at trial, and the state sought to impeach the defendant with his statements. However, the State had conceded that the statements were inadmissible under Miranda during the prosecution's case. The defendant was convicted of selling heroin to an undercover police officer. On appeal, the U.S. Supreme Court held that the failure to comply with Miranda did not prevent the state from using the defendant's statement when the defendant gave conflicting testimony at trial. The Court concluded that his credibility was appropriately impeached by use of his earlier conflicting statements. The Court indicated that Miranda did not provide a shield that permitted defendants to give false testimony at trial time.

Two state supreme courts, California and Hawaii, adopted a stricter standard and do not allow the use of the statements. In both states, the state legislatures passed statutes allowing the use of the statements for impeachment purposes as long as the statements met the voluntarily test.

In *Michigan v. Tucker*, 417 U.S. 433 (1974), during a custodial interrogation, the defendant gave police the name of an alibi witness. The witness actually gave incriminating evidence to police. A defective Miranda warning was given to the defendant prior to him making the statement. The U.S. Supreme Court noted that the respondent had been apprised of his right to counsel, that the respondent stated that he did not want one, and that the only defect was the failure to inform him that counsel would be provided free if he could not afford one. The Court held that this was a far cry from the compulsory incrimination prohibited by the Fifth Amendment, which Miranda was designed to prevent. The Court held that this failure did not require the exclusion of evidence obtained as a result of the statement, particularly where the statement itself was excluded. The Court noted the defendant's statement was not involuntary, and that the trustworthiness of the witness's evidence was not implicated by the circumstances surrounding his interrogation. **Note:** The statement was not admissible, but the evidence obtained as the result of the statement—that is, the alibi witness's testimony—was admissible.

The public safety exception was addressed in the case of *New York v. Quarles*, 467 U.S. 649 (1984). Benjamin Quarles was charged in a New York trial court with criminal possession of a weapon. The trial court suppressed the gun in question, as well as a statement made by the respondent, because the statement was obtained by police before they read the respondent his Miranda rights. That ruling was affirmed on appeal through the New York Court of Appeals. The U.S. Supreme Court reversed and concluded that under the circumstances involved in the case, overriding considerations of public safety justified the officer's failure to provide Miranda warnings before he asked questions devoted to locating the abandoned weapon.

The record showed that a woman approached two police officers who were on road patrol, told them that she had just been raped, described her assailant, and told them that the man had just entered a nearby Safeway supermarket and was carrying a gun. While one of the officers radioed for assistance, the other (Officer Kraft) entered the store and spotted Quarles, who matched the description given by the woman. Quarles ran toward the rear of the store, and Officer Kraft pursued him with a drawn gun, but lost sight of him for several seconds. Upon regaining sight of him, Officer Kraft ordered him to stop and put his hands over his head, frisked him, and discovered that he was wearing an empty shoulder holster. After handcuffing him, Officer Kraft asked him where the gun was. Quarles nodded toward some empty cartons and responded that "the gun is over there." Officer Kraft then retrieved the gun from one of the cartons, formally arrested the respondent, and read him his rights under Miranda. Quarles indicated that he would answer questions without an attorney being present and admitted that he owned the gun and had purchased it in Florida. The trial court excluded his initial statement and the gun because he had not yet been given the Miranda warnings, and also excluded the respondent's other statements as evidence tainted by the Miranda violation. Both the Appellate Division of the New York Supreme Court and the New York Court of Appeals affirmed. The U.S. Supreme Court reversed and held that the statements were admissible because the officer's actions were reasonable based on public safety.

An undercover law enforcement officer posing as a fellow inmate was not required to give Miranda warnings to an incarcerated suspect before asking questions that could elicit an incriminating response because no custodial interrogation occurred [*Illinois v. Perkins*, 496 U.S. 292 (1990)]. **Note:** In the Perkins case, the accused had not been formally charged and therefore the Sixth Amendment prohibition against interrogating a person without the accused's attorney present did not apply.

The Court in the Perkins case stated that the Miranda doctrine must be enforced strictly, but only in situations where the concerns underlying that decision are present. Those concerns are not implicated in Perkins, since the essential ingredients of a "police dominated atmosphere" and compulsion are lacking. It is Miranda's premise that the danger of coercion results from the interaction of custody and official interrogation, whereby the suspect may feel compelled to speak due to fear of reprisal for remaining silent or in the hope of more lenient treatment should a confession be made. That coercive atmosphere is not present when an incarcerated person speaks freely to someone who is believed to be a fellow inmate and who is assumed not to be an officer having official power over the incarcerated person. In such circumstances, Miranda does not forbid mere strategic deception by taking advantage of a suspect's misplaced trust.

The Court noted that the only difference between the Perkins case and *Hoffa v. United States*, 385 U.S. 293—which upheld the placing of an undercover agent near a suspect in order to gather incriminating information—was that Perkins was incarcerated. Detention, however, whether or not for the crime in question, does not warrant a presumption that such use of an undercover agent renders involuntary the incarcerated suspect's resulting confession. *Mathis v. United States*, 391 U.S. 1, held that an inmate's statements to a known agent were inadmissible because no Miranda warnings were given. When suspects do not know that they are speaking to a government agent, there is no reason to assume the possibility of coercion. *Massiah v.*

CASE STUDY: How Would You Rule?

Assume that you are the trial judge in the *State v. Allen* case in which the defendant Allen is being tried for murder. Would you allow Allen's statements to be admitted into evidence? Would you allow the gun to be admitted into evidence? If fingerprints were taken from the gun, would the fingerprints be admissible?

Facts: On the night of September 9, Sacramento Police Officer Haynes responded to a report that a father had shot his son. Haynes arrived at the intersection of East Levee Road and Northgate Boulevard, and was met by Leon Danker, an eyewitness to the shooting. Danker informed Haynes that he heard gunshots, and later saw that the victim's head was bleeding.

Danker, who was homeless, led Haynes to his campsite. Allen's son, Steve, was there, lying in a sleeping bag with his head in a pool of blood from a gunshot wound to the head. Danker's campsite was located under a tree and was covered by bushes. Allen lived in a nearby campsite. Officer Haynes was soon after joined by Officer Hill and a police dog. They searched the campsites and nearby vicinity, but were unable to find Allen or the gun.

Officers Miller and Louie heard a broadcast of the shooting and description of Allen. As these officers searched along Del Paso Boulevard, they observed Allen at a gas station pay phone, about a mile and a half from the crime scene. The officers took him into custody, but did not inform him of his Miranda rights. They performed a pat-down search of Allen and found a kitchen knife in his right front pants pocket. A search of the immediate area and the phone booth did not reveal any other weapons, but an open twelve-pack of beer was found on the ground near where Allen was arrested.

Officers Hahn and Martin, who had been at the crime scene, went to assist Officers Louie and Miller. After Allen was identified by Danker, Officers Hahn and Martin took custody of Allen, and escorted him back to the crime scene. They did not give Allen Miranda warnings, but while in the police car, Officer Martin stated to Allen that "the weapon used was supposedly a gun," but that no gun had been found. The officer then told Allen that "if the wrong person found the gun, it could hurt someone else."

Upon arriving at the crime scene, the following conversation took place between Allen and Officer Martin:

Allen: How is he? Is he going to make it?

Officer: I don't know.

Allen: I want to go see the body. He's not supposed to die.

Officer: I can't do that. The body is at UCD Med Center.

Allen: Is he still alive? Just tell me he is still alive.

Officer: I don't know. As far as I know, he is.

Allen: I think I can show you where the gun is.

Officer: Will you try? If not, someone can get hurt with that same gun.

Allen: I'm not positive because I blacked out, but I am pretty sure I can. If you and maybe one other officer go with me, I'll try. We have to walk. Its [sic] about 20 to 30 minutes [sic] walk from here. Tell me my son is not going to die. He's not supposed to die.

Officer: At this point he's being worked on at the Med Center. What his condition is, I don't know.

Allen: I don't want this to happen to someone else. I think I can show you. The gun is in a black backpack. We have to start at the bridge on Northgate south of the levee.

[To see how the U.S. Court of Appeals for the Ninth Circuit ruled on the issue, read *Allen v. Roe*, 305 F.3d 1046 (2002). Why is the case named *Allen v. Roe* rather than *State v. Allen*? Because Allen, while in a California prison, filed a writ of *habeas corpus* in federal court stating that his conviction violated his federal constitutional rights. Roe was the state prison warden, i.e., the individual restraining the freedom of Allen.]

bright-line rule / A rule that has been established by court decisions that provides clear guidance to police officers.

United States, 377 U.S. 201, and similar cases—which held that the government may not use an undercover agent to circumvent the Sixth Amendment right to counsel once a suspect has been charged—were inapplicable in Perkins, because here no murder charges had been filed at the time of the interrogation. Also, unavailing was Perkins' argument that a **bright-line rule** for the application of Miranda is desirable, since the Court noted law enforcement officers will have little difficulty applying the holding of the Perkins case.

In Perkins, the undercover officer questioned the uncharged suspect. In *Kuhlmann v. Wilson*, 477 U.S. 436 (1986), the U.S. Supreme Court noted that the Sixth Amendment did not forbid the admission in evidence of an indicted defendant's statements to a jailhouse informant who was "placed in close proximity but made no effort to stimulate conversations about the crime charged."

May Congress Overturn the Miranda Requirements?

Does the U.S. Congress have the authority to pass legislation that overturns the Miranda requirements? This question has been the subject of numerous debates among constitutional scholars. On several occasions, legislation has been introduced that would overturn the requirements. The proposals have never been enacted into law. The U.S. Supreme Court addressed this issue in *Dickerson v. United States*, 530 U.S. 428 (2000).

The Court stated that Congress may not legislatively supersede our decisions interpreting and applying the Constitution. This issue therefore turns on whether the Miranda Court announced a constitutional rule or merely exercised its supervisory authority to regulate evidence in the absence of congressional direction. The Court stated that, "relying on the fact that we have created several exceptions to Miranda's warnings requirement and that we have repeatedly referred to the Miranda warnings as 'prophylactic,' and 'not themselves rights protected by the Constitution,' the Court of Appeals in the Dickerson case [wrongly] concluded that the protections announced in Miranda were not constitutionally required." The Court noted that many of its subsequent cases have also referred to Miranda's constitutional underpinnings. The Court also stated, "Prophylactic though it may be, in protecting a defendant's Fifth Amendment privilege against self-incrimination, Miranda safeguards a fundamental trial right."

VOLUNTARINESS OF A CONFESSION

Even if the Miranda requirements are complied with, the confession or other statement taken from a suspect must meet the voluntariness test. Earlier in this chapter, the tactics used in Brown and Ashcraft to obtain a confession were discussed. While those two cases establish that there are definite limitations on police conduct in many cases, the distinction between what is permissible and what is illegal conduct is not so clear.

Several states have passed legislation or rules of criminal procedure to provide the police with a bright-line rule as to what is permissible and what is not when interrogating a suspect. A typical procedural rule is the State of New York's rule:

§ 60.45. New York Rules of evidence; admissibility of statements of defendants [NY CLS CPL § 60.45 (2006)]

1. Evidence of a written or oral confession, admission, or other statement made by a defendant with respect to his participation or lack of participation in the offense charged, may not be received in evidence against him in a criminal proceeding if such statement was involuntarily made.

2. A confession, admission, or other statement is "involuntarily made" by a defendant when it is obtained from him:
   (a) By any person by the use or threatened use of physical force upon the defendant or another person, or by means of any other improper conduct or undue pressure which impaired the defendant's physical or mental condition to the extent of undermining his ability to make a choice whether or not to make a statement; or
   (b) By a public servant engaged in law enforcement activity or by a person then acting under his direction or in cooperation with him:
      i. by means of any promise or statement of fact, which promise or statement creates a substantial risk that the defendant might falsely incriminate himself; or
      ii. in violation of such rights as the defendant may derive from the constitution of this state or of the United States.

The New York Committee that drafted this rule noted in its comments that:

The logical rule with respect to a confession or other inculpatory statement of a defendant would probably be that it is always admissible as an admission against interest, but that its weight and truth may and should be reduced or discounted in the eyes of the triers of the facts by evidence that it was involuntarily made. In the case of statements made to law enforcement and other public officials, however, it has long been a public policy doctrine that proof of involuntariness precludes admissibility thereof. Although Criminal Code § 395 [prior rule] rendered inadmissible an involuntary statement made to "a private person" as well as one made "in the course of judicial proceedings," the term *private person* is intended to embrace public officers (*People v. Rogers*, 1908, 192 NY 331, 350, 85 NE 135);

and, indeed, the only real importance of the inadmissibility rule lies in its application to statements made to public servants or to persons acting under their direction or in cooperation with them. The new rule limits its scope.

Subdivision 2 excludes from evidence every such statement obtained by any kind of pressure or under any circumstances that the courts and fair-minded people in general do or might consider coercive, unjust, improper, or in any way conducive to possible false self-incrimination.

Judicial Decisions on Voluntariness of Statements

Court decisions on the voluntariness of statements are founded on either the concept that some police misconduct may produce a confession from an innocent person or the admission of evidence obtained by such means is an affront to the integrity of the judicial system. The problem for law enforcement officers is that appellate courts differ on what constitutes misconduct sufficient to hold a statement inadmissible.

The issue of voluntariness concerns police or law enforcement tactics. If a confession is obtained without the knowledge or participation of the police, or if police participation is sufficiently limited, the confession is fully admissible at a trial [*People v. Jones* (1978, New York 2d Dept) 402 NYS2d 28, (affirmed on appeal) 393 NE2d 443 (1979)]. In the Jones case, security personnel at a major department store may have used unwarranted tactics with a suspected shoplifter, but since the police were not involved, the suspect's statement was admissible.

One court noted that in determining whether a confession was voluntary, bearing on the personal characteristics of the confessor, consideration should be given to age, education and intelligence, physical and emotional condition at the time of the interrogation, and prior experience with the police. Those factors which, on the other hand, must be looked at to determine the amount of police pressure used to induce the confession include the length of interrogation and delay in arraignment; the general conditions under which the interrogation took place; any extreme psychological or physical pressure; possible inducements, methods, and stratagems that were used by the police; and, of course, whether the confessor was apprised of the right to counsel and privilege against self-incrimination [*State v. Wallace*, 207 N.W.2d 855 Wis. (1973)].

The U.S. Supreme Court [*Rogers v. Richmond*, 365 U.S. 534 (1961)] stated that the attention of the trial judge should be focused, for purposes of the U.S. Constitution, on the question of whether the behavior of the State's law enforcement officials was such as to overbear the petitioner's will to resist and bring about confessions not freely self-determined—a question to be answered with complete disregard of whether or not the petitioner in fact spoke the truth. The employment of a standard infected by the inclusion of references to probable reliability resulted in a constitutionally invalid conviction, pursuant to which Rogers is now detained "in violation of the Constitution." A defendant has the right to be tried according to the substantive and procedural due process requirements of the Fourteenth Amendment. This means that a vital confession, such as is involved in this case, may go to the jury only if it is subjected to screening in accordance with correct constitutional standards.

Following are some examples of confessions that were considered by the courts as voluntary:

- The defendant claimed that he confessed only because God told him to confess. [*Colorado v. Connely*, 107 S.Ct. 515 (1986)]
- At the time of the confession, the defendant has a .20 blood alcohol level. [*People v. Murtishaw*, 29 Cal. 3d. 733 (1981)]
- The defendant was under the influence of drugs at the time of his confession, but his responses to the questions were coherent. [*People v. Missin*, 128 Cal. 3d 1015 (1982)]

Burden of Proof

The burden of showing that a confession of crime has not been obtained by improper means, that it is a voluntary act, uninduced by hope of favor or fear of harm, is one which the law casts upon the state (*Nicholson v. State*, 38 Md. 140; *Green v. State*, 96 Md. 384, 54 A. 104; *Bram v. United States*, 168 U.S. [532], 571, 18 S. Ct. 183, 42 L. Ed. 568; *Watts v. State*, 99 Md. 30, 57 A. 542; *Toomer v. State*, 112 Md. [285] 292,

76 A. 118). When the prosecution fails to meet this obligation, it is improper to admit the confession.

Length of Interrogation

Compare the interrogation tactics discussed earlier in the Ashcraft case with those in *People v. House*, 566 N.E. 2d 259 (1990). In House, the defendant was held in an interview room for forty-nine hours and questioned intermittently by the police. He was given his rights and did not request an attorney. He also did not complain of mistreatment during the questioning. He was not handcuffed, was allowed to use the restroom, and was fed at regular intervals. The Illinois Supreme Court found that the confession was voluntary. The state court noted:

> Although, as we have indicated, the deprivation of basic facilities is a factor to be considered against the State, the "stark environment" of the interview room is not so weighty a factor as the defendant contends. A jail cell is hardly a paradise for the senses, yet defendants properly processed and charged can be held there for lengthy periods of time.
>
> We now turn to the duration of the defendant's detention in the interview room. Although we do not believe this factor, considered with others present here, should render this defendant's statement involuntary, and although we realize that the drawing of a bright line would be unworkable given the totality-of-the-circumstances standard we must apply, this is perhaps the appropriate case to caution the police regarding brinkmanship. Given even a slightly different set of circumstances, the result might very well have been different. Having said that, we find here that the length of time the defendant was detained prior to his statements is not such a great departure from established precedents that it requires suppression of the defendant's statements.

While the length of detention is a very important consideration in determining whether statements or a confession were voluntarily made, in State v. Herrington, 165 N. W. 2d 120 (1969) the U.S. Supreme Court considered the threshold question is whether the period of detention was unreasonably long in the first instance. Statements made during a period of unreasonable detainment will be excluded in most states whether voluntary or involuntary. As to the time factor, Inbau et al. (2001, p. 596) opined that a competent interrogator will rarely require more than four hours to obtain a confession from an offender. They also contend that the suggested four-hour or less rule is less likely to be viewed by a court or jury as unreasonable than one that is extended over a longer period of time.

Psychological Coercion

In this section, we will examine how the psychological persuasion tactics used by the police affect the admission of a confession. The leading case on the use of psychological coercion is *Spano v. New York*, 360 U.S. 315 (1959).

After having been indicted in a New York State court on a charge of murder, Spano was subjected to prolonged interrogation by numerous law enforcement officers beginning in the early evening and continuing into the night and following morning. The defendant's requests to see his attorney were denied. The court held that his will, in accordance with his attorney's instructions, not to answer questions of the police, was overborne by official pressure, fatigue, and sympathy falsely aroused. In the latter respect the record disclosed that a police officer, a relative of the defendant, whom the defendant had first contacted by telephone, was instructed by his superiors to falsely state that because of this telephone call his job was in jeopardy, and that loss of his job would be disastrous to his three children, his wife, and his unborn child. At the trial, the confession was introduced in evidence over appropriate objections. The jury returned a verdict of guilty and the defendant was sentenced to death. The New York Court of Appeals affirmed the conviction over three dissents. The U.S. Supreme Court reversed and held that the confession was involuntary.

The U.S. Supreme Court noted in *Arizona v. Fulminante*, 499 U.S. 279 (1991) that a finding of coercion does not need actual physical violence by a government agent and that a credible threat is sufficient. The Court stated that "coercion can be mental as well as physical, and . . . the blood of the accused is not the only hallmark of an unconstitutional inquisition." In *Payne v. Arkansas*, 356 U.S. 560 (1958), the Court found that a confession was coerced because the interrogating police officer had promised that if the accused confessed, the officer would protect the accused from an angry mob outside the jailhouse door.

In the case of *Biscoe v. State*, 67 Md. 6, 8 A. 571, the in-custody defendant, although pressed often to make a confession, persisted in denying his guilt. It was not until he was told by the committing magistrate, "that it would be better for him to tell the truth, and have no more trouble about it," that he confessed. A Maryland appellate court held that the confession was inadmissible. The appellate court noted that a simple caution to the accused to tell the truth, if he says anything, was permissible. But where the admonition to speak the truth has been coupled with an expression importing that it would be better for him to do so, makes the confession inadmissible. The court found that the objectionable words "being that it would be better to speak the truth, because they import that it would be better for him to say something" was a warning not to remain silent.

In *United States v. Jackson*, 918 F.2d 236 1st Cir. Mass. (1990), the defendant confessed that a firearm was his. He contended on appeal that his confession was based on an indirect threat by the police that if he did not confess that his sister would be prosecuted. The U.S. Court of Appeals held that the confession was voluntary. The appellate court noted that there was no evidence that he was subjected to direct threats or promises. Moreover, even if the court were to assume that the police did use an implied "threat" or "promise" that Jackson's sister might be caused or spared harm, depending on whether or not Jackson admitted ownership of the firearm, the court still could not conclude that his will was overborne. The court noted that Congress and the courts have indicated that to determine voluntariness it is necessary to look at the totality of the circumstances, including any promises or threats made by police officers or the prosecution, in order to see whether the will of the accused was overborne.

The court also noted that there was no evidence that an especially close relationship existed between Jackson and his sister, or that Jackson was unusually susceptible to psychological coercion on that account or any other, particularly in light of Jackson's very substantial previous experience with the criminal justice system. The totality of these circumstances indicates that Jackson did not lose volitional control, nor was his will overborne.

A threat to send the suspect to prison for a more serious offense unless he admits to the present offense was considered by one court as a coercive threat [*State v.*

Harvey, 259 P. 21 (1927)]. A similar holding was reached in California, where a juvenile was threatened with prosecution as an adult and a prison term unless he admitted he committed the crime [*In re G.*, 125 Cal. Rptr. 625 Cal. App. 2d Dist. (1975)].

In the *In re G.* case, the court stated that the voluntary or involuntary nature of the *statement*, "does not depend upon the bare language of the inducement but rather upon the nature of the benefit to be derived by a defendant if he speaks the truth, as represented by the police." The court noted that while the interrogating officers used bare language informing the juvenile that they could not promise probation or parole, they made it crystal clear to him that he had no hope of anything other than incarceration if he did not confess. The interrogators sought to convey to the juvenile that as police, they had the power to determine whether he would be tried as an adult and sentenced to state prison for life, and that they would exercise that power if he did not admit his part in the crime.

In *Leyra v. Denno*, 347 U.S. 556 (1953), the U.S. Supreme Court held that a confession should be excluded. In that case, a police psychiatrist posing as a physician urged the defendant to confess to a murder of which the defendant was accused. The confession was made, but the Court barred its use as evidence at trial. The Court in that case also considered the defendant's fatigue and susceptibility to suggestion to make the method of obtaining the confession constitutionally impermissible.

When an issue of fact arises as to the influence of fear produced by threats and confessions made under inducement, it is not a question of law for the court to decide, but a question of fact for the jury under proper instructions. Where threats or inducements are conceded by the state or where facts are admitted, which as a matter of law constituted threats or inducements, it is a question of law for the court [*State v. Seablom*, 103 Wash. 53 (1926)].

In *McCalvin v. Yukins*, 2006 FED App. 0119P 6th Cir. (2006), the U.S. Court of Appeals examined the claim that Traci L. McCalvin's confession was involuntary. McCalvin was convicted of second-degree murder. During her state criminal trial, she moved to suppress her confession, but the trial court denied the motion. A federal district court found her confession involuntary because, among other things, a detective told her that if she were convicted of first-degree murder, she would not have contact with her family, including her children. The U.S. Court of Appeals reversed the district court's decision and held that the confession was admissible.

McCalvin had been interrogated for several hours before a Detective Helgert took over the interrogation for approximately the next one and one-half hours. McCalvin declined any food, coffee, or water. For the first thirty to forty-five minutes, McCalvin continued to maintain that the death was an accident. During this time, however, Helgert became more confrontational. He told McCalvin that the officers did not believe her. He gave her a "hook," a question aimed to get a defendant to admit to a crime while simultaneously shifting the blame away, by asking McCalvin if she had merely tried to scare Branch by driving toward her. McCalvin testified at her trial that Helgert told her that if she changed her story, the prosecutor might drop the charges. She also testified that Helgert told her that she could go home if she changed her story to say that she had intended to only scare Branch. Helgert never admitted to promising McCalvin anything, but he testified that he told McCalvin that if she went to prison for first-degree murder, she would spend the rest of her life in prison and would not have contact with her family, including her children.

The appellate court noted that the district court had relied on the decision in *United States v. Tingle*, 658 F.2d 1332 9th Cir. (1981), but stated that Tingle is distinguishable. In Tingle, an FBI agent told the defendant that she would not see her child "for a while" if she went to prison. However, unlike this case, the agent promised the defendant that her cooperation would be communicated to the prosecutor, but if the defendant refused to cooperate the agent threatened to tell the prosecutor that she was "stubborn or hard-headed." Finally, the defendant sobbed and was noticeably shaking for at least ten minutes before confessing. In this case, the agent testified that Tingle appeared unemotional. The appellate court stated that while it did not approve of the tactics used by the interrogator, the confession was voluntary.

In *Colorado v. Spring*, 479 U.S. 564 (1987), the U.S. Supreme Court held that the inquiry of whether a waiver of the right to remain silent is coerced has two distinct dimensions. First, the relinquishment of the right must be voluntary in the sense that it is the product of a free and deliberate choice rather than intimidation, coercion, or deception. Second, the waiver must be made with a full awareness both of the nature of the right being abandoned and the consequences of the decision to abandon it. Only if the totality of the circumstances surrounding the interrogation reveals both an uncoerced choice and the requisite level of comprehension may a court properly conclude that the Miranda rights have been waived.

Promises

In this section, we will examine the affect of promises on the question of the admissibility of a confession. A confession obtained by promises of immunity or mitigation of punishment is inadmissible [*Ashby v. State* (1976), 265 Ind. 316, 354 N.E.2d 192]. However, vague and indefinite statements by the police such as "seeing what they could do for him" or "it would be in his best interest to tell the real story" are not sufficient inducements to preclude use of a confession obtained thereby [*Ortiz v. State* (1976), 265 Ind. 549, 356 N.E.2d 1188; *Perry v. State* (1978), 176 Ind. App. 120, 374 N.E.2d 558]. The promise to "help in every way he could" is also too vague and indefinite to constitute the type of an inducement that renders a confession involuntary.

In *Freeman v. State*, 258 Ark. 617, 527 S.W. 2d 909 (1975), the prosecuting attorney had simply stated that if the defendant made the confession, "he could not make any promises but that if he had committed a crime it was probably one that would not result in more than twenty-one years incarceration." The Arkansas appellate court noted that there is a presumption that an in-custody confession is involuntary and the burden is upon the state to show the statement to have been voluntarily, freely, and understandably made, without hope of reward or fear of punishment. It was undisputed that the deputy sheriff stated, "I'll help you any way that I can," and the officer did not do anything to help him. The court held that the confession was involuntary and reversed the conviction.

The same Arkansas appellate court noted that it is often difficult to determine whether an officer's statement is a promise of reward or leniency, a statement meant to deceive, or merely an admonishment to tell the truth. In *Wright v. State*, 267 Ark. 264, 590 S.W.2d 15 (1979), the court allowed a statement by an interrogating officer that, "things would go easier if you told the truth." The court in that case noted that Wright differed from Tatum because in Tatum the promise was false. The court established the rule that when a police officer makes a false promise that misleads a suspect, and the suspect gives a confession because of that false promise, then the confession has not been made voluntarily, knowingly, and intelligently. The court also noted that for the statement to be involuntary, the promise must have been induced or influenced the confession. By the last statement, the court seems to imply that a false statement or promise of an immaterial matter would not make the statement involuntary.

In *Commonwealth v. Williams*, 388 Mass. 846 (1983), the court stated that an officer may indicate that the person's cooperation would be brought to the attention of the public officials or others involved, or may state in general terms that cooperation has been considered favorably by the courts in the past. What is prohibited is not a general statement about the value of cooperation, but a promise that cooperation by the defendant will aid the defense or result in a lesser sentence being imposed.

How Would You Rule as a Trial Judge?

The defendant was arrested for rape and murder. While being interrogated by an officer, he asked the police officer if he would be sentenced to death for his crime. The police officer stated: "Sam, to be honest with you, I would think that the courts in your situation would be very lenient. I really do. I think that they will observe the fact that you need help—you're trying to seek that help already, psychological, psychiatric help, and I think they would recommend a psychiatrist." The defendant was black and had professed a dislike for "honkies." The police used a black officer to interrogate him, hoping to obtain a psychological advantage.

Question: Taken together, does the statement of the police officer and use of the black officer establish improper psychological techniques and thus result in a confession that is not the result of the free will and rational choice of the defendant?

Court's Decision: The court held in this factual situation that the confession was admissible. The court stated that the comments were not promises of leniency and that predictions about future events are not the same as a promise of leniency. The court also stated that there is nothing inherently wrong with the police's efforts to create a favorable climate for confession and that the use of the black police officer, even though designed to gain a psychological advantage, was not improper [*Hawkins v. Lynaugh*, 844 F.2d. 1132 5th Cir. (1988)].

Trickery and Deceit

The U.S. Supreme Court has sanctioned the use of trickery and deceit in interrogation [*Frazier v. Cupp*, 394 U.S. 731 (1969)]. The Court indicated that unlike promises, trickery and deceit do not present the risk of inducing false confessions. In the Frazier case, the petitioner claimed that his confession was involuntary and that it should have been excluded for that reason. The Court held that the confession was voluntary so as to render it admissible in a state criminal prosecution. This was despite the fact that the police falsely told him that his associate had confessed, and that during the questioning the defendant stated that, "I think I had better get a lawyer before I talk any more; I am going to get into trouble more than I am in now," and the officer replied, "You can't be in any more trouble than you are in now." The Court noted: (1) the defendant received partial warnings of his constitutional rights before he made any incriminating statements, having been told that he could have an attorney if he wanted one and that anything he said could be used against him at trial; (2) the questioning was of short duration, lasting slightly more than one hour; and (3) the defendant was a mature individual of normal intelligence. The Court held that this misrepresentation was insufficient to make an otherwise voluntary confession inadmissible. The Court stated that the issue of voluntariness must be decided by viewing the "totality of the circumstances." In *People v. Afieri*, 95 Cal. 3rd 533 (1982), however, a California court held that a confession obtained after a defendant was informed that his fingerprints were found on a flashlight used in the crime was inadmissible.

In *Willis v. State*, 268 Ind. 269, 273, 374 N.E.2d 520, 523 (1978), the accused agreed to take a polygraph examination. Prior to the examination he signed a statement that included the phrase, "I understand that the results of this polygraph (lie detector) test may be used in court against me or for me, that it may become an exhibit in any trial in which I may be involved." Willis submitted to the polygraph after being informed, falsely, that his co-defendant had implicated him in the crime. He confessed after he failed the examination. The court stated that one does not easily suppose that a false confession will be elicited by a false report of an accusation. The admissibility of a confession is predicated on its reliability, not on an agreement that it may be admitted. The court stated, however, the same is not true of a stipulation to take a lie detector test. Viewed as a matter of contract, the stipulation was based on a misrepresentation of fact. One can easily imagine that an innocent suspect, confronted with a false report that a perpetrator had implicated the suspect, would agree to a lie detector test in the belief that it would exonerate the suspect. The court held that the confession was inadmissible.

NONTESTIMONIAL EVIDENCE

The Fifth and Sixth Amendments do not apply to nontestimonial evidence. In some situations, however, the Fourth Amendment restrictions on search or seizure may apply. Those restrictions are discussed in Chapter 6. Accordingly, a suspect may be forced to incriminate himself or herself by:

- submitting to a blood test
- submitting to a voice test
- giving a DNA sample
- appearing in a lineup
- producing a sample of his or her handwriting

How Would You Rule as a Trial Judge?

Timothy McVeigh was arrested for bombing the Oklahoma City federal building, which caused many deaths. A federal grand jury issued a subpoena ordering him to furnish exemplars of his handwriting. He refused, contending that the subpoena was a violation of his Fifth Amendment privilege against self-incrimination. As judge, how would you rule? [To read how the federal district court judge ruled see *United States v. McVeigh*, 896 F. Supp. 1549 W.D. Okla (1995)].

IMMUNITY

The rule against self-incrimination does not apply if the individual being questioned has been granted immunity, in which case the government may compel the testimony of a witness. The principle involved is that when immunity is granted, the witness's testimony is not self-incriminating. There are two types of immunity: (1) transactional, and (2) use and derivative use. If a person receives *transactional immunity*, he or she cannot be prosecuted for the transaction about which the witness was compelled to testify. It is the broadest type of immunity and gives the witnesses greater protection than is constitutionally required [*Kastigar v. United States*, 406 U.S. 441 (1972)].

Use and derivative use immunity restricts the government from using the testimony or any other information obtained directly or indirectly from the testimony. The government may still prosecute a person who has use and derivative use immunity as long as the government establishes that the evidence it offers at trial was derived from a legitimate independent source.

In Kastigar, the U.S. Supreme Court held that use and derivative use immunity was sufficient to compel a person to testify regarding an event. The Court noted that the burden was on the government to establish that the evidence used to convict the defendant was not obtained as a result of the compelled testimony. In *United States v. North*, 920 F.2d. 940 D.C. Cir. (1990), a court of appeals held that the government did not fulfill its burden of showing that the evidence was free from the taint of immunized testimony, where the government witnesses used at trial had seen Oliver North's immunized testimony on national television.

THE ART OF LISTENING

An important part of both interviewing and interrogating is listening to the responses. Poor listening habits frequently cause the loss of information. Wolvin and Coakley (1982, p. 6) list three approaches to effective listening: listening for comprehension, listening for empathy, and listening for evaluation.

Listening for comprehension is a method of receiving information and requires little or no feedback from the listener. Under this method, the listener's purpose is to understand and remain objective. The listener does not inspect critically each question, answer, or reaction. This approach is commonly used in the initial segment of an interview.

The *listening with empathy* approach is a method of responding beyond merely receiving the message being conveyed. Empathic listening is a total response and it reassures, comforts, and expresses warmth. It is not synonymous with showing sympathy. For example, the officer may state to a crime victim, "I understand your feelings regarding the robbery, but I need a description of the person who snatched your purse." One key to empathic listening is saying verbally and nonverbally to the aggrieved person, "I understand your feelings."

The third approach to listening is *listening for evaluation*. Evaluative listening is important, but the person must be careful and guard against expressing evaluations verbally and nonverbally during the interview if the need or desire is for the interviewee to be cooperative and disclose information.

SUMMARY

- Interviewing is a nonaccusatory questioning of an individual who may have information needed by the interviewer. Interrogation is an accusatory questioning of a suspect.

- The general purpose of an interview is to obtain information, whereas the purpose of an interrogation it to obtain a confession or evidence that can be used to convict a defendant.

- The basic objectives in both interviews and interrogations in law enforcement are to obtain accurate information, distinguish fact from fiction, identify and convict the offender, and assist the victim of a crime.

- Interviewing is an art that requires skills.

- An interview should attempt to determine what happened and why.

- The directive approach to interviewing is where the interviewer controls the pacing and question, whereas in the nondirective approach, the interviewer allows the interviewee to determine the approach and scope of the interview.

- Interviews frequently take either the sympathetic or the logical approach. In the sympathetic approach, the interviewer attempts to sympathize with the interviewee. In the logical approach, the interviewer establishes a superior psychological position and conducts a "no nonsense" interview.

- The first few minutes of an interview are critical in determining the amount of information that will be received from the interview.

- The *Terry v. Ohio* case upheld the right of a police officer to stop and question a suspicious person.

- Rutledge defines an interrogation as a "controlled questioning calculated to discover and confirm the truth from the responses of an individual, in spite of his or her intentions and efforts to conceal the truth."

- A confession is a direct acknowledgment of guilt, whereas an admission is an admission of some key facts, but is not an acknowledgment of guilt.

- Reid's "Nine Steps of Interrogation" is used by many police interrogators to obtain a confession or an admission.

- The results of polygraph and CVSA tests are normally not admissible in evidence and should be used only as a supplement to the investigation.

- Lieberman has developed techniques to identify deception. He has divided his forty-six clues into seven sections. The sections are body language, emotional states, interpersonal interactions, verbal content, how something is said, psychological profile, and general indications of deceit.

- Both the Fifth and Sixth Amendments to the U.S. Constitution limit police interrogations.

- Under the Sixth Amendment, a defendant may not be questioned without the presence or consent of an attorney if the individual has been formally charged.

- Under the Escobedo case, a suspect has the right to an attorney whenever the investigation focuses on the suspect and is no longer a general inquiry.

- Prior to conducting interrogations or functionally equivalent questioning of an individual who is in custody, the individual must be advised of Miranda rights.

- A person is in custody, for Miranda rule purposes, when the individual is deprived of freedom of action in any significant way.

- When the individual invokes Miranda rights, the questioning must stop and may not be started unless the individual initiates the questioning. This rule is to prevent the police from badgering an individual into waiving the rights.

- For a waiver of Miranda rights to be effective, the individual must understand what rights are being given up. This requirement creates problems if the individual has difficulty in understanding the English language.

- There are three major exceptions to the Miranda rule, provided the statement is otherwise voluntary: the use of the statement to impeach a defendant's testimony at trial, public safety, and questioning by undercover agents.

- To determine if a confession is voluntary, the courts use the totality of circumstances test.

- The burden of proof to establish that a confession was voluntary is on the prosecution.

- The length of the interrogation is one factor considered by the courts in looking at the issue of whether the confession was voluntarily given.

- The use of tricks and deceptions are generally permissible, but psychological coercion is not. False promises may make the confession involuntary.

- The Fifth and Sixth Amendments do not apply to nontestimonial evidence.

Classroom Discussion Questions and Activities

1. Observe interview segments on television and rate the interviews good or bad according to whether the interviewer accomplished his or her goals.

2. Divide the class into pairs and have the students practice interviewing witnesses at a crime scene.

3. Listen to a local news interview or classroom interview and identify the listening approaches being used.

4. Read an interview in *Time, Newsweek, U.S. News & World Report,* or another news magazine. Try to determine the levels of interactions used in the listening process.

Websites and Other Resources

Bureau of Justice Statistics Law Enforcement Statistics:
www.ojp.usdoj.gov/bjs/lawenf.htm

Law Enforcement: The Phoenix Police Department:
www.ci.phoenix.az.us/POLICE/policidx.html

BJA Law Enforcement Training Database:
www.bjatraining.ncjrs.gov

Federal Law Enforcement Training Center:
www.fletc.gov

Florida Department of Law Enforcement:
www.fdle.state.fl.us/index.html

Florida Department of Environmental Protection (FDEP) Information on Environmental Investigations:
www.dep.state.fl.us/law

Louisiana Commission on Law Enforcement Home Page:
www.cole.state.la.us

Robert Longley's Government Information Newsletter:
www.usgovinfo.guide@about.com

References

Hoag, T. (2006). *Prior bad acts*. New York: Bantam.

Inbau, F. E., Reid, J. E., Buckley, J. P., & Jayne, B. C. (2004). *Criminal interrogation and confessions* (4th ed.). Sudbury, MA: Jones and Bartlett.

Lieberman, D. J. (1999). *Never be lied to again*. New York: St. Martin's Press.

Lopez, F. (1975). *Personnel interviewing*. New York: McGraw-Hill.

Manual for police of New York State. (2005). N. Denny (Ed.). Flushing, NY: Looseleaf Law Publications.

Monk, L. R. (2000). *The bill of rights: A user's guide* (3rd ed.). Alexandria, VA: Close Up Publishing.

Rutledge, D. (2001). *Criminal interrogations*. Incline Village, NV: Copperhouse.

Rutledge, D. (2004, September). Does Miranda hear poisonous fruit? *Police Magazine*, pp. 82–84.

Stewart, C. J., & Cash, Jr., W. B. (1988). *Interviewing principles and practices*. Dubuque, IA: Wm. C. Brown.

Wallace, H., & Roberson, C. (2004). *Written and interpersonal communication: Methods for law enforcement* (3rd ed.). Englewood Cliffs, NJ: Prentice-Hall.

Wolvin, A. W., & Coakley, C. G. (1982). *Listening*. Dubuque, IA: Wm C. Brown.

Chapter 6

Handling Calls for Service

" I promise you a police car on every sidewalk. "

—Mayor Marion Barry Mayor of Washington, DC

CHAPTER OUTLINE

- Introduction
- The Police Service Role
- Disputes
- Suspicious Character Calls
- Prowlers
- Missing and Runaway Children
- Missing Adults
- Welfare Checks
- The Mentally Ill
- The Homeless Population
- Abandoned Vehicles
- Stalled Vehicles
- Directing Traffic
- Lost Property
- Stolen Property
- Repeat Calls
- Citizen Contacts
- Summary

OBJECTIVES

After completion of this chapter, you will be able to do the following:

- Understand the differences between the service function, order maintenance function, and law enforcement function of the police.
- Explain what is meant by the police service role.
- Discuss considerations in handling disputes.
- Describe the appropriate procedures in the investigation of suspicious characters.
- Describe the appropriate procedures in the investigation of a prowler.
- In general, describe the police response to missing children and adults.
- Understand the AMBER Alert system.
- Describe procedures in welfare check calls.
- Describe techniques that can be followed when dealing with the mentally ill.
- Understand the important elements in taking a lost or stolen property report.
- Discuss the perplexities that the police face when dealing with homeless populations.
- Describe the problems associated with stalled vehicles and abandoned vehicles.
- Describe the techniques to be followed in manual traffic control.
- Discuss the techniques the police can use in handling repeat calls.

INTRODUCTION

Imagine that you have managed to secure a ticket to see your local college basketball team play in the sweet sixteen of the NCAA regional tournament. This is the first time your school has made it to the sweet sixteen in twenty-five years and the excitement is growing beyond proportion in your community. On the day of the basketball game you decide to intentionally arrive at the arena several hours early to ensure that you can get a reasonably close parking spot. As it turns out, you manage to park about four blocks from the arena.

As you begin the walk toward the arena you reach your hand into your pocket for the ticket. It's not there! You panic, trying to remember what you did with the ticket. All of a sudden it dawns on you that you left the basketball ticket in your car above the sun visor. You turn around and briskly begin to walk back to your car. As you approach your car you reach into your coat pocket to retrieve your car keys. There're not in your pocket. Frantically, you dig into each one of your pockets, but to no avail—you can't find your car keys. You think to yourself, what a terrible day this is shaping up to be. Once back at your car you carefully examine the interior, but your keys just aren't there.

You are becoming more and more frustrated as you think to yourself that you must have dropped the keys somewhere between where you parked and the basketball arena. You backtrack and search the path you walked. No such luck. You can't locate your car keys. Did someone pick them up? Maybe someone turned them into the police? These questions quickly come to mind. There is only one thing left to do—you call the police on your cellular phone to report the lost keys.

This chapter provides an overview of the many police activities that are considered service-related, many of which are noncriminal calls. While it would be virtually impossible to cover all service-related functions of the police, this chapter will cover some of the more common service-related calls. The chapter provides a general protocol for dealing with many service-related calls; however, police officers reading this book should always refer to their departmental standard operating procedures for specific guidelines. For the student of the police reading this chapter, or the interested citizen just wanting to gain an understanding of police operations, you should come away with a fairly good idea of why police do what they do in specific service-related calls.

THE POLICE SERVICE ROLE

Throughout this book we have made it a point to emphasize that a significant amount of police work is service-related. The scenario presented in the introduction section is considered a service-related police function. Service-related calls may include lost adults or children, disputes, directing traffic, assisting a citizen, welfare checks, checking buildings, helping stranded motorists, motor vehicle accidents, abandoned vehicles, lost property, found property, and the like. Police officers deal with these types of calls on a regular basis.

Citizens often have a romanticized notion of police work, in part due to television, movies, and crime novels (Haberfield, 2002). It has been said that the police officer is not primarily a crime fighter, but a service provider to the public (O'Keefe, 2004). Many police officers begin their careers with high expectations of becoming crime fighters; that is, arresting armed robbers, catching the burglar leaving the building, and apprehending the homicide suspect still holding the smoking gun. It doesn't take long for neophyte police officers to learn that much of their time is spent with boring, mundane tasks that are anything but glamorous.

Did you know that many studies have shown that the crime-fighting role of the police only makes up between 10 and 30 percent of the police officers' on-duty time? Crime is usually only involved in the minority of calls that police are assigned to handle (Whitaker, 1982). Skolnick and Bayley (1996) made this point when they found that only about 20 percent of an officer's day is devoted to crime fighting. They also point out that the crimes that typically terrify the public—robbery, rape, burglary, and homicide—are rarely encountered by police on patrol. Professor Kenneth Peak notes that only Dirty Harry in the movies has his lunch disturbed by a bank robbery (Peck, 1999).

Cordner (1979) reviewed a number of studies that examined police workload. Cordner found that a large portion of calls to the police are handled without dispatching patrol units (30 to 70 percent), and that of all the calls dispatched to patrol units, only a small portion are crime-related or law enforcement related. According to Cordner, a large portion of dispatched radio calls are ambiguous in nature and call for craft and flexibility in problem resolution rather than single-minded enforcement of the law.

In his classic book, *Varieties of Police Behavior*, Professor James Q. Wilson (1968) wrote that the police have three primary functions: law enforcement, order maintenance, and the provision of services. Wilson thought that peacekeeping (maintaining order) constituted most of the police's activities and noted that less than 20 percent of the calls answered by police involved enforcing the law and crime control. He pointed out that the majority of an officer's time is spent with service activities. Wilson believed that in many cases the police deliberately avoided enforcing the law in an attempt just to maintain order and keep the peace.

Cole and Smith (2004) provide an apt description of the law enforcement, order maintenance, and service functions of the police. They describe order maintenance as a broad mandate to keep the peace or otherwise prevent behaviors that might disturb others, which can range from a barking dog to dealing with a fistfight. By way of description, they note that police are usually called on to handle these situations with discretion, rather than deal with them as strict violations of law,

Voices of Experience

Motorcycle Patrol

Excerpts from an interview between Cliff Roberson and former police officer, David LaRose, Manager of Training and Crime Prevention, HSS (Hospital Shared Services), Denver, Colorado. LaRose is also an adjunct instructor in criminal justice for Westwood College.

Q: *What was your most challenging or interesting assignment as a police officer?*

A: It was my assignment as a motorcycle officer. After about four years on the police force, I applied for and was selected as a motorcycle patrol officer. Generally, my duties included enforcing traffic laws, educating the public on safety issues, and duties involved with parades, community events, and escorting visiting officials. One time I was one of the officers who escorted the President of the United States. On a typical day I would be on the road by 8:00 in the morning. I would work the major traffic points and school zones, or wherever there was a high volume of traffic. My normal assignment was four ten-hour days and then off three. It was a high visibility position focused on traffic enforcement and

motorist education with a lot of public service and community awareness assignments.

When I was assigned, a senior officer bet me that I would be injured within a year. I won the bet, since my major accident occurred after about eighteen months of motorcycle duty. The accident occurred when I was initiating a traffic stop. A lady in an oncoming vehicle veered into the center lane and hit me, causing serious injury. Apparently the lady was disciplining her children, crossed over the center median, and hit me broadside. I suffered life-threatening injuries. My left arm and left leg were fractured in many locations. I was in rehab for about six months and during that time I was only interested in getting back to my motorcycle patrol. After this accident, I developed a greater sense of self-worth and since then have been more aware of my surroundings. ■

though of course their authority to deal with these situations is based on violations of law. They describe the law enforcement component as those activities based solely on cases where the law is violated and a suspect must be identified and apprehended. The most obvious instances include robbery, murder, or burglary. This is the popular notion of the main police function, but actually it is relatively uncommon.

Cole and Smith (2004) remind us that the most common police function is to provide a broad range of services not related to crime or wrong-doing. They outline the service functions as including first aid, providing tourist information, guiding the disoriented, or acting as educators (preventing drug use or similar preventions). Because police agencies are traditionally available year-round, twenty-four hours a day, citizens call the police not only in times of trouble, but also when just inconvenienced. As a result, police services may include roadside auto assistance, providing referrals to other agencies, finding lost pets or property, or checking locks on vacationers' homes.

PRACTICE HINTS

Examples of Police Functions

Law Enforcement	Order Maintenance	Service
Arresting a suspect	Dispersing rowdy juveniles and adults	Welfare checks
Investigating a crime		Giving directions to citizens
Responding to a crime in progress	Responding to noise complaints	Finding lost children and adults
Serving warrants	Performing crowd control	Assisting stranded motorists
Enforcing traffic laws (writing speeding tickets)	Quelling a public disturbance	Prevention activities
	Directing traffic	Checking buildings

Sometimes it is difficult to distinguish between the law enforcement, order maintenance, and service-related functions of the police categories. Often, these functions can be somewhat ambiguous. When the police direct traffic at an intersection where a traffic light has burned out, it can be argued that they are performing both order maintenance and service functions. The police perform an important order maintenance function in the sense that if traffic isn't manually directed by the police it would result in traffic order problems and perhaps accidents. Likewise, the police are performing an important service-related function for the general public by directing traffic at the intersection while the traffic light is being repaired. We could apply the same logic to dispersing rowdy juveniles, which may be considered not only an order maintenance function, but also a service function. Can you think of other examples where the three categories (law enforcement, order maintenance, and service) seem to overlap?

DISPUTES

Dispute or **conflict resolution** is a broad term covering any process by which a dispute between two or more parties is resolved. The nature of the disputes that police respond to are diverse and can be between neighbors, family members, spectators at sporting events, store proprietors and their customers, and a wide variety of other situations.

Most disputes are handled quickly by police officers and result in minimal official police action taken. For example, parents at a little league baseball game get into an argument over whose child is the better ball player. If the police are called to a dispute such as this, they most likely will request that both parents settle down and usually additional police action is not necessary. Oftentimes the mere police presence will be enough to quell the disagreement, however, police officers can never take a simple dispute lightly. At times, a dispute may escalate into a volatile situation. In some cases the police may be required to use physical force in order to resolve the conflict. If force is used by the police, it is imperative that the appropriate use of force policy dictated by the reasonable application of force be adhered to.

conflict resolution / Also referred to as dispute resolution. The process of resolving a dispute or a conflict by providing an equitable settlement to both side's needs and interests so that they are satisfied with the outcome. The objective of conflict resolution is to end conflicts before they start or before they escalate to physical fighting.

Officer Safety

Police officers should always consider officer safety a priority when dealing with a dispute, regardless of the perceived magnitude. Dispute calls can be deadly for officers. The Uniform Crime Report shows that between 1994 and 2003 there were ninety-eight officers killed while investigating some type of disturbance. Fifty-seven of these deaths were cases where the officer was investigating a family dispute.

When officers arrive at a reported dispute, the parties involved should be separated as quickly as possible. Separating the disputants will minimize continued conflict and provide additional safety for the officers. Officers should separate the parties in a manner that the officers never lose site of each other. This is a tactical maneuver so that officers always have a visual on each other. Officers should always stand in a bladed position with their weapon side away from the disputants. Officers should never stand with the weapon side facing a person involved in a dispute. This prevents a person who may become unruly from lunging for the officer's weapon.

Regardless of the nature and severity of a dispute, there are always appropriate ways of handling it and walking away looking like a professional. In some cases, police officers choose to handle disputes inappropriately and often do little to resolve the dispute at hand. Of course, this can lead to repeated calls to the same location for the same problem. It is always best to attempt to resolve the dispute, which will reduce the likelihood of repeated calls that take their toll on police resources.

Effective Communication

The most important skill for police officers in resolving a dispute is effective communication. Police officers should always keep in mind that what you say is not nearly as important as how you say it. Thus, in handling a dispute, effective communication skills are the best tool an officer has. As most police officers know, the tone of voice and demeanor can make the difference in either de-escalating or escalating a situation.

A police officer in one Midwest city related the following story: "I was out on a disturbance between two guys that were neighbors arguing over where one put a fence. It was a really minor thing. I had things pretty much under control until my backup arrived. He is a real asshole, an authoritarian type, and he can't communicate with anyone very well. He arrived at the scene and started ordering one of the parties around and told him that the police have better things to do then to babysit adults who can't agree on where to put a fence. I was really embarrassed. It ended up being a yelling match between him and one of the parties involved in the disturbance. When he showed up it was almost like I had a worse dispute. He really pissed the guy off. I can't say as I blame the guy."

Experts say that communication is composed of different methods that include words, voice, tone, and nonverbal clues. Of these, some are more effective in delivering a message than others. In a conversation or verbal exchange, words are 7 percent effective, tone of voice is 38 percent effective, and nonverbal clues are 55 percent effective. Nonverbal clues include body language (e.g., arms crossed, standing, sitting, relaxed, tense), and emotion of the sender and receiver (e.g., yelling, speaking provocatively, enthusiastic).

Police officers can be assertive without being perceived as overly aggressive. The first step is to declare, or state clearly, what you want the disputant to do. When you have a difficult encounter, be professional and do not lose your self-control because, simply put, it is of no use. You may actually find it helpful to acknowledge what is being said by showing an understanding of the disputant's position, or by simply replaying it (a polite way of saying "I hear what you are saying").

Next, the officer states his or her own point of view clearly and concisely with perhaps a little supporting evidence. For example, "You have to move along out of this area because it is posted no trespassing, and failing to do so can result in more serious action taken, and you don't want that, do you?" Finally, state what you want to happen next, and move it forward (e.g., "Let's get out of this field so you can go about your day and so that I can get back on patrol. Does that sound OK to you?")

Tactical Communication

Tactical communication is not a martial art, but it is a form of self-defense that will throw an opponent for a loop and assist the officer who may be handling a very tense dispute situation. Tactical communication strategies have been taught with proven success in the hardest arenas available. In law enforcement, where tensions and emotions run high, control over such encounters is necessary if everyone is to stay safe. Tactical communication has been used to calm people, demonstrate their best interests within the law, and preserve the peace. This makes police officers safer and thereby better able to handle the problem by addressing the person's needs, not simply arguing about demands.

Thompson and Jenkins (1993), writing in their groundbreaking work on tactical communication, relate that there are basically three goals of this technique. The first and most important goal is to ensure officer safety. Goal number two is to enhance the police officer's professionalism. The third goal is to increase efficiency, which will ultimately improve performance level. Increasing efficiency means saying it right the first time.

Using techniques from tactical communication can be the officer's most powerful tool or worst enemy. It would be fair to say that all of us have our biases or buttons that can be pushed; the key is the ability to control them and not let them impact the way police duties are performed. Police officers see much despair during a tour of duty. Seeing this despair can be depressing. Understandably, police officers at times may have a difficult time coping with it all. Police see society at its absolute worst. It is crucial that officers learn how to control their emotions and thoughts. If officers can't control their own emotions and thoughts, how will they effectively control others?

Police liability and accountability are stronger issues now than ever before, and to survive and be successful officers must professionally enhance the way they perform and communicate with others. When police officers deal with people in dispute situations, they must be skillful in their verbal ability. Likewise, officers should enter into a dispute with a plan of action and know exactly how to handle verbal resistance and confrontation, all the while remaining calm and in control of the situation.

Police training has historically spent an enormous amount of time training police officers in physical defense tactics; however, much less time is spent training police officers in how to communicate effectively (Birzer, 2003; Birzer & Tannehill, 2001). Most police officers don't have to qualify with their verbal skills periodically like they do with their firearms. Knowing the importance of effective communication, perhaps they should. Just as officers are trained at physical defense skills, they should also be tactically trained in the use of their presence and words. Tactical communication gives officers a system of specific tried and tested tactics and patterns of behavior that will allow them to respond professionally under all conditions.

By far the most common abuse that a police officer is faced with is the words that suspects or disputants yell out. In order to stay calm and professional under pressure you must not get drawn into words people throw at you, whether it is sarcasm or obscene language. Tactical communication is effective in allowing officers to handle this problem by utilizing some basic principles. Words and meanings are almost never the same. Tactical communication distinguishes the difference between the two, and demonstrates how to respond to what you think people mean rather than react to the words they say.

Listen and Ask Questions

Individuals involved in a dispute each have their own story about what is important and why. Listening to disputing parties is important in order to determine the true nature of the dispute. It also has the potential to give an aura of fairness, so that each side gets to tell their story. Insight into these different stories can make a great difference in the ultimate resolution of the problem. If possible, officers should frame questions in an open-ended format. Open-ended questions may assist the officer in understanding the background of the conflict better.

Questions should also be asked that probe below the surface. To probe below the surface requires redirecting the energy. Ask questions like: "Why does that seem to be the best solution to you?" "What's your real need here?" "What interests need to be served in this situation?" "What do you think needs to be done here?" and "What's the outcome or result you want?" The answers to these questions can assist the officer in developing an effective solution to the dispute, while giving the impression that the officer is genuinely interested in the disputant's problems. For a more in-depth discussion of communication skills for police officers please revisit Chapter 5.

PRACTICE HINTS

Active Listening Tips

- **Be attentive:** concentrate on what is being said
- **Be impartial:** don't form an opinion, just listen
- **Reflect back:** restating what has been said helps the other person know that you understand
- **Summarize:** pull together the important messages so that all involved recognize what was important during the conversation

Look for the Hidden Problem

The officer should make an attempt to uncover the underlying or hidden problem. In essence, the officer should look beneath the conflict and determine the facts. Fact finding is essential to resolving conflict, as often conflicts are generated by a misperception or misunderstanding of the facts involved. As difficult as this may be in some cases when dealing with boisterous and belligerent persons, the officer should try to be sensitive to the other's position and perspective. See the conflict through the other's eyes. The effective resolution of a conflict may actually involve partially empathizing with the other person, understanding the world from the other person's frame of reference. It may be helpful to try to summarize the other's argument and demands. This will assist in minimizing miscommunication and misperceptions that can play a large role in conflicts.

Resolving the Dispute

There are several techniques an officer may utilize in dispute resolution. The easiest and most convenient technique is to simply separate the parties involved and send them on their way. However, in more serious cases, where one person has assaulted the other person or some other crime has been committed, an arrest will be required. Officers should always try to counsel the parties involved in the dispute. In some cases, the actual threat of arrest will resolve the dispute in the short term. It is always best to attempt to solve the problem for the long term, if possible. Disputing parties should be referred to resources that may be more equipped to resolve their dispute. Some communities have mediation services available on a low-cost basis, while just about all communities will have services for the victims of domestic violence.

domestic violence /
Violence between adult intimate partners. An abusive behavior used by one person in a relationship to control the other. Domestic violence typically involves an assault or battery upon a member of a household including a spouse, parent, child, blood-related family member, or others domiciling in the same place.

Domestic Violence

Domestic violence is a widespread problem in the United States, endangering the victim and having an exacerbating effect on the weakening of the family. In cases of **domestic violence**, an arrest is almost always required due to the mandated arrest laws that have been enacted in most states. Domestic violence occurs when a family member, spouse, or partner physically harms the other family members, spouse, or partner. The term "intimate partner violence" is often used synonymously; other terms have included wife beating, wife battering, husband battering,

Voices of Experience

Handling Domestic Violence Calls

Excerpts from an interview between Cliff Roberson and former police
lieutenant, Richard G. Kuiters, presently a professor at Bergen Community
College, Paramus, New Jersey.

Q: *When you were a patrol officer, how did you handle
domestic violence cases?*
A: Domestic violence is one of the most terrible calls
that an officer can get. You are talking about power
control over loved ones. When I first starting handling domestic violence calls, the police at that time
considered it a family problem. We would go back to
the same home time and time again. Often we went
to the same home four or five times in the same week.
We did nothing about the problem except tell the offender to stop doing it. A common procedure was to
give the offender a ride away from the house so that
he would have cooling off time as he walked back
home. The first time we would drop him about fifteen minutes from the house and the next time about
thirty minutes. In extreme cases, we would take him
to New York City where it would take him all night to
get home.

Today we look at it as not a family problem, but
a police problem. We consider what we are going to
do for the victim and how we resolve this problem.
The three considerations now used are officer
safety, victim safety, and offender accountability.
The methods used presently include using restraining orders, special cell phones that the victims are
given, and alarms that victims can utilize to contact
the police. The police are more concerned now with
victim services. Some jurisdictions will help victims
relocate and most help develop safety plans for
the victims. Law enforcement is now more service-
oriented and is interested in providing services to
victims of abuse. ■

relationship violence, domestic abuse, spousal abuse, and family violence, with
some legal jurisdictions having specific definitions.

In many states, officers are required to make an arrest if they have probable cause
to believe that a crime of domestic violence was committed. Mandatory arrest laws
were enacted to correct the problem centering on the willingness of officers to drive an
accused abuser around the block to let him "cool off" before returning home, rather
than taking him to jail. An officer does not need to witness the crime to make an arrest,
but can rely on evidence at the crime scene. Evidence may include the victim's statement, torn clothing, victim's injuries, or destruction of property in the home,

The requirement for positive action in domestic violence cases incurs obligations at each stage of the police response. These obligations extend from initial deployment to the response of the first officer on the scene, through the whole process
of investigation, and the protection and care of affected victims and children. An
important objective of the police response is to ensure the protection of the victim
while allowing the criminal justice system to hold the offender accountable. An
effective investigation should be completed in all cases where a domestic violence
incident is reported. Officers investigating a complaint of domestic violence are responsible for protecting the victim and ensuring that the victim is no longer at risk
of violence. The officer is also responsible for arresting the offender. The officer
should be aware that domestic violence may be compounded by numerous other
factors, such as drug and alcohol abuse.

When responding to a domestic violence call officers should use all reasonable means to prevent further abuse. The officer should also practice good officer safety skills that have been stressed throughout this book. Whenever officers believe that abuse has occurred, they are required to take steps to prevent further abuse. These steps may include:

- Arranging for the victim to be taken to a medical facility for treatment or to a place of safety.
- Offering immediate and adequate information of the victim's rights, including the right to obtain a Protection of Abuse order or to begin criminal proceedings.
- Providing referrals to local domestic violence agencies.
- Providing referrals to counseling services for both the victim and the offender.
- Assisting the victim with developing a safety plan.
- Advising the victim on home security issues.

Some Dispute Calls End in Tragedy

A San Antonio police officer and a woman were shot and killed Thursday when the officer answered a domestic disturbance call on the city's west side, officials said. Officer Hector Garza, 48, was fatally shot shortly after arriving at the residence about 9:00 A.M. He had been with the force twenty-five years and is the fifth San Antonio police officer to die in the line of duty in recent months.

Police said they have arrested a suspect and are preparing capital murder and murder charges against the man, police spokeswoman Sandy Gutierrez said in a statement. Garza was shot after responding for the second time Thursday morning to a domestic disturbance call. He had been to the house accompanied by a partner on the first call about an hour earlier.

Source: San Antonio police officer, woman killed in domestic disturbance call (2001, March 30). *The Daily Texan.* Retrieved online at www.dailytexanonline.com.

SUSPICIOUS CHARACTER CALLS

Imagine for a moment that you are home alone one evening watching television. As you get up to close the living room drapes you notice a man sitting in a car that is parked on the street directly in front of your house. You don't recall seeing the car or the man in the neighborhood in the past. You watch for a few minutes, but the car doesn't leave. The man is just sitting in his car. It is getting dark, and you become a bit concerned and pick up the phone and call the police.

You inform the police dispatcher that there is a man sitting in a car in front of your house and you are a bit frightened. The dispatcher asks you several questions and assures you that two police officers have been dispatched to the area. After several minutes two patrol cars arrive and you see the officers approach the suspicious car and begin to talk to the occupant. You notice that one of the officers shines his flashlight in the car. It is getting too dark to notice anything else. After about ten minutes, the car pulls away and the officers knock on your door. The officers inform you that the person in the car was an insurance agent who was waiting on his client who lives next door to return home. You sigh with relief. The officers assure you that the person really was an insurance agent and that there is nothing to worry about.

Suspicious character calls, much like the scenario presented, are a fairly common police call. In most cases, they end up being nothing and require minimal action on the part of the officer; however, the officer must use due caution when responding to suspicious character calls because it is never certain what they will encounter. It could very well be the insurance agent waiting on his client to return home, or it may be the lookout for a burglary in progress or some other crime. The sobering statistics from the Uniform Crime Report illustrate the danger of suspicious character calls all too well. According to the Uniform Crime Report, from the years 1994–2003 there were ninety-six law enforcement officers killed while investigating suspicious persons or circumstances.

Officers should approach suspicious character calls utilizing officer safety techniques at all times. Whenever possible, two officers should respond to suspicious character calls. If the suspicious character is in a vehicle, the officers should approach from the rear of the vehicle, similar to the technique used for making a traffic stop. If it is after dark, headlights or a spotlight should be used to illuminate the interior of the vehicle under investigation. One officer should approach on the driver's side and make contact with the occupant of the vehicle while the backup officer should approach on the passenger side, illuminating the vehicle with a flashlight to control others who may be in the vehicle. If the suspicious character is on foot, the officers should maintain a secure and tactical distance (a few feet) from the suspect and stand in a bladed position with the weapon side away from the person being questioned.

If the officer has any safety concerns, and thinks that the suspicious character may be carrying a weapon, he should perform a **frisk** of the person's outer clothing. The purpose of a frisk or pat-down search is to dispel suspicions of danger to the officer and other people in the vicinity. A frisk is a search for concealed weapons and is normally justified when there are concerns of safety for the officer and for others. The Supreme Court held in the *Terry v. Ohio* decision that a police officer has the right to detain and search an individual without a warrant, or even probable cause, as long as there is a reasonable suspicion that the individual may be armed. What the officer feels through the outer clothing during the pat down may provide probable cause for the officer to complete a full search. For example, the officer performs a pat-down search of the outer perimeter of a person's coat. While performing the pat down, the officer feels a hard object that is reasonably believed to be a dangerous weapon. The officer is then justified to go into the pocket and retrieve the hard object.

frisk / Also referred to as a pat-down search. A noninvasive precautionary frisk or pat-down search of the outer clothing of a suspect. The purpose of the frisk is to protect the officer. The justification for the frisk is discussed in the case of *Terry v. Ohio*, 392 U.S. 1, 88 S.Ct. 1868, 20 1.Ed.2d 889 (1968).

Identification should be requested from the suspicious character and a records check performed to see if the person has any outstanding warrants. An explanation of why the person is in the area at that particular time should be requested. If necessary, a field interview card (FI) should also be completed on the person(s). The *field interview card* is an intelligence system used to obtain and record information on the presence of individual(s) in a given location at a specific time and date. It contains the name, address, telephone number, physical description, age, date of birth, and description of clothing worn. If an automobile is involved, the make, year, tag license, number style, and color are included. Suppose there is a burglary that occurs in a certain area at a certain time. Investigators can then perform a query for field interview

Voices of Experience

Safety Issues During Traffic Stops

Excerpts from an interview between Cliff Roberson and former police officer, Bill Lally. Professor Lally is presently Chair of the Criminal Justice Department, ITT Technical Institute, Ft. Wayne, Indiana.

Q: *What safety precautions should an officer take during a routine traffic stop?*
A: Traffic stops too many times become routine for police officers. Traffic stops are one of the most dangerous activities that a police officer engages in. When the officer stops a vehicle, he or she has no idea what he or she is about to encounter. For the most part, the overwhelming majority of traffic stops are routine, mundane types of activities. Therefore, officers tend to get into a complacency mode in which they tend not to use the precautions that they were trained to use.

I was trained to use a magic line as to my position when I approached a stopped motorist. I would draw a mental line from where the driver's side car door meets the car frame and stand behind that line facing the front of the car. From this position, I could see into the car and the driver would be required to turn his or her head to see me. By being behind this line, I could control the driver's exit from the vehicle and prevent the exit. Also, if the driver opened the door suddenly, I would not risk being pushed into traffic or be jumping back into the line of traffic passing us.

Too many times you will see officers standing right in front of the window. **Note:** In some departments troopers are taught to stand in front of the car looking into the car from the front windshield. This tends to protect the officer from other traffic while still providing the officer a view into the car and at the motorist. Myself, I prefer to use the magic line concept and ensure that no part of my body, except for maybe my hand, was in front of the magic line.

You should always retrieve items with your non-dominant hand. For example, if you are right-handed, take the driver's license or whatever else you receive from the driver in your left hand. This keeps your dominant hand free in case you need it for protection. When you walk back to your vehicle, keep an eye on the stopped vehicle. This doesn't mean that you have to walk backwards, but keep glancing over your shoulder at the stopped vehicle. Finally, be alert when writing a ticket. Don't let your eyes be glued on the ticket book. I recommend that you write the ticket while in your vehicle and using your steering wheel as the prop for the ticket book. That way your eyes are level with the stopped vehicle in front of you. ∎

cards that were completed in the area of the crime. The conscientious officer who spends a few extra minutes completing the field interview can potentially lead investigators to a suspect.

If the subject under investigation has no legitimate reason to be in the area, and if the officers have no reason to detain the individual, after the field interview has been completed, they should direct the individual to leave the area. If a complainant wishes to be contacted, the officers should make contact and get necessary information for the police report. It is a wise practice to complete either a field interview or official police report in cases of suspicious characters.

PROWLERS

Prowlers are another call that the police respond to on a frequent basis. Like the suspicious character call, it is easy for the officer to develop a laissez-faire attitude when approaching prowler calls; however, this attitude can be deadly and should be avoided.

The responding police officers have little advance knowledge of what they will encounter at the scene. There have been police officers killed investigating prowler calls. Often, the report of a prowler is merely based on caller suspicions that may have been aroused by a noise, shadow, perhaps the wind blowing, a cat scratching at the window, the fear of being home alone, or perhaps a scary movie on television.

The prowler may simply be a law-abiding citizen taking a walk, or walking his dog. It could be lonely Ms. Smith, who on a windy and stormy evening hears a noise outside of her window at 1:00 A.M. and decides to call the police. On the other hand, the prowler could be the suspect who has just committed a felony crime (murder, burglary, robbery, sexual assault) and is walking away from the crime scene. In other cases, the prowler may be the suspect who is preparing to commit a crime and is interrupted by the police. These are all more reasons for officers to approach the prowler call using stringent officer safety measures.

The primary objective of the police when investigating the report of a prowler is to verify if there is in fact a prowler, and what the prowler is doing at the location. The officers should make an effort to properly identify the prowler. Police officers have probably heard every reason known as to why prowlers are in a particular place at a particular time. A few of the typical responses that an officer may hear are:

1. "I was looking for my dog."
2. "I was taking a shortcut home."
3. "I'm lost."
4. "I was tired and decided to rest."
5. "I needed to urinate and did it out of the public's view."
6. "I was looking in the window to see if this was my friend's house."
7. "I'm trying to find a friend's house."
8. "I'm hiding from someone who wants to harm me."
9. "I live here."
10. "I was drinking and some friends kicked me out of the car."
11. "I'm just walking home. I work up the street."
12. "I couldn't sleep and decided to take a walk."

Regardless of the reason given, the officer should investigate each incident carefully. It should be determined if the prowler legitimately belongs in the area. It is important to remember that many persons suspected of being a prowler actually do belong in the neighborhood. The officer responding to the prowler call should not be provoked into overreacting.

A field interview card should be completed on the suspected prowler. Officers should never accept just any explanation of why the prowler is in a particular area such as, "I was just walking my dog," when there is no dog to be found. All explanations given by a prowler should be carefully investigated. The officer should be mindful that the prowler could be a peeping Tom with voyeuristic tendencies. "Peeping Tom" is a term used to describe someone who looks into the windows of residences, in many cases residences where females live. The peeping Tom with voyeuristic tendencies will look into windows to obtain sexual gratification by trying to get a glimpse of a female undressing or combing her hair. He often chooses a residence where a female lives alone and attempts to view the female through the window.

Officer safety is paramount when investigating a prowler and prowler calls should almost always require a two-officer response. If possible, dispatchers should keep the complainant on the telephone until officers arrive in the area. This will allow the dispatcher to obtain real-time information about activities of the prowler, which can then be radioed or sent via the mobile data computer to the responding field units. Dispatchers can obtain pertinent information about the area that would be advantageous for the responding officers to know. For example, it may be important for responding officers to know that the complainant has a large dog in her backyard, or that the backyard has a twelve-foot privacy fence with several missing links on the south side. It also allows the dispatcher to let the complainant know when officers have arrived at the scene. Police should request that complainants remain in their residence at all times during the prowler investigation.

The initial entry into the area of a prowler call is important. The officers should be stealthy during entry into the area, by avoiding a grand entry (e.g., screeching tires, sirens wailing, red lights flashing, or racing engine). Pull into the area slowly and quietly, paying attention to the surroundings. It may be a good idea to turn the headlights off when pulling into the immediate area. Of course, this should be done using due caution. There was a case where an officer was responding to a prowler call in a neighborhood that did not have street lights, which made the neighborhood very dark. The officer turned his headlights off when approaching the scene and ran into a parked car. Fortunately, the damage to the patrol car and the parked car was minimal because the officer was traveling slowly. Obviously, when an officer elects to turn the headlights off when pulling into an area, prudent judgment should be used.

Upon arrival at the location of the prowler call, park a few houses down from the location where the prowler is reported to be. When walking to the location, secure key rings and turn down the volume on the portable radio. There are differing thoughts on the use of the flashlight. One school of thought proposes making great use of the flashlight and illuminating the area as much as possible. It is thought that the mere illumination of the flashlight will naturally draw out someone who may be hiding. Others argue that it is best to limit the use of the flashlight until you are close to where the prowler is reported. This argument proposes that an officer's primary objective is to surprise the prowler. Limiting use of the flashlight tends to accomplish this objective.

There may indeed be situations where minimal use of the flashlight is recommended, while in other situations its illumination would be quite effective. Officers should use their best judgment of when to use the flashlight or illuminating devices at the scene of a prowler. Factors that should be considered in this decision include if the suspected prowler is reported to be armed, if it is suspected that a crime has been committed, or if the prowler is purposely hiding from the police, all of which would justify significantly lighting up the area.

The decision to approach the area with your handgun drawn should be driven by the information from the dispatcher. If the dispatcher advises that the prowler is a white male in his mid-thirties wearing a black sweatshirt and blue jeans and carrying what appeared to be some type of weapon, maybe a handgun, then obviously this information would dictate that the officer should approach the location with the firearm drawn. When the handgun is drawn, the finger should always be off the trigger to avoid an accidental discharge. Simply placing the trigger finger on the trigger guard will suffice.

Officers should search the area as a team and always be aware of where the other officer is searching. Once again, search the area as quietly as possible. Take into account tactical considerations by walking along trees, buildings, houses, or other structures in the event that you may need to take cover quickly. The search should be slow and methodical, as a prowler can hide just about anywhere. Police officers have found subjects hiding under porches, in cars, under cars, in garages, in trees, in sheds, in crawl spaces that are accessible from outside of a residence, and even in dog houses. These areas should be searched thoroughly. Officers should also pay close attention to fresh tracks, especially if it has recently snowed or rained. It is also a good idea to pay attention to shrubbery that appears to have been freshly trampled on.

When contact is made with the prowler, a visual inspection should be made of the suspect's demeanor and clothing, paying close attention to bulges in pockets, which could indicate that the subject is carrying a weapon. At all times the officer should watch the suspect's hands and movement. If the officer has a safety concern, or sees a bulge in the prowler's clothing, a quick frisk of the suspect's outer clothing should be performed.

As noted previously, the prowler should be checked for warrants, and the officer should demand an explanation of why the individual is in the area. A field interview card should be completed. The owner of the property where a prowler was found should be contacted to ensure that the prowler did not have permission to be there. If it is determined that a crime has not been committed, and the prowler has been properly identified and documented via a field interview, then the individual should be released.

PRACTICE HINTS

Tips for Checking Suspicious Characters and Prowlers

- Always expect the worse.
- Use a tactical approach.
- Your approach should be done in a stealthy manner.
- If after dark, decide to what extent you will illuminate the area with flashlights.
- Obtain as much information from the dispatcher as possible pertaining to the location and potential obstacles, such as dogs and fences.
- Search the area thoroughly and methodically.
- When contacting the suspect, maintain a safe distance and stand with your weapon side away from the suspect.
- Observe the suspect for unusual bulges in the clothing that could indicate a weapon or other dangerous contraband. Always watch the suspect's hands and movements.
- Control the suspect. Perform a frisk for safety, if necessary.
- Get identification on the suspect, and check for warrants.
- Demand an explanation of why the suspect is in the location.
- Complete a field interview card.
- Arrest if you have probable cause that a crime has been committed. Release the suspect if you don't.

MISSING AND RUNAWAY CHILDREN

Missing children pose a complex problem for the police. In one instance, the police may be dealing with a case where a lack of communication exists between two divorced couples over who is taking the child for the weekend. Subsequently, the mother shows up at school to pick up her child and her child is gone, only later to find the child safe at his father's house. While in other cases, a child may be kidnapped by a stranger or other estranged family member for the purpose of doing harm to the child. Police must discern the incident at hand in an expedient manner.

There are different types of missing children that police deal with including family abductions; endangered runaways; nonfamily abductions; and lost, injured, or otherwise missing children. The best national estimates for the number of missing children are from incidence studies conducted by the U.S. Department of Justice's Office of Juvenile Justice and Delinquency Prevention. In 1999, an estimated 797,500 children were reported missing. Of these missing children, 58,200 children were abducted by nonfamily members; 115 children were the victims of the most serious, long-term nonfamily abduction, called stereotypical kidnapping; and 203,900 children were the victims of family abduction.

As most police officers know, the largest number of missing children happen to be runaways; followed by family abductions; then lost, injured, or otherwise missing children; and finally, the smallest category, but the one in which the child is at greatest risk of injury or death, nonfamily abductions. There is sometimes an assumption that family abductions are not a serious matter; however, this is not true. In some cases children are told that the left-behind parent doesn't want or love them. These children may live the life of a fugitive, always on the run with the noncustodial parent and taken away from their home, friends, school, and family, which can be devastating to the child.

Responding to Missing Persons

The police agency should have an aggressive policy in place to investigate and locate lost or missing persons of any age. Officers should follow-up on any and all investigative leads that may result in the immediate location of a missing person. In all cases there should never be a waiting period for reporting a missing child.

A child who is missing under unusual circumstances is usually considered to be at risk until sufficient information to the contrary is confirmed. For example, the child tells his parents that he doesn't want to live with them anymore because he did not like what was prepared for dinner. He tells his parent that he will go and live with his friend who gets to have pizza every night. A few hours later the child is discovered missing from his room and his parents report him missing to the police. Most likely this juvenile will be found at his friend's house or will return home in a few hours.

The reporting officer should conduct a preliminary investigation and gather enough information from the reporting person to complete necessary reports. If the police agency uses a departmental missing persons report, this form along with a narrative report should be completed by the reporting officer on all missing persons. The narrative report should include any additional information received from the reporting person or others that may assist the investigation. In some cases a separate report may be used by the law enforcement agency for missing juveniles, runaways, or children in need of care.

A *Request for Assistance and Authorization for Medical Treatment* form should be completed for all juvenile missing persons and runaways or adults having a legal guardian. If the reporting person refuses to sign this form, the refusal and the reason for refusal should be duly noted in the narrative report. The following **National Crime Information Center (NCIC)** entry information should be obtained on missing persons, juvenile runaways, and kidnapped victims:

PRACTICE HINTS

Generic Definitions and Protocol—Missing Persons

- **Critical Missing:** Any person (of any age) who could be in imminent danger.
- **Reporting Person:** Person of any age reporting an individual as missing and requesting assistance.
- **NCIC Missing Person File:** A National Crime Information Center (NCIC) bound folder called "Missing Person File Data Collection/Entry Guide" containing a survey of personal descriptors on the missing person. Also referred to as an NCIC Missing Person packet.
- **Status Offender Juvenile:** A juvenile who is charged with an offense that would not be a crime if committed by an adult (e.g., curfew or tobacco infractions).

- Complete name
- Date and place of birth
- Social security, operator's license, and other identifying numbers
- Complete physical description
- Description of vehicle, if involved
- Clothing description
- Recent photograph, if available

National Crime Information Center (NCIC) / A computerized index of criminal justice information (i.e., criminal record history information, fugitives, stolen properties, missing persons). It is available to federal, state, and local law enforcement and other criminal justice agencies and is operational twenty-four hours a day, 365 days a year.

The NCIC is the United States' central database for tracking crime-related information, including wanted persons, missing persons, certain firearms, stolen property, and criminal histories. Operated by the FBI, it receives input from government agencies and all fifty state governments.

AMBER Alert

The reporting officer should make a great effort to assess the missing person's situation and determine if the person could be in danger. The reporting officer should immediately notify the on-scene supervisor if the victim may be in danger, abducted, or a victim of a crime.

In critical situations, there should be a determination made if the situation falls under AMBER Alert guidelines. If so, the watch commander should initiate an **AMBER Alert**. The AMBER Alert, named for nine-year-old Amber Hagerman, who was kidnapped from her neighborhood in Arlington, Texas and killed, is a voluntary partnership between law enforcement agencies, broadcasters, and transportation agencies to activate an urgent bulletin in the most serious child abduction cases. Broadcasters use the Emergency Alert System to air a description of the abducted child and suspected abductor. This is the same concept used during severe weather emergencies. The goal of an AMBER Alert is to instantly galvanize the entire community to assist in the search for and safe recovery of the child.

AMBER Alert / The notification to the general public, by various media outlets, that a confirmed abduction of a child has happened. AMBER is an acronym for "America's Missing: Broadcast Emergency Response," and was named for nine-year-old Amber Hagerman, who was abducted and murdered in Arlington, Texas in 1996.

Amber Hagerman

On January 13, 1996, nine-year-old Amber Hagerman was riding her bicycle in Arlington, Texas, when a neighbor heard her scream. The neighbor saw a man pull Amber off her bike, throw her into the front seat of his pick-up truck, and drive away at a high rate of speed. The neighbor called police and provided a description of the suspect and his vehicle. The Arlington Police and the FBI scoured the area interviewing neighbors and searching for the suspect and vehicle. Local radio and television stations covered the story in their regular newscasts. Four days later, the worst-case scenario became all too sobering. Amber's body was found in a drainage ditch four miles away. Her kidnapping and murder still remain unsolved.

PRACTICE HINTS

AMBER Alert Success Stories

- **August 31, 2006—San Antonio, Texas:** A two-year-old boy was left in the care of a homeless woman by his mother. When the mother could not find the woman or her child, an AMBER Alert was issued. A lead from the AMBER Alert directed authorities to the suspect and child. The suspect was arrested and the child was safely recovered.
- **August 1, 2006—Rochester, Michigan:** Three young siblings were abducted by their father when he believed they were to be taken away by social services. An AMBER Alert was issued in Michigan and Illinois, as he was believed to be heading south. When the suspect entered Illinois and saw that an AMBER Alert had been activated, he quickly returned to Michigan and turned himself in. The suspect was apprehended and the children were safely recovered.
- **July 22, 2006—Cincinnati, Ohio:** A six-month-old boy was in the backseat of his father's car when he was carjacked at gunpoint. The suspects fled with the vehicle and the child still inside. An AMBER Alert was quickly activated. The child was left in a stroller on the front porch of a woman who was aware of the AMBER Alert. She notified authorities, and the child was safely recovered.
- **June 17, 2006—Dearborn County, Ohio:** An eight-year-old boy and his one-year-old brother were abducted from their babysitter's home by their noncustodial father. Because there was a domestic

relations protection order against the man, an AMBER Alert was issued. He heard the Alert and turned himself and the children in to authorities.
- **May 31, 2006—Howard City, Michigan:** A three-year-old girl was abducted by her noncustodial father after his parental rights were terminated. An AMBER Alert was issued. The man drove to a mental health facility to turn himself in after hearing the AMBER Alert. The child was safely recovered.
- **May 13, 2006—Stockton, California:** A sixteen-year-old girl was abducted at knifepoint during a home invasion robbery. An AMBER Alert was quickly activated. When the suspects saw their own vehicle description on a changeable message sign, they called 911. The suspects were then tracked and apprehended. The child was safely recovered.
- **April 10, 2006—San Bernardino, California:** After a man shot his girlfriend, he drove her to a hospital, left her out front, and fled with his seventeen-month-old son and the woman's three-year-old daughter. An AMBER Alert was quickly issued. When the suspect heard the AMBER Alert, he dropped the children off with relatives, who quickly notified authorities. The children were safely recovered.

Source: National Center for Missing and Exploited Children, accessed online on November 28, 2006 at www.missingkids.com.

PRACTICE HINTS

Runaway/Missing Juvenile Procedures

- The reporting officer should gather information regarding: child custody court orders, parents' involvement in a divorce or child custody battle, nonfamily abduction, domestic violence, child abuse or sexual assault, past instances of running away, name and address of school, and means of transportation to and from school.
- Consider a search of the child's home or school locker. The reporting officer should continue to search even after contacting the Juvenile Unit, in cases of critical missing children.
- If the agency uses the form, *A Request for Assistance and Authorization for Medical Treatment*, it should be completed anytime a parent/guardian reports a juvenile as "runaway" or ungovernable. This form gives officers parental permission to apprehend and hold the juvenile since there is no violation of criminal law.

The Reporting Officer Should:

1. Ensure the parent(s)/guardian(s) have read the form and understand their responsibility to return the runaway from outside the jurisdictional boundaries once apprehended as circumstances indicate.
2. Fill out the form as completely as possible and sign it as a witness.
3. Have the parent(s)/guardian(s) sign the form in the officer's presence.
4. If a foster parent or other placement, include all names and phone numbers of caseworkers in the official report.
5. When the runaway is found, officers should interview the juvenile to obtain intelligence information, such as "hideout" houses.
6. Cancel the runaway report by completing the appropriate paperwork.
7. Make arrangements for the juvenile to be transported back to the parent(s)/guardian(s) or to juvenile intake.

MISSING ADULTS

Missing adults or missing persons require many of the same procedures that are followed in cases of missing children or juveniles. A missing person is someone whose whereabouts is unknown to the reporting party. A **missing person** is someone who has disappeared for a long period of time, commonly with no known reason. By the end of 2005, there were 109,531 active missing person records according to the U.S. Department of Justice. You may see their photographs posted on bulletin boards, postcards, and websites, with a phone number to call if someone sees that missing person. There is generally no waiting period for reporting a person missing. Most law enforcement agencies must accept a report of a missing person without delay and give priority to the handling of the report.

There are many reasons why people disappear. Often an individual chooses to disappear voluntarily; most such individuals return within a short period of time. Some missing persons in the United States never return home. One reason for this may be that many people leave home simply to start again in a new place

missing person / Someone who has disappeared for a long period of time, commonly with no known reason. Their photographs are often posted on bulletin boards, postcards, and websites.

under a new name. They may have had difficulties with individuals in their lives, or they may have lost someone and wish to begin a new life in a new location. In some cases, individuals choose to commit suicide in a remote location or under an assumed name to spare their families the shame of a suicide or to allow their deaths to be eventually declared, which may allow survivors to collect on insurance premiums.

A common misconception is that a person must be absent for seventy-two hours before being legally classified as missing. This is rarely the case. There is usually no time limitation as to when someone can be reported as missing. In instances where there is evidence of violence or of an unusual absence, law enforcement agencies often stress the importance of beginning an investigation promptly. Most law enforcement agencies must accept any report, including a report by telephone, of a missing person. This must be done without delay and with priority given to the handling of the report. The reporting officer investigating a missing adult should gather the following information on the person:

- Date, time, and location last seen.
- Physical condition of subject.
- Identity of anyone who may have been accompanying the subject.
- Recent photograph.
- Information about circumstances of disappearance, especially any unusual circumstances that might indicate the person was abducted or is otherwise at risk of harm.
- Identity of associates, friends, relatives, and others who might have information about the whereabouts of the person.
- Whether the subject has been reported missing or runaway on prior occasions and the degree to which this absence is different from past instances.
- Information about the extent of any search for the subject prior to being reported missing.
- Any information about where the missing person might have gone, or places the missing person frequents.
- If the subject has been involved in any recent domestic incidents; suffered emotional trauma or a life crisis; demonstrated unusual, uncharacteristic, or bizarre behavior; is dependent on drugs or alcohol; has a history of mental illness or is taking prescription medication.
- If appropriate, complete the necessary paperwork and enter the missing person into the NCIC computer system.

Recovery of Missing Persons

If the location of a missing person is discovered, competent adults cannot be forced to return home. Officers should advise the missing person that they are the subject of an investigation. The missing subject should be asked if the officer can advise the reporting party of the subject's whereabouts. Requests to not have their whereabouts revealed should be honored. This is especially true in cases involving domestic disputes where the reported missing person could be placed in imminent danger should the other half of the dispute discover the person's whereabouts.

All missing persons who are located should be checked for outstanding warrants. In all cases, the reporting person should be informed of the well-being of the missing person. The missing person's notice should be cancelled by notifying the appropriate personnel and organizations as soon as possible.

WELFARE CHECKS

You haven't seen your neighbor, Mr. Smith, for several days. Mr. Smith is eighty-one years old and lives alone. You think to yourself, "This is unusual, he always picks up his newspaper, but yet the last two morning editions are laying in his driveway." You hope Mr. Smith is OK. You slowly walk toward Mr. Smith's residence and knock on the front door. There is no reply. You knock again, louder. There is still no reply. Worried that something is terribly wrong you call the police.

After several minutes two police officers arrive and make contact with you. You explain to the officers that you have not seen Mr. Smith for several days and this is really unusual. The officers advise you that they will check it out. You observe the officers knock on the front door. There is no reply. They walk around to the back door and knock loudly while yelling Mr. Smith's name out loud. After several minutes the door opens and Mr. Smith, wearing what appears to be pajamas and a house robe, slowly steps onto the back porch. Mr. Smith explains to the officers that he has been sick the past few days and has been on bedrest. He further explains that his bedroom is in the rear of the residence and because he is hard of hearing, he can't hear if someone knocks on the front door. The officers ask if there is anyone they can call. Mr. Smith says no, and advises the officers that his son will be visiting him tomorrow.

The officers bid a good evening to Mr. Smith and then advise the neighbor of the situation. The officers further advise the neighbor that he did the right thing by calling and that it is good that neighbors look out for one another. The police, in this case, have performed what is commonly referred to as a welfare check. Welfare check calls are very common in police work.

Fortunately, in the prior scenario there was a good ending; however, in many welfare check calls this is not the case. In one particular welfare check call, an individual was not heard from or seen for several days. After arriving at the scene, a family member related to the officers that her brother had just been laid off from his job and was very depressed. She was worried about him because he had made some suicide threats. Once officers entered the residence they found the victim in his bedroom slumped over the bed. The victim committed suicide by shooting himself in the head with a 22-caliber handgun. The point here is that police officers have been called to make welfare checks and have found suicides, homicides, natural deaths, and a sundry of other situations. It is imperative that police officers always take welfare check calls seriously.

While there are many different potential outcomes for welfare check calls, what follows are some general guidelines that may be helpful for police officers when responding to these types of calls:

1. Obtain as much detail from the dispatcher as possible while driving to a welfare check call.

2. Upon arrival, talk to the reporting party first to glean as much detail as possible (e.g., when was the occupant(s) last seen, do they have family nearby, who has a key to the residence, how may cars should be in the driveway or garage, has the mail been checked, has the newspaper been picked up, how many live in the residence, has anyone noticed unusual persons coming and going, has anyone smelled any unusual odors).

3. Talk to neighbors to inquire if they have seen or heard anything unusual.

4. After the initial assessment, knock on the door. If there is no reply, walk around the residence and peer into the windows. Next, knock on the back door. If there is nothing unusual found during the initial investigation, there is probably no additional action that can be taken. You may call a relative with a key to come to the scene. The relative may wish to enter the residence.

5. In the case that an odor is smelled, such as gas coming from the residence, contact a supervisor and call the fire department.

6. If the situation is an exigent one, where a body can be seen laying on the floor by looking in the window, contact a supervisor for permission to use force to enter into the residence. A search warrant is not required here due to the exigency of this situation. In other words, it is an emergency situation and the exigency is an exception to the Fourth Amendment's requirement for a search warrant.

7. If an elderly person is found to be alone in a residence that has been the subject of a welfare check call, attempt to contact a relative or friend and explain the situation to them. If the elderly person has no relatives living in the area, other resources may be used, such as temporary shelters for the elderly, senior citizen organizations, the department on aging, and temporary care services. Of course, if the elderly person is ill and is in need of medical treatment, paramedics should be summoned to the scene.

Checking the Welfare of Children

In some cases officers are called to check the welfare of children. In these cases, if the child is being exposed to dangerous living conditions, the child should be removed from the home and taken into protective police custody. The officer should use good judgment as to the nature of dangerous living conditions. Being without water and electricity will justify taking a child into protective custody, while in other cases the justification may be physical signs of **child abuse**. Child abuse is harm to, or neglect of, a child by another person, whether adult or child. Child abuse happens in all cultural, ethnic, and income groups.

In recent years the public's increased awareness and reports of suspected child abuse have put pressure on law enforcement to improve their investigations of such cases. Police officers frequently must make a determination as to whether a child's accident or illness was caused by a parent or caretaker. However, it is often difficult even for medical personnel to discriminate between injuries and illnesses that are accidental and those that are not. Officers must determine whether the explanation for an injury is believable. Police should begin their investigation by asking the caretaker or parent for an explanation of the child's bruises or injuries. This is best done by simply asking how the accident happened. If the officer is still suspicious, specialized child abuse units or investigators should be notified and advised of the situation.

child abuse / The physical or psychological mistreatment of a child by his or her parents (including adoptive parents), guardians, or other adults. While this term emphasizes carrying out wrong acts, a related term is child neglect: not doing what is necessary, negligence. The combined problem area is often called child abuse and neglect.

All bruises and other trauma must be investigated. If bruises are found on two or more planes of a child's body, officers should be even more suspicious. For example, a child has bruises on the back and stomach. The caretaker's explanation is that the child fell backward in the living room of the family home. This might explain the bruises on the back, but not the stomach bruises. If a discrepancy exists between the reported cause of an injury and the injuries seen, officers should investigate further.

There are four major types of child abuse that officers may encounter on a welfare check call: physical abuse, sexual abuse, emotional abuse, and neglect. Physical child abuse is an injury resulting from physical aggression. This type of abuse is often the most obvious to police officers. The injury from physical child abuse may be the result of:

- beating, slapping, or hitting
- pushing, shaking, kicking, or throwing
- pinching, biting, choking, or hair pulling
- burning with cigarettes, scalding water, or other hot objects
- severe physical punishment

THE MENTALLY ILL

A mentally ill person is any person who is suffering from a mental disorder. A mental disorder may be manifested by a clinically significant behavioral or psychological syndrome or pattern and associated with either a painful symptom or impairment in one or more important areas of functioning. This may involve substantial behavioral, psychological, or biological dysfunction, to the extent that the person is in need of treatment. Police officers are increasingly coming into contact with persons suffering from mental illness (Watson, Corrigan, & Ottati, 2004). In some cases a person may exhibit obvious signs of mental illness by acting out what is perceived as strange or odd behavior, while in others cases the mental illness is not so obvious and may be latent.

There are a number of factors that have influenced the increased police contact with the mentally ill. These factors include displacement from institutional settings without adequate increases to community support, below-poverty-level disability assistance rates, homelessness, and reduced provincial and general hospital psychiatric capacities resulting in inadequate treatment stabilization.

It may surprise you to know that a fair amount of crime victims that police deal with also have a mental illness. Violence against people with mental health problems is a serious issue and a chronic problem for those who experience it. More than one-fourth of persons with severe mental illness are victims of violent crime in the course of a year, a rate eleven times higher than that of the general population, according to a study by researchers at Northwestern University. They estimated that nearly three million severely mentally ill people are crime victims each year in the United States (Teplin et al., 2005). Training to improve not only awareness, but also response strategies, to the problem of violence against people with mental health problems for the police force should be increased.

Police officers should recognize that just because a person they are called to deal with exhibits bizarre or different behavior does not necessarily mean that they are criminals. Likewise, the typical response to suspected criminal activity (containment, interrogation, detention) may not be appropriate when dealing with a person with a mental illness, especially when in crisis. Suppose that officers are called to check on a man sleeping under a blanket in the park. The officers notice that the man is acting strange, talking to himself, and rolling around in his blanket in what appears to be a jolting and violent manner. By talking to this man and asking questions, the officers determine that the man is a Vietnam War veteran who is having a flashback. By talking to this person and asking the right questions, the officers are able to resolve the situation without using force.

This book has advocated the need for police officers to become effective communicators. Likewise, when dealing with mentally ill persons effective communication can mean the difference between a potentially dangerous altercation and the successful resolution of the incident. According to Cordner (2006), police officers can resolve the most threatening of situations involving people with mental illness by maintaining a calm demeanor, using good oral and nonverbal communication, and using proper tactics. However, when communication techniques fail, it is crucial to have additional alternatives short of deadly force. Too often in the past, police officers who have encountered people experiencing mental health crises have used poor tactics, which in some cases turned immediately to the use of deadly force.

It is a good idea for police officers to become familiar with the mental health resources located in their communities and how to contact them, if needed. Officers should also get into the habit of carrying brochures that detail mental health facilities and services in their community. These brochures are also ideal because they can be disseminated to family members of mentally ill persons. It is important for officers to increasingly become more sensitive to the mentally ill, be prepared to refer them to appropriate resources, and not just jail them as a matter of routine to quickly solve a problem.

When the officer has the choice between jail and mental healthcare, the jail is almost always available, but the mental health system is not always available and is not always convenient even when it is available. Often, as a quick fix, police officers get into the habit of booking the mentally ill into the jail. However, this is problematic because it takes up needed jail space, and it does little to solve the problem in the long term. However, if the mentally ill person has committed a crime, the police officer may be left with little alternative other than jail.

Officers that have contact with persons that appear to be mentally ill should make a wholehearted effort to determine if witnesses, neighbors, and/or family have witnessed behavior that would lead a reasonable person to believe that the subject is a danger to themselves or others. The officer should pay attention to evidence at the scene that indicates that the subject is a danger to themselves or others. If the officer determines, through appropriate investigation, that an individual presents a potential danger to themselves or others, emergency care should be initiated. The officer should arrange for transportation of the subject to a treatment facility for evaluation.

THE HOMELESS POPULATION

homelessness / A situation where a person does not have a permanent place of residence. Often homeless persons live on the street or in abandoned buildings.

Homelessness is an extremely complex social problem that impacts the quality of life in the community. An estimated 842,000 adults and children are homeless in a given week, with that number swelling to as many as 3.5 million over the course of a year (Burt et al., 1999). Homeless persons suffer from high rates of mental and physical

Homeless man with cart sleeps on ground at entrance to expensive shop on Madison Avenue, NYC. Police officers frequently are required to intervene in situations involving homeless people. The officers should respect the rights of these individuals, but also recognize that many homeless people have mental problems.

health problems exacerbated by living on the streets and in shelters. Generally speaking, homeless individuals and families are those who are sleeping in places not meant for human habitation, such as cars, parks, sidewalks, and abandoned buildings, or those who are sleeping in an emergency shelter as a primary nighttime residence.

Racial and ethnic minorities, particularly African-Americans, are overrepresented among homeless populations. For example, 41 percent of the homeless are non-Hispanic whites, compared to 76 percent of the general population. Forty percent of the homeless are African-Americans, compared to 11 percent of the general population; 11 percent are Hispanic, compared to 9 percent of the general population; and 8 percent are Native American, compared to 1 percent of the general population. Homelessness continues to be a largely urban phenomenon. Seventy-one percent of the homeless are in central cities, 21 percent are in suburbs, and 9 percent are in rural areas (Burt et al., 1999).

Homelessness creates an especially perplexing problem for the police. Simply being homeless in many jurisdictions is not a crime. However, it is the lifestyle that many homeless persons lead that is a crime. Living in abandoned buildings and parks may be a violation of city ordinances and perhaps other state statutes. Homeless persons may start a fire to stay warm in an abandoned building, the fire gets out of control, and the building and surrounding buildings are damaged. The homeless person who begs for money or panhandles in a busy downtown area may be guilty of violating city ordinances. While police officers may be sensitive to the plight of the homeless person, the officer must balance this with the effective enforcement of laws that the homeless person may have violated.

The mere sight of a homeless person can create a certain amount of fear among the general citizenry. Unfortunately, as most police officers know, simply arresting the homeless person who is panhandling will do little to resolve the problem. The homeless person who is arrested will be back out of jail in a few hours or days at the most, and return to the street engaged in the same activity. It is important for the police to work with other social services to minimize the illegal activity that homeless persons may be involved in. The problem of homelessness is a pathology that goes beyond the police response. It must be realized that for persons forced to live in public spaces without access to shelter, public restrooms, and places to store their belongings, life continues to be disastrous.

Some cities have made great strides in addressing the problem of homelessness. The Public Safety and Regulatory Services Committee of the Minneapolis City Council ordered the Community Advisory Board on Homelessness to address building code issues and homelessness. The result was the creation of a Decriminalization Task Force to review all laws, policies, and practices that have the effect of criminalizing homelessness, and reporting back to the city and county with recommendations (Illegal to be Homeless Report, 2004). The Task Force sets the foundation for an increase in social services and assistance as a pathway to ending the criminalization of homelessness in Minneapolis. The following recommendations were subsequently presented to the city council for discussion and approval:

1. **Ordinance changes.** These include the repealing of an anti-camping ordinance and the rewording of other ordinances, such as trespassing, panhandling, loitering, shelter restrictions, interference with traffic, and public urination.

2. **Police protocols.** Training police to link homeless people to services will meet the needs of homeless people while ensuring the protection of their civil rights. Changes include the requirement of a complaint before police presence, a notice to campers before eviction, referrals to providers, and improvements in the handling of property belonging to those experiencing homelessness.

3. **Vagrancy charges.** Vagrancy laws are remnants of a previous era of law enforcement. Minnesota's vagrancy statute should be repealed.

4. **Public testimony.** Time should be allotted whereby public testimony is scheduled to allow advocates and people who have or are currently experiencing homelessness to come forward and speak to the city council and mayor on the issues stated previously.

These four items are part of a serious effort to address some of the immediate issues homeless people encounter on a daily basis. At the same time, a task force began dialogue between the city attorney's office, the police department, and the civil rights' department to deal with long-term issues and create constructive alternatives to the criminalization of homelessness. The task force also conducts ongoing discussions to address the following:

1. **City attorney policies and programs.** Geographic restrictions resulting in banishment in certain areas should be halted and a less punitive approach should be taken toward people experiencing homelessness.

2. **Civilian review authority.** In its role as a police watchdog body, the Civilian Review Authority should work with homeless providers to make it easier for people experiencing homelessness to report police misconduct.

3. **Police protocols.** Mental health workers should respond to calls involving those experiencing mental illness, while 911 dispatchers should review procedures to see if more calls can be directed to mental health workers.

4. **Police training and instructions.** All officers should be instructed to treat every resident, even those experiencing homelessness, with respect. In addition, officers

should undergo training on services that are available to people experiencing homelessness. Officers would also be issued resource cards to guide people to appropriate services.

5. **Police positions/services.** A police officer should be assigned to help homeless people who are perpetrators or victims of crime, and a mental health specialist position should be created to provide training and services.

New York Transit Bureau Homeless Outreach Squad

In the 1990s, the New York City Police Department (NYPD) Transit Bureau created the Homeless Outreach Squad. The NYPD Transit Bureau's Homeless Outreach Squad is a squad of police officers who address the problems of the homeless by interacting with them and providing them with transportation and access to the myriad of outreach services available in a humane and sensitive fashion. The officers of the squad continually receive additional specialized training. These factors provide the officers with the resources essential to aggressively enforce the penal law statutes and New York Code of Rules and Regulations in a consistent manner throughout the year in areas not accessible to routine patrol, such as the track and tunnel areas, as well as the emergency exits.

The innovative combination of diligent patrol, continuous reinspection of previously identified locations, placement of individuals with appropriate service agencies, and the arrest of chronically service-resistant individuals residing in the tunnel and track areas has resulted in an 86 percent reduction of homeless deaths on the transit system. The Transit Bureau's Homeless Outreach Squad has been recognized by other police agencies throughout the world, as well as by many homeless advocacy and outreach groups, as being at the forefront in implementing and successfully fulfilling its initiatives to provide transport and access to the many services available to the homeless community (Rowland, 2006).

ABANDONED VEHICLES

Imagine for a moment that you are driving through a neighborhood that you are not familiar with. As you drive through the neighborhood streets you notice several abandoned cars left parked on the street, some of them up on jacks with the wheels and tires noticeably missing. The abandoned cars probably don't leave a very good impression of the neighborhood, and perhaps create a bit of fear that the neighborhood may be full of crime.

Some car owners abandon old vehicles without caring about the consequences. This creates an eyesore and can encourage vandalism and arson, endangering lives, property, and the environment. Abandoned vehicles can lower property values and have a negative impact on the quality of life. People abandon vehicles for a variety of reasons, including the increased cost of vehicle ownership, low scrap-metal prices (meaning that people are charged by scrap dealers to take vehicles), and the desire to avoid the penalty for keeping a vehicle on the road illegally. Vehicles left abandoned on streets degrade the neighborhood, cause health hazards, and become a magnet for anti-social behavior.

The problem of abandoned vehicles in a community is a quality of life issue and should be addressed by the police. Abandoned vehicles are those vehicles that have been left on public streets and may have one or more of the following characteristics:

- Dismantled, partially or fully
- In a state of disrepair (broken windows, sitting on blocks, etc.)
- Missing license plates
- Filled with garbage
- Sitting in the same spot for several days and appearing nonoperational
- In front of a residence in which owners have moved away
- Sitting in the street on jacks with the wheels missing

Abandoned Vehicles on Public Roadways

Police officers should promptly investigate reports of abandoned vehicles on public roadways. If the vehicle is not an immediate traffic hazard, it should be marked with an orange "Vehicle Courtesy Check" sticker. The vehicle should be checked to ensure that it is not stolen, which can be done by running a check on the license tag and the vehicle identification number. The owner can be located in the same manner. The tire should be marked to determine if the vehicle has been moved when rechecked. Officers should then complete the standard departmental abandoned vehicle reports and record all pertinent information. After a specified time has elapsed (which may vary by individual state law), the officer should then determine if the vehicle has been moved. If the vehicle has not been moved, it can be towed and cited for being abandoned on the public roadway.

Abandoned Vehicles on Private Property

The police can tow an abandoned vehicle from private property when all attempts have been exhausted in locating the owner or when the vehicle is in violation of an ordinance or statute. Primarily, the same procedures should be followed as in the case of investigating an abandoned vehicle on public property; however, many police departments will require the owner of the property where the abandoned vehicle is located to sign a "hold harmless agreement" form. The hold harmless agreement basically states that the owner of the property where the abandoned vehicle is being towed from, releases and holds harmless the law enforcement agency and the governing body from any and all liability resulting from removal, towing, and storage of said vehicle(s).

STALLED VEHICLES

A single stalled vehicle can create a traffic jam of gigantic proportions. If you have ever been driving in rush hour traffic and happen to come upon a stalled vehicle, you probably have experienced the frustration of congested and slow-moving traffic. The congestion caused by a stalled vehicle can pose a potential accident hazard, so it is imperative that the police deal with stalled vehicles expediently and effectively. Vehicle traffic on the roadway must remain free-flowing and collision free.

The police officer is usually a welcome sight at the scene of a stalled vehicle. When an officer investigates a stalled vehicle the first consideration is to strategically park the patrol vehicle behind the stalled vehicle. The officer should position the patrol car just a few feet behind the stalled vehicle for protection. If the officer has traffic cones or traffic flares, they should be placed at least 50 or more yards behind the stalled car in order to alert other motorists. Traffic cones or flares can be placed in several locations. One cone should be placed 50 or so yards behind the stalled vehicle, another cone placed at 25 yards behind the stalled vehicle, and then one at 10 yards. This strategic placement offers maximum warning to approaching drivers.

If the driver is not present, and if traffic is heavy, the officer should call to have the vehicle towed in order to avoid serious traffic congestion and prevent a traffic accident. If the driver is absent from the car, but traffic is relatively light, the officer may elect to attempt to spend a few minutes locating the driver as opposed to towing the car. Once again, the traffic volume and time of day will most likely dictate the officer's decision whether to tow the vehicle immediately. If possible, the stalled car should be pushed onto the shoulder of the roadway or completely off the roadway and into a parking lot. If necessary, the officer should direct traffic until the stalled vehicle has been safely removed from the roadway.

If the location of the stalled vehicle dictates that the officer direct traffic in order to keep the traffic moving smoothly, the officer should wear a reflective orange vest that is highly visible to approaching traffic. If at night, the officer should place flares around the stalled vehicle and utilize a flashlight with an orange cone attachment. The traffic-directing LED light is an effective light used for manual traffic direction as it has four built-in ultra bright LED lights that produce an attention-getting flash pattern guaranteed to attract attention and increase the officer's visibility. The special fluorescent-coated diffuser enhances red light output. The LED light runs on two D-cell batteries that will run for 400 hours.

A stalled vehicle in a congested traffic route presents several threats. First, motorists who are frustrated by the congestion may attempt to maneuver their cars in and out of traffic in an attempt to get through traffic quickly, which increases the chances for an accident. Second, the stalled vehicle will assuredly result in motorists who just have to look as they drive by, not paying attention to what's in front of them. Invariably, while they are looking at the stalled car, they run into the rear of another car. This can result in a chain reaction.

It is also possible that **road rage** may develop in an overanxious driver who is trying to maneuver his or her way through the traffic to no avail. Road rage is a term used to refer to violent incidents caused primarily due to the inability to control one's anger while driving, which causes accidents or incidents on roadways. It is often a natural extension of aggressive driving.

road rage / The deliberate dangerous and/or violent behavior under the influence of heightened, violent emotion such as anger and frustration, with regard to the use of automobiles. Road rage is violence exhibited by drivers in traffic.

DIRECTING TRAFFIC

Most police officers don't like the idea of standing out in the middle of an intersection directing traffic, especially in the pouring rain, a snow blizzard, or the scorching heat. But, as most police officers know all too well, it's one of those necessary evils.

Traffic control is an invaluable service that is provided by the police to the general public. It is actually one of the most basic things that police do. Police officers spend maybe a day or less in the academy learning and practicing traffic control techniques. In some academies, recruits are taken to a busy intersection to practice the traffic control skills they just learned in the academy.

Police officers often encounter circumstances where manual traffic control is needed. This can be caused by any number of situations, such as a traffic collision, roadway construction, traffic signal malfunctions, or some type of natural disaster. For whatever reason, police officers need to know how to control traffic safely to reduce the likelihood of motorists becoming confused by unclear traffic directions and causing a collision.

Traffic Control Techniques

The officer assigned to direct traffic should maintain a professional attitude and demeanor while conducting traffic control duties. Any other type of attitude or demeanor is likely to create more confusion than already exists for the personnel or vehicles being controlled. The first step is to select the proper location at the scene where traffic control will be initiated in order to establish operations. Several factors must be considered in selecting this location, including the design of the intersection, traffic patterns, lighting conditions, and the degree of traffic control required.

The position of the police officer should be selected with personal safety in mind. This position must be clearly visible to drivers and should not interfere with the flow of traffic. The most commonly selected point is the middle of the intersection. However, intersection design may dictate that another spot be chosen. Some types of intersections require the officer to be positioned on one side or the other of the center, as in "T" type intersections, a one-way street, or unusually narrow roads.

Traffic control police officer wearing sunglasses and yellow-green reflective vest halts cars in one direction to let others pass in Los Angeles, CA. For most police officers, traffic control, although a necessary function, is not a popular one.

When directing traffic, police officers should stand with their face or back toward the stopped traffic and their side toward the traffic being directed to proceed. Manual traffic control signals used by police officers should be standardized for clear understanding, clearly visible, easily understood, and capable of transmitting information rapidly.

When engaged in the actual traffic control, the police officer should:

1. Give only necessary signals.
2. Leave the intersection if traffic becomes light (or when officially relieved from the post).
3. Turn the head to look toward the vehicle the officer intends to signal.
4. Give only one signal at a time.
5. Remain aware of traffic approaching from all directions.
6. Point (with the hand) to pedestrians the officer intends to direct, using minimum movement of hands and arms.
7. Repeat a signal several times to move sluggish traffic more rapidly.

There are six basic signals for manual traffic control: (1) stop, (2) go, (3) change direction, (4) right turn, (5) left turn, and (6) prohibited turn.

1. **Stop**
   - Extend the arm toward the vehicle(s) being signaled.
   - Raise the arm forty-five degrees above vertical.
   - Bend the elbow.
   - Hold the hand vertically with fingers together, extended, and with the palm facing traffic.
2. **Go—Move Along**
   - Use the hand nearest the stream of traffic being directed to go.
   - Holding the arm horizontal at shoulder height point with the index finger at the vehicle(s) being directed.
   - Bending the elbow, bring the hand back in an arc to the front of the chin to direct traffic to pass in front of the person directing traffic.
   - Using the same procedure, bring the hand back behind the ear to direct traffic to pass in back of the person directing traffic.
3. **Change of Direction**
   - Use the stop signal to stop each stream of moving traffic separately.
   - Turn ninety degrees.
   - Keep both hands in the stop signal position.
   - Give the go signal to each stream of traffic separately.
4. **Right Turn**
   - Usually made without direction from the person controlling traffic.
   - Use the right arm for traffic approaching from the right.
   - Use the left arm for traffic approaching from the left.
   - With the arm extended horizontally, point at the driver.
   - Swing the arm straight to point to where the driver is to go.
5. **Left Turn**
   - Stop opposing traffic.
   - Use the right arm for traffic approaching from the right.
   - Use the left arm for traffic approaching from the left.

- With the arm extended horizontally, point at the driver.
- Swing the arm straight to point to where the driver is to go.

6. **Prohibited Turn**
   - Shake head no.
   - Use a whistle, if necessary, to get the driver's attention.
   - Signal the driver to make the appropriate legal turn.

PRACTICE HINTS

Using Equipment in Traffic Control

Whistle
- One long blast signals traffic to stop.
- Two short blasts signals traffic to proceed.
- Several short blasts should be used to gain attention.
- The whistle should be used as needed and never to indicate frustration or anger.

Verbal Commands
- Do not shout.
- Use a loud tone.

Flashlight
- To stop traffic, swing the flashlight beam across the vehicle's path several times.
- Direct the beam downward at the pavement, being careful not to blind drivers.
- After a vehicle is stopped, use manual signals for further instructions.

Angry Driver Runs Over Worker Directing Traffic

A Davis County man was jailed Friday morning after he allegedly got impatient while driving — and ran over a construction worker who halted traffic to let school children cross.

John Thornley, 51, is accused of running over the worker near Dawson and Gentile Streets in Layton Friday morning. Police say he became agitated that flagger Samuel Allen was slowing the flow of traffic.

"He told me that after the kids were clear, he was going to go whether I liked it or not. He said he would run me over."

After the children had crossed, Allen says he glanced back to Thornley's vehicle.

"He let off the clutch and proceeded to hit me with his car," he said. "He came forward and the front bumper hit me in the knee caps. He basically just hit me and I rolled off to the side."

"The potential is there for a very serious accident," said Sgt. James Petre of the Layton Police Department. "If the flagger had gone underneath the car [instead of] going to the side of it, he could have easily been crushed by the wheels."

Thornley was later arrested and booked into jail on charges of assault and fleeing the scene of an accident.

Source: www.kutv.com; Accessed online November 29, 2006.

LOST PROPERTY

We have all lost personal property from time to time. It may be that we dropped our wallet in a restaurant only to discover it missing hours later. Perhaps we may have left our watch in the locker room at the health club. When a citizen calls the police to report lost property, the officer normally handles these types of reports in a fairly standard manner.

The first thing the officer must determine is the fact that the property has indeed been lost and not stolen. The officer proceeds with recording basic identifying information about the property. This includes a description of the property, identifying marks, serial number, model number, and any specific distinguishing marks or characteristics that would make the property readily identifiable. A distinguishing characteristic may be the owner's engraved initials on the back of a watch. It is also important to try and narrow down the location where the property was lost. When was the last time the reporting party saw the property? Did the reporting party leave the property laying somewhere? Did anyone else have possession of the property? These are all relevant questions that should be asked and answered. Once the officer obtains a thorough description of the property, a lost property case should be cut through records and a written report prepared.

STOLEN PROPERTY

A stolen property report is handled much the same way as a lost property report. The only difference is that in a stolen property report, a crime has been committed and there may be evidence at the scene to process. The officer should make a determination regarding where the property was taken from and the approximate time of the theft. In a larceny case where a lawn mower was taken from the backyard of the victim's residence, it is important to determine the approximate time of the theft. When was the last time the victim saw the lawn mower? When did the victim discover it missing? With this information, the officer can narrow down the time of the theft to between 3:00 P.M. (the last time the mower was seen) and 8:00 P.M. (when the victim discovered the lawn mower missing).

A thorough description of the property must be gathered. The description should include model and serial numbers, if known. Distinguishing marks and characteristics, and the value of the property must be determined. In some cases the victim may have a picture of the property; the officer should request a copy of the picture. Officers should, like other crime scenes, diagram or note in their report where the property was located when it was stolen. In cases of great dollar loss, photographs should be taken of the crime scene. Photographs can provide permanent documentation of where the property was located and can also depict any damage or marks created by the suspect(s) during the crime.

Victims should be asked if they know of anyone who may have committed the theft. Likewise, in the case of a larceny or burglary, the officer should conduct a neighborhood check in an effort to determine if anyone saw or heard anything unusual. If there is an abundance of evidence left at the scene, a crime lab should be called to process the scene. Evidence could include footprints in the mud left by the suspect, or blood evidence where the suspect(s) cut themselves crawling through a window. This will vary depending on the individual police agency and the dollar loss involved in the crime. In a burglary case where the dollar loss is in the tens of thousands, it is wise to call a crime lab to process the scene.

Finding Stolen Property

The best way to find property once it is lost or stolen is to have up-to-date records, pictures, or video noting serial and model numbers, if available, or to place an "owner-applied number" on items without a serial number. Unique numbers make identifying and matching items to the rightful owner easier, as a national database is used to track stolen and recovered items via serial number once the item is reported lost, stolen, or found. However, if this information is not available, a detailed description will help, as will a general idea of when and where the property was lost or stolen.

REPEAT CALLS

Repeat calls for police services take up an enormous amount of police resources. Most police officers can attest to the fact that there are always a few locations on their beats that are the subject of repeat calls. In some cases, due to the nature of the problem, there is little the police may do to prevent repeat calls. In some cases, however, repeat calls to a particular location are the result of officers haphazardly dealing with the situation. Officers may find it helpful to apply problem-solving approaches to locations that result in repeat calls for police services.

Recall from Chapter 3, problem solving works by identifying and dealing with the root causes of a problem instead of repeatedly responding to the consequences (Goldstein, 1990). The concept of problem solving is best illustrated by the following fictitious example. Suppose police have responded several times a day to calls from a neighborhood that is located near a popular bar. The calls result in the police dispersing drunk and disorderly persons who hang out in the bar's parking lot. Under the incident model, police would simply dispatch officers to the scene, take action, and maybe file a report. In itself, this would do little to resolve the long-term problems of disorder and drinking in public.

Under the problem-solving approach, police would collect some additional information. This may include surveying residents, analyzing the time of day when incidents occurred, determining how often the night club has been fined for allowing persons to leave the establishment with alcohol, and evaluating characteristics of the environment. The results of this analysis would be used to craft a customized response to the disorder and public drinking. Periodically, the effectiveness of the response would be tested and reviewed, and the response would be further optimized.

Taking a problem-solving approach to addressing specific repeat calls requires a broad inquiry into the nature of the particular problem. As part of that inquiry, police may find it useful to analyze the patterns of repeat calls relating to specific victims, locations, and offenders. Research has shown that a small minority of locations account for a fairly large amount of calls for police services. The same holds true for offenders; that is, a small number of offenders account for a fairly large amount of crime. Some researchers have found that as much as 60 percent of calls for police services come from about 10 percent of locations (Spelman & Eck, 1989). If you are a police officer reading this book, you can probably think of a few locations on your beat or within your community that take up a large portion of police resources due to repeat calls.

The SARA problem-solving model may provide an excellent tool for police officers to use to address repeat calls for services at a particular location. The SARA model is widely applicable to problems faced by many neighborhoods. In brief, the SARA model proposes that first a Scanning exercise should be undertaken, in which a clear understanding of the problem is identified. The scanning phase is followed by an Analysis phase, where a comprehensive review of the problem takes place, drawing on the data identified during the scanning phase. The analysis results will inform the Response phase of the method, where a design for intervention and crime reduction should be implemented, with appropriate structure being put in place to monitor and modify the implementation where necessary. The final Assessment stage is intended to determine whether the response worked. If the response had little or no effect, more analysis can be completed so that a more appropriate response can be applied. If the response resulted in a positive change, the officer can determine what is required, if anything, to maintain the change. Revisit Chapter 3 for a more detailed discussion of the SARA problem-solving model.

PRACTICE HINTS

SARA Problem-Solving Model at a Glance

- Scanning — identifying the problem
- Analysis — learning the problem's causes, scope, and effects
- Response — acting to alleviate the problem
- Assessment — determining whether the response worked

CITIZEN CONTACTS

Casual conversations with citizens are a vital law enforcement function. Actions such as knock and talks, conversing with persons in public, and other similar actions are encouraged, but should end when the person indicates a desire to end the contact, and the officer has no reason to detain the person under applicable legal authority. Friendly contacts with citizens in neighborhoods that have poor relations with the police are especially encouraged. If business cards are made available by the department, officers are encouraged to leave a business card with every contact who does not receive the officer's name in writing. The primary officer on a call would leave a business card, unless one is specifically requested from another officer participating in the police activity.

Officers should keep in mind that perception can create community dissension as quickly as reality. Therefore, it is important that officers take all reasonable steps to prevent giving a perception of stopping citizens without legal basis or in violation of the department's policy and procedure. Creating an appearance that the person stopped is suspected of grievous conduct when no such reasons exist should be avoided. An example of this would be an officer stopping a person for a minor traffic violation and more officers are present at the scene than necessary to safely complete the law enforcement business at hand.

When greeting citizens, police officers should be kind and deliver an appropriate greeting, such as "good morning." A verbal introduction is also a good way to make a good impression on the citizen: "Good morning, I am Officer Jones from the Somewhere in America Police Department." If the officer is stopping the citizen for some justified reason, a polite explanation of the reason for the stop should be provided by the officer. Certain tactical reasons may exist, making this greeting impractical. Officers should skip the greeting if tactical circumstances exist.

Anti-crime efforts often call for increased public contacts based on minor infractions and minor law violations. These operations are sometimes referred to as **zero tolerance**. Zero tolerance basically means that officers engage in aggressive patrolling, including stopping persons for minor violations. Such stops must always be made with reason to believe the person has been, is, or is going to commit a crime. In zero tolerance operations the officers should use great discretion in determining the appropriate level of police action necessary to reasonably assure compliance. The primary purpose of zero tolerance operations is high visibility and increased contacts. Police officers should always conduct themselves in a professional manner when involved in zero tolerance activities. If possible, citizens living in the neighborhood should be briefed on the reasons for the increase in police contacts in the neighborhood. This can go a long way in dispelling rumors of police harassment.

zero tolerance / A police tactic where officers engage in aggressive patrolling, including stopping persons for minor violations. Zero tolerance tactics are usually carried out in areas that have a high incidence of crime.

SUMMARY

- Police officers handle a significant amount of service-related calls during a typical tour of duty. The media often portrays police work as glamorous crime-fighting tasks. While police do perform their fair share of crime fighting, estimates reveal that anywhere from 60 to 90 percent of a police officer's job is service-related.

- Service-related calls may include lost adults or children, disputes, directing traffic, assisting a citizen, welfare checks, checking buildings, helping stranded motorists, motor vehicle accidents, abandoned vehicles, lost property, found property, and the like.

- Police officers are often called to mediate disputes. Some disputes are minor and may be as simple as neighbors arguing over a property issue, while other disputes may be of a more serious nature, such as domestic violence.

- Police officers should practice good officer safety skills when dealing with any dispute, regardless of the perceived magnitude. Dispute calls can be potentially dangerous for officers. Each year there are officers killed in the line of duty while investigating dispute calls.

- The most important skill for police officers in resolving a dispute is effective communication. Police

officers should always keep in mind that what you say is not nearly as important as how you say it. Thus, in handling a dispute, effective communication skills are the best tool the officer has.

- Suspicious character calls are a fairly common police call. In most cases, they require minimal action on the part of the officer. However, the officer must use due caution when responding to suspicious character calls because it is never certain what the officer will encounter. The suspicious character could be the salesman who is lost and trying to find an address or it could be the lookout person for a burglary in progress. Like most other police calls, officers should approach a suspicious character call exercising good officer safety techniques.

- Prowler calls, much like suspicious character calls, can be dangerous for police officers largely because the officers have little idea what they are getting themselves into. The prowler may simply be a law-abiding citizen walking his dog or it could be a peeping Tom who is making rounds in the neighborhood peering in windows.

- There are different types of missing children that police typically deal with: family abductions; endangered runaways; nonfamily abductions; and lost, injured, or otherwise missing children. Regardless, police officers should treat any missing child with immediacy.

- The largest number of missing children happen to be runaways, followed by family abductions; then lost, injured, or otherwise missing children, and finally, the smallest category, but the one in which the child is at greatest risk of injury or death, non-family abductions.

- In critical situations, it should be determined if the missing child falls under AMBER Alert guidelines. An AMBER Alert is a notification to the general public, by media outlets, that an abduction of a child has happened. AMBER is an acronym for "America's Missing: Broadcast Emergency Response," and was named for nine-year-old Amber Hagerman, who was abducted and murdered in Arlington, Texas in 1996.

- A missing adult or missing person requires many of the same procedures that are followed in cases of missing children or juveniles. A missing person is someone whose whereabouts is unknown to the reporting party. A common misconception is that a person must be absent for a certain amount of time before being legally classified as missing. This is rarely the case. In instances where there is evidence of violence or of an unusual absence, law enforcement agencies often stress the importance of beginning an investigation promptly.

- The nature of a welfare check call may vary. One example of a welfare check call is when police are called to check on an elderly neighbor who has not been seen for days. Sometimes police find the worst case during a welfare check call, such as suicides and homicides. Welfare check calls should always be taken seriously.

- In some cases police may encounter child abuse or abandoned children during a welfare check call. It may be that a parent(s) left their small children at home alone while they went out for a night of partying at the local night club. In the case of discovered child abuse, there are generally four types that could be encountered by police officers: physical abuse, sexual abuse, emotional abuse, and neglect.

- Mental disorders are common in the United States. An estimated 26 percent of Americans ages eighteen and older, about one in four adults, suffer from a diagnosable mental disorder in a given year. More than one-fourth of persons with severe mental illness are victims of violent crime in the course of a year, a rate eleven times higher than that of the general population. In light of these figures, police officers will inevitably come into contact with the mentally ill. Thus, officers should become familiar with the mental health resources located in their communities and how to contact them, if needed.

- Police officers should recognize that just because a person they are called to deal with exhibits bizarre or different behavior does not necessarily mean that they are criminals, they could be suffering from a serious mental illness. When dealing with mentally ill persons, effective communication can mean the difference between a potentially dangerous altercation and successful resolution of the incident.

- Abandoned vehicles are an eyesore and can give the impression that no one cares about the neighborhood. Abandoned vehicles should be addressed by the police not only as a quality of life issue for the neighborhood, but also as a potential criminal violation if the vehicle is left abandoned on a public street. If the police are called to investigate an abandoned vehicle on private property (e.g., a grocery store parking lot), a hold harmless agreement should be signed by the private property owner prior to the police impounding the vehicle.

- The congestion caused by a stalled vehicle can pose a potentially serious accident hazard. Police officers should diligently work toward removing a stalled vehicle from the roadway as expeditiously as possible in order to minimize the potential risk of an accident or other traffic-related hazards.

- Police officers may be called upon to manually direct traffic. Officers should use proper techniques and hand signals when directing traffic. If an officer directs traffic in a haphazard manner it will likely result in confusion on the part of drivers, and worse yet, may cause a traffic accident. If officers are directing traffic at night, they should wear a light reflective vest and use a lighted orange traffic cone.

- Citizens from time to time lose or misplace their property while in a public location. They often call the police to make a lost property report. It is important that the officer record accurate identifying information about the lost property. This includes a description of the property, identifying marks, serial number, model number, and any specific distinguishing marks or characteristics that would make the property readily identifiable.

- A stolen property report is handled much the same way as a lost property report. The only difference is that in a stolen property report, a crime has been committed and there may be evidence at the scene. It is important to glean an accurate and thorough description of stolen property. This greatly assists in the proper identification of the property in the event that it is recovered.

■ Repeat calls for police services can result in an enormous strain on police resources. Some repeat calls are due to the police haphazardly handling them in the first place. Police officers should proactively address the problem of repeat calls to specific locations. Problem-solving techniques should be used to diagnose and resolve repeat calls. Using a problem-solving model, such as the SARA model, may be effective in identifying why the police respond to specific locations repeatedly, and may also assist in tailoring a resolution to the problem.

Classroom Discussion Questions and Activities

1. Describe the service role of the police.

2. List at least five police calls that are considered part of the service role of the police.

3. What is the AMBER Alert system?

4. Discuss the importance of effective communication skills in handling a dispute call.

5. Describe how officers can resolve a tense and threatening situation involving a person with a mental illness who is acting aggressive.

6. Discuss a few of the guidelines police should follow when investigating a prowler call.

7. Discuss innovative approaches of how the police are beginning to handle homeless populations.

8. Think about a location in your community that is the subject of repeat police calls. From your perspective, how have the police dealt with this location?

9. Discuss the importance of applying problem-solving methods in resolving the problem of repeat calls.

10. Interview a police officer and ask the officer how dealt with a homeless person in the performance of their duties.

11. What is tactical communications?

Websites and Other Resources

Center for Problem Oriented Policing:
    www.popcenter.org/

National Center for Homeless Education:
    www.serve.org/nche/

Federal Bureau of Investigation—Uniform Crime Report:
    www.fbi.gov/ucr/ucr.htm

National Center for Missing and Exploited Children:
    www.missingkids.com/

National Center for Missing Adults:
    www.theyaremissed.org/ncma/

References

Birzer, M. L. (2003). The theory of andragogy applied to police training. *Policing: An International Journal of Police Strategies and Management, 26* (1), 29–42.

Birzer, M. L., & Tannehill, R. L. (2001). A more effective training approach for contemporary policing. *Police Quarterly, 4,* 233–252.

Burt, M. R., Aron, L. Y., Douglas, T., Valente, J., Lee, E., & Iwen, B. (1999). *Homelessness: Programs and the people they serve.* Washington, DC: Interagency Council on the Homeless.

Cole, G. F., & Smith, C. E. (2004). *The American system of criminal justice* (10th ed.). Belmont, CA: Wadsworth.

Cordner, G. W. (1979). Police patrol work load studies: A review and critique. *Police Studies, 2* (2), 50–60.

Cordner, G. W. (2006). People with mental illness. *Center for problem oriented policing.* Accessed online: www.popcenter.org.

Goldstein, H. (1990). *Problem-oriented policing.* New York: McGraw-Hill.

Haberfield, M. R. (2002). *Critical issues in police training.* Upper Saddle River, NJ: Prentice-Hall.

Illegal to be Homeless Report. (2004). *The criminalization of homelessness in the United States.* Washington, DC: National Coalition for the Homeless.

Mehrabian, A. (1972). *Nonverbal communication.* Chicago: Aldine-Atherton.

O'Keefe, J. (2004). *Protecting the republic: The education and training of American police officers.* Upper Saddle River, NJ: Prentice-Hall.

Pear, K. (1999). *Policing in America: Methods, issues, and challenges* (3rd ed.). Upper Saddle River, NJ: Prentice Hall.

Rowland, J. (2006). Homeless Outreach Squad. Accessed online at www.nyc.gov/html/nypd/html/transportation/hou.html.

Skolnick, J. H., & Bayley, D. H. (1986). *The new blue line: Police innovation in six American cities.* New York: The Free Press.

Spelman, W., & Eck, J. E. (1989). Sitting ducks, ravenous wolves, and helping hands: New approaches to urban policing. *Public Affairs Comment,* Austin, TX: School of Public Affairs, University of Texas.

Teplin, L. A., McClelland, G. M., Abram, K. M., & Weiner, D. A. (2005). Crime victimization in adults with severe mental illness: Comparison with the national crime victimization survey. *Archives General Psychiatry, 62,* 911–921.

Thompson, G., & Jenkins, J. B. (1993). *Verbal judo: The gentle art of persuasion.* New York: William Morrow.

Watson, A. C., Corrigan, P. W., & Ottati, V. (2004). Police officers' attitudes toward and decisions about persons with mental illness. *Psychiatric services, 55,* 49–53.

Whitaker, G. P. (1982). What is patrol work? *Police Studies, 4* (4), 13–22.

Wilson, J. Q. (1968). *Varieties of police behavior: The management of law and order in eight communities.* Cambridge, MA: Harvard University Press.

Forensics

" DNA technology could be the greatest single advance in the search for truth, conviction of the guilty, and acquittal of the innocent since the advent of cross-examination "

—Judge Joseph Harris in *People vs. Wesley*

CHAPTER OUTLINE

- Introduction
- Duties of a Forensic Scientist
- FBI Forensic Laboratory
- Crime Scene
- Body Fluids
- Fibers
- DNA
- Questioned Documents
- Fingerprints
- Firearms
- Digital Evidence
- Collection and Preservation of DNA Evidence
- Summary

After completion of this chapter, you will be able to do the following:

- Understand the basic concepts of forensic science.
- Explain the duties of a forensic scientist.
- Describe the duties of specialized forensic scientists.
- Describe the functions of the FBI Forensic Laboratory.
- Explain Locard's principle.
- List the basic requirements in investigating a crime scene.
- Discuss the principles involved in evaluating bloodstain patterns found at a crime scene.
- List the functions of blood in the human body.
- Explain the grouping of blood types.
- Describe how fibers are examined.
- Explain DNA identification procedures.
- Describe the process used to examine questioned documents.
- Explain how fingerprints are used for identification purposes.
- Discuss how digital evidence is preserved.

CASE STUDY: *Hudson v. State*
10th Court of Appeals—Waco, Texas
August 30, 2006 - 10-05-00172-CR

Police officers investigating the burglary of trucks found a piece of a tooth in the driver's seat of one of the trucks. About three weeks after the burglary of the trucks, an investigator identified the defendant as a potential suspect because of his prior involvement in similar cases. The defendant was in jail on other charges when he was identified as a suspect. The investigator asked jailers to bring the defendant to his office to discuss the burglary. The defendant asked for a soft drink and he was given one. He denied knowing anything about the burglary and refused to allow the investigator to look at his teeth to see if a tooth was chipped or broken. The defendant also refused the investigator's request to use a swab and obtain a DNA specimen. When jailers came to return the defendant to his cell, he smashed the soft drink can and threw it in a trash can. After the defendant left, the investigator retrieved the can and submitted it for DNA analysis. A specimen obtained from his soft drink can matched the DNA from the tooth. Based on this information, an arrest warrant was obtained, and the defendant was eventually convicted of burglary of a vehicle. The defendant argued that the seizure of his DNA specimen was unlawful because it was done without a warrant, probable cause, or reasonable suspicion.

(continued)

Held: Conviction affirmed. The Fourth Amendment does not prohibit the seizure of property that has been abandoned voluntarily. Property is considered to have been abandoned voluntarily if: "(1) the defendant intended to abandon the property, and (2) the decision to abandon the property was not due to police misconduct." Here, the defendant was about to be taken from the investigator's office when he threw the can in the trash of his own volition. This conduct indicated intent on the defendant's part to abandon the can and there was nothing in the record to indicate that the defendant's decision to throw the can away was induced by police misconduct.

INTRODUCTION

forensic / An adjective relating to law courts or to public debate; based on a Latin word meaning "pertaining to law."

forensic science / The study and application of scientific facts and techniques to legal problems.

anthropometry / A personal identification method based on eleven body measurements.

The purpose of this chapter is to introduce the basic concepts of forensic science to future law enforcement personnel. **Forensic** is based on a Latin word meaning "pertaining to law" and is defined by one dictionary as an adjective relating to law courts or to public debate. **Forensic science** is defined as the study and application of scientific facts and techniques to legal problems (*The New Lexicon Webster's Dictionary of the English Language*, 1988, p. 369).

The most famous forensic scientist is probably the fictional Sherlock Holmes. Arthur Conan Doyle published the first of his Sherlock Holmes novels, *A Study in Scarlet*, in 1887. Holmes, in the novels, used many different scientific means to analyze the evidence left behind at a crime scene. In 1879, Alphonse Bertillon published the first book on anthropometry. **Anthropometry** is a personal identification method based on eleven body measurements. This is generally thought to be the first system of personal identification used by the police. Later, when a case demonstrated that

Arthur Conan Doyle published the first of his Sherlock Holmes novels, *A Study in Scarlet*, in 1887. His fictional Sherlock is the most famous forensic scientist.

Edmond Locard established the first police crime laboratory in 1910 in Lyon, France. He originated the "Locard principle" which states that "every contact leaves a trace."

two different persons had the same anthropometry measurements the system was abandoned.

In 1892, Francis Galton published *Fingerprints*. In his book, he explained how police departments could use fingerprints as a means of personal identification. The book discussed the many different characteristics of fingerprints and how the combinations are used to form a unique fingerprint for each person.

The first police crime laboratory was established in 1910 in Lyon, France by Edmond Locard. Locard is famous for some of the cases he solved. He solved a case involving the counterfeiting of gold coins by analyzing metal scrapings on the suspect's clothing. He solved a strangulation case by analyzing fingernail scrapings from the victim. He also solved numerous cases by using fingerprint evidence. In investigating a case, the first thing he wanted to study was the suspect's clothing. He originated the **Locard principle**, which states that "every contact leaves a trace."

Locard principle / A principle that holds that every contact leaves a trace.

The first police crime laboratory in the United States was established in 1924 by the Los Angeles Police Department. In 1925, the New York Police Department established a Bureau of Forensic Ballistics. In 1915, Leone Lattes discovered a method for typing dried bloodstains based on the pioneering work of Karl Landsteiner. His method has been used to determine the blood types of mummies.

DUTIES OF A FORENSIC SCIENTIST

Unlike the popular TV series, *CSI Miami*, the forensic scientist does not run around investigating crimes to catch the criminal. The role of the forensic scientist is to analyze physical evidence. Normally, the scientist is an expert in one scientific area.

Voices of Experience

Field Forensics

Excerpts from an interview between Cliff Roberson and former police officer, Albert D. Bettilyon, currently criminal justice school chair for ITT, Tucson, Arizona.

Q: *When we talk about "field forensics" what are we referring to?*

A: There are two parts of forensics, the laboratory setting, which involves scientists working in crime labs; and field forensics, which involves trained evidence technicians going to a crime scene when summoned there by police and evaluating the scene, locating evidence, recording evidence, processing evidence, packaging the evidence, working within the law enforcement agencies going to the scene collecting, recording, and presenting that evidence in court for trial.

Q: *How realistic are the* CSI *television shows?*

A: The television shows are designed for entertainment. The programs basically take the highlights of field forensics work. Rarely in the real world does evidence become identified in a short period of time. While the programs hire law enforcement personnel to help them in writing the programs, the process is much more difficult, time consuming, and the results are not as information yielding as they are on television. While confessions and positive evidence identification are obtained in forty-four minutes on the *CSI* shows, in my 1,400 unnatural death investigations the quickest time to identify a suspect took four days.

Q: *Walk us through one of your death investigations.*

A: The case I selected occurred in suburban Chicago. A middle-aged medical doctor reported that while he was at home washing his car in the driveway, his wife, who had been depressed, committed suicide in the home. He stated that he came inside to assist her, carried her into the bathroom, and attempted to perform life-saving maneuvers. However, the evidence we recovered and processed at the scene told a different story. The wife had been stabbed. It was noted that in only 4 percent of suicides involving women, will the woman actually use a knife. The trajectory of the knife suggested that it would have been difficult for the woman to have stabbed herself in the manner indicated by the wound. Generally, in suicides where knives are used in the abdomen, the knife trajectory is upward into the body. In this case, the knife's trajectory as it entered the body was downward. In addition, the bloodstain patterns did not fit the doctor's version of the facts. The bloodstain patterns also indicated that the victim had been carried about 15 feet across the bedroom before the body was taken into the bathroom. Prior to talking to the doctor, we had examined the scene and made some findings regarding the death. The doctor's statement did not agree with our initial findings. ■

Most scientists have degrees in biology, chemistry, or physics. Recently, many of them are graduates of forensic science programs at universities.

When the scientist receives the evidence it is the scientist's role to analyze it and give conclusions to investigators regarding identification, comparison, probability, and reliability of the results of the examination. Frequently, examiners must testify in court regarding their examination and conclusions. When testifying as an expert witness, examiners may give their opinions. Ordinary witnesses generally are not allowed to express opinions when testifying.

POLICE IN ACTION: Specialized Forensic Scientists

Medical examiner: A physician who is authorized by state statutes to investigate unexpected, suspicious, or unnatural deaths within the state.

Forensic pathologist: A physician trained in determining the causes of death.

Odontologist: A forensic dentist who applies the science of dentistry to police investigations.

Forensic toxicologist: A scientist who is trained to detect the presence of poisons or drugs in body fluids, tissues, and organs.

Forensic psychiatrist: A medical doctor who specializes in the application of psychiatry to law.

Forensic engineer: An engineer who analyzes bridges and buildings by applying engineering principles to law.

Forensic entomologist: An individual who studies insects and applies that study to law.

Forensic anthropologist: Performs specialized examinations of human skeletal remains or badly decomposed bodies for identification purposes.

FBI FORENSIC LABORATORY

FBI Forensic Services

"The successful investigation and prosecution of crimes require, in most cases, the collection, preservation, and forensic analysis of evidence. Forensic analysis of evidence is often crucial to determinations of guilt or innocence."
—FBI *Handbook of Forensic Services*, 2003, pp. 2–4.

The FBI has one of the largest and most comprehensive forensic laboratories in the world. The forensic services of the FBI Laboratory Division and the Investigative Technology Division are available to:

- FBI field offices and legal attachés.
- U.S. attorneys, military tribunals, and other federal agencies for civil and criminal matters.
- State, county, and municipal law enforcement agencies in the United States and territorial possessions for criminal matters.

All forensic services, including expert witness testimonies, are rendered free of cost; however, the following limitations apply:

- No examination will be conducted on evidence that has been previously subjected to the same type of examination. Exceptions may be granted when there are reasons for a reexamination. These reasons should be explained in separate letters from the director of the laboratory that conducted the original examination, the prosecuting attorney, and the investigating agency.

Toxicologist doing some testing. Nebraska State Crime Lab.

- No request for an examination will be accepted from laboratories having the capability of conducting the examination. Exceptions may be granted upon approval of the FBI Laboratory Assistant Director or a designee.
- No testimony will be furnished if testimony on the same subject and in the same case is provided for the prosecution by another expert.
- No request for an examination will be accepted from a nonfederal law enforcement agency in civil matters.

CRIME SCENE

Locard Principle: "Every contact leaves a trace."

As discussed in Chapter 4, crime scene analysis is important in the crime-solving process. In addition, rapid technological advances have greatly expanded the amount of information that can be obtained from the analysis of physical evidence from a crime scene. Chapter 4 looked at crime scene investigation from the police officer's point of view. In this chapter, we examine the crime scene as a forensic investigator would. In order to take advantage of these new opportunities, the investigator is required to use sound scene-processing practices to recover useful evidence. Critical to the administration of a crime is the objective recognition, documentation, collection, preservation, and transmittal of physical evidence for analysis.

The investigator may need a search warrant in order to legally enter and collect physical evidence. There are exceptions to the warrant requirements, as will be discussed in Chapter 8. Caution is recommended in this area. Nothing is more frustrating than the collection of evidence that cannot be admitted into evidence. The four most common exceptions to the requirements for a warrant are:

- **Emergency.** If the police are responding to a situation where it appears that persons are in danger, no warrant is required.

- **Destruction of evidence.** If the police have a reasonable basis for concluding that entry is needed to prevent the destruction of evidence, under most conditions the police may enter without a warrant.

- **Consent.** If consent is obtained from a person who is authorized to give consent, the police do not need a warrant to enter.

- **Lawful arrest.** If the police arrest an individual, generally they may search the area in which the individual was arrested.

The basic steps that an investigator should take at any crime scene are:

1. Ensure that you have legal clearance to enter the area.
2. Secure and protect the crime scene.
3. Conduct a search of the area using a "search pattern."
4. Document and record the items found at the scene.
5. Collect and package the evidence.
6. Transmit the evidence to the crime lab.

Voices of Experience

Forty-One Years of Police Experience

Excerpts from an interview between Cliff Roberson and retired police officer, John Maxwell. Professor Maxwell is currently a faculty member at Drexel University, Philadelphia, Pennsylvania.

Q: *I understand that you retired from the Philadelphia Police Department (PPD) after almost forty-two years of service. Under what circumstances were you hired as a police officer?*

A: I was hired under an innovative program at the age of eighteen. The program was called the police adjunct program. The PPD solicited students who had just graduated from high school. Out of the thousands of high school seniors who took the test, only twelve of us were selected. We were attached to the police academy for the next twenty-four months. We would go to a block of training and work with an operational bureau within the department. We were not allowed to carry a gun or to work on the streets. We were actually interns in the various departments. After a period of time we would go back to the academy and share experiences. After additional classroom work, we would be placed in a different operational unit. We would rotate so that each of us was placed in different units. By the end of the twenty-four months, we had trained in all the major bureaus. All twelve individuals completed the program and stayed with the department until they had been promoted at least one time.

The program was disbanded after several classes. I am not sure of the actual reasons it was disbanded, but I have heard of several, including the fact that many of the individuals were drafted into the military and did not return to the police department when they were released from the military. I also heard that apparently it was too costly with the twenty-four month training period. In addition, because of the department's needs for manpower, the minimal entry age for regular officers was lowered. At the time I was hired, the entry requirement for regular police officers was twenty-three years old. This was later reduced to twenty-one. ■

Police officers from a tactical team searching through a house when serving a search warrant. Kansas City, MO, PD Street Narcotics Unit TAC.

A crime scene should be searched in a systematic manner. Generally, an initial walk-through will be made and then followed by a more thorough search. There are four standard search patterns currently in use by law enforcement: strip, grid, spiral, and quadrant. A spiral search, as shown in Figure 4.1, is used by a single investigator at an outdoor crime scene. It is also used frequently in underwater searches. In a spiral search, the investigator starts a distance from the crime scene and works his or her way via a spiral to the spot where the crime occurred.

When an item found at a crime scene is introduced into evidence at a court proceeding, the party introducing the evidence, generally the prosecution, must establish that the item was the exact item found at the scene. This authentication may be accomplished in two ways—by use of a chain of custody or a description of the article that establishes that it is the same article. The party must also establish that the item has not been altered. The easiest and most practical method to meet these requirements is by use of a chain of custody. Often it is hard to establish by description alone that an article, such as a match, was the same article found at the scene. A *chain of custody* is a document that records the date, time, and the person who had possession of the evidence from the time it was collected until the time it is offered as evidence in a trial. When the item is transferred from one officer to another, the chain of custody must reflect the date and time of the transfer and the person to whom it was transferred.

The steps involved in securing and preserving a crime scene until the scene may be turned over to specialized crime scene investigators are outlined in the U.S. Department of Justice handbook, *Crime Scene Investigation: A Reference for Law Enforcement Training,* June 2004, NCJ 200160.

Securing the Crime Scene

Initial Response/Receipt of Information

a. Note or log dispatch information. **Note:** The responding officer is expected to obtain this key information, from dispatch or direct citizen complaint to officer, or officer observation onsite.
   1. Address
   2. Location (e.g., storefront, second-floor rear, garage, mile marker, compass direction)
   3. Time
   4. Date
   5. Type of call
   6. Parties involved
   7. Weapons involved
   8. Ongoing and/or dangerous scene

b. Be aware of any persons or vehicles leaving the crime scene. Note: The officer is expected to, as soon as possible, write down information.
   1. Note arrival time
   2. Describe vehicles (make, model, color, condition, license plate number, age)
   3. Describe individuals (height, weight, race, age, clothing, sex, distinguishing features)
   4. Describe direction of travel (from first observation)

c. Approach the scene cautiously.
   1. Scan the entire area to thoroughly assess the scene
   2. Note any possible secondary crime scenes (e.g., different areas where evidence/activity is observed)
   3. Be aware of any persons in the vicinity who may be related to the crime
   4. Be aware of any vehicles in the vicinity that may be related to the crime

d. Assess the scene for officer safety.
   1. Assess the scene for ongoing dangerous activity
      Note: Look, listen, smell (e.g., downed power lines, animals, biohazards, chemicals, weapons)
   2. Ensure officer safety before proceeding.
      Note: Discretion is advised. Unreasonably dangerous scenes should not be entered (e.g., anthrax, bomb scene)

e. Remain alert and attentive.
   1. Assume crime is ongoing until determined to be otherwise (keep looking, listening, smelling)

f. Treat location(s) as a crime scene until determined to be otherwise.
   1. Use all information initially received
   2. Use all senses
      Note: The scene may not be what it initially appears to be

Safety Procedures

a. Evaluate the scene for safety concerns.
   1. Scan the area for present dangers (look, listen, smell)
   2. Check for hazardous materials (e.g., gasoline, natural gas, electrical lines, biohazards)

    3. Check for weapons

    4. Check for radiological or chemical threats

    5. Notify appropriate support agencies to render the scene safe (prior to entry) (e.g., fire department, HazMat, bomb squad)

b. Approach the scene with caution.

    1. Ensure officer safety

    2. Reduce risk to victim(s)

    3. Reduce risk to witnesses

    4. Reduce risk to others

c. Survey the scene for dangerous persons and control the situation.

    1. Be aware of violent persons

    2. Be aware of potentially escalating conflicts

    Note: Remember that officers' actions can contribute to the escalation or de-escalation of the situation

    3. Apply communication and defensive training skills

d. Notify supervisory personnel and call for assistance/backup.

    1. Follow departmental guidelines for notification of supervisors

    2. Call for assistance/backup as appropriate

Emergency Care

a. Assess the victim(s) for injury.

    1. Assess medical needs/signs of life

    2. Administer emergency first aid (if needed)

b. Call for medical personnel.

    1. Follow departmental guidelines/practices for notification of emergency medical personnel

    2. Continue to assist the victim(s) as necessary

c. Guide medical personnel to the victim(s) at the scene.

    1. Choose pathways to minimize contamination/alteration of the crime scene

    2. Direct medical personnel along the chosen pathway

    3. Remain with emergency medical personnel, if possible

d. Point out potential physical evidence to medical personnel.

    1. Instruct emergency medical personnel to avoid contact with evidence items/material

    2. Instruct emergency medical personnel to preserve all clothing (avoid altering bullet holes, knife tears, etc.)

    Note: Altering includes cutting, tearing, ripping through existing bullet holes.

    3. Document movement of injured persons by emergency medical personnel

    4. Document movement of scene items by emergency medical personnel (e.g., furniture, blankets, weapons)

e. Instruct emergency medical personnel not to "clean up" the scene.

    1. Avoid removal of items originating from the scene (e.g., removal of trace and other physical evidence by adherence to emergency medical equipment and personnel cleaning the victim's skin surface)

    2. Avoid alteration of items originating from the scene

    Note: Alterations to the scene can include additions of items by emergency medical personnel

f. Document emergency medical responder(s) at the scene.
  Note: This is for future investigative purposes (e.g., information about scene alteration and/or to obtain elimination and/or standard/reference samples).
  1. Name(s)
  2. Unit(s)
  3. Agency name and business telephone numbers
  4. Name/location of medical facility to which the victim(s) is being transported
g. Obtain "dying declaration" as appropriate.
  Note: Review jurisdictional law regarding dying declarations.
  1. Assess victim's level of injury (life-threatening injury)
  2. Note any statement
h. Document statements and comments.
  Note: Documentation should include to whom and under what circumstances statements/comments were made.
  1. Document statements and comments made by victims
  2. Document statements and comments made by suspects
  3. Document statements and comments made by witnesses
i. Document statements and comments made during transport.
  1. Accompany the injured person(s) to the medical facility, if possible
  2. Document statements and comments made by the injured person(s) during transport
  3. If law enforcement is unavailable, request that medical personnel who accompany the injured person(s) to the medical facility document statements and comments
  Note: Remind medical personnel to preserve evidence

Secure and Control Persons at the Scene

a. Control all persons at the scene.
  1. Restrict movement of persons at the scene
  2. Prevent persons from altering physical evidence
  3. Prevent persons from destroying physical evidence
  4. Continue to maintain safety at the scene
  5. Restrict areas of movement within the scene
  6. Continue to control the scene by maintaining officer presence
b. Identify all persons at the scene. **Note:** Identify means to obtain verifiable personal information.
  1. Identify suspects (secure and separate)
  2. Identify witnesses (secure and separate)
  3. Identify bystanders (remove from the scene)
  4. Identify victims/family members/friends (control while showing compassion)
  5. Identify medical and assisting personnel
c. Exclude unauthorized/nonessential personnel from the scene.
  1. Law enforcement officials not working the case
  2. Politicians
  3. Media
  4. Other nonessential personnel (i.e., any persons not performing investigative or safety functions at the scene)

Establish and Preserve Scene Boundaries

a. Establish scene boundaries by identifying the focal point(s) of the scene and extending outward.
   Note: Be aware of trace and impression evidence during scene assessment.
   1. Secure areas where the crime occurred
   2. Secure areas that are potential points and paths of entry/exit of suspects/ witnesses
   3. Secure areas where victim(s)/evidence may have moved or been moved
   4. Initially secure a larger area, since it is easier to contract than to expand the boundaries

b. Set up physical barrier(s).
   1. Set the physical perimeter for established scene boundaries (with crime scene tape, rope, cones, vehicles, personnel, etc.)
   2. Set the physical perimeter for established scene boundaries by using existing structures (walls, rooms, gated areas, etc.)

c. Document entry of all people entering and exiting the scene.
   1. Record the names of persons entering the scene
   2. Record the names of persons exiting the scene

d. Maintain integrity of the scene by controling the flow of personnel and animals entering and exiting the scene.

e. Attempt to preserve/protect evidence at the scene.
   1. Protect evidence from environmental elements, if possible
   2. Protect evidence from manmade intrusions (e.g., shoe or tire impressions)
   3. Protect evidence from mechanical devices (e.g., sprinklers, helicopters)
   4. Protect evidence from animals

f. Document the original location of the victim(s) or objects at the scene that were observed being moved. **Note:** Care should be taken to use nondestructive techniques to document locations.
   1. Document point of origin of the victim(s) or items at the scene.
   2. Document alternate location.

g. Follow jurisdictional laws related to search and seizure by determining the need for obtaining consent to search or a search warrant.

Transfer Control of the Scene to the Investigator(s) in Charge

a. Brief the investigator(s) taking charge of the scene.

b. Assist in controlling the scene.

c. Transfer control of entry/exit documentation.

d. Remain at the scene until relieved of duty.

Processing the Crime Scene

Conduct Scene Assessment

a. Talk to the first responders regarding their observations and/or activities.
   1. Introduce yourself and explain your role
   2. Obtain information regarding the incident
   3. Ascertain established scene boundaries
   4. Ascertain previously chosen pathway

b. Evaluate safety issues for personnel entering the scene.
   1. Reevaluate and modify, as necessary, current safety practices
   2. Require personal protective equipment (PPE) as appropriate
c. Evaluate search and seizure issues.
   1. Determine the need for obtaining consent to search
   2. Determine the need for obtaining a search warrant
   3. Determine the need for prosecutorial/legal resources
d. Evaluate/establish the path of scene entry/exit.
   1. Establish pathway by reassessing and modifying, as necessary, the chosen pathway
   2. Ensure that authorized personnel are informed of any modifications to the established pathway
e. Evaluate initial scene boundaries.
   1. Determine appropriateness of the initial scene boundaries
   2. Ensure that the areas where the crime occurred are secure
   3. Ensure that the areas that are potential points and paths of entry/exit of suspects/witnesses are secure
   4. Ensure that areas where victim(s)/evidence may have moved or been moved are secure
   5. Make modifications as necessary
f. Determine/prioritize the scene investigation(s).
   1. Determine the size and number of scene(s)
   2. Prioritize the steps in the scene investigation(s)
   3. Allocate current resources
g. Establish a staging area for consultation and equipment.
   1. Identify an area in close proximity to the scene
   2. Identify an area not involved in the incident
   3. Secure the staging area and limit access
h. Establish communication between individuals at multiple scenes (as necessary).
   1. Establish the type of communication equipment to be used
      Note: When selecting equipment, consider security of communication
   2. Update with current information as necessary
i. Establish a secure area for temporary evidence storage.
   1. Evaluate environmental factors that could effect degradation/loss of evidence when selecting a secure area for temporary evidence storage
   2. Establish a secure area for temporary storage for evidence. **Note:** Consider rules of evidence/chain of custody.
j. Determine additional resource requirements.
   1. Determine the need for additional investigative resources
   2. Determine the need for specialized units
   3. Determine the need for legal consultation
   4. Determine the need for specialized equipment/supplies
   5. Request additional resources as determined
k. Ensure scene integrity/security.
   1. Maintain scene entry/exit documentation
   2. Prevent unauthorized access to the scene

l. Ensure that witnesses to the incident are identified and separated.
   1. Ascertain potential witnesses
   2. Separate witnesses from each other and from others present
   3. Obtain valid identification from witnesses
   4. Document witness identification(s)

m. Ensure that the surrounding area is canvassed.
   1. Assign appropriate personnel to conduct the canvass
   2. Ensure that results of the canvass are documented
      Note: Documentation should also include locations where persons are not found for future follow up.

n. Ensure preliminary documentation/photography. **Note:** The purpose of this section is to ensure that the presence and/or appearance of items, persons, and conditions that are likely to be lost if not immediately documented or photographed are recorded.
   1. Photograph or document items that may change
   2. Photograph or document conditions that may change
   3. Photograph or document persons, including injuries or lack thereof

Conduct Scene Walk-Through and Initial Documentation

a. Minimize scene contamination.
   1. Use established entry/exit points and pathways
   2. Determine the need for personal protective equipment prior to entry
   3. Conduct walk-through with individuals responsible for processing the scene, if available

b. Prepare preliminary documentation.
   Note: Document factual observations, not opinions.
   Document the scene as first observed (e.g., preliminary photograph, rough sketch, notes).

c. Identify and protect fragile/perishable evidence.
   1. Evaluate crowds/hostile environment(s) and ensure that evidence is secure, as necessary
   2. Evaluate weather conditions and ensure that evidence is protected, as necessary
   3. Identify fragile/perishable evidence
   4. Ensure documentation/photography of fragile/perishable evidence (immediately, if possible)
   5. Ensure collection of fragile/perishable evidence, as appropriate

Document the Scene

a. Determine the type of documentation necessary for the specific scene.
   1. Determine if photographs, videos, sketches, or measurements are needed
   2. Determine if forms are needed to supplement note taking (e.g., photo logs, checklists, evidence log, chain of custody forms)

b. Coordinate documentation of the scene.
   Note: Assign or prioritize documentation; ensure that all documentation ultimately bears the unique identifier(s) assigned to the case.
   1. Coordinate photographing of the scene
   2. Coordinate videotaping of the scene

3. Coordinate sketching of the scene
4. Coordinate measurements of specific scene items
5. Coordinate notes

c. Photograph the scene.
   Note: Ensure that photographs taken depict a fair and accurate representation of the scene/items photographed.
   1. Take overall scene photographs
   2. Take medium-range scene photographs
   3. Take close-up scene photographs
   4. Photograph evidence with and without measurement scales and/or evidence identifiers
      Note: Instruct when to photograph with and without measurement scale and/or identifiers with appropriate evidence items.
   5. Photograph victims, suspects, witnesses, crowds, and vehicles at the scene as relevant
   6. Photograph from various perspectives as relevant (e.g., aerial, witness's view, area under body once body is removed)

d. Videotape the scene as an optional supplement to photographs. **Note:** Consider switching audio off according to jurisdictional requirements.
   1. Determine if videotaping is needed (e.g., at a homicide, a large scene, an officer-involved incident, or a large amount of evidence)
   2. Ensure that new tape is used
   3. Break off write-protect tab after taping to prevent accidental overwrite

e. Prepare preliminary sketch(es) and take measurements.
   1. Measure the immediate area of the scene
   2. Indicate "North" on the sketch
   3. Indicate that the sketch is "not to scale"
   4. Measure the relative location of evidence for future correlation with evidence records
      Note: Instruct on particular measurement techniques (e.g., triangulation, coordination, use of a legend).
   5. Measure the evidence prior to movement
   6. Measure rooms, furniture, and other objects relevant to the scene
   7. Measure the distance to adjacent buildings or other landmarks (e.g., mile markers, bridges, manhole covers, silos)
   8. Consider additional sketches that may be useful to focus attention on a particular area or item

f. Generate notes at the scene (e.g., photo logs, checklists, evidence log, chain of custody forms, detailed conditions of the items).
   1. Document the scene location
   2. Document time of arrival at the scene
   3. Document time of departure from the scene
   4. Document scene appearance
   5. Record transient evidence (e.g., smells, sounds, sights)
   6. Record environmental conditions (e.g., weather, temperature)
   7. Document circumstances that require departures from usual procedures (e.g., safety, environmental, traffic issues)

Bloodstains at the Crime Scene

"Due to the fact blood is a fluid; the analysis of the splatter can be evaluated with some of the basic laws of physics. These laws are Newton's Second Law and Projectile Motion."

—Jamie Coon, 2004

bloodstain pattern analysis / The study of blood as it comes in contact with a surface.

Bloodstain pattern analysis is the study of blood as it comes in contact with a surface. At crime scenes where there are blood splatters, the analysis of splatter is important because it can provide significant clues to help reconstruct the crime. The position and appearance of blood marks on the body and its immediate surroundings can help reconstruct the crime. The size and shape of the blood patterns left behind at the crime scene can also determine the source of the blood and movement that might have occurred after the bloodshed began.

Blood has known properties that allow experts to analyze and reproduce the patterns made at the crime scene. From the reconstruction of the blood patterns, investigators can determine if a crime was committed or if the wound was self-inflicted. They can also determine if the victim crawled or was pulled away from the location where the point of impact occurred. Blood splatter evidence is admissible in court because it is verified by the basic laws of physics and basic principles of biology, chemistry, and math. In *People v. Avila*, 133 P.3d 1076, 38 Cal.4th 491, 43 Cal.Rptr.3d 1 (Cal. 05/15/2006) the court affirmed the defendant's conviction and stated in its opinion, "Based on the crime scene evidence, including blood splatter evidence, and the position of Medina's body, authorities concluded that when she was shot Medina was lying in the position in which she was found, and that she probably was shot in the temple first and in the forehead second."

In *People v. Ochoa*, No. E037937 (Cal. App. Dist.4 04/24/2006) the court stated in its opinion:

> As discussed earlier, the circumstances, including the manner of the killing and the condition of the victim's body, supported a finding of intent to inflict extreme and prolonged pain. There were pools of blood and blood splatter on the floor and walls of the hallway and bedroom. There also was blood splatter on the bedroom ceiling. The blood splatter evidence, along with the wood splinters, indicated that the victim was at about five different locations in the hallway and bedroom during the course of the attack. The height of the blood splatter on the walls indicated that the victim was at times standing, sitting, and on the ground. Based on the evidence, the jury reasonably could have found that Ochoa pursued Gallardo as he attempted to avoid his attacker.

As one California court noted in discussing blood splatter evidence: "The methods employed are not new to [science] or the law, and they carry no misleading aura of scientific infallibility" [*People v. Stoll* (1989) 49 Cal. 3d 1136, 1157 (265 Cal. Rptr. 111, 783 P.2d 698)].

When analyzing blood patterns at a crime scene, the key variables involved are:

- spot size
- quantity
- shape
- distribution

- location
- angle of impact
- target surface

Source: Marieb, E. M. (2001). *Human anatomy and physiology* (5th ed.). Englewood Cliffs, NJ: Pearson Education, pp. 650–680.

Some common terms used in studying blood at a crime scene are:

- **Angle of Impact:** The acute angle formed between the direction of a blood drop and the plane of the surface it strikes.
- **Cast-Off Pattern:** A bloodstain pattern created when blood is released or thrown from a blood-bearing object in motion.
- **Drip Pattern:** A bloodstain pattern that results from blood dripping into blood.
- **Flight Path:** The path of the blood drop, as it moves through space, from the impact site to the target.
- **Flow Pattern:** A change in the shape and direction of a bloodstain due to the influence of gravity or movement of the object.
- **Impact Pattern:** Bloodstain pattern created when blood receives a blow or force resulting in the random dispersion of smaller drops of blood.
- **Misting:** Blood that has been reduced to a fine spray, as a result of the energy or force applied to it.
- **Projected Blood Pattern:** A bloodstain pattern that is produced by blood released under pressure as opposed to an impact, such as arterial spurting.
- **Spatter:** Blood that has been dispersed as a result of force applied to a source of blood. Patterns produced are often characteristic of the nature of the forces that created them.
- **Target:** A surface upon which blood has been deposited.
- **Transfer/Contact Pattern:** A bloodstain pattern created when a wet, bloody surface comes in contact with a second surface. A recognizable image of all or a portion of the original surface may be observed in the pattern.
- **Wipe Pattern:** A bloodstain pattern created when an object moves through an existing stain, removing and/or altering its appearance.

Source: Forensic Serology: Bloodstain Pattern Analysis. Accessed online at www.policensw.com/info/forensic/forensic6c.html on May 12, 2006.

BODY FLUIDS

Blood

The average human body contains about five liters of blood. Blood has five main functions for the human body. First, it acts as a transport, transporting oxygen from the lungs to the cells and carbon dioxide back to the lungs. It transports chemical messengers released by the body, as well as nutrients and waste mate-

Blood Types in Humans

Blood Type	Antigen Present in Red Blood Cells
A+	A, D
A-	A
B+	B, D
B-	B
AB+	A, B, D
AB-	A, B
O+	D
O	None

rial. Second, the circulation of blood helps maintain the body temperature. Third, blood maintains the body's pH level by using carbon dioxide to buffer the system. Fourth, it carries toxins to the kidneys where enzymes break them down and they are excreted from the body in urine or sweat. **Note:** the kidneys filter your entire volume of blood about 1.5 times per hour. Fifth, the blood helps control the balance of the body's electrolytes, including salt.

Blood is mostly water containing three different types of cells: erythrocytes (red blood cells, RBC), leukocytes (white blood cells), and thrombocytes (platelets). Red blood cells contain hemoglobin, which is needed to transport oxygen from the lungs to the cells. White blood cells constitute a major part of our immune system. The body uses protein tags to identify its own cells and keep the immune system from mistaking them for invading organisms and attacking them. The red blood cells can have A or B protein tags, antigens, on them for identification purposes. Red blood cells with no identification are called type O. There is a protein tag, D antigen, which controls the Rh factor. If the D antigen is present, the person is Rh-positive. If the D antigen is missing the person is Rh-negative.

When blood is present at the scene of a crime, four basic questions need to be answered:

1. Is it blood?
2. Is it human blood?
3. What type of blood is it?
4. Who does it belong too?

Blood contains an enzyme, peroxidase, which makes its identification easy. Many chemicals react with peroxidase to give certain visible colors indicating that the liquid is blood. Benzidine makes the stain turn blue if it is blood and phenolphthalein makes the bloodstain turn red. Most agencies now use luminol (aminophthalhydrazide), which is more sensitive, comes in handy aerosol spray cans, and glows in the dark. Luminol can detect blood in trace amounts of 1:5,000,000 parts. This is especially important where someone has attempted to remove blood stains by using cleaning agents and water. **Note:** Sometimes horseradishes, radishes, oranges, lemons, and grapefruits will give a false positive.

The standard test to determine if the blood is human is the precipintin test. In conducting the precipintin test, human blood cells are injected into a laboratory animal. The animal's immune system creates antibodies that specifically bind to human blood cells. The antibodies are then put in a test tube and then some of the suspected human blood is added to the test tube. The formation of a dark ring at the interface indicates the blood is human.

Semen

In sexual crimes, the most important evidence that an investigator can find is the presence of seminal fluid. **Note**: The absence of seminal fluid does not mean that the sexual crime did not occur. Semen (seminal fluid) is the liquid portion of the male ejaculation. It is composed of 95 percent seminal fluid and about 5 percent spermatozoa. The average male ejaculation is less than four milliliters (about one teaspoon), but contains about 200 million spermatozoa.

In trying to locate semen at a crime scene, generally the investigator will use ultraviolet (UV) light because semen stains fluoresce under UV light. Suspected stains may then be tested using a piece of filter paper moistened with a solution of sodium naphthol phosphate or Fast Blue B. Both of these chemicals react with the acid phosphatase present in the seminal fluid by changing color. At the crime lab, the scientist generally looks for the presence of a protein labeled p30. The presence of p30 or prostate specific antigen (PSA) indicates the presence of seminal fluid. **Note**: Once the seminal fluid dries out it becomes quite brittle and can disintegrate with handling.

FIBERS

Based on Locard's principle that every contact leaves a trace, fibers are a good source of evidence. The more violent the contact between the offender and the victim, the more likely that fibers will be transferred from one to the other. Because fibers are lost

The Use of Fibers to Convict a Serial Killer

Wayne Williams was believed to have killed at least twenty-nine children in Atlanta between July 1979 and May 1981. On May 22, 1981, Williams was stopped by an Atlanta police officer because he was illegally parked on a bridge. He was cited and released. Two days later when the body of Nathaniel Carter was found in the river near the bridge, the police obtained a search warrant and searched Williams' car. There were yellow-green nylon carpet fibers on the body. These fibers matched the carpet in Williams' car. An expert testified that the probability of carpet fiber being present at random was 0.00013.

Eventually, there were twenty-eight different fibers that were used to associate Williams with the victims and the crime scenes. Williams was convicted on February 27, 1982, and sentenced to two life imprisonments for the murder of two of the victims, Carter and Jimmy Payne. Two days later, the Atlanta "child murder" task force announced that he was responsible for twenty-three of the thirty murdered children. The task force was then disbanded. The other seven cases were never solved.

On May 6, 2005, DeKalb County, Georgia, Police Chief Louis Graham ordered the reopening of the murder cases of four boys killed in DeKalb County between February and May 1981 that were attributed to Williams. Chief Graham stated that Williams may be innocent of all of the murders. However, the authorities in neighboring Fulton County, Georgia, where the majority of the murders occurred, refused to reopen the cases under their jurisdiction. Williams has always vehemently denied the charges. The reopened cases were eventually closed for the lack of new evidence.

In November 2005, British rock band Deep Purple's album featured a song called "Wrong Man," which was sung from Williams' point-of-view—a protest of innocence.

natural fibers / Fibers from animal fur, silkworms, or plants.

manufactured fibers / Fibers that are either regenerated fibers or fibers made from substances created in a laboratory.

microspectrophotometer / An instrument used to analyze the chemical identity of the fiber and any dyes used to color the fiber.

with the passage of time, any victim fibers found on a suspect or the reverse generally indicates contact between the two within the last twenty-four hours.

Fibers are classified as natural or manufactured. **Natural fibers** include fibers from animal fur, silkworms, or plants. **Manufactured fibers** are either regenerated fibers or fibers made from substances created in a laboratory. Manufactured fibers include nylon, polyester, acrylic, olefin, and aramid. Fibers are identified by their shape, size, and optical properties when studied under a microscope. In addition, a **microspectrophotometer** may be used to analyze the chemical identity of the fiber and any dyes used to color the fiber.

DNA

DNA / DNA is a long polymer of nucleotides (a polynucleotide) and encodes the sequence of the amino acid residues in proteins using the genetic code, a triplet code of nucleotides.

Deoxyribonucleic acid (DNA) is a nucleic acid, usually in the form of a double helix, that contains the genetic instructions specifying the biological development of all cellular forms of life, and many viruses. **DNA** is a long polymer of nucleotides (a polynucleotide) and encodes the sequence of the amino acid residues in proteins using the genetic code, a triplet code of nucleotides. DNA is thought to date back to between approximately 3.5 to 4.6 billion years ago.

DNA is not a single molecule, but rather a pair of molecules joined by hydrogen bonds. It is organized as two complementary strands, head-to-toe, with the hydrogen bonds between them. Each strand of DNA is a chain of chemical "building blocks," called nucleotides, of which there are four types: adenine (A), cytosine (C), guanine (G), and thymine (T). These allowable base components of nucleic acids can be polymerized in any order, giving the molecules a high degree of uniqueness. Every person's DNA, their genome, is inherited from both parents. The mother's mitochondrial DNA, together with twenty-three chromosomes from each parent, combines to form the genome of a zygote, the fertilized egg. As a result, with certain exceptions such as red blood cells, most human cells contain twenty-three pairs of chromosomes, together with mitochondrial DNA inherited from the mother (Watson, 2003, pp. 42–44).

To identify individuals, forensic scientists scan thirteen DNA regions that vary from person to person and use the data to create a DNA profile of that individual (sometimes called a DNA fingerprint). There is an extremely small chance that another person has the same DNA profile for a particular set of regions.

Only one-tenth of a single percent of DNA (about three million bases) differs from one person to the next. Scientists can use these variable regions to generate a DNA profile of an individual, using samples from blood, bone, hair, and other body tissues and products.

In criminal cases, this involves obtaining samples from crime-scene evidence and a suspect, extracting the DNA, and analyzing it for the presence of a set of specific DNA regions (markers). The markers in a DNA sample are found by designing small pieces of DNA (probes) that will each seek out and bind to a complementary DNA sequence in the sample. A series of probes bound to a DNA sample creates a distinctive pattern for an individual. These samples are compared to determine whether the suspect's sample matches the evidence sample. A marker by itself usually is not unique to an individual; if, however, two DNA samples are alike at four or five regions, odds are great that the samples are from the same person. If the sample profiles don't match, the person did not contribute the DNA at the crime scene.

Figure 7.1   The Replication of DNA

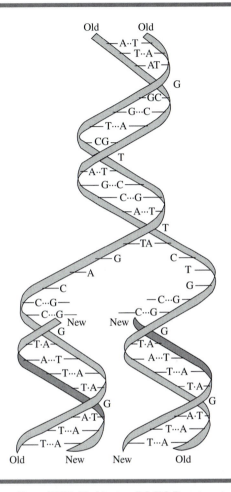

Source: Forensic DNA Analysis and Issues (1991). Washington, DC: U.S. Department of Justice, p. 3.

If the patterns match, the suspect may have contributed the evidence sample. While there is a chance that someone else has the same DNA profile for a particular probe set, the odds are exceedingly slim. Most experts consider that using DNA forensic technology is far superior to eyewitness accounts, where they consider the odds for correct identification based on eyewitness identification are about 50:50 (Humane Genome Project).

The more probes used in DNA analysis, the greater the odds for a unique pattern and against a coincidental match, but each additional probe adds greatly to the time and expense of testing. Four to six probes are recommended. Testing with several more probes will become routine, observed John Hicks (Alabama State Department of Forensic Services). He predicted that DNA chip technology (in which thousands of short DNA sequences are embedded in a tiny chip) will enable much more rapid, inexpensive analysis using many more probes, and raising the odds against coincidental matches.

Compulsory Requirement to Give DNA Blood Sample?

In 2004, Adrian Lamo entered a guilty plea in a U.S. District Court to a violation of 18 U.S.C. section 1030, computer fraud, a Class D felony. Mr. Lamo was placed on probation for a period of thirty months. Lamo had a reputation as an accomplished computer hacker.

Lamo was informed by the U.S. Probation Office that the office needed to obtain a blood sample from him for DNA testing. The blood was to be extracted from him at the U.S. Probation Office. He expressed grave concerns about the procedure based on reasons of religion. Lamo believes the blood of man to be both dear and sacred. He expressed these concerns to his probation officer and to defense counsel. On April 26, 2006, Lamo reported to the U.S. Probation Office, as directed in a letter dated April 5, 2006. He did so and presented hair samples as well as offered fingernail clippings and cheek swabs. However, the probation office requested a blood sample from him. He declined to provide a blood sample at that time based on his understanding that he would be able to raise his concerns in Court. The District Court denied his request and ordered him to submit to the blood test. (*U.S. v. Lamo*, No. CR S-05-022-FCD)

The first individual sent to jail as the result of DNA testing was Colin Pitchfork. In 1983, Lynda Mann, a 15-year-old schoolgirl, was raped and murdered in the Narborough, England, area. Using forensic science techniques available at the time, a semen sample taken from her body was found to belong to a person with type A blood and an enzyme profile that matched only 10 percent of males. With no other leads or evidence, the case was left open. In 1986, Dawn Ashworth, another 15-year-old who lived in the nearby town of Enderby, was found strangled and sexually assaulted in the same area. The *modus operandi* matched that of the first attack, and semen samples revealed the same blood type.

The prime suspect was a local boy, Richard Buckland, who revealed knowledge of Ashworth's body and admitted the crime under questioning, but denied the rape and murder of Lynda Mann. The town carried out a mass screening of its 1,400 male residents in an attempt to find a match. Later, it was learned that one individual, Colin Pitchfork, who had not yet been tested, tried to persuade someone else to give him a DNA sample. The police then retrieved a sample from Pitchfork and the DNA matched the DNA profile in the semen found in Lynda Mann's body. As of July 2006, Pitchfork was still in an English prison for the rape and murder with a scheduled release date of 2017. **Note**: to read a fascinating book on the case, read *The Blooding*, by Joseph Wambaugh.

DNA was first introduced as evidence in the United States in a state courtroom in 1987 (News Brief, *Police Magazine*, April 2006, p. 16). As of May 2006, statutes in five states and the federal government required the taking of DNA profiles of all persons arrested for a felony. If the person is acquitted or charges are drop, then the profile is deleted (Willing, 2006).

The FBI's Combined DNA Index System (CODIS) was first created to catalog violent criminals and sexual predators, but the 2004 Justice for All Act expanded the system to include samples from all newly convicted federal felons, including drug offenders and white-collar criminals.

A Case Study on the Use of DNA Evidence

On October 25, 1998, a Houston, Texas woman was taken from her apartment at gunpoint. She was raped and then dumped in a field in the next county. On October 30, 1998, she identified 16-year-old Josiah Sutton, a local high school football star, as one of her attackers. He was tried and convicted in July 1999. At his trial, a Houston Police Department (HPD) crime analyst testified that the DNA evidence found on the victim matched Sutton's DNA profile. He was convicted and sentenced to twenty-five years confinement in the Texas prison system.

In December 2002, the Houston Crime Laboratory was the subject of an independent audit because of numerous problems. The HPD suspended DNA testing and started retesting evidence from hundreds of cases.

In July 2003, retests in the Sutton case discredited the original analyses and established that Sutton's DNA was not present in the sample. Sutton was released from prison on bond pending retrial. In May 2004, the Texas governor granted Sutton a pardon based on the governor's belief that Sutton was innocent. Sutton received a payment of $118,000 in reparations from the state for his four years of confinement.

In March 2005, Donnie Young was convicted of possession of a controlled substance and sentenced to serve prison time. Texas law requires that all persons serving time in a state prison submit DNA samples. Young's DNA profile was entered into the Texas database. In May 2006, it was determined that Young's DNA matched the DNA obtained from the victim in 1998. Based on the DNA match, Young was indicted in June 2006 for the aggravated sexual assault of the victim (Khanna & Glenn, 2006).

On June 21, 2006, Houston Chief of Police Harold Hurtt announced that a national forensic association has recertified Houston's DNA division after a four-year lapse that began when an audit discovered numerous problems at the lab. The flaws included unqualified personnel, botched test results, and a leaky roof that contaminated evidence. The final cost for the independent audit and reexamination of the DNA cases for the city of Houston will likely exceed $6 million. The chief stated that the city has a moral duty to make sure no innocent persons remain in prison because of the slipshod and possibly malicious actions of former lab personnel.

Press Conference of Chief Hurtt, Houston City Hall, June 21, 2006.

QUESTIONED DOCUMENTS

"Although not all handwriting is identifiable to a specific writer, the examination of handwriting characteristics can sometimes determine the origin or authenticity of questioned writing. Traits such as age, sex, personality, or intent cannot be determined from handwriting examinations."

—FBI *Handbook of Forensic Services*, p. 158

A **questioned document** is generally considered as any signature, handwriting, typewriting, or other mark whose source or authenticity is in dispute or doubtful. The most common questioned documents include letters, checks, driver's licenses, contracts, wills, voter registrations, passports, petitions, threatening letters, suicide notes, and lottery tickets (Brunelle, 1982).

questioned document / Generally considered as any signature, handwriting, typewriting, or other mark whose source or authenticity is in dispute or doubtful.

The profession of questioned document examination (QDE) can be traced back to 1870. Famous cases involving QDE include the Dreyfus affair, Bruno Hauptmann and the Lindbergh kidnapping, the Hitler Diary profiling controversy, and Clifford Irving's forgery of Howard Hughes' signature and Mormon documents.

In 1910, Albert Osborn's book, *Questioned Documents*, was published. This is probably the first book on QDE. Osborn's basic principles regarding handwriting comparison as evidence of individual characteristics is summarized as follows:

- The most identifying characteristics are those that are most divergent from the regular system or national average.
- Repeated characteristics that are inconspicuous should be sought first and given the most weight.
- Regular or national system similarities alone are insufficient to base judgments on.
- It is the combination of particulars, common and uncommon, that identifies false documents.
- It is impossible to discover how all strange and peculiar characteristics were developed.
- People do unaccountable things in their speech, gestures, and writing.
- An individual characteristic may be the survival of an error overlooked by a teacher.
- Many characteristics are outgrowths or copies of an at-one-time-admired design.

The Questioned Documents Unit of the FBI has the mission to examine and compare data appearing on paper and other evidentiary materials. The surface data includes handwriting, hand printing, typewriting, printing, erasures, alterations, and obliterations. Impressions in the surface of paper, such as those from indented writing or use of a check writer or dry seal, are also routinely evaluated by unit examiners, as are shoeprint and tire tread impressions. In addition to data contained on the surface of documentary evidence, data within paper or other surfaces—watermarks, safety fibers, and other integral features—may be components of document examinations. Unit examiners also match the torn or perforated edges of items such as paper, stamps, or matches. Other unit examinations include analyses of typewriter ribbons, photocopiers, facsimiles, graphic arts, and plastic bags. The unit also maintains a number of databases: the Anonymous Letter File, the Bank Robbery Note File, the National Fraudulent Check File, the Watermark File, and the Shoeprint File (FBI *Handbook of Forensic Services*, 2003, pp. 3–4).

The Questioned Documents Unit of the Michigan State Police provides the following summary of document analyses:

Writing and Printing: Writing and printing are identifiable. Writing and printing can be compared with known writing of individuals to determine if they did or did not write a document in question.

Inks: Inks can be examined to determine if different inks were used to produce a particular document in question. Inks that have been obliterated or destroyed through fading, burning, water, overwriting, chemicals, or other means can often be recovered and made legible. Although the Michigan State Police Questioned Documents Unit does not offer ink dating at the present time, arrangements can be made to have this type of examination conducted at a federal laboratory.

Paper: Paper can be compared with known samples to determine if the document in question is similar to a known sample. Paper can sometimes be dated or traced to a particular source or manufacturer. Paper can also be reconstructed, such as matches reconstructed to their match books, shredded or torn documents, cut documents, and so on. Paper that has been burned or watersoaked can often be restored.

Typewriters: Typewritten documents can be identified with a particular typewriter to the exclusion of all others. Typewriting can also be classified to determine what type of machine was used to produce the document. In addition, typewriter ribbons, correction ribbons, and correction materials can be examined to determine if these materials were used to produce the document in question.

Photocopiers, Printers, Mechanical Devices: Items used to produce documents can be examined and compared with the actual device (or known samples of the device) to determine if the particular device was used to produce a document in question.

FINGERPRINTS

As noted in the beginning of this chapter, in 1892 Francis Galton published *Fingerprints*. In his book, he explained how police departments could use fingerprints as a means of personal identification. Fingerprints, palm prints, and footprints are impressions of the friction ridge skin present on the palm side of the hand and soles of the feet. When a person touches, grabs, or walks barefoot on a surface, an impression of the friction ridge skin may be left behind. These unintentional impressions are called *latent prints*.

The importance of latent print evidence is its ability to identify an individual. Latent prints can be identified to a single person because the friction ridge skin possesses two key properties: permanence and uniqueness. With the exception of injury, a person has the same fingerprints, palm prints, and footprints from sixteen weeks' gestation until decomposition after death. Additionally, the friction ridge skin has unique characteristics that allow even a small portion of a latent print to be identified to a single person.

Latent prints left on a surface can be visualized through a variety of chemical and physical development techniques. Once visible, the latent print can be photographed and compared to the known inked fingerprints (or palm prints or footprints) of an individual. Through careful analysis and comparison of the friction ridge skin characteristics in both the unknown latent print and the known inked print, a person can be identified, or eliminated, as having made the print (Arkansas State Crime Laboratory website).

Latent fingerprints may be searched through the Automated Fingerprint Identification System (AFIS). AFIS is a computer-based system that compares fingerprints entered into the system with those already in the system.

FIREARMS

Gunshot Residue

In crimes involving firearms, the detection of gunshot residue (GSR) can provide critical evidence. The presence of GSR on the victim indicates that the victim was shot at close range; the absence of it indicates that the victim was not shot at a close range. In establishing whether the victim was murdered, committed suicide, or the shooting was in self-defense, the distance between the victim and the weapon is very important. Often the distances can be estimated by reproducing the blast pattern. Distances are generally described as contact, near contact, or intermediate contact. If the distance exceeds three feet, the distance is difficult to determine.

A *contact shot* is often used in execution-type shootings or in suicides. Because of the hot expanding gases, it causes a star-shaped tear in the fabric or skin. Other indications of a contact shot include a circular bruise that develops over the skin as the result of the pressure of the gases. The heat of the expanding gases often burns the skin or fabric.

A *near-contact shot* is often indicated by a concentration of GSR and considerable stippling (the presence of small abrasions caused by the unburned powder hitting the skin). The *intermediate contact shot* has a wider and lighter GSR pattern and the bullet hole tends to be more irregular, as the bullet tumbles in flight.

An entrance wound is smaller and has inverted margins (skin is bent inward) when compared with an exit wound. The exit wound is larger and has everted margins (skin is bent outward).

Two tests are commonly used to determine if a person has recently fired a firearm. One is an atomic absorption spectroscopy (AAS). In an AAS analysis, the backs of a suspect's hands are rubbed with a cotton swab moistened with a dilute solution of nitric acid. The backs of both hands are swabbed and the swabs are kept in separate packages. In addition, the hands are dipped into separate packages filled with dilute nitric acid. The samples are then introduced into the AAS to determine the presence of lead, barium, or antimony from the blow-back of the weapon when a firearm discharges.

The second and newer test is with the use of a scanning electron microscope equipped with an energy-dispersive X-ray attachment (SEM/EDX). This test is becoming more popular because it allows for the detection of GSR on a shooter's hand for a longer period of time after the weapon has discharged. In this test, a metal stud is pressed against the hand of the suspected shooter. The adhesive on the end of the stub picks up any GSR residue from the primer blast embedded in the skin. **Note:** On firearms that use a rim fire cartridge (generally a 22-caliber gun), no GSR will be present because the cartridge has no central primer that is pressed into the bottom and no gases escape.

Identification of Firearms

According to Heather Harrelson of the Birmingham Laboratory, Alabama Department of Forensic Sciences, the primary tool of the firearms' examiner, the comparison microscope, has changed little since it was adopted in 1925. She notes that the instrument is justifiably considered the most significant contribution to the field, because without it firearms identification would be impossible. The comparison microscope is actually composed of two individual microscopes connected by an optical bridge. This allows the examiner to view two objects simultaneously with one-half of the field of view magnified by one microscope while the other half is magnified by the second microscope. As a result of this development, identification of fired bullets and cartridge cases became as conclusive as fingerprints (Alabama Department of Forensic Science website).

Identification of fired ammunition to a specific firearm is made possible by distinguishing marks left by the gun on the surface of both the bullet and the cartridge case. The markings fall into two categories: class characteristics and individual characteristics. *Class characteristics* include general features, such as the number of lands and grooves and their width, direction of twist, and bullet diameter. Because many firearms are built to the same specifications, the variation of these characteristics will be nominal from multiple guns of the same make and model. However, the *individual characteristics* imparted to a bullet or cartridge case are different for every firearm and make it possible for an examiner to positively identify a round of fired ammunition as coming from a specific gun (Alabama Department of Forensic Science website).

The National Integrated Ballistics Information Network (NIBIN) was developed by a partnership between the FBI and the ATF. Each agency had its own imaging system with networked search capabilities; however, the systems were incompatible. The FBI and ATF acknowledged the need for the two competing systems to be interoperable so that an image captured by one system could be analyzed and correlated on the other system. In May 1997, the NIBIN Board was created to unify efforts of developing a national imaging system. After extensive research, they decided to pursue the joint development of one system. In December 1999, the FBI and ATF signed a memorandum of understanding defining their role in the NIBIN program. The FBI is responsible for providing the communications network and the ATF is responsible for field operations.

Through the NIBIN program, Integrated Ballistics Identification System (IBIS) equipment is used to compare firearms-related evidence stored in the database. IBIS digitally captures the images of fired bullets and fired cartridge cases from crime scenes and test fires from recovered firearms. When a new image is entered, the system searches the existing database for a match. When a possible match is observed, a firearms examiner must compare the actual evidence with a comparison microscope. Once identification has been made by the examination of the actual evidence, a "hit" is noted in the system. A hit is defined as a linkage of at least two different crime investigations where there previously had been no known connection. NIBIN allows for links between investigations across jurisdictional boundaries (Alabama Department of Forensic Science website).

DIGITAL EVIDENCE

Digital evidence is information stored or transmitted in binary form that may be relied on in court. The term *digital evidence* refers to evidence that exists in a digital format, such as computer-generated files. It is important to remember that other forensic disciplines might be able to recover other evidence, such as fingerprints on the hard drive, hair or fibers in the keyboard, and handwritten disk labels or printed material. In these instances, procedures should be developed to determine the order and manner in which examinations should be performed to reap full evidentiary value.

digital evidence / Information stored or transmitted in binary form that may be relied on in court.

To assist law enforcement agencies and prosecutorial offices, the National Institute of Justice (NIJ) has developed a series of guides dealing with digital evidence. The guides discuss the handling of digital evidence from the crime scene through analysis and finally into the courtroom. The guides summarize information from a select group of practitioners who are knowledgeable about the subject matter. These groups are more commonly known as technical working groups. The guides are available through the National Institute of Justice website at www.ojp.usdoj.gov/nij/pubs. In this section, a brief summary of guides is presented. **Note:** Because of the complex issues associated with digital evidence examination, the guides may not be feasible in all circumstances and their recommendations are not legal mandates or policy directives, nor do they represent the only correct courses of action. Rather, the recommendations represent a consensus of the diverse views and experiences of the technical working group members who have provided valuable insight into these important issues. The NIJ expects that law enforcement offices will be able to use these recommendations to spark discussions and ensure that its practices and procedures are best suited to its unique environment.

When dealing with digital evidence, the following general forensic and procedural principles should be applied:

- Actions taken to secure and collect digital evidence should not affect the integrity of that evidence.
- Persons conducting an examination of digital evidence should be trained for that purpose.
- Activity relating to the seizure, examination, storage, or transfer of digital evidence should be documented, preserved, and available for review.

Through all of this, the examiner should be cognizant of the need to conduct an accurate and impartial examination of the digital evidence.

How Should Digital Evidence Be Processed?

Assessment: Computer forensic examiners should assess digital evidence thoroughly with respect to the scope of the case to determine the course of action to take.

Acquisition: Digital evidence, by its very nature, is fragile and can be altered, damaged, or destroyed by improper handling or examination. Examination is best conducted on a copy of the original evidence. The original evidence should be acquired in a manner that protects and preserves the integrity of the evidence.

Examination: The purpose of the examination process is to extract and analyze digital evidence. Extraction refers to the recovery of data from its media. Analysis refers to the interpretation of the recovered data and putting it in a logical and useful format.

Documenting and Reporting: Actions and observations should be documented throughout the forensic processing of evidence. This will conclude with the preparation of a written report of the findings.

Voices of Experience

Computer-Related Investigations

Excerpts from an interview between Cliff Roberson and former police officer, Mark R. McCoy, currently a professor at the University of Central Oklahoma. Professor McCoy also served as a deputy inspector for the Oklahoma State Bureau of Investigation (OSBI) where he specialized in computer-related investigations.

Q: *Tell us about the Computer Crime Unit of the Oklahoma State Bureau of Investigation (OSBI).*
A: In about 1996, the state bureau decided it had a need for agents trained to investigate computer-related crimes. At that time I and another agent were provided specialized training. We were sent to the International Association of Computer Investigative Specialists, a group that provided training in digital forensics. Then we attended courses at the National White Collar Crime Center and the courses provided by the companies that produced forensics software. For about the first four years, the other agent and I were the only investigators specially trained for computer-related investigations. But as the number of cases involving computers grew, the bureau created a computer crime unit and I was promoted and assigned as head of the unit. I had agents assigned to different parts of the state and their focus was the investigation of computer crime and the forensic examination of digital evidence. We found computers used in just about all types of crimes. Later, we started examining cell phones, BlackBerry devices, and other electronic devices for evidence. We also testified in court as expert witnesses regarding the results of our investigations.

Q: *What is considered as digital forensics?*
A: Digital forensics is the examination of computers or electronic devices in a manner so that the evidence may be used in court. Sound forensic methods must be used to handle digital evidence so it is not altered or destroyed. First, we would make exact duplicates of the data, whether it was data on a cell phone, hard drive, or other storage device. Then we would conduct an examination of the duplicate, protecting the original evidence. Often we found data on a device that was important evidence in our case. We recovered items users thought that they had deleted or had hidden. We can also track Internet activity of the computer user, locate segments of electronic chat conversations and email

messages, and in some cases find documents related to the case. In one case involving narcotics, we found that the dealer's little black book was computerized. In child pornography cases, we have been able to recover deleted images of child photos.

Q: *What about Internet crimes against children?*
A: The OSBI received a federal grant to investigate Internet crimes against children. With the advent of the Internet, pedophiles have been able to work out of their homes more anonymously and look for children that are online in chat rooms. They groom the children online and arrange to meet them for sexual purposes. Investigators would go online and pretend to be children, using the same type of language that a young child would use. The pedophiles that we identified came from all walks of life. In one case, an investigator from Illinois who indicated that he had identified a pedophile in Oklahoma contacted us. Later it was determined that the pedophile was a police chief from a small town in Oklahoma. The chief had sent child pornography to the investigator in Illinois. As the results of the investigation, we served a search warrant on the chief's home and recovered evidence on his computer including nude pictures of himself that he had sent to children. At the time we searched his home, he was not home. He found out that his home had been searched. He took off and was a fugitive for about a year.

Generally, we obtained our leads by creating a screen name that would match that of a twelve- or thirteen-year-old youth. There are chat rooms for pedophiles, where they discuss having sex with children. There are chat rooms for young kids and these chat rooms are monitored by many pedophiles. We would go into chat rooms and pretend to be a child. It would not take long before we were approached by a pedophile. While teaching classes, I have gone online in class and allowed the students to observe pedophiles hitting upon our "twelve-year-old girl." ∎

Evidence Acquisition

Principle: Digital evidence, by its very nature, is fragile and can be altered, damaged, or destroyed by improper handling or examination. For these reasons, special precautions should be taken to preserve this type of evidence. Failure to do so may render it unusable or lead to an inaccurate conclusion.

Procedure: Acquire the original digital evidence in a manner that protects and preserves the evidence, according to the following basic steps:

- Secure digital evidence in accordance with departmental guidelines. In the absence of such guidelines, useful information can be found in "Electronic Crime Scene Investigation: A Guide for First Responders," at www.ojp.usdoj.gov/nij/pubs-sum/187736.htm.
- Document the hardware and software configuration of the examiner's system.
- Verify operation of the examiner's computer system to include hardware and software.
- Disassemble the case of the computer to be examined to permit physical access to the storage devices.
- Take care to ensure equipment is protected from static electricity and magnetic fields.
- Identify storage devices that need to be acquired. These devices can be internal, external, or both.
- Document internal storage devices and hardware configuration.
- Document drive condition (e.g., make, model, geometry, size, jumper settings, location, drive interface).
- Document internal components (e.g., sound card; video card; network card, including media access control (MAC) address; personal computer memory card international association (PCMCIA) cards).
- Disconnect storage devices (using the power connector or data cable from the back of the drive or from the motherboard) to prevent the destruction, damage, or alteration of data.
- Retrieve configuration information from the suspect's system through controlled boots.
- Perform a controlled boot to capture CMOS/BIOS information and test functionality.
- Boot sequence (this may mean changing the BIOS to ensure the system boots from the floppy or CD-ROM drive).
- Perform a second controlled boot to test the computer's functionality and the forensic boot disk.
- Ensure the power and data cables are properly connected to the floppy or CD-ROM drive, and ensure the power and data cables to the storage devices are still disconnected.
- Place the forensic boot disk into the floppy or CD-ROM drive. Boot the computer and ensure the computer will boot from the forensic boot disk.

- Reconnect the storage devices and perform a third controlled boot to capture the drive configuration information from the CMOS/BIOS.

- Ensure there is a forensic boot disk in the floppy or CD-ROM drive to prevent the computer from accidentally booting from the storage devices.

- Drive configuration information includes logical block addressing (LBA); large disk; cylinders, heads, and sectors (CHS); or auto-detect.

- Power system down.

- Whenever possible, remove the subject storage device and perform the acquisition using the examiner's system. When attaching the subject device to the examiner's system, configure the storage device so that it will be recognized.

- Exceptional circumstances, including the following, may result in a decision not to remove the storage devices from the subject system:
  - **RAID (Redundant Array of Inexpensive Disks).** Removing the disks and acquiring them individually may not yield usable results.
  - **Laptop systems.** The system drive may be difficult to access or may be unusable when detached from the original system.
  - **Hardware dependency (legacy equipment).** Older drives may not be readable in newer systems.
  - **Equipment availability.** The examiner does not have access to necessary equipment.
  - **Network storage.** It may be necessary to use the network equipment to acquire the data.

When using the subject computer to acquire digital evidence, reattach the subject storage device and attach the examiner's evidence storage device (e.g., hard drive, tape drive, CD-RW, MO).

- Ensure that the examiner's storage device is forensically clean when acquiring the evidence.

- Write protection should be initiated, if available, to preserve and protect original evidence.

- The examiner should consider creating a known value for the subject evidence prior to acquiring the evidence (e.g., performing an independent cyclic redundancy check (CRC), hashing). Depending on the selected acquisition method, this process may already be completed.

- If hardware write protection is used:
  - Install a write protection device
  - Boot system with the examiner's controlled operating system

- If software write protection is used:
  - Boot system with the examiner-controlled operating system
  - Activate write protection

- Investigate the geometry of any storage devices to ensure that all space is accounted for, including host-protected data areas (e.g., nonhost specific data, such as the partition table, matches the physical geometry of the drive).

- Capture the electronic serial number of the drive and other user-accessible, host-specific data.

- Acquire the subject evidence to the examiner's storage device using the appropriate software and hardware tools, such as:
  - Stand-alone duplication software
  - Forensic analysis software suite
  - Dedicated hardware devices
- Verify successful acquisition by comparing known values of the original and the copy or by doing a sector-by-sector comparison of the original to the copy.

Data Hiding Analysis

Data can be concealed on a computer system. Data hiding analysis can be useful in detecting and recovering such data and may indicate knowledge, ownership, or intent. Methods that can be used include:

- Correlating the file headers to the corresponding file extensions to identify any mismatches. Presence of mismatches may indicate that the user intentionally hid data.
- Gaining access to all password-protected, encrypted, and compressed files, which may indicate an attempt to conceal the data from unauthorized users. A password itself may be as relevant as the contents of the file.
- Steganography.
- Gaining access to a host-protected area (HPA). The presence of user-created data in an HPA may indicate an attempt to conceal data.

Ownership and Possession

In some instances it may be essential to identify the individual(s) who created, modified, or accessed a file. It may also be important to determine ownership and knowledgeable possession of the questioned data. Elements of knowledgeable possession may be based on the analysis described previously, including one or more of the following factors:

- Placing the subject at the computer at a particular date and time may help determine ownership and possession. (timeframe analysis)
- Files of interest may be located in nondefault locations (e.g., user-created directory named "child porn"). (application and file analysis)
- The file name itself may be of evidentiary value and also may indicate the contents of the file. (application and file analysis)
- Hidden data may indicate a deliberate attempt to avoid detection. (hidden data analysis)
- If the passwords needed to gain access to encrypted and password-protected files are recovered, the passwords themselves may indicate possession or ownership. (hidden data analysis)
- Contents of a file may indicate ownership or possession by containing information specific to a user. (application and file analysis)

Documenting and Reporting

Principle: The examiner is responsible for completely and accurately reporting findings and the results of the analysis of the digital evidence examination. Documentation is an ongoing process throughout the examination. It is important to accurately record the steps taken during the digital evidence examination. All documentation should be complete, accurate, and comprehensive. The resulting report should be written for the intended audience.

Examiner's Notes: Documentation should be contemporaneous with the examination, and retention of notes should be consistent with departmental policies. The following is a list of general considerations that may assist the examiner throughout the documentation process:

- Take notes when consulting with the case investigator and/or prosecutor.
- Maintain a copy of the search authority with the case notes.
- Maintain the initial request for assistance with the case file.
- Maintain a copy of chain of custody documentation.
- Take notes detailed enough to allow complete duplication of actions.
- Include in the notes dates, times, descriptions, and results of actions taken.
- Document irregularities encountered and any actions taken regarding the irregularities during the examination.
- Include additional information, such as network topology, list of authorized users, user agreements, and/or passwords.
- Document changes made to the system or network by or at the direction of law enforcement or the examiner.
- Document the operating system and relevant software version and current, installed patches.
- Document information obtained at the scene regarding remote storage, remote user access, and offsite backups.

During the course of a digital examination, information of evidentiary value may be found that is beyond the scope of the current legal authority. Document this information and bring it to the attention of the case agent because the information may be needed to obtain additional search authorities.

COLLECTION AND PRESERVATION OF DNA EVIDENCE

Forensically valuable DNA can be found on evidence that is decades old. However, several factors can affect the DNA left at a crime scene, including environmental factors (e.g., heat, sunlight, moisture, bacteria, and mold). Therefore, not all DNA evidence will result in a usable DNA profile. Further, just like fingerprints, DNA testing cannot tell officers when the suspect was at the crime scene or for how long.

POLICE IN ACTION: Fictional Case Study

The following below fictional case of a digital evidence case was presented in U.S. Department of Justice Office Publication NCJ 199408 (April 2004), "Forensic Examination of Digital Evidence: A Guide for Law Enforcement," pp. 23–24.

Case Brief

SUBJECT owned a roofing company. SUBJECT gave his laptop computer to an employee to take to Mom & Pop's Computer Repair for monitor problems. Upon repairing the laptop, Mom of Mom & Pop's started the laptop to ensure the monitor had been fixed. A standard procedure of Mom & Pop's was to go to the Recent menu on the Start Bar of Windows® 98 systems and select files for viewing. Mom was presented with what appeared to be an image of a young child depicted in a sexually explicit manner. Mom telephoned the county sheriff. A sheriff's deputy responded and observed the image and confirmed it to be a violation of a State statute. The laptop was seized because it contained contraband. The seizure was performed in a manner consistent with recommendations found in *Electronic Crime Scene Investigation: A Guide for First Responders*. The laptop was entered into evidence according to agency policy, and a search warrant was obtained for the examination of the computer. The computer was submitted for examination.

Objective: To determine whether SUBJECT possessed child pornography. This was complicated by the number of people who handled the laptop.

Computer type: Generic laptop, serial # 123456789.

Operating system: Microsoft® Windows® 98.

Offense: Possession of child pornography.

Case agent: Investigator Johnson.

Evidence number: 012345.

Chain of custody: See attached form.

Where examination took place: Criminal investigations unit.

Tools used: Disk acquisition utility, universal graphic viewer, command line.

Assessment: Reviewed the case investigator's request for service. The search warrant provided legal authority. The investigator was interested in finding all information pertaining to child pornography, access dates, and ownership of the computer. It was determined that the equipment needed was available in the forensic lab.

Acquisition: The hardware configuration was documented and a duplicate of the hard drive was created in a manner that protected and preserved the evidence. The CMOS information, including the time and date, was documented.

Examination: The directory and file structures, including file dates and times, were recorded. A file header search was conducted to locate all graphic images. The image files were reviewed and those files containing images of what appeared to be children depicted in a sexually explicit manner were preserved. Shortcut files were recovered that pointed to files on floppy disks with sexually explicit file names involving children. The last accessed time and date of the files indicated the files were last accessed ten days before the laptop was delivered to Mom & Pop's.

Documentation and reporting: The investigator was given a report describing the findings of the examination. The investigator determined that he needed to conduct interviews.

Next step: The employee who delivered the laptop computer to Mom & Pop's Computer Repair was interviewed, and he indicated that he had never operated the computer. Further, the employee stated SUBJECT had shown him images of a sexual nature involving children on the laptop. SUBJECT told the employee that he keeps his pictures on floppy disks at home; he just forgot this one image on the laptop.

The State's Attorney's Office was briefed in hopes of obtaining a search warrant for SUBJECT's home based on the examination of the digital evidence and the interview of the employee. A warrant was drafted, presented to a judicial officer, and signed. During the subsequent search, floppy disks were discovered at SUBJECT's house. Forensic examination of the floppies revealed additional child pornography, including images in which SUBJECT was a participant. This resulted in the arrest of SUBJECT.

Case Brief Report

Report of Media Analysis Memorandum for:

Subject:

1. **Status:** Closed.
2. **Summary of Findings:** Anytown County Sheriff's Police Investigator Johnson, USA 01234
   Forensic Media Analysis Report SUBJECT: DOE, JOHN
   Case Number: 012345
   - 327 files containing images of what appeared to be children depicted in a sexually explicit manner were recovered.
   - 34 shortcut files that pointed to files on floppy disks with sexually explicit file names involving children were recovered.
3. **Items Analyzed:**
   TAG NUMBER: ITEM DESCRIPTION:
   012345   One Generic laptop, Serial # 123456789
4. **Details of Findings:**
   Findings in this paragraph related to the Generic Hard Drive, Model ABCDE, Serial # 3456ABCD, recovered from Tag Number 012345, One Generic laptop, Serial # 123456789.

   The examined hard drive was found to contain a Microsoft® Windows® 98 operating system.

   The directory and file listing for the media was saved to the Microsoft® Access Database TAG012345.MDB.

   The directory C:\JOHN DOE\PERSONAL\FAV PICS\ was found to contain 327 files containing images of what appeared to be children depicted in a sexually explicit manner. The file directory for 327 files disclosed that the files' creation date and times are 5 July 2001 between 11:33 P.M. and 11:45 P.M., and the last access date for 326 files listed is 27 December 2001. In addition, the file directory information for one file disclosed the last access date as 6 January 2002.

   The directory C:\JOHN DOE\PERSONAL\FAV PICS TO DISK\ contained 34 shortcut files that pointed to files on floppy disks with sexually explicit file names

(continued)

involving children. The file directory information for the 34 shortcut files disclosed the files' creation date and times are 5 July 2001 between 11:23 P.M. and 11:57 P.M., and the last access date for the 34 shortcut files was listed as 5 July 2001.

The directory C:\JOHN DOE\LEGAL\ contained five Microsoft® Word documents related to various contract relationships John Doe Roofing had with other entities.

The directory C:\JOHN DOE\JOHN DOE ROOFING\ contained files related to operation of John Doe Roofing.

No further user-created files were present on the media.

5. **Items Provided:** In addition to this hard copy report, one compact disk (CD) was submitted with an electronic copy of this report. The report on CD contains hyperlinks to the above-mentioned files and directories.

IMA D. EXAMINER   May 17, 20xx
Released by   Computer Forensic Examiner

DNA evidence can be collected from virtually anywhere. DNA has helped solve many cases when imaginative investigators collected evidence from nontraditional sources. One murder was solved when the suspect's DNA, taken from saliva in a dental impression mold, matched the DNA swabbed from a bite mark on the victim. A masked rapist was convicted of forced oral copulation when his victim's DNA matched DNA swabbed from the suspect's penis six hours after the offense. Numerous cases have been solved by DNA analysis of saliva on cigarette butts, postage stamps, and the area around the mouth opening on ski masks. DNA analysis of a single hair (without the root) found deep in the victim's throat provided a critical piece of evidence used in a capital murder conviction.

Investigators and laboratory personnel should work together to determine the most probative pieces of evidence and to establish priorities. Every officer should be aware of important issues involved in the identification, collection, transportation, and storage of DNA evidence. These issues are as important for the first responding patrol officer as they are for the experienced detective and the crime scene specialist. Biological material may contain hazardous pathogens such as the human immunodeficiency virus (HIV) and the hepatitis B virus that can cause potentially lethal diseases. Given the sensitive nature of DNA evidence, officers should always contact their laboratory personnel or evidence collection technicians when collection questions arise.

Only a few cells can be sufficient to obtain useful DNA information to help your case. Remember that just because you cannot see a stain does not mean there are not enough cells for DNA typing. Further, DNA does more than just identify the source of the sample; it can place a known individual at a crime scene, in a home, or in a room where the suspect claimed not to have been. It can refute a claim of self-defense and put a weapon in the suspect's hand. It can change a story from an alibi to one of consent. The more officers know how to use DNA, the more powerful a tool it becomes.

As with fingerprints, the effective use of DNA may require the collection and analysis of elimination samples. It often is necessary to use elimination samples to determine whether the evidence comes from the suspect or from someone else. An officer must think ahead to the time of trial and possible defenses while still at the crime scene. For example, in the case of a residential burglary where the suspect may have drunk a glass of water at the crime scene, an officer should identify appropriate people, such as household members, for future elimination sample testing. These samples may be needed for comparison with the saliva found on the glass to determine whether the saliva is valuable evidence. In homicide cases, be sure to collect the victim's DNA from the medical examiner at the autopsy, even if the body is badly decomposed. This may serve to identify an unknown victim or distinguish between the victim's DNA and other DNA found at the crime scene.

When investigating rape cases, it may be necessary to collect and analyze the DNA of the victim's recent consensual partners, if any, to eliminate them as potential contributors of DNA suspected to be from the perpetrator. If this is necessary, it is important to approach the victim with extreme sensitivity and provide a full explanation of why the request is being made. When possible, the help of a qualified victim advocate should be enlisted for assistance.

To Avoid Contamination of Evidence That May Contain DNA Evidence

- Wear gloves. Change them often.
- Use disposable instruments or clean them thoroughly before and after handling each sample.
- Avoid touching the area where you believe DNA may exist.
- Avoid talking, sneezing, and coughing over the evidence.
- Avoid touching your face, nose, and mouth when collecting and packaging evidence.
- Air-dry evidence thoroughly before packaging.
- Put evidence into new paper bags or envelopes, not into plastic bags. Do not use staples.

SUMMARY

- Forensic science is the study and application of scientific facts and techniques to legal problems.

- Anthropometry, a personal identification method based on eleven body measurements, is generally thought to be the first system of personal identification used by the police.

- Francis Galton, who published *Fingerprints*, is considered as the developer of the fingerprint identification process.

- Edmond Locard originated the Locard principle, which states that "every contact leaves a trace."

- The role of a forensic scientist is to analyze physical evidence. Normally, the scientist is an expert in one scientific area.

- The FBI has one of the largest and most comprehensive forensic laboratories in the world.

- Crime scene analysis is important in the crime-solving process. Critical to the administration of a crime is the objective recognition, documentation, collection, preservation, and transmittal of physical evidence for analysis.

- The investigator may need a search warrant in order to legally enter and collect physical evidence.

- An investigator should take the following steps at the crime scene: (1) ensure that you have legal clearance to enter the area, (2) secure and protect the crime scene, (3) conduct a search of the area using a "search pattern," (4) document and record the items found at the scene, (5) collect and package the evidence, and (6) transmit the evidence to the crime lab.

- A crime scene should be searched in a systematic manner using one of four standard search patterns: strip, grid, spiral, and quadrant.

- Blood has known properties that allow experts to analyze and reproduce the bloodstain patterns at the crime scene in order to reconstruct the crime.

- Blood contains an enzyme, peroxidase, which makes its identification easy. Many chemicals react with peroxidase to give certain visible colors indicating that the liquid is blood. When blood is present at the scene of a crime, four basic questions should be answered: Is it blood? Is it human blood? What type of blood is it? Whom does it belong to?

- Because the Locard principle states that every contact leaves a trace, fibers are a good source of evidence. The more violent the contact between the offender and the victim, the more likely that fibers will be transferred from one to the other.

- DNA is a long polymer of nucleotides (a polynucleotide) and encodes the sequence of the amino acid residues in proteins using the genetic code, a triplet code of nucleotides. Forensic scientists scan thirteen DNA regions that vary from person to person and use the data to create a DNA profile of that individual (sometimes called a DNA fingerprint).

- A questioned document is considered as any signature, handwriting, typewriting, or other mark whose source or authenticity is in dispute or doubtful. The most common questioned documents include: letters, checks, driver's licenses, contracts, wills, voter registrations, passports, petitions, threatening letters, suicide notes, and lottery tickets.

- Fingerprints, palm prints, and footprints are impressions of the friction ridge skin present on the palm side of the hand and soles of the feet. When a person touches, grabs, or walks barefoot on a surface an impression of the friction ridge skin may be left behind.

- The importance of latent print evidence is its ability to identify an individual. Latent prints can be identified to a single person because the friction ridge skin possesses two key properties: permanence and uniqueness.

- With the exception of injury, a person has the same fingerprints, palm prints, and footprints from sixteen weeks' gestation until decomposition after death. Additionally, the friction ridge skin has unique characteristics that allow even a small portion of a latent print to be identified to a single person.

- The presence of gunshot residue (GSR) on the victim indicates that the victim was shot at close range. The absence of it indicates that the victim was not shot at a close range. In establishing whether the victim was murdered, committed suicide, or the shooting was in self-defense, the distance between the victim and the weapon is very important.

- Often the distances can be estimated by reproducing the blast pattern. Distances are generally described as contact, near contact, or intermediate contact.

- The primary tool of the firearms examiner is the comparison microscope, which has changed little since it was adopted in 1925.

- The comparison microscope is actually composed of two individual microscopes connected by an optical bridge. This allows the examiner to view two objects simultaneously with one-half of the field of view magnified by one microscope while the other half is magnified by the second microscope. As a result of this development, identification of fired bullets and cartridge cases became as conclusive as fingerprints.

- Identification of fired ammunition to a specific firearm is made possible by distinguishing marks left by the gun on the surface of both the bullet and the cartridge case.

- The term *digital evidence* refers to evidence that exists in a digital format. For the most part we are talking about computer-generated files. The National Institute of Justice guides discuss the handling of digital evidence from the crime scene through analysis and finally into the courtroom.

- Actions taken to secure and collect digital evidence should not affect the integrity of that evidence.

- Persons conducting an examination of digital evidence should be trained for that purpose.

- Activity relating to the seizure, examination, storage, or transfer of digital evidence should be documented, preserved, and available for review.

Classroom Discussion Questions and Activities

1. Interview a local fingerprint examiner and report the results to the class.
2. Determine what forensic laboratory the local police department uses.
3. Create a mock crime scene and have members of the class inspect the scene.
4. How important is DNA to law enforcement?
5. Should individuals be forced to provide DNA profiles? Under what conditions?
6. How can digital evidence be safeguarded?
7. Why are bloodstain patterns at a murder scene important?

Websites and Other Resources

Alabama State Department of Forensic Sciences
www.adfs.state.al.us/index.htm

Arkansas State Crime Laboratory
www.arkansas.gov/crimelab/sections/latents

Electronic Crime Scene Investigation: A Guide for First Responders
**www.ojp.usdoj.gov/nij/
pubs-sum/187736.htm**

"Forensic Serology: Bloodstain Pattern Analysis."
**www.policensw.com/info/forensic/
forensic6c.html**

Humane Genome Project
**www.ornl.gov/sci/techresources/
Human_Genome/elsi/forensics.shtml#1**

Michigan Crime Lab
**www.michigan.gov/msp/0,1607,
7-123-1593_3800-15887—,00.html**

References

Brunelle, R. L. (1982). Questioned document examination. In R. Saferstein (Ed.), *Forensic science handbook*. Englewood Cliffs, NJ: Prentice-Hall.

FBI Handbook of Forensic Services. 2003.

Khanna, R., & Glenn, M. (2006, June 22). HPD makes arrest in iconic DNA case. *Houston Chronicle*, p. A1.

Marieb, E. M. (2001). *Human anatomy & physiology* (5th ed.). Englewood Cliffs, NJ: Pearson Education, pp. 650–680.

News brief. (2006, April). *Police Magazine, 30*(28) 16.

New lexicon Webster's dictionary of the English language, encyclopedic edition. (1988). New York: Lexicon Publishing, p. 369.

Osborn, A. (1910). *Questioned documents*. Albany: Boyd Printing Company.

U.S. Department of Justice handbook. (June 2004). *Crime scene investigation: A reference for law enforcement training*, NCJ 200160.

Wambaugh, J. (1989). *The blooding*. New York: Morrow.

Watson, J. D. (2003). DNA: *The secret of life*. New York: Knopf, pp. 42–44.

Willing, R. (2006, May 1). Officials increase DNA profiles. *USA Today*, p. A1.

Chapter 8

Legal Constraints That Impact Police Operations

" I looked out at the class of astonishingly smug and overconfident first-year law students: 'Can anyone tell me why the law permits law enforcement agents to use deceit at the investigative stage, when they're not even sure of a suspect's guilt, but strictly forbids them from lying during the testimonial stage, when they're absolutely sure the suspect is criminal?' "

—Fictional character in *Judge and Jury* by James Patterson

CHAPTER OUTLINE

OBJECTIVES

After completion of this chapter, you will be able to do the following:

- Explain the restraints placed on the police by the Fourth Amendment.
- Define what constitutes a search within the meaning of the Fourth Amendment.
- Describe what is required before a search or arrest warrant will be issued.
- Explain the concept of probable cause.
- Explain what is protected by the Fourth Amendment.
- Define what constitutes "standing" to object to evidence.
- Explain the requirements for a Terry stop.
- Define the actions necessary to constitute an arrest.
- Explain the general rules regarding the use of force by police officers.
- Explain when the police may use deadly force.

INTRODUCTION

In this chapter, the legal constraints that impact police operations will be discussed. Those constraints include search and seizure, civil liability, and the use of force by police officers. These subjects are complex and a complete coverage of each would result in volumes of text. Accordingly, only the basics of each subject will be covered. Our goal is to provide the reader with a working knowledge of legal constraints that impact police operations. The discussions will focus on the general legal rules within the United States. In some jurisdictions, state constitutions, statutes, court rules, and local practices may vary. In actual practice, when in doubt, consult the local police legal advisor.

SEARCHES

Any study of the restrictions on police searches must begin with a review of the elements of the Fourth Amendment of the U.S. Constitution. The Fourth Amendment, with its convoluted word structure, is not a model of clarity. The amendment has two key phrases: the first phrase protects individuals from unreasonable searches and seizures of their homes, papers, and effects. The second phrase, known as the warrant clause, sets forth the requirements for and restrictions on issuing a warrant. **Note:** While an arrest is a seizure within the meaning of the Fourth Amendment, arrests will be discussed in a separate part of this chapter.

   Note: The amendment does not prohibit all searches and seizures, but only the "unreasonable" ones. What constitutes an unreasonable search will be discussed later in the chapter. Note that only persons, houses, papers, and effects are protected by the amendment. Also note that while the warrant clause describes the requirements

Police officers from tactical team searching through house when serving search warrant. Kansas City, MO, PD Street Narcotics Unit TAC.

The Fourth Amendment Outlined

- The right of the people to be secure in their
  - persons
  - homes
  - papers
  - effects

  against unreasonable searches and seizures, shall not be violated.

- No warrant shall issue, but
  - upon probable cause
  - supported by oath or affirmation
  - particularly describing the
    - place to be searched
    - the persons or things to be seized

and limitations of a warrant, it does not require that a warrant be issued before conducting a search. The warrant requirement will also be discussed later in this chapter. As a general rule, the U.S. Supreme Court has held, regarding searches, that you must get a warrant unless certain circumstances exist.

What Constitutes a Search?

Unless the incident qualifies as a search or seizure, it is not restricted by the Fourth Amendment. The U.S. Supreme Court presently uses the *privacy approach* in deciding what constitutes a search.

The *privacy approach* was first formulated by the Court in the case of *Katz v. United States*, 389 U.S. 347 (1967). In Katz, federal agents suspected illegal activities and installed an electronic listening device outside a public telephone booth that Katz frequently used. At trial, when Katz moved to exclude intercepted conversations, the government argued that there was no search of a person, house, papers, or effects, and therefore the Fourth Amendment did not apply. The government also contended that the telephone booth was a public place and not subject to the amendment's restrictions.

The Court held that listening to private conversations between people constituted a search. The Court stated that the Fourth Amendment protects people, not property. The Court stated: "What a person knowingly exposes to the public, even in his own home or office, is not a subject of the Fourth Amendment protection . . . But what he seeks to preserve as private, even in an area accessible to the public, may be constitutionally protected."

Therefore, a **search** is a government intrusion into an area or interest where a person has a reasonable expectation of privacy. So, would the results in the Katz case have been different had the government, rather than placing a listening device outside the telephone booth, positioned an undercover agent dressed as a homeless person near the booth in such a manner that the agent could hear the conversation? Under this scenario, the government's actions would probably not be considered a search, because talking on a telephone within the hearing distance of another person (the apparent homeless person) would not constitute a reasonable expectation of privacy.

In the Katz case, federal agents attached the listening device to the telephone booth. What would have been the results if Katz's girlfriend had placed the listening device in an attempt to catch him cheating on her? What if after the girlfriend intercepted the messages she turned them over to the federal agents? (**Note:** A prohibited search is based on a "government intrusion.") Because under this scenario there was no government intrusion, the intercepted conversations would not be prohibited by the Fourth Amendment. If, however, the federal agents had influenced the girlfriend to place the listening device in the booth, this would constitute a government intrusion based on the concept that the girlfriend was acting as an agent for the government.

One of the defined requirements noted earlier was the requirement of a *reasonable expectation of privacy*. Included within the reasonable expectation of privacy is the requirement that society accept the expectation as reasonable. The expectation of privacy is an objective expectation.

Consider this scenario: John lives in a suburban area. He has purchased a large amount of illegal drugs and is in the process of dividing them into smaller bags for retail sales. Does John have a reasonable expectation of privacy if he is dividing and repackaging the drugs in his front room with the windows open and he can be observed from the sidewalk? It is unlikely that a court would hold that his expectation of privacy was objectively reasonable.

Instead of dividing the drugs in his living room, John does the work in his bathroom. There is only one small window in the bathroom and an officer was required to stand upon a drainage pipe in order to look into the bathroom window. In this situation, a court would probably hold that John had a reasonable expectation of privacy.

search / A government intrusion into an area or interest where a person has a reasonable expectation of privacy.

Houses

Houses are one of the protected items specifically listed in the Fourth Amendment. The U.S. Supreme Court has always protected the sanctity of the home. As discussed later in the chapter, except under limited exceptions, the police must have a warrant

CASE STUDY: *United States v. Shanks*
No. 96-1578 (10/9/1996)
U.S. Court of Appeals (7th Cir. 1996)

Booker T. Shanks ("Shanks") was convicted by a jury of knowingly and intentionally possessing with the intent to distribute heroin and of knowingly and intentionally possessing with the intent to distribute heroin within 1,000 feet of a school, in violation of 21 U.S.C. sec. 841(a)(1) and 21 U.S.C. sec. 860(a). On appeal, Shanks challenged the constitutionality of the warrantless search that discovered the drugs.

After receiving an anonymous tip that someone was dealing drugs from Shanks' residence, located on the upper floor of a two-story duplex condominium, the police attempted to corroborate the tip by looking for evidence of drug activity in the garbage containers located next to the garage, which was approximately 20 feet away from Shanks' residence. The garbage containers were located on the narrow strip of land that occupied the space between the garage and the alley. The police confiscated the garbage containers in the early hours of the morning and replaced them with identical containers so that no one would notice. They then investigated the contents of the confiscated garbage containers, including opaque bags that were either tied or sealed with metal twist ties. Inside these bags the police discovered drug paraphernalia and other incriminating evidence, including pieces of aluminum foil that tested positive for the presence of heroin. The police subsequently used this evidence along with the informant's tip to secure a search warrant for the Shanks' household. Shanks challenged the search of his garbage can, which provided the police with probable cause to obtain a warrant to search his home. According to Shanks, if the search of the cans was illegal, then the warrant to search the home was fruit of the poisonous tree.

Supreme Court's Decision: In *California v. Greenwood*, 486 U.S. 35, 37 (1988), the Supreme Court held that the Fourth Amendment does not prohibit the warrantless search and seizure of garbage left for collection outside the curtilage of the home. The garbage containers in Greenwood were located at the curb in place for collection at a fixed time. As in this case, the evidence that was collected from Greenwood's garbage was found inside sealed, opaque bags. The Court held that any expectation of privacy in the garbage was not objectively reasonable because of the extent to which the garbage was exposed to the public. Specifically, the Court noted that, "it is common knowledge that plastic garbage bags left on or at the side of a public street are readily accessible to animals, children, scavengers, snoops, and other members of the public." Moreover, the garbage was placed at the curb, "for the express purpose of conveying it to a third party, the trash collector, who might himself have sorted through the respondents' trash or permitted others, such as the police, to do so."

In the present case, the magistrate and district judges found that the garbage containers also lay outside the curtilage and that Shanks had no reasonable expectation of privacy in his garbage. Shanks appears to argue that his garbage containers did lie within the curtilage of his home because they were located next to his garage. But Shanks' garbage containers were also located adjacent to the alley, and thus, we reject his argument and note that this case is not significantly distinguishable from the situation presented in Greenwood, where the Supreme Court found that curbside garbage was located outside the curtilage of the defendant's home.

Even assuming that the garbage containers were within the curtilage of Shanks' home, see *United States v. Pace*, 898 F.2d 1218, 1228 (7th Cir. 1990) ["A home's

curtilage is the area outside the home itself, but so close to and intimately connected with the home and the activities that normally go on there that it can reasonably be considered part of the home."], Shanks cannot show that the district court's additional finding (that he did not hold a reasonable expectation of privacy in the garbage) is clearly erroneous. Indeed, the mere intonation of curtilage does not end the inquiry. In *United States v. Hedrick*, 922 F.2d 396 (7th Cir. 1991), we noted that Fourth Amendment issues do not depend solely on curtilage. Still, we refrained from establishing a *per se* rule justifying all garbage can searches: A determination, however, that garbage placed in cans for ultimate collection is unprotected by the Fourth Amendment would allow police officers to inspect cans placed next to the garage or the house itself without any showing of probable cause or any warrant, and without regard to the accessibility of the cans to the public as a whole.

Thus, we found that the relevant inquiry is "whether the garbage cans were so readily accessible to the public that they exposed the contents to the public for Fourth Amendment purposes." We further explained that where garbage is readily accessible from the street or other public thoroughfares, an expectation of privacy may be objectively unreasonable because of the common practice of scavengers, snoops, and other members of the public in sorting through garbage.

Because the garbage cans in this case were readily accessible and visible from a public thoroughfare, the alley, and because it is common for scavengers to snoop through garbage cans found in such alleys, we agree that Shanks could harbor no reasonable expectation of privacy because the garbage was essentially exposed to the public. Furthermore, Shanks cannot claim an expectation of privacy (that society would accept as objectively reasonable) merely because it was the police, rather than the regular garbage service, who rummaged through his garbage. Once he placed his contraband-containing bags in the garbage containers located adjacent to a public thoroughfare, he exposed them to the public-at-large, including the police.

curtilage / The area outside the home itself, but so close to and intimately connected with the home and the activities that normally go on there that it can reasonably be considered part of the home.

to search a home. The Court has expanded the protection of "house" to include the actual structure and the living space surrounding the home. The protected living space is considered the home's curtilage.

The tradition of expanded protection of the home existed in English common law prior to the adoption of the U.S. Constitution. William Pitt, in his 1763 address before the House of Commons in England, stated: "The poorest man may in his cottage bid defiance to all forces of the Crown. It may be frail; its roof may shake; the wind may blow through it; the storm may enter; but the King of England cannot enter—all his force dares not cross the threshold of the ruined tenement" (Hendrie, 1998, pp. 25–28).

In *United States v. Dunn*, 480 U.S. 294 (1987), the Supreme Court described the curtilage as the "area to which extends the intimate activity associated with the sanctity of a person's home and the privacies of life." The Court, in Dunn, established four factors to consider in determining whether an area was within the curtilage:

- What is the proximity of the area to the home?
- Is the area within the same enclosure as the home?
- What is the nature of the use to which the area is put?
- What steps have been taken by the resident to prevent the area from being viewed by passersby?

Voices of Experience

Defensive Tactics

Excerpts from an interview between Cliff Roberson and former police officer, Richard M. Hough Sr., presently the Criminal Justice Coordinator, University of West Florida, Chipla Campus.

Q: *I understand that one of your many police assignments included the teaching of defensive tactics in the police academy. Tell us about that assignment.*

A: The classes provide aspiring officers with hands-on training in control and restraint techniques, as well as the policy and legal implications. I spent a number of years also teaching RPT writing and I would always tell recruits that I wasn't quite sure which topic was most important. Eventually, I introduced a method to practice defensive tactics and then immediately write a RPT on the simulated action. This was great practice for the real world of patrol. While the methods taught in academies help officers, they cannot prepare an officer for every situation. When affecting an arrest, an officer is trying to restrain a person who may be fighting and is not observing any rules. This is why you will often see several officers "wrestling" with a subject; they are trying not to hurt that person.

The use of force in law enforcement is seen as a major category of discretion, probably the most important category of discretion. I view discretion as the essence of policing. It can provide the right solution for the right situation, but may also lead to tragedy and liability if that discretion is misused. A suspect injured by the strikes of officers subsequent to the suspect being handcuffed may invoke a claim that the officers did not have sufficient training in proper use of force. A passively resisting suspect who refuses to cooperate, but does not physically resist or evade an officer and who is then struck with a baton or stunned by an electronic device, may reasonably claim that the officer involved failed to use alternate methods before utilizing that level of force.

I got satisfaction from knowing that the training I provided new and in-service officers helped keep them from harm and insulated them from certain aspects of liability. Over the years I have also taught special procedures to deal with multiple suspects or suspects armed with various weapons or who are barricaded in awkward places. The study and practice of physical skills of using force, and when not to use force, are critical to the contemporary officer. Verbal intervention training plays a big part in training new officers. How we can resolve or de-escalate a situation without anyone being hurt is the critical question. ■

In the Dunn case, the Court held that a barn was not within the curtilage of the house. The barn was located on a 198-acre ranch, and was 60 yards from the house and 50 yards from a second fence surrounding the home. The Court noted that there was no indication that the barn was being used for those intimate activities normally associated with the home. In Dunn, law enforcement officers had smelled the odor of precursor chemicals normally used in the manufacture of illegal drugs. The officers had approached the barn from an open field and noticed suspicious activity. Using this information, the officers obtained a search warrant and searched the barn. The officers discovered evidence that was used to convict defendants of manufacturing illegal drugs. The Court held that the evidence was admissible.

CASE STUDY: *Kirk v. Louisiana*
536 U. S. 635 (2002)

On an evening in March 1998, police officers observed the petitioner's apartment based on an anonymous citizen complaint that drug sales were occurring there. After witnessing what appeared to be several drug purchases and allowing the buyers to leave the scene, the officers stopped one of the buyers on the street outside the petitioner's residence. The officers later testified that, "because the stop took place within a block of the apartment, they feared that evidence would be destroyed and ordered that the apartment be entered." Thus, "they immediately knocked on the door of the apartment, arrested the defendant, searched him thereto, and discovered the cocaine and the money." Although the officers sought and obtained a search warrant while they detained the petitioner in his home, they only obtained this warrant after they had entered his home, arrested him, frisked him, found a drug vial in his underwear, and observed contraband in plain view in the apartment.

Supreme Court's Decision: Police officers entered the petitioner's home, where they arrested and searched him. The officers had neither an arrest warrant nor a search warrant. Without deciding whether exigent circumstances had been present, the Louisiana Court of Appeals concluded that the warrantless entry, arrest, and search did not violate the Fourth Amendment of the U.S. Constitution because there had been probable cause to arrest the petitioner. The court's reasoning plainly violates our holding in *Payton v. New York*, 445 U. S. 573, 590 (1980), that "absent exigent circumstances," the "firm line at the entrance to the house . . . may not reasonably be crossed without a warrant." We thus grant the petition for a *writ of certiorari* and reverse the Court of Appeal's conclusion that the officers' actions were lawful, absent exigent circumstances.

"The Fourth Amendment to the U.S. Constitution has drawn a firm line at the entrance to the home, and thus, the police need both probable cause to either arrest or search and exigent circumstances to justify a nonconsensual warrantless intrusion into private premises. . . . Here, the defendant was arrested inside an apartment, without a warrant, and the state has not demonstrated that exigent circumstances were present. Consequently, the defendant's arrest was unconstitutional, and his motion to suppress should have been granted." [The decision was issued **per curiam**, which means that all justices agreed and there was no principal author of the opinion.]

per curiam decision / A court decision where all the justices agree and there is no principal author of the opinion.

Selected Fourth Amendment Decisions from 1914 to Present Requiring Suppression of Evidence Seized in a Private Home Following an Illegal Arrest or Search

Weeks v. United States, 232 U. S. 383 (1914) [Adoption of the exclusionary rule for federal courts.]

Amos v. United States, 255 U. S. 313 (1921) [Excluded evidence in federal courts obtained as the result of an unconstitutional warrantless arrest and search.]

Byars v. United States, 273 U. S. 28 (1927) [Evidence excluded in federal courts because of an invalid warrant.]

United States v. Berkeness, 275 U. S. 149 (1927) [Evidence excluded in federal courts because of an insufficient affidavit to support the search warrant.]

Taylor v. United States, 286 U. S. 1 (1932) [Evidence excluded in federal courts because of a warrantless search.]

Elkins v. United States, 364 U. S. 206 (1960) [Evidence excluded in federal courts because of a search beyond scope of warrant.]

Silverman v. United States, 365 U. S. 505 (1961) [Evidence excluded in federal courts because of the warrantless use of an electronic device.]

Chapman v. United States, 365 U. S. 610 (1961) [Evidence excluded where police used false statement to gain entry to the home for a warrantless search.]

Mapp v. Ohio, 367 U. S. 643 (1961) [Exclusionary rule applied to state prosecutions for the first time to exclude a warrantless search.]

Stanford v. Texas, 379 U. S. 476 (1965) [Evidence excluded in state prosecutions because of defects in the warrant.]

Riggan v. Virginia, 384 U. S. 152 (1966) [Evidence excluded in state prosecutions because of an insufficient affidavit to support the warrant.]

Bumper v. North Carolina, 391 U. S. 543 (1968) [Evidence excluded in state prosecutions because the consent to search was obtained by false information.]

Chimel v. California, 395 U. S. 752 (1969) [Evidence excluded in state prosecutions because the search incident to arrest exceeded the scope of authority.]

Connally v. Georgia, 429 U. S. 245 (1977) [Evidence excluded in state prosecutions because the warrant was issued by a magistrate judge who was not neutral.]

Franks v. Delaware, 438 U. S. 154 (1978) [Results of search excluded because the affidavit that supported the warrant contained false statements.]

Welsh v. Wisconsin, 466 U. S. 740 (1984) [Evidence excluded because the warrantless entry into the home was without exigent circumstances.]

Thompson v. Louisiana, 469 U. S. 17 (1984) (*per curiam*) [Warrantless search.]

Arizona v. Hicks, 480 U. S. 321 (1987) [Evidence excluded because of an unreasonable search.]

Kyllo v. United States, 533 U. S. 27 (2001) [A thermal-imaging device aimed at a private home from a public street to detect relative amounts of heat within the home constituted a "search" within the meaning of the Fourth Amendment. Warrantless use of heat-imaging technology.]

Standing

standing / Based on the rule that defendants generally must assert their own legal rights and interests, and cannot rest their claim to relief on the legal rights or interests of another person.

The legal concept of **standing** is based on the rule that defendants generally must assert their own legal rights and interests, and cannot rest their claim to relief on the legal rights or interests of another person. This rule assumes that the party with the right has the appropriate incentive to challenge (or not challenge) governmental action and to do so with the necessary zeal and appropriate presentation. It represents a concern that if the claim is brought by someone other than one at whom the constitutional protection is aimed, the courts might be called upon to decide abstract questions of wide public significance, even though other governmental institutions may be more competent to address the questions and even though judicial intervention may be unnecessary to protect individual rights [*Warth v. Seldin*, 422 U. S. 490, 498 (1975)].

To have standing to object to a search, your constitutional rights must be violated. For example, Covington's home was illegally searched and the evidence was used to convict Brown of receiving stolen merchandise. Brown could not object to the illegal search of Covington's home because Covington's constitutional rights, not Brown's, were violated.

Whitmore v. Arkansas, 495 U.S. 149 (U.S. Supreme Court, 1990) examined the question of whether a third party had standing to challenge the validity of a death sentence imposed on a capital defendant, Simmons, who refused to appeal his death sentence. The petitioner was a Catholic priest who counseled inmates at the Arkansas Department of Correction. The priest contended that the Eighth and Fourteenth Amendments prevented the State of Arkansas from carrying out the death sentence imposed on Simmons without first conducting a mandatory appellate review of Simmons' conviction and sentence. The Supreme Court held that the priest lacked standing to contest the decision to execute Simmons and dismissed the petition.

In *Rakas v. Illinois*, 439 U.S. 128 (U.S. Supreme Court, 1978) the defendants were convicted of armed robbery and their convictions were affirmed on appeal. At their trial, the prosecution offered into evidence a sawed-off rifle and rifle shells that had been seized by police during a search of an automobile in which the petitioners had been passengers. Neither defendant was the owner of the automobile and neither had ever asserted that he owned the rifle or shells seized. The Illinois Appellate Court held that the petitioners lacked standing to object to the allegedly unlawful search and seizure and denied their motion to suppress the evidence. The court stated that: "We believe that the defendants failed to establish any prejudice to their own constitutional rights because they were not the persons aggrieved by the unlawful search and seizure. . . . They wrongly seek to establish prejudice only through the use of evidence gathered as a consequence of a search and seizure directed at someone else and fail to prove an invasion of their own privacy."

Defendants urged the U.S. Supreme Court to relax or broaden the rule of standing enunciated in *Jones v. United States*, 362 U.S. 257 (1960), so that any criminal defendant at whom a search was "directed" would have standing to contest the legality of that search and object to the admission at trial of evidence obtained as a result of the search. Alternatively, they argued that they had standing to object to the search because they were "legitimately on the premises" at the time of the search.

The Supreme Court refused to extend the rule of standing in Fourth Amendment cases in the manner suggested by the defendants. The Court stated that the "Fourth Amendment rights are personal rights which, like some other constitutional rights, may not be vicariously asserted."

The Court noted that persons who are aggrieved by an illegal search and seizure only through the introduction of damaging evidence secured by a search of a third person's premises or property have not had any of their Fourth Amendment rights infringed upon. Because the exclusionary rule is an attempt to effectuate the guarantees of the Fourth Amendment [*United States v. Calandra*, 414 U.S. 338, 347 (1974)], it is proper to permit only defendants whose Fourth Amendment rights have been violated to benefit from the rule's protections. The Court concluded that there was no reason to think that parties whose rights have been infringed upon will

A police officer searches a male suspect leaning against the back of his pickup truck along the side of a road during an arrest in Texas.

not, if evidence is used against them, have ample motivation to move to suppress it. Even if such persons were not defendants in the action, they may be able to recover damages for the violation of their Fourth Amendment rights or seek redress under state law for invasion of privacy or trespass.

WARRANT CLAUSE OF THE FOURTH AMENDMENT

probable cause / Exists where the facts and circumstances within the officers' knowledge and of which they have reasonably trustworthy information are sufficient to warrant a person of reasonable caution in the belief that an offense has been or is being committed.

As noted earlier in this chapter, the Fourth Amendment states that no warrant shall issue but upon probable cause supported by oath or affirmation and particularly describing the place to be searched and the persons or things to be seized. A search warrant must be issued by a neutral and detached magistrate. It is the magistrate, not the police, who makes the determination that **probable cause** exists. In determining whether probable cause exists to issue a warrant, magistrates base their decisions upon the facts, not opinions, contained in a sworn affidavit submitted by the officer requesting the warrant.

A Search Warrant

In 2006, an exotic dancer accused several members of Duke University's top-ranked lacrosse team of rape. The following documents were filed by Durham police in the North Carolina Superior Court involving that case. In April 2007, all charges were dismissed by the district attorney.

STATE OF NORTH CAROLINA   IN THE GENERAL COURT OF   I
JUSTICE
DURHAM COUNTY   DISTRICT COURT DIVISION

ATTACHMENT FOR APPLICATION FOR SEARCH WARRANT

IN THE MATTER OF: 610 N. Buchanan Blvd. Durham, NC 27701

  I, Investigator Benjamin Himan being a duly sworn officer, request that the
COURT issue a warrant to search the place, person, vehicles, and any other items or
places described in this application; and to find and seize the property described in this
application.

<u>Description of items to be seized</u>

1. Any DNA evidence to include hair, semen, blood, salvia related to the suspects
    and victim.

2. Blue bathroom carpet/ rug

3. Any clothing related to the suspects and the victim

4. Any documentation identifying the suspects

5. Collection of latent prints identifying persons in the residence

6.   Documentation of ownership of residence

7. Property belonging to ▓▓▓▓▓▓ ▓▓▓▓▓▓ to include but not limited to a purse,
    wallet, make-up and make-up bag, cellular camera telephone, and a shoe

8. Still photographs, video footage and digital recordings of the party

9. Any cameras or video devices which could contain photographs or footage of the
    party on 03/13/2006 to 3/14/2006

10. Artificial Fingernails with a reddish color polish

11. United States Currency totaling $400.00 or portions of said currency (all twenty
    dollar bills)

MAGISTRATE/ JUDGE

DATE: 3-16-06

APPLICANT

DATE: 3/16/06

(continued)

STATE OF NORTH CAROLINA
JUSTICE
DURHAM COUNTY

IN THE GENERAL COURT OF

DISTRICT COURT DIVISION

2

ATTACHMENT FOR APPLICATION FOR SEARCH WARRANT

Description of items to be seized - Continued

12. Any electronic data processing and storage devices, computers and computer systems including central processing units; internal and peripheral storage devices such as fixed disks, external hard disks, floppy disk drives and diskettes, tape drives and tapes, cartridges, optical storage devices or other memory storage devices; peripheral input/output devices such as keyboards, printers, video display monitors, optical reader/write devices, and related communications devices such as modems; together with system documentation, operating logs and documentation, software and instruction manuals Any e-mail correspondence, other electronic communications, memos, or documents of any type referring to *First Degree Rape, Robbery, Kidnapping, First Degree Sexual Offense, Hate Crimes, Felony Strangulation, and Assault on a female.*

Description of Crimes

First Degree Forcible Rape (N.C.G.S. 14-27.3), First Degree Kidnapping (N.C.G.S.14-39), First Degree Forcible Sexual Offense (N.C.G.S. 14-27.4), Common Law Robbery (N.C.G.S. 14-87.1), Felonious Strangulation (N.C.G.S. 14-32 4(b))

Description of Premises to be Searched

The residence to be searched is located at 610 North Buchanan Blvd. in Durham, North Carolina. From the Durham Police District 2 Substation located at 1058 W. Club Blvd, officers will turn left traveling south on Guess Rd which turns into North Buchanan. The residence is on the east side of the street just after W. Markham. The premise to be searched is a one story single family dwelling white in color with black shutters. The shutters are only on the front and right side of the home if looking at the residence from the street. The front door faces west towards the street. There is a green motor vehicle parked in the garage on the East side of the dwelling. The numbers 610 are black and are on the front door of the residence. There are two brick chimney protruding from the roof of the dwelling. A chain link fence runs along the East side of the dwelling.

MAGISTRATE / JUDGE
DATE: 3/16/06

APPLICANT
DATE: 3/14/06

STATE OF NORTH CAROLINA   IN THE GENERAL COURT OF   **3**
JUSTICE
DURHAM COUNTY   DISTRICT COURT DIVISION

ATTACHMENT FOR APPLICATION FOR SEARCH WARRANT

Description of Vehicle to be Searched

1996 Green Honda Accord, Virginia License Plate Number JBM-5999
VIN: 1HGCD5654TA199992
And / or
Any vehicle on the curtilage

Description of Person to be Searched

Not applicable

IN THE MATTER OF: 610 N. Buchanan, Durham N.C.

Probable Cause Affidavit

The affiant swears to the following facts to establish probable cause for the issuance of a search warrant. I, Inv. B.W. Himan, am a sworn law enforcement officer and have been since 2003. I have been employed as a sworn police officer with the Durham City Police Department since 2003. I am currently an investigator with the Durham City Police Department's Criminal Investigation Division Violent Crimes Unit.

The Criminal Investigations Division has the responsibility of follow-up investigations of the crimes committed by adults and juveniles involving crimes against person and property. The primary objectives of this Division are to provide both investigative and general support to the other Divisions of the Durham Police Department in the accomplishment of establishing departmental goals and objectives. The Violent Crimes and Property Crimes Units are a part of the District 2 Criminal Investigations Division, dedicated to investigation matters of the people within the city of Durham, NC concerning persons.

I have been assigned to the Criminal Investigations Division as an Investigator in District 2. I have been involved in numerous investigations to include domestic violence assaults, robberies, sexual assaults, and homicide investigations. I have received specialized training in the area of criminal investigation over my years with the Durham City Police Department. I have attended the following classes related to Law enforcement:

Interview and Interrogation, Police Law Institute, Field Training Officers School, Street Drug Enforcement for Patrol Officers, and Child Death Investigation. These classes are in addition to hundreds of hours of In-Service Training with the Durham Police

MAGISTRATE / JUDGE

DATE: 3/6-06

APPLICANT

DATE: 3/16/06

(continued)

STATE OF NORTH CAROLINA
JUSTICE
DURHAM COUNTY

IN THE GENERAL COURT OF   4

DISTRICT COURT DIVISION

ATTACHMENT FOR APPLICATION FOR SEARCH WARRANT

     On 3/14/06 at 1:22am Durham City Police Officers were called to the Kroger on Hillsborough Road. The victim reported to the officers that she had been sexually assaulted at 610 North Buchanan Blvd. The investigation revealed that the victim and another female had an appointment to dance at 610 North Buchanan Blvd. The victim arrived at the residence and joined the other female dancer. The victim reported that they began to preform their dance in master bedroom area. After a few minutes, the males watching them started to get excited and aggressive. The victim and her fellow dancer decided to leave because they were concerned for their safety. As the two women got into a vehicle, they were approached by one of the suspects. He appoligized and requested they go back inside and continue to dance. Shortly after going back into the dwelling the two women were seperated. Two males, Adam and Matt pulled her into the bathroom. Someone closed the door to the bathroom where she was, and said "sweet heart you can't leave." The victim stated she tried to leave and the three males (Adam, Bret, and Matt) force fully held her legs and arms and sexually assaulted her anally, vaginally and orally. The victim stated she was hit, kicked and strangled during the assault and she attempted to defend herself, but was overpowered. The victim reported she was sexually assaulted for an approximate 30 minute time period by the three males. Police went to the residence in the early morning hours shortly after the victim reported the event. The Green Honda was parked at the residence at that time. Officers documented that vehicle was present, and no one would come to the door.

     This Affiant is requesting the COURT to issue a warrant to search the residence, outbuildings, trash, and any vehicles on the curtilage of 610 North Buchanan Blvd Durham, North Carolina. In order to search and seize any evidence described under "Evidence to be Seized" from inside the residence of 610 North Buchanan Blvd. Durham, North Carolina.

MAGISTRATE / JUDGE

DATE: 3-16-06

APPLICANT

DATE: 3-16-06

STATE OF NORTH CAROLINA
In The General Court of Justice
☐ District   ☐ Superior Court Division

Durham County

| File No. |
| Film No. |

| In the Matter of |
| Name |
| 610 N. Buchanan Blvd. |
| Date of Search |
| 3/16/06 |

INVENTORY OF SEIZED PROPERTY

G.S. 15A-254,-

I, the undersigned officer, executed a search of:

610 N. Buchanan Blvd   Durham, NC

Person, place or vehicle searched
610 N. Buchanan

This search was made pursuant to:
xx☒ a search warrant issued by: Tammy Drew

☐ a consent to search given by:

☐ other legal justification for the search:

The following items were seized:

1. make up bag with ID 2. Laptop - Dell serial # H5U XU31

3. P.C. Card - Motorola - serial # 03UT17415856 4. Dell Latitude Laptop serial # 7GCX011

5. Motorola Notebook adapter serial # 145901426807 24 6. Web Cam - Creative serial # CDUF00

621000. 7. Digital Camera Case - Sony - serial # 3515746 8. Micro Cassette

Recorder - Olympus 9. Verizon cellphone - 406KSYU009960 2 10. Apple Laptop Mac Probook

11 Verizon cell phone - VX9900 12. Sony Hard Drive - 3043053

AOC-CR-206   Original - File   Copy - person whose property was seized

Seized Items Continued:
13 Apple Laptop - I Book 14. Canon Digital camera PC1158 15. Sony Camera Dsc P8
16 Canon Digital Camera, 17. Large Rectangle green bath rug 18. Small Bath Mat, 19 white floor
cleaning wipe, hand towel with initials, 21 Swabbings 22. 5 fingernails, 23 Dish Rag 24 Green Rug
25 plastic Bag with wet paper towel 26. Large Rug 27, Paper Towels 28. Pills, 29. #160 30. KY Jelly Bottle
Photograph

☐ I am leaving a copy of this Inventory with the person named below, who is:
    ☐ the owner of the place searched
    ☐ the owner of the vehicle searched

(continued)

X the person in apparent control of the place searched	
□ the person in apparent control of the vehicle searched	
□ the person from whom the items were taken	
□ As no person was present, I am leaving a copy of this Inventory:	
□ in the place searched, identified on the reverse	
□ in the vehicle searched, identified on the reverse.	

Name and Address of Person to Whom A Copy Of This Inventory Was Delivered

Dan Flannery   Durham, NC
610 N. Buchanan

The law enforcement agency identified below will hold the seized property subject to Court Order.

SWORN AND SUBSCRIBED TO BEFORE ME	Signature of Law Enforcement Officer
Date *3/22/06*	Title of Law Enforcement Officer *Investigator*
Signature	Name and Address of Agency *505 W. Chapel Hill St*
□ Deputy CSC □ Asst. CSC □ Clerk of Superior Court □ Magistrate	*Durham, NC 27701*

Acknowledgment of Receipt

I, the undersigned, received a copy of this inventory

Date *3/22/06*
Signature of Recipient

Probable Cause

As noted earlier, the Fourth Amendment provides that "no warrant shall issue but upon probable cause." In addition, the U.S. Supreme Court has required probable cause before many authorized warrantless searches may be made. Generally, when we discuss probable cause it is in reference to a search or arrest warrant, but there are four basic situations when the probable cause is an issue: arrests with warrants, arrests without warrants, searches and seizures with a warrant, and searches and seizures without warrants.

What constitutes probable cause is difficult to explain. As the Pennsylvania Supreme Court noted in *Commonwealth v. One 1958 Plymouth Sedan*, 211 A.2d 536 (Pa. Sup. Ct. 1965): "Probable cause is exceedingly difficult to explain and to apply to the facts and circumstances of a particular case." Justice Rutledge in *Brinegar v. U. S.*, 338 U.S. 160 (1949) stated that in "dealing with probable cause . . . as the very name implies, we deal with probabilities. These are not technical; they are the factual and practical considerations of everyday life on which reasonable and prudent men, not legal technicians, act."

As noted by the Pennsylvania Supreme Court in *McCarthy v. De Armit*, 99 Pa. 63 (1920): "The substance of all the definitions of probable cause is a reasonable ground for belief of guilt." The U.S. Supreme Court stated in *Carroll v. United States*, 267 U.S. 132 (1925): "Probable cause exists where the facts and circumstances within the officers' knowledge and of which they had reasonably trustworthy information are sufficient in themselves to warrant a man of reasonable caution in the belief that an offense has been or is being committed."

The Pennsylvania Court also noted in *De Armit* that: "Many years ago this court stated that probable cause depends upon the honest and reasonable belief of the officer and must be judged by the totality of the circumstances existing at the time of the search and seizure." The Pennsylvania Court noted that probable cause has been said to exist where the facts and circumstances within the arresting officers' knowledge and of which they had reasonably trustworthy information are sufficient in themselves to warrant a person of reasonable caution in the belief that an offense has been or is being committed and that the person to be arrested has committed or is committing the offense.

> ### General Rules Involving Probable Cause That Apply to Both Searches and Arrests
>
> - The magistrate, not the police, makes the determination as to whether probable cause exists in warrant applications.
> - Probable cause may be based on hearsay information.
> - The phrase "person of reasonable caution" does not refer to a person with special legal training, it refers to the average person who under the circumstances would believe that the individual being arrested had committed the offense or that the items to be seized would be found in a particular place.
> - Probable cause requires an "honest and reasonable belief."
> - Proof beyond a reasonable doubt is not required to establish probable cause.
> - Probable cause may be established by an officer's own knowledge of certain facts and circumstances, by information given by informants, or information plus corroboration.
> - Probable cause cannot be based on the results of the search or arrest. For example, if the search of a person reveals the presence of drugs, that cannot be used to justify the search in the first place. Probable cause must exist before the search or the arrest.
> - The experience of the officer may be considered as one factor in establishing probable cause, but cannot be the sole factor justifying the arrest or search.
> - If the facts used to establish probable cause are provided by an informant, additional corroboration is required because of the inherent unreliability of informants.

Judge Learned Hand, speaking for the U.S. Court of Appeals, Second Circuit in *U. S. v. Heitner*, 149 F. 2d 105, 106 (2nd Cir. 1945), noted that it was well-settled that an arrest or search may be based on hearsay evidence; and, indeed, the probable cause necessary to support an arrest or search does not demand the same strictness of proof as the accused's guilt upon a trial.

Duties of the Magistrate in Issuing a Warrant

The courts have insisted that magistrates must perform their duties in a neutral and detached function. A **magistrate** may not serve merely as a rubber stamp for the police. As the U.S. Supreme Court stated in *Lo-Ji Sales, Inc. v. New York*, 442 U.S. 319 (1979): "A magistrate failing to manifest that neutrality and detachment demanded of a judicial officer when presented with a warrant application and who acts instead as an adjunct law enforcement officer cannot provide valid authorization for an otherwise unconstitutional search."

In *Franks v. Delaware*, 438 U.S. 154 (1978), the U.S. Supreme Court noted that the deference accorded to a magistrate's finding of probable cause does not preclude inquiry into the knowing or reckless falsity of the affidavit on which that determination

magistrate / A judicial officer or judge with the authority to issue warrants.

was based. When a defendant alleges that the police made deliberate false statements or the police were reckless regarding the use of information used to establish probable cause, the trial court should hold a **Franks hearing**.

A *Franks hearing* looks at the issue of police misconduct in production of the affidavit used to support the finding of probable cause. As noted in *United States v. Stanert*, 762 F.2d 775 (1985), to void an otherwise valid search warrant because of false or misleading statements by the police, the defendant must make "a substantial showing that the officer intentionally or recklessly omitted facts required to prevent technically true statements in the affidavit from being misleading." **Note:** If the information used by the police in the affidavit was false, but the police acted in an honest and reasonable manner and did not know that the information was false, the inaccuracy will not void the warrant.

Franks hearing / A hearing that looks at the issue of police misconduct in production of the affidavit used to support the finding of probable cause.

Execution of a Search Warrant

At common law, unless otherwise provided, searches were required to be conducted during daylight hours. As a general rule, most warrants provide guidelines as to when the search may be conducted. In some states, state statutes regulate the hours when a search warrant may be executed. The general rules regarding the execution of a search warrant include:

- Search warrants have only a limited life. Unlike an arrest warrant, generally a search warrant must be executed without unnecessary delay.
- Unnecessary damages to a house during execution of a search warrant may result in a Fourth Amendment claim under 42 U.S.C. sec. 1983 [*DiCesare v. Stuart*, 12 F.3d 973 (10th Cir. 1993)].
- Under federal law: "A search warrant relating to offenses involving controlled substances may be served at any time of the day or night if the judge . . . is satisfied there is probable cause to believe that grounds exist for the warrant and for its service at such time" (21 U.S.C. sec. 879). A nighttime search under this statute "requires no special showing . . . other than a showing that the contraband is likely to be on the property or person to be searched at that time" [*Gooding v. United States*, 416 U.S. 430 (1974)].
- The Federal Rule of Criminal Procedure 41(h) defines "daytime" as "the hours from 6:00 A.M. to 10:00 P.M. according to local time."
- Generally, officers executing a search warrant must announce their authority and purpose before entering a dwelling without consent (18 U.S.C. sec. 3109). There is, however, an exception to this "knock-purpose" rule when exigent circumstances exist [*Sabbath v. United States*, 391 U.S. 585 (1968)].
- Police may enter without knocking "when the officers reasonably believe the persons to be apprehended might destroy evidence during a delay in police entry" [*United States v. Tracy*, 835 F.2d 1267 (8th Cir. 1988)].
- After the search is completed, the officer in charge of the search is required to make a "return" to the court. This "return" should include a list of the property taken.
- The scope of the search and its duration must relate directly to the magistrate's previous determination of probable cause.
- The police may not use extraordinary force in conducting the search.

May a Civilian Participate in the Execution of a Warrant?

Many cases have considered the analogous issue of whether a civilian may participate in the execution of a search warrant. In executing a search warrant, government officials must ensure that the search is conducted in a way that minimizes unwarranted intrusions into an individual's privacy. If the civilian participating in the execution of a search warrant was the victim of a theft who has been requested by police to point out property that has been stolen from the victim, the courts have unanimously held that the civilian's presence did not affect the propriety of the search [*United States v. Robertson*, 21 F.3d 1030 (10th Cir. 1994)]. A carjacking victim's presence in a defendant's residence was permitted to help identify items covered by warrant in *People v. Superior Court*, 598 P.2d 877, 878 (Cal. 1979).

Most courts have required that the civilian's role must be to aid the efforts of the police. In other words, civilians cannot be present simply to further their own goals. In *Wilson v. Layne*, 526 U.S. 603 (1999), the U.S. Supreme Court held that inviting media to "ride along" on the execution of a warrant violated the defendant's Fourth Amendment rights. The Court noted that the officer must be in need of assistance. Police cannot invite civilians to perform searches on a whim; there must be some reason why a law enforcement officer cannot conduct the search and some reason to believe that postponing the search until an officer is available might raise a safety risk. The civilians must be limited to doing what the police have authority to do.

The use of civilians in the execution of federal search warrants is governed by statute 18 U.S.C. sec. 3105 (A search warrant may in all cases be served by any of the officers mentioned in its direction or by an officer authorized by law to serve such warrant, but by no other person, except in aid of the officer on his requiring it, he being present and acting in its execution).

- A warrant that authorizes covert and surreptitious entry without any provisions for post-search notification to the residents is unconstitutional [*United States v. Freitas*, 800 F.2nd 1451 (9th Cir. 1986)].

Eavesdropping

The first U.S. Supreme Court case on electronic eavesdropping was *Olmstead v. United States*, 277 U.S. 438 (1928). This case involved the interception of a telephone conversation. In *Olmstead*, the Court held that wiretapping was not covered by the Fourth Amendment. The *Olmstead* decision was overruled by the Court in *Berger v. New York*, 388 U.S. 41 (1967). In *Berger*, the Court held that conversations were protected by the Fourth Amendment.

Following are some general rules regarding electronic eavesdropping:

- Electronic surveillance by agents of the government is a search and seizure under the Fourth Amendment.
- In most cases, a warrant is needed for the surveillance.
- Intercepted conversations on a cordless or cell phone do not invade the reasonable expectation of privacy and no warrant is needed [*United States v. Mathis*, 96 F.3d. 1577 (11th Cir. 1996)].
- The Fourth Amendment does not apply to telephone company billing records.
- A pen register that records all the numbers dialed from a particular telephone is not a search within the meaning of the Fourth Amendment [*Smith v. Maryland*, 442 U.S. 735 (1979)].

CASE STUDY: *Muehler v. Mena*
1544 U.S. 93 (U.S. Supreme Court, 2005)

Do the Police have a right to detain an individual in handcuffs during the search of a home and to question her about her immigration status?

Respondent Mena and others were detained in handcuffs during a search of the premises the respondents occupied. Mena sued the officers in civil court under 42 U. S. C. sec. 1983. The District Court found in her favor. The Ninth Circuit affirmed, holding that the use of handcuffs to detain Mena during the search violated her Fourth Amendment rights and that the officers' questioning about her immigration status during the detention constituted an independent Fourth Amendment violation. The U.S. Supreme Court reversed the case.

Decision by Chief Justice Rehnquist: Mena's detention in handcuffs for the length of the search did not violate the Fourth Amendment. That detention is consistent with *Michigan v. Summers*, 452 U. S. 692, in which the Court held that officers executing a search warrant for contraband have the authority "to detain the occupants of the premises while a proper search is conducted." The Court there noted that minimizing the risk of harm to officers is a substantial justification for detaining an occupant during a search and ruled that an officer's authority to detain incident to a search is categorical and does not depend on the "quantum of proof justifying detention or the extent of the intrusion to be imposed by the seizure."

Because a warrant existed to search the premises, and Mena was an occupant of the premises at the time of the search, her detention for the duration of the search was reasonable under *Summers*. Inherent in *Summers'* authorization to detain is the authority to use reasonable force to effectuate the detention. The use of force in the form of handcuffs to detain Mena was reasonable because the governmental interest in minimizing the risk of harm to both officers and occupants, at its maximum when a warrant authorizes a search for weapons and a wanted gang member resides on the premises, outweighs the margin intrusion. Moreover, the need to detain multiple occupants made the use of handcuffs all the more reasonable. Although the duration of a detention can affect the balance of interests, the two- to three-hour detention in handcuffs in this case does not outweigh the government's continuing safety interests.

The officers' questioning of Mena about her immigration status during her detention did not violate her Fourth Amendment rights. The Ninth Circuit's holding to the contrary appears premised on the assumption that the officers were required to have independent reasonable suspicion in order to so question Mena. However, this Court has "held repeatedly that mere police questioning does not constitute a seizure" [*Florida v. Bostick*, 501 U. S. 429, 434]. Because Mena's initial detention was lawful and the Ninth Circuit did not hold that the detention was prolonged by the questioning, there was no additional seizure within the meaning of the Fourth Amendment, and, therefore, no additional Fourth Amendment justification for inquiring about Mena's immigration status was required.

EXCEPTIONS TO THE FOURTH AMENDMENT

Searches Without a Warrant

The U.S. Supreme Court has stated that searches without a warrant are illegal, unless the search was conducted under one of the recognized exceptions to the warrant requirement. The general rule is that you must get a warrant unless you can't. When items obtained as the result of a search warrant are offered into evidence there is a presumption that the search was legal and the party objecting to the search has the burden of proving its illegality. When the search was conducted without a warrant, the presumption is that the search was illegal and the burden of establishing the legality of the search is on the party that is offering the evidence.

The two most frequent situations in which the police may search without a warrant are vehicle searches and where exigent circumstances prevent the police from having time to obtain a search warrant. **Note:** In both cases the police will need probable cause to search.

The courts have upheld the warrantless searches of vehicles on public roads or public property based on the concept that there is a lesser expectation of property in a vehicle than in a home and the mobility of the vehicle makes the logistics of obtaining a warrant difficult. The relaxing of the warrant requirement does not dispense with the need for probable cause. **Note:** if the vehicle is not in a public place (e.g., parked in a private garage), a warrant will probably be needed to search it. The general rules involved in a warrantless search of an automobile include:

- A traffic or vehicle code violation will usually provide sufficient basis to detain and search a vehicle.
- If the officer has probable cause to search a vehicle, generally the officer will have probable cause to search any container in the vehicle. However, if the probable cause is based on the possible presence of a large object or person, then the search of a small container probably would not be authorized under the concept that you cannot find an elephant in a matchbox.
- If there is an arrest of the occupant of a vehicle, the officer may search the vehicle.
- In most states during a routine traffic violation stop, the officer may order all occupants out of the vehicle.
- Generally, officers must have at least "reasonable suspicion" to stop a vehicle on a public road; however, officers may stop motorists and briefly detain vehicles on a public road for sobriety checkpoint roadblocks. **Note:** Officers do not have the discretion as to which car they will stop. They generally must stop all vehicles. If after the brief stop an officer has reasonable suspicion that the driver is under the influence, then the officer may develop this stop into a more detailed stop.
- If a driver is arrested and the vehicle is detained by the police, the police may conduct an inventory of the vehicle.

The basis for searches based on exigent circumstances is that for some reason it is impractical for the police to get a warrant. The factors that a court will consider in determining the existence of exigent circumstances include:

- It must be impractical to obtain a warrant.
- The emergency that justifies the warrantless search also acts to limit the scope of the search.
- All exigency searches need probable cause.

Plain View Doctrine

As discussed earlier, a search constitutes a government intrusion into an area where the individual has a reasonable expectation of privacy. If the item is in plain view, then there has not been a search within the meaning of the Fourth Amendment.

Where Exigent Circumstances Permitted the Warrantless Entry into a Home

Note: *Payton v. New York*, 445 U. S. 573, 586 (1980) held that to enter a home, police must have a warrant or exigent circumstances. In the following cases, the U.S. Supreme Court held that sufficient exigent circumstances existed.

Mincey v. Arizona, 437 U. S. 385 (1978): Undercover officer shot inside. Police could enter to rescue someone from imminent harm.

Michigan v. Tyler, 436 U. S. 499 (1978): Home on fire. Law enforcement officers could enter in an attempt to put out the fire.

Ker v. California, 374 U. S. 23 (1963): Destructible narcotics. Police could enter to prevent destruction of evidence.

Warden v. Haden, 396 U.S. 1027 (1970): Fresh pursuit of a dangerous felon. Police chased a fleeing robber into the house.

U.S. v. Santana, 427 U. S. 38 (1976): Drug suspect. Arrest started in public place (front yard) and suspect ran back into her house.

Brigham City v. Stuart, 126 S.Ct. 1943 (2006): Police may enter a home without a warrant when they have an objectively reasonable basis for believing that an occupant is seriously injured or imminently threatened with such injury.

This statement assumes that officers have a right to be where they were when the viewing took place. For example, after breaking into an apartment, the officer could not claim that the stolen TV was in plain view.

An item is still considered to be in plain view even when common means of enhancing the vision are used (e.g., binocular or flashlight). In *Texas v. Brown*, 460 U.S. 730 (1983), the U.S. Supreme Court noted that it was "beyond dispute" that the action of a police officer in shining his flashlight to illuminate the interior of a car, without probable cause to search the car, was not a search of the car. In *United States v. Lee*, 274 U.S. 559 (1927), the officers' use of the beam of a flashlight, directed through the essentially open front of the respondent's barn, did not transform their observations into an unreasonable search within the meaning of the Fourth Amendment. On the other hand, if the police engage in a much more intense form of surveillance, especially from places not ordinarily used by the public, this may constitute a search under *Katz* (LaFave, 1987, pp. 433–434). It would probably be considered a search if a high-powered telescope was used to determine what a person was reading in a high-rise apartment.

In *Arizona v. Hicks*, 480 U.S. 321 (1987), the police were lawfully on the premises and noticed new stereo equipment. An officer moved the equipment so that he could look at the serial number. It was later determined that the equipment had been stolen. The court held that the plain view doctrine did not apply and that the search was invalid. The court noted that until the officer moved the equipment, the serial number was not in plain view and that looking at the serial number was an illegal search because the officer had no probable cause to believe that the equipment had been stolen.

Open Fields

In the 1920s, Mr. Hester lived on his parents' farm in South Carolina. Hidden in the woods on the family farm was Hester's equipment for making illegal whiskey. The equipment was well hidden in the woods and away from the family house. Government agents entered the farm without a warrant and discovered the equipment. When Hester was prosecuted for his whiskey-making activities, he claimed that the evidence was taken as the result of an illegal search. Both parties agreed that the agents had trespassed on the property and that the equipment was well hidden in the woods. The U.S. Supreme Court held that **open fields** were not protected by the Fourth Amendment. Justice Oliver Holmes stated that the special protection accorded by the Fourth Amendment to the people in their "persons, houses, papers, and effects," is not extended to the open fields. The distinction between the latter and the house is as old as the common law [*Hester v. United States*, 265 U.S. 57 (1924)].

open fields / The portion of a premises that is outside the curtilage of the home or business. "Open fields" are not protected by the Fourth Amendment.

In *Oliver v. United States*, 466 U.S. 170 (1984), acting on reports that marijuana was being raised on the farm of petitioner Oliver, two narcotics agents of the Kentucky State Police went to the farm to investigate. Arriving at the farm, they drove past the petitioner's house to a locked gate with a "No Trespassing" sign. A footpath led around one side of the gate. The agents walked around the gate and along the road for several hundred yards, passing a barn and a parked camper. At that point, someone standing in front of the camper shouted: "No hunting is allowed, come back up here." The officers shouted back that they were Kentucky State Police officers, but found no one when they returned to the camper. The officers resumed their investigation of the farm and found a field of marijuana over a mile from the petitioner's home. The Court noted that the field itself was highly secluded; bounded on all sides by woods, fences, and embankments; and could not be seen from any point of public access.

The Court concluded that this was not a field that invited casual intrusion. However, according to the Court, open fields do not provide the setting for those intimate activities that the amendment is intended to shelter from government interference or surveillance. There is no societal interest in protecting the privacy of those activities, such as the cultivation of crops that occur in open fields. Moreover, as a practical matter, these lands usually are accessible to the public and the police in ways that a home, an office, or commercial structure would not be. The Court noted that fences or "No Trespassing" signs, which effectively bar the public from viewing open fields in rural areas, do not prevent the field from being legally considered an open field.

Searches of Parolees and Persons on Probation

A usual condition of parole is that the individual submit to being searched at any time and with no requirements for probable cause. A similar clause is in most probation contracts. If such an agreement exists, then the parolee or person on probation may be searched at any time unless otherwise restricted by state case law or statute. If the agreement does not exist, then the normal rules of search and seizure apply.

Searches Incident to Lawful Arrest

If the police make a lawful arrest, probable cause is not needed to search the arrested individual. In addition, the officer may search any area within the immediate control of the arrestee. If the arrest is determined to be illegal or without authority, any evidence found on the body of the arrested person or discovered in the immediate vicinity of the individual is generally not admissible in evidence. General rules regarding searches incident to lawful arrest include:

- The search will be valid as an incident to arrest only if the search and arrest are carried out contemporaneously, although either may precede the other.
- If the arrest is proper, the officer may search without probable cause.
- Under most circumstances, if a person is arrested in a vehicle, the entire passenger compartment of the vehicle may be searched. There is a conflict among the states and the courts as to whether the trunk of the vehicle may also be searched.
- If a person is arrested within a home, generally only the immediate room that the individual was in when arrested may be searched. This is under the concept that the police may search the area under the immediate control of the arrestee. **Note:** As a general rule, the police may not search the entire home.
- The courts in a few states will not admit evidence discovered in a search pursuant to an arrest if it appears to the court that the arrest was a pretext in order to have authority to search the individual. Most courts, however, do not consider the motive of the officers arresting an individual as long as the officers had probable cause to arrest.

Consent

Persons may waive their rights under the Fourth Amendment and consent to a search. Even if officers have in their possession a search warrant, the officers should first ask permission to search. If permission is given, then the legality of the warrant is immaterial. If permission is denied, then the officers may search pursuant to the warrant. Unlike in-custody interrogation, an officer is under no obligation to advise the individual of the right to refuse the requested search or to seek an attorney.

The issue as to whether or not consent was voluntary depends on the surrounding circumstances. Undercover police officers may deceive an individual regarding their identity in order to obtain permission to enter the premises. The fact that the consent was given by mistake or as a direct result of police deception as to identity does not make the entry unlawful unless the deception was unreasonably fraudulent. For example, consent based on an officer's false statement that the officer has a search warrant is not a valid consent. However, the officer may advise individuals that if they refuse to consent, then the officer will obtain a warrant.

To be effective the consent must be given by someone who possesses common authority or apparent common authority to give permission. For example, a live-in girlfriend's consent to search an apartment was considered as effective. Once consent is given, it may be withdrawn. If withdrawn, the officers are under an obligation to stop the search. **Note:** Anything discovered prior to the withdrawal of consent is generally admissible in evidence and may also be used to provide probable cause to obtain a search warrant. The mere fact of a person's refusal to consent may not be considered in establishing probable cause.

CASE STUDY: *Georgia v. Randolph*
126 S.Ct. 1515, 164 L.Ed.2d 208 (U.S. Supreme Court, 2006)

Is consent given by one occupant to search a house valid where another physically present occupant objects to the search?

Respondent Scott Randolph and his wife, Janet, separated in late May 2001, when she left the marital residence in Americus, Georgia, and went to stay with her parents in Canada, taking their son and some belongings. In July, she returned to the Americus house with the child, though the record does not reveal whether her object was reconciliation or retrieval of remaining possessions.

On the morning of July 6, she complained to the police that after a domestic dispute her husband took their son away, and when officers reached the house she told them that her husband was a cocaine user whose habit had caused the family financial troubles. She mentioned the marital problems and said that she and their son had only recently returned after a stay of several weeks with her parents. Shortly after the police arrived, Scott Randolph returned and explained that he had removed the child to a neighbor's house out of concern that his wife might take the boy out of the country again; he denied cocaine use, and countered that it was in fact his wife who abused drugs and alcohol. Scott refused to give the police permission to search the house.

Janet Randolph was asked to consent to a search, which she readily gave. She led the officer upstairs to a bedroom that she identified as Scott's, where the officer noticed a section of a drinking straw with a powdery residue that was later determined to be cocaine.

Decision by Justice David Souter: To the Fourth Amendment rule ordinarily prohibiting the warrantless entry of a person's house as unreasonable *per se*, *Payton v. New York*, 445 U. S. 573 (1980); one "jealously and carefully drawn" exception recognizes the validity of searches with the voluntary consent of an individual possessing authority. That person might be the householder against whom evidence is sought [*Schneckloth v. Bustamonte*, 412 U. S. 218 (1973)], or a fellow occupant who shares common authority over property, when the suspect is absent and the exception for consent extends even to entries and searches with the permission of a co-occupant whom the police reasonably, but erroneously, believe to possess shared authority as an occupant. None of our co-occupant consent-to-search cases, however, has presented the further fact of a second occupant physically present and refusing permission to search, and later moving to suppress evidence so obtained.

This case invites a straightforward application of the rule that a physically present inhabitant's express refusal of consent to a police search is dispositive as to him, regardless of the consent of a fellow occupant. Scott Randolph's refusal is clear, and nothing in the record justifies the search on grounds independent of Janet Randolph's consent. The State does not argue that she gave any indication to the police of a need for protection inside the house that might have justified entry into the portion of the premises where the police found the powdery straw . . . Nor does the State claim that the entry and search should be upheld under the rubric of exigent circumstances, owing to some apprehension by the police officers that Scott Randolph would destroy evidence of drug use before any warrant could be obtained. [The judgment of the Supreme Court of Georgia, which held that the search was illegal, was affirmed.]

Student Drug Testing

One of the leading cases on testing students for drugs is *Vernonia School District 47J v. Acton*, 515 U. S. 646 (1995). In that case, school officials, motivated by the discovery that athletes were leaders in the student drug culture and concerned that drug use increases the risk of sports-related injury, petitioned the school district (District) to adopt the Student Athlete Drug Policy (Policy), which authorized random urinalysis drug testing of students who participate in its athletics programs. Respondent Acton was denied participation in his school's football program when he and his parents refused to consent to the testing. They then filed this suit, seeking

Consent to Search a Computer

The *Trulock v. Freeh* case [275 F.3d 391 (4th Cir. 12/28/2001)] presented an interesting issue regarding a third party's consent to search a computer. Linda Conrad and Notra Trulock, an unmarried couple, lived together and shared the same computer. Each individual had password-protected files. Conrad gave government agents permission to search the computer. The agents took the computer and accessed the password-protected files of Trulock.

The Court stated that although Conrad had authority to consent to a general search of the computer, her authority did not extend to Trulock's password-protected files. Trulock's password-protected files are analogous to the locked footlocker inside the bedroom. By using a password, Trulock affirmatively intended to exclude Conrad and others from his personal files. Moreover, because he concealed his password from Conrad, it cannot be said that Trulock assumed the risk that Conrad would permit others to search his files. Thus, Trulock had a reasonable expectation of privacy in the password-protected computer files and Conrad's authority to consent to the search did not extend to them. The Court held that Trulock had alleged a violation of his Fourth Amendment rights.

declaratory and injunctive relief on the grounds that the Policy violated the Fourth and Fourteenth Amendments and the Oregon Constitution. The U.S. Supreme Court held that the Policy was constitutional under the Fourth and Fourteenth Amendments.

The Court noted that the first factor to be considered in determining reasonableness was the nature of the privacy interest on which the search intruded. Here, the subjects of the Policy were children who had been committed to the temporary custody of the State as schoolmaster; in that capacity, the State may exercise a degree of supervision and control greater than it could exercise over free adults. The requirements that public school children submit to physical examinations and be vaccinated indicate that they have a lesser privacy expectation with regard to medical examinations and procedures than the general population. Student athletes have even less of a legitimate privacy expectation, for an element of communal undress is inherent in athletic participation, and athletes are subject to preseason physical exams and rules regulating their conduct.

The privacy interests compromised by the process of obtaining urine samples under the Policy are negligible, since the conditions of collection are nearly identical to those typically encountered in public restrooms. In addition, the tests look only for standard drugs, not medical conditions, and the results are released to a limited group.

The nature and immediacy of the governmental concern at issue, and the efficacy of this means for meeting it, also favored a finding of reasonableness. The importance of deterring drug use by all this nation's schoolchildren cannot be doubted. Moreover, the Policy is directed more narrowly to drug use by athletes, where the risk of physical harm to the user and other players was high. The Fourth Amendment does not require that the "least intrusive" search be conducted, so the respondent's argument that the drug testing could be based on suspicion of drug use, if true, would not be fatal; and that alternative entails its own substantial difficulties.

Stop and Frisk

Prior to *Terry v. Ohio*, 392 U.S. 1 (1968), any restraint of an individual amounting to a seizure for the purposes of the Fourth Amendment was invalid unless justified by probable cause. The U.S. Supreme Court in Terry created a limited exception to this general rule: certain seizures are justifiable under the Fourth Amendment if there is articulable suspicion that a person has committed or is about to commit a crime. In that case, a stop and a frisk for weapons were found unexceptionable. *Adams v. Williams*, 407 U.S. 143 (1972), applied the same approach in the context of an informant's report that an unnamed individual in a nearby vehicle was carrying narcotics and a gun.

In Terry, the policeman who detained and "frisked" the petitioner had for thirty years been patrolling the area in downtown Cleveland where the incident occurred. His experience led him to watch the petitioner and a companion carefully, for a long period of time, as they individually and repeatedly looked into a store window and then conferred together. Suspecting that the two men might be "casing" the store for a "stick-up" and that they might have guns, the officer followed them as they walked away and joined a third man with whom they had earlier conferred. At this point, the officer approached the men and asked for their names. When they "mumbled something" in response, the officer grabbed the petitioner, spun him around to face the other two, and "patted down" his clothing. This frisk led to the discovery of a pistol and to the petitioner's subsequent weapons conviction.

The Court held that the "stop and frisk" in Terry was justified by the probability, not only that a crime was about to be committed, but also that the crime "would be likely to involve the use of weapons." The Court confined its holding to situations in which the officer believes that "the persons with whom he is dealing may be armed and presently dangerous" and "fears for his own or others' safety."

In *Pennsylvania v. Mimms*, 434 U.S. 106 (1977), while on routine patrol, two Philadelphia police officers observed respondent Harry Mimms driving an automobile with an expired license plate. The officers stopped the vehicle for the purpose of issuing a traffic summons. One of the officers approached and asked the respondent to step out of the car and produce his owner's card and operator's license. The respondent got out of the car, whereupon the officer noticed a large bulge under the respondent's sports jacket. Fearing that the bulge might be a weapon, the officer frisked the respondent and discovered in his waistband a .38-caliber revolver loaded with five rounds of ammunition. The other occupant of the car was carrying a .32-caliber revolver. The respondent was immediately arrested and subsequently indicted for carrying a concealed deadly weapon and for unlawfully carrying a firearm without a license. The Court held that once a motor vehicle has been lawfully detained for a traffic violation, the police officers may order the driver to get out of the vehicle without violating the Fourth Amendment's proscription of unreasonable searches and seizures.

Terry Stops

The **Terry stop** must be a temporary stop and not an arrest. It must be a reasonable suspicion, based on articulable facts, that criminal activity is involved. After the stop, if the officer has reason to fear that there is a danger involved, the officer may pat down the clothes of the person being stopped. The pat down is only for the safety of the officer and for detecting any weapons.

Terry stop / A temporary stop with reasonable suspicion based on articulable facts that criminal activity is involved.

ARRESTS

When a police officer has contact with a citizen, the contact may be classified as a consensual encounter, a detention, or an arrest. An arrest (seizure of a person) is the taking of a person into custody so that the person may be held to answer for the commission of a crime. The primary difference between a detention and an arrest is that to be classified as a detention, the stop must be relatively brief. If the detention continues for more than a brief period, it will develop into arrest.

An arrest requires four essential elements:

- **Intention to arrest.** There must be intent to arrest the person. The police cannot accidentally arrest an individual. Because this is a subjective requirement, it is often difficult to establish in court unless the police officer's actions clearly indicate that the officer intended to arrest the individual.

- **Authority to arrest.** The individual making the arrest must have the authority to arrest. Authority to arrest distinguishes an arrest from a false imprisonment or kidnapping.

- **Seizure and detention.** There must be a seizure and detention of the person. The seizure and detention may be actual, such as handcuffing a person, or constructive when the individual submits without the use of force. Mere words do not constitute an arrest. Merely telling a person "you are under arrest" is not an arrest unless it is accompanied by an actual seizure or by submission of the individual to the officer's will and control.

- **An understanding by arrestees that they are being arrested.** Persons detained must understand that they are being arrested. Normally, the understanding is conveyed through words, such as "you are under arrest." Sometimes the understanding is conveyed by actions of the police, such as handcuffing of an individual. If the accused persons are too drunk, drugged, insane, or unconscious to understand that they are being arrested, then the understanding element is excused. The test used by the courts in these situations is: Would individuals with normal facilities understand that they are being arrested?

Arrests are grouped into *arrests with a warrant* and *arrests without a warrant*. The courts have demonstrated a bias toward arrests with warrants. An arrest with a warrant is presumed to be legal unless the contrary is established. An arrest without a warrant is presumed illegal until the contrary is established.

The seizure and detention element requires that there be a submission by the person being arrested. The submission, however, may be implied by the individual merely going with the police officer. The detention may be a "constructive restraint" under some circumstances. For example, in one case the accused was seriously injured in an automobile accident allegedly caused by his driving under the influence of alcohol. The police officer at the scene informed the accused that he was under arrest. The defendant lapsed into unconsciousness. He was taken by ambulance and given a blood test while unconscious. The officer then proceeded to assist other injured persons and did not accompany the accused to the hospital. Several days thereafter, the accused was released from the hospital with a notice to appear in court. The accused contended that he was never arrested and therefore pursuant to state law there was no authority to take a blood sample from him without his permission

Police officers arrest several young male suspects kneeling with their hands behind their heads outside a building.

or a court order. There was a state statute that permitted the taking of a blood sample from an individual who is arrested for driving under the influence. The appeals court held that the officer had constructively arrested the individual. The court stated that: "We deem it wholly unreasonable under the circumstances . . . to require the officer to closely attend that person to the exclusion of the officer's duty to obtain aid for the accident victims, and to prevent further traffic pileups and injuries" [*People v. Logue*, 35 Ca. 1 (1973)].

The authority to arrest is generally determined by state statute. Private persons may under certain circumstances have the authority to arrest an individual (often referred to as *citizen's arrest*). The validity of an arrest is determined by the law of the jurisdiction where the arrest was made. Because an arrest is also a seizure of the person, it must comply with Fourth Amendment standards to be legal. The Fourth Amendment requirements may not be overlooked by classifying the arrest as only a "detention."

In most states, an officer may arrest a person without a warrant whenever the officer has reasonable cause to believe that the person to be arrested has committed a felony, whether or not a felony has been committed by the defendant or anyone. A felony need not have been committed within the presence of the officer. An officer may arrest a person without a warrant if the officer has probable cause to believe that the person has committed a misdemeanor in the officer's presence. Absent of statutory authority, an officer may not arrest without a warrant for a misdemeanor not committed in the officer's presence.

Most states give officers authority to arrest for traffic offenses that occurred out of the presence of the officer. Suppose an individual driving under the influence has an accident. When the officer arrives on the scene, the crime has already been committed. In some states this may be a misdemeanor. Most states' traffic codes provide authority to arrest in such cases. Other common exceptions include misdemeanors committed on school property and crimes committed by juveniles.

For an arrest warrant to be valid, it must be issued by a magistrate (judicial officer) based on facts presented to the officer establishing the existence of probable cause. The magistrate must be "neutral and detached." In a few states, the warrant may be issued by a court clerk if empowered to do so by state law. Because an arrest is the seizure of a person, most of the rules discussed earlier in this chapter regarding a search warrant are applicable to arrest warrants.

CASE STUDY: Excerpts from *United States v. Mark B. Harris*
1993.DC.178, 629 A.2d 481 (D.C. Cir. 1993)

Warrantless, nonconsensual searches or seizures within the home are presumptively unreasonable under the Fourth Amendment [*Payton v. New York*, 445 U.S. 573 (1980)] . . . A warrantless, nonconsensual entry into the home to make an arrest may be justified, however, where there are "exigent circumstances."

The U.S. Supreme Court has not attempted a comprehensive definition of the exigent circumstances exception to the warrant requirement. The leading cases in which the Court has upheld warrantless, nonconsensual entries into the home to make an arrest remain *United States v. Santana*, 427 U.S. 38 (1976), and *Warden v. Hayden*, 387 U.S. 294 (1967). In both of these cases, police were in "hot pursuit" of suspects whom they had probable cause to arrest. But the Court has intimated that exigent circumstances may exist even where police are not in hot pursuit of the suspect . . . In concluding that exigent circumstances justified a warrantless entry to apprehend an armed robbery suspect approximately four hours after the crime, the U.S. Court of Appeals for the District of Columbia developed seven different factors. As later summarized in *United States v. Lindsay*, 165 U.S. App. D.C. 105 (1974), the factors are:

- that a grave offense is involved, particularly a crime of violence
- the suspect is reasonably believed to be armed
- a clear showing of probable cause
- a strong reason to believe that the suspect is in the dwelling
- the likelihood of escape if not swiftly apprehended
- a peaceful entry as opposed to a "breaking"
- the time of entry (night or day)

General rules regarding an arrest warrant are as follows:

- An arrest warrant must describe the offense charged and contain the name of the accused, or if name is unknown, a description of the accused.
- The warrant must indicate the time of issuance, the city or county and state where it is issued, and the duty of the arresting officer to bring the arrested person before the magistrate.
- Arrest warrants, unlike search warrants, are valid until they are recalled by the court.

- When making an arrest pursuant to a warrant, the officer need not have the warrant in his or her presence, as long as the officer is aware of its contents.

- If the officer has the warrant, the officer must display it if requested.

- If the officer does not have the warrant, the officer must explain to the defendant the reason for the arrest.

- Suspects may be arrested in a public place at any time providing there is authority to arrest.

- Traditionally, a person's home is that person's castle. Accordingly, absent exigent circumstances, an arrest warrant is necessary in order to arrest someone inside the individual's home. **Note:** A home or dwelling includes any place the suspect resides (e.g., a tent, boat, mobile home, van, or hotel room).

- To arrest someone in a third person's home—absent exigent circumstances, consent, or other exceptions—a search warrant is needed (to search for the suspect). Exigent circumstances are emergency situations requiring immediate action to prevent imminent danger to life or serious damage to property, or to prevent the escape of a felon.

- Rules regarding consent to enter the home to arrest a suspect are similar to the rules regarding consent to search.

- Federal arrest warrants are valid in all states.

- A state arrest warrant is valid only within the jurisdiction of the state. There is a "hot pursuit" exception whereby officers may cross state lines to arrest an individual if in "hot pursuit."

> ### Excerpts from a Supreme Court Decision
> ### *Kaupp v. Texas*, 538 U. S. 626 (2003)
>
> Although certain seizures may be justified on something less than probable cause [*Terry v. Ohio*, 392 U. S. 1 (1968)], we have never sustained against Fourth Amendment challenge the involuntary removal of a suspect from his home to a police station and his detention there for investigative purposes . . . absent probable cause or judicial authorization. *Hayes v. Florida*, 470 U. S. 811 (1985) cf. *Payton v. New York*, 445 U. S. 573 (1980) . . . The police may not seek to verify mere suspicions by means that approach the conditions of arrest. . . . The police can stop and briefly detain a person for investigative purposes if the officer has a reasonable suspicion supported by articulable facts that criminal activity may be afoot, even if the officer lacks probable cause. Such involuntary transport to a police station for questioning is "sufficiently like arrest to invoke the traditional rule that arrests may constitutionally be made only on probable cause."

EXCLUSIONARY RULE

The **exclusionary rule** has been applied in federal criminal cases since 1914, when the rule was first adopted to protect the rights secured by the Fourth Amendment [*Weeks v. United States*, 232 U.S. 383 (1914)]. Since 1961, when the U.S. Supreme Court decided *Mapp v. Ohio*, 367 U.S. 643 (1961), the states have been compelled to exclude from the State's case-in-chief evidence obtained in violation of the Fourth Amendment. The exclusionary rule is a judicially created remedy that originated as a means to protect the Fourth Amendment right of citizens to be free from unreasonable searches and seizures.

exclusionary rule / A rule of evidence that excludes evidence from being admitted in a criminal trial on the question of the defendant's guilt or innocence that was obtained in violation of the defendant's constitutional rights.

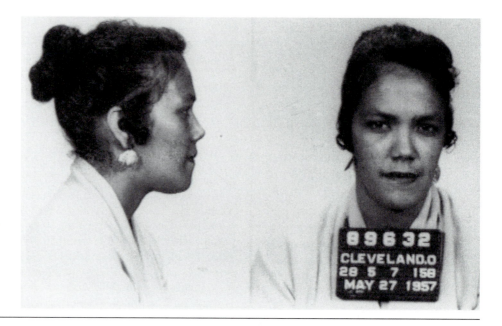

Police photo of Dollree Mapp, aka, Dolly Mapp (1961). The U.S. Supreme Court in *Mapp v. Ohio* required states to apply the exclusionary rule in cases involving illegal searches.

The exclusionary rule was not designed to "make whole" a citizen who has been subjected to an unconstitutional search or seizure. Rather, the aim of the rule is to deter police misconduct. The deterrent purpose of the exclusionary rule necessarily assumes that the police have engaged in willful, or at the very least, negligent, conduct, which has deprived the defendant of some right. By refusing to admit evidence gained as a result of such conduct, the courts hope to instill in those particular investigating officers, or in their future counterparts, a greater degree of care toward the rights of an accused.

General rules regarding the exclusionary rule:

- There are at least five exceptions to the exclusionary rule: (1) good-faith exception, (2) purged taint exception, (3) independent source exception, (4) inevitable discovery exception, and (5) impeachment of the defendant at trial.

- The U.S. Supreme Court has been more reluctant to apply the exclusionary rule to Miranda violations involving confessions and admissions, than to search and seizure issues.

- The exclusionary rule does not apply to noncriminal trial proceedings.

- The U.S. Supreme Court, holding that the exclusionary rule does not apply to grand jury proceedings, implied that the Fourth Amendment exclusionary rule should apply only in those circumstances in which its remedial objective of deterrence will be most efficaciously served.

- An individual must have a legal standing to object before the exclusionary rule may be applied. For example, the violation of the Fourth Amendment rights of one individual cannot be used to exclude information used to find evidence against a co-defendant.

- The exclusionary rule does not apply to deportation hearings.

CASE STUDY: *Hudson v. Michigan*
No. 04-1360 (U.S. Supreme Court, 2006) 2006 WL 1640577

Does the exclusionary rule require the suppression of evidence when the police violate the "Knock and Announce" Rule?

Detroit police executed a search warrant for narcotics and weapons and entered Hudson's home in violation of the Fourth Amendment's "knock-and-announce" rule. The trial court granted Hudson's motion to suppress the evidence seized, but the Michigan Court of Appeals reversed and Hudson was convicted of drug possession.

Justice Anthony Scalia delivered the opinion of the U.S. Supreme Court, concluding that violation of the "knock-and-announce" rule does not require suppression of evidence found in a search.

Majority Opinion: This case is before us only because of the method of entry into the house. When the police arrived to execute the warrant, they announced their presence, but waited only a short time—perhaps "three to five seconds"—before turning the knob of the unlocked front door and entering Hudson's home. Hudson moved to suppress all the inculpatory evidence, arguing that the premature entry violated his Fourth Amendment rights. The common-law principle that law enforcement officers must announce their presence and provide residents an opportunity to open the door is an ancient one.

This Court has rejected "indiscriminate application" of the exclusionary rule, *United States v. Leon*, 468 U.S. 897, holding it applicable only where its deterrence benefits outweigh its substantial social costs . . . Exclusion may not be premised on the mere fact that a constitutional violation was a "but-for" cause of obtaining the evidence. The illegal entry here was not the but-for cause, but even if it were, but-for causation can be too attenuated to justify exclusion. Attenuation can occur not only when the causal connection is remote, but also when suppression would not serve the interest protected by the constitutional guarantee violated.

The interests protected by the knock-and-announce rule include human life and limb (because an unannounced entry may provoke violence from a surprised resident), property (because citizens presumably would open the door upon an announcement, whereas a forcible entry may destroy it), and privacy and dignity of the sort that can be offended by a sudden entrance. But the rule has never protected one's interest in preventing the government from seeing or taking evidence described in a warrant. Since the interests violated here have nothing to do with the seizure of the evidence, the exclusionary rule is inapplicable. . . .

The social costs to be weighed against deterrence are considerable here. In addition to the grave adverse consequence that excluding relevant incriminating evidence always entails—the risk of releasing dangerous criminals—imposing such a massive remedy would generate a constant flood of alleged failures to observe the rule, and claims that any asserted justification for a no-knock entry had inadequate support. Another consequence would be police officers refraining from timely entry after knocking and announcing, producing preventable violence against the officers in some cases, and the destruction of evidence in others. Next to these social costs are the deterrence benefits. The value of deterrence depends on the strength of the incentive to commit the forbidden act. That incentive is minimal here, where ignoring knock-and-announce can realistically be expected to achieve nothing but the prevention of evidence destruction and avoidance of life-threatening resistance, dangers which suspend the requirement when there is "reasonable suspicion" that they exist (*Richards v. Wisconsin*, 520 U. S. 385, 394). Massive deterrence is hardly necessary. Contrary to Hudson's argument that without suppression there will be no deterrence, many forms of police misconduct are deterred by civil-rights suits, and by the consequences of increasing professionalism of police forces, including a new emphasis on internal police discipline.

Note: Do not read too much into this decision. The U.S. Supreme Court did not eliminate the knock-and-announce rule as stated by many scholars. All the Court did was to hold that this was not a ground to exclude the evidence. It is still a violation of the Fourth Amendment not to comply with the rule where compliance is not excused by exigent circumstances. As Devallis Rutledge commented: "The exclusion is gone, but potential liability remains" (Rutledge, 2006, p. 96).

"Fruit of the Poisonous Tree" Doctrine

The "fruit of the poisonous tree" doctrine is used by the courts to suppress evidence that was discovered as the result of an illegal search or discovered because information obtained during an illegal search directed the police to the location or existence of other evidence.

The U.S. Supreme Court has held that not all evidence is "fruit of the poisonous tree" simply "because it would not have come to light but for the illegal actions of the police" [*Wong Sun v. United States*, 83 S.Ct. 407 (1963)]. The Court stated that the "more apt question" is "whether, granting establishment of the primary illegality, the evidence . . . has been come at by exploitation of that illegality or instead by means sufficiently distinguishable to be purged of the primary taint."

The Court noted in *Murray v. United States*, 108 S.Ct. 2529 (1988) that the exclusionary rule prohibits introduction into evidence of tangible materials seized during an unlawful search and of testimony concerning knowledge acquired during an unlawful search. Beyond that, the exclusionary rule also prohibits the introduction of derivative evidence, both tangible and testimonial, that is the product of the primary evidence, or that is otherwise acquired as an indirect result of the unlawful search, up to the point at which the connection with the unlawful search becomes "so attenuated as to dissipate."

CIVIL LIABILITY

> Every person who, under the color of any statute, ordinance, regulation, custom, or usage of any State . . . subjects or causes to be subjected any citizen . . . to the deprivation of any rights, privileges, or immunities secured by the Constitution and laws shall be liable to the party injured in an action at law. . . . **42 USC 1983**

A police officer, department, or city may be subject to civil litigation in one of three situations:

- A civil action based on an intentional tort (battery, false arrest, infliction of mental distress, conversion of property).
- A civil action based on negligence (negligent driving, negligent discharge of a firearm, negligence in the use of lawful force to effect an arrest).
- A civil action based on an infringement of a constitutional right (illegal search, denial of right to counsel, illegally preventing a person from exercising a constitutional right) (*Police supervision: A manual for police supervisors*, 1985).

The majority of civil litigation against police agencies and individual officers is based on violations of constitutional rights that are filed pursuant to Title 42, U.S. Code, Section 1983. Many states have similar statutes. Section 1983 became effective in 1871. For the first ninety years, there was relatively little action under Section 1983. It appears that there were only six reported cases involving law enforcement agencies and persons during its first ninety years.

In 1961, the U.S. Supreme Court in *Monroe v. Pape* 365 U.S. 167 (1961) held that when a police officer is alleged to have acted improperly in conducting an illegal

CASE STUDY: *Wilson v. State*

Department of Corrections, 127 P.3d 826 (Alaska, 2006)

Merle Wilson sued the State of Alaska when he was released from a correctional institution because the State did not return him to the "place of arrest." Alaska Statute 33.30.081(b) and 22 Alaska Administrative Code (AAC) 05.585(a) required the State of Alaska to transport a released prisoner to the "place of arrest." Merle Wilson argued that, because he was arrested at his home, the statute and regulation required the state to return him to his home on Columbia Cove, 3.5 miles from Tenakee Springs, when it released him from prison in May 2002. There are no roads to Columbia Cove; it is accessible only by boat, footpath from Tenakee Springs, or floatplane. A chartered flight to Columbia Cove from Juneau would have cost about $350. The state had denied his request, agreeing to take him to Tenakee Springs on a regularly scheduled flight, at a cost of about $79.

Court Decision: We conclude that the state's policy of transporting released prisoners to the community nearest the exact location of their arrest is, under the particular circumstances of this case, a reasonable interpretation of the statute and regulation. Because it was not unreasonable for the state to conclude that Columbia Cove was within the community of Tenakee Springs, the statute and regulation were satisfied when the state offered to transport Wilson to the community of Tenakee Springs. We consequently affirm the superior court order denying Wilson's appeal.

search, the officer can be sued in federal court by alleging that the officer deprived the injured party of that individual's constitutional rights. After the *Pape* case was published, the number of court filings increased significantly. It was estimated that in the calendar year 2005, over 7,500 court actions were filed alleging civil liability under section 1983.

While Section 1983 of the U.S. Code creates civil liability for public officials, including police officers, who violate a person's constitutional rights while acting "under color of law," the U.S. Supreme Court has recognized two kinds of immunity that shield some official actions from liability that might otherwise arise under Section 1983. The most common type of immunity is qualified immunity, which protects officials from liability when reasonable officials in the defendant's position would not have understood their actions to violate a person's constitutional rights [*Harlow v. Fitzgerald*, 457 U.S. 800 (1982)].

More limited in application, but certainly broader in protection, is absolute immunity, which the U.S. Supreme Court has held applies to the performance of certain functions when those functions are integral to the functioning of our adversarial judicial system [*Briscoe v. LaHue*, 460 U.S. 325 (1983)]. The Court has carefully restricted absolute immunity because it protects an official from liability even when the official acted with knowledge of the constitutional violation. Testimony at adversarial judicial proceedings is the most historically grounded of these functions which merit absolute immunity. In restricting absolute immunity, the Court restricted it to only those situations that advance the furtherance of our adversarial legal system.

Those functions more "intimately associated with the judicial phase of the criminal process" are more likely to merit careful consideration for absolute immunity. In contrast, those functions more "investigative" in nature—searching for "clues and corroboration"—are more removed from the judicial process and merit only qualified immunity.

Key issues involving civil liability of the police, as extracted from court decisions, include:

- Section 1983 is not itself a source of substantive rights, but merely provides a method for vindicating federal rights elsewhere conferred [*Albright v. Oliver*, (1994) 510 U.S. 266].

- All witnesses—police officers as well as lay witnesses—are absolutely immune from civil liability based on their testimony in judicial proceedings [*Briscoe v. LaHue*, 663 F.2d 713 (7th Cir.1981)].

- A police officer who makes an arrest on the basis of a facially valid arrest warrant will in most cases be entitled to qualified immunity [*Hamill v. Wright*, 870 F.2d 1032 (5th Cir. 1989)].

- In *Griffin v. Maryland*, 378 U.S. 130 (1964), the U.S. Supreme Court found state action when an amusement park security guard who had been deputized as a sheriff of the county, wore a badge, and identified himself as a deputy sheriff, arrested black park patrons who refused to leave the park in response to his order. The Court there declared, "If an individual is possessed of state authority and purports to act under that authority, his action is state action. It is irrelevant that he might have taken the same action had he acted in a purely private capacity or that the particular action which he took was not authorized by state law."

- The Constitution and laws of the United States do not guarantee an accused the right to Miranda warnings, they only guarantee the accused the right to be free from self-incrimination. The Miranda decision does not even suggest that police officers who fail to advise arrested persons of their rights are subject to civil liability; it requires, at most, only that any confession made in the absence of such advice of rights be excluded from evidence. "No rational argument can be made in support of the notion that the failure to give Miranda warnings subjects a police officer to liability under the Civil Rights Act" [*Bennett v. Passic*, 545 F.2d 1260 (10th Cir. 1976)].

- A police officer is absolutely immune from a section 1983 civil action for his testimony, even if false, before the grand jury [*Kelly v. Curtis*, 21 F.3d 1544, (11th Cir. 1994)]. According to the Court, the reason is that, "Police officers testify in scores of cases every year, and defendants often will transform resentment at being convicted into allegations of perjury by the state's official witnesses." If a police officer witness "could be made to answer in court each time a disgruntled defendant charged him with wrongdoing, his energy and attention would be diverted from the pressing duty of enforcing the criminal law."

- Police officers are not entitled to qualified immunity in a Section 1983 claim based on an officer's false statements in an affidavit submitted to a magistrate judge for arrest warrant at warrant hearing [*United States v. Martin*, 615 F.3d 318 (5th Cir. 1980)].

- The law prohibits a police officer from knowingly making false statements in an arrest affidavit about the probable cause for an arrest in order to detain a citizen. The qualified immunity will not shield an officer from liability for such false statements, if such false statements were necessary to the probable cause [*Jones v. Cannon*, 174 F.3d 1271 (11th Cir. 1999)].

- An arrest without probable cause is unconstitutional, but officers who make such an arrest are entitled to qualified immunity if there was arguable probable cause for the arrest [*Lindsey v. Storey*, 936 F.2d 554, 562 (11th Cir. 1991)].

- Claims of excessive force by police officers in effecting an arrest are justifiable under Section 1983 because they implicate the Fourth Amendment's guarantee to "the people" of the right "to be secure in their persons . . . against unreasonable searches and seizures." In an excessive force case the "reasonableness" inquiry is an objective one. The question is whether the officers' actions are objectively reasonable in light of the facts and circumstances confronting them, without regard to their underlying intent or motivation. An officer's evil intentions will not make a Fourth Amendment violation out of an objectively reasonable use of force; nor will an officer's good intentions make an objectively unreasonable use of force constitutional [*Hernandez v. City of Pomona*, 138 Cal. App. 4th 506 (2006)].

USE OF FORCE

"Although most police activities do not involve the use of force, those that do reflect important patterns of interaction between officer and citizen."
— Geoffrey Alpert, University of South Carolina, 2002

The U.S. Supreme Court in *Graham v. Connor*, 490 U.S. 386 (1989), held that the key in determining if an officer's use of force is appropriate is whether or not the force is reasonable in light of the facts and circumstances that are present. The reasonableness of a particular use of force must be judged from the perspective of a reasonable officer on the scene, rather than with the 20-20 vision of hindsight. The Court ruled that the measure of reasonableness must factor in allowances for the fact that police officers are often forced to make split-second decisions in circumstances that are tense, uncertain, and rapidly evolving, and that such factors are important in determining the amount of force that is necessary in a particular situation.

An officer's conduct is evaluated under an objective reasonableness standard [*Greiner v. City of Champlin*, 27 F.3d 1346 (8th Cir. 1994)]. The Court in *Champlin* held that claims that law enforcement officers used excessive force in making an arrest are analyzed under the Fourth Amendment, and the test is whether the amount of force used was objectively reasonable under the particular circumstances.

In *Smith v. Freland* 954 F.2d 343 (6th Cir. 1992), the Court stated that: "We must avoid substituting our personal notions of proper police procedure for the instantaneous decision of the officer at the scene. We must never allow the theoretical, sanitized world of our imagination to replace the dangerous and complex world that policemen face every day." What constitutes reasonable action may seem quite different to someone facing a possible assailant than to someone analyzing the question at leisure.

Use of Deadly Force

The use of deadly force during an arrest is governed by the U.S. Supreme Court decision in *Tennessee v. Garner*, 471 U.S. 1 (1985). In Garner, the father of a 15-year-old burglary suspect who was slain by a police officer, filed suit against the officer, the Memphis Police Department, the city of Memphis, and other public officials, alleging

Voices of Experience

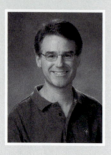

Officer-Involved Shooting

Excerpts from an interview between Cliff Roberson and former police officer, Scott W. Phillips, currently a professor at Buffalo State College, Buffalo, New York.

Q: *While you were serving as a police officer in Houston, Texas, it is my understanding that you were involved in a shooting incident. Tell us about it.*

A: It was a shooting of an 18-year-old youth. He was seen using a gun to break into a vehicle. I got into a foot chase with him. He turned with an object in his hand. I thought he was going to shoot me, so I fired one shot at him. He was hit and he went down. I called for emergency services and a supervisor. The shot did not kill him, but it is my understanding that because the bullet lodged in a sensitive part of his body the doctors left it in. To the best of my knowledge he is still living.

I was wearing black sneakers that night rather than the regulation-type shoes. My biggest concern was not about the shooting. I was convinced that the shooting was good. I was more concerned about changing my shoes before the supervisor showed up. Some months later, the sergeant from internal affairs called me and stated that he had no problems with the shooting, but that the chief wanted to do a re-enactment of the shooting on videotape. After months of not hearing from anyone in internal affairs, I called them. Finally one year, one month, and one day after the shooting, I received a letter that stated that the shooting was justified. I told my partner that I did not have that luxury of time in my work. For over a year this matter hung over my head. ■

Citizens Complained More Than 26,000 Times in 2002 about Excessive Police Force—Evidence in about 8 Percent of Complaints Justified Disciplinary Action

WASHINGTON—Large state and local law enforcement agencies with 59 percent of the nation's sworn officers received 26,556 citizen complaints about the police use of force during 2002, the Justice Department's Bureau of Justice Statistics (BJS) announced today. The rate was 6.6 complaints per 100 full-time sworn officers. Eighty-four percent were made against large municipal departments, BJS said.

About 8 percent of the complaints were officially sustained; that is, there was sufficient evidence to justify disciplinary action against the officer or officers; 34 percent were not sustained; 25 percent were unfounded, meaning the complaint was not supported by facts or the alleged incident did not occur; 23 percent ended in exonerations because the police actions were lawful and proper, and 9 percent ended in other dispositions, such as complaint withdrawal.

The percentage of officially sustained complaints ranged from 6 percent among county police departments to 12 percent among sheriffs' offices. However, the BJS report said, caution must be exercised when interpreting complaint data because volumes, rates, and dispositions may well vary by agency characteristics, such as the size and type of the agency as well as the policies and procedures related to the handling of complaints. Approximately 19 percent of large municipal police departments had a civilian complaint review board or agency within their jurisdictions.

The report, "Citizen Complaints About Police Use of Force" (NCJ-210296), was written by BJS statistician Matthew Hickman. The report can be found at: www.ojp.usdoj.gov/bjs/abstract/ccpuf.htm.

Bureau of Justice Statistics' press release, accessed online June 25, 2006, at www.ojp.usdoj.gov/bjs.

Voices of Experience

Use of Force

Excerpts from an interview between Cliff Roberson and former police officer, Leon R. Kutzke, presently residential faculty member at Chandler Gilbert Community College, Chandler, Arizona.

Q: *In your many years as a police officer, how often and when were you required to use force?*
A: The use of force is a critical aspect of policing. With the advent of cameras within cell phones and other video-type recorders it is likely that any use of force will end up on a website. The use of force must be appropriate and within the law. This is not to mean to detract from the officer's ability to protect himself or herself and others in the community. In my thirty years of policing, the use of force was not as frequent as one would suppose after watching TV shows. I probably used force other than just hand-cuffing people and putting them in a cruiser only about six or seven times a year. I anticipated using my weapon only about three times in my entire career. In short, while the use of force is very important, it is also infrequent for the average patrol officers unless they work in high crime areas.

Even though police officers are not using use of force skills regularly, it is important that officers continually train on them because they may be needed without warning. The officers also need to keep up with the changes in the law on the use of force. It is a simple concept: you can use reasonable and necessary force to accomplish whatever is necessary, but once you begin to move into retribution, that is wrong. So the police officer needs to be an individual who is calm and able to control his or her emotions. As Sir Robert Peel stated in 1829, a good police officer has to be one who is quiet and in control of his emotions, and is able to deal with situations in a reasonable and effective fashion and that includes physical force as well. ■

that the shooting violated the Fourth, Fifth, Sixth, Eighth, and Fourteenth Amendments to the U.S. Constitution.

Officer Hymon shot the youth when he refused to stop. The Court noted that in using deadly force to prevent Garner's escape, the officer was acting pursuant to the authority of a Tennessee statute which provided that "if, after notice of the intention to arrest the defendant, he either flees or forcibly resists, the officer may use all the necessary means to effect the arrest" [Tenn. Code Ann. sec. 40-7-108 (1982)]. Although the police department's policy was more restrictive than the state statute, it also authorized the use of deadly force in cases of burglary.

The Court held that the Tennessee statute was unconstitutional as applied and that deadly force may not be employed to prevent the escape of a suspected felon unless the police officer has probable cause to believe that the suspect poses a significant threat of serious harm or death to the officer or others. A key issue often overlooked in a discussion of the *Garner* case is that while the City was held liable for the death, the individual officer (Hymon) was not because the officer was acting pursuant to a statute and his reliance on the statute was reasonable.

Officer Thomas Pappas was terminated by the New York City Police

County of Sacramento v. Lewis
118 S. Ct. 1708 (1998)

The police, on occasions calling for fast action, have obligations that tend to tug against each other. Their duty is to restore and maintain lawful order, while not exacerbating disorder more than necessary to do their jobs. They are supposed to act decisively and to show restraint at the same moment, and their decisions have to be made in haste, under pressure, and frequently without the luxury of a second chance.

Department (NYPD). At the time of his termination he worked as a computer operator in the NYPD information systems division. Prior to his transfer to information services, he spent five years as a patrol officer. He was a commissioned officer. On at least two occasions, he received letters from an auxiliary police department soliciting charitable contributions. Pappas responded by filling the enclosed return envelopes with racist and anti-Semitic materials and returning them anonymously. Nowhere in the mailings did he identify himself or his affiliation with the NYPD. Apparently he responded to charitable solicitations from other, non-police-related organizations in a similar manner.

The Nassau County Police Department initiated an investigation to identify the sender. The department sent out a similar charitable solicitation enclosing coded return envelopes. Pappas used the coded envelope to send a batch of racist and anti-Semitic literature. The Nassau County Police Department was thus able to trace the literature's source to a post office box rented by Pappas. This investigative technique was repeated several more times with similar results, first by the Nassau County Police Department and later by the NYPD Internal Affairs Bureau.

The NYPD charged Pappas with violation of a departmental regulation forbidding dissemination of defamatory materials through the mail. After a disciplinary trial, he was found guilty of violating this regulation and was dismissed from the NYPD. He brought a 42 U.S. Code sec. 1983 claim in the Southern District of New York contending that the dismissal violated his First Amendment rights.

The district court dismissed his claim, finding that the speech at issue did not constitute speech on a matter of public concern. A sharply divided U.S. Court of Appeals for the Second Circuit, in an opinion written by Judge Pierre N. Leval, upheld the district court's actions. The court reasoned that because a police department cannot function effectively without public perception that it enforces the law in an unbiased manner, the state's interest in promoting the efficiency of its services outweighs the officer's interest as a citizen in commenting on matters of public concern. Judge Colleen McMahon (United States District Court for the Southern District of New York, sitting by designation) filed a separate concurring opinion reasoning that the court need not reach this balancing analysis because the officer's mailings did not constitute speech on a matter of public concern [*Pappas v. Giuliani*, 290 F.3d 143 (2d Cir. 2002)].

SUMMARY

- Unless the incident qualifies as a search or seizure, it is not restricted by the Fourth Amendment.

- The U.S. Supreme Court presently uses the "privacy approach" in deciding what constitutes a search.

- A search is a government intrusion into an area or interest where a person has a reasonable expectation of privacy.

- Houses are one of the items specifically listed in the Fourth Amendment. The U.S. Supreme Court has always protected the sanctity of the home. The Court has expanded the protection of "house" to include the actual structure and the living space surrounding the home.

- The legal concept of standing is based on the rule that defendants generally must assert their own legal rights and interests, and cannot rest their claim to relief on the legal rights or interests of another person.

- The magistrate, not the police, makes the determination as to whether probable cause exists in warrant cases.

- Probable cause may be based on hearsay information.

- The phrase "person of reasonable caution" does not refer to a person with special legal training, it refers to the average person who under the circumstances would believe that the individual being arrested had committed the offense or that the items to be seized would be found in a particular place.

- A *Franks hearing* looks at the issue of police misconduct in production of the affidavit used to support the finding of probable cause.

- To void an otherwise valid search warrant because of false or misleading statements by the police, the defendant must make "a substantial showing that the officer intentionally or recklessly omitted facts required to prevent technically true statements in the affidavit from being misleading."

- The two most frequent situations in which the police may search without a warrant are vehicle searches and where exigent circumstances prevent the police from having time to obtain a search warrant.

- Persons may waive their rights under the Fourth Amendment and consent to a search. Unlike in-custody interrogation, an officer is under no obligation to advise the individual of the right to refuse the request or to seek an attorney.

- An arrest requires four essential elements:
  - intention to arrest
  - authority to arrest
  - seizure and detention
  - an understanding by the arrestees that they are being arrested

- The *exclusionary rule* is a judicially created remedy that originated as a means to protect the Fourth Amendment right of citizens to be free from unreasonable searches and seizures.

- The U.S. Supreme Court has held that not all evidence is "fruit of the poisonous tree" simply because it would not have come to light but for the illegal actions of the police. The "more apt question" is "whether, granting establishment of the primary illegality, the evidence . . . has been come at by exploitation of that illegality or instead by means sufficiently distinguishable to be purged of the primary taint."

- A civil action against an agency or officer may be based:
  - On an intentional tort (battery, false arrest, infliction of mental distress, conversion of property).
  - On negligence (negligent driving, negligent discharge of a firearm, negligence in the use of lawful force to effect an arrest).
  - On an infringement of a constitutional right (illegal search, denial of right to counsel, illegally preventing a person from exercising a constitutional right).

- The key in determining if an officer's use of force is appropriate is whether or not the force is reasonable in light of the facts and circumstances that are present. The reasonableness of a particular use of force must be judged from the perspective of a reasonable officer on the scene, rather than with the 20-20 vision of hindsight.

Classroom Discussion Questions and Activities

1. What does the Court mean when it states that it uses the "privacy approach" to determine if an activity is a search within the meaning of the Fourth Amendment?

2. In a recent case, the trial court overruled a defendant's objections to the admission of evidence discovered as the result of a warrantless search of a home. The trial judge held that the defendant "lacked standing to object." What did the judge mean by that ruling?

3. What are the differences between a search warrant and an arrest warrant?

4. Draft an affidavit that could be used to support a search warrant to search the home of a drug dealer.

References

Hendrie, E. M. (1998, April). Curtilage: The expectation of privacy in the yard. *FBI Law Enforcement Bulletin*, pp. 25–28.

LaFave, W. (1987). *Search and seizure* (2nd ed.), Vol. 1, sec. 2.4(b) St. Paul, MN: West.

Patterson, J. (2006). *Judge and jury.* New York: Little, Brown.

Police supervision: A manual for police supervisors. (1985). Arlington, VA: IACP.

Rutledge, D. (2006, August). Knock-notice after Hudson. *Police Magazine* pp. 96–98.

Chapter 9

Police Reports and Other Correspondence

" Put it before them briefly so they will read it, clearly so they will appreciate it, picturesquely so they will remember it, and above all, accurately so they will be guided by its light. "

—Joseph Pulitzer

CHAPTER OUTLINE

- Introduction
- Field Notes
- Report Writing
- Chain of Custody Reports
- Special Reports
- Writing Styles
- Computerized Reports
- Recording Witness Recollections
- Records
- Testifying in Court
- Summary

OBJECTIVES

After completion of this chapter, you will be able to do the following:

- Explain the importance of taking fair and accurate notes.
- Describe the appropriate procedures for taking field notes.
- Identify and discuss the six basic questions in any law enforcement investigation: who, what, where, when, why, and how.
- Understand the process of writing police reports.
- Describe the purpose and importance for chain of custody reports.
- Describe the preferred writing styles used in police reports.
- Explain the importance of proofreading your reports.
- Identify the recommended steps to use when dictating reports.
- Explain why an essential element of any police investigation is the recording of witness recollections.
- Describe the manner in which an officer should testify in court.

INTRODUCTION

"Almost everything that a police officer does must be reduced to writing."
—O. W. Wilson and Roy C. McLaren, 1972

"There is no distinct 'right way' to complete a police report."
—Anonymous

In the book *Written & Interpersonal Communication*, Wallace and Roberson (2004) defined writing as a method of recording and communicating ideas by means of a system of visual marks. Notice that the first part of the definition states that it is the recording of ideas. **Writing**, unlike oral communication, is a permanent form of communication. We forget spoken words, whereas writing is a permanent record of our thoughts and ideas. Writing is a method of communicating. One problem with written communication when compared to oral communication is there is a lack of instant feedback. This limits the writer's ability to correct, refine, or focus the information into a more understandable format.

Note that the final part of the definition is that writing is a system of visual marks. This presents problems with written communication in the area of legibility and correct use of symbols. The writer's handwriting is often difficult to decipher, and symbols used by the writer could mean one thing to that person and another thing to the reader (Wallace & Roberson, 2004).

writing / A method of recording and communicating ideas by means of a system of visual marks.

Writing is an important part of every police officer's job. Consider this part of the Ocala, Florida, Police Department's job description for police officers:

Writes and dictates reports in a narrative form, describing activities, events, investigations, and enforcement action taken. Completes short incident reports to record events and action taken. Prepares arrest warrants for suspects, presenting sufficient information to record the warrant. Writes application for search warrants, presenting sufficient information to gain legal approval to proceed. Makes field notes in notebook to document activities, conditions, and other necessary information. Completes departmental forms to record time worked, overtime, and leave requests. Takes personal notes on assignments and information given by supervisors, and other information such as stolen vehicles and securities.

In this chapter, we will examine police reports and other correspondence that police officers are required to compose. In many cases, the police reports will consist of completing standard forms such as the State of Montana Initial Offense Report depicted in Figure 9.1

Figure 9.1 State of Montana Initial Offense Report

Initial Offense Report
General Nature of Charges:

Time of Offense:	Location of Offense:

Name of Accused:

Age of Accused:	Residence of Accused:

Name of Victim:

| Sex Offense? *If so, name should not be included.* |
| Confidentiality Requested? *If so, name should not be included.* |

Name of Witness:

| Confidentiality Requested? *If so, name should not be included.* |
| Report Date: |
| Reporting Officer: |

FIELD NOTES

Field notes are considered to be the basis for most police incident reports. Field notes should be taken as soon as practicable after an incident and should be made in a notebook. Some organizations have prescribed notebook types that the officer must use for field notes. Most officers prefer to use a loose-leaf notebook that is easy to organize with pages that can be removed for use in writing other reports and to use when testifying in court. Field notes are made for the purpose of compiling facts in the order in which they presented themselves. Because they are taken at the time the officer learned or observed the facts, they tend to be taken as the most accurate report of the incident. Alterations in field notes, however, are viewed with suspicion. It is important that the field notes contain an unbiased report of the facts.

      Effective field notes are noted for their accuracy, brevity, clarity, and completeness. It is essential that the field notes provide a clear picture of what happened during an incident or at a crime scene. In addition, the notes must be readable. Notes that cannot be deciphered after a period of time are worthless. Notes, like police reports in general, should answer the six basic questions of who, what, where, when, why, and how. As noted in the *Manual for Police of New York State* (2005, 2-14-1): "Field notes are essential to good report writing and your report will only be as thorough as the notes taken during the investigation."

field notes / Notes made at the scene of a crime for the purpose of compiling facts in the order in which they presented themselves.

Voices of Experience

Need for Accurate Reports

Excerpts from an interview between Cliff Roberson and retired Sheriff's lieutenant, Gregg W. Etter, Senior. Professor Etter is currently a faculty member at the University of Central Missouri, Warrensburg, Missouri.

Q: *Any advice for officers in writing their field reports?*
A: Yes. The most important factor in report writing is to pay attention to detail. Small, seemingly insignificant details may not mean anything at the time, but often those small details have great importance in the investigation. For example, in one case, the entire investigation turned on a minor detail in a miscellaneous field report. A female prostitute had been kidnapped by some drug dealers because they thought that she had cheated them on a marijuana deal. She had managed to escape. After she escaped, she was taken to a hospital because she had been beaten up pretty badly and had a broken arm. I went to the hospital to take her statement. She told me this wild statement about being stuffed into the trunk of a car. That she had been tortured and sexually assaulted. And that they had taken her to her boyfriend's apartment, killed his tropical fish, and shot him. When I got back to the office, I was looking through the reports that had been filed that week and found a miscellaneous field report filed by a road deputy. According to the field report, the officer had taken a call from a male who was deemed to be mentally ill. The male talked about this lady who was put in the trunk of the car. Since there were no report of any missing person fitting the description, the deputy questioned the validity of the report. [The prostitute did not turn up until five days later.] The road deputy was given a key ring by the mentally ill person, which the deputy had noted in his report and turned in. The key ring had the prostitute's first name on it. The mentally ill person was able to give a description of the car and sufficient identification to identify the individuals involved in the kidnapping and shooting. ■

Excerpts from Commonwealth of Virginia Department of Criminal Justice Police/Sheriff's Department General Order 2-14
July 1, 1999

Field Notes
All formal reports begin with field notes. Field notes are important for the following reasons:

1. To create a permanent record of events.
2. To aid the investigation.
3. To ensure accurate testimony in court.
4. To protect the officer from false accusations.

Retention of Field Notes

Most agencies have written policies regarding the retention of field notes. The courts have disagreed on this question. Consider the following two cases. In the *Wisconsin* case, the court held that the destruction was not error, whereas the *Guam* court thought otherwise. Unless your agency prescribes otherwise, you should retain your field notes until the case is final, including an appeal. Why give the accused an additional issue to appeal?

CASE STUDY: *State of Wisconsin v. Charles Garven*
1997.WI.0001032

Defendant Garven argued that his due process rights to present a complete defense were violated by the detective's destruction of field notes. The detective interviewed Garven at his residence for approximately one and one-half to two hours. During the interview, Garven denied touching the child's breast. The detective made handwritten notes of the interview. A day or two later, he typed up a four-page report from his notes and threw the handwritten notes away.

Wisconsin Supreme Court Decision: Garven argued that his due process rights to present a complete defense were violated by the detective's destruction of his field notes. We disagree. A two-pronged analysis is employed to determine whether the destruction of evidence violates due process. Consider the finding of *State v. Greenwold*, 189 Wis.2d 59 (Ct. App. 1994): (1) If the evidence destroyed is apparently exculpatory and of such a nature that the defendant would be unable to obtain comparable evidence by other reasonably available means, its destruction violates due process, or (2) if the evidence was potentially exculpatory and was destroyed in bad faith, its destruction also violates due process. The Wisconsin due process clause is the substantial equivalent of its federal counterpart.

Garven failed to show that any information of substance contained in the field notes was not also contained in the typewritten report. He pointed to no discarded information that would have any probable effect on the outcome. The evidence is material only if there is a reasonable probability that, had the evidence been disclosed to the defense, the result of the proceeding would have been different [*United States v. Bagley*, 473 U.S. 667 (1985)]. Here, the detective testified that the typewritten report was a summation of his notes and contained some direct quotes of Garven. We conclude that Garven failed to demonstrate that the notes were exculpatory in any material way.

Garven further argued that the notes were potentially exculpatory and that the officer destroyed the notes in bad faith. This claim must also fail. There is no indication that the notes were potentially exculpatory. There is no suggestion that the officer acted in bad faith. The officer testified that he worked for the police department for nineteen years and it was his practice to type up his reports from his handwritten notes and throw the notes away because they were hard to read. Also, the officer's report typed from the notes was made available to Garven.

People v. Laxamana
2001 Guam 26 (Guam 12/13/2001)

Court's Decision: Because field notes may contain information that can be discovered, they must be preserved. "The duty of disclosure is operative as a duty of preservation" [*United States v. Bryant*, 439 F.2d 642 (D.C. Cir. 1971)] (overruled on other grounds by *Arizona v. Youngblood*, 488 U.S. 51). The state has the duty to employ regular procedures to preserve such discoverable evidence [*People v. Hitch*, 12 Cal. 3d 641 (1974)]. The obligation of the prosecution to disclose certain items is rendered meaningless without a corresponding obligation on the part of the prosecution to preserve those potentially discoverable items. Simply put, the prosecution cannot disclose what it no longer possesses.

Perhaps even more significant is the notion that failure by a state agency to preserve potentially discoverable material usurps a judicial function. Determining the scope of discovery is a role traditionally reserved for the court. Final decision as to production must rest within the good sense and experience of the district judge. Allowing a government agency to institute a procedure of regularly destroying potentially discoverable material vitiates the court's authority, leaving the judiciary with the awkward task of guessing. Whenever potentially exculpatory evidence is permanently lost, courts face the treacherous task of divining the import of materials whose contents are unknown and, very often, disputed. Common sense dictates that the court cannot properly perform its inquiry if the material is destroyed.

Not only does such a procedure impede on the court's authority, but it simultaneously undercuts a defendant's statutory rights. Preservation ensures that a defendant's future right to discovery is not diluted at another, less visible stage.

Lastly, some critics question whether a defendant who receives a final police report incorporating an officer's field notes is entitled to receive both the field notes and the police report. The U.S. Court of Appeals for the Ninth Circuit found that the notes are producible even if it affirmatively appeared that the entire contents of the notes were included in a document that was turned over to the defense [*United States v. Johnson*, 521 F.2d 1318 (9th Cir.)]. The D.C. Circuit came to the same conclusion, reasoning that even the most conscientious agent can err. And certainly we cannot consider it beyond the bounds of possibility that a report be distorted because of overzealousness on the part of the agent preparing it. A glance over the shoulders of government agents may be required to safeguard and foster the search for truth in a criminal trial.

REPORT WRITING

Joseph Davis (2004), in discussing a police report or narrative that a police officer has to write after completing an investigation, notes that reports take many different forms. According to Davis, any documentation recorded on a departmental form, or other approved medium (computer disks), and maintained as a permanent record is considered to be a report.

It is of the utmost importance that a police report accurately reflects all the facts discovered by an officer. Consider the following actual situation: On March 3, 1991, Rodney King, while driving a car in Los Angeles, California, didn't stop when signaled by a police car behind him, but instead, he increased his speed. One estimate said that King drove at 100 miles per hour for 7.8 miles. When police

Police Officer Interview Checklist

The following checklist is often used by military personnel when obtaining information from a civilian police officer regarding an incident involving a military person either as a witness, victim, or suspect. It is included in the text to provide the readers with an example of using a checklist to ensure that all the information needed is collected.

1. General guidelines
   a. Always identify yourself and your status.
   b. Ask the officer to visit the scene.
   c. Always ask the officer to bring a copy of the accident report and any field notes. Remember that the notes may have information not in the report.
   d. If photos were taken, ask for a copy (you may have to pay for them).
   e. Try to get off to a good start with the interview. Remember that most police officers are professionals and assume that you are too. Also, many police officers are former military personnel (or in the Reserves or Army National Guard). It should be easy to begin the interview if you start off with polite inquiries about any military background.
2. Personal data
   a. Full name
   b. Address
   c. Office, station, or barracks address/telephone number
   d. Badge number
3. Law enforcement background
   a. Years working for police force.
   b. Jobs held, dates; supervisor's name and address/telephone number.
   c. Other law enforcement-related jobs held, dates, supervisor's name and address/telephone number.
   d. Law enforcement training and education (start from high school). What institution/organization, type of course, grades?
   e. Inquire specifically about experience/education in accident, investigation/reconstruction. If the officer identifies himself or herself as an accident reconstructionist, ask for the officer's qualifications.
   f. Has the officer testified in court or deposition about an accident scene investigation he or she conducted? How many times and when? Determine if the court was criminal or civil.
4. Parties
   a. Does the officer know the claimant, the claimant's family, or any witnesses or their families? Get specific details.
   b. Has the officer received inquiries or been interviewed about the accident by anyone else? If relevant, get specifics to include the identity of the person(s) making the inquiry.
   c. Note any obvious bias the officer may have. Inquire discreetly about it.
5. Events prior to the accident
   a. How long had the officer worked that day? Was it the officer's normal shift? Had the officer worked other accident scenes that day?
   b. Was the officer alone in the car or was a partner along? Find out how to contact the other officer.

    c. How did the officer learn of the accident (radio call, witness the crash, came onto scene)?

    d. How far away was the scene? How long did it take to respond?

6. At the scene

    a. Were other emergency vehicles already present or called? Who called them? Get full identification of the services called to the scene.

    b. What did the officer do and in what sequence? Get general descriptions of the officer's actions at the scene.

    c. What witnesses were identified? Be sure to ask the officer to examine field notes to determine whether there are other names.

    d. If photos were taken, who took them?

    e. If you are at the scene, have the officer identify key locations, such as point of impact and the final resting point of each vehicle.

    f. Have there been other accidents at the scene? Is it identified as a problem? Is any corrective action pending? If the officer does not know the answers to these questions, ask how you can find out.

    g. Is the accident scene different now? How and why? (For example, the foliage has changed due to change of seasons.)

    h. Witnesses.

        (1) What did the witnesses tell the officer?

        (2) What did the claimant and our driver say?

    i. What other investigation did the officer perform?

    j. Traffic signals.

        (1) Were the traffic signals functioning properly?

        (2) If not, did the officer watch the lights change and time the traffic lights?

        (3) Was any corrective action taken on the lights? Who knows about it?

    k. Who maintains the intersection and the lights?

7. Enforcement action

    a. Was anyone cited? Is enforcement action pending?

    b. If no one was cited, and it appears someone (including our driver) should have been, ask why no one was.

    c. If someone was cited, ask why.

8. Vehicles

    a. Were they moved before the accident was investigated?

    b. Were the vehicles retained in police custody?

    c. Was any lab or reconstructionist work done on the vehicles? If so, get copies of the reports and the name of the person doing the analysis.

    d. Where are the vehicles now (if you do not already know)?

9. What is the officer's opinion as to fault and why?

finally stopped the car, they delivered fifty-six baton blows and six kicks to King in a period of two minutes, producing eleven skull fractures, brain damage, and kidney damage.

    The officers, unaware that the incident had been videotaped, filed inaccurate reports, not mentioning the fact that force was used on Rodney King. As the result of this one incident, four Los Angeles police officers were indicted, and eventually two of those officers were convicted and sentenced to thirty months in prison. The

Voices of Experience

Report Writing

Excerpts from an interview between Cliff Roberson and former police officer,
Leon R. Kutzke, presently residential faculty member at Chandler Gilbert
Community College, Chandler, Arizona.

Q: *What advice can you give to a new officer regarding report writing?*

A: I have taught report writing to police officers and sometimes it is not an easy task. Officers should constantly work to sharpen their report writing skills. The major complaints that I hear from police administrators are that we need to teach people how to write. Our investigators go out into the field and do a wonderful job investigating crime, but when you read their reports you realize that they fail to document the results of their investigations in the reports. The reports contain grammatical errors, bad sentence construction, missing data, and often give incomplete pictures of what occurred. These faulty reports hamper prosecution of criminals. Students in criminal justice need to concentrate on their writing skills. More and more law enforcement agencies are evaluating a job applicant's written communication skills in making hiring decisions. Police officer's reports are read by prosecutors, judges, and other justice agencies. The reputation of your department and you will be judged to some degree based on your writing skills and it is important that your department and you be viewed as professionally competent. Not only must the reports be readable, but above all they must be accurate. ■

incident eventually led to six days of riots in Los Angeles, where fifty-four people were killed, 2,383 were known to have been injured, and 13,212 were arrested (Lepore, 2004).

One experienced police officer was quoted by Nicholas Meier in *Plain English for Cops* (1999) saying, "All reports need to be complete and accurate." The officer

Rodney King, with a scarred head, speaks at a podium with his lawyer, Steven Lerman, at his side regarding his arrest on March 3, 1991.

notes that officers die slow and agonizing deaths on a witness stand far more often than from some criminal's gun or knife in "real" life on the streets. According to the officer, you risk dire consequences when cutting reports short in a number of ways.

The covers, information sheets, or first pages used by various agencies in their standard police reports vary, depending on many factors, including different state and local legal requirements. The computer software programs and computer hardware available are also different among the agencies. In addition, individual department leaders have different preferences. However, the narrative section for each state is basically the same.

Narrative Section

The *narrative section* is used to report facts of incidents. This section will focus on the narrative portions rather than the cover or information section of reports. The narrative section is a blank portion of the report that the officer uses to clarify the cover sheet information. It provides a chronological history of the officer's involvement. Joseph Davis (2004) states that writing the narrative should be the easiest part of report writing. According to him, if you have properly taken notes and organized them, the writing of the narrative is anticlimactic.

The first rule in writing the narrative section is that the police report must be factual. It is essential that the integrity of the officer and the agency should never be questioned. Therefore, under no circumstances should the facts be enhanced by adding events that did not occur. Nothing important should ever be omitted from a report. The report should contain accurate facts even if that means that someone goes unpunished for their actions. As a veteran prosecutor once informed a rookie police officer, "Every word that you write in your report, you must be able to justify in a court of law" (Wallace & Roberson, 2004, p. 28).

Building Blocks of Information

The officer should use certain **building blocks** of information to ensure that everything is included. These building blocks ensure that the officer covers **who, what, when, where, why,** and **how** in each report. In *Written and Interpersonal Communications,* Wallace and Roberson (2004) explain the five "w's" and the "h" in detail.

The "**who**" is much broader than who committed the crime. Answering the question of who involves identifying the complaining party, the victim, the suspect, the witnesses, and any involved law enforcement personnel. This identification should include home and work addresses, telephone number, physical descriptions, and occupations, when appropriate.

The officer must also cover the broad information covered by the query of "**what**" crime was committed, such as: What evidence was obtained? What was done with any evidence? What agencies responded to the call? What agency has jurisdiction? What section or officers will conduct any necessary follow-up investigation? (Wallace & Roberson, 2004).

The question of "**when**" is more than the date, day, and time of the offense. Once the officer has answered the question of what persons were observed at the scene of the crime, the officer must take this query further by answering the following questions: When did they arrive? How long did they stay? When did they leave? Next,

building blocks / Memory tools designed to ensure that the officer covers **who, what, when, where, why,** and **how** in each investigative report.

the officer must answer the question concerning when law enforcement officers arrived at the scene of the crime. The report also needs to include when the officer contacted the victim, the witnesses, or other parties to take their statements (Wallace & Roberson, 2004).

"**Where**" refers to the requirement that the locations and activities of the police should also be carefully recorded. Where they interviewed victims, witnesses, and suspects will be important. Where they arrest the suspect may also be critical. If it was inside a residence, were they lawfully there? Where the evidence was collected, marked, and stored is important to follow-up investigators. Thus, simply listing where the crime occurred is only the beginning of answering the query of **where**. (Wallace & Roberson, 2004).

"**How**" the offense was committed is also very important for *modus operandi* files. What tools were used and how they were used are often critical pieces of evidence that may tie the offense to similar crimes. When answering the how question, the officer must report how it was discovered and how it was reported. The officer must also report how a victim was transported, how the suspect arrived and departed the scene, and how all witnesses happened to be at the location. How the officer identified the victim, suspect, and the witnesses, as well as how the officer located these individuals is also important information (Wallace & Roberson, 2004).

Finally, the officer's narrative should attempt to answer the question of motive, or "**why**" the person committed the crime. Traditionally, jurors and prosecutors want to know why the crime was committed, therefore, officers should attempt to answer this question, if possible. Why was the offense reported? Was it to seek revenge, or for other reasons? The officer should report, if available, why the suspect committed the crime in that manner and why the witnesses came forward (Wallace & Roberson, 2004).

Using this method to complete the narrative section should ensure that there are no gaps or missing pieces of information in the report. Gathering this information is only the first step in writing a complete report. Once the information is obtained, the officer must then organize and report it in a clear and concise manner.

Outline Format

Another method for police report narratives is by the *outline format*. This method varies from the standard chronological report by steering away from the order of events and writing the report with the use of headings. These headings are used to break the report into an easy-to-read outline. Generally, the department will have certain headings that are required to be in every report. One police department requires the following headings in a police report involving an arrest:

- **Source of Activity:** This section documents the officer's reason for being at the location of the incident.
- **Observations:** This section describes the reporting officer's observations. In this section the officer would record such things as reasonable suspicion, search and seizure, use of force, and any other acts providing probable cause for the arrest.
- **Arrest:** This section is used to describe the reporting officer's actions at the time of arrest.
- **Statements:** This section is used to summarize any formal statements made by the arrestee, witnesses, or victims.

- **Booking:** This section is used to record the location of booking along with the charges and transporting officer.
- **Evidence:** This section is used to recap previously mentioned seized property and indicate a disposition of the items.
- **Additional Information:** This section is used to record any facts that are not included in one of the previous sections.

A similar format may also be required for incident and information reports. The use of the headings helps ensure that all the information is obtained. These headings also assist the detectives and prosecutors by pointing out the different areas of the report, making the report quicker and easier to read.

Many experienced officers in the process of organizing their report will organize the events in a chronological order before starting with the narrative section. Using this procedure at a crime scene you may organize the events as follows:

- Victim parked her car behind the store.
- Victim returned at (time) and noticed that her car was gone.
- Police were called.
- Arrived at the scene.
- Noticed that a street light was unlit.
- Received statement from victim.
- Searched area and discovered (or did not discover) evidence.
- Made a crime broadcast.
- Completed field notes.
- Car was entered into stolen vehicle system.

From the outline, you can then write a cohesive narrative and plug in the facts that you have collected.

Completing the Report

Get it all, get it right, and write it clear.

Once the officer has gathered the necessary information, the next step is to ensure that the report is accurate, complete, and fair. Accuracy in a police report includes the requirement that it be written objectively. The officer must either verify information contained in the report or note which facts are not verified.

Completeness is essential in all police reports. A prosecutor should be able read a police report and answer all the who, what, when, where, why, and how questions discussed earlier. While the report must be complete, it must not be so detail oriented as to confuse the reader. Completeness includes the principle of conciseness. The officer must learn when to leave information in the main body of the report and when to place it in a supplemental report. Likewise, the report should not be so lengthy and full of details that the reader must wade through the unimportant to find the useful information (Wallace & Roberson, 2004).

The police report must be completed in a fair and impartial manner. An officer has the obligation to be fair to everyone involved in the criminal justice system, including the suspect. Fairness in a police report requires combining accuracy and completeness to ensure that all relevant information is reported. The officer's credibility and reputation will outlive any single report; therefore, integrity should never be compromised on any case (Wallace & Roberson, 2004).

Practical Tips to Improve Your Reports

According to Dan Pasquale (2006), a detective for the City of Tracy Police Department in northern California, one of the easiest ways to improve any report is by simply collecting all of the contact information for everyone involved in an incident. Anyone who has ever had to go back and re-contact victims or suspects without the aid of current information knows the value of this. Every day investigators have to spend hours attempting to track down witnesses and related people who were at the scene, but left without giving full contact information. Sometimes the involved parties withhold their information, but most of the time it is the officers' fault that the information was not contained in the reports. Officers tend to get overwhelmed with the number of people at a scene or they hurry off to the next call; as a result, they get only the basics, such as name, birth date, and address (Pasquale, 2006).

Another commonly overlooked piece of information that officers should add to their reports are email addresses of each contact person. Later the officer or the prosecutor can use email to correspond with witnesses and victims. An email may work if the officer just needs to ask a simple question. An added benefit to email interviews is that you can print out the responses and attach them to your report if needed (Pasquale, 2006).

Often at a busy scene, officers hand out statement forms, go about their business, then collect them and move on. The officer should take the extra time to read over the statement and make sure all the information is there. If there are questions, the officer can write them on the statement form in a question and answer format. This way the officer can quickly and easily clarify and nail down details that would have been missed. Because victims and witnesses tend to forget the little details of a case after they leave the scene, getting them to give a complete statement at the scene gives the investigators the benefit of fresh information and prevents "tainting," which happens when witnesses talk about the incident with each other after the officers leave (Pasquale, 2006).

CHAIN OF CUSTODY REPORTS

A *chain of custody report* accompanies items of evidence. For each item of evidence, there should be a separate chain of custody report. An example of a chain of custody form, used in the state of Wisconsin when blood and urine are collected, is shown in Figure 9.2. The report should accurately reflect the route and timing of the movement of the item of evidence. The report should also contain precise information as to who had possession of the item and any person who had access to it. Suppose that an officer searches a driver who has been stopped for driving under the influence of drugs and finds a bag of marijuana on the driver. The officer should mark the evidence and transfer it according to established procedures to the evidence locker. The bag will probably be sent to a crime laboratory for analysis and then returned to

Figure 9.2 Wisconsin State Laboratory of Hygiene Chain of Custody Form

WISCONSIN STATE LABORATORY OF HYGIENE
2601 Agriculture Drive
Madison, WI 53718

CHEMICAL EMERGENCY RESPONSE: CLINICAL SAMPLE
EVIDENCE / CHAIN-OF-CUSTODY FORM

Patient's Name (Last)	(First)	(MI)	Collection Date MO DAY YR	Patient Label
				** Patient information on the label does not need to be reentered in the gray portion of this form

Collection Time
__AM
__PM

Hospital ID # / Information

Specimen Type / Source
Blood
EDTA – Purple top tubes
Green top tubes
Gray top tubes
Urine   Approx. Volume   mL

Please include two blank containers from the same lot # for each container type used for sample collection

Comments:

Method of Shipment: Dunham Express
                             Hospital Courier

Hospital Contact / Address

Date: Time:

1. Collected by: _____/_____
                    (Printed Name):   (Signature)

   Reason: _____

Date: Time:

2. Received by: _____/_____
                    (Printed Name):   (Signature)

   Reason: _____

Date: Time:

3. Received by: _____/_____
                    (Printed Name):   (Signature)

   Reason: _____

Date: Time:

4. Received by: _____/_____
                    (Printed Name):   (Signature)

   Reason: _____

Date: Time:

5. Received by: _____/_____
                    (Printed Name):   (Signature)

   Reason: _____

Date: Time:

6. Received by: _____/_____
                    (Printed Name):   (Signature)

   Reason: _____

WSLH Use Only — Sample Condition Upon Receipt (or other comment)

WSLH – Ag Drive ID#_____   WSLH – Henry Mall ID# 1_____   #2 _____

South Carolina Department of Health and Environmental Control Chain of Custody form modified by the WSLH on 12/10/04

Figure 9.2 Continued

INSTRUCTIONS FOR COMPLETING CHAIN OF CUSTODY FORMS:

NOTE – Two Chain of Custody Forms are required for each patient: one for the blood samples and one for the urine sample.

A. Collector insures that patient information and date and time of specimen collection appears on the Chain of Custody Form by affixing a patient label in the indicated area. If a patient label is not available, complete the gray shaded area on the Chain of Custody Form.

B. Collector completes Specimen Type / Source information on the Chain of Custody Form.

C. Collector begins the "chain of custody" by providing printed name, signature, date, time and reason for specimen collection on line 1 of the Chain of Custody Form. Each person who takes control of the specimens after the sample collector, continues the chain by providing the appropriate information on the Chain of Custody Form.

D. Place completed Chain of Custody Forms in a plastic zip lock bag on top of the appropriate specimens before closing the lid of the shipping container.

---

the locker. Several months later, when the driver is being tried for the possession of the bag, the prosecutor will need to establish to the court that this is the same bag that the officer found on the driver. The chain of custody report should provide that information because it reflects who has had possession of the bag from the moment that it was taken by the officer until the moment the prosecutor offers it into evidence. The report will also reflect who had access to the bag in case an issue arises as to whether the bag has been tampered with.

> ### State v. Johnson
> **90 N.J. Super. 105, 216 A.2d 397 (App. Div. 1965)**
>
> ---
>
> **Excerpts from the Court's Decision:** A party seeking to introduce an item of physical evidence must prove that the item was that which was taken from a particular person or place which makes the item relevant as evidence in the trial. Such proof is provided by testimony identifying the item as having been taken from that person or place, and by evidence tracing custody of the item from the time it was taken until it is offered in evidence. This latter evidence is necessary to avoid any claim of substitution or tampering.

SPECIAL REPORTS

In addition to incident reports, arrest reports, use of force reports, and crime reports, agencies have a wide variety of special reports. Some agencies have a special report for every conceivable type of offense. For example, one law enforcement agency had

Figure 9.3   Montana Notice of Officer Hire/Termination Slip

MONTANA PEACE OFFICERS STANDARDS AND TRAINING ADVISORY COUNCIL
3075 N. Montana, PO BOX 201408, Helena, MT 59620-1408
Phone 444-3605 Director, Administrative Support 444-4108 or 444-4763, FAX 444-4722

NOTICE OF OFFICER HIRE/TERMINATION SLIP

Please indicate your field of employment:

☐ Peace Officer   ☐ Public Safety Communication Officer   ☐ ADULT Probation & Parole Officer
☐ Corrections / Detention Officer   ☐ Motor Carrier Services Officer   ☐ JUVENILE Probation & Parole Officer
☐ Coroner   ☐ Deputy Coroner   ☐ Other

AGENCY NAME:

ADDRESS:

HIRE	**TERMINATION**
Officer's Last Name First Name MI	Officer's Last Name First Name MI
Date of Birth _____	Date of Birth _____
SSN _____	SSN _____
Date of Hire _____	Dates of Employment: _____ to_____
Rank/Title: _____	
Previous Employer: _____	Rank/Title: _____
	Class of Termination:
Dates Employed at Previous Agency:	☐ Resigned ☐ Deceased
	☐ Retired ☐ Medical Disabled
From _____ to _____	☐ Involuntary

I certify the above information is true and meets requirements of the State of Montana and the Board of Crime Control.

_____
Official Name (Sheriff, Police Chief, Mayor, etc.)   *Date _____*

This form is to be completed and forwarded to the POST
Advisory Council with 10 days of hire or termination
per 7-32-303, MCA.

Revised 12/31/03 SM & CF

over forty-seven different types of forms including dead body reports, obscene telephone reports, bad check reports, advisement of rights forms, computer crime reports, abandoned vehicle reports, and discharge of firearms reports. Each agency has different policies on reporting incidents. An example of a special report is the Montana Notice of Officer Hire/Termination Slip, which is shown in Figure 9.3.

WRITING STYLES

Police reports were traditionally written in a very formal style and filled with technical words and phrases. Realizing that the overly formalistic style of writing tends to take more time and was difficult to read, most agencies today encourage their officers to use an informal style of writing. An informal style does not, however, excuse substandard or idiomatic language. It may be described as writing in conservational and proper English. The style encourages the use of short sentences and words that are short and direct. Informal writing has been described as direct, sincere, and credible. Your reports will have greater credibility because the report sounds like you—human and understandable.

Stephen King has written many fictional bestsellers, but his most important book is not about fiction, it's about writing. In *On Writing*, King explains the process of writing. He states that, "Good writing is often about making good choices when it comes to picking the tools you plan to work with" (King, 2000, p. 128). To King, words are the tools of writing and he has two rules for becoming a better writer: read a lot and write a lot. King states that writing narrative is writing that moves the reader from point A to B and finally to point Z.

Wallace and Roberson (2004, p. 33) emphasize the importance of punctuation by asking students to punctuate the following sentence: "Woman without her man is a savage." They reported that in one English class one male student punctuated as follows: "Woman, without her man, is a savage." Whereas a female student wrote: "Woman! Without her, man is a savage."

For years, the use of the first person was considered as lacking in credibility and subjective. Even though many agencies still require writing in the third person, most agencies now allow the use of the first person "I" or "We" in reports because it makes the report clearer and easier to read with less chance for misinterpretations. Reports should also be written in the active voice. Active voice is where the subject of the sentence is doing the acting (e.g., Jim purchased a weapon). The passive voice is where the subject is being acted on (e.g., The weapon was purchased by Jim). Avoid using, if possible, the passive voice. General rules involved in good report writing include:

- Write in an informal style.
- Use the active voice.
- Use clear and concise language.
- Avoid jargon and all but the most common abbreviations.
- Reread every report for the following:
  - Correct and clear language
  - Completeness
  - Does it make sense?
  - Does it reflect a clear picture of the incident?

One of the biggest problems is the use of abbreviations. For example what does P.C. mean? To many it may mean personal computer or politically correct. It may also mean probable cause or penal code. While the use of abbreviations may reduce the length of your report, it can also cause confusion. As a general rule, unless the abbreviation is clear (e.g., FBI), leave it out or the first time it is used indicate its meaning. For example, the probable cause (PC) for the arrest is set forth in the affidavit for a warrant.

Proofreading

After you have finished the narrative part of the report, your next step should probably be to proofread the entire report. Check for misspelled words, inappropriate grammar, and anything that may make the report difficult to understand. After you have proofread the report, ask yourself if this is the best you can do. Are you ready for a judge or jury to read your report? Would you feel comfortable in showing your report to the police chief? Items to check in the proofreading phase include:

- Is the report in the correct form and format?
- Is the active voice used when possible?
- Is the spelling correct?
- Was appropriate grammar used?

Dictation

The practice of dictating your report can save you valuable time. We can talk faster than we can write. Many officers, however, have problems in trying to dictate their reports. In one law enforcement agency that required the officers to dictate their reports, some of the officers would write out their report and then read it into the dictation machine. Dictation takes practice, but the more you dictate, the easier it gets. Finally, it will become second nature and will be much more efficient than writing the report. General rules regarding dictation include:

- Prior to dictating, try to eliminate background noise.
- Give the transcriber adequate instructions about the type of report or memo and other key items.
- Develop an outline prior to dictating and then dictate from the outline.
- Talk slowly, clearly, and distinctly.
- Specify the grammar and punctuation needed.
- Stay focused and do not talk to others or do other things while dictating.

COMPUTERIZED REPORTS

Most police departments are currently using laptops or other computerized data entry devices to assist the officer in writing or developing the required reports. For example, one such program is the Automated Law Enforcement Incident report (ALEIR) software package. It is advertised as a complete Windows-based computerized police records management and police dispatch system designed for law enforcement agencies. According to the advertisements, the program combines the technologies of word processing and data processing into one program. Whether the officer uses a computer-assisted program or manually enters the information, the principles regarding accuracy, completeness, and fairness must be upheld.

Officers in the Smyrna, Georgia, Police Department prepare their reports on in-car computers. They save a copy on the hard drive and then copy the reports onto a disk. That disk is brought to headquarters and downloaded on one of two workstations. The officers print their reports, which are given to the patrol supervisor and then to records management. All other officers prepare reports from their desk personal computer and follow the same procedure. The department is working on taking the disk from the officer and placing the files directly into a records computer folder and having the supervisors approve the reports in that file. Then the file will be handled by the records clerks for printing, filing, and any further processing. The records department will be able to email or fax reports upon request to officers or the public.

Prior to the implementation of its present system, Alexandria, Virginia, police officers used to write an average of 26,000 accident and incident reports by hand. Data entry was delayed from four to six months because it took records personnel approximately forty-five minutes to review and enter information from each report into the central database. None of the operational, tactical, or administrative information was immediately accessible to detectives or patrol officers (Samarra & Craige, 2004).

The department now uses a wireless and completely automated system where all reports are completed, reviewed, printed, and downloaded directly into the department's records management system. The department uses cellular digital packet data (CDPD) and a tactical computer system that combines laptop computers, software, and institutional practices. Alexandria's system gives officers access to a wide variety of software tools such as word processing, forms creation, customized database queries, intranet capabilities, and much more. In addition, the computers function equally well inside or outside the patrol vehicle. Officers are no longer required to respond to the police station to complete their work because many functions historically requiring the officer's presence at the station can now be completed on the street (Samarra & Craige, 2004).

Incident reports are National Incident Based Reporting System (NIBRS) compliant and also contain all data elements necessary to satisfy Virginia reporting requirements. All reports are now entered within twenty-four hours, and a records clerk can process about eighteen electronic reports in the same time it formerly took to process one handwritten report. Report information is immediately available to officers and detectives in the station and on the street (Samarra & Craige, 2004).

Computerizing a Small-Sized Police Department

The Pratt, Kansas, Police Department, a small department, created a partnership with the IBM Corporation to computerize their report writing and records retention functions. Pratt is a small city situated between Dodge City and Wichita. The population of Pratt is 6,500. The police department was limited in its ability to manage case records and field communications. Steve Holmes, the chief of police, states: "We were quickly running out of space in our building for record storage. Our time on paperwork has essentially been cut in half." The Pratt Police Department has fourteen officers and five dispatchers and its jurisdiction covers twelve square miles.*

At the time that the new system was adopted, the department used basically a pencil-and-paper system, with all forms having to be filled in from scratch, one at a time, with each incident. Also, because of the workload, there was always the possibility that, over time, many details of a case would fall through the cracks or be forgotten. The department had insufficient capability for tracking all law enforcement, dispatching, and jail-related activities—not to mention limited ability to coordinate and communicate with other agencies.

The present system now uses IBM Lotus Notes, Lotus Domino Server, and Enterpol Solutions for Public Safety. **Enterpol** is a suite of applications primarily for small- to medium-size police departments, but which can also handle larger agencies. The suite assists in dispatching, information management, and facility records, from initial 911 call to booking and release or incarceration. Enterpol is an IBM Lotus Domino-based solution, based on the Domino platform.

Much of the funding for the Pratt solution came from federal grants and from money acquired by the state in drug-related forfeiture cases. Pratt used some of its grant money to provide the Pratt County Sheriff's Department with an Enterpol installation and a central database, which both departments can share.

The Pratt Police Department has received the following benefits from their computerized system:

Enterpol / A suite of computer applications designed primarily for small- to medium-size police departments, but which can also handle larger agencies. The suite assists in dispatching, information management, and facility records, from initial 911 call to booking and release or incarceration. Enterpol is an IBM Lotus Domino-based solution, based on the Domino platform.

- Officers can manage incidents more efficiently, and coordinate with other state agencies.
- Paperwork was cut in half.
- Improved interagency coordination and communication.
- Officers now spend more time in the field and less in the office.
- Efficiency improvements equivalent to having an additional officer on the force at no cost.

In a typical scenario for an incident using Enterpol, the dispatch center might receive a 911 call reporting a domestic disturbance. Enterpol dispatch is interfaced with the 911 phone system, which displays the name and address of the call location. This information is displayed, even if the caller hangs up. Dispatch creates an incident report with the click of a mouse and sends officers to respond. Officers are assigned the call by a simple "drag and drop," or by use of keyboard functions. Dispatch times, arrival times, and any memos associated with the call are placed in the call history record, which is created automatically in Enterpol.

Officers can complete required reports quickly and easily. If the subjects involved have been previously entered in the database, no keyboarding is involved. The subject's personal information is filled in by simply selecting the name from the central name database. Once the required information has been entered into Enterpol, all Kansas standardized reports (offense, arrest, and accident) and all jail-booking information, including any bond, for example, can be generated and printed, or sent electronically to the state.

*Information obtained from website: www-306.ibm.com/software/success/cssdb.nsf/cs/ JKIN-6QTQV7?OpenDocument&Site=wp; accessed online August 1, 2006.

Handwritten statements and other documents can be scanned and attached to the incident in Enterpol. This makes the case file available to any computer terminal on the network, even police cars in the field, via a wireless network. Officers can even view a booking photo on scene if identity is an issue. Criminal history for a subject is available with a single inquiry from any network computer.

Before Enterpol, the dispatcher would receive the call and have to write by hand all the name and address information. Other information, such as call assignment and arrival times, was added by hand to the handwritten call log. The dispatcher would type the information in the official radio log as time permitted, sometimes well after the call had been completed.

Officers often would have to type subject information three or four times to complete the reports, requiring at least twice as much office time. A paper case file would have a case number assigned and be filed. Criminal history involved a manual search.

Upgrading a Large Metropolitan Police Department

The Las Vegas Metropolitan Police Department (LVMPD) provides law enforcement services to one of the fastest growing regions in the nation. Its 2,297 officers serve a population of 1.5 million residents that is bolstered by 35 million tourists annually. An increase of 5,000 new residents a month challenges government agencies to update aging technologies that would support improved services.

MDTs / Mobile data terminals located in a patrol vehicle.

The LVMPD introduced **mobile data terminals (MDTs)** to its patrol vehicle fleet for the first time in the mid-1970s and upgraded them in 1986. After fifteen years of service, the MDTs became outdated and incapable of performing the full range of functions necessary for patrol officers. The mortality rate of the MDTs was high, replacement parts were unavailable, and maintenance had reached the point of diminished return. These "**dumb terminals**," as they are often called, were limited to basic functions and did not allow officers direct access to criminal justice databases, automated field reporting, or the department's intranet and wireless network.

dumb terminals / Computer terminals that are limited to basic functions and do not allow officers direct access to criminal justice databases, automated field reporting, or the department's intranet and wireless network.

The detectives recognized the potential benefits of having laptop computers in the field. Detectives had no automated field reporting capabilities and were limited to mobile communications or a telephone to access **CAD/RMS** (Computer Assisted Dispatch/Records Management System) information or to make criminal justice database inquiries. The LVMPD believed that mobile laptop technologies in the field would greatly improve the ability of detectives to perform their duties.

CAD/RMS / Computer Assisted Dispatch/Records Management System that provides access to criminal justice database inquiries.

The LVMPD's goals were to improve patrol officers' safety and their ability to engage in community policing activities by replacing aging mobile data terminals. In addition, detectives and the cadet corps would have investigative and report writing tools available in the field. The following objectives were developed to accomplish this goal:

- Update and replace mobile data hardware and software in patrol vehicles.
- Provide detectives with mobile data technologies in the field.
- Make mobile data field reporting available to cadets.

- Improve the overall efficiency and effectiveness of patrol and detectives.
- Provide officers instantaneous access to various criminal justice databases and the department's intranet.
- Improve the ability of patrol officers to identify and respond to neighborhood problems.

A Community Oriented Policing Services (COPS) Technology grant funding was used to purchase 236 mobile laptop computers for detective vehicles. The computers were mounted on brackets on the front seat floorboard between the driver and passenger seats and are removable. Automated field reporting software allows detectives and cadets to complete reports in the field. The wireless network provides detectives the ability to access RMS and various criminal justice databases in the field. In addition, detectives are able to take and access field notes and use other desktop computer applications as the situation dictates.

Technology funding was used to purchase an additional ninety-two mobile data terminals for patrol vehicles. This purchase helped the department complete its replacement of the fleet's aging mobile data equipment. The funding was also used to upgrade the operating system for 340 of the patrol's 450 vehicles. The system upgrade provided quicker access to existing databases and reduced downtime that often was a result of the age of the equipment. A wireless network also allowed officers access to the department's intranet, which housed such important information as resource guides for community groups, a complete version of the Nevada Revised Statutes, and departmental general orders and administrative notices. Permanent and temporary restraining orders were also accessible to officers through the intranet.

Grant-funded mobile data terminals were also installed in vehicles used by police cadets. The LVMPD cadet program provides employment to eighteen- to twenty-one-year-olds interested in a career in law enforcement. Cadets are trained to respond to nonemergency calls for service and write police reports that are noninvestigative in nature. Their primary role is to provide patrol officers with more time to engage in higher priority police matters, including community policing. Many cadets become police officers after reaching their twenty-first birthday.

The LVMPD reported that COPS funding contributed significantly to the modernization of mobile computing for its patrol fleet and for the first time made these technologies available for detectives and cadets. Patrol officers and plainclothes detectives now have a variety of resources available to them that previously required lengthy radio communications or departure from the field. For example, patrol officers responding to a domestic disturbance can access the department's intranet through MDTs and provide victims with a variety of community resources in a timelier manner. Officers can also access neighborhood conflict mediation tools that provide dispute remedies such as statutory relief or referral to appropriate agencies.

The ability of cadets to take reports in the field has increased patrol officers' availability. In addition, updates to the operating system allow officers to file reports directly to RMS, thus freeing civilian staff from the time-consuming task of re-entering report data.

Detectives have noted the substantial benefits of MDTs as well. Previously, detectives relied on radio or telephone communications to conduct business in the field. The instantaneous access to criminal justice databases and field reporting has reduced travel time to the office and allowed detectives to conduct more in-depth investigations in the field. Finally, detectives have access to calls for service data and are able to assist patrol officers.

[Information obtained from LVMPD's grant report to COPS (Community Oriented Policing Services), U.S. Department of Justice, posted on website www.copsreportsfromthefield.org/reports/NV-TECH-LasVegas.pdf. Accessed online August 1, 2006.]

RECORDING WITNESS RECOLLECTIONS

Principle: **The record of the witness's statements accurately and completely reflects all information obtained and preserves the integrity of this evidence.**

Policy: **The investigator shall provide complete and accurate documentation of all information obtained from the witness.**

(NIJ Technical Working Group for Eyewitness Evidence, October 1999)

An essential element of any police investigation is the recording of witness recollections. During, or as soon as reasonably possible after the interview, the investigator should:

- Document the witness's statements (e.g., audio or video recording, stenographer's documentation, witness's written statement, written summary using witness's own words).
- Review written documentation; ask the witness if there is anything that should be changed, added, or emphasized.

Complete and accurate documentation of the witness's statement is essential to the integrity and success of the investigation and any subsequent court proceedings. Point-by-point consideration of a statement may enable judgment on which components of the statement are most accurate. This is necessary because each piece of information recalled by the witness may be remembered independently of other elements.

The investigator should review the individual elements of the witness's statement to determine the accuracy of each point. After conducting the interview, the investigator should:

- Consider each individual component of the witness's statement separately.
- Review each element of the witness's statement in the context of the entire statement. Look for inconsistencies within the statement.
- Review each element of the statement in the context of evidence known to the investigator from other sources (e.g., other witnesses' statements, physical evidence).

A point-by-point consideration of the accuracy of each element of a witness's statement can assist in focusing the investigation. This technique avoids the common misconception that the accuracy of an individual element of a witness's description predicts the accuracy of another element (NIJ Technical Working Group for Eyewitness Evidence, October 1999).

RECORDS

For years, law enforcement agencies used filing cabinets full of thousands of reports. Presently, most agencies have replaced filing cabinets with computerized data. Each law enforcement agency has a different structure for its records system. For the most part, the records system is the nerve center or the memory bank of the agency.

Most agencies' records systems contain the originals of police reports that are retained for a length of time, normally one to two years. The reports are generally backed up immediately on computerized disks or CDs. After a specified time, the originals are destroyed and the computerized copies are retained. Agencies generally keep crime files where each offense is classified according to the Uniform Crime Reports classification system. The agencies then file annual reports to the FBI regarding the crime data.

Agencies also keep records of all arrests made by the agency. Arrest records are alphabetically arranged by the names of the arrestees and the offenses for which they have been arrested. Agencies also retain offender registration files of convicted felons, parolees, probationers, convicted arsonists, and registered sex offenders. Generally, offender registration files include not only the name and address of the offenders, but also their photos, fingerprints, and DNA profiles. In many cases, the offender register files are available to the public. For example, anyone can go to the website www.registeredoffenderslist.org to find the registered sex offenders in their neighborhood. The State of Texas, like most other states, has a website that provides information regarding individuals' criminal history. Some parts of the website are restricted to law enforcement agencies, other parts are open to the public. The website, maintained by the Texas Department of Public Safety, may be accessed at www.records.txdps .state.tx.us. The website also contains stolen motor vehicles and equipment registry.

TESTIFYING IN COURT

"Think as wise men do, but speak as common people do."
—Aristotle

Cliff Roberson, while teaching at California State University, frequently would sit as judge *pro tem* (temporary judge) in the California Superior and Municipal Courts. One day while sitting as judge in a jury case, he heard the following testimony from a local police officer:

> I alighted from my unit and observed the target walking toward a unit operated by the county. I explained to the target that this incident occurred within the city limits and therefore he should have talked to this officer rather than the county officer. Then I 10-20ed my location to my dispatcher. [The officer continued testifying in this manner for the next forty-five minutes. At no time during the officer's testimony did he look at the jury.]

Consequences of One False Statement in Court

Dr. Park Dietz has testified in numerous cases regarding forensic psychiatry issues.

Dr. Park Dietz was a well-known psychiatrist who testified frequently in criminal cases. His creditability as a witness was forever tarnished because of his mistaken testimony in a case where Andrea Yates was being prosecuted for drowning two of her five children. She allegedly drowned all five, but was charged with only two of the murders. She was found guilty, but the conviction was reversed on appeal because of Dr. Dietz's testimony. She was later retried and found not guilty by reasons of insanity. Following are excerpts from her first trial:

Yates v. Texas
171 S.W.3d 215 (Tex. CA, 1st Dist. 2005)

The tenth psychiatrist, Dr. Park Dietz, who interviewed the appellant and was the State's sole mental-health expert in the case, testified that the appellant, although psychotic on June 20, knew that what she did was wrong. Dr. Dietz reasoned that because the appellant indicated that her thoughts were coming from Satan, she must have known they were wrong; that if she believed she was saving the children, she would have shared her plan with others rather than hide it as she did; that if she really believed that Satan was going to harm the children, she would have called the police or a pastor or would have sent the children away; and that she covered the bodies out of guilt or shame.

On cross-examination, the appellant's counsel asked Dr. Dietz about his consulting work with the television show, *Law & Order*, which the appellant was known to watch. The testimony was as follows:

Q: Now, you are, are you not, a consultant on the television program known as *Law & Order*?
A: Two of them.

Q: Okay. Did either one of those deal with postpartum depression or women's mental health?
A: As a matter of fact, there was a show of a woman with postpartum depression who drowned her children in the bathtub and was found insane and it was aired shortly before the crime occurred.

The second mention of *Law & Order* came during Dr. Lucy Puryear's testimony. Dr. Puryear, a defense expert witness, was cross-examined by the State regarding her evaluation of the appellant. The State specifically asked about her failure to inquire into whether or not the appellant had seen *Law & Order*. Dr. Puryear testified as follows:

Q: You know she watched *Law & Order* a lot; right?
A: I didn't know. No.
Q: Did you know that in the weeks before June 20th, there was a *Law & Order* episode where a woman killed her children by drowning them in a bathtub, was defended on the basis of whether she was sane or insane under the law, and the diagnosis was postpartum depression and in the program the person was found insane, not guilty by reason of insanity? Did you know that?
A: No.
Q: If you had known that and had known that Andrea Yates was subject to these delusions, not that she was the subject of a delusion of reference, but that she regularly watched *Law & Order* and may have seen that episode, would you have changed the way you went about interviewing her, would you have interviewed whether she got the idea somehow she could do this and not suffer hell or prison?
A: I certainly wouldn't have asked her that question. No.
Q: Would you have—you didn't have to ask her that question, but you could have explored that?
A: If I had known she watched that show, I would have ask[ed] her about it, yes.

[The producers of the show furnished affidavits that no such incident was ever portrayed in the TV series.]

Do you understand what the officer was testifying about? How many jurors do you think would understand? This case involved a direct conflict regarding a statement made by the defendant at the scene. The officer had claimed that the defendant had admitted his guilt. The defendant claimed he did not make such a statement. The jury acquitted the defendant. Roberson believed that had the officer testified in conservational English and looked at the jury when he testified, the results would have been different. Some general rules regarding testifying in court:

- Prior to going to court, review reports on the incident in question.
- Tell the truth. Above all other things, honesty comes first.
- Dress like a professional.
- Testifying is not an easy, natural experience, but when on the witness stand try to look as natural as possible.
- Give loud and audible answers. Everything you say will be recorded. Do not nod your head or give other signs unless specifically requested to do so.
- Don't be cocky or sarcastic.
- Don't make jokes on the stand; testifying is a serious business.
- Be courteous and always address the judge as "Your honor."
- Do not lose your temper or demonstrate displeasure with the defense counsel.
- If asked if you have discussed your testimony with the prosecutor, admit it freely if you have done so. [**Note:** When Cliff Roberson was a prosecutor he would always advise the police officers to admit that they had discussed the case with the prosecutor and that the prosecutor had stressed the importance of telling the truth.]

SUMMARY

- Writing is a method of communicating. One problem with written communications when compared to oral communication is there is a lack of instant feedback. This limits the writer's ability to correct, refine, or focus the information into a more understandable format. The final part of the definition is that writing is a system of visual marks.

- Field notes are considered as the basis for most police incident reports. Field notes should be taken as soon as practicable after an incident.

- Field notes are made for the purpose of compiling facts in the order in which they presented themselves. Because they are taken at the time the officer learned or observed the facts, they tend to be taken as the most accurate report of the incident.

- Effective field notes are noted for their accuracy, brevity, clarity, and completeness. It is essential that the field notes provide a clear picture of what happened during an incident or at a crime scene.

- It is of the utmost importance that a police report accurately reflects all the facts discovered by an officer.

- The narrative section is used to report facts of incidents. This section will focus on the narrative portions rather than the cover or information section of reports. The narrative section is a blank portion of the report that the officer uses to clarify the cover sheet information.

- The first rule in writing the narrative section is that the police report must be factual. It is essential that the integrity of the officer and the agency should never be questioned.

■ The officer should use certain building blocks of information to ensure that everything is included. These building blocks ensure that the officer covers **who**, **what**, **when**, **where**, **why**, and **how** in each report.

■ Another method for police report narratives uses an outline format. This method varies from the standard chronological report by steering away from the order of events and writing the report with the use of headings.

■ Accuracy in a police report includes the requirement that it be written objectively. The officer must either verify information contained in the report or note which facts are not verified.

■ Completeness is essential in all police reports. A prosecutor should be able to read a police report and answer all the who, what, when, where, why, and how questions.

■ A chain of custody report accompanies items of evidence. For each item of evidence, there should be a separate chain of custody report. The report should accurately reflect the route and timing of the movement of the item of evidence.

■ Police reports were traditionally written in a very formal style and filled with technical words and phrases.

■ Most police departments are currently using laptops or other computerized data entry devices to assist the officer in writing or developing the required reports.

■ An essential element of any police investigation is the recording of witness recollections. During or as soon as reasonably possible after the interview, the investigator should document the witness's statements (e.g., audio or video recording, stenographer's documentation, witness's written statement, written summary using witness's own words).

■ The investigator should also review written documentation and ask the witness if there is anything that needs to be changed, added, or emphasized.

■ Complete and accurate documentation of the witness's statement is essential to the integrity and success of the investigation and any subsequent court proceedings.

■ Presently, most agencies have replaced filing cabinets with computerized data. Each law enforcement agency has a different structure for its records system. For the most part, the records system is the nerve center or the memory bank of the agency.

■ Most agencies' records systems contain the originals of police reports that are retained for a length of time, normally one to two years. The reports are generally backed up immediately on computerized disks or CDs.

Classroom Discussion Questions and Activities

1. Establish a mock trial where students act as judge, prosecutor, defendant, and a police officer testifying on the stand. After the exercise, have the rest of the class evaluate the effectiveness of the testimony.

2. Write field notes on an incident. Review the field notes for possible improvement.

3. Draft a police report using the five W's and H.

4. Draft a police report using the outline format.

5. Describe the general rules for writing an accurate and clear police report.

6. Discuss why it is important for all reports to be accurate and not contain any false data.

7. Discuss what steps witnesses may take to make their testimony more believable to a jury.

8. What are the advantages of using computerized records compared with physical filing cabinets?

9. What actions should an officer take prior to being called into the courtroom to testify?

10. Should officers retain their field notes? Why? For how long?

References

Davis, J. N. (2004). *Painless police report writing*. Upper Saddle River, NJ: Pearson-Prentice Hall.

King, S. (2000). *On writing*. New York: Simon & Schuster.

Lepore, M. (2004, February 26). The 1991 Rodney King police brutality case and the Los Angeles riots. *Crimsonbird.com nonfiction book reviews*. www.crimsonbird.com/history/rodneyking.htm

Manual for police of New York state. (2005). N. Denny (Ed.). Flushing, NY: Looseleaf Law Publications.

Meier, N., & Adams, R. J. (1999). *Plain English for cops*. Durham, NC: Carolina Academic Press.

NIJ Technical Working Group for Eyewitness Evidence. (October 1999). *Research report: Eyewitness evidence: A guide for law enforcement*. Washington, DC: National Institute of Justice.

Pasquale, D. (2006, July). Report writing tune-up. *Police Magazine*.

Samarra, C. E., & Craige, J. (2004, April). Special focus: The Alexandria police department tactical computer system. *The Police Chief, 71* (4).

Wallace, H., & Roberson, C. (2004). *Written & interpersonal communications*. Upper Saddle River, NJ: Pearson-Prentice Hall.

Wilson, O. W., & McLaren, R. C. (1972). *Police administration*. (3rd ed.). New York: McGraw-Hill.

Chapter 10

Police Communications

" Changes in how we manage resources and expect services to be delivered cooperatively have caused communications needs to evolve internally within organizations and externally between them. For example, decentralized decision making and accountability—key principles in community policing—require that information be readily available to officers who are often widely dispersed throughout jurisdictions. "

—U.S. Department of Justice, *Draft Copy of Law Enforcement Tech Guide for Communications Interoperability*, 2006, p. 15

CHAPTER OUTLINE

- Introduction
- Police Language
- Radio Communications
- Telephone Communications
- Special Communications Issues
- Computer Systems
- Data Communications
- Computer Networks
- Summary

OBJECTIVES

After completion of this chapter, you will be able to do the following:

- Explain the elements of a communication.
- Describe the importance of police communications.
- Describe the advantages and disadvantages of using police jargon.
- Explain the importance of using correct radio procedure.
- Describe the functions of a 9-1-1 response system.
- Identify the correct procedures to use when using the 9-1-1 system.
- Explain the issues involved in using emails.
- Identify the issues involved in police communications.

INTRODUCTION

We take communications for granted. In fact, the mere reading of this text is a form of communication. It is estimated that 70 percent of the time that we are awake, we are involved in some sort of communications (Wallace & Roberson, 2004, p. 2). Often we hear the statement that communications may be either verbal or written. The correct statement should be that communications may be oral, written, or nonverbal. Remember that **verbal communications** (meaning language) may be either written or oral.

verbal communications / Language that is either written or oral.

Wallace and Roberson noted that there are at least ninety-four different definitions of communications, but regardless of the definition, all communications encompass three essential elements:

- It is a process, not an isolated event.
- It involves at least two persons.
- Its primary purpose is the exchange of information.

The reason that communications is not an isolated event is that it requires at least five basic steps:

- the transmitting of an idea or information
- the sending of the idea through a medium
- receiving the message
- understanding the idea
- providing feedback to the sender

The concept of transmitting an idea implies the formation of one or more thoughts and the desire to express these thoughts. Suppose you are a section chief and you see an officer in your section who looks very tired. If you make a comment to the officer that he looks tired, then you are communicating information to the officer. If, however, you decide not to say anything, then the information was not transmitted and therefore there was no communication. To be a communication, you needed to send the idea or information to the officer via a medium, such as an oral comment. If the officer did not hear you or did not understand it, then there was no communication. If the officer in the example heard you and understood you, then the officer would provide feedback. **Note:** Ignoring a communication is technically a form of feedback.

Communications cannot occur in a vacuum. There must be at least two people involved. If you go into the woods and shout and no one hears you, you are making a noise, but you are not communicating. Frequently, when I have difficulty in writing a letter, I will read the draft to myself out loud. [If anyone hears me, I always comment that seldom do I get a chance to talk to someone so brilliant.] This is not a form of communication because only I am involved. When I mail the letter to someone else, it then becomes a communication.

communication / A transmission whose primary purpose is to transmit information.

The primary purpose of the **communication** must be to transmit information. If I make a statement to see how my voice will sound in a forest, I am not making the noise to transmit information and therefore it is not a communication. Sometimes the actual words used in the communication are not the information being transmitted, but the information is more subtle. Suppose a suspect wants to convey to the officer that he or she is not intimidated by the officer. The suspect may say something like, "I could care less." In this example, it is the tone of the message that is transmitting the message to the officer, not the words.

Communication is critical in a law enforcement agency. Officers need the ability to communicate internally regarding policies and procedures that affect the agency's operations. Likewise, the ability of officers to communicate externally to groups or individuals within the community is also critical. Both oral and written communications are addressed in this chapter. **Note:** Written law enforcement reports were covered in Chapter 9.

Communications within a law enforcement agency may be horizontal, downward, or upward. A downward communication could be a message from the chief to all officers. An upward communication would be from an officer to the chief. Communications are also horizontal or lateral, perhaps from one officer to another. Communications may also be considered as formal or informal. A formal communication would be a memo from the chief. A classical type of informal communication is the "rumor mill."

POLICE LANGUAGE

All professions have their own jargon and slang that they use on a daily basis. Frequently, to outsiders they refer to it as technical language, but actually it is the jargon and slang of the profession. Police officers also speak a unique language—one that is often considered by others as slang. In police "lingo" cars become "units" and perpetrators become "perps." It's interesting to note that sometimes police language is different in different parts of the country—a criminal is a "perp" in New York and a "suspect" in California.

Police jargon or slang serves a useful purpose. It helps communicate concepts unique to law enforcement more efficiently to other officers. One officer can transmit information to another officer quicker using police jargon. It also helps soften the harsh edge of daily reality. The biggest handicap with the use of jargon is that it is often used when an officer is dealing with members of the community-at-large who may not understand the jargon and therefore its use may create barriers to effective communications.

RADIO COMMUNICATIONS

In the 1920s, when the police first started using radio communications, it was strictly one-way communications broadcast on standard low wattage AM radios. The dispatcher broadcasted service calls and hoped an officer would respond to the calls. If the officers wanted to communicate with the dispatcher or the station, they were required to do so by telephone or police call-boxes.

A Short History of LAPD Radio Communications

In May of 1924, Los Angeles Police Chief R. Lee Heath attended an Amateur Radio show. He observed a contest demonstrating home-built automobile-mounted radio receivers potentially suitable for police use. He was impressed with the results, and the following year, at the National Radio Exposition, he organized a demonstration of an airplane with an officer aboard following a "suspect's" car, radioing its movements to listeners below on a low wattage radio station. In 1929, Chief of Police James E. Davis, who had succeeded Heath, ordered his staff to investigate the use of radio to "more quickly dispatch officers to where they are needed." Several years of testing followed, with the help of some local broadcasters and inventors. Like Heath, however, Davis's term as chief was cut short due to the politics of the era. The tests started by Heath and Davis proved successful. Under new Police Chief Roy Steckel, and with strong support from the City Council President, the Los Angeles Police Department (LAPD) was granted its first radio license from the Department of Commerce Radio Bureau (predecessor of the Federal Communications Commission [FCC]) in February of 1931. Finishing work was then done on the transmitter, and receiving sets were installed in several patrol cars. The final tests of the radios and the dispatch system were accomplished in April 1931, and the LAPD Radio Station went into service on May 1, 1931.

In 1936, the FCC issued an "Experimental Service" radio license to LAPD–W6XPA for testing of 100-watt mobile transmitters in four police cars, to study the properties and usefulness of two-way radio. Limited funding for 200 cars was approved by the Los Angeles City Council in 1938. Because their budget did not allow for purchasing new radios, the Radio Technical Division personnel built 210 transmitter sets in their shop, which was located in the basement of the Lincoln Heights Jail. These "home brew" radios ended up operating for more than a decade in the city.

Source: "A Short History of LAPD Radio Communications" by Harry Marnell from "An Unofficial History of the Los Angeles Police Department's Communications Division" posted at http://harrymarnell.com/kma367.htm. Used by permission of Harry Marnell.

Connecticut State Police's First Use of Two-Way Radios

In 1939, Edward J. Hickey, Commissioner of the Connecticut State Police, asked Daniel Noble, a professor of electrical engineering at the University of Connecticut, to design a mobile-radio system for the state police. A one-way system was suggested, but Noble, who had designed two-way AM units and FM broadcast stations, recommended a two-way, FM system. Receiving the go-ahead from Hickey, Noble drew up a circuit design and specifications, from which a practical unit was built by Fred Budelman, chief engineer of the Fred M. Link Company. Noble later said that the success of the system was due to choosing phase modulation, selecting proper station sites, using rooftop antennas on the cars, and employing different transmitting frequencies for the base stations and mobile units. The system began operations at Hartford in 1940, signaling the nationwide switch from AM to FM.

Source: Institute of Electrical and Electronics Engineers' website: www.ieee.org/web/aboutus/history_center/police_radio.html. Accessed August 30, 2006.

Today, most patrol officers are dispatched by radio. Most law enforcement agencies have at least three or more frequencies. The three common frequencies are the primary channel, which carries the bulk of the traffic including dispatch; an administrative channel to handle administrative matters; and a car-to-car channel to allow uninterrupted communications between individual patrol units. The larger police agencies, like the Chicago Police Department, use over one hundred frequencies and many of their police divisions, bureaus, and specialized units have their own channels.

Ohio State Highway Patrol Sgt. Burnett Hughs using an early speed radar device in the 1950s. Note the size of the unit compared to the units used today.
Photo courtesy of Ohio State Police.

Interdepartmental Operations Channel

Presently, most states have an interdepartmental operations channel that is assigned to law enforcement agencies for use by mobile/mobile police radio communications between state law enforcement agencies. For example, New York State operates a channel (155.370 MHz) that is restricted to communications between state police agencies. The use of this channel for noninterdepartmental operations is a violation of FCC rules and regulations. The Tucson, Arizona, Police Department provides detailed instructions on the use of police radio, as shown in Figure 10.1.

Figure 10.1 **Tucson Police Department General Orders Volume 6 Communications, Section 6200, Use of Police Radio**

Law enforcement agencies in most cases have detailed instructions regarding the use of police radios. The Tucson, Arizona, Police Department's general order on the use of police radios is a good example of detailed instructions regarding the use of police radios.

TUCSON POLICE DEPARTMENT GENERAL ORDERS		VOLUME 6 COMMUNICATIONS
Revised: July 2006		6200 USE OF POLICE RADIO Issued May 2001

6200   USE OF POLICE RADIO

6210   GENERAL [CALEA 81.2.5 a]

According to the rules and regulations of the Federal Communications Commission (FCC), all radio communications, regardless of their nature, shall be restricted to the minimum practicable transmission time. As a result, voice and data radio discipline shall be maintained. Field supervisors are responsible to monitor radio and data traffic to ensure appropriate discipline. FCC regulations make it unlawful to:

☐ Transmit superfluous communications of any kind

☐ Use profane, indecent or obscene language

☐ Make unnecessary or unidentified transmissions

6211   Responding to Calls for Service

Members shall respond to all radio assignments promptly and return to service as soon as possible.

When a member encounters an on-sight situation while en route to an assigned call, they shall advise the dispatcher of the situation. If the situation demands immediate attention, the member shall advise the dispatcher and request that the original call be reassigned. If the original call is of a higher priority, the member shall request that another unit be dispatched to handle the on-sight situation.

Similarly, when an officer is en route to an assigned call and the officer decides to divert to another call or situation, the officer shall inform the dispatcher of the expected

Figure 10.1 Continued

delay in response, or the need to re-dispatch the call. That notification must be done on the radio even if the officer has already accomplished the change utilizing available computer commands.

All officers shall monitor their assigned frequency and respond when called or if needed for priority situations. When called by a dispatcher, officers shall respond by giving their designator and location. Officers who do not have mobile computer systems shall record the initial call information as it is being dispatched.

In non-emergency calls, and when practicable for emergency calls, members will utilize the computer system to identify when they have arrived at an assigned call. In extreme emergencies, on-site situations or when no computer system is available, members shall advise the dispatcher when they arrive at an assigned call. Members may request other resources or back-up whenever necessary. Field supervisors shall monitor calls for service and staffing levels. Field supervisors are responsible for the tactical deployment of police resources, and they may cancel or delay response to a call. Those field supervisors are then responsible for notification of the complainant.

RADIO DESIGNATORS

Identification [CALEA 81.2.5 c]

Members using a Department radio shall identify themselves through the use of a designator. Members not assigned a designator shall use their payroll numbers. Designators shall be created to reflect the specific assignment of the individual wherever possible. Designators will also be used as specific unit identifiers for computer-aided dispatching. The following assignments have established designators:

~ Office of the Chief of Police
 - Command 1   Chief of Police
 - Command 2   Deputy Chief of Police
 - Command 3   Assistant Chief of Police
 - Command 4   Assistant Chief of Police
 - Command 5   Assistant Chief of Police
 - Command 6   Assistant Chief of Police
 - 12C(Charlie) 1   Chief of Staff
 - 12C2   Executive Officer
~ Professional Standard Division
 - 14C1   PSD Captain
 - 14C2   OIA Lieutenant
 - 14C4   Accreditation/Audit Lieutenant
~ Operations Bureaus
 - 1C(Charlie) 1   ODS Captain
 - 1C2-1C4   ODS Lieutenant
 - 2C1   ODW Captain
 - 2C2-2C   ODW Lieutenant
 - 3C1   ODM Captain
 - 3C2-3C4   ODM Lieutenant
 - 4C1   ODE Captain
 - 4C2-4C4   ODE Lieutenant

- 5C1	ODD Captain
- 5C2-5C4	ODD Lieutenants
- 15C1	Field Support Captain
- 15C2	Traffic Lieutenant
- 15C3	Tactical Support Lieutenant
- 7C1	Specialized Response Division Captain

Members who are assigned to these bureaus and are authorized to use the police radio shall use designators conforming to their assignment or shall use their payroll numbers to identify themselves.

6230   MOBILE COMPUTER COMMUNICATIONS

Police vehicles may be equipped with Mobile Data Terminals (MDT) or Mobile Tactical Computers (MTC). For purposes of this section, the terms are interchangeable. Instructions for using the equipment can be found in the MDT training manual. This equipment shall be used for job-related messaging only. The use of this or any communications equipment for personal or non job-related purposes is prohibited.

6240   CALL PROCESSING [CALEA 81.2.4 a-j; 81.2.5 b]

Communications, in concert with the mission and goals of the Department and working with a users committee shall establish a call priority system. Calls for police service are entered into the computer system and assigned individual numbers. Associated information and data is automatically included. Communications personnel update information on calls as necessary, including the status of officers. The service operator assigns priorities to calls for service based on established guidelines, as follows:

- **LEVEL 1 EMERGENCY RESPONSE** – An incident posing an immediate threat to life where the threat is present and on-going; and/or an incident posing an immediate threat to life involving the actual use or threatened use of a weapon. The mere presence of a weapon alone, however, without any indication of use or threat of use does not support or justify a Level 1 call.

- **LEVEL 2 CRITICAL RESPONSE** – An incident involving a situation of imminent danger to life or a high potential for a threat to life to develop or escalate. This incident must be in progress or have occurred within the past five (5) minutes.

- **LEVEL 3 URGENT RESPONSE** – Crimes against persons or significant property crimes where a rapid response is needed and the incident is in progress, has occurred within the past 10 minutes or is about to escalate to a more serious situation.

- **LEVEL 4 GENERAL RESPONSE** – Other crimes or matters requiring police response, generally occurring more than 10-minutes prior to dispatch and having a complainant.

- **LEVEL 5 INFORMATION RESPONSE** – Call to relay information or notify officers about a situation. Calls are sent to beat books/briefing and are not dispatched by Communications.

- **LEVEL 6 BEAT CALL RESPONSE** – Calls that require a police response but are not time critical and are most suitably handled by a beat officer. Level 6 calls are not dispatched by Communications. Clearance may be satisfied with conversion to a Level 5 call.

Figure 10.1 Continued

6241 Major Incidents [CALEA 81.2.5 e]

The number of members assigned to a call will be determined by the known or expected seriousness of the situation taking into account officer safety and the size and scope of the incident. Officers and supervisors can request more or fewer people at their discretion.

High-priority dispatches may be preceded by an alert tone. Units close to the location shall advise the dispatcher of their location and await assignment. It is the responsibility of the on-duty field supervisor or Incident Commander to ensure that assignments are adequate and appropriate. During such incidents, radio traffic may be restricted to priority transmissions. Except in an emergency, all officers not involved in the incident shall remain in service and off the radio until the emergency aspect of the event has been resolved. Units assigned to the call shall advise the dispatcher they are en route. If additional units are required, units close to the location of the event will utilize the MDT "AE" command to show themselves en route instead of utilizing the radio.

If immediate police action (not routine or administrative business) is required on a situation not related to the major incident, officers may switch radio frequencies to conduct the necessary business. The respective dispatchers shall be notified.

6241.1 Major Incident In Progress

When a major incident is occurring, the dispatcher may activate the "major incident in progress tone," and when appropriate have the responding units switch to a different channel or talk group. This is an audible tone that occurs automatically in the background of each transmission so listeners will be aware that an incident is in progress. During the time that this tone is activated, officers shall remain in service and off the radio unless they have information pertinent to the emergency. Any officer involved in a major incident may request the activation of the tone. The tone will be deactivated as soon as practicable to allow for normal traffic, but the tone can remain in effect as long as is necessary for the safety of those involved.

6241.2 Briefing of Communications

A Communications supervisor will be notified as soon as possible of a major ongoing incident to allow briefing of Communications personnel. A Communications supervisor is responsible for updating the major incident log at Communications. A Communications supervisor shall also be contacted for any pre-planned event that has a high-risk potential (e.g., search warrant service) or other event that may involve a greater than usual deployment of personnel (e.g., parades, DUI deployment, Safe Streets, etc.).

6242 Officers Working Special Duty

Officers who are working Special Duty police assignments shall notify the dispatcher via radio or computer prior to the start of their assignment. The officer will advise the dispatcher of their designator and the location of the Special Duty assignment. The dispatcher will verify the designator, name, and assignment location with the Special Duty listing at their dispatch console. The officer will further advise the dispatcher via radio or computer when the Special Duty assignment has been completed.

6243   Callback Investigations [CALEA 81.2.14]

Non-emergency calls for service may be generated from emergency or 911 calls. The callback operation is decentralized, and under the administrative supervision of the Operations Bureaus. Callback operators shall disregard division boundaries when responding to callbacks. Every effort will be made to respond to callbacks in a timely manner. Callbacks will be handled as follows:

- Emergency calls will be routed to the 911 system.
- Runaway, walk away and missing person calls will be given priority handling or dispatched.
- Calls not requiring police presence will be designated as callback.
- Calls older than 24 hours will be given priority.
- Calls over 72 hours old will be cleared after three reasonable attempts at contact.
- Callback lists will be automatically generated for each workday.

Source: "Tucson Police Department General Order 6200 Use of Police Radio" Reprinted by permission of the Tucson Police Department, Tucson, Arizona.

Basics of Radio Communications

Radio communications use radio waves at different frequencies, grouped within bands that are part of the radio spectrum.

The **radio wave** is the basic building block of radio communications. Like waves on a pond, a radio wave is a series of repeating peaks and valleys. The entire pattern of a wave, before it repeats itself, is called a cycle. The number of cycles, or times that a wave repeats in a second, is called frequency. Frequency is measured in the unit hertz (Hz), referring to a number of cycles per second. One thousand hertz is referred to as a kilohertz (kHz), one million hertz as a megahertz (MHz), and one billion hertz as a gigahertz (GHz).

The **radio spectrum** is the complete range of frequencies from approximately 30 kHz up to more than 300 GHz that can be used for radio communications. Frequencies are often grouped in ranges called bands. Bands of interest to public safety include HF (high frequency), VHF (very high frequency), UHF (ultra high frequency), and most recently SHF (super high frequency). The FCC regulates use of the non-federal spectrum, including that used by state and local public safety agencies.

radio wave / The basic building block of radio communications. Like waves on a pond, a radio wave is a series of repeating peaks and valleys.

radio spectrum / The complete range of frequencies from approximately 30 kHz up to more than 300 GHz that can be used for radio communications.

Spectrum Allocations/Regulations

Spectrum allocations for state and local public safety are fragmented into many distinct slices of the radio spectrum. Regulation of specific frequencies for federal agency use occurs within the National Telecommunications and Information Administration, while the FCC regulates the spectrum for non-federal users (see "Radio Spectrum," National Institute of Justice Publication 212975, dated February 2006).

Radio Procedures

Listening and talking on the radio are acquired skills that take practice to become proficient. As a veteran police officer once advised, when using the radio always assume that most of the people in the city are listening to you. In addition, most agencies keep recordings of all radio traffic. Accordingly, keep your radio traffic professional. Each officer with a radio is assigned a call sign. Use the call signs rather than an officer's name. Always identify yourself to the dispatcher by the call sign.

Radio time is limited, so don't waste it. Think out your message in advance. Your radio transmission should convey the information in a calm, clear, accurate, and concise manner. If your message must be long and time-consuming, pause every 20–30 seconds so that if another unit has an emergency, the unit can break in.

Most law enforcement agencies use a code system as a shorthand method of transmitting information. For example, in most agencies the code 10-20 refers to location. The 10 code (e.g., 10-20 for location) is the most widely used system. It is also the code adopted by the Association of Public Safety Officers. The 10 code is set forth later in the chapter. Many law enforcement agencies also use the 11 code for a wide variety of traffic-related situations. In one agency a code 11-15 means children playing in the street.

Agencies also code the radio calls by "status" codes. Generally, the lowest status code is Code 0 which is routine, Code 2 is priority, and Code 3 the highest priority. Some departments, like the LAPD, also subdivide the status codes such as "Code 3 high" for life and death situations or "Code 2 high", which could be a robbery or other violent crime.

Rolling File Check Procedure
[Manual for Police of New York State, 2-3-5]

The following procedure is recommended for patrol units and dispatchers before a traffic stop is made:

Mobile Radio Operator: Call your dispatcher for a rolling file check when you want a file check on a registration plate number **before** you stop the vehicle.

Dispatcher: After receipt of a request for a rolling file check, make inquiry into the DMV computer using the function code: RALL. This will give you a file check on the plate, VIN, and registrant.

Silent Scanners

For more than half a century, the media and the general public have been able to tune in to emergency communications by using relatively inexpensive scanners. The squawking of one, or more typically several, scanners has been a staple in the newsroom for as long as most journalists can remember.

Many police agencies are trying to prevent citizens from listening to police scanners. The Winter Park Police Department (in central Florida) was one of the first law enforcement agencies to encrypt all its radio communications. The City of Philadelphia's Police Department has also switched to encrypted communications, but it wasn't long before those willing to pay for expensive decoders could get them. Those agencies generally argue that the shielding of communications is necessary to prevent criminals, drug dealers especially, from monitoring in order to keep tabs on the police's whereabouts. Police agencies have always had the ability to conduct sting operations in silence or on special radio channels, but if anyone can afford the expensive technology designed to get around encryption, it's drug dealers. As a newspaper noted, blanket encryption in the Flagler County, Florida, Sheriff's Office's case—where most crime doesn't fall in the category of urban murders and drug dealing—will end up shutting out mostly those who listen to police communications for good purposes. The *Florida News Journal* claims that essentially the greater majority of the county will be, for most residents, under the equivalent of police-radio silence (July 24, 2006, p. A-1).

According to the newspaper, listening to police scanners isn't just a hobby or a strange way to add some white noise. Many people listen to police scanners for genuinely legitimate and commendable reasons. There are those who want to know what's happening in their neighborhood—crime, fires, ambulance calls—though just as often as not it's cats hung up in trees and false alarms bothering a few square blocks. A mildly trained ear listening to scanner transmissions can have virtually the whole story, uncut and unfiltered. There are also those who like to make sure that law enforcement and public safety agencies are doing their jobs, answering dispatch calls promptly and knowledgeably. The trained ear listening to a scanner can pick up on those nuances. And, of course, it should be said that there are those who depend on scanner transmissions to stay on top of breaking events in the community, so readers and viewers can be informed promptly. Police news is usually among the most sought-after by newspaper readers and television viewers alike.

Police communications, according to the newspaper, are public records. As such, they should be accessible to the public rather than hidden from it as effectively as the technology allows. If the Sheriff's Office in Flagler County, Florida, or others aren't about to turn back, state law still compels the agencies to record their dispatch communications and to keep the recordings at least thirty days before discarding them. This provides an oversight window for those who truly want to keep tabs on their police agency, but it doesn't replace the live element of monitoring activity as it is happening. For that, scanner buffs and others will have to invest in more expensive technology that outwits encryption. Ultimately, according to the paper, it's worth noting that keeping tabs on police work is a much greater public service than dissimulating it.

In 2005, the Wichita Falls, Texas, Police Department encrypted their scanners. More than a month after the new encrypted police scanners went silent for the media and public the news organizations reached an agreement with the city to allow access to the communications. The media outlets had threatened to sue for the same access to real-time police and fire communications they had in the past. The media claimed that by listening to scanners, reporters find out about car accidents, crimes, fires, road closures, and public safety threats.

As the result of the agreement, the city will allow television stations and newspapers each to buy as many as two programmed digital radios. The radios are programmed to receive dispatching information from the Wichita Falls Fire Department, as well as the police department's primary traffic channel. For weeks,

Wichita Falls officials insisted that the media and other outside parties should not have access. Officials claimed that officers' safety was at risk if the public knew where police were going. They also claimed that information that officers need to give to each other during an incident, such as someone's health condition or criminal activities, cannot be broadcast with others listening (*The Daily Texan*. After refusing initially, city gives media police scanners. Austin, Texas, June 8, 2005, p. A3).

Radio Call Signs and Codes

Police agencies generally use identification designations for call signs. This may be very simple in a small agency—"Unit Paul 1" may be the chief of police and "Unit Paul 2" the deputy chief. The larger agencies, like the Los Angeles Police Department (LAPD), frequently use codes that identify the unit by either geographic location or function. From 1968 to 1975, NBC ran a popular television show, *Adam-12*, about police officers in Los Angeles. The program concentrated on the daily activities of a pair of LAPD officers whose call sign was 1-Adam-12. At the time, LAPD was divided into eighteen divisions. The "1" referred to LAPD's central district, "Adam" designated a two-officer patrol, and the "12" was the actual unit number. The call signs of the two lead actors in the television series, *CHIPS*, a series about the California Highway Patrol, were "LA Mary 6 and Mary 7." They were fictional motorcycle patrol officers assigned to the LA division of the California Highway Patrol. The call sign "6 FB-12" in LAPD refers to a foot patrol unit in the sixth district (Hollywood) and "12" is the actual unit number. "14-Mary-Queen-4" is a motorcycle officer assigned to the Motor Task Force. "4-King-25" is a robbery homicide investigator working for LAPD Investigative Services.

Almost all law enforcement agencies use radio codes to save air time and make communications more effective. The **phonetic alphabet** was designed to avoid confusion between letters that sound alike. The phonetic alphabet is a list of words used to identify letters in a message transmitted by radio or telephone. Spoken words from an approved list are substituted for letters. For example, the word "Navy" would be "November Alfa Victor Yankee" when spelled in the phonetic alphabet. This practice helps to prevent confusion between similar sounding letters, such as "m" and "n," and to clarify communications that may be garbled during transmission.

The phonetic alphabetic has been used widely by the military. An early version of the phonetic alphabet appeared in the 1913 edition of *The Bluejackets' Manual*. Found in the Signals section, it was paired with the Alphabetical Code Flags defined in the International Code. Both the meanings of the flags (the letter which they represent) and their names (which make up the phonetic alphabet) were selected by international agreement (U.S. Navy, 1913).

phonetic alphabet / List of words used to identify letters in a message transmitted by radio or telephone.

Virginia State Police Ban 10 Codes

In November 2006, the Virginia State Police banned the use of 10 Codes by the state police in radio transmissions. The 10 Codes have been used by generations of officers since the 1920s and are considered a part of police culture. Under the new regulations, the state police will stop using language such as, "What's your 10-20?" Instead, they will simply ask, "What is your location?" The movement to plain English is expected to help officers in times of stress.

Source: Press release by Virginia Governor Timothy Kaine, November 9, 2006.

Each agency may have its own codes, but generally the following codes are used:

Partial List of Standard Radio Codes Used by Many Agencies

10-1 Signal weak
10-2 Signal good
10-3 Stop transmitting
10-4 Message received
10-5 Relay
10-6 Busy
10-7 Out of service
10-8 In service
10-9 Repeat
10-10 Fight in progress
10-11 Animal problem
10-12 Stand by
10-13 Report conditions
10-14 Prowler report
10-15 Civil disturbance
10-16 Domestic problem
10-17 Meet complainant
10-18 Urgent
10-19 Go to station
10-20 Location
10-21 Phone ___
10-22 Disregard
10-23 Arrived at scene
10-24 Assignment complete
10-25 Report to ___
10-26 Detaining suspect
10-27 Driver's license information
10-28 Vehicle registration information
10-29 Check for wants/warrants
10-30 Unauthorized use of radio
10-31 Crime in progress
10-32 Person with gun
10-33 Emergency, stand by
10-34 Riot
10-35 Major crime alert
10-36 Correct time
10-37 Investigate suspicious vehicle
10-38 Stop suspicious vehicle
10-39 Use lights and siren
10-40 Respond quickly
10-41 Beginning shift
10-42 Ending shift
10-43 Information
10-44 Permission to leave
10-45 Dead animal
10-46 Assist motorist
10-47 Emergency road repair
10-48 Traffic control
10-49 Traffic signal out

10-50 Traffic accident
10-51 Request tow truck
10-52 Request ambulance
10-54 Livestock on roadway
10-55 Intoxicated driver
10-56 Intoxicated pedestrian
10-57 Hit-and-run accident
10-58 Direct traffic
10-59 Escort
10-60 Squad in vicinity
10-61 Personnel in vicinity
10-62 Reply to message
10-63 Prepare to copy
10-64 Local message
10-65 Network message
10-66 Cancel message
10-67 Clear for network message
10-68 Dispatch information
10-69 Message received
10-70 Fire alarm
10-71 Advise of nature of fire
10-72 Report progress of fire
10-73 Smoke report
10-74 Negative
10-75 In contact with ___
10-76 En route to ___
10-77 E.T.A.
10-78 Request assistance
10-79 Notify coroner
10-80 Pursuit in progress
10-81 Breathalyzer report
10-82 Reserve lodgings
10-83 School crossing detail
10-84 E.T.A.
10-85 Arrival delayed
10-86 Operator on duty
10-87 Pick up
10-88 Advise of telephone number
10-89 Bomb threat
10-90 Bank alarm
10-91 Pick up subject
10-92 Illegally parked vehicle
10-93 Blockage
10-94 Drag racing
10-95 Subject in custody
10-96 Detain subject
10-97 Test signal
10-98 Escaped prisoner
10-99 Wanted

Phonetic Alphabet

There are two general phonetic alphabets used in the United States. Law enforcement agencies generally use the one on the left, while fire agencies primarily use the one on the right.

Law Enforcement					Fire and Military			
A	Adam	N	Nora		A	Alpha	N	November
B	Boy	O	Ocean		B	Bravo	O	Oscar
C	Charlie	P	Paul		C	Charlie	P	Papa
D	David	Q	Queen		D	Delta	Q	Quebec
E	Edward	R	Robert		E	Echo	R	Romeo
F	Frank	S	Sam		F	Foxtrot	S	Sierra
G	George	T	Tom		G	Golf	T	Tango
H	Henry	U	Union		H	Hotel	U	Uniform
I	Ida	V	Victor		I	India	V	Victor
J	John	W	William		J	Juliet	W	Whiskey
K	King	X	X-ray		K	Kilo	X	X-ray
L	Lincoln	Y	Young		L	Lima	Y	Yankee
M	Mary	Z	Zebra		M	Mike	Z	Zulu

Crime Broadcasts

When an officer arrives at the scene of a crime, one of the officer's first responsibilities is to broadcast information about the crime to dispatch and other patrol units. While each agency has its own format for crime broadcasts, generally the broadcasts are in the following order: type of crime, time delay, location, any weapons used, loss or injury involved, suspects if any, type and description of vehicle the suspects may be in, and possible direction of travel. A typical crime broadcast may be: armed robbery at 2116 Main; at 10:15 A.M.; weapon used described as a blue-steel revolver; loss was one hundred and ten dollars; suspect is a male Caucasian estimated height about six feet and heavyset; vehicle may have been a 1990 Black Ford Mustang with California plates; last seen northbound on Main Street.

TELEPHONE COMMUNICATIONS

Most citizens contact the police by telephone. Agencies generally have set policies for answering telephone calls. Many agencies have the goal of answering every telephone call within a specified number of rings. In the larger agencies, the telephones are usually answered by a dispatcher. In the smaller agencies, officers often provide relief assistance for the dispatcher. The general rule is that each call will be handled in an efficient and proficient manner. The 9-1-1 system is used for emergencies and a different line is for non-emergencies; however, many emergency calls are received on non-emergency lines. When that happens, the dispatcher or officer needs to know how to handle the call.

Cellular telephones (cell phones) are commonly used for communications and the number of individuals using cell phones is increasing each year. A big problem with cell phones is that conversations on these phones are not secure communications. Officers using cell phones to pass information to headquarters or other officers should assume that the public, the press, and even some sophisticated criminals may be listening to the conversations. Of course, this also works to the police's advantage. One of the largest Medicare fraud cases in New York State was broken because the criminals were talking on cell phones that the federal agents were monitoring. [As mentioned in Chapter 6, monitoring a cell phone is not a search under the Fourth Amendment and therefore does not require a warrant.]

Federal ENHANCE 9-1-1 Act of 2004

In December 2004, the "Ensuring Needed Help Arrives Near Callers Employing 9-1-1 Act of 2004" (ENHANCE 9-1-1 Act of 2004) was enacted by the federal government. [This act has to be one of the most uniquely titled acts in American history.] The act established a national 9-1-1 Implementation Coordination Office (ICO) whose functions include:

- Actions to improve federal coordination and communication on 9-1-1 activities.
- Developing, collecting, and disseminating information concerning practices, procedures, and technology used in the implementation of 9-1-1 services.
- Administering a grant program designed to provide funding to 9-1-1 call centers to upgrade their equipment and operations to receive 9-1-1 calls with automatic phone number and location identification.

The National 9-1-1 Office is housed in the Office of Emergency Medical Services at the National Highway Traffic Safety Administration (NHTSA). NHTSA, along with the National Telecommunications and Information Administration (Department of Commerce), are partners in this effort.

9-1-1 Communications

9-1-1 is the official national emergency number in the United States and Canada. The 9-1-1 network is also part of the nation's emergency response and disaster preparedness system. Although the term "9-1-1" has come to mean the entire public safety communications system, in fact, it's simply a dedicated telephone system for relaying calls from the public.

When the 9-1-1 number was inaugurated in Haleyville, Alabama, as the result of an AT&T proposal, it was intended as an easily remembered, no-coin method of reaching the correct law enforcement, fire, and EMS agencies. However, since 9-1-1 procedures are under the control of local agencies, many different policies have developed for the proper use of 9-1-1 since its first use. Today, officials estimate that over 270,000 calls are made to 9-1-1 each day in the United States.

A 9-1-1 system is considered either Basic or Enhanced. A Basic 9-1-1 system provides three-digit dialing, no coin is required from pay telephones, and there is intelligent routing to the Public Safety Answering Point (PSAP) that handles the area where the phone is located. An Enhanced 9-1-1 system adds the ability to display the caller's address and telephone number at the PSAP for the dispatcher's reference. Some 9-1-1 systems also have the ability to automatically ring-back the caller on hang-up, lock a line open for tracing, or transfer callers to other agencies or telephone numbers with a single button.

Enhanced 9-1-1 Wireless Services: One of the chronic problems with 9-1-1 systems is the growing use of cell phones that do not automatically provide a location where the call is being made. To overcome this problem, the FCC established rules for a wireless Enhanced 9-1-1 (E9-1-1). These rules seek to improve the effectiveness and reliability of wireless 9-1-1 service by providing 9-1-1 dispatchers with additional information on wireless 9-1-1 calls. The wireless E9-1-1 program is divided into two parts: Phase I and Phase II. Phase I requires carriers, upon valid request by a local PSAP, to report the telephone number of a wireless 9-1-1 caller and the location of the antenna that received the call. Phase II requires wireless carriers to provide far more precise location information, within 50–300 meters in most cases.

The deployment of E9-1-1 requires the development of new technologies and upgrades to local 9-1-1 PSAPs, as well as coordination among public safety agencies, wireless carriers, technology vendors, equipment manufacturers, and local wireline carriers.

Federal Communications Commission's Recommendations for the Public's Use of 9-1-1

- Do not program 9-1-1 into your auto-dial telephone. You won't forget the number, and programming the number invites accidental dialing of the number. Also, please do not dial 9-1-1 to "test" your phone or the system. This needlessly burdens the dispatchers and system with non-emergency calls.
- If you live in a region that is subject to natural disasters (earthquake, tornado, hurricane, etc.), pre-plan a method of communicating with family, friends, and relatives before an incident occurs. Choose any emergency contact outside the area that will be affected by the disaster. Make them the relay point for those who want to contact you. After the disaster hits, you can make just one telephone call to your contact, and have that information relayed to all those you care about.
- Dial 9-1-1 only for an emergency. An emergency is any serious medical problem (chest pain, seizure, bleeding), any type of fire (business, car, building), or any life-threatening situation (fights, person with weapons, etc.). Most jurisdictions also urge citizens to use 9-1-1 to report crimes in progress, whether or not a life is threatened.
- Do not dial 9-1-1 for a non-emergency. Instead, dial the agency's listed seven-digit non-emergency telephone number. A non-emergency incident is a property damage accident, break-in to a vehicle when suspect is gone, theft of property (when suspect is gone), vandalism (when suspect is gone), panhandlers, intoxicated persons who are not disorderly, or cars blocking the street or alleys.
- Do not pick up the telephone and put it down if you don't hear a dial-tone—you'll tie up the telephone network and delay obtaining a line. Stay on the line until you hear the dial-tone. If you hear a fast-busy, all circuits are busy—try again later. If you reach a recording, the telephone system isn't available for your call—try again later.
- In many large cities, 9-1-1 calls are answered by a dispatcher if one is available. However, if all call-takers

are busy on other calls, the 9-1-1 call is answered by a call distributor that holds the call, and then automatically routes it to the first available call-taker. Do not hang up if you reach a recording and try to call back. Stay on the line and your call will be answered in order. If you hang up, your call will be delayed because you will be placed at the end of other callers.

- Your 9-1-1 call will automatically be routed to the police, fire, or EMS agency that handles the area where the telephone is located. In general, 9-1-1 calls are answered by the area's law enforcement agency, who either handles the call or transfers it immediately to the appropriate agency.

- If you dialed 9-1-1 in error, do not hang up the telephone. Instead, stay on the line and explain to the dispatcher that you dialed by mistake and that you do not have an emergency. If you hang up, a dispatcher will call back to confirm that there is no emergency. If you don't answer, a police officer or deputy must be dispatched to confirm that you are OK. This will needlessly take resources away from genuine emergencies.

- Briefly describe the type of incident you are reporting. For example, "I'm reporting an auto fire," or "I'm reporting an unconscious person," or "I'm reporting a shoplifter." Then stay on the line with the dispatcher—do not hang up until the dispatcher tells you to. In some cases, the dispatcher will keep you on the line while the emergency units are responding to ask additional questions or to obtain ongoing information.

- If your call is answered by a law enforcement agency and you are reporting a fire or medical emergency, the call-taker will transfer your call—stay on the line while the call is transferred. The call-taker who answers will need information about the incident.

- Let the call-taker ask you questions—they have been trained to ask questions that will help prioritize the incident, locate it, and speed an appropriate response. Your answers should be brief and responsive. Remain calm and speak clearly. If you are not in a position to give full answers to the call-taker (the suspect is nearby), stay on the phone and the dispatcher will ask you questions that can be answered "yes" or "no."

- Be prepared to describe your location and the location of the emergency. Although an Enhanced 9-1-1 system will display your telephone number and location, the dispatcher must confirm the displayed address or may ask you for more specific location information about the victim or suspects.

- If you are a cellular caller, your telephone number and location will not be displayed for the dispatcher's reference. You must be able to describe your location so emergency units can respond. Be aware of your current city or town, address, highway and direction, nearby cross-streets or interchanges, or other geographic points of reference.

- Cellular 9-1-1 calls are frequently routed to a central PSAP that could be many miles from your location. Be prepared to give the dispatcher your complete location—city or town, address or location, inside or outside, what floor or room, and so on.

- Be prepared to describe the persons involved in any incident. This includes their race, sex, age, height and weight, color of hair, description of clothing, and presence of a hat, glasses, or facial hair.

- Be prepared to describe any vehicles involved in the incident. This includes the color, year, make, model, and type of vehicle (sedan, pick-up, sport utility, van, tanker truck, flatbed, etc.). If the vehicle is parked, the dispatcher will need to know the direction it's facing. If the vehicle is moving or has left, the dispatcher will need to know the last direction.

- Be patient as the dispatcher asks you questions. While you are answering the dispatcher's questions, the dispatcher is entering or writing down the information. If you are reporting an emergency, most likely a response is being made while you are still on the line with the dispatcher.

- Listen to the dispatcher's instructions for assistance if you are in danger yourself. The dispatcher may tell you to leave the building, secure yourself in a room, or take other action to protect yourself.

- Don't hang up until the call-taker tells you to. Follow any instructions the dispatcher gives you, such as meeting the officers at the door, or flagging down the firefighters at the curb.

- If you are able and have training, apply first aid to any patients who need it. Give the victim reassurance that help is on the way. Secure any dogs or other pets that may interfere with the emergency response. Gather any medications the patient is taking that the medical crew will need to take with the patient.

Source: FCC website www.fcc.gov/fcc-bin/bye?http://www.9-1-1dispatch.com/9-1-1_file/9-1-1tips.html. Accessed on line August 16, 2006.

Procedures for Answering 9-1-1 Calls

Recommended procedures for 9-1-1 calls by Technical Working Group for Eyewitness Evidence, 1999 (reformatted).

Policy: As the initial point of contact for the witness, the 9-1-1/emergency call-taker or dispatcher must obtain and disseminate, in a nonsuggestive manner, complete and accurate information from the caller. This information can include the description/identity of the perpetrator of a crime. The actions of the call-taker/dispatcher can affect the safety of those involved as well as the entire investigation.

Procedure: During a 9-1-1/emergency call—after obtaining preliminary information and dispatching police—the call-taker/dispatcher should:

1. Assure the caller the police are on the way.
2. Ask open-ended questions (e.g., "What can you tell me about the car?"); augment with closed-ended questions (e.g., "What color was the car?").
3. Avoid asking suggestive or leading questions (e.g., "Was the car red?").
4. Ask if anything else should be known about the incident.
5. Transmit information to responding officer(s).
6. Update officer(s) as more information comes in.

Summary: The information obtained from the witness is critical to the safety of those involved and may be important to the investigation. The manner in which facts are elicited from a caller can influence the accuracy of the information obtained.

Washington State Enhanced 9-1-1 (E9-1-1) Unit

The Washington State Enhanced 9-1-1 (E9-1-1) Program was established as a result of voter referendum approval in 1991. The referendum directed that E9-1-1 emergency communications systems be in place in every county of the state by December 31, 1998. It provided for a state E9-1-1 coordination office to facilitate local planning and installation of such systems. Funding provisions were included in the referendum for county and state excise taxes to support implementation of E9-1-1 plans and systems. The state's role was clearly defined as supporting those counties that could not implement E9-1-1 with funds collected by their own county. Stakeholders of the state E9-1-1 Program are the citizens of the state, the county governments responsible for implementation and operation of the systems, and public safety service agencies. The Washington Utilities and Transportation Commission (WUTC) and other legislative committees have a continuing interest in the E9-1-1 Program.

The Enhanced 9-1-1 (E9-1-1) Unit of the Emergency Management Division works with counties and communications companies to ensure the E9-1-1 system is operational and available to all the citizens in the State of Washington. The Unit also provides technical assistance on the acquisition and installation of

equipment and linking both public and private telephone systems to the E9-1-1 system.

The E9-1-1 State Coordinator has the responsibility to provide oversight of statewide 9-1-1 wireline and wireless activities. The E9-1-1 Office interacts with telecommunications companies and the WUTC to ensure lifesaving 9-1-1 calls are routed and received correctly in accordance to national standards. The E9-1-1 State Coordinator sets standards for wireless E9-1-1 operation and rules for fiscal assistance to counties. Assistance to counties includes technical, database/GIS, national issues, financial, operations, training, administration, accessibility, contingency planning, wireless, and public education.

During the 2001–2003 biennium, over five million calls to 9-1-1 were answered at sixty-eight Public Safety Answering Points (PSAPs) statewide. Of those calls, two million were made from wireless telephones. In calendar year 2004 alone over 6.2 million calls to 9-1-1 were answered at sixty-three Public Safety Answering Points (PSAPs) in Washington state's thirty-nine counties. Of those calls, 2.3 million were reported made from wireless phones.

Source: Washington Military Department, Emergency Management Division, website: www.emd.wa.gov/2-e911/911-idx.htm. Accessed on line August 15, 2006.

Ad for Oakland, California, Police Department Position
Police Communication, Dispatcher

The Position

Under the general supervision of a Police Communications Supervisor or Sergeant of Police, Police Communications Dispatchers receive and transmit routine and emergency telephone and radio voice messages, dispatch required equipment, perform responsible clerical work of moderately high difficulty, operate complex teletype and video terminals for automated information retrieval, and receive and direct all other 9-1-1 calls.

Police Communications Dispatchers receive approximately one year of on-the-job training and must attend a POST-certified basic dispatcher course. During training, working hours and days off vary. After successful completion of training, dispatchers are eligible to draw for permanent shift assignment, based on seniority. New dispatchers are often assigned the 3:00 P.M.–11:00 P.M. shift or the 11:00 P.M.–7:00 A.M. shift, including weekends and holidays. There is a twelve-month probationary period. Dispatchers may be scheduled to work any of three shifts in a twenty-four hour period; may be required to work a schedule with rotating days off; and often work weekends, holidays, and overtime as required by emergencies or departmental needs.

Typical duties may include, but are not limited to, the following:

- Answer phone calls on 9-1-1 lines and non-emergency lines in the Police Communications Division, interview callers to obtain essential information, and record data and critical information on incidents as they develop.
- Analyze calls for priority level of emergency response and take or recommend an effective course of action to protect life and property.
- Provide information to police field units, order services requested by field units, dispatch and/or cancel field unit back-up assistance, and monitor field units for service availability.
- Operate sophisticated computer-aided dispatch radio and phone systems and accurately enter information into the computer, including brief descriptions of crimes, incidents, or other emergencies.
- Broadcast calls for service to police officers, command personnel, and civilian employees working in the field; carefully and simultaneously track the activities of police officers and civilians to determine their status and ensure their safety.
- Maintain composure and professionalism when dealing with hostile or frightened callers during stressful or rapidly changing situations.

Source: Reprinted from Job Announcement, Oakland, California, Police Department, dated July 12, 2006.

SPECIAL COMMUNICATIONS ISSUES

This section discusses special communications issues that occur because of cultural, language, or physical difficulties preventing or hindering communications between a law enforcement officer and a witness, victim, or suspect. Communicating with persons from other cultures or encountering an individual speaking a foreign language has become more common during routine patrol. Officers must be prepared to communicate effectively in our present multicultural environment.

Non-English-Speaking Individuals

On any court day in Los Angeles County, California, there are interpreters available for seventy-eight different languages and yet, there are days when an interpreter is needed for another language. How many languages are spoken in the United States today? According to Sondra Thiederman (2006), there are over 400 distinct languages being spoken in the United States today. If we add to this the fact that languages other than English are spoken in at least 14 percent of all homes, we begin to see the impact that language diversity has on our lives.

The 2000 U.S. Census noted unprecedented changes in the number and distribution of foreign-born people living in the United States. More than 11 percent of the total population—over 31 million people—had been born beyond the nation's borders. Compared to earlier immigrants, these new arrivals tend to be more geographically dispersed. The major port cities of New York and Los Angeles are no longer the favored entry ports, and suburban areas and "second cities" are increasingly common destinations. Suburban areas, in particular, have had to reinvent their public safety and justice delivery systems to incorporate the needs of new immigrants. A law enforcement agency cannot economically afford to provide for interpreters for all possible language situations that an officer may encounter in the field.

Bismarck, North Dakota, Police Stumped by Language Barrier

In 2006, Bismarck, North Dakota, police, in trying to break up a fight at a Chinese restaurant also had to overcome a language barrier. None of the four people involved in the fight spoke English. From what officers could gather, two women, ages forty-two and twenty-eight, had been arguing, and two men, ages fifty and thirty-eight, tried to intervene. The two men apparently started shoving each other. Police contacted three Chinese translators, but the translators could not understand any of the people involved in the scuffle. The four people might have been speaking Chinese dialects that were unknown to the translators. One of the individuals gave a written statement, but it was written in a version of Chinese that no one could read.

Source: Boston Globe, May 23, 2006, p. A12.

As noted in a Vera Institute Report (2006), in a moment of crisis, the inability to communicate with police officers and other members of the criminal justice system can have distressing consequences. According to the report, a large and growing number of immigrants in the United States who have limited English proficiency (LEP) experience this problem regularly as they struggle to describe a perpetrator to a police officer, attempt to defend themselves against accusations, try to follow conditions of probation, or stumble through communications with a parole officer. As a result, many victims fail to report crimes and communication is impaired when a family member or an untrained staff member acts as an interpreter.

When an officer arrives on the scene of a crime or accident and one or more individuals involved does not speak English, the officer is still required to gather information quickly and accurately. Frequently, the officer will turn to other family members or neighbors who are present and are bilingual. If this occurs, it is important that the officer also include in the report the name and address of the interpreter. There are inherent problems with using family members or neighbors as interpreters because they may not be proficient in both languages and are probably biased.

Survival Spanish

Hispanics are one of the largest minority groups in the United States. The lack of communication between the police and the Hispanic population can have grave

What an Officer Can Do to Be Understood by Non-Native English Speakers

1. **Talk in a normal volume—do not shout.** Shouting interferes with effective communications because it can intimidate listeners who may already have inadequate feelings regarding their language abilities. Shouting is also demeaning to the listener.

2. **Speak distinctly and at a deliberate pace.** Speaking fast is considered by many as a sign of brightness, but it makes it more difficult to understand what you are saying. Be aware of your speech and carefully enunciate even the most commonplace words.

3. **Allow pauses in the conversation.** Silence is not a sign of failure or lack of communication. Many other cultures regard silence as a demonstration of strength, as a way of communicating respect for what the speaker has just said, and as an opportunity to formulate well-thought-out comments and questions. The Japanese proverb, "He who speaks does not know; he who knows does not speak" exemplifies the perspective found in many Far Eastern countries. Give the listener time to digest what you have said and formulate a response.

4. **Stop and check for understanding frequently.** Do not let too much material go by before stopping to check on whether the listener understands you.

5. **Be precise in your choice of words.** Use words that are simple and easy to understand.

6. **Keep your message simple and short.** Do not use complex or compound sentences. Short sentences are easier to understand.

7. **Avoid idioms, slang, and jargon.** Idioms, slang, and jargon are serious blocks to our ability to communicate across language barriers.

8. **Use positive phrasing when possible.** Sentences with negative phrases are more likely to be misunderstood.

9. **Watch for nonverbal signs.** Nonverbal signals can be helpful in assessing how much has been understood. However, body language is by no means universal throughout the world. The avoidance of eye contact can indicate that the person is not following you, but can also be an indication of respect. When a listener narrows the eyes, stays focused on the speaker, and nods and smiles in appropriate spots, then the individual is generally grasping what you are saying. However, perpetual nodding and smiling that does not relate directly to what you are saying might reflect a desire to please and often indicates very little real comprehension.

10. **Notice a lack of interruptions.** A complete lack of interruptions often means that the material is not being understood.

11. **The absence of questions.** The absence of questions often means that the listener is not grasping what you are saying.

12. **Inappropriate laughter.** Inappropriate laughter is often a sign of poor comprehension.

consequences. Many Hispanic residents don't report crime because they think the police don't speak their language or they fear being deported.

The reality is that the police do offer services in several languages and do not have the capacity to deport undocumented immigrants. To equip officers with the ability to handle individuals whose primary language is Spanish and who do not understand English, many law enforcement agencies are offering courses of studies in the Spanish language. Many of these courses are called "Survival Spanish." The Criminal Justice Center at Sam Houston State University started offering "Survival Spanish" in 1986. The program was a cooperative effort between the police academy and a faculty member of the university's Spanish department. When the program was first started, it concentrated on language; later a cross- cultural training component was added when the individuals involved realized that cultural barriers were just as important as the language barrier (Blair & Slick, 1990, p. 42).

Basic Survival Spanish for Arizona Law Enforcement Officers

Problem Identification: Hispanic Americans are the fastest-growing minority population in the United States. Arizona shares a border with Mexico and, as such, has welcomed increasing numbers of Spanish-speaking motorists. Law enforcement agencies in Arizona are aware of communication problems, exacerbated by cultural differences, between law enforcement officers and motorists who speak only Spanish. The problems are particularly acute while performing field sobriety tests (FSTs), during which an officer may not be able to properly explain the tests. In the most extreme situations, impaired motorists have been released because the police officer could not communicate with the driver.

Goals and Objectives: The goal of the Basic Survival Spanish for Law Enforcement and Driving Under the Influence/Driving While Intoxicated (DUI/DWI) Protocols program is to increase successful apprehensions of Arizona motorists who are driving while impaired by alcohol. This goal will be addressed through the following objectives:

- Focusing special DUI/DWI programs on Spanish-speaking drivers
- Providing law enforcement officers with basic Spanish language skills
- Developing a Spanish language DUI enforcement training course
- Developing a Spanish language DUI/DWI protocol training course

Strategies and Activities: In 1998, the Arizona Governor's Office of Highway Safety developed a two-part program designed to resolve the communication problems between law enforcement officers and drivers apprehended for impaired driving, who speak only Spanish. The program consists of two multi-hour training courses.

During the first course, officers are trained in basic survival Spanish, with emphasis on DUI enforcement and FST administration. Officers are selected to participate in the training course based on their proven skills in detecting and apprehending an impaired driver. These officers are most often chosen from among those assigned to the statewide DUI Task Forces. Upon completion of the twenty-four-hour Basic Survival Spanish for Law Enforcement Officers course, officers are able to produce Spanish sounds correctly, pronounce necessary Spanish words intelligibly, recognize and work effectively with cultural differences among the driving public, and conduct specific law enforcement protocols in Spanish. Specific law enforcement protocols include:

- Stopping and searching a suspect
- Serving an arrest or search warrant
- Making a traffic stop
- Booking a suspect
- "Mirandizing" a suspect

Upon completion of the eight-hour training course, Survival Spanish for DUI/DWI Protocols, officers will be able to use Spanish to conduct the following law enforcement protocols:

- DUI/DWI initial contact
- Four FSTs (horizontal gaze nystagmus, walk and turn, one leg stand, finger to nose)
- Results of the FST
- Medical emergencies

Results: Since 1998, more than 350 law enforcement officers have participated in the two Spanish language training courses. Based on the popularity and expressed value of the original two training classes, a third eighty-hour training class has been developed, entitled Spanish Immersion Program.

Source: Information obtained from a handout by the Arizona Department of Public Safety, 2004.

Communicating with Deaf or Hard of Hearing Citizens

In *Edwards v. City of Houston*, No. H-98-1369 (S.D. Tex.), Edwards sued the City of Houston and contended that when he was questioned by a City of Houston police officer, he was not provided with a sign language interpreter. The officer then arrested him and he was incarcerated at the city jail. Edwards alleges that he was not provided with the effective communication he needed in order to receive life-sustaining medications, and that he was not allowed to use a telecommunication device for the deaf (TDD) to call an attorney or his family. During his first court appearance at the City of Houston municipal court, Edwards alleges that he was not provided with an interpreter. Edwards also alleges that he was not provided a sign language interpreter when he needed to report a criminal act against him. The case was settled by agreement between the parties. As a result of this case, and based on the settlement agreement, the National Association of the Deaf (NAD) developed model policies, in conjunction with the U.S. Department of Justice, and city and county police departments, to ensure that police and sheriff departments take the necessary steps to interact with persons who are deaf and hard of hearing.

Specifically, the settlement agreement provides comprehensive practices and procedures for law enforcement personnel to ensure effective communication with deaf and hard of hearing individuals. These model policies apply when police officers and sheriff's deputies receive citizen complaints; interrogate witnesses; arrest, book, and hold suspects; operate telephone 9-1-1 emergency centers; provide emergency medical services; and enforce laws. The model policies provide for important protections:

- First and foremost, these model policies recognize that law enforcement personnel must take the appropriate steps to ensure that persons who are deaf and/or hard of hearing can communicate effectively. This includes the importance of providing auxiliary aids and services and reasonable accommodations when necessary for "effective communication" as required by the Americans with Disabilities Act, Section 504 of the Rehabilitation Act, and state laws.

- Law enforcement personnel must provide auxiliary aids and services without charge, including sign language interpreters, following notice and request, when necessary to ensure effective communication with deaf and/or hard of hearing individuals.

- Law enforcement personnel must post notices that auxiliary aids and services are available in locations near public entrances and processing areas in the city and county jails, in courthouse buildings, and in pretrial and related offices.

- When law enforcement personnel learn that a person is deaf and/or hard of hearing, they must ask that person whether auxiliary aids and services are necessary to ensure effective communication and will inform the person that these services are available without charge.

- Law enforcement personnel must use their best efforts to provide auxiliary aids and services in a timely manner.

- Law enforcement personnel must conduct interviews, medical screenings, and hearings through sign language with a qualified sign language interpreter when the deaf and/or hard of hearing person's primary means of communication is sign language.

- Persons who are deaf and who communicate in sign language cannot communicate when they are handcuffed. The model policies provide that law enforcement personnel will remove the handcuffs of booked and classified detainees who are deaf to allow for effective communication if the removal of the handcuffs does not result in a direct threat to the health and safety of any person in a jail or cause an undue burden or fundamental alteration of the custodial activity.

- Law enforcement personnel must have TTYs available so that equivalent phone service is available at no cost to the deaf person.

- Appropriate training must be provided for law enforcement personnel on the obligation to accommodate and provide auxiliary aids and services.

COMPUTER SYSTEMS

"President Johnson, in his 1968 State of the Union Message to Congress, announced a grand plan: 'To bring the most advanced technology to the war on crime in every city and county in America.' In less than ten months, Congress and the President had put into law the Omnibus Crime Control and Safe Streets Act of 1968. Among other initiatives, this law created the Law Enforcement Assistance Administration, LEAA, specifically to deliver on the President's promise of technological assistance."

(White, Radnor, & Jansik, 1975, p. 10)

The first real-time police computer system in the United States was installed in the St. Louis Police Department in the mid-1960s. The use of computer technology by the police has expanded rapidly since then. A number of factors have fueled this growth. Given the labor-intensive nature of police work and the tradition of devoting only a very small percentage of departmental resources to research and development, interest focused in the 1960s on improving police services by allocating dollars for equipment and technology. Recommendations in 1967 from the President's Commission on Law Enforcement and the Administration of Justice (The Crime Commission) suggested that technology might be an important tool for police work, and federal funding from the Law Enforcement Assistance Administration (LEAA) provided added resources to purchase such equipment (Colton, 1979).

Today, there is an incredible network of computer information available to law enforcement and others. Most officers with computers in their patrol vehicles have available national databases on individuals, including wanted persons, missing persons, probation and parolee information, and traffic and criminal histories; vehicles, including registered owners; other types of property; and hazardous property. These readily available databases provide officers a primary source of information to assist in making discretionary decisions concerning the handling of criminal suspects, drivers, and witnesses at the scene of an incident.

Along with the easy access of information comes the ability to misuse that information. In one case, a veteran police officer used a police computer to help her drug-dealing boyfriend identify undercover agents posing as drug buyers. The officer would run license numbers to determine if the owner of the vehicle was a police officer or if the car belonged to a law enforcement agency. An audit of the officer's computer revealed that more than fifty uses of the computer were for no apparent legitimate police use (Miller, 2000, p. 109). In most jurisdictions, the unauthorized use of a computer database by an officer is a crime.

Official Emails

Communicating by email is now more popular than using regular U.S. Mail (snail mail). Unfortunately, many times individuals use official email for unofficial uses.

Police officer uses computer to check driver's license numbers in his police car, IA. This in-car computer allows the officer to determine the validity of the license on the scene.

For example, in 2005 a police officer in Topeka, Kansas sent an email over the police net to a newspaper columnist criticizing a column that the columnist had written in the local newspaper. The veteran officer with a previously unblemished record was disciplined for his actions in using the police net. Attorneys will tell you that the "e" in email stands for "evidence" because merely deleting the email does not delete all records of it. Generally, the servers that transmit the email and the servers that receive it retain copies in the servers' permanent files. In one case, where a Midwestern University was investigating a professor for misconduct, the investigators were able to restore all the emails that the professor had received and transmitted for the previous year, even though the emails had been deleted by the professor.

In-Car Systems

In most agencies, police use in-car systems to check on license plates and people's criminal records. They also can file incident and arrest reports from their cars. The computers communicate with the police station on a radio network.

LAPD Used Police Computer Systems to Look Up Celebrities

The City of Los Angeles, California, paid Los Angeles police officer's ex-girlfriend $387,500 to settle a lawsuit alleging that the officer had used police computers to investigate her and hundreds of others, and sold the data to tabloids for a tidy profit.

According to the lawsuit, for six years the officer used Los Angeles Police Department computers to look up confidential law enforcement records on celebrities and other high-profile people, including Sharon Stone, Courteney Cox Arquette, Sean Penn, and Halle Berry.

The same officer was involved in another lawsuit, which was settled out of court. The lawsuit alleged that the officer had accessed the records to sell the information to tabloids. The officer claimed that he was just carrying out orders from superiors. According to internal LAPD documents, between 1994 and 2000 the officer tapped computer files on scores of celebrities, including Meg Ryan, Kobe Bryant, O. J. Simpson, Larry King, Drew Barrymore, Dionne Warwick, Farrah Fawcett, Cindy Crawford, and Elle Macpherson.

Source: LAPD used police computer systems to look up celebrities (2003, April 8). *Los Angeles Times,* A-1.

How the California Department of Motor Vehicles (DMV) Protects Your Information (From a California DMV press release dated June 2006)

The DMV has security measures in place to protect against loss, misuse, unauthorized access, or alteration of the information under its control. Information that is physically located within the DMV is protected by various security measures, which may include the following: access to confidential or sensitive information only by authorized individuals; secured entry to the different divisions that maintain the information; storage of confidential information in locked desks, files cabinets, and/or rooms; storage of confidential data files on floppy disks, which are then stored in locked desks or file cabinets; saving confidential files to a private drive on the Local Access Network (LAN); and computer password protection of confidential data files.

Department employees, consultants, contractors, and student assistants responsible for handling and protecting information maintained by the DMV department are required to sign an annual information security and disclosure statement that includes the following:

- A DMV employee may only access information when necessary to accomplish the DMV's mission and objectives. Information is not to be accessed or used for personal reasons.
- A DMV employee may only disclose information from DMV files or databases to individuals who have been authorized to receive it through appropriate DMV procedures.
- A DMV employee may not enter false or incomplete data or delete existing valid data in any database or file or take an unauthorized action that would cause

the interruption or denial of services, or the destruction or alteration of data or software.

- A DMV employee must take reasonable precautions to maintain the secrecy of any password used to access information.
- A DMV employee must take reasonable precautions to protect equipment from unauthorized access.
- Failure to comply with these policies will result in disciplinary action in accordance with state and federal laws and regulations and/or civil or criminal prosecution.

Notification When Your Information Is Released

California Vehicle Code (CVC) section 1810 allows the public to obtain your DMV information by filling out the Request for Driver License/Identification Card Information or the Request for Vehicle/Vessel Registration Information form (INF 70D/70R) and submitting the appropriate fee (provided on form) for each request.

Any request for information submitted on forms INF 70D or INF 70R, CVC section 1810 (b) requires the department to notify the record subject of the request. CVC sections 1808.21 and 1810.2 allow government and commercial requesters who have an account with the department that has been approved to obtain DMV record information for a legitimate business use to access your information without notifying you. CVC section 1808.22 (c) requires the department to notify you when the DMV releases your residence address to an attorney for a motor-vehicle-related incident.

In 2006, the police in Keene, New Hampshire discovered that their in-car computers interfered with a popular donut chain's computers. Officers, when obtaining donuts and coffee at the donut shop's drive-up window, were required to disable their computer modems to avoid interfering with the donut shop's computer system (*Boston Globe*, January 19, 2006, p. C-1).

DATA COMMUNICATIONS

Data networks help tie together public safety communications systems from beginning to end. Data networks include the automatic number identification/automatic location identification (ANI/ALI) data arriving with an initial 9-1-1 call for service through the responder's final status code transmission from a mobile data computer.

Data communications started with the World Wide Web; now it pervades our homes, offices, and even vehicles. The Internet and private networks are powered by a suite of protocols known as the Transmission Control Protocol/Internet Protocol (TCP/IP). TCP/IP connects physical components together in standardized ways.

The broad adoption of Internet protocols has also supported the growth of the Extensible Markup Language (XML). XML is the universal language of data communications, particularly for data that crosses system and jurisdictional boundaries.

COMPUTER NETWORKS

As the result of the Internet, there is an incredible amount of information that can be obtained on law enforcement by the average network user. In addition, most law enforcement agencies have their own website that may be located by doing a computer search. The reported decisions of most courts and federal and state statutes and regulations are available online. Listed in this section are some of the more popular websites:

Administrative Offices of the U.S. Courts: www.uscourts.gov

American Academy of Forensic Sciences: www.aafs.org

American Bar Association: www.abanet.org

Center for Problem-Oriented Policing: www.popcenter.org

Community Oriented Policing Services (COPS), U.S. Department of Justice: www.cops.usdoj.gov

Community Policing Consortium: www.communitypolicing.org

Denver, Colorado, Police Department: www. denvergov.org/Police

Drug Enforcement Administration: www.usdoj.gov/dea

Federal Bureau of Investigation: www.fbi.gov

Federal Judicial Center: www.fjc.gov

Fresno, California, Police Department: www.fresno.gov/fpd/policing

International Association of Chiefs of Police: www.theiacp.org

Justice Information Center: www.ncjrs.org

Kansas City, Kansas, Police Department: www.kckpd.org/copps.htm

Latest Crime and Justice News: www.crimenews.info

Links to Law Enforcement Agencies Nationwide: www.police.sas.ab.ca

List of Community Policing and Problem-Solving Programs: www.faculty.ncwc.edu/toconnor/comlist.htm

Metropolitan Washington Airports Authority Police Department: www.mwaa.com/authority/police

National Center for Community Policing, Michigan State University: www.cj.msu.edu/-people/cp/webpubs.html

National Center for Women and Policing: www.womenandpolicing.org

National Crime Prevention Council: www.ncpc.org/

New York Regional Community Policing Institute: www.jjay.cuny.edu/rcpi

Police Structure and Organization: A State-by-State Guide to Federal Agencies, State/County/Municipal Law Enforcement Agencies: www.faculty.ncwc.edu/toconnor/polstruct.htm

Policing in Canada: www.psepc.gc.ca/policing

Tampa, Florida, Police Department: www.tampagov.net/dept_police

U.S. Bureau of Alcohol, Tobacco, Firearms and Explosives (ATF): www.atf.gov

U.S. Bureau of Justice Assistance: www.ojp.usdoj.gov/BJA

U.S. Department of Justice: www.usdoj.gov

U.S. Treasury Department: www.ustreas.gov

Vancouver, British Columbia Police Department: www.city.vancouver.bc.ca/police

SUMMARY

- Communications encompasses three essential elements: it is a process, not an isolated event; it involves at least two persons; and its primary purpose is the exchange of information.

- Communications is not an isolated event in that it requires at least five basic steps: the transmitting of an idea or information, the sending of the idea through a medium, receiving the message, understanding of the idea, and providing feedback to the sender.

- The concept of transmitting an idea implies the formation of one or more thoughts and the desire to express these thoughts.

- Communications cannot occur in a vacuum. There must be at least two people involved.

- The primary purpose of the communication must be to transmit information.

- Communications within a law enforcement agency may be horizontal, downward, or upward. Communications may also be considered as formal or informal.

- Police officers speak a unique language—one that is often considered by others as slang. Police jargon or slang serves a useful purpose. It helps communicate concepts unique to law enforcement more efficiently to other officers. The biggest handicap with the use of jargon is that it is often used when an officer is dealing with members of the community-at-large who may not understand the jargon.

- Most law enforcement agencies use at least three or more radio frequencies. The three common frequencies are the primary channel, an administrative channel, and a car-to-car channel. Some larger police agencies use over 100 frequencies and many

of their police divisions, bureaus, and specialized units have their own channels.

- A radio wave is the basic building block of radio communications. The entire pattern of a wave, before it repeats itself, is called a cycle. The number of cycles, or times that a wave repeats in a second, is called frequency. Frequency is measured in the unit hertz (Hz), referring to a number of cycles per second.

- Radio spectrum is the complete range of frequencies from approximately 30 kHz up to more than 300 GHz that can be used for radio communications. Frequencies are often grouped in ranges called bands. Bands of interest to public safety include HF (high frequency), VHF (very high frequency), UHF (ultra high frequency), and most recently SHF (super high frequency). The Federal Communications Commission (FCC) regulates use of the non-federal spectrum, including that used by state and local public safety agencies.

- Listening and talking on the radio are acquired skills that take practice to become proficient. Keep your radio traffic professional. Each officer with a radio is assigned a call sign. Use the call signs rather than an officer's name.

- Most law enforcement agencies use a code system as a shorthand method of transmitting information. The 10 code is the most widely used system. It is also the code adopted by the Association of Public Safety Officers.

- Police agencies generally use identification designations for call signs.

- When an officer arrives at the scene of a crime, one of the officer's first responsibilities is to broadcast information about the crime to dispatch and other patrol units.

- Most citizens contact the police by telephone. Agencies generally have set policies for answering telephone calls. In the larger agencies, the telephones are usually answered by a dispatcher. In the smaller agencies, officers often provide relief assistance for the dispatcher. The general rule is that each call will be handled in an efficient and proficient manner.

- The 9-1-1 system is used for emergencies and a different line is for non-emergencies. However, many emergency calls are received on non-emergency lines. 9-1-1 is the official national emergency number in the United States and Canada. The 9-1-1 network is also part of the nation's emergency response and disaster preparedness system. Although the term 9-1-1 has come to mean the entire public safety communications system, in fact, it's simply a dedicated telephone system for relaying calls from the public.

- Communicating with persons from other cultures or encountering an individual speaking a foreign language has become more common during routine patrol. Officers must be prepared to communicate effectively in our present multicultural environment.

Classroom Discussion Questions and Activities

1. The police in New Jersey stop two different drivers after the police had randomly checked their license plate numbers. The lawyer representing both drivers claims that unrestricted use of computers in police cars to check on vehicle registration and driving records is an unreasonable search and seizure. The New Jersey Attorney General's office asserted that the computers are a valid crime-fighting tool and using them is not an illegal search. All vehicles entering or leaving the City of London or British seaports are being watched by robot automatic number plate scanners, which feed the data to the Police National Computer (PNC) in Hendon. The PNC replies within five seconds if the vehicles are "of interest" to police. Should there be restrictions on such police activities? If so, what should they be?

2. Should law enforcement agencies attempt to eliminate the use of jargon by their officers?

3. Should citizens be allowed to monitor police radio communications?

4. Go on the Internet and listen to a police department scanner. You can access and listen to the New York Police Department general radio traffic or other major police departments at: www.dxzone.com/catalog/Internet_and_Radio/Police_Scanners/

References

Blair, G. B., & Slick, S. L. (1990, January). Survival Spanish: Needed training for Police. *The Police Chief, 57*, pp. 42–47.

Colton, K. W. (1979, January). The impact and use of computer technology by the police. *Social Impacts of Computing, 22* (1), pp. 10–11.

Marnell, H. *An unofficial history of the Los Angeles Police Department's communications division.* Posted at website: www.harrymarnell.com/kma367.htm. Accessed August 13, 2006.

Miller, M. R. (2000). *Police patrol operations* (2nd ed.). Incline Village, NV: Copperhouse.

National Institute of Justice Publication No. 212975. (2006, February). *Radio spectrum.*

Technical Working Group for Eyewitness Evidence (1999, October). *Eyewitness evidence: A guide for law enforcement.* Washington, DC: National Institute of Justice.

Thiederman, S. Language barriers: Bridging the gap. Posted at website: www.diversityworking.com/diversityManagement/language_barriers.php. Accessed August 17, 2006.

U.S. Navy. (1913). *The bluejackets' manual.* Annapolis: Naval Institute Press.

Vera Institute Report. (2006, August). *Translating justice: Overcoming language barriers.* New York.

Wallace, H., & Roberson, C. (2004). *Written and interpersonal communications methods for law enforcement.* (3rd ed.). Upper Saddle River, NJ: Prentice-Hall.

White, M., Radnor, M., & Jansik, D. (1975). *Management and policy science in American government: Problems and prospects.* Lexington, MA: D. C. Heath.

Chapter 11

Gangs and Drugs

" We need to send a clear message to gang members that violent crime will not be tolerated. "

—Tim Bishop Congressman,
1st District, New York

CHAPTER OUTLINE

O B J E C T I V E S

After completion of this chapter, you will be able to do the following:

- Discuss the history of gangs.
- Identify the role gangs play in the community.
- Understand why individuals join gangs.
- Identify the major gangs and their general locations.
- Identify the role that gangs play in illegal substance abuse.
- Discuss the problems that face our society as a result of drugs and alcohol.
- Distinguish between the crimes of possession, possession for sale, and sale of controlled substances.
- Be able to list the different types of alcohol-related crimes.
- Be familiar with the various proposed alternative solutions to these offenses.
- Describe the procedures involving in testing police officers for substance abuse.
- Explain the relationship between drugs and gangs.

I N T R O D U C T I O N

This chapter will cover both gangs and illegal substance abuse. While they are two separate topics, because gang members are generally involved in substance abuse as users, distributors, or pushers, there is considerable overlap in the two topics. This does not mean to imply that trafficking in illegal drugs necessarily includes gangs. Patrol officers generally deal with both gangs and substance abuse on a daily basis. Also included in this chapter are discussions on solutions to the substance abuse problems, alcohol-related crimes, and the drug testing of police officers.

GANGS

"Once found principally in large cities, violent street gangs now affect public safety, community image, and quality of life in communities of all sizes in urban, suburban, and rural areas. No region of the United States is untouched by gangs. Gangs affect society at all levels, causing heightened fears for safety, violence, and economic costs."
—2005 National Gang Threat Assessment, National Alliance of Gang Investigators Associations

What constitutes a "criminal gang?" A criminal gang is defined under the Nevada Revised Statutes (193.168, Section 6) as any combination of persons, organized formally or informally, so constructed that the organization will continue its operation even if individual members enter or leave the organization, which (a) has a common name or identifying symbol; (b) has particular conduct, status, and customs indicative of it; and (c) has as one of its common activities engaging in criminal activity punishable as a felony, other than the conduct that constitutes the primary offense.

The California Department of Justice requires that a group meet all of the following criteria to be considered a gang (Allnut & Pennell, 2000, p. 13):

- Have a name and identifiable leadership.
- Claim a territory, turf, neighborhood, or criminal enterprise.
- Associate on a continuous or regular basis.
- Engage in delinquent or criminal behavior.

To be documented as a gang member by the California Department of Justice, an individual had to meet at least one of the following criteria:

- Admit gang membership.
- Have tattoos or wear or possess clothing or paraphernalia associated with a specific gang.
- Be observed participating in delinquent or criminal activity with known gang members.
- Be known to the police as having a close association with known gang members.
- Be identified by a reliable informant as a gang member.

Bloods and Crips gang truce after Los Angeles riots in 1992. Unfortunately, the truce did not last very long.

On April 20, 2005, Stephen Johnson, Senior Policy Analyst for Latin America at the Kathryn and Shelby Cullom Davis Institute for International Studies, testified before the Subcommittee on the Western Hemisphere, U.S. House of Representatives, regarding the status of gangs in the United States. Johnson noted that throughout history, gangs have flourished when there were population shifts and unstable neighborhoods. According to Johnson, gang membership has increased exponentially since the 1960s. He noted that the gangs that flourished in Los Angeles in the 1960s have expanded to other cities in the United States and into Mexico and Central America.

Johnson stated that gang membership represented only a faction of the general population. He estimated that there are 700,000 street gang members, compared to some 280 million American residents. (One congressperson noted that 700,000 did not seem like a small faction to him.) Johnson expressed concern over the disproportionate growth and violence of gangs. The number of cities reporting gang problems increased from 270 in 1970 to more than 2,500 by 1998; an increase of approximately 800 percent. The National Youth Gang Survey (NYGS, 2005) estimated that there were 21,500 gangs and 731,500 active members in the United States. It is also estimated that U.S.-based gangs have fraternal links to some 300,000 gang members in Mexico and Central America. NYGS estimated that 85 percent of the gang members reside in large cities.

Johnson (2005) stated that most of the trouble starts with unstable neighborhoods. He also indicated that broken homes, violent role models, and access to drugs feed gang growth. Some of his conclusions include:

- Youths living where acquaintances were in trouble with law enforcement were three times more likely to join gangs.
- Children living in single-parent families with other adults were three times more likely to join gangs than children living in two-parent families.
- Youths with low academic achievement were more than three times as likely to join gangs.
- Poor academic performance and low commitment to school correspond to gang membership.
- Youths who used marijuana frequently were almost four times as likely to join a gang as youths who did not use marijuana or who only experimented with it.
- Youths who engage in early violent behavior were more than three times as likely to join gangs.

There are regional differences in gang structure and activities. The larger cities typically have more gangs, larger gangs, and gangs that have been in existence for longer periods of time. The large cities also tend to have gangs that are more involved in serious criminal activity, are more highly organized, and have a more identifiable leadership structure. Delinquent gangs are more common in smaller cities and tend to be more loosely organized, with ephemeral leadership. The smaller cities' gangs are generally newer and lack historic roots. Delinquent gangs appear to be the most typical among Southeast and Midwest cities. In the Western States, violent gangs are the most common. Income-generating gangs (including drug-dealing gangs) are reported most commonly in the Northeast (Reed & Decker, 2002, p. 43).

Anti-Gang Tactics

"Police have tried a wide variety of measures to address the problem of gangs at the local level. They have employed situational crime prevention, for example, altering the flow of vehicular traffic to reduce gang-related violence; enforcing anti-loitering statutes to keep gangs from intimidating and menacing community members; using civil injunctions to keep gang members out of areas where they cause trouble; setting up traffic checkpoints; carrying out aggressive curfew and truancy enforcement; and cracking down on weapons violations, often using federal laws that impose stiffer penalties. Some jurisdictions have used a technique known as 'lever pulling,' targeting specific chronic offenders with warrants, close supervision of probation conditions, and other measures."

Source: Taken from Reed & Decker, 2002, p. 66. **Note:** Internal citations omitted.

anti-gang tactics / Tactics targeted to reduce gang problems; includes mediation, situational crime prevention, working with families, and other strategies.

Law enforcement approaches to controlling the gang problems vary among the communities. Many agencies have integrated **anti-gang tactics** into community or problem-oriented approaches to gangs. The anti-gang tactics include mediation, situational crime prevention, working with families, and other strategies (Reed & Decker, 2002, p. 66). Many researchers, including Klein (1997), contend that anti-gang tactics that involve only law enforcement will solidify gangs by increasing cohesion among gang members. It appears that policing strategies are most effective when teamed with intervention programs, such as providing economic opportunities, job training, remedial education, and other services and community involvement (Reed & Decker, 2002, pp. 66–67). These diverse strategies may be necessary to deal with highly versatile and adaptive gangs.

Anti-Gang Legislation

Most states have found traditional criminal law to be adequate in prosecuting most of the crimes committed by gang members (ILJ, 1994). However, some gang-related offenses, like drive-by shootings, also are not adequately covered. Many states have enacted new statutes that target criminal street gang activity.

Subject matter state statutes that have been enacted since the 1960s in efforts to control gangs or were promoted as anti-gang legislation include:

- Possessing a dangerous weapon on school property or in a vehicle at school.
- Discharging a firearm out of a motor vehicle.
- Aiming a firearm at a human being or discharging a weapon where a person might be endangered.
- Imposing an additional penalty for the procurement or solicitation of a minor to commit certain violations as an agent.
- Establishing additional penalties for committing certain violations at or near schools, school bus stops, or recreational facilities for minors.
- Creating penalties for felonies committed on a school bus.
- Increasing the penalty for felonies committed to promote activities of a criminal gang (referred to as the "gang sentencing enhancement statute").

The primary federal statutes used to prosecute street gangs are:

- The Racketeer Influenced and Corrupt Organizations (RICO) Act
- The Continuing Criminal Enterprise (CCE) statutes that are part of the Comprehensive Drug Abuse Prevention and Control Act of 1970.

These two acts are designed to attack the conspiratorial nature of gangs and require prosecutors to present evidence of multiple criminal acts committed by various gang members to establish a pattern of criminal activity by the gangs. For RICO prosecutions the prosecutor must establish evidence of racketeering acts, known as predicate acts.

A **RICO predicate act** can include any substantive criminal act such as illegal drug distribution, fraud, theft, or illegal gambling. In addition to establishing the predicate act or acts, the prosecutor must also establish that the enterprise (company or gang) was involved in the activities that resulted in the criminal acts being committed. An advantage of prosecuting a gang and its members under RICO is that the prosecutor, in establishing the predicate acts, can show the full range of the gang activities, whereas if the gang members were prosecuted for a distinct crime, such as murder, the prosecutor would be limited in presenting evidence of other crimes committed by the gang. Accordingly, a prosecution under RICO allows the prosecutor to convey a clear overall picture of a gang's criminal activity. Prosecutions under the CCE statutes are very similar to the RICO prosecutions, with the additional requirement that the predicate acts must be in violation of a substance abuse statute. RICO also has provisions for civil actions to obtain forfeitures of gang property.

RICO predicate act / A basic criminal act; can include any substantive criminal act such as illegal drug distribution, fraud, theft, or illegal gambling.

Gang Prosecution

"Many states use existing criminal statutes to address gang crime rather than enact separate gang legislation. These include accessory, aiding and abetting, racketeering, habitual offender, harassment, and witness intimidation statutes. Even in states with anti-gang legislation, prosecutors' familiarity with existing criminal codes may predispose them to proceed with normal charging practices, avoiding the complexities and difficulties of some anti-gang statutes."

—Reed & Decker, 2002, p. 191

Anti-gang legislation helps prosecutors in plea-bargaining negotiations. By requiring a prison sentence and a doubling of the prison term, the threat of conviction under a gang sentencing enhancement statute is a powerful inducement to encourage a defendant to enter a guilty plea. In addition, the threat of a gang sentencing enhancement conviction is often brought up in a subtle, less direct manner in plea bargaining negotiations.

Many cities and counties have established special gang prosecution units. A typical unit is the Clark County, Nevada, Gang Prosecution Unit, which is designed to reduce the level of gang violence in the community (Las Vegas) and to enhance communication among law enforcement agencies (federal, state, county, and school police), prosecutors' offices, community-based organizations, probation departments, schools, community leaders, and family members of gangs and potential gang members. The Clark County unit uses both a proactive and reactive approach to increase gang intelligence and investigation. The unit works closely with the Special

Officer Dan Robbins of the Los Angeles Police Department on Friday, January 26, 2007, pictured at the 77th Division central booking with Jose Covarrubias, a gang member arrested on suspicion of having drug paraphernalia.

Enforcement Detail of the Las Vegas Police Department to compile information on currently active gang members and associates in the community. The gang prosecution staff meets regularly with this police unit to discuss use of particular informants, constitutional issues, and victim/witness support resources (Reed & Decker, 2002, p. 177).

The Clark County unit adopted the following tactics to achieve its goals:

- Using a computerized gang offender-based tracking system to monitor gang activity.
- Prosecution of gang-related crime through vertical prosecution. (Vertical prosecution is where the same team of prosecutors takes the case from start to finish.)
- Taking a "team approach" to improve interagency coordination of gang intelligence and facilitate multijurisdictional investigations.
- Monitoring parole and probation for gang members to facilitate revocations for offenders who continue to participate in gang-related activities.
- Establishing a gang hotline through the Las Vegas Metropolitan Police Department to increase gang intelligence and contact with victims and witnesses of gang activity.
- Establishing a victim/witness protection program that provides physical security against potential threats and violence by gang members.

National Gang Threat Assessment

Note: The material for this section was taken directly from the National Gang Threat Assessment Report (2005).

The 2005 National Gang Threat Assessment was a collaborative effort of the U.S. Department of Justice and state and local individuals involved in anti-gang activities. Funding for the effort was provided by a grant from the U.S. Department of Justice, Bureau of Justice Assistance (BJA). Surveys were mailed to hundreds of investigators who are members of the fifteen state and regional gang investigators associations that comprise the National Alliance of Gang Investigators Associations (NAGIA). These responses from local law enforcement officers form the basis for the assessments contained in this section. To this information on gang activity was added intelligence generated by the Federal Bureau of Investigation (FBI), National Drug Intelligence Center (NDIC), and local intelligence collection organizations.

The 2005 National Gang Threat Assessment revealed several new trends in gang activity and gang migration:

- Hispanic gang membership is growing, especially in the Northeast and South.
- Gangs are more sophisticated in their use of technology and computers and are using these tools to perpetrate criminal acts.
- Respondents reiterated that gangs remain a constant threat, that they are still growing in membership and violence, and that denial by communities is a gang's greatest ally.

As gangs migrate across the country, they bring with them crime and violence. Reasons for migration range from expansion of territories to families moving because of jobs or incarceration. As families move, they bring with them children, associates, and long-distance ties to gangs. The migration of gang members leads to the establishment of gangs in neighborhoods previously gang-free and may bring new arrivals into potentially deadly conflict with local gangs. Many times the migratory pattern, as well as the genesis and growth of home-grown gangs, is indirectly aided by official denial. This allows the gangs to work with anonymity, establishing gang turfs that support narcotics networks and neighborhood drug dealing. Gang members returning from prison also have an impact on neighborhoods. Jurisdictions with returning members have documented notable increases in violence and drug trafficking. Lack of community-assistance programs for these individuals only compounds the problem.

General Trends with Gangs

Law enforcement respondents to the 2005 National Gang Threat Assessment noted several trends that were prevalent across the country:

- Gangs remain the primary distributors of drugs throughout the United States.
- Gangs are associating with organized crime entities, such as Mexican drug organizations, Asian criminal groups, and Russian organized crime groups. These groups often turn to gangs to conduct low-level criminal activities, protect territories, and facilitate drug-trafficking activities. Financial gain is the primary goal of any association between these groups.
- Gang members are becoming more sophisticated in their use of computers and technology. These new tools are used to communicate, facilitate criminal activity, and avoid detection by law enforcement.

- Few gangs have been found to associate with domestic terrorist organizations.
- The susceptibility of gang members to any type of terrorist organization appears to be highest in prison.
- Prison gangs pose a unique threat to law enforcement and communities.
- Incarceration of gang members often does little to disrupt their activities. High-ranking gang members are often able to exert their influence on the street from within prison.
- Hispanic gang membership is on the rise. These gangs are migrating and expanding their jurisdictions throughout the country. Identification and differentiation of these gangs pose new obstacles for law enforcement, especially in rural communities.
- Migration of California-style gang culture remains a particular threat. The migration spreads the reach of gangs into new neighborhoods and promotes a flourishing gang subculture.
- While the number of all-female gangs remains low, the role of women in gangs is evolving. Women are taking more active roles, assisting in the movement of drugs and weapons, and gathering intelligence from other gangs.
- Indian Country is increasingly reporting escalating levels of gang activity and gang-related crime and drug trafficking. The remote nature of many reservations and a thriving gang subculture make youth in these environments particularly vulnerable to gangs.
- Outlaw motorcycle gangs (OMGs) are expanding their territory and forming new clubs. This is reflected in increased violence among OMGs as they battle over territories.
- Approximately 31 percent of survey respondents indicated that their communities refused to acknowledge the gang problem. Several communities only began to address gang issues when high-profile gang-related incidents occurred.
- Forming multi-agency task forces and joint community groups is an effective way to combat the problem. However, decreases in funding and staffing to many task forces have created new challenges for communities.

While general trends were apparent across the nation, each region also noted specific trends affecting their communities.

Northeast

- Neighborhood or home-grown gangs and hybrid gangs are being seen with increasing frequency.
- A growth of gangs within Hispanic immigrant communities has occurred recently, bringing increased violence and crime to many communities.
- The frequency of incidents of gang-related violence and drug trafficking on Indian reservations has increased.
- Gang members display a lack of respect for their community and for law enforcement.
- This region is particularly vulnerable to drug distribution by gangs because of the compact nature of the region and the well-developed transportation infrastructure.

- Gangs are reported to be most frequently involved in crimes relating to vandalism and graffiti, firearms possession, assault, and homicide.

South

- Mara Salvatrucha (MS-13) is one of the newest threats to the region, especially in Washington, DC, Virginia, and the surrounding areas.
- The growth of gangs within the Hispanic community has brought increased levels of violence and crime to the region.
- Communities are noting increases in graffiti and tagging.
- Neighborhood or home-grown gangs are reported throughout the region.
- Gangs in this region are most likely to be involved in the distribution and sale of marijuana and cocaine.

Midwest

- Gang activity around schools and college campuses has increased.
- Gangs are concealing their affiliations and colors to hide from law enforcement.
- Gangs are substantially involved in both the wholesale and street-level distribution of drugs in this region.
- Gangs are increasingly cooperating with each other to facilitate crime and drug trafficking.
- Gang and drug activity in Indian Country has increased.
- Indian Country is being affected by the high level of drug trafficking. Hispanic street gangs are reportedly using Native Americans to transport narcotics onto reservations.

West

- Gangs are employing an increased level of sophistication in the planning and execution of criminal acts, especially against law enforcement officers.
- Street gangs are frequently involved in the distribution of both marijuana and methamphetamine.
- The number of cases of identity and credit card theft perpetrated by gang members has increased.
- Reports indicate an increased use of firearms by gang members.
- Approximately three-quarters of respondents to this survey reported moderate to high involvement of gangs in the street-level distribution of drugs.
- More than 90 percent of respondents in this region reported some level of gang involvement in vandalism and graffiti.

HISPANIC GANGS

Note: The material for this section was taken directly from the National Gang Threat Assessment Report (2005).

Hispanic gangs are not a new phenomenon in the United States; however, they have increasingly become a concern for law enforcement agencies in recent years.

The Hispanic population in the United States in 2003 was reported to be 39.9 million; an increase of 13 percent from the 2000 census. As a result of the continuous growth in the Hispanic population throughout the United States, Hispanic gang membership is also increasing. The 2001 National Youth Gang Survey reported that 49 percent of all gang members were Hispanic/Latino, an increase of 2 percent from 1999 survey results. As Hispanic men and women migrate, both legally and illegally, to rural and urban areas in the United States, they are confronted by language challenges, limited employment options, and victimization by gangs already operating in the area. Faced with these obstacles, gang membership is often viewed as a viable option. As Hispanic gang membership rises throughout the United States, law enforcement pays more attention to it. More gang members are being arrested than ever before.

Another aspect of Hispanic gang membership impacting law enforcement efforts concerns the implications rising from illegal immigrant arrests and deportations. Deported individuals often maintain their ties to gangs in the United States, resulting in the extension of criminal enterprises into other countries. Hispanic gang members find it easier to access drugs and weapons in their home countries and courier the items back to the United States rather than to conduct their operations within the United States. U.S. currency used to pay for drugs and weapons is easily exchanged and has a much higher value in many foreign countries.

In addition, gangs identified and targeted by law enforcement may migrate to areas where law enforcement is unfamiliar with them and they are freer to continue their criminal activity. Hispanic gang members take advantage of the language and cultural obstacles posed to law enforcement in areas where there has not been a very large Hispanic population in the past.

The following sections define and describe some of the most recent issues affecting law enforcement efforts to identify and dismantle Hispanic gangs.

Prominent Hispanic Gangs

Law enforcement agencies were asked to report the presence of several Hispanic gangs in their region. Of the reporting agencies, more than 50 percent indicated that Los Sureños (Sur 13) was present in their region. Nearly 40 percent of agencies reported moderate to high Sur 13 gang activity. The presence of Sur 13 was reported in 87.8 percent of jurisdictions reporting in the Western region. Approximately 45 percent of law enforcement agencies also reported the presence of the Latin Kings, with 16.7 percent indicating moderate or high gang activity.

The identification and differentiation of Hispanic street gangs poses obstacles for law enforcement across the nation. These prominent street gangs are described briefly here.

Sur 13: During the 1980s, California street gangs were divided into Sureños (Southerners) and Norteños (Northerners)—umbrella terms for Hispanic street gangs in California. These terms are used to distinguish whether the gang is from the northern or southern part of the state. Southern gangs are closely associated with the Mexican Mafia and often use the number 13 in their gangs and tagging, as M is the thirteenth letter of the alphabet.

As various southern California gang members migrated from the state, many began to unite under the name Sureño. Additionally, as a result of the gang's close connection to the Mexican Mafia, the group retained the use of the number 13 in its name. Thus, as gang members began to appear in the Southwest and on the East Coast, they referred to themselves as both **Sur 13** and Los Sureños.

It is important to note that hundreds of Hispanic gangs identify with the Sureño philosophy and use the number 13 as part of their gang identifiers. The presence of the number 13 does not necessarily indicate affiliation with the Mexican Mafia. Claiming Sureño merely indicates that the gang resides or originated in southern California; in some cases the gang may not be from southern California, but simply identifies with the Sureño gang style. Many Sureño gangs are rivals of each other. For example, Florencia 13 is a Sureño gang, but is an enemy of MS-13 in some areas.

Northern California street gangs are considered Norteños and use the number 14, as N is the fourteenth letter of the alphabet. Norteño gangs are rivals of Sureño gangs, but just as Sureño gangs are not all aligned with each other, Norteño gangs are not necessarily aligned with other Norteños.

California is redefining the ways that law enforcement traditionally considers Norteño and Sureño alliances and rivalries. After observing increasing numbers of Sureño gangs from southern California migrating to northern California, law enforcement noted the following trends:

- Local northern California gangs, typically in conflict with each other over drug trafficking and territorial issues, are now collaborating in order to resist the Sureño gangs migrating from the South.

- The Sureños migrating from the South are conflicting with their counterparts who reside in northern California because they believe they are more like Norteños than Sureños.

- Hispanic gangs in northern California are negotiating with an outlaw motorcycle gang to acquire drugs in exchange for allegiance against another OMG, which has aligned with southern Hispanic gangs.

In light of these trends, law enforcement must recognize that the terms Norteños and Sureños are no longer sufficient to describe California street gangs. When documenting gang members in their local areas, law enforcement must deliberately note not only an individual's gang affiliation, but also where the individual is from and the gang's local allies and rivals.

Sur 13 was reported to be present in every region and in thirty-five states across the country. More than 50 percent of law enforcement respondents indicated the presence of Sur 13 in their jurisdictions, with 39.5 percent of agencies reporting moderate to high activity. It must be noted that there are no national Los Sureños or Sur 13 hierarchical gangs. While there may be loose connection among some gangs using the Los Sureños or Sur 13 name, most of these gangs are not connected to one another. They simply may have latched onto the name for their local group from media sources or gang-connected relatives. They may not even be aware of other Sureños.

Mara Salvatrucha (MS-13): **MS-13**, a primarily El Salvadoran street gang, originated in Los Angeles in the 1980s. Since then, the gang has successfully migrated from southern California to the East Coast, establishing a significant presence in Virginia, Maryland, North Carolina, and New York. MS-13 formed in the Rampart area of Los Angeles, which was heavily populated by Mexican-American gangs. After being constantly victimized by the dominant Mexican gangs, El Salvadoran immigrants banded together for protection, thus enlarging their membership and force. The group called itself Mara Salvatrucha, or MS, and as it grew in size, it aligned with the

Sur 13 / Southern gangs that are closely associated with the Mexican Mafia and often use the number 13 in their gangs and tagging, as M is the thirteenth letter of the alphabet.

MS-13 / A primarily El Salvadoran street gang that originated in Los Angeles in the 1980s.

Mexican Mafia under the Los Sureños umbrella. Once aligned with the Mexican Mafia, the group incorporated the number 13 in its name. MS-13, while maintaining independent leadership and organization, remains affiliated with the Mexican Mafia.

The presence of MS-13 was reported in the jurisdictions of 145 law enforcement agencies across the country, although only 12.1 percent of respondents indicated that this gang had moderate to high activity. MS-13 was present in thirty-one states.

18th Street / An Hispanic gang formed in the 1960s, composed of individuals with mixed racial backgrounds.

18th Street: **18th Street**, formed in the 1960s, is a Hispanic gang composed of individuals with mixed racial backgrounds. One of the largest and oldest Hispanic gangs, 18th Street's acceptance of immigrants and its lack of racial barriers enabled this group to grow and expand substantially. Originating in Los Angeles, the gang has migrated up the West Coast and over the Midwest to the East Coast. 18th Street is calculated in its expansion and recruitment, reportedly recruiting in elementary and middle schools. It is also known to have counterparts in Mexico and throughout Central America. 18th Street is known to maintain ties with the Mexican Mafia on the West Coast and to have rivalries with MS-13.

Law enforcement officials reported activity by 18th Street in 31.4 percent of jurisdictions. Regionally, while only 22 percent of reporting agencies in the Northeast indicated the presence of 18th Street, 60.9 percent of law enforcement respondents from the West Coast reported its presence.

Latin Kings / An Hispanic gang, also known as the Almighty Latin King Nation (ALKN), formed in Chicago in the mid-1960s.

Latin Kings: The **Latin Kings**, also known as the Almighty Latin King Nation (ALKN), formed in Chicago in the mid-1960s. In the 1980s, after a lengthy power struggle with members of the Chicago faction, the Connecticut- and New York-based Latin Kings chapters separated and formed the Almighty Latin Charter Nation and the Almighty Latin King and Queen Nation (ALKQN), respectively. Both regional factions have operated autonomously from the Chicago faction and abide by their own constitutions. State contingencies generally exercise allegiance to one of these three major factions. Gang membership consists predominately of Puerto Rican males, although individuals of other ethnicities—including Spanish, Portuguese, Italian, and South American—are allowed to become members. The Latin Kings have regional chapters across the Midwest, the East Coast, the central states, Texas, and California, with an estimated 25,000 to 50,000 members nationwide and nearly 20,000 members residing within Chicago alone. In particular, the New York, New Jersey, and Connecticut regions are hotbeds for Latin Kings activity, including drug-related crime and bitter gang turf wars.

Nearly half of reporting agencies—44.8 percent—documented the presence of the Latin Kings in their jurisdictions. Seventy percent of law enforcement respondents in the Northeast reported the presence of the Latin Kings, while 56.9 percent of respondents in the Midwest reported their presence.

Migration of Sureños into the Southwestern United States

Sureño gang members are migrating out of California into the southwestern part of the United States and have been well-documented in Arizona, New Mexico, and Texas. Information suggests that members of Sureño street gangs are migrating out of California as a result of prison transfers and to avoid the state's tough three-strikes laws. Once outside California, the members assimilate under the name Sureños or

Sur 13. While some gangs continue to pay taxes to the Mexican Mafia and assist in its drug distribution, others cut ties to California and operate as a local gang. It is not uncommon for gangs in these other states to form using the name Sureños—when they have no ties to California other than an affinity for the name—so they can bask under the reputation of the Sureños style.

The migration of Sureño gangs from California poses a threat in terms of drug trafficking and violence because of their extensive criminal networks. These networks not only facilitate the expansion of drug-trafficking enterprises, they also allow gangs to easily replace local leaders in the event of arrest or death. Law enforcement should closely monitor their criminal activity and their contact with gang members in California, both on the street and in correctional institutions.

Identifying and Distinguishing Hispanic Gangs

The ability to identify and distinguish Hispanic gangs and cliques creates a unique challenge for law enforcement; however, it is essential for anticipating criminal activity and rivalries, as well as for preventing gang expansion and recruitment.

For example, while Sur 13 and MS-13 street gangs use similar identifiers in their tags and tattoos, the gangs differ greatly in composition, typical *modus operandi*, and allies and rivals. In order to effectively target and dismantle violent criminal enterprises, law enforcement officials must be aware of the subtle differences between these groups.

Gang Coordination and Alliances

Recent information suggests that law enforcement officials are seeing an increased effort on the part of some Hispanic gangs to organize their members into a criminal enterprise. The different ALKQN cliques in the New York area came together several years ago under one leader in New York and attempted to align with one of their largest rivals, the Bloods. More recently, information gleaned by law enforcement indicates that MS-13 clique leaders from the United States and Central America have been holding meetings in an attempt to coordinate all MS-13 members under one leadership umbrella. There has also been some speculation that MS-13 leaders would like to bring 18th Street and MS-13 together to become the strongest Hispanic gang in Central America and the United States. Recent violence occurring between MS-13 and 18th Street, and within the gangs themselves in several jurisdictions, indicates that attempts to align the two gangs have not yet been successful.

Although some Hispanic gangs have developed extensive networks, most Hispanic gangs are not coordinated. Hispanic gang behavior in one jurisdiction may not carry over to another. Members adapt to the area in which they operate, and this may differ from location to location.

Foreign Law Enforcement Efforts to Combat Gangs

Hispanic gangs have also become the focus of numerous law enforcement efforts abroad. In Central America, approximately 30,000 gang members, particularly in

Honduras, El Salvador, and Guatemala, are being targeted for a major law enforcement crackdown. Many of these members are affiliated with MS-13 and 18th Street, two of the most prominent gangs in Central and North America. In August 2003, Honduras implemented anti-gang laws, making it illegal to participate in a gang formed to perpetuate criminal activity. The penalty carries a maximum prison sentence of twelve years. El Salvador declared a state of emergency, enacting an anti-gang initiative in July 2003. While similar legislation is pending enactment in Guatemala, all three countries have initiated anti-gang operations.

As a result of the Central American anti-gang initiatives, the United States may become fertile ground for international gangs fleeing newly established or reformed anti-gang laws. While the United States is aggressive in deporting convicted gang members of international origin, gang members are reportedly using the Bureau of Immigration and Customs Enforcement's Temporary Protective Status (TPS) to remain in the United States and avoid gang prosecution in Central America.

TPS was established for Central American nationals as a result of the natural disasters occurring in Honduras and El Salvador. The status allows migrants from these two areas to remain in the United States for a designated period of time and apply for work. Under TPS, a migrant can only be deported if convicted of a felony or more than one misdemeanor.

FEMALE GANGS

Note: The material for this section was taken directly from the National Gang Threat Assessment Report (2005).

Young women continue to take active roles in gangs. Although the number of female gangs is increasing, street gangs are still predominately made up of males. The 2000 National Youth Gang Survey revealed that only 6 percent of the nation's gang members were female. All-female gangs continue to be an anomaly, as most female gang members tend to be affiliated with male gangs. In fact, the 2000 National Youth Gang Survey respondents reported that 39 percent of all youth gangs had female members; however, 82 percent of respondents reported that none of the gangs in their jurisdictions were predominately composed of females.

The responsibilities of females in gangs are evolving. While they continue to assume the traditionally subordinate functions of providing emotional, physical, and sexual support to male gang members, females are taking more active roles in gangs, as some female gang members have graduated from affiliate status to membership.

This elevation in status also involves an elevation in risk. Females now assist in the movement of drugs and weapons for male gang members and gather intelligence from rival gangs. Others are committing drug sales, robberies, assaults, and drive-by shootings on behalf of male gang members. Respondents to the 2005 National Gang Threat Assessment Survey reported that female gang members in their jurisdictions most often:

- Assist male gang members in committing crimes
- Carry drugs and weapons and provide safe houses for contraband
- Commit assaults and larcenies and intimidate other female students in schools
- Engage in prostitution
- Engage in drug sales, vandalism, and credit card and identity theft

Although female gang members can be just as violent as their male counterparts, violence committed by female gang members is still relatively low compared to that of male gang members. One Chicago-based study found that although females in gangs may fight as much as males, they use weapons less frequently and are less likely to kill. A large number of fights and assaults involving female gang members occur within the school setting.

Some females commit violent crimes to gain status and prove themselves worthy of the gang; however, male gang members rarely grant women the same power or status as men in the gang. There have also been numerous reports of females being sexually exploited by males within the gang. Female gang members are often "sexed in" (rather than "jumped in") to the gang, an initiation ritual that involves sex with several gang members, often for an extended period of time.

Although female gang membership in male-dominated gangs is increasing, the prevalence of predominately female gangs continues to be a rare phenomenon. The most recent data from the 2005 National Gang Threat Assessment reveals that 10 percent of law enforcement agencies are now reporting exclusively female gangs. Female gang members are generally more inclined to commit property crimes and drug offenses, and most of their assaults and fights occur within a school setting and without weapons.

Although female gang members commit relatively little violent crime, violence among girls in gangs is on the rise, and law enforcement should be concerned about their increasing brutality and their roles as weapons carriers. Traditionally, female gangs have received less attention from researchers and law enforcement, and most efforts have focused on intervention programs designed to provide an alternate refuge for girls attempting to escape abusive environments. Furthermore, law enforcement officials are less likely to recognize or stop female gang members, and they have experienced difficulty in identifying female involvement in gang-related activity.

INDIAN COUNTRY GANGS

Note: The material for this section was taken directly from the National Gang Threat Assessment Report (2005).

The consistent growth of the gang subculture as a national phenomenon has touched communities of every size across the country. While still perceived by some to be an urban-based social problem, gang activity has steadily affected parts of the country that were once believed to be immune from this behavior. Such is the case with Indian Country and the emergence of the gang subculture not only on reservations across the country, but among certain urban-based Native Americans as well.

Although most youth in Indian Country are not involved in gang activity, those who are involved tend to be young, primarily between the ages of twelve and twenty-four. These youth become involved in gangs either by connecting to existing gang structures or by starting their own gang sets. Gang behavior is more about group cohesiveness, predatory activities, and a party atmosphere than it is about organized criminal behavior with a profit motive.

Most gangs in Indian Country are small and autonomous. Structurally, leadership tends to be decentralized, with collective decisions being the common theme. Although some of these gangs will claim turf, gang alignment tends to revolve around which gang is perceived to be the most influential at any given time.

Native-American gangs will often take on the characteristics of urban street gangs in terms of signs, symbols, and other forms of gang representation. While some gangs identify themselves by names unique to the Indian culture or a specific area (such as Shanob Mob, Nomadz, Wild Boyz, Native Mob, Native Outlawz, and Dark Side Family), others align themselves with nationally recognized gangs (such as Indian Bloods, Native Gangster Disciples, Indian Gangster Disciples, Native Mob Vice Lords, Igloo Housing Crips, and Insane Cobra Folk Nation). This national affiliation, often evidenced by body markings, is not indicative of a relationship between Native-American gangs and other gang structures; rather, it is utilized for purposes of notoriety and intimidation. Most gang crimes occurring in Indian Country are property based, such as graffiti and vandalism; however, the extent of violent crime connected to gang activity is increasing.

Over the past decade, Indian reservations across the country have increasingly reported escalating levels of gang violence, as well as drug usage and distribution. Although not all of the violence is connected to gang activity, gangs are considered one of the factors in the escalating violence.

When studying the growth of gangs in Indian Country, it is essential to consider the illicit drug trade. The remote nature of many reservations is conducive to the proliferation of methamphetamine labs, the growth of marijuana, and the distribution of a wide variety of illegal substances. The proximity of many reservations to the Mexican border also provides easy access to these drugs, a fact only exacerbated by the extent of alcohol and drug abuse already occurring in many parts of Indian Country.

Female involvement in Indian-Country gangs is another important consideration. Twenty percent of females are engaged in some level of gang activity, compared to the national rate of 6 percent for female gang involvement. The significance of female involvement must not be underestimated, as gang-involved females are allowing themselves to be physically and sexually abused and will sometimes escalate their own behavior to prove they can be as violent or antisocial as their male counterparts.

Gang activity among Native Americans in prison is increasing due to the general influence of gang activity in correctional facilities, as well as the tendency for some Native-American gang members to feel a sense of pride in serving time. The rate of prison incarceration per capita among Native Americans is approximately 38 percent higher than the national rate, and the number of youth in custody in the Federal Bureau of Prisons has increased 50 percent since 1994. This trend may account for the emergence of Native-American prison gangs, such as Indian Brotherhood, Red Brotherhood, Indian Posse, Warlords, Bear Paw Warrior Society, and similar structures. Native-American gang members released from these facilities often return to their communities and bring the gang lifestyle with them, contributing to the growth of the gang problem.

The absence of an aggressive gang-prosecution initiative in Indian Country has allowed gang activity to flourish and grow. Law enforcement in Indian Country lacks a comprehensive and sustained law enforcement model that emphasizes identification of active gang members and directed enforcement activity to deal with the behavior. A lack of gang intelligence, including gang trends, membership numbers, and alliances and rivalries, places law enforcement officials at a disadvantage, as they are unable to have a clear understanding of the depth of the gang problem. Additionally, many Native-American youth involved in gang- and drug-related crime perceive that little or no retribution for criminal behavior will occur at the tribal court level.

An increasing number of tribes have recognized the need to curb the growth of the gang problem over the past several years, despite the historic denial of the presence of gangs in Indian Country. Efforts have been made to educate tribal authorities and educators in gang recognition and effective resource allocation. Finally, some tribes are returning to the traditional practice of banishment as a means of dealing with gang and criminal behavior. Although used by only a handful of tribes across the country, the practice is an alternative available to tribes as they seek solutions to deal with the growing problem of gang activity.

OUTLAW MOTORCYCLE GANGS

Note: The material for this section was taken directly from the National Gang Threat Assessment Report (2005).

Outlaw motorcycle gangs (OMGs) have been in existence for more than fifty years. The growth of OMGs and their increasing criminal endeavors have made them the subject of numerous criminal investigations by law enforcement. These criminal activities include, but are not limited to, murder, assault, kidnapping, prostitution, money laundering, weapons trafficking, motorcycle and motorcycle-parts theft, intimidation, extortion, arson, and the production, smuggling, transportation, and distribution of drugs. While drug trafficking is still the primary SRC of income for OMGs, the other criminal activities represent an increasing SRC of funds.

Each of the **major OMGs**—the Hell's Angels, Bandidos, Outlaws, and Pagans—has been identified as being involved in murder, bombings, extortion, arson, and assault. The Hell's Angels, Bandidos, and Outlaws have also been involved in weapons trafficking, prostitution, money laundering, explosives violations, motorcycle and motorcycle-parts theft, intimidation, insurance fraud, kidnapping, robbery, theft, stolen property, counterfeiting, and contraband smuggling.

major outlaw motorcycle gangs / The Hell's Angels, Bandidos, Outlaws, and Pagans. These gangs have been identified as being involved in murder, bombings, extortion, arson, and assault.

Individual club members are also involved in all types of criminal activity apart from the activities of the club. In some cases, the club sanctions these criminal activities, while in other cases the criminal activities are carried out by individual OMG members on their own. In many cases, individual members conduct the same type of criminal activity conducted by the club.

While OMGs have long been involved in violence and drugs, their ties to organized crime represent a relatively new phenomenon. In addition to reports that OMGs are performing some menial tasks for organized crime, there are also indications that OMGs may be attempting to take over many of the activities of traditional organized crime entities.

The Outlaws are major producers and distributors of methamphetamine, although they are also involved in the transportation and distribution of marijuana, cocaine, and prescription drugs. Their involvement in drugs has been long-standing, and two of their former international presidents, Henry Bowman and Frank Wheeler, were imprisoned for drug distribution, among multiple other charges.

The Pagans are involved in the distribution of marijuana, methamphetamine, and PCP in the United States. Generally, they are not directly involved in the retail distribution of drugs, preferring instead to use puppet clubs and female associates to handle retail distribution. Successful law enforcement efforts against the Pagans have reduced their drug-trafficking activities; however, a resurgence of drug activity by the Pagans to cover the cost of the escalating conflict with the Hell's Angels is possible. Much of this increased activity would likely be carried out by puppet clubs and newly recruited members.

Outlaw Motorcycle Gang Expansion

Violence among OMGs has escalated. In the United States, this is largely due to the efforts of the major clubs, particularly the Hell's Angels, to expand their territory and establish new clubs. Expansion efforts involve not only adding members to existing clubs, but also adding chapters in new areas. Frequently, one club attempts to move into an area that another club claims as its territory, and conflicts ultimately arise.

The major OMGs have been in an expansion mode for the past several years. As of 2005, Hell's Angel's chapters numbered 218—more than double the number seen in the previous five years. Between 1999 and 2000, the Bandidos more than tripled their size. Although they have only 152 chapters, their estimated membership of more than 2,000 makes them a potential threat to surpass the Hell's Angels in size. The Outlaws added twenty-eight chapters in the United States between 1999 and 2002. Their 1,200 members make them third in size; however, arrests of Outlaw's members in Canada and the United States have severely crippled the club. The Pagans are attempting to add and retain members, but due to recent arrests and the defection of current members, their numbers have been falling. It is possible they may fall below the Sons of Silence, currently ranked fifth in size in the United States.

In the ongoing turf battles between rival motorcycle clubs, the major clubs are aligning against the Hell's Angels. In general, the Hell's Angels have adversarial relationships with the Pagans and the Mongols and clash over territory with the Bandidos and the Outlaws. The Hell's Angels were at odds with the Outlaws as a result of recent expansion of Outlaws into Hell's Angels–controlled states, including Connecticut, Massachusetts, New Hampshire, and New York.

Intelligence reports from California, however, indicate that the Mongols may be losing members due to a "green light," or hit, placed on them by the Mexican Mafia. Intelligence reports state that the Mongols are abandoning their patches and may be returning to the street gangs from which they were recruited.

NATIONAL GANGS

This section contains a brief description of the gangs that are considered to be national gangs, as their presence is found in all states, **Note:** The material for this section was taken directly from the National Gang Threat Assessment Report (2005).

MS-13

The Mid-Atlantic Regional Gang Investigators Network (MARGIN) reports that MS-13 is the largest and most dangerous threat in the Mid-Atlantic area. Specifically in Virginia and Washington, DC, MS-13 has solidified itself as the largest Hispanic gang. MS-13 has also been expanding into North Carolina and Virginia. Intelligence reporting in 2002 indicated that MS-13 members trafficked in powdered cocaine, marijuana, heroin, and methamphetamine throughout the South, including Texas, Virginia, and Maryland. Consistent with this intelligence, more than 50 percent of law enforcement officials in the current survey reported the presence of the Bloods, with 24 percent reporting high or moderate activity.

Crips

Like the Bloods, the Crips are also present throughout the South. Crips sets in this region operate autonomously and are not formally affiliated with West Coast Crips. In North Carolina, the Crips show signs of a Midwest influence in their adoption of the traditional Gangster Disciples' signs and symbols, such as pitchforks and six-pointed stars. Crips follow drug-trafficking patterns similar to those that the Bloods follow: "Members of Crips sets transport cocaine, marijuana, heroin, methamphetamine, and PCP primarily from southern California, Texas, and Florida for distribution throughout the southeastern states." In the 2005 survey, 30 percent of officials reported moderate or high Crips activity, and an additional 25 percent reported a low level of activity by the gang.

Latin Kings

Law enforcement officials report a significant presence of the Latin Kings in North Carolina, Florida, Virginia, and Texas. This information is further corroborated by the current survey, wherein 47 percent of law enforcement officials reported the presence of the Latin Kings.

Asian Gangs

Approximately 31 percent of officials in the southern region reported the presence of Asian gangs. This is consistent with intelligence reporting that documents the West Coast, Chicago, and New York City as major areas for Asian gang activity.

OMGs

Although Sureño street gangs originated in southern California—in fact, in California their name is used as an umbrella term for all southern California street gangs—they have been documented in almost every region of the United States through tattoos, graffiti, and interviews with sources. Most Sureño gangs outside of California merely documented the presence of the Hell's Angels, Outlaws, and Pagans, and Virginia also noted increasing numbers of the Bandidos. Additional intelligence indicates the presence of OMGs in the following areas:

- Hell's Angels: South Carolina, Maryland, Kentucky, and North Carolina
- Sons of Silence: Florida, Arkansas, Kentucky, and Louisiana
- Bandidos: Texas, South Carolina, Kentucky, Oklahoma, Alabama, Arkansas, and Louisiana

Many southern states have chapters of OMGs, but because their membership numbers are smaller than those of street gangs and because OMGs receive less political attention, many jurisdictions do not consider them as great a threat as other street gangs. In the current survey, more than 30 percent of officials in the region reported the presence of the Outlaws. Officials reported the presence of the Hell's Angels and Pagans as well, with a low level of activity.

Gangster Disciples

Gang intelligence reports indicate the Gangster Disciples (GD) transport and distribute "multikilogram quantities of powdered and crack cocaine and multipound quantities of marijuana throughout the southeastern region, particularly Tennessee and Georgia." Gangster Disciples in North Carolina are self-contained and have no association with GD members on a national level. The gang has also been documented in Florida and Virginia.

In the current survey, almost 40 percent of investigators in the southern region reported the presence of the Gangster Disciples. Maryland and Washington, DC, have also documented the Gangster Disciples, although the gang calls itself the Crips while adopting the Gangster Disciples signs, symbols, and ideology. This phenomenon was also reported in North Carolina; however, investigators there classified the gangs as Crips.

DRUG ENFORCEMENT

The use of illegal substances is considered as one of the major crime problems in the United States. Cocaine is believed to be the most prevalent drug for the majority of male and female users. About 20 percent of individuals arrested for suspected drug involvement tested positive for two or more drugs. Other popular drugs that are used include marijuana, heroin, amphetamines, and PCP.

Twenty-seven percent of all felons on probation for drug offenses were rearrested for a subsequent drug violation. Probation department records revealed that 53 percent of all probationers had a drug abuse problem, 22 percent were occasional users, and 31 percent were frequent users. In addition, probationers with a drug abuse problem were more likely to be rearrested than nonabusers.

Not only do drug abusers have a higher recidivism rate than other offenders, they are more likely to be arrested and convicted than other criminals. Narcotic offenses not only clog our jails and institutions, but they also cause serious problems for our law enforcement agencies. From a law enforcement perspective, the most pressing threat to our society is the violence associated with street-level drug dealing—particularly crack cocaine (Blair, 1987, p. A-1). A majority of this violence can be attributed to youth gangs (Juvenile Gangs, 1988). This violence has become a way of life for many street gangs throughout the United States.

Another problem for law enforcement is the close link between drug use and street crime. The studies cited previously clearly indicate that a majority of all criminals are heavily involved in drug use and abuse. Thus, controlling drug use may be a method for reducing robberies, burglaries, and petty thefts.

Scholars have pointed out that drug use undermines the health, economic well-being, and social responsibility of drug users. In addition, drug trafficking threatens the civility of city life and undermines parenting. Finally, law enforcement professionals acknowledge that the police can accomplish little by themselves. The drug problem will require more resources than simply putting more cops on the street (Moore, 1989). The offenses may be simple, but they affect every segment of our society.

Aerial view of a customs official with dog checking cargo for drugs, bombs, and other threats. The use of dogs to detect for drugs and bombs is important in attempting to control the drug traffic and reducing the danger from terrorist attacks.

Narcotics

Narcotic offenses have been widely publicized in the media. This publicity ranges from multimillion-dollar drug busts to stories of drug overdoses by young children. These crimes are relatively simple to define, but debate rages about both the causes and cures of drug-related offenses. Narcotic offenses run the gamut from simple possession of marijuana to the sale of heroin. Offenders vary from a neighbor supplying marijuana for an afternoon party to a Miami drug lord planning distribution of heroin throughout the United States. Today many segments of our society use or have used narcotic drugs.

narcotic offenses / Drug-related crimes that run the gamut from simple possession of marijuana to the sale of heroin.

Narcotics and their use are not a new phenomenon in our society. Opium was used by such noted physicians as Hippocrates. [Hippocrates was an early Greek doctor who at one time was believed to have written the Hippocratic Oath. This oath pledges service to the patient and establishes high moral and ethical standards for those in the medical profession.] Widespread use of these narcotics led to a serious drug abuse problem in the United States as early as 1924. The use and abuse of drugs has continued since then.

FOCUS ON DRUGS AND ALCOHOL: SOME DEFINITIONS

The following paragraphs describe some of the more common drugs used in our society. It is not intended to cover all the various types of drugs encountered by law enforcement officials. Rather, it should be used as an introduction to the vast array of drugs that are available on the streets of our nation.

Common Drugs Used in the United States

Central Nervous System Stimulants
- Cocaine
- Crack
- Amphetamines
- Methamphetamine
- Ice

Central Nervous System Depressants
- Alcohol
- Barbiturates
- Tranquilizers

Hallucinogens
- LSD
- Peyote

Narcotic Analgesics
- Morphine
- Codeine
- Heroin
- Methadone
- Demerol

Phencyclidine

Cannabis
- Marijuana
- Hashish
- Hash oil

Central Nervous System Stimulants

Central nervous system stimulants are drugs that increase the functional state of the central nervous system.

Cocaine is a psychoactive alkaloid produced from the coca leaf. The coca shrub thrives in several regions of the South American Andes. It was first discovered by Albert Niemann of Germany in 1860. It is a very powerful natural drug whose use produces euphoria, restlessness, and excitement. Cocaine can be sniffed into the nostrils or injected. The resulting euphoria is short-lived, and heavy users must constantly snort the drug to maintain the feeling. *Speedballing* is the practice of mixing cocaine and heroin for the purpose of obtaining a distinct high. *Freebasing* refers to the conversion of street cocaine to freebase, or pure cocaine. This substance is then sprinkled on a cigarette or smoked in a pipe. Freebase enters the bloodstream through the lungs and the high is felt before the smoke is exhaled.

Crack is refined cocaine that comes in rock form. Crack is an off-white color resembling pieces of soap. The word "crack" comes from the crackling sound made when it is smoked, or from its occasional resemblance to cracked plaster. The popularity of crack is that it renders cocaine smokable. When smoked, it produces an immediate high.

Amphetamines are synthetic drugs that stimulate the central nervous system. The use of these drugs produces an intense physical reaction, including increased blood pressure, breathing rate, and elevation of mood. Some of the more commonly used amphetamines are benzedrine, dexedrine, and methedrine. Extended use of this drug can result in exhaustion, anxiety, and depression.

Methamphetamine is a form of amphetamine that has been called the poor man's cocaine. It has various street names including meth, speed, or crystal. It has been produced illegally for decades and may be manufactured in homemade laboratories. It may be injected, inhaled, or taken orally.

Ice is smokable methamphetamine. Ice was initially reported in Hawaii in 1985 and supposedly has become its greatest drug problem. The slang term "ice" was due to the drug's appearance, generally a clear, crystal-shaped form that looks like glass. In some areas this narcotic is also known as *crank*. Ice has the same properties as methamphetamine, but through a recrystallization process, the rocklike crystals can be smoked. The ice form of methamphetamine is highly addictive.

Central Nervous System Depressants

Central nervous system depressants are drugs that decrease the functional state of the central nervous system.

Alcohol refers to ethanol, which is a psychoactive ingredient found in alcoholic beverages. Consumed orally, it produces a wide range of symptoms depending on the individual and the amount ingested. These symptoms can range from euphoria to aggressive behavior.

Barbiturates are defined as barbituric acid derivatives used in medicine as sedatives and hypnotics. Barbituric acid was discovered by Adolf Baeyer in Germany in 1864. Some of the more commonly abused barbiturates are amobarbital (Amytal), known on the street as blues or blue devils; pentobarbital (Nembutal), known as nembies, yellows, or yellow jackets; and secobarbital (Seconal), known as reds, red devils, or Seccy. Barbiturate use can produce a state of intoxication. There may be an initial loss of inhibition, euphoria, and behavioral stimulation. They may also produce drowsiness and sleep.

Tranquilizers are antipsychotic agents generally used to treat schizophrenia and acute psychosis. However, many lay persons use the term to refer to the benzodiazepine drugs, Librium and Valium. These drugs were originally manufactured to treat various symptoms of anxiety. Their use produces drowsiness, light-headedness, and other impairments of mental and physical activities.

Hallucinogens

LSD is a synthetic drug also known as lysergic acid diethylamide-25. This substance stimulates cerebral sensory centers and promotes a full range of visual hallucinations. The drug may induce feelings of anxiety and panic, and some users have experienced flashbacks even after discontinuing use of the substance.

Peyote is a small cactus that grows naturally in Mexico and the southwestern portion of the United States. It contains *mescaline*, a hallucinogenic substance named after the Mescalero Apaches, who first used it. Peyote produces a wide range of hallucinations including colors, geometric patterns, and out-of-body sensations.

Narcotic Analgesics

Narcotic analgesics are drugs that depress the central nervous system and relieve pain without producing loss of consciousness. The most common narcotics are derivatives of opium. Similar to coca leaves, opium has a long history of use. Long before 4000 B.C., opium was known for its medicinal qualities, and it was used as a narcotic in Sumerian and European cultures 6,000 years ago. Opium is produced from the opium poppy flower. People first learned to smoke opium in China, and the practice quickly spread to many parts of the world.

Morphine is the principle psychoactive alkaloid in opium. It was first produced in 1805 and was named after the Greek god of dreams, Morpheus. Morphine is ten times stronger than opium and is used by physicians to relieve pain. It produces an elevation of spirits and then drowsiness. Morphine is a highly addictive drug.

Codeine is another derivative of opium that may be used legally under a doctor's orders. It is present in many pain-relieving prescription drugs. It can produce drug dependence of the morphine type and therefore is considered highly addictive.

Heroin was first produced in 1874 by an Englishman, D. P. Wright, and is twenty-five times stronger than morphine. It is one of the more commonly used drugs in the United States. Users quickly build up a tolerance and must use more of the drug to obtain the same effect. It is sold as a powder and mixed before being injected into the bloodstream. There are numerous forms of heroin: "Mexican Brown" is sold in the western United States and is pink-brown in color. It is usually a fine powder with dark brown flecks. The color may vary from light brown to chocolate. "Persian Heroin" is tan or reddish in color. It is not water soluble; rather lemon juice or vinegar is added prior to cooking in the traditional spoon. "Black Tar Heroin" began appearing in the United States about 1979. This drug is especially desired on the streets because of its purity, about 93 percent. There are numerous street names for Black Tar, including gum, goma, and Mexican Mud.

Methadone is a synthetic drug that is used to assist heroin users in breaking their habit. Some states have established methadone clinics where heroin users may

Voices of Experience

D.A.R.E. Program

Excerpts from an interview between Cliff Roberson and former police officer, Robert Boyer. Professor Boyer is currently a professor of criminal justice at Luzerne County Community College, Nanticoke, Pennsylvania. He also continues to work as a part-time police officer in Pennsylvania. In addition, he is the mayor of Wyoming, Pennsylvania.

Q: *What is the D.A.R.E. program?*

A: The D.A.R.E. [Drug Abuse Resistant Education] program was pioneered by the Los Angeles school district and the Los Angeles Police Department. It was targeted to grade school students. The program provides instruction to the students by specially trained police officers on drugs and related issues. The program starts out instructing the students on safety and how to call for emergency assistance. D.A.R.E. then bridges to the point where drug awareness is taught in a manner that provides students with accurate drug information. Scare tactics are not used. The students are exposed to the consequences of drug use. It is more than just saying "don't use drugs" or "just say no." It teaches kids how to say no. They get a chance to practice saying no in skits where the students are involved in role playing. It gives kids a really positive interaction. The program builds a feeling of trust in the officers. The kids bond with the police officers. ■

go to obtain the drug legally in lieu of purchasing heroin on the streets. Methadone is considered highly addictive. The withdrawal following extended use of methadone is more prolonged but less intense than that of heroin.

Demerol is a synthetic drug that is used by the medical profession. It is usually administered before and after operations as a method of controlling pain.

Phencyclidine

Phencyclohexyl piperidine (PCP), monohydrochloride, is a synthetic drug. It was first discovered in 1956 by researchers at Parke, Davis, and Company. The PCP sold in the United States is made in illegal laboratories. PCP in its pure state is a clear liquid. In solid form, it is a powder that may be white or have a yellowish or brownish tint. It may act as a depressant, a stimulant, a psychedelic, and a tranquilizer. It also removes the feeling of physical pain. The user's pain threshold is dramatically increased, and therefore traditional police restraints may be ineffective against a person under the influence of PCP.

Key Substance Abuse Terms

Cannabis: A group of drugs produced from the leaves of *Cannabis sativa*, including marijuana, hashish, and hash oil.

***Cannabis sativa* L.:** Proper name for the marijuana plant.

Central Nervous System Depressants: A group of drugs that depress the functional state of the central nervous system, including alcohol, barbiturates, and tranquilizers.

Central Nervous System Stimulants: A group of drugs that increase the functional state of the central nervous system, including cocaine, crack, amphetamines, methamphetamine, and "ice."

Crop Eradication: The systematic effort to destroy plants that produce the raw material that is manufactured into a narcotic drug.

Crop Substitution: Effort to motivate farmers in foreign countries to grow domestic food crops for commercial markets instead of poppies, coca bushes, or cannabis plants.

Crucial Alcoholic Phase: Point when the drinker's loss of control becomes complete, there is isolation from others, and life becomes centered around alcohol.

Final or Bottom Alcoholic Phase: Point when a drinker experiences emotional disorganization or impaired thinking.

Hallucinogens: A group of drugs that produce hallucinations, including LSD and peyote.

Intermediate Alcoholic State: Point when an individual who drinks has occasional blackouts coupled with a compulsion to drink and lose control.

Narcotic Analgesics: A group of drugs that depress the central nervous system and relieve pain without producing loss of consciousness, including morphine, codeine, heroin, methadone, and Demerol.

Phencyclidine: A synthetic drug that removes the feeling of physical pain and may act as a depressant, stimulant, psychedelic, or tranquilizer. Also known as PCP.

Prealcoholic Phase: Point when a person has an occasional drink as a means of reducing tension.

Under the Influence: Condition where alcohol or drugs have affected the nervous system, brain, or muscles so as to impair to an appreciable degree the ability to operate a motor vehicle in a manner like that of ordinary, prudent, and cautious persons in full possession of their faculties using reasonable care and under like circumstances.

Usable Form: Substance of a quality and quantity suitable for use as a narcotic.

Cannabis

Cannabis is produced from the leaves of *cannabis sativa*, a weedlike plant that is grown throughout the world. The active ingredient in cannabis is tetrahydro-cannabinol (THC). Prolonged use can cause distortion in auditory and visual perception. Small doses produce a "high" or excitement that gives way to drowsiness.

Marijuana is produced from the leaves of cannabis. It is called pot, dope, and other names. Normally it is smoked as a cigarette or in a pipe.

Voices of Experience

Undercover Narcotics Officer

Excerpts from an interview between Cliff Roberson and former police lieutenant, Richard G. Kuiters, presently a professor at Bergen Community College, Paramus, New Jersey.

Q: *Tell us about your experiences as a narcotics undercover officer.*

A: I remember the day I started. I got called into the chief's office. There were three administrators and three captains in the office. My first thoughts were, "What did I do now?" The chief informed me that he would like to start an undercover narcotics unit and wanted me to be a part of it. My first assignment was to go to Newark, New Jersey. I went into the area and was a white man in a mostly black and Hispanic territory. By watching the street dealers, I picked up a lot of tips on how to operate on the street. I became proficient at dealing on the street. But, I knew that sooner or later I was going to be identified as a cop.

After a while, I decided to change my approach and go after the big boys. If it was going to be a big deal, you are not going to do that with the street dealers. I changed my pace. I shaved my beard and cleaned up. Our approach then was to do it as a big business and let the money do the talking. The first time we sat down and acted like we had money, the suppliers demanded that we show them at least $40,000 in cash. We had to go to the New Jersey Treasury Department to get the $40,000. The state sent three troopers to accompany the cash. I had the opinion that the troopers could care less about me and were only interested in protecting the cash. We showed them the money and along came a purchase of 200 pounds of marijuana, a kilo of co-

caine, and ten thousand pills. That was the start of a new revolution in the narcotics task force. We learned that it was all about the money.

We found that as we caught these individuals and debriefed them, we obtained a wealth of information regarding other criminal activities. Once these individuals were caught, they were ready to bargain for reduced sentences. One thing we started doing in the task forces was to conduct a debriefing of the suspects in all cases. We had no problems getting them to talk because when they realized they were going to jail, they wanted to make the best deal possible for themselves—remember they are dealers. The first-timers are the easiest targets, but even the career criminal will bargain as it gets close to his court date.

One of the problems in dealing with street-level undercover work is that the supervisor has to watch his or her squad because you do not want them relating to or going over to the other side. You do not want them to become a part of the problem. The bottom line is that the undercover officer should never use drugs. If they do, then their creditability in the courtroom is destroyed. Myself, I always pretended that I had a cough and therefore could not smoke or take the drugs at that time. One time a dealer offered me a smoke and I stated that I could not because of my cough. He goes into the back room and comes back with black tar pitch opium to swallow to soothe my throat to stop the cough. I then arrested him for distribution of opium. ▪

Hashish is a concentrated form of cannabis that is produced from the unadulterated resin from the female plant. It is also called hash.

Hash oil is a liquid form of hashish that is considered a very powerful form of the drug. The concentration of THC in this oil may be as high as 90 percent.

DRUG LEGISLATION

Uniform Controlled Substances Act

Almost all states have adopted the Uniform Controlled Substances Act. A typical act, which is based on the Uniform Controlled Substances Act, is the California Controlled Substances Act (referred to as the Act) which is set forth in the California Health and Safety Code (H&S), Sections 11000–11853.

The following definitions are set forth in the Act:

Controlled Substances: A drug, substance, or immediate precursor which is listed in any section of the Act (H&S 11007).

Drug

(a) A substance recognized as drugs in the official United States Pharmacopoeia of the United States or official National Formulary, or any supplement to any of them;

(b) substances intended for use in the diagnosis, cure, mitigation, treatment, or prevention of disease in man or animals;

(c) substances (other than food) intended to affect the structure or any function of the body of man or animals; and

(d) substances intended for use as a component of any article specified in subdivisions (a), (b), and (c).

Drugs do not include devices or their components, parts, or accessories (H&S 11014).

Marijuana: Marijuana means all parts of the plant *Cannabis sativa* L., whether growing or not; the seeds thereof; the resin extracted from any part of the plant; and every compound, manufacture, salt, derivative, mixture, or preparation of the plant, its seeds or resin. It does not include the mature stalks of the plant, fiber produced from the stalks, oil or cake made from the seeds of the plant, any other compound, manufacture, salt, derivative, mixture, or preparation of the mature stalks (except the resin extracted therefrom), fiber, oil, or cake, or the sterilized seed of the plant which is incapable of germination (H&S 11018).

Because California does not draw distinction among different types of marijuana, it is not necessary for the prosecutor, in prosecution for possession or sale of marijuana, to specify and prove species of marijuana subject of charge; no reasonable doubt exists in this section and Sec. 11360 as to what plants are subject of prosecution and no violation of due process exists because of description of the plants (*People v. Hamilton*, 105 Cal.App.3d 113).

Narcotic Drug: Narcotic drug means any of the following whether produced directly or indirectly by extraction from substances of vegetable origin, or independently by means of chemical synthesis, or by a combination of extraction and chemical synthesis:

(a) Opium and opiate, and any salt, compound, derivative, or preparation of opium or opiate.

(b) Any salt, compound, isomer, or derivative, whether natural or synthetic, or the substances referred to in subdivision (a), but not including the isoquinoline alkaloids of opium.

(c) Opium poppy and poppy straw.

(d) Coca leaves and any salt, compound, derivative, or preparation of coca leaves, but not including decocainized coca leaves or extraction of coca leaves which do not contain cocaine or ecgonine.

(e) Cocaine, whether natural or synthetic, or any salt, isomer, derivative, or preparation thereof.

(f) Ecgonine, whether natural or synthetic, or any salt, isomer, derivative, or preparation thereof.

(g) Acetyfentanyl, the thiophene analog thereof, derivatives of either, and any salt, compound, isomer, or preparation of acetylfentanyl or the thiophene analog thereof (H&S 11019).

Opiate: Opiate means any substance having addiction-forming or addiction-sustaining liability similar to morphine or being capable of conversion into a drug having addiction-forming or addiction-sustaining liability (H&S 11020).

Opium Poppy: Opium poppy means the plant of the species *Papaver somniferum* L., except its seeds (H&S 11021).

Schedules

The Uniform Controlled Substances Act divides the controlled substances into five different schedules.

Schedule I: Those drugs classified as Schedule I controlled substances are listed in H&S 11054. Substances classified under Schedule I include:

1. opiates, unless specifically listed in another schedule
2. heroin
3. LSD (lysergic acid diethylamide)
4. mescaline
5. marijuana
6. hallucinogenic substances, unless specifically listed in another section
7. morphine methylbromide
8. peyote

9. cocaine base
10. methaqualone

Note: This is not a complete list of all Schedule I substances.

Schedule II: H&S 11055 contains a list of those substances classified as Schedule II. The list includes:

1. opium
2. codeine
3. cocaine, except that classified as Schedule I
4. pentobarbital
5. morphine
6. methadone
7. amphetamines
8. methylphenidate

Note: This is not a complete list of substances under Schedule II.

Schedule III: Schedule III controlled substances are listed in H&S 11056. The list of Schedule III substances includes:

1. phencyclidine (PCP)
2. methaqualone
3. barbiturates
4. stimulants, unless specifically listed under another schedule
5. depressants, unless specifically listed under another schedule
6. secobarbital
7. lysergic acid
8. chorthexadol

Note: This is not a complete list of substances under Schedule III.

Schedule IV: Schedule IV substances are listed in H&S Section 11057 and include the following substances:

1. veronal
2. luminal
3. chloral hydrate
4. valmid
5. placidyl
6. barbital
7. chloral betaine
8. pipradrol

Note: This is not a complete list of substances under Schedule IV.

Schedule V: The Schedule V controlled substances listed in H&S 11058 include:

1. not more than 200 milligrams of codeine per 100 milliliters or per 100 grams
2. not more than 100 milligrams of opium per 100 milliliters or per 100 grams
3. not more than 100 milligrams of dihydrocodeine per 100 milliters or per 100 grams

Reporting Requirements: The Act requires certain reports be submitted regarding the manufacture, sale, or delivery of controlled substances. Reports required include:

1. (H&S 11100) Any manufacturer, wholesaler, retailer, or other person who sells, transfers, or otherwise furnishes certain controlled substances shall submit a monthly report to the State Department of Justice of all of those transactions. Those substances include:
   a. phenyl-2-propanone
   b. methylamine
   c. ethylamine
   d. D-lysergic acid
   e. ergotamine tartrate
   f. diethyl malonate
   g. malonic acid
   h. ethyl malonate
   i. barbituric acid
   j. piperidine
   k. N-acetylanthranilic acid
   l. pyrrolinine
   m. penylacetic acid
   n. anthranilic acid
   o. morpholine
   p. ephedrine
   q. pseudoephedrine
2. (H&S 111000.1) Any manufacturer, etc., who receives the controlled substances listed above from outside the state shall make a report of the transaction to the State Department of Justice.
3. (H&S 11103) Reports are required to be made on the thefts or loss of any of the controlled substances listed under Section 11100.

ALCOHOL-RELATED OFFENSES

Until several years ago, alcohol offenses were looked upon as "victimless" crimes, since everyone had a drink now and then. The formation of MADD (Mothers Against Drunk Driving) and the ensuing publicity surrounding the effects of driving and drinking have raised the public's awareness regarding not only "drunk driving" but other alcohol-related offenses. This section will briefly examine some of the more common alcohol-related crimes.

The Alcohol Problem

There is no doubt that we as a society have an alcohol problem. The extent of the consumption of alcoholic beverages is staggering. There are approximately 100 million Americans who occasionally drink an alcoholic beverage and between nine and ten million individuals who can be classified as alcoholics (Liska, 1990, p. 218). Of this startling figure, an estimated eighteen million American adults and several million children are experiencing physical, mental, and social problems related to the consumption of alcohol. These problems include cirrhosis of the liver, certain types of cancers, emotional disorders, interpersonal conflicts, and alcohol-related violence (Howard, Ganikos, & Taylor, 1990).

Public Drunkenness

Public drunkenness has been present in American society since the establishment of the colonies. The Puritans stocked their ship the *Arabella* with 10,000 gallons of wine, 42 tons of beer, and only 11 tons of water (Lee, 1963).

A person does not normally become a chronic drunk in one or two days. While numerous models describe the transition from occasional drinker to public drunk, one of the most accepted is E. M. Jellinek's medical model. The stages of alcoholism include the prealcoholic phase, when the person has an occasional drink as a means of reducing tension; the intermediate stage, when an individual drinks and has occasional blackouts coupled with a compulsion to drink and loss of control; the crucial phase, when the loss of control becomes more complete, the drinker is isolated from others, and life becomes centered around alcohol; and the final or bottom phase, when the drinker experiences emotional disorganization or impaired thinking (Jellick, 1960).

Being Intoxicated: Simply having a few drinks before the football game does not make a person a drunk. There are degrees of intoxication. For this aspect of the offense to be satisfied, the level of intoxication must reach the degree set forth in the next element.

To the Degree That One Is Unable to Care for Oneself: The consumption of alcohol must reach a level where the person cannot function. Normally, the individual will have slurred speech, stagger while attempting to walk, or, more commonly, pass out from the consumption of alcohol. The offender will have severely impaired reasoning and be unable to function in a normal manner.

In a Public Place: It is not a crime to become this severely intoxicated in the privacy of your own home, the offense must be committed in a public place. Subways, bus stations, streets, alleyways, and empty fields are common locations where police will find persons so intoxicated that they are classified as public drunks.

We have come to accept public drunkenness as a disease instead of a crime. In order to treat rather than punish, some states do not classify public drunkenness as a criminal offense. Police officers who discover a person who is drunk may contact a social service agency and place the person in its care until the individual has sobered. Other jurisdictions treat the offense as a civil matter and commit the person to a detoxification center to "dry out." Whether it is classified as a crime or a civil matter, public drunkenness is a serious issue that we must address within our society.

Driving Under the Influence

Every state has a law that prohibits driving a motor vehicle while under the influence of alcohol or drugs. The purpose of these statutes is to protect every person lawfully on a public road or highway and to reduce the hazards of prohibited operation of a motor vehicle to a minimum. Unlike public drunkenness, which requires the person to be extremely intoxicated, driving under the influence requires only that the driver be influenced in his or her mental or physical operation of the vehicle.

Driving or Operating a Motor Vehicle: The defendant must be the driver or engaged in the operation of a motor vehicle. Simply being intoxicated while a passenger in an automobile is insufficient for purposes of this element. Driving usually is defined as movement of the vehicle in some direction and means steering and controlling the vehicle while it is in motion.

It may be an offense, depending on the wording of the statute, simply to "operate" the vehicle while under the influence of alcohol or drugs. Operation may include sitting in a vehicle with its engine running and the transmission in park. Some cases have held that the vehicle need not be in motion to constitute operation [*Gallagher v. Commonwealth*, 205 Va. 666, 139 S.E.2d 37 (1964)].

Some statutes define *motor vehicle* very broadly for purposes of this crime. Many states prohibit the driving or operation of motorcycles, motorbikes, motor homes, bicycles, boats, and even horses. The purpose behind this broad prohibition is to ensure that other drivers are protected from any activity that may cause an accident or injury.

Upon a Public Street or Highway: The offense must be committed upon a public street, road, or highway to satisfy this element of the offense. A public road or street is one that is open for use or is used by the public for motor vehicle or pedestrian traffic. Courts have found public park roads or thoroughfares in fairgrounds open to the public and therefore public streets within the meaning of the statutes.

While Under the Influence of Alcohol or Drugs: Many statutes define "under the influence" in a variety of ways. One example states that the defendant is under the influence if it can be proved that the alcohol or alcohol and drugs have affected the nervous system, brain, or muscles so as to impair to an appreciable degree the ability to operate a motor vehicle in a manner like that of ordinary, prudent, and cautious persons in full possession of their faculties using reasonable care and under like circumstances.

Proof that the defendant was under the influence may be given by the officer's testimony. The officer would testify regarding the defendant's driving pattern, behavior, and performance on any field sobriety test. While this method may result in a conviction, the more common method of proving this element of the crime involves establishing the defendant's blood alcohol level. *Blood alcohol level* is a legal and medical term that is expressed in milligrams of alcohol per milliliter of blood.

This level has been translated into the ability or fitness to operate a motor vehicle based upon several broad categories or zones of impairment.

Law enforcement agencies utilize a variety of tests to establish the blood alcohol level. The three most common are blood, breath, and urine tests. Blood tests involve drawing a sample of blood from the defendant and having it chemically analyzed. Breath tests require the defendant to blow into a machine that analyzes the alcohol content of the breath. Urine tests utilize a urine specimen taken from the defendant and then analyzed like a blood sample. Each of these tests is voluntary in that the police cannot obtain the sample without the defendant's consent. Many states, however, provide for loss of the defendant's driver's license if he or she refuses to provide a sample of blood, breath, or urine for analysis.

Some states have enacted presumptions that shift the burden of proving this element. If the driver of the vehicle has tested for a certain blood alcohol level and it can be shown that this level existed during the operation of the vehicle, offenders must prove they were not under the influence. This level varies from state to state, but many statutes establish .08 to .10 blood alcohol level as a presumptive indication that the defendant was under the influence of alcohol and/or drugs at the time of the operation of the motor vehicle. Driving under the influence is an offense that can be just as destructive as use of drugs. Thousands of innocent citizens are killed or maimed each year as a direct result of drunk drivers. State legislatures have responded to calls for reform by such groups as MADD and have increased penalties for this offense and shifted the burden of proof to the offender by lowering the blood alcohol level as it relates to the presumption of driving while under the influence.

This section has examined the alcohol problem and offenses that involve consumption of alcohol. Drug and alcohol crimes continue to occupy a high percentage of law enforcement's time and energy. Local, state, and federal elected officials have all sounded the call to battle against these types of crimes. The next section will examine some of the proposed solutions to drug and alcohol offenses.

SOLUTIONS TO DRUG AND ALCOHOL ABUSE

The solutions to drug and alcohol abuse are complex and subject to wide-ranging debate. The following discussion is not intended to provide a comprehensive examination of all possible intervention techniques available to society, rather, it is an effort to list some of the more common initiatives that are presently being utilized by law enforcement agencies and public and private institutions.

Legalization

The legalization of some or all illegal drugs is an emotional issue that has its proponents and opponents. Each side presents statistics and theories to support its position. Neither side is strictly liberal or conservative, rather, their ranks include scholars, police officers, and elected members of local, state, and national legislatures. Several states have legalized marijuana for medical use and several others are considering it.

This creates problems, because it is still a violation of federal law to import marijuana or to take marijuana across state lines.

The advocates of legalization, including certain law enforcement officials and other prominent scholars, believe that we have lost the "war on drugs." They claim we must explore new and previously unthinkable alternatives in our efforts to stop the spread of illegal drugs. These authorities insist that legalization of illegal drugs will benefit innocent victims as well as society (*Law Enforcement News*, 1988; Trebach, 1987).

The opponents of legalization insist that we are winning the battle against illegal drugs. They point out that our society is built on the premise of protecting those who cannot protect themselves. These authorities raise the actual and potential damage that legalized drugs will have on society (Tully & Bennett, 1989, pp. 57–64).

The following paragraphs summarize the position of each group regarding legalization of drugs. The prior arguments are simplified versions of the more sophisticated positions set forth by the proponents and opponents of legalization. No matter which position one takes, there will be a vocal and emotional response by the other side. Legalization and its effects will continue to be hotly debated in universities, law enforcement agencies, and other institutions for the foreseeable future.

Attacking the Drug Problem

In the United States and other countries, fear, concern, and disgust have caused governments and private businesses to attempt to find a solution to the drug abuse problem. This is no easy task, as high profits from the growing and sale of drugs, organized criminal activities, and old-fashioned greed play an important part in opposing any meaningful reform. The following is a brief discussion of the more important strategies being used to counter drug abuse.

International Agreements: As early as 1912, nations were enacting international agreements to prohibit certain types of drugs. The International Opium Convention was signed at the Hague, the Netherlands, in 1912. The League of Nations enacted conventions similar to the 1912 agreement in 1925, 1931, and 1936. In 1961, the United Nations Single Convention on Narcotic Use consolidated most of these earlier agreements.

In addition to these international conventions, there are numerous other treaties, agreements, protocols, and resolutions between various nations designed to reduce the supply of illegal drugs. These agreements include the Permanent Secretariat of the South American Agreement on Narcotic Drugs and Psychotropic Substances, initiatives by the Organization of American States, the South Pacific Commission, and the Pan-Arab Bureau for Narcotic Affairs of the League of Arab States, just to name a few. The purpose of all these agreements is to combat the growth, distribution, and sale of prohibited drugs.

Prevention of Illicit Demand: Prevention and reduction of the demand for illegal drugs involves a multifaceted approach that combines law enforcement activities, intervention in the workplace, and education.

Law Enforcement Activities: The main purpose of law enforcement activities in the United States is to reduce the demand, control supply, and suppress trafficking in illegal drugs. Any law enforcement administrator will tell you that police working by themselves cannot stop the sale of illegal drugs. Therefore, other measures have been employed by our government to wipe out drug usage.

Education: We have undertaken a concerted effort to educate our young children on the dangers of using drugs. This information is taught in our classrooms and transmitted into our homes by television. Many of us have seen the television commercial of the egg frying in the pan and the admonition regarding drug usage. "Just Say No to Drugs" is a common phrase that can be heard throughout our school system.

Testing in the Workplace: The federal government has passed mandatory drug testing for certain federal employees. We have all seen the signs in various businesses: "Drug Free Workplace." Many businesses are now requiring as a condition of employment that prospective employees submit to a drug test prior to being hired.

Control of Supply: By attempting to control the supply of illegal drugs, nations are focusing their efforts on the growers of the raw material. Growers of opium poppies, coca bushes, and cannabis plants are the targets of these efforts. However, controlling the supply of such goods is a complex and difficult task.

Crop Eradication: Eradication refers to the systematic effort to destroy those plants that produce the raw material that is manufactured into narcotic drugs. In addition, there are planned activities that search out and destroy cannabis plants. These plants are destroyed either by physically uprooting them or by spraying them with herbicide. These efforts are taking place both domestically and internationally (Whitehead, 1986).

Crop Substitution: Substitution seeks to motivate farmers in foreign countries to grow domestic food crops for the commercial market instead of poppy, coca, or cannabis plants. Most of these programs have been failures. The main reason for such a lack of success is the difference in price between the prohibited plants and regular farm produce—sometimes as much as 50 to 1 (Painter, 1989).

Rural Economic Development: Crop substitution alone does not appear to be effective in controlling the narcotic problem. Some countries are attempting to combine this measure with rural economic development programs aimed at controlling the supply of drugs. These programs offer redevelopment activities within areas controlled by the state. Thus, local police are better able to monitor the activities of the farmers. In addition, the farmers can live closer to home and enjoy the benefits of civilization. Colombia and Thailand are two of the countries that are actively engaged in these types of programs (Where poppies once stood, 1984).

Suppression of Illicit International Trafficking: Drug traffickers have employed and continue to employ every conceivable organizational, strategic, and tactical measure to transport their product to market. Some authorities have suggested certain methods to suppress these efforts.

Interdiction of Major Drug Networks: International treaties permit states to stop the entry of drugs inside their boundaries by extraterritorial means. The U.S. Coast

Guard, the Border Patrol, and the Drug Enforcement Administration target known routes of drug dealers. The theory behind this strategy is to cut the lines of supply and make it more expensive to purchase the drugs on the streets.

Forfeiture of Assets: Federal law allows law enforcement agencies to seize as contraband certain classes of property used by persons found to possess or deal drugs. Items subject to seizure include cars, homes, apartment complexes, commercial establishments, and boats, to name a few. State and local agencies may participate in these activities. The items seized are auctioned off and the proceeds are funneled back to the various law enforcement activities for specified purposes.

Extradition: Drug traffickers habitually seek haven in a country that has no extradition treaty with a principle consuming nation. The United States has entered into several extradition treaties aimed at apprehending drug leaders and bringing them to trial. Colombia's Medellin cartel suffered a major defeat when one of their ringleaders, Carlos Lehder, was successfully extradited to the United States in 1987. The seizure and transportation of President Noriega of Panama to the United States for trial in 1991 is a striking example of the government's attempt to bring to trial those who are ringleaders in the international trade of narcotics.

Numerous initiatives are being undertaken on both the international and national levels to attack the drug problem, ranging from traditional law enforcement activities to drug education programs. The profit from dealing drugs is enormous, and the need for drugs by an addict is overpowering. This war on drugs will continue, grow, and adopt new strategies as long as narcotics continue to invade our shores and harm our citizens.

Prevention of Alcohol Abuse

Some authorities believe that alcohol-related crimes are only symptoms of a much larger problem. They argue that we as a society must address alcohol abuse and its causes if we are to stop the carnage that is occurring on our nation's roads and highways as a result of drunk drivers. What causes alcoholism is a multifaceted issue that is beyond the scope of this text. However, we can address some of the programs that are aimed at preventing alcohol abuse. There are numerous theories regarding how to prevent alcohol abuse. Jan Howard, Mary Ganikos, and Jane Taylor set forth the following typology of some of the more common prevention strategies (Howard, Ganikos, & Taylor, 1990, p. 19).

Socialization Approaches: Socialization approaches are based upon the theory that the transfer of knowledge, values, and norms from one group to another person will cause the recipient to internalize what has been taught and act accordingly through self-control mechanisms.

School-Based Interventions: These programs include instruction in the hazards of alcohol consumption, refusal skills, and social skills. They normally are taught in grammar and high schools. In general, school-based programs have had very limited success (Moskowitz, 1989, p. 54).

Driver Education Programs: There are two primary types of educational interventions that focus on the prevention of drinking and driving: the school-based program aimed at primary prevention and programs for drunk driving offenders, a form of secondary prevention.

Media Interventions: Mass communication is a common approach to the prevention of alcohol problems. Historical data indicate that counter advertising on television concerning smoking practices was an effective strategy (Office on Smoking and Health, 1989, p. 461).

Health Warning Labels: The new warning labels on alcoholic beverages may act as a form of deterrence. These labels express the official concern of the U.S. government regarding the consumption of alcoholic beverages.

Primary Health Care Providers: There is some authority to support the theory that providers of care could play an important role in preventing alcohol abuse (Dupont, 1983, p. 1003). These efforts may be effective in patients with emerging problems, where health intervention might detect the problem, offer counseling, and give treatment.

Social-Control Approaches: Social-control approaches target self-control; however, they do so by establishing external situations that allow for restricted choice.

Economic Disincentives: There are a number of studies to indicate that increases in the price of alcoholic beverages directly correlate with decreases in the number of alcohol-related traffic accidents (Coate & Grossman, 1987, p. 23). The surgeon general has recommended increased taxation as a means of reducing the drunk driving problem (Office of the Surgeon General, 1989, pp. 8–11). Other economic disincentives include the availability of civil lawsuits for the sale of alcoholic beverages at public facilities to persons who are under the influence. If these persons are subsequently in an accident, the victims may have a right to sue the tavern owner who served the drunk driver the last drink or drinks.

Restricted Availability: A number of authorities have stated that restrictions on the availability of alcoholic beverages reduces alcohol problems (Abadinsky, 1993, p. 34). Other interventions include restrictions on the number and type of establishments that are allowed to sell alcoholic beverages.

Punishment: Violations of alcohol-related laws are punishable by license revocation, fines, and imprisonment. The revocation of an offender's driver's license is usually an administrative matter and may be carried out independent of any criminal charges. Some states have established minimum sentences for drunk drivers that require them to spend a certain number of days in jail. (See Figure 11.1 as an example.)

The above typology sets forth a brief analysis of some approaches to solving or combating the alcohol problem that faces our society. This is a complex problem that will take a determined effort not only by law enforcement departments, but by state, local, and national agencies as well. We must continue this "war on alcoholism" if we are to prevent further death and destruction on our roads and highways.

Figure 11.1 Connecticut OWI Chart

TWO WAYS TO LOSE YOUR LICENSE:

There are two laws to protect the citizens of Connecticut from the impaired driver:

• DRIVER'S LICENSE SANCTIONS
• CRIMINAL PENALTIES

The DRIVER'S LICENSE SANCTIONS (license suspension periods) outlined below have been revised recently and will be imposed IN ADDITION TO CRIMINAL PENALTIES. In most cases, the driver's license sanctions will be imposed much earlier. IN ALL CASES, they will be imposed in addition to criminal penalties and will appear on your driving record.

ADMINISTRATIVE SANCTIONS

Blood Alcohol Level	First Offense	Second Offense	Third Offense
Refusal to submit to a blood, breath or urine test	6 months	1 year	3 years
Test results of .02 or higher and you are under twenty-one years of age	90 days	9 months	2 years
Test results of .08 or higher; up to, but not including, .16	90 days	9 months	2 years
Test results of .16 or higher	120 days	10 months	2½ years

CRIMINAL LAW

Under Connecticut's criminal law, the driver arrested for DUI will receive both a summons and a court date. If the court proceedings result in a **conviction,** the following penalties must be imposed:

	First Offense Test results of .08 or higher	Second Offense (within 10 years) Test results of .08 or higher	Third Offense (within 10 years of last conviction) Test results of .08 or higher
Fine:	$500 to $1,000	$1,000 to $4,000	$2,000 to $8,000
Jail:	6 mo., 48 hrs minimum mandatory or 6 mo., suspended with 100 hrs. community service	2 yrs., 120 days minimum mandatory and 100 hrs. of community service	3 yrs., 1 yr. minimum mandatory and 100 hrs. of community service
Suspension:	One year	Three years (or until you are 21 years of age, whichever is longer)	Permanent Revocation

DRUG TESTING OF POLICE OFFICERS

The widespread use of illegal drugs is apparent in every segment of American life, including police employees. Because police work can be stressful and traumatic, it is no surprise that a few officers may use drugs as a means of coping. Accordingly, illegal drug use by police officers is a concern of every police chief. Approximately 73 percent of police departments conduct drug screening of applicants. In addition, most departments have written policies and procedures for conducting drug screening tests when there are reasons to suspect that an officer has been using illegal drugs.

One issue regarding drug tests is whether the establishment of a drug testing program is a change in working conditions and therefore subject to collective bargaining. The union concerns in this area include:

- the standards for drug concentration levels present in the urine
- the confidentiality of results
- procedural safeguards

> ## Model Drug Testing Policy
> ### (International Association of Chiefs of Police)
>
> The International Association of Chiefs of Police (IACP) has developed a model drug testing policy. (McEwen, Manili, & Connors, 1986). The policy recommends:
>
> - Testing of all applicants for drugs and narcotics use.
> - Testing present employees who are having performance difficulties or other indications of a potential drug problem.
> - Testing employees when involved in the use of excessive force, suffering or causing on-duty injury.
> - Routine testing of all employees assigned to "high-risk" assignments, such as narcotics and vice.

When an officer tests positive and further investigation determines that the officer is a drug abuser, the question then is should the officer be treated for the abuse problem, fired, or both. If the police keep a known drug abuser as a police officer, there is a potential for civil liability if the officer is involved in misconduct or an accident. If the drug use is caused, however, by job stress, is it fair to fire the officer? The present trend in handling this situation appears to be that taken by the City of Boston. In that city, assistance programs are available for officers who have problems with drugs. Employees who voluntarily enter the program are provided confidential counseling and their participation in the program is also confidential. If the officers do not voluntarily seek assistance, they may be fired. Other cities have similar programs. For example, the City of New York has a drug awareness program and a drug awareness workshop included in their training programs. The police employees' association in Philadelphia (Fraternal Order of Police) produced a videotape program that encourages officers with drug or alcohol problems to seek professional help. In addition, the association provides limited counseling in this area.

Should the police hire individuals who have used drugs in the past? There appears to be no uniform treatment by departments regarding the handling of applicants who either admit or are discovered to have used drugs. Almost all departments screen out individuals who have had serious past drug incidents. Individuals who have only experimented with drugs are screened out in some jurisdictions and not in others. The trend appears to be against automatic exclusion of applicants who have only experimented with drugs. Most departments who accept applicants with a history of drug incidents conduct more in-depth background investigations on those applicants than they do on other applicants. In addition, even the experimental use of drugs is considered as a negative factor in evaluating a person's application.

GANGS AND DRUGS

What Is the Relation Between Drugs and Gangs?

Note: The material for this section was taken from the National Drug Intelligence Center's pamphlet: NDIC Product No. 2005-L0559-001, "Drugs and Gangs Fast Facts, Questions and Answers," published by the U.S. Department of Justice, 2005.

Street gangs, outlaw motorcycle gangs (OMGs), and prison gangs are the primary distributors of illegal drugs on the streets of the United States. Gangs also smuggle drugs into the United States and produce and transport drugs within the country.

Street gang members convert powdered cocaine into crack cocaine and produce most of the PCP available in the United States. Gangs, primarily OMGs, also produce marijuana and methamphetamine. In addition, gangs increasingly are involved in smuggling large quantities of cocaine and marijuana and lesser quantities of heroin, methamphetamine, and MDMA (also known as ecstasy) into the United States from foreign sources of supply. Gangs primarily transport and distribute powdered cocaine, crack cocaine, heroin, marijuana, methamphetamine, MDMA, and PCP in the United States.

Located throughout the country, street gangs vary in size, composition, and structure. Large, nationally affiliated street gangs pose the greatest threat because they smuggle, produce, transport, and distribute large quantities of illicit drugs throughout the country and are extremely violent. Local street gangs in rural, suburban, and urban areas pose a low, but growing threat. Local street gangs transport and distribute drugs within very specific areas.

These gangs often imitate the larger, more powerful national gangs in order to gain respect from rivals. Some gangs collect millions of dollars per month selling illegal drugs, trafficking weapons, operating prostitution rings, and selling stolen property. Gangs launder proceeds by investing in real estate, recording studios, motorcycle shops, and construction companies. They also operate various cash-based businesses, such as barbershops, music stores, restaurants, catering services, tattoo parlors, and strip clubs, in order to commingle drug proceeds with funds generated through legitimate commerce.

What Is the Extent of Gang Operation and Crime in the United States?

There are at least 21,500 gangs and more than 731,000 active gang members in the United States. Gangs conduct criminal activity in all fifty states and U.S. territories. Although most gang activity is concentrated in major urban areas, gangs also are proliferating in rural and suburban areas of the country as gang members flee increasing law enforcement pressure in urban areas or seek more lucrative drug markets. This proliferation in non-urban areas increasingly is accompanied by violence and is threatening society in general.

According to a 2001 Department of Justice survey, 20 percent of students aged twelve through eighteen reported that street gangs had been present at their school during the previous six months. More than a quarter (28 percent) of students in urban schools reported a street gang presence, and 18 percent of students in suburban schools and 13 percent in rural schools reported the presence of street gangs. Public schools reported a much higher percentage of gang presence than private schools.

What Are the Dangers Associated with Gang Activity?

Large street gangs readily employ violence to control and expand drug distribution activities, targeting rival gangs and dealers who neglect or refuse to pay extortion fees. Members also use violence to ensure that members adhere to the gang's code of conduct or to prevent a member from leaving. In November 2004 a 19-year-old gang member in Fort Worth, Texas, was sentenced to thirty years in prison for fatally shooting a childhood friend who wanted to leave their local street gang.

Authorities throughout the country report that gangs are responsible for most of the serious violent crime in the major cities of the United States. Gangs engage in an array of criminal activities including assault, burglary, drive-by shooting, extortion, homicide, identification fraud, money laundering, prostitution operations, robbery, sale of stolen property, and weapons trafficking.

What Are Some Signs That Young People May Be Involved in Gang Activity?

Changes in behavior such as skipping school, hanging out with different friends, or, in certain places, spray-painting graffiti and using hand signals with friends can indicate gang affiliation.

In addition, individuals who belong to gangs often dress alike by wearing clothing of the same color, wearing bandannas, or even rolling up their pant legs in a certain way. Some gang members wear certain designer labels to show their gang affiliation. Gang members often have tattoos. Also, because gang violence frequently is glorified in rap music, young people involved in gangs often try to imitate the dress and actions of rap artists. Finally, because substance abuse is often a characteristic of gang members, young people involved in gang activity may exhibit signs of drug or alcohol use.

Drug Trends in Gangs

Street gangs have a high level of involvement in the distribution and sale of drugs. Respondents to the 2005 National Gang Threat Assessment Survey indicated that more than 50 percent of gangs had at least moderate involvement in street-level distribution, whereas at the wholesale level of distribution, gangs were more likely to have a lower level of involvement. Survey respondents indicated that gang involvement was highest with regard to the distribution and sale of marijuana and cocaine.

In Florida, drugs enter Miami via the Caribbean. Cocaine is transported throughout the Northeast and Midwest, with distribution at the wholesale and retail levels varying by jurisdiction. In Houston, Mexican criminal groups are the primary distributors of drugs at the wholesale level, whereas gangs, such as the Black Gangster Disciples, the Crips, the Latin Kings, and MS-13, control most retail distribution.

While the primary markets for methamphetamine remain in the central and western regions of the United States, the South is still greatly affected by the distribution and availability of this drug. Reports indicate that in such areas as Atlanta, Miami, Mississippi, New Orleans, and Tennessee, availability is increasing.

Such gangs as the Vice Lords and Sur 13 are known to be distributors of methamphetamine in the South, especially in Florida. OMGs and various local street crews are also highly involved in the distribution of methamphetamine at the retail level. Atlanta, Miami, and Houston remain primary markets for cocaine in the South. In Atlanta, wholesale Mexican traffickers transport the cocaine into the city for further distribution to drug markets throughout the southeastern and northeastern regions.

SUMMARY

- A criminal gang is generally defined as an organization that has a common name or identifying symbol; has particular conduct, status, and customs indicative of it; and has as one of its common activities engaging in criminal activity punishable as a felony, other than the conduct that constitutes the primary offense.

- Gang membership has increased exponentially since the 1960s. The gangs which flourished in Los Angeles in the 1960s have expanded to other cities in the United States and into Mexico and Central America.

- The National Youth Gang Survey estimated that there were 21,500 gangs and 731,500 active members in the United States. It is also estimated that U.S.-based gangs have fraternal links to some 300,000 gang members in Mexico and Central America. It is estimated that 85 percent of the gang members reside in large cities.

- The larger cities typically have more gangs, larger gangs, and gangs that have been in existence for longer periods of time. The large cities also tend to have gangs that are more involved in serious criminal activity, are more highly organized, and have a more identifiable leadership structure.

- Delinquent gangs are more common in smaller cities and tend to be more loosely organized, with ephemeral leadership. The smaller cities' gangs are generally newer and lack historic roots.

- Anti-gang tactics include mediation, situational crime prevention, working with families, and other strategies.

- Many researchers contend that anti-gang tactics that involve only law enforcement will solidify gangs by increasing cohesion among gang members.

- Most states use traditional criminal law in prosecuting most of the crimes committed by gang members. However, some gang-related offenses, like drive-by shootings, also were not adequately covered. New statutes were enacted to combat these deficiencies.

- The primary federal statutes used to prosecute street gangs are RICO and the CCE statutes, which are part of the Comprehensive Drug Abuse Prevention and Control Act of 1970.

- The two acts are designed to attack the conspiratorial nature of gangs and require prosecutors to present evidence of multiple criminal acts committed by various gang members to establish a pattern of criminal activity by the gangs.

- For RICO prosecutions the prosecutor must establish evidence of racketeering acts, known as predicate acts. A predicate act can include any substantive criminal act such as illegal drug distribution, fraud, thefts, or illegal gambling. In addition to establishing the predicate act or acts, the prosecutor must also establish that the enterprise (company or gang) was involved in the activities that resulted in the criminal acts being committed.

- As gangs migrate across the country, they bring with them crime and violence. Reasons for migration range from expansion of territories to families moving because of jobs or incarceration.

- Gangs remain the primary distributors of drugs throughout the United States.

- Gangs are associating with organized crime entities, such as Mexican drug organizations, Asian criminal groups, and Russian organized crime groups. These groups often turn to gangs to conduct low-level criminal activities, protect territories, and facilitate drug-trafficking activities. Financial gain is the primary goal of any association between these groups.

- Gang members are becoming more sophisticated in their use of computers and technology. These new tools are used to communicate, facilitate criminal activity, and avoid detection by law enforcement.

- Hispanic gangs are not a new phenomenon in the United States; however, they have increasingly become a concern for law enforcement agencies in recent years. As a result of the continuous growth in the Hispanic population throughout the United States, Hispanic gang membership is also increasing.

- Young women continue to take active roles in gangs. Although the number of female gangs is increasing, street gangs are still predominately made up of males.

- Most gangs in Indian Country are small and autonomous. Structurally, leadership tends to be decentralized, with collective decision making the common theme. Although some of these gangs will claim turf, gang alignment tends to revolve around which gang is perceived to be the most influential at any given time.

- Native-American gangs will often take on the characteristics of urban street gangs in terms of signs, symbols, and other forms of gang representation.

- Outlaw motorcycle gangs (OMGs) have been in existence for more than fifty years. The growth of OMGs and their increasing criminal endeavors have made them the subject of numerous criminal investigations by law enforcement. These criminal activities include, but are not limited to, murder, assault, kidnapping, prostitution, money laundering, weapons trafficking, motorcycle and motorcycle-parts theft, intimidation, extortion, arson, and the production, smuggling, transportation, and distribution of drugs.

- The use of illegal substances is considered as one of the major crime problems in the United States. Cocaine is believed to be the most prevalent drug for the majority of male and female users. Other popular drugs that are used include marijuana, heroin, amphetamines, and PCP.

- Another problem for law enforcement is the close link between drug use and street crime. The studies cited above clearly indicate that a majority of all criminals are heavily involved in drug use and abuse.

- Narcotics and their use are not a new phenomenon in our society. Opium was used by such noted physicians as Hippocrates.

- There is no doubt that U.S. society has an alcohol problem. The extent of the consumption of alcoholic beverages is staggering. An estimated 18 million American adults and several million children are experiencing physical, mental, and social problems related to the consumption of alcohol.

- The solutions to drug and alcohol abuse are complex and subject to wide-ranging debate.

- Most law enforcement departments have written policies and procedures for conducting drug screening tests when there are reasons to suspect that an officer has been using illegal drugs.

- Street gangs, outlaw motorcycle gangs, and prison gangs are the primary distributors of illegal drugs on the streets of the United States. Gangs also smuggle drugs into the United States and produce and transport drugs within the country.

Classroom Discussion Questions and Activities

1. The following problems examine various factual situations that involve driving or operating a motor vehicle. For purposes of these problems, you should assume that the defendant is intoxicated to the degree that all other elements of the offense have been satisfied.

Problem 1

In a state that requires the driving of a vehicle as part of the offense, an officer observed a vehicle, with its motor running, on the side of a deserted road approximately ten miles from the nearest residence. The defendant was passed out in the backseat.

ISSUE: Do these facts establish driving? The courts in these situations will look to determine if there was sufficient evidence to establish that the defendant was in control of the vehicle and had driven it to that location. The fact that the incident occurred on a deserted road and the defendant was in the car normally will carry weight. The defendant must then rebut this evidence and put forth facts that raise a reasonable doubt in the minds of the judge or jury. Normally, defendants in these situations contend that someone else was the driver and they were merely intoxicated passengers. However, the location of the defendant in the car will be considered vital in establishing this element. What if the defendant was passed out in the passenger's side of the front seat? What if he was slumped over the wheel? [*State v. Blaine*, 148 Vt. 272, 531 A.2d 933 (1987)]

Problem 2

In a state that prohibits operation of a vehicle while under the influence, an officer observed a vehicle moving on a public road in an erratic manner. After stopping the car and approaching the driver's side, the officer observed a ten-year-old behind the wheel and the defendant in the passenger seat. The defendant was obviously intoxicated and stated that the minor was her son.

ISSUE: Was the defendant operating the vehicle within the meaning of the statute? In this situation, the courts will hold the defendant was not "operating" the vehicle. She may have legal custody or control of the vehicle by virtue of the relationship with the driver and may be charged with contributing to the delinquency of a minor, but she will probably not be convicted of DUI. [*State Dept. of Public Safety v. Juncewski*, 308 N.W.2d 316 (1981)]

Problem 3

Under the same statute as in problem 2, the officer discovered the defendant in the vehicle with its engine running, but the gear shift was in the park position and the emergency brake was on.

ISSUE: Was the defendant operating the vehicle within the meaning of the statute? Courts may find this element of the offense has been satisfied in these types of factual situations. The vehicle does not have to be in motion for the defendant to be operating it within the meaning of these statutes if the accused set in motion the operative machinery of the vehicle for purposes of putting it in motion. [Compare *State v. Hedding*, 122 Vt. 379, 172 A.2d 599 (1961) and *Commonwealth v. Plowman*, 28 Mass. App. Ct. 230, 548 N.E.2d 1278 (1990), upholding convictions, with *Ferguson v. City of Doraville*, 186 Ga. App. 430, 367 S.E.2d 551 (1988), which stated merely occupying a parked car is not sufficient for this element.]

2. What actions can be taken to combat the gang problem or to reduce the level of violence associated with gang activities?

3. Should the drug problem be treated as a "medical" problem?

4. Should law enforcement officers be subject to random and unannounced drug tests? Justify your position.

References

Abadinsky, H. (1993). *Drug abuse*, Chicago: Nelson-Hall.

Allnut, D., & Pennell, S. (2000). Crime in the San Diego region: Mid-year report. San Diego, CA: San Diego Association of Governments.

Blair, W. G. (1987, March 8). Study urges new measures to combat drugs. *New York Times*, p. A-1.

Coate, D., & Grossman, M. (1987). Change in alcoholic beverage prices and legal drinking ages: Effects on youth alcohol use and motor vehicle mortality. *Alcohol Health Res. World 22*.

DuPont, R. L. (1983). Teenage drug use: Opportunities for the pediatrician. *J. Pediatr. 102*(6), 1003–1007.

Egley, Jr., A. (2002, February). National youth gang survey trends from 1996 to 2000. OJJDP Fact Sheet. Washington, DC: U.S. Department of Justice, Office of Justice Programs, Office of Juvenile Justice and Delinquency Prevention, p. 2, at www.ncjrs.org/pdffiles1/ojjdp/fs200203.pdf. Accessed online September 25, 2006.

Egley, Jr., A., Howell, J. C., & Major, A. K. (2004). Recent patterns of gang problems in the United States: Results from the 1996–2002 national youth gang survey. In *American youth gangs at the millennium*, F.-A. Esbensen, S. G. Tibbetts, & L. Gaines. Long Groves, IL: Long Groves Press, pp. 103–104.

Fatal Accident Reporting System 1989: A Decade of Progress. (1991). Washington DC: Government Printing Office, Table 2-2, p. 2-2.

Garcia, M. (2005, February 1). N.Y. using terrorism law to prosecute street gang. *The Washington Post*, p. A-3.

History of Youth Gangs: Department of Justice, Office of Juvenile Justice and Delinquency Prevention. (1998, August). Youth gangs: An overview. Juvenile Justice Bulletin, at www.ojjdp.ncjrs.org/jjbulletin/9808/history.html. Accessed online December 3, 2004.

Howard, J., Ganikos, M. L., & Taylor, J. A. (1990). Alcohol prevention research. In *Drug and alcohol abuse prevention*, R. R. Watson (Ed.). Clifton, NJ: Humana Press.

Institute of Law and Justice (ILJ). (1994). Gang prosecution in the United States. Final Report Submitted to the National Institute of Justice, Washington, DC.

Jellick, E. M. (1960). *The disease concept of alcoholism*. New Brunswick, NJ: College and University Press.

Johnson, S. C. (2005, April 20). Testimony before the Subcommittee on the Western Hemisphere, U.S. House of Representatives. Posted at www.heritage.org Accessed online September 25, 2006.

Juvenile gangs: Crime and drug trafficking. (1988, September). *Juv. Just. Bull.* Washington, DC: Office of Juvenile Justice and Delinquency Prevention.

Katz, C. M. (2001). The establishment of a police gang unit: An examination of organizational and environmental factors. *Criminology, 39*(1), 37–73.

Klein, M. (1997). The problem of street gangs and problem-oriented policing. In *Problem-oriented policing: Crime-specific problems critical issues and making POP work*, T. O. Shelley & A. C. Grant (Eds.). Washington, DC: Police Executive Research Forum, pp. 57–88.

Law Enforcement News. (1988, April 30). John Jay College of Criminal Justice, City University of New York.

Lee, H. (1963). *How dry were we: Prohibition revisited*. Englewood Cliffs, NJ: Prentice-Hall.

Liska, K. (1990). *Drugs and the human body* (3rd ed.). New York: Macmillan, p. 218.

McEwen, J. T., Manili, B., & Connors, E. (1986, October). National Institute of Law Enforcement and Criminal Justice Research Project. Employee drug testing policies in police departments: A summary report. Washington, DC: Government Printing Office.

Moore, M. H., & Kleiman, M. A. R. (1989, September). The police and drugs. Perspectives on Policing, U.S. Department of Justice.

Moskowitz, J. M. (1989). The primary prevention of alcohol problems: A critical review of the research literature. *J. Stud. Alcohol 50*, 54–88.

National Drug Intelligence Center. (2005). Pamphlet: NDIC Product No. 2005-L0559-001, Drugs and gangs fast facts, questions and answers. Washington, DC: U.S. Department of Justice.

National Gang Threat Assessment Report. (2005). Grant Number 2003-DD-BX-031, Washington, DC: Bureau of Justice Assistance, U.S. Department of Justice.

National Youth Gang Survey. (2005). Juvenile Justice Clearinghouse, Office of Juvenile Justice and Delinquency Prevention, Rockville, MD.

Office of the Surgeon General. (1988, December 14–16). Surgeon general's workshop on drunk driving proceedings. Washington, DC: Government Printing Office, pp. 8–11.

Office on Smoking and Health. (1989). Smoking control policies. In *Reducing the health consequences of smoking: 25 years of progress*. A report of the Surgeon General's Centers for Disease Control. Rockville, MD: DHHS Publication No. [CDC] 89-8411, pp. 461–536.

Painter, J. (1989). Bolivia's new president faces an old problem: How to control coca growing. Latinamerica Press.

Reed, W. L. & Decker, S. H. (Eds.). (2002). Responding to gangs: Evaluation and research. NCJ 190351 Research Publication. Washington, DC: Department of Justice.

Rosenzweig, P. (2006). The gang act needs modification. Heritage Foundation Web Memo at www.heritage.org/ Research/Crime/wm494.cfm. Accessed online September 25, 2006.

Trebach, A. S. (1987). *The great drug war*. New York: Macmillan.

Tully, E. J., & Bennett, M. (1989, August). A law enforcement response to legalizing illicit drugs. *Police Chief*, 57–64.

U.S. Department of Justice, (2004). *Sourcebook of criminal justice statistics*. Washington, DC: Government Printing Office.

Where poppies once stood. (1984). *Far Eastern Econ. Rev. 10*.

Whitehead, J. (1986). U.S. international narcotics control programs and policies. *Dept. of State Bull.*

Police Operations in Culturally Diverse Communities

" The communities of the United States in which the police operate have been constructed from people from many different shores. "

—Ronald Takaki, A Different Mirror:
A History of Multi-cultural America, 1993.

CHAPTER OUTLINE

- Introduction
- Changing Demographics
- Skeletons in the Closet
- Contemporary Problems
- Police–Minority Relations Today
- Dangerous Traits and Behaviors
- Improving Police–Minority Relations
- The Culturally Competent Police Officer
- Hate and Bias Crimes
- Summary

OBJECTIVES

After completion of this chapter, you will be able to do the following:

- Describe demographic changes taking shape in the United States.
- Discuss how past events, such as police abuses, impact the state of police–minority relations today.
- Discuss how contemporary problems, such as racial profiling, can exacerbate police–minority relations.
- Discuss the current state of police–minority relations.
- Identify dangerous behaviors and traits that police officers should avoid pertaining to their views of race and ethnicity.
- Discuss strategies for improving police–minority relations.
- Discuss how being culturally competent can enhance beat management.
- Describe specific strategies for responding to hate and bias crimes.
- Describe the three types of hate and bias offenders.

INTRODUCTION

A sixteen-year-old African-American male named Marcus is walking home late one autumn evening. There is a bitter chill in the air as he hurries to get home. He works at the local supermarket sacking groceries. It's his first job and he puts in about twenty hours a week so that he can make some spending cash for clothes and shoes, which he would otherwise go without. Marcus lives with his mother in the **ghetto** area of the community.

Marcus is about two blocks from home when he notices headlights creeping up behind him. He continues walking without looking back. He knows that in the inner city it is sometimes a matter of survival to mind your own business.

Suddenly there is a loud bellow from the police car that has been following: "STOP, POLICE: WE WANT TO TALK WITH YOU!" There are two white police officers in the patrol car. The officers ask Marcus for identification and begin to pepper him with questions: "Where have you been?" "What are you doing out walking in this area?" "Where are you going?" "Do you have any drugs or firearms on you?"

A fear of the police was instilled in Marcus at an early age. Growing up, he heard stories of police harassment and excessive use of force. Marcus was taught not to give the police a hard time, and to do everything that is requested or he may end up beaten, in jail, or dead. After several minutes of being questioned he is released.

ghetto / An area within a city in which members of a particular cultural, ethnic, religious, or national group live in high concentration. The term *ghetto* is now commonly associated with notions of deprivation, unemployment, and social exclusion and is sometimes used interchangeably with the term *inner city*.

Marcus continues walking home. The police stops have become so common that he thinks nothing of it, he is numbed to the experience, and he simply goes through the routine. It's an everyday part of living in the inner city. To him, the police are seen as people to fear, the representatives of a system that more often than not is unfair to minorities. Ironically, this fear has been perpetuated through generations of minorities living in the United States. Bell (2000) argues that from the earliest time in our history, a primary role of the police was to keep African-Americans under control and that this dates back to slavery.

Police officers will increasingly interact with racially and ethnic diverse populations. Police relations with minority communities have always been somewhat strained, and continue to be today.

This chapter discusses police operations in culturally diverse communities. While the chapter discusses operational guidelines that the police can utilize to foster better police–minority relations, this book seeks to place police–minority relations within a broader, historical framework. This makes it necessary, as painful as it may be, to examine the skeletons in the closet. By so doing, police officers who work in minority neighborhoods will be in a better position to make more informed decisions that impact the neighborhood, as well as having a conceptual understanding of why many in the minority community still look upon the police with an aura of suspicion. Furthermore, students of the police can begin to critically think about how the past has a direct impact on the current state of police–minority relations. In order to assist you in understanding the ever-evolving cultural diversity in the United States, we begin the chapter with a brief look at the changing demographics.

Children stand before old slum houses in a small Vermont town where unemployment is high due to decline in industrial jobs. This town, with many tenement dwellings like this one, had the highest unemployment rating in the state. Generally the area will also be a high crime area.

CHANGING DEMOGRAPHICS

The United States is distinguished by the size and diversity of its racial and ethnic populations. From all indications, these trends promise to endure. In fact, some demographers project that by the year 2050 the United States will likely have no single majority group.

The ever-evolving diversity trends in the United States have implications for policing in a variety of areas, including recruiting to ensure adequate representation of women and minorities in the ranks, training of police officers, as well as the type and quality of policing services offered in diverse communities. Furthermore, the changing demographics associated with increased life expectancy, an aging population, retirement of the baby boomers, more immigrants, changes in the ethnic makeup, and generational diversity are all expected to create new demands on police operations.

Throughout history, the ethnic and cultural diversity of the United States' population has grown constantly. During much of that time, established American groups assumed that newcomers would be assimilated into existing cultural patterns; this is referred to as the **melting pot** model. In the twenty-first century, the melting pot model has been recognized as neither a good description of what has happened nor a plausible prediction of what can happen as our population continues to diversify rapidly.

melting pot / A place where immigrants of different ethnicity or cultures form an integrated and homogenous society.

A more appropriate way to refer to what has occurred in the United States is **pluralism**. A pluralistic society is one in which members of diverse ethnic, racial, religious, or social groups maintain an autonomous participation in and development of their traditional culture. Pluralism is the concept that various groups in society have mutual respect for one another's culture, a respect that allows minorities to express their own culture without suffering prejudice or hostility (Schaefer, 2000). The religious and cultural patterns of American society are now more varied than ever, and police must continually strive to develop appropriate methods to police a pluralistic society.

pluralism / The notion that various groups in a society have mutual respect for one another's culture, a respect that allows minorities to express their own culture without suffering prejudice or hostility.

Police officers entering the policing profession in the twenty-first century face both a citizen population and a set of professional values that require skills for negotiating cultural difference. **Multiculturalism** is a definition that has taken on different meanings over the years. A multicultural society is one that is made up of many different ethnic and racial groups.

multiculturalism / A term used to describe many cultures learning to get along with one another with mutual respect.

The population of the United States continues to grow increasingly diverse. In recent years, Hispanics have grown faster than the population as a whole. Chideya Farai in her book, *The Color of our Future* (1999), revealed that America's racial composition is changing more rapidly than ever and the number of immigrants in America is the largest in any post-World War II period. The proportion of African-Americans has been rising gradually, and by 2020 they are predicted to comprise about 12.9 percent of our total population. Similarly, by 2020 Asian-Americans will represent about 6.5 percent of the American population and Hispanics will be responsible for more than 37 percent of our total population.

By the year 2030, it is projected that one out of four U.S. residents will be Hispanic or Asian in ethic makeup. According to the U.S. Census Bureau, the current total U.S. population is estimated at 281,421,906, and is based on current growth rates applied to the 2000 Census figures.

Voices of Experience

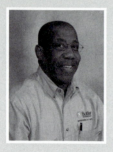

Cultural Awareness Training

Excerpts from an interview between Cliff Roberson and Jeffery L. Tymony.
Professor Tymony has held numerous positions in the criminal justice field
and is currently a professor at Butler Community College, El Dorado, Kansas.

Q: *I notice that you are a cultural awareness trainer. What does cultural awareness training include?*

A: It includes creating cultural sensitivity for others. For law enforcement, cultural sensitivity is a couple of things. First, the officer should be sensitive to the needs of the community he or she is serving. Most law enforcement officers are men and most are white. They are generally not of the same racial or social background as the many individuals in the communities they serve and they cannot impose their value systems on the people they are suppose to protect and serve. That is one component of the training.

The second component of the training is learning how to communicate with different cultures. The officers must accept the training. If the training is touchy, feely type training, the officers won't listen. You have to ease them into it. Explain that it may save their lives or keep them out of a lawsuit. For example, in Los Angeles, when an individual was arrested the officers required him or her to kneel and put the hands behind the head. Many officers did not understand why the Asian-Americans, especially those of Laotian or Vietnamese ancestry, were upset at this type of handling and many would resist being arrested. The officers failed to understand that to these Americans, the kneeling and putting your hands behind your head was the "assassination position."

Who the officers talk to first when he or she answers a dispatch to a home is a cultural issue. With Asian-Americans, the officers should first talk to the elders. When talking to Hispanic youths, as a general rule, because of cultural background, they will not look you in the eye. This doesn't mean they are trying to hide something or are not involved, it's a cultural thing. In the United States, we have pockets of subcultures. It is in the best interest of the officers to be sensitive to the cultural differences of the various cultures.

The length of the program varies. Normally we train about four hours at a time. There is not a lot of lecture; it is an interactive series of exercises where you put them in a scenario where they are a member of a minority culture. One exercise that we use is called "shelter." The training group has to come to a consensus regarding the exercise. Under the scenario, the world is about to be hit by a comet. There is going to be a period of darkness and it will be cold. You are in a safe position as long as you are in the shelter, but to survive you need individuals with certain skills. The group has to decide who is going to be in the shelter when it closes. Only about five people out of the fifteen can be in the shelter. I give them a list of people that the group can choose from. The list has people of all ages, races, and skills. The argument comes down to who will help them survive when they come out of the shelter. They stop thinking about race, religion, background, and start thinking about what is needed to survive. In the critique we discuss how they made their decisions, and it is normally based on survival skills. Their biases disappear. There are other exercises about value clarification. I am not trying to change their values, but only to create an awareness of cultural differences. ■

Racial and ethnic diversity has always been central to American society. Immigration from different parts of the world, and the different fertility and mortality rates among recent migrants, has kept the racial and ethnic composition in flux. In 1999, African-Americans were the largest minority in the United States, accounting for 12.1 percent of the population. However, according to the U.S. Census (2000), the Hispanic population grew at nearly four times the rate of the U.S. population

Diversity in the United States in 2000

	Total Population	Percent of Population
Total Population	281,421,906	100
White	211,460,626	75.1
Black or African-American	34,658,190	12.3
American Indian and Alaska Native	2,475,956	0.9
Asian	10,242,998	3.6
Native Hawaiian and other Pacific Islander	398,835	0.1
Other race	15,359,073	5.5
Two or more races	6,826,228	2.4
Hispanic or Latino	35,305,818	12.5

Note: Percentages add up to more than 100 percent because Hispanics may be of any race and are therefore counted under more than one category and because of rounding error.

Source: U.S. Census Bureau, Census 2000, p. 132.

overall during the last two years, cementing the Latinos' position as the country's largest minority group.

By 2025, Hispanics will account for 18 percent of the U.S. population, while only 13 percent of the population will be African-American. Over the same period, the percentage of whites will decline by ten percentage points, to 62 percent. If current trends continue, almost half of the U.S. population will be non-white by 2050. The Population Reference Bureau projected significant racial and ethic changes to the landscape of the United States by the year 2025. They compare projected 2025 data with 1999 data.

Growing Diversity: Prediction as to How the Population Will Change

	1999 (%)	2025 (%)
White	71.9	62.0
Black	12.1	12.9
Hispanic	11.5	18.2
Asian/other	4.5	7.0

Note: White, Black, and Asian/other categories exclude Hispanics, who may be of any race. The Asian/other category includes American Indians, Eskimos, Aleuts, and Pacific Islanders. Totals may not add to 100 due to rounding error.

Source: Population Reference Bureau. Accessed online at www.prb.org/ on November 11, 2006.

SKELETONS IN THE CLOSET

One of the major concerns in law enforcement is gaining the community's support and acceptance of law enforcement and its agents (Coffey, Eldefonso, & Hartinger, 1982). Many of the tensions and mistrust of minorities toward the police have been passed along from generation to generation. Much of the distrust between the police and minority communities can be, at least in part, explained by historical events. In order to illustrate the historical significance, some selected events are discussed. The objective of these examples is to place the chapter's discussion within a broader historical framework. By providing an historical framework, the state of police–minority relations can be better understood. In fact, we don't have to glance that far back in history to get a not-so-glamorous look at police–minority relations gone astray.

Watts Riot

The Watts Riot in Los Angeles, California, erupted on August 13, 1965, as the result of a routine arrest of a drunk driver. A Los Angeles police officer flagged down motorist Marquette Frye, whom he suspected of being intoxicated. When a crowd of primarily African-American onlookers began to taunt the police officer, a second officer was called in. According to eyewitness accounts, the second officer struck crowd members with his baton, and news of the act of police brutality soon spread throughout the neighborhood. The incident, combined with escalating racial tensions, overcrowding in the neighborhood, and a summer heat wave, sparked violence on a massive scale. Despite attempts the following day aimed at quelling anti-police sentiment, residents began looting and burning local stores.

The rioting lasted five days and more than thirty-four people died, at least 1,000 were wounded, and an estimated $200,000 million in property was destroyed. An estimated 35,000 African-Americans took part in the riot, which required 16,000 national guardsmen, county sheriff's deputies, and police to end. Although city officials initially blamed outside persons for the insurrection, subsequent studies showed that the majority of participants had lived in Watts all their lives. Studies also found that the protesters' anger was directed primarily at white shopkeepers in the neighborhood and at members of the nearly all-white Los Angeles Police Department. The rioters left African-American churches, libraries, businesses, and private homes virtually untouched.

Zoot Suit Riots

The zoot suit riots were a series of riots that erupted in Los Angeles, California, during World War II, between servicemen stationed in Los Angeles and Mexican-American youths, recognized because of the zoot suits they favored.

The riots began in the racially charged atmosphere of Los Angeles, where servicemen returning from the war had increasingly come into conflict with the local Mexican "zoot suiters." On June 3, 1943, a group of servicemen on leave complained that they had been assaulted by a gang of Mexican-American youth (also referred to at the time as *Pachucos*). Pachucos were Mexican-American youth who developed their own subculture during the 1930s and 1940s, primarily in the Southwestern United States. In response, the servicemen gathered and proceeded to downtown and East Los Angeles, which was largely inhabited by the Mexican-Americans. They attacked all the men they found wearing zoot suits, often ripping off the suits and burning them in the streets. In many instances, the police intervened by arresting beaten-up Mexican-American youths for disturbing the peace.

The Detroit Riots

The Detroit Riots of 1967 started when Detroit vice officers executed a raid on an after-hours drinking club in a predominantly African-American neighborhood. The officers expected to round up a few patrons, but instead found eighty-two people inside the club holding a party for two returning Vietnam veterans.

The officers made multiple arrests at the scene. While they waited for the arrival of prisoner transportation vehicles, a crowd gathered around the establishment and began to protest the arrests. After the last police car left the area, a small group of African-American men who were confused and upset because they were kicked out of the club lifted up the bars of a clothing store located next door, and broke the windows. Looting and fires then spread rapidly through the northwest side of Detroit. The disorder then spread to the east side of Detroit. Within forty-eight hours, the National Guard was mobilized, to be followed by the 82nd airborne on the riot's fourth day. As police and military troops sought to regain control of the city, violence escalated. At the conclusion of the rioting, which lasted five days, forty-three people were dead, well over 1,100 injured, and over 7,000 people had been arrested.

There have been many explanations of why the riots occurred. Some of these explanations include political, economic, and social factors; police abuse; lack of affordable housing; urban renewal projects; economic inequality; African-American militancy; and rapid demographic change.

It is well known that in the 1960s some members of the Detroit Police Department routinely harassed African-Americans, including using racial epithets and excessive force. Such excessive use of force was manifested in the 1962 police shooting of an African-American prostitute who was shot in the back while fleeing from the back of a patrol car. Other cases of police brutality in Detroit included the severe beating of a prostitute, and the beating of an African-American teenager for allegedly disturbing the peace.

Tulia, Texas

In one other case that gained national attention, nearly 10 percent of the African-American residents of small town Tulia, Texas, were arrested and indicted on bogus drug charges. In the Tulia case, an eighteen-month drug sting led to the arrest of forty-six of the town's 4,699 residents. Coordinated by the Panhandle Regional Narcotics Trafficking Task Force, the operation netted thirty-eight narcotics trafficking convictions with defendants receiving sentences as long as ninety years in prison.

The sting operation earned undercover officer Tom Coleman the coveted "Outstanding Lawman of the Year" award, presented by the Texas Narcotic Control Program. Subsequently, a state district court judge ruled that all thirty-eight convictions should be overturned due to revelations that Coleman, the sole undercover officer in the sting, fabricated evidence and perjured himself while testifying against the defendants. Twelve of those convicted were immediately released. The remaining defendants have already been paroled or released since the judge's ruling.

Other Incidents

On April 29, 1992, Los Angeles police officers pulled over Rodney King, an African-American male, for a traffic violation. According to the officers, King emerged from his automobile in an aggressive manner that suggested he might have been high on drugs. Before handcuffing King, the police delivered some fifty-six blows and kicks and a number of shocks from a Taser stungun to the fallen body of the suspect while almost twenty other officers stood by and watched. A man named George Holliday, standing on the balcony of a nearby building, videotaped the incident. The next day, he gave his eighty-one-second tape to Los Angeles TV channel five. By the end of the day, the video was being broadcast by TV stations around the world. Four days later, all the charges were dropped against King and four officers were charged with felony assault and other beating-related charges.

The Independent Commission on the Los Angeles Police Department came out three months later documenting the "systematic use of excessive force and racial harassment in the LAPD." It also noted management problems and condemned the department's emphasis on crime control rather than crime prevention, which served to isolate the police from the public.

On April 29, 1992, the four police officers were found not guilty of committing any crimes against Rodney King. After the announcement of the verdict, the local police were caught fleeing the area where large-scale riots had erupted. The National Guard was then called in. The riots ended six days after they began and resulted in the deaths of forty-two people, the burning of 700 structures, the arrest of nearly 5,000 people, and almost one billion dollars in property damage. Because of the riots, the U.S. Justice Department resumed the investigations that had begun due to the King beating.

Spray-painted graffiti about police brutality. This graffiti indicates an act of misconduct by the police can seriously damage the community's respect for the police.

Recently in Los Angeles, an African-American car theft suspect whose video-taped beating by a Los Angeles police officer drew comparisons to the infamous assault on Rodney King, reached a $450,000 settlement with the city. The suspect was kneed and then struck eleven times with a large metal flashlight by a police officer. The beating, captured by a television news crew in a helicopter, occurred at the end of a high-speed, twenty-one-mile car chase that began in South Los Angeles. Los Angeles Police Chief William J. Bratton fired the officer shortly after a three-person Board of Rights found the officer guilty of using unnecessary force. Bratton also announced that the department would phase out the use of the large metal flashlights. The car theft suspect was not charged with any crimes (Krikorian, 2006).

A Necessary Examination

For some readers of this chapter, the events discussed previously are not new to you, and for many, you were probably not born when these events transpired. A discussion of these past police abuses isn't taken up in this chapter to keep living in the past, but is to place the suspicions that many minority communities hold toward the police into a proper historical context. In essence, the skeletons in the closet have to be pulled out, acknowledged, and examined in order to effectively understand the complex nature of contemporary police–minority relations.

By critically examining injustices of the past, police authorities can move toward reconciliation and a more harmonious relationship with the minority community. However, this is a "two-way street." In order to make police–minority relations work, the minority community must also be willing to engage in productive dialogue with the police, as opposed to just verbalizing concerns. A recent Police Executive Research Forum (2001) report suggests that minority community members can get involved by:

- Engaging in dialogue about solutions, rather than about blame.
- Encouraging one another to apply for employment with the police department, and supporting those who go through the process.
- Developing a broad understanding of professional police practices (perhaps through contacts with national and state police organizations), in order to form an objective standard by which to judge police actions.
- Acknowledging police officers who promote positive police–community relationships with awards or other commendations.

CONTEMPORARY PROBLEMS

There are a number of problems that have an affect on the state of police–community relations in the United States. To casual observers there may be the general appearance that everything is OK, and that police relations with the minority community is so far removed from their lives that a certain sense of apathy prevails. Perhaps there is even the thought that if everyone would simply follow the rules, they wouldn't have problems with the police. This viewpoint, of course, is somewhat narrow in the sense that there are a number of factors that should be placed in proper context, especially if you are a minority citizen living in the inner city.

Undeniably, the plight of the inner-city residential complexes across the United States has become an intensely debated topic. The problem of high concentrations of poor and poorly educated minority families in substandard housing, many of whom are out of work, in an environment rife with crime, dysfunctional families, and domestic violence, has created a host of problems for the police. Blight, high crime, business deterioration, and white flight have combined to create inner-city landscapes that give the appearance of war zones rather than neighborhoods.

The police are caught in the nonenvious position between enforcing the law while doing so in a manner as to avoid the appearance of targeting the inner-city community for disproportionate law enforcement. While police authorities continue to struggle with how to best provide services in minority communities, the accusations that some police officers disproportionately stop minorities simply because of the color of their skin has exacerbated the problem.

Racial Profiling

One of the more perplexing issues facing the criminal justice system today is the allegation that some contemporary police practices are motivated by bias and racism. Some observers have accused the police of systematically stopping minority motorists simply because of the color of their skin, while the police themselves emphatically deny these allegations. This alleged practice has come to be known as **racial profiling**.

racial profiling / The practice of constructing a set of characteristics or behaviors based on race and using that set of characteristics to decide whether an individual might be guilty of some crime and therefore worthy of a stop, investigation, or arrest.

Racial profiling is "any police-initiated action that relies on the race, ethnicity, or national origin rather than the behavior of an individual or information that leads the police to a particular individual who has been identified as being, or having been, engaged in criminal activity" (Ramirez, McDevitt, & Farrell, 2000, p. 3). Racial profiling, whether real or perceived, can have a devastating impact on police–minority relations.

Recently, the United States Commission on Civil Rights (2000) set forth recommendations to improve the quality of police protection while ensuring the protection of civil rights for all Americans. The commission's report asserted that the issue of racial profiling remains the highest priority and recommended the enactment of legislation to prosecute violators and increased efforts to eliminate its practice in all law enforcement activities.

Anecdotal evidence suggests that many minorities believe that the police routinely stop and search them because of the color of their skin (Harris, 1999; Weitzer & Tuch, 2002). Often, this evidence is dismissed as isolated experiences of angry, overly sensitive, or disgruntled minorities. Some statistical evidence, however, tends to confirm the anecdotal accounts of minority citizens that they are indeed being singled out for traffic stops and searches.

Antonovics and Knight (2004) reviewed vehicle search data from the Boston Police Department. They discovered that more than 43 percent of all searches were of African-American motorists, even though these motorists represented only 33 percent of the cars that were stopped by the police.

A study in Ohio found that African-Americans were twice more likely to be stopped by the police than non-African-Americans. In the study, traffic citation information was examined from four of the largest municipal court systems in Ohio. It was discovered that in Akron, African-Americans received 37 percent of all citations for moving violations; in Toledo, they received 31 percent; in Dayton, the number was 50 percent; and in Franklin County, which includes Columbus, the figure was 25 percent (Harris, 1999).

In San Diego, African-American and Hispanic drivers were found to be over-represented in vehicle stops. African-American drivers had about a 60 percent greater chance of being stopped by the police when compared to whites, and Hispanic drivers about a 37 percent chance of being stopped (Cordner, Williams, & Velasco, 2002).

Citizens also seem to think that racial profiling indeed occurs. A 1999 Gallup poll of citizens found that 59 percent of Americans believe that race-based profiling was widespread (Newport, 1999). Consistent with national polls, qualitative assessments by the Police Executive Research Forum (2001) reveals a theme that citizens believe that racial profiling occurs on a fairly widespread basis.

CASE STUDY: Selected Racial Profiling Cases

United States v. Miller, 821 F.2d 546 (11th Cir. 1987)

The defendant was stopped on I-95 primarily because he matched the police officers' "drug courier profile" (which considers race). After his motion to suppress evidence was denied by the trial court, the defendant was convicted of possession of cocaine with intent to distribute. The 11th Circuit, on appeal, held that driving "cautiously" and failing to look at a trooper on the side of the road, both part of the "drug courier profile," did not constitute probable cause to stop a car for a drug search. The court also held that any consent given was the product of the illegal detention (thus not voluntary) and that the taint of the unreasonable stop was not sufficiently attenuated. This case resembled another involving the same officer who had used the same drug profile to illegally stop and search a vehicle [*U.S. v. Smith*, 799 F.2d 704 (11th Cir. 1986)].

Ferguson v. City of Montgomery, 969 F.Supp. 674 (N.D.Ala. 1997)

The plaintiff was stopped at the Montgomery, Alabama, Greyhound station because police had received an anonymous tip that a "black male" who was acting as a "drug mule" was on his bus. Though the race and gender descriptions matched, the height and weight descriptions did not. The plaintiff was patted down and officers found a pistol, which the plaintiff told them he was carrying because he was a member of the Los Angeles School Police. After the officers realized the plaintiff wasn't the "drug mule," they then believed him to be an escaped prisoner from Pickens County. The Pickens County Sheriff informed them that the plaintiff was not the escaped prisoner and the officers arrested the plaintiff for impersonating a peace officer and for carrying a pistol without a license. Both charges were later dismissed. The plaintiff

subsequently filed claims under 42 U.S.C. secs. 1981, 1986, and 1983 (violation of constitutional rights under the Fourth, Fifth, Sixth, Eigthth, and Fourteenth Amendments) against the arresting officers.

The plaintiff later requested that the Eighth Amendment claim be dismissed, which it was. The court dismissed the section 1981 claim for failure to state the claim in the complaint. The court held that in order to bring the section 1986 claim, there must be an implied section 1985 claim that expressly states discrimination due to race or some other class. The plaintiff failed to express such a claim, so he was given ten days to amend his complaint. The 11th Circuit uses a two-prong test to determine whether officers are exempt from qualified immunity from Fourth Amendment claims and held that since the officers passed this test, they dismissed the plaintiff's Fourth Amendment claim.

The court held that the plaintiff did not provide sufficient detail for defendants to prepare adequate response to his Fifth, Sixth, and Fourteenth Amendment claims, thus giving the plaintiff ten days to amend his complaint to provide such detail.

United States v. Pruitt, 174 F 3d 1215 (11th Cir. 1999)

Hispanic motorists who were convicted of drug possession appealed on the basis that the officers had no authority to search their car as the traffic stop was only for speeding. Citing the Supreme Court decision in Knowles, the 11th Circuit agreed with the defendants, reversing their convictions. The court discussed the fact that the defendants' Hispanic appearance and out-of-state license plates resulted in a racial profile "fishing expedition" that would not alone have warranted a stop.

Responding to Racial Profiling

In response to allegations of racial profiling, many jurisdictions have begun to track information about those who are stopped, searched, ticketed, and/or arrested by law enforcement officers (Engel & Calnon, 2004). In 1999, under pressure to address minority complaints about police treatment, U.S. Attorney General Janet Reno called for police departments to collect more hard data to see whether and where racial profiling may be occurring. As a result, the U.S. Department of Justice prepared a resource guide on racial profiling data collection systems with the objective to assist law enforcement agencies with data collection (Ramirez, McDevitt, & Farrell, 2000).

President George W. Bush, in his February 27, 2001 address to a Joint Session of Congress, declared "that racial profiling is wrong and we will end it in America." He directed the attorney general to review the use of race by federal law enforcement authorities as a factor in conducting stops, searches, and other law enforcement investigative procedures.

In 1997, U.S. Congressman John Conyers first introduced the Traffic Stops Statistics Act, which requires the collection of several categories of data on each law enforcement traffic stop, including the race of the driver and whether a search was performed. The bill passed in the U.S. House of Representatives, but was not considered by the Senate. It has been reintroduced each congressional session since then, but as of 2006 has not been approved by both houses.

Many individual states have passed data collection acts that call for law enforcement to collect driver data pertaining to age, race, gender, ethnicity, reason for stop and alleged violation, date, time, location, license plate number, warning given, citation given, arrest made, personal search conducted, search of vehicle conducted, contraband found, items seized for forfeiture, and authority for search.

Data collection efforts are an attempt to provide the tangible numbers that will enable police and community leaders to better understand their policing activities. With this understanding, police departments will be able to examine and revamp policing strategies based on effectiveness, reconfigure deployment of police resources, or take other measures. Data collection includes both the collection of the numbers and objective analysis of the data, which is often done through a partnership between the police department and outside experts.

Data collection has the potential to allow researchers and police authorities to gauge the proportionality of traffic stops based on racial factors. However, simply collecting race-based data alone may do little to assist a law enforcement agency in answering questions about its practices. In addition, the law enforcement agency must arrange for the analysis and interpretation of what the data means. This analysis process may lead to more questions than answers, which can be frustrating for both the police and the community.

One other potential problem with data collection efforts that police supervisors and commanders should remain aware of is if law enforcement officers believe they are being monitored, they may disengage from police activity. In other words, officers would selectively reduce their traffic stops in order to avoid any behavior that might be perceived as racially biased. Proper training and standard operating procedures should minimize this to a certain extent.

It is crucial that law enforcement objectives be carried out without the consideration of race. However, we point out that the situation is different when a police officer acts on the personal identifying characteristics of potential suspects, including

Denver Police Department Mission Statement

To promote and enhance a healthy relationship between the Denver Police and the community through mutual accountability, which promotes open communication and fosters respect and trust.

In order to accomplish this we will do the following:

- Ensure that bias profiling does not occur
- Compile statistical data as to the nature of police contacts
- Develop policies that reflect this position
- Create training programs for the community and the police
- Develop standards and monitor compliance
- Value safe neighborhoods and support policing to ensure the safety of elders, youth, disabled, and all individuals.

Source: www.Denvergov.org. Accessed online October 20, 2006.

PRACTICE HINTS

Data Collection Records Should Include at a Minimum:

- Location of the stop
- Date and time of the stop
- Age, race/ethnicity, and gender of the driver
- Traffic violation or reason for the stop
- Disposition of a stop (arrest, citation, warning, or no action)
- Whether a search was conducted of the driver, passengers, or vehicle
- If a search was conducted, was any contraband discovered or seized and the nature of the contraband
- Whether the officer knew the race/ethnicity of the driver before the stop

age, sex, ethnicity, or race. Obviously, when a victim or witness describes the assailant as being of a particular race, authorities may properly limit their search for suspects to persons of that race. Thus, it is important to remember that in conducting activities in connection with a specific investigation, police officers may consider race and ethnicity only to the extent that there is trustworthy information, relevant to the locality or time frame that links persons of a particular race or ethnicity to an identified criminal incident.

The Police Executive Research Forum (2001) presented a model policy statement as a guide for law enforcement agencies that addressed racial profiling. The policy, in part, reads:

> Officers shall not consider race/ethnicity in establishing either reasonable suspicion or probable cause. Similarly, officers shall not consider race/ethnicity in deciding to initiate even these nonconsensual encounters that do not amount to legal detentions or to request consent to search (p. 52).

University of Texas at Austin Campus Police Racial Profiling Statement

During the 77th Texas Legislative Session, a state statute was enacted to address the state legislators' growing concern regarding the practice of racial profiling in the law enforcement profession. Specifically, the statute mandated that police agencies in the State of Texas shall implement a policy that complies with Texas Code of Criminal Procedure, Articles 2.131, 2.133, and 2.134.

The University of Texas at Austin Campus Police Department (UTPD) in compliance instituted a policy that addressed racial profiling and provided a compliant process for those who believe they have been stopped or searched based on racial, ethnic, or national origin profiling.

Policy Statement

Two of the fundamental rights guaranteed by the United States and Texas constitutions are equal protection under the law and freedom from unreasonable searches and seizures by government agents. The right of all persons to be treated equally and to be free from unreasonable searches and seizures must be respected. Racial profiling is an unacceptable patrol tactic and will not be condoned.

It is the practice of UTPD to police in a proactive and responsible manner and to enforce state and federal laws without regard to race, ethnicity, or national origin. All University of Texas at Austin police officers are expected to conduct themselves in a dignified and respectful manner when dealing with the public.

UTPD will accept complaints from any person who believes he or she has been stopped or searched based on racial, ethnic, or national origin profiling. Complaints should be directed to the University Police Department shift commander at 512-471-4441 or the internal affairs investigator at 512-475-6711. All complaints will be investigated in a thorough and timely manner.

Source: University of Texas at Austin website at www.utexas.edu.police. Accessed online November 8, 2006.

PRACTICE HINTS

Racial Profiling

- In making routine or spontaneous law enforcement decisions, such as ordinary traffic stops, police officers should never use race or ethnicity to any degree.
- Police officers should never use race as a basis for any law enforcement decision.
- Police officers may rely on race and ethnicity in a specific suspect description.
- In conducting activities in connection with a specific investigation, police officers should consider race and ethnicity only to the extent that there is trustworthy information, relevant to the locality or time frame that links persons of a particular race or ethnicity to an identified criminal incident.

Police Crackdowns

A police crackdown is any dramatic increase in police officer presence, sanctions, and threats of apprehension either for specific offenses or for all offenses in specific areas of a community. Crackdowns usually involve high-risk visibility and numerous arrests. They may use undercover or plainclothes officers working with uniformed police, and may involve other official actions in addition to arrests. Because the inner city usually has a disproportionate amount of crime, such as drugs and gangs, the police have utilized crackdowns as an operational strategy. Police should be cautious about conducting crackdowns.

Improperly conducted crackdowns can worsen police–community relations and thereby undermine police legitimacy. Many of the urban riots of the 1960s were at least partly due to widespread crackdowns in minority communities. When crackdowns are aimed at street activity, they can be criticized for their disparate impact on the poor, who typically spend more time on the street than do the affluent. Also, when police use highly aggressive tactics, such as using military strategies, weapons, and attire for relatively routine enforcement and patrol activities, they risk heightening fear among offenders and casual observers.

Police should use careful planning when conducting crackdowns and engage in dialogue with the affected neighborhoods about why there is a need for a crackdown. Studies have shown that when police explain the purpose and scope of crackdowns to the public ahead of time, as well as to the people they stop during crackdowns, they can gain public support, which continues while the crackdown is in effect (Eck & Maguire, 2000).

POLICE–MINORITY RELATIONS TODAY

Progress in the area of race relations in the United States has made great strides in recent years. However, in spite of this improvement many in the minority community still have a great distrust for the police. Many minority citizens view the police with considerable suspicion. In addition, there is some scholarship that has shown that minority neighborhoods offer the greatest hostility toward the police (Feagin, Vera, & Batur, 2001). The accusation of the police engaging in the practice of racial profiling has further exacerbated the already strained and complex relationship between the police and members of the minority community. One study found that minorities were less likely to have favorable attitudes toward the police as a result of racial profiling (Weitzer & Tuch, 2005).

Contacts with the police also tend to have stronger and longer-lasting effects on the views of African-Americans when compared to whites (Tyler & Hugo, 2002). African-Americans are more likely than whites to leave an encounter with the police upset or angry (Bordua & Tifft, 1971).

Animosity toward the police can clearly be seen when examining racial dimensions. For example, Webb and Marshall (1995) found that African-American communities hold less favorable attitudes toward the police than do white Americans. There is a vast literature base that points to a clear history of negative attitudes that African-Americans hold toward the police when compared to other racial and ethnic groups (Priest & Carter, 1999).

Studies have shown that African-Americans consistently give poor performance ratings to the police when compared to white Americans (Davis, 1990). Whites not only tend to hold more favorable opinions of the police when compared to African-Americans, but they are also more prone to favor aggressive law enforcement, as well as being more skeptical of criticisms of the police (Weitzer & Tuch, 2004).

In one recent study, African-Americans reported that they were mistreated by the police five times more than whites had reported (Weitzer & Tuch, 1999). Some scholars have attempted to explain these racial differences with the group-position thesis. The group-position thesis holds that when the police are criticized, whites may perceive their group interests indirectly threatened, which may explain in part why whites are dubious or dismissive of allegations of police misconduct when compared to African-Americans (Bayley & Mendelsohn, 1969).

There is some speculation that the hostility that some minority communities hold toward the police is rooted in a very complex and troubling history that dates back to slavery (Alexander & Gyamerah, 1997). The following is a telling description of this history:

> The fact that the legal order not only countenanced but sustained slavery, segregation, and discrimination for most of our nation's history—and the fact the police were bound to uphold that order—set a pattern for police behavior and attitudes toward minority communities that has persisted until the present day. That pattern includes the idea that minorities have fewer civil rights, that the police have little responsibility for protecting them from crime within their communities (Williams & Murphy, 1990, pp. 4–5).

Professor David Carter (1985) found several reasons that Hispanic crime victims did not report crime to the police. First, because they felt the police would do little or nothing, and their previous experience with the police was bad, some reported that they did not want to bother the police, and some related that they were afraid of the police.

DANGEROUS TRAITS AND BEHAVIORS

There are a number of dangerous traits and behaviors that have no place in police work. These traits and behaviors can be disastrous in terms of police–minority relations, and in potential liability for police agencies. Police supervisors have an obligation to monitor their police officers for signs of bias or other behavioral problems or traits, especially officers that work in minority areas of the community.

Stereotyping

stereotyping / Unreliable generalizations about all members of a group that do not take into account individual differences within the group.

Stereotyping is not only harmful in its own right, it does damage by fostering prejudice and discrimination. Common stereotypes include a variety of allegations about groups based on race, ethnicity, gender, and nationality. Stereotyping is the process of assuming a person or group has one or more characteristics because most members of that group have (or are thought to have) the same characteristics.

Stereotypes are based on simplification, exaggeration or distortion, generalization, and presentation of cultural attributes as being natural. It is the simplification and generalization process that helps people categorize and understand their world, but at the same time it often leads to errors. When stereotypes are inaccurate and negative (as they often are between groups in conflict) they lead to misunderstandings that make resolving the conflict more difficult. Stereotyping is sometimes the result of fear and may directly lead to prejudice. A police department and a community that can respect cultural differences are much less likely to be fearful of other cultures that are different from their own.

Stereotypes of Hispanics

1. Some police officers consider Hispanics foreigners, without care to their ancestry. Some comment that they should go back to Mexico when, in fact, they are of Cuban heritage.
2. Some officers believe that young Hispanics with low-riding cars are either gang members or school dropouts. While many do ride around in groups, this does not imply gang affiliation.
3. Lazy. This stereotype has developed out of a misunderstanding of Hispanics' laid-back behavior.
4. Many officers presume that Hispanics can only speak Spanish. When arriving on the scene, therefore, they might address comments to whichever person is able to speak English.

Source: Jackson, M. S. (2006). *Policing in a diverse society: Another American dilemma.* Durham, NC: Carolina Academic Press.

Self-Fulfilling Prophecy

In some situations we may act upon negative stereotypes with the result that false accusations become true. This is called a **self-fulfilling prophecy**. Self-fulfilling prophecy occurs when a person or group described as having a particular characteristic(s) begins to display the very traits attributed to them. Put another way, self-fulfilling prophecy is a phenomenon by which people's expectations about future events lead them to behave in particular ways and, on occasion, can cause the expected event to occur. People tend to find what they are looking for. More than that, they may even tend, unwittingly, to create what they seek. For example, social prejudice believes other people are less capable than us.

self-fulfilling prophecy / The tendency of individuals to respond to and act on the basis of stereotypes, a predisposition that can lead to the validation of false definitions.

Self-Fulfilling Prophecy

- The police officer forms certain expectations of people or events.
- The officer communicates those expectations with various cues.
- People tend to respond to these cues by adjusting their behavior to match them.
- The result is that the original expectation becomes true.

Prejudice

Prejudice is a negative attitude that rejects an entire group. Prejudice and discrimination are negative manifestations of integrative power. *Prejudice* is an attitude that one may have about another group, while *discrimination* is behavior that deprives a

prejudice / A negative attitude that rejects an entire group.

group of certain rights or opportunities. Prejudice does not necessarily coincide with discrimination. For example, a person may have negative attitudes and feelings about another group but never act upon those attitudes and feelings, which would deprive another person of certain rights and opportunity.

Instead of bringing people together, prejudice and discrimination pushes them apart. People show prejudice when they form a negative opinion without knowing all the facts. Prejudice in any form, racial or social, is destructive and costly to society. *Social prejudice* believes other people are less capable. A police officer may think that female police officers or African-American police officers are less capable; thus, the officer will often act on this belief. If a female officer subsequently leaves the police service because of the prejudice, then it is reinforced by the prejudiced officer.

A police agency that allows prejudiced officers who blatantly act on their prejudices to remain on the job can have dire consequences. Officers that exhibit prejudiced behavior should be identified and dealt with expediently by police management. Unfortunately, for many years society accepted racial prejudice. Thus, many racial groups, primarily African-Americans who were the disproportionate target of racial prejudice, rebelled, and society in general came to the realization of the destructive force of prejudice. In essence, prejudicial behaviors may force good minority and female police officers to leave police work with a "failure label" that often follows them from law enforcement job to law enforcement job.

racism / A doctrine that one race is superior. Racism may be expressed individually and consciously, through explicit thoughts, feelings, or acts; or socially and unconsciously, through institutions that promote inequality between races.

Racism

Racism is the hatred of one person by another or the belief that another person is less than human because of skin color, language, customs, place of birth, or any factor that supposedly reveals the basic nature of that person. Put another way, when a person or group thinks that they are superior to another person or group because of their race, the person or group is guilty of racism. When racist belief is applied in practice, it takes forms such as prejudice, discrimination, segregation, or subordination. Racism involves having the power to carry out systematic discriminatory practices. An example of this would be a racist police officer who elects to work in a Hispanic neighborhood so that he can act on his racist tendencies by using the official position of police officer to stop and harass Hispanic citizens.

When People Act on Their Prejudices

You may recall the sobering news headlines that shocked the world in 1998. The sadistic murder of a middle-aged African-American man in Texas is an indication of the savagery that some still hold toward persons simply because of the color of their skin. James Byrd, Jr., forty-nine years old, was beaten unconscious, chained to the back of a pick-up truck, and dragged for miles over rural roads outside the town of Jasper. It is believed that Byrd survived through most of this experience, that is, until he was decapitated. The suspects, three white men, John William King, Shawn Berry, and Lawrence Brewer Jr., were arrested and subsequently convicted of the crime. Berry gave a confession that implicated the other two as the principal assailants. Both King and Brewer had links to white supremacist groups. In the course of the killing, one of the perpetrators reportedly made a reference to the *Turner Diaries*, a fascistic novel that was in the possession of Timothy McVeigh when he was arrested for his role in the Oklahoma City bombing.

Authoritarian Personality

Authoritarian personality theory views prejudice as an isolated incident that anyone may possess. The authoritarian personality centers on an adherence to conventional values, uncritical acceptance of authority, and a concern for power. This personality is in turn aggressive toward persons who do not conform to conventional norms or authority structures. In essence, police officers who are raised in authoritarian environments will then later treat others as they have been raised. Discrimination would then be acted out against persons or groups who celebrate customs or cultures that are different from the conventional.

authoritarian personality / A psychological construct of a personality type likely to be prejudiced and to use others as scapegoats.

Scapegoating

Scapegoating contends that prejudiced people believe they are society's victims. The scapegoating theory suggests that individuals, rather than accepting responsibility for some failure, transfer the responsibility for failure to some susceptible group. This is often seen when unsuccessful applicants assume that the minority candidate or woman gets the job that they were denied.

scapegoating / When a person or group is blamed irrationally for another person's or group's problems or difficulties.

Labeling Theory

Police officers should avoid labeling a person based on one or several characteristics. An example of this would be a police officer who labels a young African-American male from the inner city a gang member, solely because he is wearing sagging jeans. The **labeling theory**, a concept introduced by sociologist Howard Becker, is an attempt to explain why certain people are viewed as different from or less worthy than others. Labeling theory views deviance as a label assigned to behavior and individuals by particular figures of authority. Suppose an Hispanic youth from the inner city misbehaves; according to the labeling theory, he may be considered and treated as a delinquent by police officers. On the other hand, another youth from a white, middle-class family, who commits the same sort of misbehavior, might be given another chance before being arrested by a police officer.

labeling theory / A sociological approach introduced by Howard Becker that attempts to explain why certain people are viewed as deviants and others engaging in the same behavior are not.

IMPROVING POLICE–MINORITY RELATIONS

Community Policing

Some contemporary police practices are attempting to mend strained relationships with minority communities. Strategies such as community-oriented policing have been thought to improve the current state of police–minority relations (Reisig & Parks, 2004). Community policing presents the idea that the police and community work in partnership to solve crime and other social problems.

As noted in Chapter 3, community policing is a philosophy based on the concept that the police and citizens working together in creative ways can solve contemporary community problems related to crime, fear of crime, social and physical disorder, and general neighborhood conditions. This philosophy is founded on the belief that achieving these goals requires the police to develop a new relationship with citizens, allowing them the power to set local police priorities and involving them in efforts to improve the overall quality of life in their community. Community-oriented policing

community policing / A philosophy in which the police are seen as members of the community, with police officers being part of where they live and work. Community policing often entails a three-pronged approach: (1) partnerships, (2) problem solving, and (3) organizational transformation. Police agencies that subscribe to this philosophy tend to do much more community work than traditional police departments.

ebonics / Distinctive dialect with a complex language structure found among many African-Americans.

shifts the focus of police work from just handling random crime calls to addressing community concerns.

Community policing encourages the use of non-law-enforcement resources within a law enforcement agency. Volunteerism involves active citizen participation with their law enforcement agency. The law enforcement organization educates the public about ways that they can partner with the organization and its members to further community policing, and provides an effective means for citizen input. Volunteer efforts can help to free up officer time and allow sworn personnel to be more proactive and prevention-oriented.

For many years, the police have employed strategies within communities in the same uniform standard, regardless of the social demographics and general makeup of the community. This has been problematic for the minority community, as needs may be significantly different for citizens living in the inner city when compared to citizens living in an affluent suburb. Police officers should be sensitive to demographic differences in these communities and tailor police strategies accordingly. Recognizing the importance of these differences, instead of a one-size-fits-all approach, puts the police and the community in a better position to realize the potential benefits of community policing (Thomas & Burns, 2005).

The community-policing strategy calls for the tailoring of problem-solving approaches to fit the needs of the specific neighborhood. An inner-city neighborhood that is plagued with open sales of drugs on the street corner and gang activity will require different policing strategies when compared with perhaps a more affluent area of the community. Addressing the inner-city drug and gang problems may involve not only enforcement, but also education and intervention strategies. Officers may find it beneficial to solicit the leadership structures within these communities.

It has been well-documented that the African-American church has been an important agency of social control and organization among African-Americans (Hill, 2003). The African-American church provided one of the earliest and most recognizable vehicles to begin to develop networks of support and control. It would help police officers working in predominantly African-American neighborhoods to get to know the church leaders in these neighborhoods and solicit their help in tailoring solutions to problems inherent within the neighborhood. This is probably something that most police officers don't often think about.

Other key organizations that police officers may find it beneficial to become familiar with and form partnerships with are the Boy's and Girl's Clubs, the Urban League, and the local branch of the National Association for the Advancement of Colored People (NAACP). Organizations such as these can play pivotal roles in assisting police officers who work in minority neighborhoods.

Ronnie Carter (1995) describes how community-policing strategies can forge a bond between officers and the community. Two white community police officers in Charlotte, North Carolina assigned to a housing development devoted many of their off-duty hours to performing improvement projects in the neighborhood. During a robbery attempt, an African-American subject killed the two officers. The city's African-American community, especially the residents of the housing project, reacted with outrage and helped the police department apprehend the assailant. In addition, the housing project tenants recommended that several of the streets and a park in the area be renamed in memory of the slain officers. Media coverage of the officers' funerals showed African-American children and adults in the community grieving along with police officers. This incident illustrates how much impact individual officers can have on a community.

With the use of the community-policing philosophy, it is anticipated that police–community relations will improve as the police and citizens have more contact with each other. This is crucial in those areas of the community, such as minority neighborhoods, where police–community relations have been strained. Community policing is said to improve police–community relations in the following areas:

- Closer relations with underprivileged and minority groups, where the need is greatest for police understanding and involvement.
- More effective and more open communication between the police and the community.
- Increased citizen involvement in crime prevention and solving of social problems as a means of reducing crime.
- Improved understanding between the police and the community, with both gaining recognition of each other's problems.
- Creation of awareness among police–community relations problems and encouragement of officers to help solve them.
- Direction of all department efforts toward improving relations with the total community, whether these involve crime prevention, public relations, or neighborhood problem solving.

Citizen Police Academies

Citizen police academies have increasingly become popular among police departments as a means to foster and improve police–community relations through education. The program is designed to provide a working knowledge and background of the law enforcement agency and to foster a closer relationship between the agency and the community. It provides an avenue for community involvement and firsthand experience of policing. Interested citizens apply for the citizen police academy and if accepted, complete a specified amount of time ranging usually from a few weeks to several weeks, one or two evenings a week.

Objectives of the Citizen Police Academy in Police–Minority Relations

- Enhances understanding of the inner workings of the police department.
- Develops realistic expectations of the police department's response.
- Builds trust and a sense of cooperation between the police department and the community.
- Provides a venue for police–citizen exchange and dialogue.
- Dispels suspicions and misconceptions.

The academy creates well-informed citizens who possess greater insight into police practices and services. Graduates of the academy are encouraged to share their knowledge and experiences with the community as the opportunity arises. Everyone benefits from enhancing citizen understanding of the role and function of the police department, which can be seminal in fostering better police–minority relations.

Relationship Building

Police agencies should undertake a critical self-assessment to determine which aspects of its current operations are the source of tensions between their departments and minority neighborhoods in order to improve relations. Where problems are identified, appropriately focused remedies should be developed.

Retired Police Captain Robert Shusta and his colleagues (2002) suggest specific activities that individual police officers can do to improve relations:

- Make positive contact with community group members from diverse backgrounds. Don't let them see you only when something negative has happened.
- Allow the public to see you as much as possible in a nonenforcement role.
- Make a conscious effort in your mind, en route to every situation, to treat all segments of society objectively and fairly.
- Remember that all groups have some bad, some average, and some good people within them.
- Go out of your way to be personable and friendly with minority group members. Remember, many don't expect it.
- Don't appear uncomfortable with or avoid discussing racial and ethnic issues with other officers and citizens.
- Take responsibility for patiently educating citizens and the public about the role of the officer and about standard operating procedures in law enforcement. Remember that citizens often do not understand "police culture."
- Don't be afraid to be a change agent in your organization when it comes to improving cross-cultural relations within your department and between police and the community. It may not be a popular thing to do, but it is the right thing to do.

Develop Community Contacts

As noted earlier in this chapter, it is a good practice for police officers to establish rapport with the local minority organizations, such as the NAACP, the Urban League, Boy's and Girl's Clubs, the minority faith community, Hispanic coalitions, and Asian or Indo-Chinese community centers and coalitions. Developing contacts with organizations such as these will keep officers informed about concerns in the minority community. Police organizations can meet the challenges of promoting and managing a diverse workforce by using the following strategies:

1. Developing training programs that promote awareness of cultural differences.
2. Promoting positive attitudes toward racial and cultural differences among ethnic groups.
3. Recognizing common links between different ethnic groups.
4. Using alternative channels of communication to maximize understanding between ethnic/cultural groups.
5. Expressing organizational concerns.
6. Identifying the concerns and needs of ethnic groups in decision-making processes.
7. Recognizing that no "one-size-fits-all" solutions exist.
8. Challenging all stereotypes and assumptions about ethnic groups.
9. Including members of all ethnic groups in all after-work organization-sponsored events.

A police officer talks to a class of fourth graders at an elementary school about the dangers of drugs. The officer is taking part in the D.A.R.E. program designed to teach the problems with using drugs.

Cultural Diversity Training

Knowledge of cultural diversity is important for police officers in the twenty-first century. It has only been in the recent past that police agencies have begun to include diversity training as part of pre-service and post-service training requirements. Education that helps familiarize officers with ethnic and cultural groups in their community is invaluable. Police officers cannot effectively address the community's needs if they do not understand the cultural traditions, mores, and values of that community (DeGeneste & Sullivan, 1997).

Multicultural training can reduce the number of lawsuits, as well as the possibility of civil disorder, but can only succeed with the acceptance and management of cultural diversity. Historically, strategies employed by police in dealing with minorities and minority issues have differed from those of other groups. While improvements in those strategies have occurred in the last decade, further improvements are needed. Although these improvements have often focused on African-Americans, many cultural diversity issues have similar implications on other racial and ethnic groups. Chief of Police Gary Coderoni, who serves with the Muscatine, Iowa, Police Department, writes:

> Cultural diversity training helps police break free from their traditional stance of being "apart from" the community to a more inclusive philosophy of being "a part of" the community. Realizing the difficulty of becoming a part of something that they do not understand causes a desperate need for an intense and ongoing educational process for developing an understanding of cultural differences and how those differences affect policing a free and culturally diverse society (Coderoni, 2002, p. 34).

There are four primary factors associated with achieving a more culturally aware police organization. First, police officers need to understand how their own cultural background molds their values and behavioral patterns. Second, officers must understand that cultural assimilation no longer is the norm in the United States. Law enforcement officers must learn about the different cultural, ethnic, and racial groups in the neighborhoods they patrol. Third, it is critical that officers understand the effective use of cross-cultural communication. Police officers who have a deeper insight into the beliefs, behaviors, and value orientations of various **ethnic groups** will rely less often on authority and force to resolve problematic situations. Finally, law enforcement officers must develop cross-cultural communicative, analytical, and interpretive skills (Weaver, 1992).

ethnic group / A group set apart from others because of its national origin or distinctive cultural patterns.

Police officers can make their jobs easier by taking the time to learn about various cultures that they will come into contact with. Knowledge of minority concerns, diversity, and historical backgrounds of the various races and groups in a community will enhance and facilitate the crime-fighting and peace-keeping functions of the police (Birzer & Tannehill, 2001). Consider the case of an officer called to the home of an Asian-American family regarding a miscellaneous complaint. In Asian-American families, the relationship and communicating patterns tend to be quite hierarchical, with the father as the identified head of the household. While many of the decisions and activities may appear to be decided by the father, many other people may come into the picture. Generally, if there are grandparents, the father would still act as the spokesperson of the family; however, chances are that he will consult with the grandparents prior to making a decision.

It is equally important and well-justified for the police to posses a contextual understanding of those racial and ethic groups represented in the United States. Consider the following information pertaining to the African-American experience in the United States:

- The experience of slavery and racism, as well as cultural differences, have shaped African-American culture.

- For many African-Americans, particularly those in the lower-socioeconomic rungs of society, the history of slavery and later discrimination continues to leave its psychological scars.

- There is tremendous diversity among African-Americans, which includes individuals at all socioeconomic levels, a number of religions, different regions of the country (rural as well as urban), and various countries of origin.

- The changing terms that African-Americans have used to refer to themselves reflect stages of racial and cultural growth, as well as empowerment.

- African-Americans react as negatively to stereotypes that they hear about themselves as officers do when they hear such statements as: "Police officers are biased against blacks" or "All police officers are capable of brutality."

- The predominance of households headed by women, particularly in the inner city, coupled with the myth of women as the head of the household, has created situations where officers have dismissed the importance of the father.

- Young African-American males, in particular, and their parents (of all socioeconomic levels) feel a sense of outrage and injustice when officers stop them for no apparent reason.

- The use of African-American varieties of English does not represent any pathology of deficiency and is not a combination of random errors, but rather reflects patterns of grammar from some West African languages.

- People in positions of authority have often misunderstood aspects of African-American nonverbal communication, including what has been termed the "cool pose."

- Cultural differences in verbal communication can result in complete misinterpretation.

- The existence of excessive force and brutality is still a reality in policing in the United States, even if it is a minority officer who commits these acts. When there is police brutality, everyone suffers, including officers and entire police departments.

- A dynamic exists between some officers and African-Americans, particularly in poor urban areas, whereby both the officer and the citizen are on the "alert" for the slightest sign of disrespect (Shusta et al., 1995, pp. 188–190).

Recruitment of Minority Police Officers

A top priority for many police executives is recruiting and retaining a workforce that reflects their community's diverse culture. The recruitment of women and minorities is essential for the police organization. In recent years there has been significant progress in increasing minorities in the ranks of sworn officers and this must continue.

Increasing the representation of minorities in police departments will foster good police–community relations. Better representation of minorities in policing sends the right message that the police service is open. Increasing diversity within police agencies is important in light of the projections that by the year 2010 more than one-third of all American children will be African-American, Hispanic, or Asian-American.

Courtesy and Professionalism

Police officers' contact with minority citizens has the potential to yield a relationship in the direction of understanding and cooperation; or conversely, one of suspicion, hostility, and hate. Police officers can improve relations with the minority community by being courteous and professional when interacting with minority citizens. Research has shown that minority citizens are much more likely to suspect that a police stop was racially motivated if they were treated discourteously or not informed of the reason rather than being treated with respect and told why they were being stopped (Police Executive Research Forum, 2001). Contacts with the police tend to have stronger and longer-lasting effects on the views of minorities when compared to whites (Tyler & Hugo, 2002), and minorities are more likely than whites to leave an encounter with the police upset or angry.

The Police Executive Research Forum (2001, pp. 61–62) suggests that an officer who detains a minority citizen can minimize the potential of fear and hostility by following some simple guidelines:

1. Be courteous and professional.

2. Introduce yourself to the citizen (providing name and agency affiliation), and state the reason for the stop as soon as practical, unless providing this information will compromise your safety or public safety. In vehicle stops, provide this information before asking the driver for the license and registration.

3. Ensure that the detention is no longer than necessary to take appropriate action for the known or suspected offense, and that the citizen understands the purpose of reasonable delays.

4. Answer any questions the citizen may have, including explaining options for traffic citation disposition, if relevant.

5. Provide your name and badge number when requested, in writing or on a business card.

6. Apologize and/or explain if you determine that the reasonable suspicion was unfounded (e.g., after the investigative stop).

THE CULTURALLY COMPETENT POLICE OFFICER

Police officers should know the racial and ethnic makeup of their communities and especially the areas they patrol. If police officers have this information they place themselves in an advantageous position to be proactive as problems arise, and thus enhance the relationship that the officers have with the community. Understanding and appreciating diversity ultimately promotes clearer communication, breaks down barriers, strengthens relationships between the officer and the community, and yields tangible results. Simply put, police officers should be culturally competent; that is, able to effectively operate within different cultural contexts within the community.

culture / A system of shared beliefs, values, customs, and behaviors that the members of different groups use to cope with their world and with one another, and that are transmitted from generation to generation.

The term **culture** can be applied to various population categories, but is normally associated with race and ethnicity. Likewise, culture is a system of shared beliefs, values, customs, and behaviors that the members of different groups use to cope with their world and with one another, and that are transmitted from generation to generation. Diversity of race and ethnicity both entices and obstructs a police officer's involvement and interaction with other persons, groups, and cultures (Wallace & Roberson, 2004).

Why should police officers be culturally competent? First, understanding culture will help the officers to understand how others interpret their environment. Culture shapes how people see their world and how they function within that world. Culture shapes personal and group values and attitudes, including perceptions about what works and what doesn't work, what is helpful and what isn't helpful, what makes sense and what doesn't make sense. Secondly, understanding culture helps police officers avoid stereotypes and biases that can undermine effective policing. Finally, being culturally competent will assist the officers when dealing with problems on their beats.

Officers should be aware that most minorities have developed a sharp sense for detecting condescension, manipulation, and insincerity. There is no substitute for compassion as the foundation and sincerity as its expression in carrying out law enforcement services equally and fairly. The first contact minorities have with the police will either confirm or dispel suspicions as to how they will be treated. When working with immigrant, refugee, or native populations, an officer will find it helpful to learn a few words of greeting from that culture. This willingness to go beyond what is comfortable and usual conveys the officer's intent to communicate. Suppose that a police officer works in an area of the community that has a large population of Hispanics. It would be beneficial for the officer to learn a little about Hispanic culture by:

- understanding relevant Hispanic cultural characteristics, traits, and values.
- having greater awareness of the officer's attitudes and behaviors, and the impact these have on the Hispanic community that the officer serves.
- recognizing the verbal and nonverbal aspects of communication that may impede working relationships.
- learning some basic phrases in Spanish and responding effectively in encounters with Hispanic citizens.

Cross-Cultural Communication

The way people communicate varies widely between, and even within, cultures. One aspect of communication style is language usage. Across cultures, some words and phrases are used in different ways. When communicating across cultures never assume the other party has understood. Be an active listener and summarize what has been said in order to verify it. Police officers should develop some understanding of cross-cultural communication. To be professionally competent, officers should be able to communicate across cultures. In an exchange with ethnic minorities, cultural differences can cause communication problems. Officers should be patient, if the situation permits. Officers should respond slowly and carefully in cross-cultural exchanges, not jumping to the conclusion that they know what is being thought and said. However, officer safety should always be a priority.

Eye Contact

You may have heard the adage, "look me in the eye when I'm talking to you." We often assume that when someone doesn't look us in the eye that they are being deceptive; however, this may not be the case at all. Don't read into a situation just because the other person does not look you in the eyes during the contact. While eye contact is a direct and powerful form of nonverbal communication, in some cultures it is considered disrespectful to look someone directly in the eye in communication. Some Hispanics may not make eye contact. This is a sign of respect and should not be taken as an affront. Similarly, Nigerians, Asians, and Pacific Islanders may avert their eyes during conversation as a sign of respect. On the other hand, Western cultures value direct eye contact as a sign of sympathy or respect. Thus, we tend to engage in direct eye contact when communicating.

Social Space

Persons from different cultures use, value, and share space differently. Officer safety demands that police officers keep a safe distance when communicating. However, officers should know that in some cultures it is considered appropriate for people to stand very close to each other while talking, while in other cultures people like to keep farther apart. Social distance may vary with different groups of people. For example, Hispanics often view Americans as being distant because they prefer more space between speakers. Americans often view individuals who come too close as invading their social space. Generally, between 1.5 and 4 feet is considered the personal zone when communicating, and the social zone—that is, walking around in public—is between 4 and 12 feet.

Touching

Officer safety dictates that officers should never allow someone to touch them. If they are close enough to touch you, then they are too close. Nevertheless, officers should recognize that some cultures touch when communicating. For instance, in Hispanic and other Latin cultures, two people engaged in conversation often touch and sometimes embrace when greeting each other. In other cultures, people are more restrained in their greetings. In the Asian/Vietnamese cultures, for example, it is not customary to shake hands with individuals of the opposite sex.

HATE AND BIAS CRIMES

hate crime / A crime where the offender chooses the victim based on the victim's race, ethnicity, or religion.

Because the United States is rich in racial and ethic diversity, and because some members of society engage in racist and prejudiced behavior, police officers will be called to investigate the incidence of **hate crimes**. The Federal Hate Crime Statistics Act defines hate or bias crime as crime "motivated, in whole or in part, by hatred against a victim based on his or her race, religion, sexual orientation, ethnicity, national origin, or disability." Federal laws and state statutes protect individuals from hate and bias crimes and provide a basis for prosecution of offenders.

The fundamental cause of hate crimes in the United States is the persistence of racism, anti-Semitism, and other forms of bigotry. The attempt to eliminate these prejudices requires that Americans develop respect for differences and begin to establish dialogue across ethnic, cultural, and religious boundaries. While bigotry cannot be outlawed, effective response by public officials and law enforcement authorities to hate violence can make a difference in deterring and preventing these crimes.

Hate crimes are actions intended to harm or intimidate people because of their race, ethnicity, sexual orientation, religion, or other minority group status. They are also referred to as *bias crimes*. Recently, in Texas, two white teens brutally beat and sodomized an Hispanic teenager simply because he was Hispanic. The perpetrators screamed racial epithets and doused the victim with bleach in an attempt to hide their fingerprints. The attack on the victim is an example of the growing incidence of hate crimes based on race in the United States. The U.S. Department of Justice reports that most hate crimes are motivated based on the race of the victim (especially anti African-American crimes), rather than on ethnicity, religion, or sexual orientation.

According to the Southern Poverty Law Institute, a nonprofit organization that tracks hate crimes, there are over 500 hate groups operating in the United States. Hate crimes do more than threaten the safety and welfare of the citizenry, these crimes inflict on victims incalculable physical and emotional damage and tear at the very fabric of society. Crimes motivated by atrocious hatred toward particular groups not only harm individual victims, but send a powerful message of intolerance and discrimination to all members of the group to which the victim belongs.

The FBI collects data about both single-bias and multiple-bias hate crimes. For each offense type reported, law enforcement must indicate one bias motivation. A single-bias incident occurs when one or more offense types within the incident are motivated by the same bias. A multiple-bias incident occurs when more than one offense type occurs in the incident and at least two offense types are motivated by a different bias. In 2005, 12,417 law enforcement agencies submitted hate crime data to the uniform crime program.

Single-Bias Hate Crime Incidents Reported in 2005 Revealed:

- 54.7 percent were racially motivated
- 17.1 percent were motivated by religious bias
- 14.2 percent resulted from sexual-orientation bias
- 13.2 percent stemmed from ethnicity/national origin bias
- 0.7 percent were prompted by disability bias

Source: Uniform Crime Reports, 2005, p. 137.

Responding to Hate Crime

Because of their unique psychological impact on the victim, hate crimes can have a more devastating effect than other crimes both in terms of the victim and the victim's community. Police officers play a critical role in responses to hate crimes. As the responding officer to allegations of hate crimes, the officer can document overt signs of hate motivation and set the tone with victims and witnesses that can impact their cooperation.

Hate crimes are considered message crimes, crimes that send a message of fear and terror, based on a foundation of bigotry. These crimes have a significant impact on the victim's community. As a result, a seemingly insignificant incident can exacerbate existing tension within the community, with the potential for reprisals and escalating violence. Therefore, hate crimes demand a special response from law enforcement and victim assistance professionals. The victims of hate crime often suffer serious and long-lasting traumatic stress that can be made worse by an inappropriate response.

When a police officer is called to the scene of a crime and subsequently discovers what is believed to be a hate crime, the officer should follow sound preliminary crime scene investigative procedures. In conducting the initial investigation, the handling police officer should first, if necessary, restore order, taking any necessary actions to gain control of the situation. As suggested throughout this book, police officers should always refer to their department's standard operating procedures for specific response and investigative guidelines regarding hate and bias crimes. Procedural steps in responding to hate and bias crime scenes may include:

- Protect and secure the scene.
- Collect and photograph evidence such as hate literature, spray paint cans, threatening letters, and symbolic objects used by the groups (e.g., swastikas, crosses).

- Identify any injured parties and take steps to provide for medical assistance.
- Determine whether any suspect(s) are present and, if so, take appropriate enforcement measures.
- Identify witnesses or others who have knowledge of the crime.
- Express empathy for the victim and show a sincere interest in the victim's well-being.
- Express the police agency's official position on the importance of hate and bias crimes, the measure that will be taken to apprehend the suspect(s), and the officer's and department's interest in the victim's well-being.
- Assist the victim in identifying and contacting community-based individuals or agencies that may provide support and assistance. These may include family members or close acquaintances, religious community, or agencies that provide counseling, shelter, food, clothing, child care, or other related services as needed.

PRACTICE HINTS

Bias Crime Indicators

- The race, religion, ethnicity/national origin, disability status, gender, or sexual orientation of the victim differs from that of the offender.
- The victim is a member of a group that is overwhelmingly outnumbered by members of another group in the area where the incident occurred.
- The incident coincided with a holiday or date of particular significance to the victim's group.
- The victim, although not a member of the targeted group, is a member of an advocacy group that supports the victim's group, or the victim was in the company of a member of the targeted group.
- Animosity exists between the victim's group and the offender's group.
- The perpetrator's comments, gestures, or written statements reflect bias, including graffiti or other symbols.
- Bias-related drawings, markings, symbols, or graffiti were left at the scene of the incident.
- Absence of any other motive, such as economic gain.

When conducting the follow-up investigation to a hate or bias crime, officers should:

- Interview victim(s) and witnesses thoroughly and respectfully.
- Secure evidence by taking photos of offensive graffiti or other symbols of bias.
- Document the circumstances and apparent motives surrounding the event.
- Locate and arrest any suspected perpetrators not apprehended at the scene.
- Provide the district or shift supervisor with information that can be responsibly reported to the media.

- Inform victim(s) of what is likely to happen during the continuing investigation.
- Appeal to witnesses to come forward by canvassing the community.
- Offer rewards for information about the incident, when possible.
- Coordinate with other law enforcement agencies in the area to assess patterns of hate crimes and determine if organized hate groups are involved.
- Collaborate with the responding officers to complete any written reports required by their department, state, and federal agencies.
- Notify the FBI if further assistance with investigations is needed.

Type of Hate/Bias Offenders

Professors Jack Levin and Jack McDevitt of Northeastern University (1993) have identified three general types of hate/bias offenders: thrill-seeking offenders, reactive offenders, and mission offenders. Hate and bias crimes sometimes don't specifically fit into categories; nevertheless, Professors Levin and McDevitt's typology provides a general framework in the investigation of hate/bias crimes.

Thrill-Seeking Offenders: Groups of teenagers who go outside their "turf" and spontaneously vandalize property or attack members of groups they consider to be inferior to them (as well as vulnerable). These offenders are not typically associated with a hate group and their manifested hatred of the victim is superficial. Such offenders may often be deterred from repeating the crimes if the community responds with a strong condemnation of their actions.

Reactive Offenders: These individuals have a sense of entitlement with regard to their rights and privileges that does not extend to their victims. They victimize individuals or groups of individuals on their own "turf" whom they consider to be a threat to their way of life, community, place of work, or privilege, and then apply the rationale that their aggression is a justifiable defensive action. Rarely are they affiliated with an organized hate group, although they may approach such a group for assistance in mitigating the perceived threat. If the perceived threat subsides, the criminal behavior generally subsides.

Mission Offenders: These individuals are often psychotic and suffer from mental illnesses that cause them to hallucinate and impair their ability to reason. They typically perceive their victim groups as evil or subhuman, believe that they have been empowered by a higher force to rid the world of evil, and feel intense paranoia and a sense of urgency that they carry out their mission. Generally operating alone, their crimes are violent in nature and may be carried out indiscriminately against any member of the target group in the community.

In 1998, the International Association of Chiefs of Police (IACP) held a hate crimes summit. As a result of the summit, there were a number of recommendations made to advance understanding of hate crime, prevent hate crime, and improve the effectiveness of response to this complex social problem. According to the IACP, law enforcement agencies must assume a central role in implementing the hate crime prevention, response, and performance measurement strategies. To encourage and enable law enforcement agencies to lead community-wide endeavors, summit participants recommended twelve actions:

1. Establish a "zero-tolerance" atmosphere in every law enforcement agency.

2. Encourage local jurisdictions to conduct hate crime summits.

3. Participate in collaborative development of coordinated approaches to prevent and respond to hate crimes.

4. Sponsor and participate actively in community events, forums, and activities concerning diversity tolerance, bias reduction, conflict resolution, and hate crime prevention.

5. Respond to and support the individual victims of hate crimes and their communities.

6. Employ community-policing strategies to prevent and respond to hate crimes.

7. Continuously investigate, track, and deal appropriately with the activities of organized hate groups.

8. Identify and report all bias-related incidents and hate crimes completely and accurately.

9. Ensure that all law enforcement professionals are trained to recognize and respond appropriately to hate crimes.

10. Assist schools and colleges to design and deliver hate crime prevention curricula and develop response protocols.

11. Engage the media as partners in preventing hate crimes and restoring victimized communities.

12. Collaborate in defining measurable outcomes of efforts to prevent and respond to hate crimes (International Association of Chiefs of Police, 1998, pp. 8–10).

SUMMARY

- America's racial and ethnic makeup is changing rapidly. In 1999, African-Americans were the largest minority in the United States, accounting for 12.1 percent of the population. However, according to the 2000 U.S. Census report, the Hispanic population grew at nearly four times the rate of the U.S. population overall during the last two years, cementing the Latinos' position as the country's largest minority group. As American communities become more racially and ethnically diverse, the nature of police–community relations increasingly becomes challenging.

- Police–community relations have at times been less than congenial, especially in minority communities. Likewise, relationships between minority communities and the police have been slow to develop.

Not only do minorities have distrust toward the police, but research shows that they possess more negative attitudes toward the police when compared with white Americans.

- The past injustices inflicted on minorities have had a profound effect on the nature of police–minority relations. Past incidents of real or perceived police abuse have sparked civil unrest, including costly and violent uprisings, and a lingering distrust between racial minority communities and the police.

- Many in the minority community feel that they have been unfairly stopped by the police simply because of the color of their skin. There is some evidence suggesting that the police disproportionately target and stop minority citizens for traffic-related stops.

- Racial profiling is any police-initiated action that relies on the race, ethnicity, or national origin rather than the behavior of an individual, or information that leads the police to a particular individual who has been identified as being, or having been, engaged in criminal activity. Racial profiling has a devastating effect on police–minority relations.

- Many states have responded to allegations of racial profiling by requiring police officers to record data pertaining to age, race, gender, ethnicity, reason for stop and alleged violation, date, time, location, license plate number, warning given, citation given, whether an arrest was made, if there was a personal search conducted, if a search of a vehicle was conducted, whether contraband was found, if items were seized for forfeiture, and the authority for the search.

- Police officers' actions should be professional at all times. There are several behaviors that police officers should avoid: scapegoating, self-fulfilling prophecy, prejudice, racism, and labeling. These traits and behaviors can be disastrous in terms of police–minority relations and in potential liability.

- Many police departments have responded to deteriorating relations with minorities with strategies such as community policing. Community-policing efforts have the potential to serve as powerful conduits for such community access. By actively embracing community input toward crime and disorder reduction, police can demonstrate the benefits of mutual respect and open communication. With community policing, citizens are viewed by the police as partners who share responsibility for identifying priorities, and developing and implementing responses to neighborhood problems.

- Community policing encourages the use of non-law-enforcement resources within a law enforcement agency. Volunteerism involves active citizen participation with their law enforcement agency. The law enforcement organization educates the public about ways that they can partner with the organization and its members to further community policing, and provides an effective means for citizen input.

- With the use of the community-policing philosophy, it is anticipated that police–community relations will improve as the police and citizens have more contact with each other. This is crucial in those areas of the community, such as minority neighborhoods, where police–community relations have been strained.

- Citizen police academies are another tool that may improve police relations in the minority community.

The purpose of the citizen police academy is to foster better communication between citizens and police through education. The program is designed to provide a working knowledge and background of the law enforcement agency and to foster a closer relationship between the agency and the community.

- Recruiting more minorities into police service is necessary to improve police–minority relations. For example, in California, in an effort to improve police–community relations in the minority community, police departments are concentrating on including diverse members of their community into programs and decision making.

- Police agencies should undertake a critical self-assessment to determine which aspects of its current operations are the source of tensions between their departments and minority neighborhoods in order to improve relations. Where problems are identified, appropriately focused remedies should be developed.

- Knowledge of cultural diversity is important for police officers in the twenty-first century. It has only been in the recent past that police agencies have begun to include diversity training as part of their pre-service and post-service training requirements. Education that helps familiarize officers with ethnic and cultural groups in their community is invaluable. Police officers cannot effectively address the community's needs if they do not understand the cultural traditions, mores, and values of that community.

- Police officers should focus on establishing rapport with local minority organizations, such as the NAACP, Urban League, Boy's and Girl's Clubs, minority faith community, Hispanic coalitions, and Asian or Indo-Chinese community centers and coalitions. Developing contacts with organizations such as these will keep officers informed about concerns in the minority community. This also has the potential to improve communication between the police and these organizations, which may assist in fostering better relations with the minority community.

- Police officers should know the racial makeup of their communities and especially the areas that they patrol. If police officers take some time and learn a little about cultural differences in the community, they place themselves in an advantageous position to be proactive, address problems, and enhance the relationship they have with the community.

- Understanding and appreciating cultural differences ultimately promotes clearer communication, breaks down barriers, strengthens relationships between the officer and the community, and yields tangible results. Simply put, police officers should be culturally competent—that is, be able to effectively operate within different cultural contexts within the community.

- According to the Southern Poverty Center, a non-profit organization that tracks hate crimes, there were over 500 hate groups operating in the United States in 1998. The Federal Hate Crime Statistics Act defines hate or bias crime as crime "motivated, in whole or in part, by hatred against a victim based on his or her race, religion, sexual orientation, ethnicity, national origin, or disability."

- Hate and bias crimes are considered message crimes, crimes that send a message of fear and terror, based on a foundation of bigotry. These crimes have a significant effect not only on the victim, but also the victim's community. As a result, a seemingly insignificant incident can exacerbate existing tension within the community, with the potential for reprisals and escalating violence.

- Hate crime offenders have been classified as thrill-seeking offenders, reactive offenders, and mission offenders.

Chapter Discussion Questions and Activities

1. Interview members of various minority groups regarding their perceptions of the police. Share and discuss the findings with the entire class.

2. Interview a police officer regarding the officer's perception of the current state of police–minority relations.

3. Discuss as a class ways that the police can improve relations in the minority community.

4. Discuss sources of police–community tensions.

5. Discuss what it means to be a culturally competent police officer.

Websites and Other Resources

Southern Poverty Law Center:
www.splcenter.org/

Uniform Crime Report, Hate Crimes Statistics:
www.fbi.gov/ucr/ucr.htm#hate

Anti Defamation League:
www.adl.org/default.htm

International Association of Chiefs of Police:
www.theiacp.org/

Community Relations Service:
www.usdoj.gov/crs/

References

Alexander, R., & Gyamerah, J. (1997). Differential punishing of African Americans and whites who possess drugs: A just policy or a continuation of the past. *Journal of Black Studies, 28*, 97–111.

Antonovics, K. L., & Knight, B. G. (2004). *A new look at racial profiling: Evidence from the Boston Police Department*. Cambridge, MA: National Bureau of Economic Research.

Bayley, D., & Mendelsohn, H. (1969). *Minorities and the police*. New York: Free Press.

Bell, D. (2000). Police brutality: Potential disaster and discomforting divergence. In J. Nelson (Ed.), *Police brutality: An anthology* (pp. 88–101). New York: W.W. Norton and Company.

Birzer, M. L., & Tannehill, R. L. (2001). A more effective training approach for contemporary policing. *Police Quarterly, 4* (2), 233–252.

Bordua, D., & Tifft, L. (1971). Citizens interviews, organizational feedback, and police community relations decisions. *Law and Society Review, 6*, 155–182.

Carter, D. (1985). Hispanic perception of police performance: An empirical assessment. *Journal of Criminal Justice, 11*, 213–227.

Carter, R. A. (1995, December). Improving minority relations. *FBI Law Enforcement Bulletin, 64*: 14–17.

Coderoni, G. R. (2002, November). The relationship between multicultural training for police and effective law enforcement. *The FBI Law Enforcement Bulletin, 11*, 12–14.

Coffey, A., Eldefonso, E., & Hartinger, W. (1982). *Human relations: Law enforcement in a changing community* (3rd ed.). Englewood Cliffs, NJ: Prentice Hall.

Cohn, E. G. (1996). The citizen police academy: A recipe for improving police-community relations. *Journal of Criminal Justice, 22* (3), 265–271.

Cordner, G., Williams, B., & Velasco, A. (2002). *Vehicle stops in San Diego: Executive report*. Retrieved January 10, 2006, from www.sandiego.gov/police/pdf/stoprpt.pdf.

Davis, J. R. (1990). A comparison of attitudes toward the New York City Police. *Journal of Police Science and Administration, 9*, 233–242.

DeGeneste, H. I., & Sullivan, J. P. (1997). *Fresh perspectives: Policing a multicultural community*. Washington, DC: PERF Publications.

Eck, J., & Maguire, E. (2000). Have Changes in Policing Reduced Violent Crime? An Assessment of the Evidence. In A. Blumstein and J. Wallman (Eds.), *The Crime Drop in America*. New York: Cambridge University Press.

Engel, R. S., & Calnon, J. M. (2004). Comparing bench mark methodologies for police citizen contacts: Traffic stop data collection for the Pennsylvania State Police. *Police Quarterly, 7*, 97–110.

Farai, C. (1999). *The color of our Future*. New York: William Morrow and Company.

Feagin, J. R., Vera, H., & Batur, P. (2001). *White racism* (2nd ed.). New York: Routledge.

Federal Bureau of Investigations. (2005). Uniform Crime Reports, 2005. Washington, DC: U.S. Government Printing Office.

Flanagan, T. J., & Maguire, K. (Eds.) (1992). *Sourcebook of criminal justice statistics*. Washington, DC: U.S. Government Printing Office.

Harris, D. A. (1997). Driving while black and all other traffic offences: The Supreme Court and pretextual traffic stops. *Journal of Criminal Law and Criminology, 87*, 544–582.

Harris, D. A. (1999). The stories, the statistics, and the law: Why driving while black matters. *Minnesota Law Review, 84*, 265–281.

Hill, A., & Scott, J. (1992, July). Ten strategies for managers in a multicultural workplace. *Resource Focus Magazine*.

Hill, R. B. (2003). *The strengths of black families*. Lanham, MD: University Press of America.

International Association of Chiefs of Police. (1998). *Responding to hate crimes: A police officers' guide to investigation and prevention*. Available at www.theiacp.org.

Johnson, J. B., & Secret, P. E. (1990). Race and juvenile court decision making revisited. *Criminal Justice Policy Review, 4*, 159–187.

Judy, R. W., & D'Amico, C. (1997). *Workforce 2020: Work and workers in the 21st century*. Indianapolis, IN: Hudson Institute.

Krikorian, G. (2006, October 7). Police beating victim settles suit. *Los Angeles Times*, p. 8–9.

Levin, J., & McDevitt, J. (1993). *Hate crimes: The rising tide of bigotry and bloodshed*. New York: Plenum.

Newport, F. (1999, October 9). *Racial profiling is seen as widespread, particularly among young black men*. Retrieved August 30, 2005, from www.gallup.com.

Parker, L. (2004, March 31). Texas scandal throws doubt on anti-drug task forces. *USA Today*, p. 3A.

Police Executive Research Forum. (2001). *Racially biased policing: A principled centered response*. Washington, DC: Police Executive Research Forum.

Priest, T. B., & Carter, D. B. (1999). Evaluations of police performance in an African American sample. *Journal of Criminal Justice, 27*, 457–465.

Ramirez, D., McDevitt, J., & Farrell, A. (2000). *A response guide on racial profiling data collection systems: Promising practices and lessons learned*. Washington, DC: U.S. Department of Justice.

Reisig, M. D., & Parks R. B. (2004). Can community policing help the truly disadvantaged? *Crime and Delinquency, 50*, 139–167.

Schaefer, R. T. (2000). *Racial and ethnic groups* (4th ed.). Upper Saddle River, NJ: Prentice Hall.

Shusta, R. M., Levine, D. R., Harris, P. R., & Wong, H. Z. (1995). *Multicultural law enforcement: Strategies for peace keeping in a diverse society*. Upper Saddle River, NJ: Prentice Hall.

Shusta, R. M., Levine, D. R., Harris, P. R., & Wong, H. Z. (2002). *Multicultural law enforcement: Strategies for peace keeping in a diverse society* (2nd ed.). Upper Saddle River, NJ: Prentice Hall.

Thomas, M., & Burns, P. F. (2005). Repairing the divide: An investigation of community policing and citizen attitudes toward the police by race and ethnicity. *Journal of Ethnicity in Criminal Justice, 3*, 71–90.

Tyler, T., & Hugo, H. (2002). *Trust in the law*. New York: McGraw Hill.

Uniform Crime Reports, 2005.

U.S. Census Bureau, 2002 Data Profiles. Web posted at www.census.gov/. Accessed October 17, 2006.

U.S. Commission on Civil Rights. (2000). *Revisiting who is guarding the guardians: A report on police practices and civil rights in America*. Retrieved January 11, 2006 from www.usccr. gov/ pubs/guard/ main. htm.

Wallace, H., & Roberson, C. (2004). *Written and interpersonal communication methods for law enforcement*. Englewood Cliffs, NJ: Prentice Hall.

Weaver, G. (1992, September). Law enforcement in a culturally diverse society. *FBI Law Enforcement Bulletin, 9*, 1–7.

Webb, V. J., & Marshall, C. E. (1995). *The relative importance of race and ethnicity on cohorts*. New York: Plenum Press.

Weitzer, R., & Tuch, S. A. (1999). Race, class, and perceptions of discrimination by the police. *Crime and Delinquency, 45*, 494–507.

Weitzer, R., & Tuch, S. A. (2002). Perceptions of racial profiling: Race, class, and personal experience. *Criminology, 40*, 435–456.

Weitzer, R., & Tuch, S. A. (2004). Race and perceptions of police misconduct. *Social Problems, 51*, 305–325.

Weitzer, R., & Tuch, S. A. (2005). Racially biased policing: Determinants of citizen perceptions. *Social Forces, 83*, 1009–1030.

Williams, H., & Murphy, P. V. (1990). *The evolving strategies of police: A minority perspective*. Washington, DC: National Institute of Justice.

Chapter 13

Crime Mapping and Analysis

" Computers have revolutionized the art of crime mapping. Once just an exercise of sticking pins into a map glued to a bulletin board, crime mapping is now built on a foundation of geographic information systems. "

—Diamond, 2004, p. 42

" Geography has become increasingly important in law enforcement and crime prevention. Criminology has long focused on individual propensities toward crime, but it was only during the last few decades that the criminogenic features of *settings* began to take on importance in research and practice. "

—Cohen, 2006, p. 124

CHAPTER OUTLINE

OBJECTIVES

After completion of this chapter, you will be able to do the following:

- Explain the role of crime analysts.
- Briefly discuss the history of crime mapping.
- Explain how computerization changed the concepts involved in crime mapping.
- Illustrate how geographic information systems are currently used in crime mapping.
- Identify the four subparts of a geographic information system.
- Discuss the types of information that crime maps can provide the police.
- Explain what constitutes a hot spot and the issues with hot spots.
- Discuss hot spot theories on crime.
- Discuss the merits of whether crime information should be made public.
- Explain the privacy issues involved in crime mapping.

INTRODUCTION

What locations are hot for auto theft right now? Assume you are a crime analyst employed by a major metropolitan police department. How would you answer that question if it was posed to you by your chief?

This chapter contains an overview of crime mapping. It is not designed to make you proficient in the art. Readers who are interested in further study in crime mapping may refer to three excellent publications that may be obtained without charge from the U.S. Department of Justice: Ronald Clarke and John E. Eck's, "Crime Analysis for Problem Solvers in 60 Small Steps"; Jacqueline Cohen's, "Development of Crime Forecasting and Mapping Systems for Use by Police"; and Keith Harries', "Mapping Crime: Principle and Practice."

CRIME ANALYSTS

Many police agencies do employ one or more crime analysts, but some of the largest and more advanced police organizations do not. When employed, the job of the crime analyst is often narrowly limited to tabulating crimes that occur. In others, it extends to identifying patterns of crimes, with the primary objective of identifying the likely offenders so that they can be apprehended. In its more ambitious form, the crime analyst's job may include identifying factors contributing to a crime pattern, but the job of deciding how to respond to these factors is usually deferred to operational personnel, who then tend to use traditional means for dealing with them.

Meanwhile, the field of crime analysis itself has grown much more sophisticated. A strong literature on its potential is now available. The ability to electronically capture, store, and retrieve massive amounts of data that police routinely collect is infinitely greater than it was just a decade ago. The capacity to map crime geographically is stunning, and is now a major, indispensable tool in crime analysis. Standard approaches have been developed for the collection, analysis, and dissemination of intelligence across jurisdictional lines, but problem analysis is not the exclusive domain of technicians. Everyone in a police agency, from officers on the beat to police executives, and, more broadly, those in both the public and private sector concerned about crime should incorporate the line of thinking set forth here into the perspectives they bring to their work (Clarke & Eck, 2003, v–vi).

CRIME MAPPING

Evidence from clay tablets found in Iraq indicates that crime maps have been around for several thousand years—perhaps tens of millennia (Harries, 1999, p. 4). The French cartographers in the nineteenth century used national maps in attempts to identify crime patterns. European cartographers conducting studies on the social ecology of crime studied the locations of crime in an attempt to provide a number of important insights regarding crime. The studies began with the work of Guerry in France in 1833, Quetelet in Belgium in 1833, and Greg in the Netherlands in 1835. They examined reported incidents of crime and mapped the incidents on topographic maps.

In the 1920s, Parks and Burgess (followed by Shaw and McKay) studied crime rates in Chicago by mapping the reported crimes on a map. They divided the map using concentric zones to support their social disorganization theories of crime causation (Roberson & Wallace, 1998, p. 98).

Shaw and McKay's mapping efforts produced a classic analysis on juvenile delinquency in Chicago. Their work is generally recognized as the landmark piece of research involving crime mapping in the first half of the twentieth century. Shaw and McKay mapped thousands of incidents of juvenile delinquency and analyzed relationships between delinquency and various social conditions (Harries, 1999, p. 6).

Crime mapping has long been an integral part of the process known today as *crime analysis*. The New York City Police Department, for example, has traced the use of maps back to at least 1900 (Vann & Garson, 2003, p. 1). The traditional crime map was a jumbo representation of a jurisdiction with pins stuck in it. The old pin maps were useful for showing where crimes occurred. However, the maps had several serious limitations. When they were updated, the prior crime patterns were lost. While raw data could be archived, maps could not, except perhaps by photographing them. The maps were static; they could not be manipulated or queried. It would have been difficult to track a series of robberies that might overlap the duration (a week or month) of a pin map. Also, pin maps could be quite difficult to read when several types of crime, usually represented by pins of different colors, were mixed together. Pin maps occupied considerable wall space. One researcher noted that to make a single wall map of the 610 square miles of Baltimore County, twelve maps had to be joined, covering 70 square feet. Pin maps had limited value—they could be used effectively, but only for a short time. Pin maps are, however, sometimes used today because their large scales allow patterns to be seen over an entire jurisdiction in detail. The manual approach of pin mapping has generally been replaced by computer mapping (Harries, 1999, p. 3).

Probably the first use of computerized crime mapping in applied crime analysis occurred in the mid-1960s in St. Louis, Missouri, by McEwen and Research Management Associates, Inc. One of the early contributors to computerized crime mapping was Lloyd Haring, who organized a seminar on the geography of crime at Arizona State University around 1970. Early computer mapping efforts used line printers as their display devices, so their resolution was limited to the physical size of the print characters. This precluded the use of computer maps for the representation of point data, at least until plotters that were able to draw finer lines and point symbols came into more general use (Harries, 1999, p. 22). According to Harries (1999, p. 23), even as late as 1980 it was necessary to wait for improvements in desktop computer capacity, printer enhancements, and price reductions before desktop mapping could become an everyday, broadly accepted phenomenon.

Presently, **geographic information systems (GIS)** are used in most major police departments for crime mapping. GIS are computerized systems that consist of a constellation of hardware and software that integrate computer graphics with a relational database for purposes of managing and displaying data about geographic locations. GIS are designed to respond to interactive queries by analyzing and displaying spatial data.

GIS were first developed as tools to manage natural resources and land and to monitor variables about forests, wildlife, and other factors affecting our ecological systems. A Canadian, Roger Tomlinson, is credited with developing the first system in 1963 to help manage Canada's national land inventory (Vann & Garson, 2003, p. 8). By the late 1960s, computer crime mapping began with the use of large mainframe computers and punch cards.

Generally, a GIS has four subsystems: data input, date storage and retrieval, manipulation and analysis, and reporting. The manipulation and analysis subsystem has two aspects: the database management system and the geographic or spatial analysis system.

geographic information systems (GIS) / Computerized systems that consist of a constellation of hardware and software that integrate computer graphics with a relational database for purposes of managing and displaying data about geographic locations.

Using Crime Maps

Constructing a crime map involves taking a set of data and making decisions consistent with the hypothetic–deductive process. Decisions need to be made about the kind of map to be prepared, how symbols or shading will look, how statistical information will be treated, and so forth. These decisions must be based on the objective to be achieved, including consideration of the target audience.

Maps can provide a rich variety of information, including, but not limited to, location, distance, and direction, as well as pattern for maps displaying point or area data. Each type of data means different things to different users.

Location may be the most important of all the types of information to be represented on, or gleaned from, a map from the perspective of a crime analyst. Where things have happened, or may happen in the future, is the most sought after and potentially useful piece of information because it has so many implications for

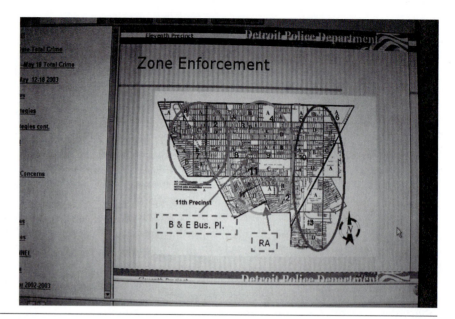

Zone enforcement computer map. Law enforcement often divide a city up into zones depending on crime rates. Different zones will need different approaches to crime prevention and having it divided makes it easier to plan and execute. This is an example of crime mapping.

investigators and for the allocation of patrol and community resources, in addition to utility in the realms of planning and politics.

Distance is not much use as an abstract piece of information. It comes to life when translated into some kind of relationship: How far did the victim live from the place where she was robbed? What is the maximum distance police cars can travel within a specific urban environment to provide acceptable response times? How far could a suspect have gone in a particular time period?

Direction is most useful when considered in conjunction with distance, although it is not typically an important piece of map information in crime analysis unless it relates to other relevant processes or conditions. It is generally used in a broadly descriptive context, such as "the hot spot of burglaries is spreading to the west," or "serial robberies are moving southeast," or "the east side is becoming a high-crime area" (Harries, 1999, p. 19).

Pattern is a useful concept in crime analysis, as so much of what crime analysts do involves describing or analyzing the pattern of crime occurrences. Pattern can be a powerful investigative tool because the way points are arranged may tell us something about the process driving that arrangement. Patterns are usually classified as random, uniform, clustered, or dispersed. In a *random arrangement*, points are just as likely to be at any place on the map as at any other. Points are distributed haphazardly around the map. A *uniform pattern* has points that are equally spaced. Alternatively, it can be said that in a uniform distribution the distance between neighboring points is maximized. In a *clustered pattern*, points are clumped together with substantial empty areas. In a dispersed pattern, the points are scattered over the area.

Harries (1999, p. 19) cautions against assuming that the nonrandom distributions (uniform and clustered) automatically mean that some interesting underlying process is at work, providing useful information about crime. This may or may not be true. Harries noted that burglaries may show up in a cluster, suggesting a hot spot, but further investigation shows that the cluster corresponds to a neighborhood with a dense population, so the high frequency is no more than an expression of the geography of risk. The terms describing the types of patterns are subject to some semantic confusion. For example, what does *dispersed* mean? A dispersed pattern could be random or uniform. Is "less dispersed" the same as "clustered"?

Harries (1999, p. 32) notes that maps are often thought of solely as display tools. In fact, maps have a wide-ranging role in the process of research, analysis, and presentation. Mapping is most effective when those broad capabilities are recognized and used to their fullest extent. The map is the end product of a process that starts with the first-responding officer's report that is processed by data entry personnel, entered into a database, and transformed into a symbol on paper. In this narrow interpretation, a map is merely a picture or part of a database.

In visual thinking, the map is used to generate ideas and hypotheses about the problem under investigation. By inspecting a map, we may notice a relationship, or correlation, between environmental factors that otherwise might have gone unnoticed. This correlation may be vertical in the sense that we see connections between different phenomena, such as crimes, land uses, and demographics. Alternatively, we may see a horizontal relationship in which we recognize a common factor across a particular crime type, such as graffiti in similar types of crime locations. Visual thinking is a private activity involving exploration and confirmation.

In the exploratory phase, maps may be crude and are not intended for display or publication. A computer-printed map of burglary patterns for the most recent week might be marked with handwritten information provided by investigators or with other data not in digital form. Information might be transcribed from a mental map to a paper map.

Another possibility, noted by Harries (1999, p. 22), is that the tools of exploratory spatial data analysis (ESDA) are used to find anomalies in data, such as an unexpected cluster of incidents, that could point to unexpected relationships. At this stage, the analyst may generate a formal hypothesis, or educated guess, to explain the process producing the observed crime pattern. Did the observed cluster of burglaries pop up by chance? Is there some recognizable cause? Is a serial burglar operating in the area? Do officers in the field have insight to offer? By developing a hypothesis, the analyst is in the mainstream of scientific research, using a venerable methodology.

Using GIS

There are numerous GIS programs or software that may be used by a crime analyst. The National Institute of Justice has a free program that may be downloaded and used as crime mapping software or as a training aid at www.schoolcopsoftware.com. The program, referred to as the **School COP Program**, does mapping with bitmap images. It contains a setup program that allows you to establish different locations on the image. Incidents (crimes) are geo-coded when you pick the location where they occurred. After the data is entered, you can map all incidents or any subset of incidents.

The Crime Mapping Research Center was established in 1997 by the National Institute of Justice. Its mission is to promote the use of crime mapping in law enforcement. The center was later renamed the National Institute of Justice's

School COP Program / A computer program that does mapping with bitmap images. Incidents (crimes) are geo-coded when you pick the location where they occurred. After the data is entered, you can map all incidents or any subset of incidents.

Mapping and Analysis for Public Safety. Its website may be accessed at www.ojp .usdoj.gov/nij/maps. The website also offers free software, including CrimeStat (spatial statistical tools). It has a Crime Mapping Tutorial, which is a self-paced course that will help you produce crime maps. Many police departments have websites that provide crime pattern and trend data for their jurisdictions. The Oakland, California, Police Department has a **Crimewatch** website that allows individuals to map a selection of various crimes. The crimes may be displayed by police beat, district, or street address. The Oakland website address is www.city .oakcc.com/maproom/crimewatch. The City of Chicago has a similar site at www .cityofchicago.org/CAPS.

Crimewatch / An Oakland, California, Police Department website that allows individuals to map a selection of various crimes. The crimes may be displayed by police beat, district, or street address.

Crime mapping and geographic information systems (GIS) are popular applications within the law enforcement community. In the past decade, law enforcement agencies have shown an increasing interest in a variety of information technologies. Police operations are information driven. Police officers and administrators are more comfortable with technology and its use for analysis and decision making than ever before. Police would like to use technology such as the Internet to reduce requests on staffing, yet still provide services to the community. Expanded functionality in computer-aided dispatch and record management systems, mobile data terminals, the Internet, and GIS have allowed law enforcement to more easily share data and partner with people and organizations in problem solving (Wartell & McEwen, 2001, p. 1).

GIS-based information-sharing systems are increasingly being used by other countries. Crime and Disorder Reduction Partnerships (CDRPs) in England and Wales are used to support their efforts to reduce crime and disorder and improve community safety. At present, there are in excess of twenty major systems distributed at either the regional, county, and/or district level in England and Wales that service CDRPs, with new systems in the planning stages (Chainey, 2006).

Why Map Crime?

As noted by the National Institute of Justice's *Briefing Book on Crime Mapping* (2002), crimes are human phenomena; therefore, their distribution across the landscape is not geographically random. For crimes to occur, offenders and their targets—the victims and/or property—must, for a period of time, exist at the same location. Several factors, from the lure of potential targets to simple geographic convenience for an offender, influence where people choose to break the law. Therefore, an understanding of where and why crimes occur can improve attempts to fight crime. Maps offer crime analysts graphic representations of such crime-related issues.

Mapping crime can help law enforcement protect citizens more effectively in the areas they serve. Simple maps that display the locations where crimes or concentrations of crimes have occurred can be used to help direct patrols to places they are most needed. Policy makers in police departments might use more complex maps to observe trends in criminal activity, and maps may prove invaluable in solving criminal cases. Detectives may use maps to better understand the hunting patterns of serial criminals and to hypothesize where these offenders might live.

Using maps that help people visualize the geographic aspects of crime, however, is not limited to law enforcement. Mapping can provide specific information on crime and criminal behavior to politicians, the press, and the general public.

Police Officer in City of London Traffic Control Room. Similar control rooms are used in all major cities in the United States. The control room is used to allocate police resources.

Hot Spots

Crime is not spread evenly across maps, it clumps in some areas and is absent in others. People use this knowledge in their daily activities. They avoid some places and seek out others. Their choices of neighborhoods, schools, stores, streets, and recreation are governed partially by the understanding that their chances of being a victim are greater in some of these places than in others. In some places people lock their cars and secure belongings, in other places they do not. Along some streets people walk swiftly and view approaching strangers with suspicion. Along other streets they casually stroll, welcome the next interesting person they might meet, and notice others making the same choices in the same areas (Eck et al., 2005).

Areas of concentrated crime are often referred to as **hot spots**. Researchers and police use the term in many different ways. Some refer to hot spot addresses, others refer to hot spot blocks, and others examine clusters of blocks. Like researchers, crime analysts look for concentrations of individual events that might indicate a series of related crimes. They also look at small areas that have a great deal of crime or disorder, even though there may be no common offender. Analysts also observe neighborhoods and neighborhood clusters with high crime and disorder levels and try to link these to underlying social conditions (Eck et al., 2005).

hot spots / Areas of concentrated crime.

Though no common definition of the term *hot spot* of crime exists, the common understanding is that a hot spot is an area that has a greater than average number of criminal or disorder events, or an area where people have a higher than average risk of victimization. This also suggests the existence of *cool spots*—places or areas with less than the average amount of crime or disorder. It also suggests that some hot spots may be hotter than others; that is, they vary in how far above average they are (Eck et al., 2005, p. 6).

Eck states that if hot spots are merely areas with an above average amount of crime or disorder, why do practitioners and researchers use the term in such a variety of ways? He notes that with recent developments in crime mapping, one can find hot spots of any size—from hot spot places to hot regions. Although all of these perspectives on hot spots have something in common—concentrations of crime or disorder separated by areas with far less crime or disorder—they differ in the area covered by the hot spots. More importantly, according to Eck, the factors that give rise to hot spot places are different from the factors that give rise to hot spot streets, hot spot neighborhoods, or hot spot cities. Further, the actions one takes to deal with a hot spot place will be different from the actions needed to address a hot spot street, hot spot neighborhood, or hot spot city (Eck et al., 2005, p. 11).

Police departments frequently use computer-mapped crime locations to delineate hot spots, or areas with high concentrations of crime. Highlighting such areas helps police direct patrols where they are most needed, thereby optimizing the deterrent effect of police presence. Although concentrations of crime locations may be discernible on a relatively simple point-map of crime locations, multiple crimes occurring at a single address may deceivingly be represented by a single point on such a map. Hot spot analysis is frequently performed using special software, such as the Spatial and Temporal Analysis of Crime (STAC) program developed by the Illinois Criminal Justice Information Authority, which draws ellipses based on the densest concentrations of mapped incidents.

The following map shows locations of residential burglaries and attempted burglaries that occurred over a two-month period in Washington, DC. Using this data, elliptical hot spots were drawn to highlight places of approximately a 1- to 4-block size where concentrations of the crimes occurred. [**Note:** Information and map taken from National Institute of Justice's *Briefing Book on Crime Mapping* (2002).]

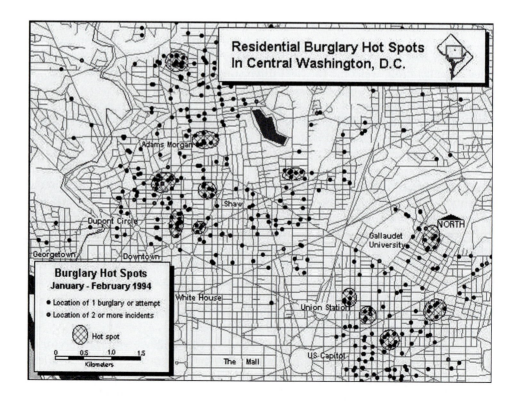

Recovery Locations

Many crime analysts consider the locations where stolen vehicles are recovered to be more relevant in solving crimes than the locations from where they are stolen. Unless a thief has an alternate mode of transportation, a stolen automobile will likely be left close to some desired destination—quite possibly a chop shop, where stolen cars are stripped down for parts. A density map can show the number of automobiles recovered per square mile.

Proximity

The applications of spatial crime analysis extend beyond the production of maps displaying crime locations for police; they provide analytical functions of interest to the general community as well.

The map on the next page of an anonymous small town with a population slightly above 6,500, locates the residences of registered child sex offenders whose addresses have been made public by the local government. These locations were compared with the locations of the town's schools. One-thousand-foot buffers were drawn around the schools to make it easier to observe how close the known offenders live to these potential target areas. Four of the twelve total offender residences fall within the buffered school zones on the map, and several of the others live just outside their perimeters. [**Note:** Information and map taken from National Institute of Justice's *Briefing Book on Crime Mapping* (2002).]

Tracking Serial Offenders

Crime maps can aid in the apprehension of serial criminals. These maps, called **criminal geographic targeting (CGT) models**, help investigators in their attempt to determine where serial criminals most likely reside given the locations of their crimes.

The CGT model adheres to the assumption that a distance relationship exists between the residences of serial offenders and where they choose to commit their crimes. Serial criminals, like everybody else, conduct their routine activities (traveling to and from work, shopping, etc.) within a certain space with which they have become familiar. Within this routine activity space, most people identify with a single anchor point, or place of central importance in their lives, usually the home. The CGT model assumes that serial criminals commit their crimes within their areas of routine activity, but at the same time they are careful not to conduct this activity in the immediate proximity of their residences.

A crime analyst using a CGT model would delineate a hunting area, the region where serial offenders seek out or encounter potential victims. With the aid of special software, each point within this area is assigned a probability of being the residence of the offender. If crime analysts have a significant number of crime locations with which to work, a serial offender's residence can be narrowed down to a small number of probable locations using a CGT model.

Possible residences of serial offenders may be estimated using a three-dimensional map, with the vertical axis representing the probability that each location is the

criminal geographic targeting (CGT) models / Computer-generated models that help investigators determine where serial criminals most likely reside given the locations of their crimes. The CGT model adheres to the assumption that a distance relationship exists between the residences of serial offenders and where they choose to commit their crimes.

Registered Child Sex Offender Representation, "Small" City—March 1997

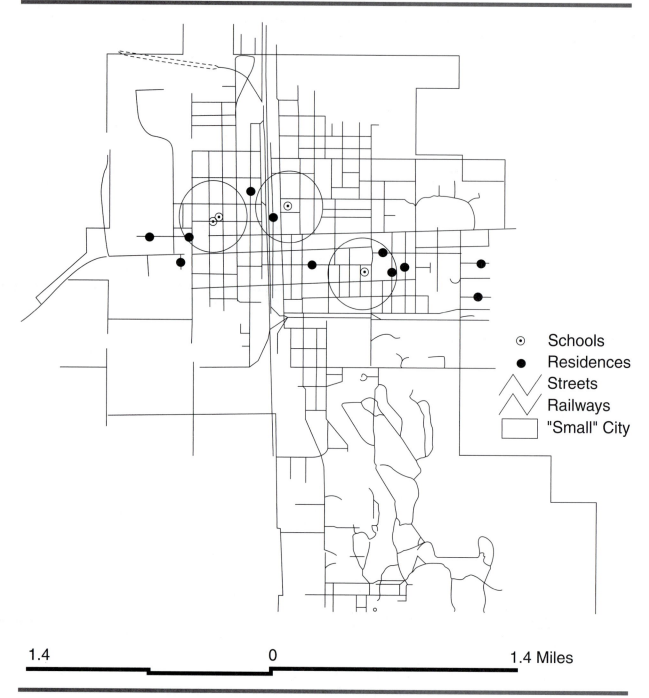

Schools
Residences
Streets
Railways
"Small" City

1.4   0   1.4 Miles

Note: The buffer contains 1,000 ft of the area.
Source: Submitted by Priyamvadha Srinivasan 03/20/97. Fair County Law Enforcement Agencies—March 1997.

residence of the offender. The "peaks" on the map are the most probable locations and correspond with the red and yellow areas on the smaller, two-dimensional inset map in the top right corner. A crime analyst would then overlay this two-dimensional map onto a street map of the area. After comparing the CGT map with other geographic factors, such as land use, police can use the map to concentrate their efforts in certain high-probability areas (Rossmo,1995).

Mapping Prisoner Reentry

Crime mapping is now being used to address a wide range of criminal justice problems, from allocating police resources to understanding the underlying causes of crime. The mapping of prisoner reentry has been accomplished in only a few cities and only recently. Even fewer cities have attempted to link incarceration and reentry data with other indicators of community well-being. The Urban Institute (UI) in 2002 launched the Reentry Mapping Network (RMN), a partnership of cities engaged in creating community change through the mapping and analysis of reentry and other community indicator data at a highly localized level.

RMN partners use mapping to pinpoint neighborhoods that experience high concentrations of returning prisoners and to examine the extent to which such communities are equipped to address the challenges that prisoner reentry creates. RMN partners use the findings from their mapping and analyses to help mobilize community members and leaders to devise targeted responses to effectively address reentry-related problems. These activities are intended to help corrections officials, community organizations, and service providers develop a better understanding of the dynamics and correlates of prisoner reentry at the local level; engage local

Emergency service operator. The operator will answer the 911 calls and direct the appropriate police, medical, or fire units to provide assistance.

stakeholders and practitioners in developing strategies to identify opportunities to address reentry-related challenges; facilitate greater coordination and collaboration among state and local agencies and organizations around this work; and expand the knowledge of how to involve communities in using data to identify and address incarceration- and reentry-related challenges.

Mapping can help identify neighborhoods that experience high geographic concentrations of prisoners returning home. Mapping the last known addresses of released inmates (available through the departments of correction in most states) can pinpoint concentrations within cities and neighborhoods, right down to the city block (La Vigne, 2004).

Crime Mapping Software

CrimeStat / A spatial statistics program for the analysis of crime incident locations.

There are many crime mapping software programs available. One of the leading is National Institute of Justice supported software, CrimeStat III. **CrimeStat** is a spatial statistics program for the analysis of crime incident locations, developed by Ned Levine & Associates under a grant from the National Institute of Justice. The program is Windows-based and interfaces with most desktop GIS programs. The program provides supplemental statistical tools to aid law enforcement agencies and criminal justice researchers in their crime mapping efforts. CrimeStat is being used by many police departments around the country, as well as by criminal justice and other researchers. The present version is 3.0 (CrimeStat III) and is available on the Internet for downloading free of charge.

The program inputs incident locations (e.g., robbery locations) in 'dbf', 'shp', ASCII, or ODBC-compliant formats using either spherical or projected coordinates. It calculates various spatial statistics and writes graphical objects to ArcView® MapInfo®, Atlas*GIS™, Surfer® for Windows, and ArcView Spatial Analyst©.

The statistics cover spatial description and distance analysis (for describing the general spatial pattern of crimes), hot spot analysis (for identifying concentrations of crashes), interpolation (for visualizing crime concentrations over a large area), space–time analysis (for understanding temporal and spatial interaction in offender behavior), and journey-to-crime estimation (for estimating the likely residence location of a serial offender). New in version 3.0 is a module for crime travel demand modeling, widely used in transportation planning. It allows a crime analyst to model crime trips over a metropolitan area and to make reasonable guesses at the travel mode and likely routes taken. It can also be used to model possible interventions.

CrimeStat III is accompanied by sample data sets and a manual that gives the background behind the statistics and examples. The software is available for free download, along with full documentation, from NACJD (National Archive of Criminal Justice Data) at ICPSR.

The MAPS program is overseeing the development, by the University of Virginia's (UVA) Systems & Information Engineering Department, of a regional scale spatial data repository for analysis and planning that can support spatial data sharing across agencies and jurisdictions, during critical incident events, as well as in their more routine needs. This repository is called the Geospatial Repository for Analysis & Safety Planning (GRASP) system. GRASP specifically addresses regional issues that relate to standard technologies, shared projections and coordinated systems, seamlessness, multiple data formats, complementary data and types, data sharing policies, and linkages to the larger spatial data infrastructure.

School COP

Developed by Abt Associates, the School Crime Operations Package (School COP) is a software application designed for entering, analyzing, and mapping incidents that occur in and around schools. Target users are persons responsible for enforcing discipline and safety regulations, investigating crime and other incidents, and planning violence prevention initiatives at elementary, middle, and high schools. School COP can be used at a single school or at the school district level. School COP includes a sample database of incidents that illustrate the package's search, reporting, and mapping capabilities. Online help is also available.

School COP runs on Windows 95, 98, NT, 2000, and XP computers and is available for download. The package is free. Abt Associates Inc. developed School COP under a cooperative agreement with the National Institute of Justice (Award No. 1999-LT-VX-K017). More details and software download for School COP are available from Abt Associates Inc.

CASE (Crime Analysis Spatial Extension)

Crime Analysis Spatial Extension (CASE) was developed by NLECTC–Rocky Mountain's Crime Mapping & Analysis Program (CMAP). CMAP, a program of the National Law Enforcement and Corrections Technology Center–Rocky Mountain Region (NLECTC-RM), was released in January 2005, CMAP CASE (Crime Analysis Spatial Extension) for ESRI's ArcGIS 8/9 GIS software.

CMAP CASE contains the spatial functions that many analysts and investigators use to find where offenders live and where they may strike next. CMAP CASE is freely available from their website at www.crimeanalysts.net. It contains a robust help file and supporting documentation explaining how these spatial functions are used to analyze crime. CMAP CASE is made available free to law enforcement agencies.

CompStat

CompStat is a crime-control model and is based on computer-driven statistics. It has been described as "a comprehensive, continuous analysis of results for improvement and achievement of prescribed outcomes" (McDonald, 2002, p. 8). Prior to 1994, the New York Police Department (NYPD), like most major police departments, was organized around avoiding risk and failure. Officers were constrained by regulations and procedures. With the implementation of the CompStat system, the NYPD is now using crime statistics and regular meetings of key enforcement personnel to direct its enforcement efforts. Under the CompStat system, there were major changes in the management style of the NYPD. Precinct commanders were granted more latitude in initiating their own operations and running their precincts. Officers were authorized to assertively enforce quality-of-life laws.

CompStat / A crime-control model based on computer-driven statistics. It has been described as "a comprehensive, continuous analysis of results for improvement and achievement of prescribed outcomes."

NYPD commanders now have daily turn-around on CompStat numbers (crime statistics) and can observe weekly trends in order to take corrective actions. Crime statistics are not the bottom line as to how the police are doing, but they are analyzed on both a precinct-by-precinct and citywide basis. CompStat implementation is based on five basic principles:

1. **Specific objectives:** Examples of crime-specific objectives are decreasing street robberies, drug sales to youths, vandalism, and carjackings.

2. **Timely and accurate intelligence:** If the police are going to respond effectively, officers at all levels must have accurate knowledge of when particular types of crime are occurring, where the crimes are occurring, and how they are being committed.

3. **Effective strategies and tactics:** The tactics must be comprehensive, flexible, and adaptable to the changing crime trends that are identified and monitored.

4. **Rapid deployment of personnel and resources:** Once tactical plans are developed, an array of personnel and other necessary resources should be promptly deployed.

5. **Relentless follow-up and assessment:** An ongoing process of rigorous follow-up and assessment is considered necessary to ensure that the desired results are actually being achieved (McDonald, 2002, p. 8–9).

Despite the national attention that has been paid to the NYPD's CompStat program, there has been little systematic analysis of the programs in policing (Weisburd et al., 2004). Weisburd and others, in a Police Foundation report, noted that only about 33 percent of police departments with more than 100 sworn officers had adopted some form of CompStat and only 11 percent of those departments with less than 100 officers had adopted it. The report concluded that the specific motivations for adopting CompStat varied across police agencies, but most expressed a desire to reduce serious crime and increase management control over field operations. The report noted that larger police agencies were more likely to adopt the NYPD model than the smaller agencies.

Analysis and Planning Level

crime early warning system (CEWS) / A computer program that maps crime forecasts by geographic area to provide a jurisdiction-wide scan for areas perhaps needing changes in tactical deployment of police.

A **crime early warning system (CEWS)** maps crime forecasts by geographic area to provide a jurisdiction-wide scan for areas perhaps needing changes in tactical deployment of police (Cohen, 2006, p. 156).

Time series data, the most frequently used series of measurements, consist of repeated measurements for a fixed observation unit (e.g., census tract, grid cell, car beat, or precinct) and fixed time interval (such as month, quarter, or year), sequenced by time period. Time series methods are the most widely researched and used forecast methods.

At the macro (policy/planning) level, police use crime mapping primarily for the design of precinct and car beat boundaries, in response to changing population and crime patterns (and perhaps budget limitations). The tasks are to design boundaries and staffing levels by precinct and car beat for the purpose of balancing workloads and achieving acceptable response times to calls for service. The corresponding planning horizon is three to five years, requiring long-range forecasts based on demographic trends and forecasts.

The meso-level of decision making corresponds to monthly CompStat meetings for precincts (or similar meetings). While CompStat meetings may be held weekly to accommodate review of a large number of precincts, such as in New York City, each precinct is reviewed only once per month. Hence, the planning horizon is a month and monthly time series data are most relevant.

The purpose of CompStat meetings is manyfold, but two major purposes relative to crime analysis are: (1) to evaluate last month's crime prevention and enforcement performance, and (2) to plan for next month's crime analysis and police activities. Time series forecasting has the potential to play an important role for both of these purposes, providing the basis for evaluation and forecasts of areas with potential crime increases next month. It is here at the meso-level that crime forecasting fits best into crime analysis.

Evaluation of performance within a specific area and month requires making a counterfactual forecast; that is, a forecast of crime level for "business as usual conditions" and no changes in policies or practices from historical conditions. Then if police intervened in special ways for prevention or enforcement during the month for evaluation, or just worked smarter and harder, the difference in the actual crime level from the counterfactual forecast can be attributed to police efforts. Alternatively, changes in the wrong direction might be attributed to changes in criminal activity (e.g., a gang war flare up).

An effective counterfactual forecast is a univariate forecast. Univariate methods capture the existing seasonal and time trend patterns in a time series and then extrapolate or extend them into the future, assuming no pattern changes. For example, the counterfactual forecast for January 2005 would be based on historical data for January 2000 through December 2004, would extend the estimated mean number of crimes for December 2004 by the estimated growth rate (or decline rate) per month to January, and adjust this value for the estimated January seasonal effect. All estimates are based on the historical data.

CompStat does not use univariate forecasts for evaluation, but rather uses the CompStat method. For this method, the counterfactual value for evaluating January 2005 crimes is January 2004 crimes for the same crime type and location. The virtue of this method is that it provides some information on the changes in crime levels over a year's time and at the same seasonal point. Its problems are first that the counterfactual value is a single data point, which is noisy and can yield false information.

The implementation of time series forecasting for use by police takes the form of a crime mapping system called crime early warning system (CEWS). It serves both the meso- and micro-levels of crime analysis.

Micro-level crime analysis includes the familiar day-to-day tasks of crime analysts: reading crime reports, identifying patterns in data, mapping crime points, identifying hot spots, and so on. CEWS includes the point data and records that support these activities (Cohen, 2006).

Crime MAPS allows you to select a jurisdiction (city, unincorporated area in the county, neighborhood, or political district) and a location of interest. The location can be a school, hospital, zip code, tourist attraction, major shopping center, neighborhood, address, or intersection. Except for a zip code or neighborhood, a radius ranging from 500 feet to one mile can be selected to generate an orange shaded area

CASE STUDY: San Diego County, California, Crime Maps

San Diego County, using the Automated Regional Justice Information System (ARJIS), has established a public website at www.mapping.arjis.org/main.aspx. By visiting this site, you can enter a street address, shopping center, or other place and find out what crimes have been reported for that location in recent months.

The law enforcement agencies in San Diego County take reports for all crime cases, arrests, citations, and some traffic collisions within the county. The reports are entered into the ARJIS, which provides the incident data for Crime MAPS. Agencies that provide data to ARJIS include the San Diego County Sheriff, all city police departments in San Diego County, the San Diego Harbor Police, the San Diego Unified School District Police, and the San Diego Community College Police.

Some city police departments and the county sheriff also provide data for some universities and community colleges in their jurisdictions, including: University of San Diego, Point Loma Nazarene, MiraCosta, and Southwestern. Data from UCSD, SDSU, CSU-San Marcos, Cuyamaca, Grossmont, and Palomar are not provided. Also, federal and state law enforcement agencies (military police, FBI, Border Patrol, and CHP) do not provide data to ARJIS.

around the selected location on the resulting map. Incidents will be mapped both inside and outside (twice the radius) this area. Note that neither an entire city nor an unincorporated county can be selected.

Types of Incidents Mapped: Various types of crimes, arrests, citations, and traffic-related incidents are available. Crime types include: aggravated assault, arson, commercial burglary, homicide, malicious mischief/vandalism, rape, residential

Voices of Experience

College Education

Excerpts from an interview between Cliff Roberson and former police officer, John M. Boal. Currently, Professor Boal is a full-time faculty member in the Criminal Justice Program at the University of Akron.

Q: *How important is a college education to a police officer?*
A: I believe education helps you develop your problem-solving abilities. Someone coming out of high school may not have had to face a lot of situations where they were required to use their problem-solving abilities. It also helps with the ability to engage in critical thinking. This is especially important to a first responder to an emergency situation who needs to make a critical assessment of the situation and determine the resources needed. The officer will need the necessary skills to make a critical assessment. ■

burglary, robbery, sex crimes other than rape, simple assault, theft, vehicle break-in, and vehicle theft. Domestic violence-related assault data are currently not included. Arrest and citation types include: curfew violation, deadly weapon possession, drunk in public, narcotics, prostitution, and truancy. Traffic-related incident types include: DUI, citations, and collisions.

Only incidents with a valid street address or intersection are included. In some cases victims may not know where the crime occurred (e.g., if their pocket was picked somewhere downtown). Such a crime will not have an address and therefore will not be included.

Time Periods of the Incident Data: Crime MAPS is updated with new data every week on Monday. This data includes reports that have been entered in ARJIS up through the previous Saturday. Some law enforcement agencies may be several weeks behind on their data entry, so if you are not getting the expected number of incidents for the most recent week, either search farther back in time or contact your local agency to clarify.

Any time period of ninety-one days or less within the past twelve months can be searched. The period can be defined by start and end dates, times of the day, and days of the week. If you are searching an area with a large number of incidents, you may want to limit your time period to fewer than ninety-one days.

Incident Attributes: The map's *Identify* feature can be used to determine the following attributes or characteristics for each incident or map location at which incidents are mapped: type of incident; hundred-block address or street intersection; and date, day, and time of occurrence. Earliest and latest dates and times are included because some crimes have a range of when they might have occurred. For instance, a car was parked at 10:00 P.M. on the third and discovered missing at 7:00 A.M. on the fourth.

Not all offenses within one report can be queried and mapped. A crime report may contain more than one offense (e.g., a robbery and an assault). Only the primary offense type can be queried and mapped. In this example, the map will show a robbery because it is the more serious offense.

Victim names and exact address data have been removed to protect the privacy of victims. Although the symbols are mapped using the specific address, when the incidents are identified, the addresses only show the hundred-block numbers, not exact addresses.

Incident Locations on the Map: All incidents are mapped at specific street addresses or intersections. The symbols are shown on the streets at those locations. This means that incidents that occur in parks, on school grounds or campuses, at shopping malls, or other such locations are mapped on a street and not at the actual location of the incident in the area. Also, when multiple incidents occur at one address or intersection, the map will show only one symbol. Each symbol can be checked with the map's *Identify* feature to see how many are at the same location.

Comparison with Incident Descriptions in the Media: Some offenses may be shown differently than initially reported in the media. For example, if the victim of a robbery was seriously wounded, the offense may be recorded (and therefore mapped) initially as a robbery, but then changed to a homicide if the victim later dies.

Comparison with Published Law Enforcement Agency Data: There are several reasons why the incident data mapped on this website may not match that published by the various law enforcement agencies. The main one is that not all incidents can be mapped, such as those without a valid street address. For official crime statistics, click on *Crime Statistics* on the ARJIS website (www.arjis.org) or contact your local agency.

Different Results on Different Days: ARJIS is continually receiving police reports for recent as well as older incidents so the incident database is subject to change over time. There can be delays in discovering and reporting crimes (e.g., a home burglary

Learning from Unsuccessful Attempts

The Chula Vista, California, Police Department was aware that the city's building boom could worsen the residential burglary problem. The new houses were intended for affluent couples who would be out during the day when burglaries were most likely to happen. The police, therefore, decided to examine the effectiveness of existing security precautions to see if any of these could be built into new homes or suggested to homeowners. Cathy Burciaga, one of the department's crime analysts, compared completed burglaries with unsuccessful attempts for an eighteen-month sample of 569 homes in the city. This indicated that deadbolts should be installed on both the side and front doors of new houses. Interviews conducted with 250 victims and 50 burglars revealed that not one burglar had tried to enter a house by breaking a double-glazed window. This led to the recommendation that all windows in new housing be double-glazed and meet strict forced-entry standards. The results of Burciaga's study are shown in the following table.

Protective Step	Completed Burglaries	Unsuccessful Attempts	Effective?*
Dusk to dawn light	28%	29%	No
Indoor light on	26%	29%	No
Indoor timer light	9%	11%	No
Deadbolt on front door	28%	25%	No
Deadbolt front and side doors	15%	29%	Yes
Outdoor motion detector	23%	36%	Yes
Radio/TV left on	9%	18%	Yes
Alarm company sign	19%	36%	Yes

* "Yes" means present in a larger percentage of unsuccessful attempts than successful ones.

Source: Research study reported in Clarke & Eck, 2003.

may not be discovered until a person returns from vacation). A robbery may become a homicide if the victim dies later. There can also be delays in entering reports into the ARJIS. In the case of a homicide, it might take several days for the medical examiner to determine that the death was unlawful.

School and Shopping Center Data: The menu of schools includes the public and private school sites in the San Diego Association of Government's (SANDAG) school database: www. sandag.org/resources/maps_and_gis/gis_downloads/downloads/metadata/schoolsdoc.htm. Not included are colleges, universities, and other institutions of higher education. If a school of interest is not listed, use its street address or the nearest street intersection.

Only major shopping centers are included. These are defined by SANDAG in one of its activity center layers. For the selection criteria, see www.sandag.org/resources/maps_and_gis/gis_downloads/downloads/metadata/majattrsdoc.htm. For smaller shopping centers, use the street address of a specific store or the nearest street intersection.

Help File: A HELP file has been created to guide users through each step of the mapping process. It explains the various options in selecting locations, incidents, and time periods, as well as the use of the various buttons on the map screen. You can see the file by clicking on the HELP button at the top of the Location, Incidents, and Time Period screens, and under Information on the Map screen.

SHOULD CRIME INFORMATION BE MADE PUBLIC?

Note: The following section was taken from *A Guide for Sharing Crime Maps and Spatial Data*, Institute for Law and Justice, NCJ 188739, pp. 4–5. (Citations omitted.)

Why should a law enforcement agency make crime data and crime maps available to researchers, other agencies, and the public?

There are many advantages, including:

1. Providing crime maps through the Internet or another convenient mechanism actually may reduce police workload; that is, fewer calls may be made to the crime analysis section for special requests if the maps are readily available. The Tempe, Arizona, Police Department put a variety of crime maps and information on the Internet to "provide timely information with nearly instantaneous updates and conserve time and resources by reducing mailings and virtually eliminating printing and duplicating costs." In addition, making crime maps and statistics accessible will alleviate common citizen calls such as, "Is this neighborhood safe?" by allowing the agency to refer the citizens to the Internet to make their own judgments.

2. Many police departments have found that the more the community knows about crime and safety issues, the more willing it is to work with the police to solve those problems. In addition, potential victims of a crime pattern may protect themselves better if they are aware of the problem.

3. Maps can assist in community policing and problem solving by showing where problems do and do not exist. While researching gang territories, George Tita, formerly with Carnegie Mellon University, mapped various activity spaces and found that only small portions of a neighborhood were affected. When he shared his maps and results with community developers and gang street workers, their response was that if this information was shared with everyone, people would understand that the whole neighborhood was not gang-infested, and businesses might be more likely to operate and invest in the area.

4. Maps can increase public awareness about neighborhood problems. On one hand, residents of higher crime areas may not want their problems highlighted. On the other hand, some welcome the attention. As an unnamed citizen once stated: "I know that I live in a high-crime area, and [your] publishing the information has only confirmed my opinions. However, it is satisfying that the local council is working in partnership with the police to accurately identify crime hot spots and as a result target crime prevention resources to those areas that most need it, rather than to the middle-class areas where people are more likely to sit on some local committee, shout the loudest, and get funds allocated to an area that in reality is of low priority."

5. Maps facilitate partnerships with researchers and other agencies. If researchers lack accurate, current data they cannot assist departments and the policing field in analyzing and solving crime and disorder problems. Most people recognize the advantage of sharing data among law enforcement agencies and across jurisdictions (because criminals do not usually respect city boundaries). In addition, agencies outside of law enforcement, such as public housing, schools, hospitals, parks and recreation departments, and urban planning divisions can work toward community safety if they are better informed about crime.

6. By providing maps and data, a police department can be sure the data are presented accurately. If the department does not provide maps and data, someone else (such as the media or a neighborhood group) eventually will—then the department risks having its data interpreted and displayed by someone less familiar with them. One nongovernmental website that currently displays crime maps and data is APBnews.com at www.apbnews.com/resource center. Its data contain information and ratings from the CAP Index, a privately developed crime-risk database.

7. Providing maps and data to the public is a means to hold the police department accountable. By making information public, law enforcement agencies are less likely to risk altering the statistics to make themselves look better. In addition, the more the public knows about crime, the more likely it is that someone or some group will ask what the police or, in a true police–community partnership, they can do about it. The concern by officers that the public may have access to up-to-date crime information has led to more internal requests for maps and use of Internet sites by the officers themselves. Officers do not want to be confronted by a community member who is more aware of crime in the neighborhood than they are.

Providing crime maps and data also poses several potential and actual disadvantages, such as:

1. The information might be used for commercial purposes (e.g., alarm companies calling burglary victims), which many citizens may find a violation of privacy or a nuisance. Many departments already release lists of crime incidents to the media, and companies will still not be able to identify specific households from the map, but they could target general areas.

2. Potential offenders may use crime maps to identify areas that have not been targeted and therefore may not be receiving much police attention.

3. Crime maps could conceivably harm a high-crime area by reducing property values or increasing insurance rates. However, no definitive study of the property value concern has been made, and insurance companies (at least in California) have already been using zip code crime information for years to define rates. Taxi drivers, pizza deliverers, and other service people sometimes hesitate to go to high-crime areas, but their reticence is often based more on reputation than on hard data. Crime maps could alleviate concerns.

4. Crime maps are open to misinterpretation by viewers if the maps are too complex or view ers do not understand statistics or crime data. Further, map shading sometimes suggests that an entire area (e.g., beat, neighborhood) has a crime problem, when in fact all the crimes may be concentrated in one or two blocks.

There may also be privacy issues involved in making crime data public, such as:

1. If a map shows the exact location of an offense, such as the victims' residence, or the incident address is released, the victims may be retraumatized by the fear that criminals will see them as an easier target.

2. Victims may decline to assist in investigations and prosecutions if they believe offenders or their associates can find out where they live by looking at crime maps.

3. If persons are victimized again, they may decide not to report the offense because of concerns about publicity through a crime map. An increase in unreported crimes makes it harder for police to respond to public safety concerns.

4. Incident-specific details associated with a map could be misused. If specific addresses are identifiable, all privacy is essentially eliminated.

DOES HOT SPOT PATROLLING SIMPLY CAUSE CRIME TO MOVE AROUND THE CORNER?

Does the concentration of policing resources on hot spots prevent crime? Weisburd and others (2005) studied this question. They concluded that hot spots policing approaches have strong impacts upon crime in targeted sites. They noted that often there is a concern that focusing police resources on hot spots will simply displace the crime to nontargeted areas. According to the researchers, when immediate spatial displacement has been examined, the findings generally support the position that displacement is small and that diffusion of crime control benefits is more likely.

They concluded that there was little evidence of immediate spatial displacement, and strong evidence for diffusion of benefits beyond the targeted areas. This finding, in the context of a controlled study that was designed to directly study displacement and diffusion effects, adds strong support to a policy approach that focuses police resources at crime hot spots. They opined that concentration on hot spots is likely to lead to strong crime prevention benefits not only in targeted sites, but also in areas close to them.

HOT SPOT THEORIES ON CRIME

Note: This discussion on Hot Spot Crime Theories was taken from *Mapping Crime: Understanding Hot Spots* (August 2005), NCJ 209393, by John Eck et al.

Place Theories

place theories / Theories that explain why crime events occur at specific locations.

Place theories explain why crime events occur at specific locations. They deal with crimes that occur at the lowest level of analysis—specific places. They involve looking at specific incidents and asking such questions as, "At what places are burglaries occurring and at what places are they not occurring?" Crime phenomena at this level occur as points, so the appropriate units of analysis are addresses, street corners, and other very small places, which are typically represented on maps as dots. Police action, such as warrants, which specify exact addresses (not blocks or neighborhoods), is very precise at this level.

Street Theories

street theories / Theories that deal with crimes that occur at a slightly higher level than specific places; that is, over small, stretched areas such as streets or blocks.

Street theories deal with crimes that occur at a slightly higher level than specific places; that is, over small, stretched areas such as streets or blocks. A prostitution stroll is an example. At this level of analysis analysts ask such questions as, "On which streets are prostitutes found and on which streets are they not found?" The appropriate units of analysis can be street segments, paths, and sections of highways, which would be represented on maps as straight, bent, or curved lines. Police action is still relatively precise, although not as precise as at the place level. Concentrated patrolling occurs at this level, as well as efforts to change traffic and street patterns.

Neighborhood Theories

Some theories of crime attempt to explain neighborhood differences. At a higher level than place or street, neighborhood theories deal with large areas. Here analysts are interested in such questions as, "What areas are claimed by gangs and what areas are not?" The appropriate units of analysis are quite varied and can include square blocks, communities, and census tracts, to name a few. Two-dimensional shapes such as ellipses, rectangles, and other polygons are used on maps to represent crime phenomena at this level. At this level, police action is far less precise because the areas are typically too large for effective concentrated patrolling. Nevertheless, depending on neighborhood characteristics, relevant action might include efforts to engage residents in collective action against crime and disorder. If offenders are mobile throughout an area, rather than concentrated at a few places, then efforts to deter them should occur at this level.

Other Large Area Theories

Still other theories attempt to explain differences in crime patterns at much higher levels of aggregation. For example, theories of crime differ among cities and regions. On the city level, suggested actions may include citywide changes in economic, transportation, education, welfare, and recreation policies, to name a few. On the multijurisdictional or multistate regional levels, suggested actions against concentrations of crime could include even broader scale policies or social change. Although these are interesting theories, they are far less useful for local police agencies, thus they are not examined here.

Repeat Victimization Theories

Finally, **repeat victimization theories** pertain to questions of why the same victims are targeted repeatedly. They can operate at any of the three levels discussed—points, lines, or polygons—however, not all repeat victimization can be shown on maps.

repeat victimization theories / Theories that pertain to questions of why the same victims are targeted repeatedly.

Types of Hot Spots

The most basic form of a hot spot is a place that has many crimes. A place can be an address, street corner, store, house, or any other small location, most of which can be seen by a person standing at its center. Places typically have a single owner and a specific function—residence, retail sales, recreation, school. Crime often is concentrated at a few places, even in high-crime areas. Although hot spots are often concentrated within areas, they often are separated by other places with few or no crimes.

Routine activity theory helps to explain why crime often is concentrated at specific places. In particular, routine activity points to how behavior is regulated at the location by place managers—owners of places or people acting on an owner's behalf.

SUMMARY

■ Most law enforcement agencies have one or more crime analysts, but some of the largest and more advanced police organizations do not. The job of the crime analyst is often narrowly limited to tabulating crimes that occur. In others, it extends to identifying patterns of crimes, with the primary objective of

identifying the likely offenders so that they can be apprehended.

■ Crime maps have been around for several thousand years—perhaps tens of millennia. European cartographers studying the social ecology of crime studied the locations of crime in an attempt to provide a number of important insights regarding crime.

- Parks and Burgess, starting in the 1920s, and later, Shaw and McKay, studied crime rates in Chicago by mapping the reported crimes on a map. They divided the map using concentric zones to support their social disorganization theory of crime causation.

- Presently, GIS are used in most major police departments for crime mapping. GIS are computerized geographic information systems that consist of a constellation of hardware and software that integrate computer graphics with a relational database for purposes of managing and displaying data about geographic locations.

- Areas of concentrated crime are often referred to as *hot spots*. Researchers and police use the term in many different ways. Some refer to hot spot addresses, others refer to hot spot blocks, and others examine clusters of blocks.

- CompStat is a crime-control model and is based on computer-driven statistics. It has been described as a comprehensive, continuous analysis of results for improvement and achievement of prescribed outcomes.

- Concentration on hot spots is likely to lead to strong crime prevention benefits not only in targeted sites, but also in areas close to them. Apparently, crime does not move around the corner.

Classroom Discussion Questions and Activities

1. Go to one of the public crime sites and examine the types of crime maps displayed at the site.

2. Plot a crime map involving incidents in your home community.

3. Visit a local law enforcement agency and determine what crime maps the agency keeps and whether some maps are still kept manually.

4. Determine if there are any "auto theft hot spots" near your home.

5. Check and determine how many registered sex offenders live within one mile of your current residence or your school dorm.

References

Block, R., & Block, C. (1995). Space, place and crime: Hot spot areas and hot places of liquor-related crime. In J. E. Eck & D. Weisburd (Eds.), *Crime and place*, Crime Prevention Studies, Vol. 4, pp. 145–184. Monsey, NY: Criminal Justice Press.

Capone, D. L., & Nichols, Jr., W. W. (1975). *Crime and distance: An analysis of offender behavior in space.* Proceedings of the Association of American Geographers, Vol. 7, pp. 45–49.

Chainey, S. (2006). *Review of GIS-based information sharing systems.* London: British Home Office.

Clarke, R. V., & Eck, J. E. (2003). *Crime analysis for problem solvers in 60 small steps.* Washington, DC: U.S. Dept. of Justice, Office of Community Oriented Policing Services.

Cohen, J. (2006 January). *Development of crime forecasting and mapping systems for use by police.* Washington, DC: U.S. Dept of Justice, NCJRS.

Cohen, L., & Felson, M. (1977). Social change and crime rate trends: A routine activities approach. *American Sociological Review, 44,* 588–608.

Diamond, J. (2004, April). Connecting the dots. *Police Magazine,* pp. 42–47.

Eck, J. E., Chainey, S., Cameron, J. G., Leitner, M., & Wilson, R. E. (2005 August). *Mapping crime: Understanding hot spots.* NCJ 209393, Washington, DC: U.S. Department of Justice.

Harries, K. (1999 December). *Mapping crime: Principle and practice.* NCJ 178919, Washington, DC: U.S. Department of Justice.

La Vigne, N. (2004). Why map prisoner reentry? *Crime Mapping News, 6* (4).

McDonald, P. P. (2002). *Managing police operations: Implementing the New York crime control model–CompStat.* Belmont, CA: Wadsworth.

National Institute of Justice. (2002). *Briefing book on crime mapping*. Washington, DC: U.S. Government Printing Office.

Roberson, C., & Wallace, H. (1998) *Introduction to criminology*. Incline Village, NV: Copperhouse.

Rossmo, D. K. (1995). Place, space, and police investigations: Hunting serial violent criminals. In J. E. Eck & D. Weisburd (Eds.), *Crime and place, crime prevention studies,* Vol. 4. Monsey, NY: Criminal Justice Press.

Vann, I. E., & Garson, G. D. (2003). *Crime mapping: New tools for law enforcement*. New York: Peter Lang.

Wartell, J., & McEwen, J. T. (2001). *A guide for sharing crime maps and spatial data*. Institute for Law and Justice, NCJ 188739.

Weisburd, D., Mastrofski, S. D., Greenspan, R., & White, J. J. (2004, April). *The growth of CompStat in American policing*. Washington, DC: Police Foundation.

Weisburd, D., Wyckoff, L. A., Ready, J., Eck, J. E., Hinkle, J., & Gajewski, F. (2005, October). *Does crime just move around the corner?* Washington, DC: U.S. Dept of Justice, NCJRS.

Chapter 14

Handling Terrorism and Natural Disasters

" All disasters are essentially local. There is no such thing as a Homeland Security Department disaster or an FBI disaster; there are only New York City, Los Angeles, Chicago, or even Des Moines disasters. Yes, their impact matters and relates to the larger community. If we are to be successful in developing a more productive anti-terrorist environment, both the public police sector and the private security sector need to change their client culture from one of mere security awareness or knowledge to that of security ownership and responsibility. *"*

—Charles P. Connolly, former Assistant Commissioner,
New York City Police Department, 2005

CHAPTER OUTLINE

- Introduction
- Terrorism and the Police Officer
- War on Terrorism
- Terrorism Alerts
- Assessing Terrorist Threats
- Anti-Terrorist and Disaster Recovery Agencies
- Bomb Threats
- Hostages
- Summary

O B J E C T I V E S

After completion of this chapter, you will be able to do the following:

- Explain a police officer's duty as a "first responder."
- Describe the duties and responsibilities of a first responder.
- Explain the differences between ordinary criminal acts and terrorist acts.
- Recognize terrorism alerts.
- Define and explain how terrorist threats are assessed.
- Describe the critical infrastructure.
- Explain terrorist risk assessment calculation.
- Describe the federal government agencies' involvement in anti-terrorism programs.
- Describe how bomb threats should be handled.
- Explain actions to take in hostage situations.

I N T R O D U C T I O N

A patrol officer's reaction to any disaster can be learned. Each disaster, no matter how different from the others, shares many common characteristics. Also, like each domestic disturbance call, each disaster can threaten your survival. The preparation for handling any disaster begins in your head. Patrol officers should think about what disasters they could encounter and how they would respond to each. For example, patrol officers in Kansas probably know how to react to a tornado, officers in the coastal states probably know how to react to a hurricane, and officers in California know how to react to an earthquake. In addition to the natural disasters, patrol officers in all states need to think about how they would react in case of a terrorist attack.

Whether it's an act of terrorism or a natural disaster, it is likely that a patrol officer will be the **first responder**. The primary responsibilities of a first responder arriving at the scene are to:

- protect life
- maintain order
- conduct traffic control
- protect property from further damage
- help establish communications
- assist in the coordination of the response of other emergency personnel

first responder / Individuals or groups responding directly to the scene of an incident, such as firefighters, law enforcement, and emergency medical service.

David Griffith

Editor, *Police* Magazine
Now we're fighting the Global War on Terrorism. What the hell does this mean? Terrorism isn't an enemy. It isn't even the name of an enemy force. Terrorism is a tactic in which vile human beings attack innocents to intimidate them and exert their political will. How do you fight that?

Source: Griffith, 2006, p. 12.

One of the officer's first responsibilities as a first responder at the scene of an emergency is to assess the situation and communicate the assessment to the officer's supervisors. The initial situation assessment normally includes:

- type of emergency or situation
- location of emergency or situation
- type of assistance needed
- number of casualties involved
- special equipment needed
- other information that would be helpful

What Is a First Responder?

A first responder is defined as individuals or groups responding directly to the scene of an incident, such as firefighters, law enforcement, and emergency medical services. It may include other city or county responders who report to the scene to assist with response or recovery actions, such as public works and utility personnel. Volunteer groups who are brought to the scene under authority of the Incident Commander, such as the Salvation Army or the Red Cross, also may be included.

Source: State of Texas Pamphlet: Strategies for Texas first responder preparedness, 2002, p. 19.

TERRORISM AND THE POLICE OFFICER

How does terrorism differ from traditional crime?
Do terrorist organizations use traditional crime to support their terrorist activities?
Why discuss terrorism in a book on police operations?

terrorism / Criminal acts caused by persons or groups motivated by political or social goals, ideological justification, and considerable forethought and planning.

Traditional crime is characterized by spontaneity, lack of planning, and pecuniary or personal motives. In contrast, **terrorism** generally involves persons or groups motivated by political or social goals, ideological justification, and considerable forethought and planning.

In recent years, there has been a marked decline in state-sponsored terrorism. This has led a number of terrorism scholars to conclude that terrorist organizations are increasingly turning to criminal activity as an alterative means of financial support. Although the criminal methods used by terrorist groups range from the highly sophisticated to the most basic, they all serve a common purpose: the crimes provide logistical support for terrorism. Crimes are committed to supply terrorists with money, material, personnel, training, communication systems, safe havens, and travel. Far from being mere accoutrements strapped onto the terrorist's agenda, these crimes are the lifeblood of terrorist organizations (Ham, 2005, p. 1).

Common crimes, such as the creation of false identities for group members, thefts to procure funding for the group, and thefts of weapons or explosive materials, are designed to support later terrorist acts. The presence of these crimes may serve as pro-incident indicators that may assist law enforcement agencies in early interdiction and prevention of terrorist incidents (Smith, Damphousse, & Roberts, 2006, p. 2). Money laundering is probably the most sophisticated crime engaged in by terrorist groups.

WAR ON TERRORISM

According to Louise Richardson (2006, p. 1), the United States can't win a war on terrorism, any more than it could win a war against armed robbery or tornadoes. What it must do, according to her, is contain the threat to the nation caused by terrorists. Richardson, who was born in Ireland to Catholic parents, learned at an early age about terrorism. She states that governments are invariably placed under enormous pressure to react forcibly and fast in the wake of a terrorist attack. She claims that this response is not likely to be most conducive to long-term success against terrorists. After interviewing all the terrorists she could contact, and studying transcripts of captured terrorists and other source material, her main conclusion is that "terrorists are not nuts." She concludes that terrorists are human beings who think like we do and have goals they are trying to achieve (Richardson, 2006, p. 53).

Richardson contends that terrorists' motivations can be summed up in a three-word phrase: revenge, renown, and reaction. According to her, terrorism is a tactic, and thus cannot be defeated; what can be defeated, or at least contained, are individual groups of terrorists. She has six rules for fighting terrorism:

1. Have a defensible and achievable goal, such as stopping the spread of Islamic militancy.
2. Live by your principles.
3. Know your enemy.
4. Separate the terrorists from their communities.
5. Engage others in countering terrorists with you.
6. Have patience and keep your perspective.

TERRORISM ALERTS

Note: The material for this section was taken from the FBI's *Terrorism Quick Reference Card*, 2003.

First responding officers should be aware of suspicious factors that may indicate a possible terrorist threat. These factors should be considered collectively in assessing a possible threat.

Suspicious Factors to Consider

- Possible Suicide Bomber Indicators
  - An individual who is alone and nervous.
  - Repeated patting of upper body or rearranging clothing excessively.
  - Wearing an inordinate amount of perfumes, colognes, or other scents that may be used to mask "chemical"-type odors.
  - Wearing loose and/or bulky clothing.
  - Clothing that does not fit weather conditions.
  - Individual may be sweating, mumbling, or may exhibit unusually calm and detached behavior.
  - Exposed wires from clothing, possibly through sleeve.
  - Rigid mid-section (explosive device or may be carrying a rifle).
  - Hands tightened (may be holding a detonation device).

- Passport History
  - Recent travel overseas to countries that sponsor terrorism.
  - Multiple passports with different countries/names.
  - Altered passport numbers or photo substitutions.
  - Pages have been removed.

- Other Identification—Suspicious Characteristics
  - No current or fixed address; fraudulent/altered social security cards, visas, and licenses.
  - Multiple IDs with names spelled differently.
  - International driver's ID: there are no international or UN drivers' licenses—they are called permits.
  - Official international drivers' permits that are over one year old. They are only valid for one year after entry into the United States.
  - Laminated or off-color international drivers' permits. They are not laminated and are paper-gray in color.
  - Individual shows unusual interest or prolonged interest in security measures or personnel, entry points and access controls, or perimeter barriers, such as fences or walls.
  - Individual actively engages in "boundary probing," beginning with physical approaches to measure possible access restrictions and/or law enforcement presence and responses.
  - Discreet use of cameras or note taking at nontourist-type locations, such as airports, bridges, and chemical plants.

- Employment/School/Training
  - No obvious signs of employment.
  - Possesses student visa, but not English proficient.
  - An indication of military-type training in weapons or self-defense.

- Unusual Items in Vehicles/Residences
  - Training manuals; flight, scuba, explosive, military, or extremist literature.
  - Blueprints with no apparent affiliation to architecture.
  - Photographs/diagrams of specific high-profile targets or infrastructures, including entrances/exits of buildings, bridges, power/water plants, routes, security cameras, subway/sewer, and underground systems.
  - Photos/pictures of known terrorists.
  - Numerous prepaid calling cards and/or cell phones.

- Global positioning satellite (GPS) unit.
- Multiple hotel receipts.
- Financial records indicating overseas wire transfers.
- Rental vehicles—cash transactions on receipts; living locally but renting vehicle.
- Vehicles with excessively darkened/tinted windows or temporary window covering that prevents viewing vehicle's interior.
- Vehicles that exhibit signs of recent modification.
- Vehicle contains unmarked packages or unusual items such as PVC pipe, magnets, compressed gas cylinders, or fire extinguishers within the passenger compartment.

■ Potential Props
- Baby stroller or shopping cart.
- Suspicious bag/backpack, golf bag.
- Bulky vest or belt.

■ Hotel/Motel Visits
- Unusual requests, such as refusal of maid service.
- Asking for a specific view of bridges, airports, military/government installations.
- Electronic surveillance equipment in room.
- Suspicious or unusual items left behind.
- Use of lobby or other pay phones instead of room phones.

■ Thefts, Purchases, or Discovery of
- Weapons/explosive materials.
- Camera/surveillance equipment.
- Vehicles (including rentals—fraudulent name or failure to return vehicle).
- Radios: short-wave, two-way, and scanners.
- Identity documents.
- Unauthorized uniforms.

ASSESSING TERRORIST THREATS

Note: The material for this section was taken from *Assessing and Managing the Terrorism Threat*, September 2005, NCJ Report 210680.

The Department of Homeland Security (DHS) defines **threat assessment** as follows: A systematic effort to identify and evaluate existing or potential terrorist threats to a jurisdiction and its target assets. Due to the difficulty in accurately assessing terrorist capabilities, intentions, and tactics, threat assessments may yield only general information about potential risks. These assessments consider the full spectrum of threats, such as natural disasters, criminal activity, and major accidents, as well as terrorist activity.

According to the DHS, threat assessments must be compiled from comprehensive and rigorous research and analysis. Law enforcement cannot function unilaterally. Threat assessments that do not incorporate the knowledge, assessments, and understanding of state, local, and private organizations and agencies with the potential threats being assessed are inherently incomplete. For example, a threat assessment of

threat assessment / a technique used by law enforcement authorities for the purpose of evaluating and describing the nature and degree of a threat. Involves efforts to identify, assess, and manage individuals and groups who may pose threats of targeted violence.

water-district facilities should include the most comprehensive data available from local police, sheriff, and fire departments; health services; emergency management organizations; and other applicable local, state, and federal agencies that may be affected by an attack on the water district's infrastructure. The threat assessment should also assimilate germane, open-source, or nonproprietary threat assessments, as well as intelligence information. Lastly, the assessment must provide a high level of awareness and understanding regarding the changing threat and threat environment faced by a government entity.

It is important to consider what can be threatened and what must be protected by state and local law enforcement agencies and their counterparts who provide security in the private sector. Those infrastructures and assets deemed most critical to national public health and safety, governance, economic and national security, and retaining public confidence have been refined and expanded. The critical infrastructure now includes:

- agriculture
- banking and finance
- chemical and hazardous waste
- defense industrial base
- energy
- emergency services
- food
- information and telecommunications
- transportation
- postal and shipping services
- public health
- water
- national monuments and icons
- nuclear power plants
- dams
- government facilities
- commercial assets

Calculating Criticality

A five-point scale can be used to estimate the impact of loss of life and property, interruption of facility or other asset use, or gain to be realized by an adversary:

- **Extreme (5):** Substantial loss of life or irreparable, permanent, or prohibitive costly repair to a facility. Lack of, or loss of, a system or capability would provide invaluable advantage to the adversary (press coverage, the political or tactical advantage to carry out further plans).
- **High (4):** Serious and costly damage to a facility or a positive effect for the adversary. No loss of life.

- **Medium (3):** Disruptive to facility operations for a moderate period of time; repairs, although costly, would not result in significant loss of facility capability. No loss of life.

- **Low (2):** Some minor disruption to facility operations or capability; does not materially advantage the enemy. No loss of life.

- **Negligible (1):** Insignificant loss or damage to operations or budget. No loss of life.

Calculating Vulnerability

The DHS defines **vulnerability assessment** as follows: The identification of weaknesses in physical structures, personnel protection systems, processes, or other areas that may be exploited by terrorists. The vulnerability assessment also may suggest options to eliminate or mitigate those weaknesses.

    Vulnerability is difficult to measure objectively. Progress is being made by agencies, such as the National Institute of Justice in partnership with the U.S. Department of Energy's Sandia National Laboratories, as well as by studies conducted by the National Infrastructure Protection Center of DHS, to assist with these assessments.

    Essential data to collect for analysis prior to conducting a threat assessment include:

vulnerability assessment / The identification of weaknesses in physical structures, personnel protection systems, processes, or other areas that may be exploited by terrorists.

- **Type of adversary:** Terrorist, activist, employee, other.
- **Category of adversary:** Foreign or domestic, terrorist or criminal, insider and/or outsider of the organization.
- **Objective of each type of adversary:** Theft, sabotage, mass destruction (maximum casualties), sociopolitical statement, other.
- **Number of adversaries expected for each category:** Individual suicide bomber, grouping or "cells" of operatives/terrorists, gangs, other.
- **Target selected by adversaries:** Critical infrastructure, governmental buildings, national monuments, other.
- **Type of planning activities required to accomplish the objective:** Long-term "casing," photography, monitoring police and security patrol patterns, other.
- **Most likely or "worst case" time an adversary could attack:** When facility/location is fully staffed, at rush hour, at night, other.
- **Range of adversary tactics:** Stealth, force, deceit, combination, other.
- **Capabilities of adversary:** Knowledge, motivation, skills, weapons, and tools.

To accomplish the intelligence mission of processing a threat assessment, a law enforcement executive must ensure that an officer or unit is trained and assigned to identify potential targets and can recommend enhancements for security at those targets. Action must be taken by all departments, including those with limited resources. Ideally, the entire patrol force should be trained to conduct intelligence gathering and reporting.

The Maritime Transportation Anti-Terrorism Act of 2002

With nearly 300 U.S. ports and about 25,000 miles of navigable waterways, protecting the nation's maritime system from terrorists presents a challenge with as many twists and turns as the nation's coastline.

The Maritime Transportation Anti-Terrorism Act of 2002 established a comprehensive national system to increase anti-terrorism security at U.S. ports and waterways. According to the American Association of Port Authorities (AAPA), the nation's ports and waterways witness over two billion tons of domestic and import/export cargo traffic annually, and that amount could triple by the year 2020. The transporting of basic commodities like apples, corn, lumber, iron ore, steel, potatoes, and plastics relies on ports and waterways. About two-thirds of all U.S. wheat and wheat flour, one-third of soybean and rice production, and almost two-fifths of U.S. cotton production is exported via U.S. ports.

"Just as airports have stepped up security, many seaports now have greater access controls, lighting, gates, fencing, ID systems, and additional personnel working to protect their facilities," said Kurt J. Nagle, President of the AAPA. The Coast Guard has also added security measures, including the inspection of all baggage, vessel escorts by armed guards, dock sweeps prior to ship arrivals, and elimination of curbside baggage check-in.

One section of the Act requires the Coast Guard to carry out vulnerability assessments for U.S. ports and any high-risk facilities in a port. Diverse frameworks of port environments make it impossible to standardize vulnerability assessments. The Port of South Louisiana is the largest tonnage port in the Western Hemisphere, stretching fifty-four miles along the Mississippi River.

The Secretary of Transportation's office was tasked with developing a national maritime transportation anti-terrorism planning system and coordinating national maritime terrorism response actions to deter and minimize damages from emergencies. The Act also provided for increased anti-terrorism efforts at foreign ports.

The Act requires assessments of foreign ports, including the screening process of cargo, the security measures used to restrict access to secure areas, and additional security on board. If a foreign port is deemed ineffective in its anti-terrorism measures and is not willing to cooperate in maintaining the efforts, the Under Secretary of Transportation may implement conditions of entry into the United States for any vessel arriving from that particular port, or any vessel carrying cargo originating from or transshipped through that port.

Source: The Maritime Transportation Anti-Terrorism Act of 2002 (2002, Spring). *Journal of Counterterrorism & Homeland Security International,* 8(3).

Photo of warning sign on Alaska pipeline. The Department of Homeland Security and the State of Alaska have taken steps in an attempt to prevent a terrorist act on the pipeline.

Voices of Experience

First Responder to a Terroristic Attack

Excerpts from an interview between Cliff Roberson and former police officer, John M. Boal. Currently, Professor Boal is a full-time faculty member in the Criminal Justice Program at the University of Akron.

Q: *What are the functions of a first responder to a terroristic attack?*
A: First, handle the emergencies and then try to determine the extent of the damage and get an assessment of the situation. Determine how big a threat it is and how many units are needed. Once the emergencies are handled, the officer should try to preserve the evidence and control the scene.

Q: *For the officers on patrol, are there any indicators or clues that a terroristic event may be in the planning stages?*

A: They should be aware of their surroundings as most of them are aware—just anything out of the ordinary. A lot of people say that police officers have a sense that others don't have regarding things like this. What it really amounts to is the ability of police officers to pay attention to detail and find things that are not normal or things that don't fit; especially in places that are likely targets, like a water storage area, utility plant, or where large numbers of people are gathered. ■

New York City's Fight Against Terrorism

New York City leaders, after having suffered two devastating attacks, decided that the city had to take more responsibility for its own security, and that New York's first line of defense was not the military, the CIA, or the FBI, it was the New York Police Department (NYPD). The NYPD has approximately 37,000 officers and is larger than the standing armies of eighty-four countries. Since September 2001, the NYPD has transformed itself from a traditional crime-fighting organization into one that places a strong emphasis on fighting terrorism. Over a thousand officers have been assigned to work exclusively on a new "terrorism beat." And, in an unprecedented move, New York has even stationed its own cops overseas. (As reported by Ed Bradley on CBS's *60 Minutes*, March 19, 2006.)

In 2002, NYPD Police Chief Ray Kelly created a Counter-Terrorism Bureau, expanded the Intelligence Division, and increased the number of cops working on terrorism with the FBI from 17 to 120. Kelly also ordered the NYPD's 37,000 officers to undergo training in how to handle chemical, biological, and radiological attacks, and mandated that the Emergency Services Unit be prepared to respond to scenarios like an attack on the subway.

The NYPD also conducts a counterterrorism operation called "a surge." About 100 police cars from all over the city swarm into an area like Times Square. These happen unannounced all over the city. The surge begins with an officer briefing, not only on their specific assignments, but on a subject you might not expect—terrorist developments thousands of miles away. A "surge" results in a simultaneous deployment of about 200 cops to potential terrorist targets—and a visible demonstration to terrorists and New Yorkers of the widespread changes the NYPD has implemented since 9/11. In addition, teams of heavily armed cops show up unannounced at train stations, office buildings, and other potential targets throughout the city (Hill, 2005, p. A17).

Photo of New York City sign honoring those who died in 9/11 attacks. As a result of the attacks, the New York City Police Department increased their activities to attempt to prevent or lessen the damage of future attacks.

The NYPD requires its detectives to take courses, like one titled "Global Jihad," that covers subjects ranging from the history of Islam to the mind of a suicide bomber. It's taught in the Counter-Terrorism Bureau, which collects information on potential threats. Civilian analysts do research on everything from radical Islam and militant terrorist organizations to detailed analysis of bomb-making techniques and terrorist attacks. Security checks and bag searches on the city's subways and trains are routine. Every day, the Harbor Unit patrols landmarks from the Statue of Liberty to the Staten Island Ferry. Every day, police divers check the base of the Brooklyn Bridge for explosives. And every day, helicopters with high-tech cameras monitor the city, looking for anything out of the ordinary. The cyber unit drawn from the police department's own resources, NYPD officers from Middle Eastern and South Asian backgrounds, monitor online chat rooms for information that may indicate terrorist activities (Hill, 2005, p. A17).

ANTI-TERRORIST AND DISASTER RECOVERY AGENCIES

Department of Homeland Security

The National Strategy for Homeland Security and the Homeland Security Act of 2002 established the Department of Homeland Security (DHS). A primary goal in the establishment of the DHS was to provide a unifying core for the national network of organizations and institutions involved in efforts to secure the nation. Presently, there are 180,000 individuals employed or under the direct supervision of the DHS.

In the event of a terrorist attack, natural disaster, or other large-scale emergency, the DHS is expected to assume primary responsibility for ensuring that

Should the Police Be Allowed to Conduct Surveillance of Political Groups in its Anti-Terrorism Campaign?

The New York Police Department (NYPD) was restricted in its surveillance of political groups because a federal consent decree prevents it from investigating political groups, unless the department possesses specific information about a crime. The original lawsuit was brought by civil liberties advocates who contend that New Yorkers had a right to engage in political activity without fear of being spied upon by the police [*Handschu v. Special Services Div.*, 605 F. Supp. 1384, 1985 U.S. Dist. LEXIS 22007 (S.D.N.Y. 1985)].

The consent decree in question, known as the Handschu decree, has been in place since 1985, when the city settled a class-action lawsuit brought by political groups like the Black Panthers. The groups had been infiltrated and monitored because of their dissident views. The decree, named for attorney Barbara Handschu, required the police department to rely on specific information of criminal activity before it can investigate a political group. Investigating officers must present the information to a three-member panel, known as the Handschu Authority, for approval. Violating the decree subjected the city to contempt proceedings.

After September 2001, the NYPD argued that it can no longer live by these standards. In various court papers, it has described the Handschu guidelines as "unworkable" and outdated rules that "dangerously" limit the police department's ability to uncover and prevent terrorist attacks. Although the Handschu Authority's yearly reports show that the panel hardly ever denied a request for an investigation, city officials contended that the mere presence of the guidelines had a chilling effect and prevented officers from making requests (Perrotta, 2003, p. 1).

The federal court judge granted the NYPD's motion to modify the Handschu Guidelines, on the condition that the NYPD include in its Patrol Guide an adapted version of the FBI Guidelines approved by the Court [*Handschu v. Special Servs. Div.*, 2003 U.S. Dist. LEXIS 6790 (S.D.N.Y., Apr. 21, 2003) and *Handschu v. Special Servs. Div.*, 2006 U.S. Dist. LEXIS 41940 (S.D.N.Y. June 20, 2006)].

Presently, the guidelines state:

- For the purpose of detecting or preventing terrorist activities, the NYPD (Intelligence Division) is authorized to visit any place and attend any event that is open to the public, generally on the same terms and conditions of members of the public generally.
- Pursuant to Modified Handschu Guidelines, the investigation of political activity may only be initiated by and conducted under the supervision of the Intelligence Division. Therefore, members of the service not assigned to the Intelligence Division may not use video recording or photography for the purpose of investigating political activity, without the express written approval of the Deputy Commissioner, Intelligence.

emergency response professionals are prepared for any situation. This includes providing a coordinated, comprehensive federal response to any large-scale crisis and mounting a swift and effective recovery effort. The DHS is tasked with prioritizing the issue of citizen preparedness, including educating the public on how best to prepare their homes for a disaster and tips for citizens on how to respond in a crisis.

DHS Vision Statement: Preserving our freedoms, protecting America . . . we secure our homeland.

DHS Mission Statement: We will lead the unified national effort to secure America. We will prevent and deter terrorist attacks and protect against and respond to threats and hazards to the nation. We will ensure safe and secure borders, welcome lawful immigrants and visitors, and promote the free-flow of commerce.

DHS Strategic Goals

Awareness: Identify and understand threats, assess vulnerabilities, determine potential impacts, and disseminate timely information to our homeland security partners and the American public.

Prevention: Detect, deter, and mitigate threats to our homeland.

Protection: Safeguard our people and their freedoms, critical infrastructure, property, and the economy of our nation from acts of terrorism, natural disasters, or other emergencies.

Response: Lead, manage, and coordinate the national response to acts of terrorism, natural disasters, or other emergencies.

Recovery: Lead national, state, local, and private-sector efforts to restore services and rebuild communities after acts of terrorism, natural disasters, or other emergencies.

Service: Serve the public effectively by facilitating lawful trade, travel, and immigration.

Organizational Excellence: Value our most important resource, our people. Create a culture that promotes a common identity, innovation, mutual respect, accountability, and teamwork to achieve efficiencies, effectiveness, and operational synergies.

History: Who Became Part of the DHS? The agencies of the DHS are housed in one of four major directorates: Border and Transportation Security, Emergency Preparedness and Response, Science and Technology, and Information Analysis and Infrastructure Protection.

The *Border and Transportation Security* directorate brings the major border security and transportation operations under one directorate, including:

- The U.S. Customs Service (Treasury)
- The Immigration and Naturalization Service (part) (Justice)
- The Federal Protective Service
- The Transportation Security Administration (Transportation)
- Federal Law Enforcement Training Center (Treasury)
- Animal and Plant Health Inspection Service (part) (Agriculture)
- Office for Domestic Preparedness (Justice)

The *Emergency Preparedness and Response* directorate oversees domestic disaster preparedness training and coordinates government disaster response. It will bring together:

- The Federal Emergency Management Agency (FEMA)
- Strategic National Stockpile and the National Disaster Medical System (HHS)
- Nuclear Incident Response Team (Energy)
- Domestic Emergency Support Teams (Justice)
- National Domestic Preparedness Office (FBI)

The *Science and Technology* directorate utilizes all scientific and technological advantages when securing the homeland. The following assets are part of this effort:

- CBRN Countermeasures Programs (Energy)
- Environmental Measurements Laboratory (Energy)
- National BW Defense Analysis Center (Defense)
- Plum Island Animal Disease Center (Agriculture)

The *Information Analysis and Infrastructure Protection* directorate analyzes intelligence and information from other agencies (including the CIA, FBI, DIA, and NSA) involving threats to homeland security and evaluates vulnerabilities in the nation's infrastructure. It brings together:

- Federal Computer Incident Response Center (GSA)
- National Communications System (Defense)
- National Infrastructure Protection Center (FBI)
- Energy Security and Assurance Program (Energy)

The Secret Service and the Coast Guard are located in the Department of Homeland Security, remaining intact and reporting directly to the Secretary. In addition, the INS adjudications and benefits programs report directly to the Deputy Secretary as the U.S. Citizenship and Immigration Services.

National Response System (NRS): The National Response System (NRS) is the government's mechanism for emergency response to discharges of oil and the release of chemicals into the navigable waters or environment of the United States and its territories. Initially, this system focused on oil spills and selected hazardous polluting substances discharged into the environment. It has since been expanded by other legislation to include hazardous substances and wastes released to all types of media.

The NRS functions through a network of interagency and intergovernment relationships that were formally established and described in the National Oil and Hazardous Substances Pollution Contingency Plan (NCP). The NCP establishes three high-level organizations and four special-force components that are described in the following paragraphs.

Federal On-Scene Coordinators (FOSC). The FOSC is a federal official, predesignated by the EPA for inland areas and by the Coast Guard for coastal or major navigable waterways. These individuals coordinate all federal containment, removal, disposal efforts, and resources during an incident. The FOSC also coordinates federal efforts with the local community's response. Anyone responsible for reporting releases should be aware of which FOSC has responsibility for the affected area. For locations near the coast or a major waterway, there may be both a Coast Guard and EPA FOSC with assigned responsibilities within jurisdictional boundaries of various state or local entities.

National Response Team (NRT) / A planning, policy, and coordinating body providing national-level policy guidance prior to an incident but not responding directly to an incident.

National Response Team (NRT). The National Response Team's membership consists of sixteen federal agencies with interest and expertise in various aspects of emergency response to pollution incidents. The **National Response Team (NRT)** is a planning, policy, and coordinating body providing national-level policy guidance prior to an incident but not responding directly to an incident. They can provide assistance to an FOSC during an incident, usually in the form of technical advice or access to additional resources and equipment at the national level.

Regional Response Team (RRT). The RRTs are the next organizational level in the federal response system. Currently, there are thirteen RRTs, one for each of the ten federal regions, plus one each for Alaska, the Caribbean, and the Pacific Basin. Each team maintains a Regional Contingency Plan and both the state and federal governments are represented. The RRTs are primarily planning, policy, and coordinating bodies. They provide guidance to FOSCs through the Regional Contingency Plans and work to locate assistance requested by the FOSC during an incident. RRTs may also provide assistance to state and local governments in preparing, planning, or training for emergency response.

The four special force components are:

- Coast Guard National Strike Force (NSF)
- Coast Guard Public Information Assist Team (PIAT)
- EPA Environmental Response Team (ERT)
- Scientific Support Coordinators (SSC)

The *Coast Guard National Strike Force* (NSF) is composed of three strategically located strike teams and a coordination center. The strike teams have specially trained personnel and are equipped to respond to major oil spills and chemical releases. The coordination center maintains a national inventory listing of spill response equipment and assists with the development and implementation of an exercise and training program for the National Response System. NSF capabilities are especially suited to incidents occurring in the marine environment, but also include site assessments, safety, action plan development, and documentation for both inland and coastal zone incidents.

The *Coast Guard Public Information Assist Team* (PIAT) is a highly skilled unit of public affairs specialists prepared to complement the existing public information capabilities of the Federal On-Scene Coordinator.

The *EPA Environmental Response Team* (ERT) is a group of specially trained scientists and engineers based in Edison, New Jersey, and Cincinnati, Ohio. Its capabilities include multimedia sampling and analysis, hazard assessment, cleanup techniques, and technical support.

The *National Oceanic and Atmospheric Administration* (NOAA) provides *Scientific Support Coordinators* (SSCs) in coastal and marine areas. The SSC serves on the FOSC staff as the lead of a scientific team. This support team provides expertise in environmental chemistry, oil slick tracking, pollutant transport modeling, natural resources at risk, environmental tradeoffs of countermeasures and cleanup, information management, contingency planning, and liaison to the scientific community and the natural resource trustees.

The primary function of the *National Response Center* (NRC) is to serve as the sole national point of contact for reporting all oil, chemical, radiological, biological, and etiological discharges into the environment anywhere in the United States and its territories. In addition to gathering and distributing spill data for Federal On-Scene Coordinators and serving as the communications and operations center for the National Response Team, the NRC maintains agreements with a variety of federal entities to make additional notifications regarding incidents meeting established trigger criteria. The NRC also takes Terrorist/Suspicious Activity Reports and Maritime Security Breach Reports.

The NRC is staffed by Coast Guard personnel who maintain a 24-hour-per-day, 365-day-per-year telephone watch. NRC watch standers enter telephonic reports of pollution incidents into the Incident Reporting Information System (IRIS) and immediately relay each report to the predesignated Federal On-Scene Coordinator (FOSC). The NRC also provides emergency response support to the FOSCs. This includes extensive reference materials, state-of-the-art telecommunications, and operation of automated chemical identification and chemical dispersion information systems. A wide range of technical systems support is provided to the NRC by the Space and Naval Warfare Systems Command (SPAWAR) Charleston—National Capital Region.

Some Acronyms Used by Anti-Terrorist Agencies

CBRNE Chemical, Biological, Radiological, Nuclear, and Explosive

COG Continuity of Government

EMAC Emergency Management Accreditation Program Emergency

EOC Emergency Operations Center

EOD Emergency Ordnance Disposal

HAN Health Alert Network

HAZMAT Hazardous Materials

HLSEM Homeland Security and Emergency Management

HSIN Homeland Security Information Network

HSOC Homeland Security Operations Center

HSPD Homeland Security Presidential Directive

LEATAC Law Enforcement Administrator's Telecommunications Advisory Committee

LEIN Law Enforcement Intelligence Network

MHz Megahertz

NIMS National Incident Management System

NIPP National Infrastructure Protection Plan

NRP National Response Plan

ODP Office for Domestic Preparedness

SAA State Administrative Agent

SNS Strategic National Stockpile

SWAT Special Weapons and Tactics

VRR Veterinary Rapid Response

USAR Urban Search and Rescue

sure images clearly record damage. Supplement with better quality photos when necessary.

- Make notes and voice recordings to accompany photographs.
- Assign staff to keep written records of contacts with insurance agents and other investigators, and staff decisions on retrieval and salvage.
- Make visual, written, and voice records for each step of the salvage procedures.

Retrieval and Protection

- Leave undamaged items in place if the environment is stable and area secure. If not, move them to a secure, environmentally controlled area.
- If no part of the building is dry, protect all objects with loose plastic sheeting.
- When moving collections, give priority to undamaged items and those on loan. Separate undamaged from damaged items.
- Until salvage begins, maintain each group in the same condition you found it; that is, keep wet items wet, dry items dry, and damp items damp.
- Retrieve all pieces of broken objects and label them.
- Check items daily for mold. If mold is found, handle objects with extreme care and isolate them.

Damage Assessment

- Notify insurance representative or risk manager. You may need an on-site evaluation before taking action.
- Make a rough estimate of the type of materials affected and the extent and nature of damage. A detailed evaluation can slow recovery now.
- Look for threats to worker safety or collections. Determine status of security systems.
- Look for evidence of mold. Note how long the materials have been wet and the current inside temperature and relative humidity.
- SEE DOCUMENTATION SECTION. Documenting the damage is essential for insurance and will help you with recovery.

Salvage Priorities

Establish salvage priorities by groups of materials, not item-by-item. A library might use subject areas or call numbers; archives, record groups; and a museum, material groupings.

Focus first protection efforts and salvage work on:

- Vital institutional information; employee and accounting records, accession lists, shelf list, and database backups.
- Items on loan from individuals or other institutions.
- Collections that most directly support the institution's mission.
- Collections that are unique, most used, most vital for research, most representative of subject areas, least replaceable, or most valuable.
- Items most prone to continued damage if untreated.
- Materials most likely to be successfully salvaged.

Historic Buildings: General Tips

- Contact architectural conservators, historic preservation agencies, FEMA, and/or structural engineers before cleanup, especially for buildings on the National Register of Historic Places.
- Follow the Secretary of the Interior's *Standards for Treatment of Historic Properties* (pp. 17–59).
- Remove standing water from basement and crawl spaces. Contact a structural engineer before pumping water; pumping can collapse the foundation when groundwater is high.
- Remove flood-soaked insulation, wallboard, and non-historic wall coverings. Support loose plaster with plywood and wood "T" braces.
- Clean historic elements first. Use non-abrasive household cleansers.
- If you treat non-historic features, do not harm historic elements.
- Inventory found items, loose decorative elements, furnishings, and collections. Save for reuse or as restoration models.
- Air dry with good ventilation. Never use systems that pump in super-dry air.

FBI

As part of its national security mission, the FBI has provided awareness information to reduce the vulnerability of U.S. persons, corporations, and institutions to intelligence and terrorist activities since the early 1970s. The initial focus of this program was the protection of classified government information, property, and personnel. In the 1990s, foreign intelligence services expanded their targeting to include private sector proprietary economic information.

National Security Branch (NSB): The FBI is the lead agency for exposing, preventing, and investigating terrorist intelligence activities on U.S. soil. The National Security Branch (NSB) was established under the FBI on September 12, 2005, in response to a presidential directive to establish a "National Security Service" that combines the missions, capabilities, and resources of the counterterrorism, counterintelligence, and intelligence elements of the FBI under the leadership of a senior FBI official.

NSB Mission Statement: To optimally position the FBI to protect the United States against weapons of mass destruction, terrorist attacks, foreign intelligence operations, and espionage by:

- Integrating investigative and intelligence activities against current and emerging national security threats.
- Providing useful and timely information and analysis to the intelligence and law enforcement communities.
- Effectively developing enabling capabilities, processes, and infrastructure, consistent with applicable laws, Attorney General and Director of National Intelligence guidance, and civil liberties.

NSB Vision Statement: To the extent authorized under the law, build a national awareness that permits recognition of a national security threat, sufficiently early to permit its disruption. This will be a discerning process that promotes the collection of relevant information and minimizes the accumulation of extraneous data that unnecessarily distracts from the analytical process.

Critical Incident Response Group (CIRG): The FBI has established a Critical Incident Response Group (CIRG) to respond to critical incidents. The Operations Support Branch (OSB) of CIRG consists of the Crisis Negotiation Unit (CNU), Crisis Management Unit (CMU), and Rapid Deployment Logistics Unit. The OSB has various functions, including the rapid delivery of personnel to a scene, whether it is a bombing or crimes against children investigation. The OSB also stresses training and international law enforcement cooperation to ensure the most impressive capability.

Crisis Management Unit (CMU): The mission of the FBI's Crisis Management Unit (CMU) is to operationally support FBI field and headquarters entities during critical incidents or major investigations. The CMU also conducts crisis management training and related activities for the FBI, and other international, federal, state, and local agencies or departments. Thus, the CMU assists in the FBI's response to, and management of, worldwide incidents. In support of this mission, the CMU conducts several regional field training exercises each year. Each exercise involves multiple field offices and hundreds of employees. Liaison is also maintained with other federal agencies, including the Federal Emergency Management Agency, Department of Energy, Environmental Protection Agency, Health and Human Services, Bureau of Prisons, and the Department of Defense. In addition, the CMU maintains contact with international, state, and local agencies as required.

Crisis Negotiation Unit (CNU): The FBI's Crisis Negotiation Unit (CNU) is part of the FBI's Critical Incident Response Group. As such, the CNU is responsible for the FBI's Crisis (Hostage) Negotiation Program. The mission of the CNU is fourfold:

- operations
- training
- research
- program management

The CNU maintains an immediate operational response capability to conduct and manage on-scene negotiations during any significant crisis event in which the FBI is involved. This response capability is available 24-hours-a-day, seven-days-a-week. As part of the CNU's operational mission, negotiators deploy overseas to assist in the management of kidnapping situations involving U.S. citizens. The FBI is considered the negotiation arm of the U.S. government for international incidents. Since 1990, the CNU has deployed to over 100 such incidents worldwide. CNU negotiators also routinely provide telephone assistance to both FBI field negotiators and domestic police negotiators during domestic crisis situations.

Critical Incident Negotiation Team (CINT): In 1985, the FBI's Crisis Management Unit at the FBI Academy in Quantico, Virginia, established a Critical Incident Negotiation Team (CINT). This is a small, mobile team of highly trained and experienced FBI negotiators. Since its inception, the CINT has negotiated approximately forty-five bank robberies and hijacking hostage incidents each year. The FBI deploys CINT negotiators both within and outside the United States.

Hostage Rescue Team (HRT): The FBI's Hostage Rescue Team (HRT) is a full-time, national-level tactical team, headquartered in Quantico, Virginia. The mission of the HRT is to be prepared to deploy to any location within four hours of notification by the Director of the FBI or his designated representative, and conduct a successful rescue of U.S. persons and others who may be held illegally by a hostile force, either terrorist or criminal in nature. The HRT is also prepared to deploy to any location and perform other law enforcement activities as directed by appropriate authorities.

Awareness of National Security Issues and Response Team (ANSIR): The FBI's Awareness of National Security Issues and Response Team (ANSIR) disseminates unclassified national security threat and warning information to U.S. corporations, law enforcement, and other government agencies. ANSIR email provides this information at no charge to any interested person meeting the subscription prerequisites. In addition to making potential targets of intelligence and terrorist activities less vulnerable through awareness, the FBI has the response capability to act when these activities are identified.

State Homeland Security Agencies

Since September 11, 2001, most states have established a state homeland security agency. New York State probably has the largest state agency. A typical state agency is the one established by the State of Iowa, which will be discussed here.

Voices of Experience

Hostage Negotiation

Excerpts from an interview between Cliff Roberson and former police officer, John M. Boal. Currently, Professor Boal is a full-time faculty member in the Criminal Justice Program at the University of Akron.

Q: *How do you go about handling a hostage negotiation?*
A: First, you should be concerned with the safety of everybody involved. You want to establish contact with the hostage takers as soon as possible and find out what their demands are. Make sure that no one is injured or about to be injured and if anyone needs medical treatment. In most cases, the police negotiator is in charge to a point where people start getting injured and then it becomes a tactical situation and is then handled by a tactical unit. The negotiator has to get a feeling for the situation and build rapport with the hostage takers and find out what they want. The negotiator tries to get the hostage takers to come to the agreement that the negotiator's solution is the correct solution to solve their problems without anyone getting hurt. Dealing with a career criminal in a hostage situation is different from dealing with someone who has a mental problem or someone who has a cause because in the latter case you have less negotiating room. A career criminal generally knows what's coming down the road and will take a more realistic view of the possible solutions. During the negotiations, the negotiators want to get as much information about the hostage takers as they can to assist in the negotiation and in case the situation is turned over to a tactical unit. An effective negotiator needs to be a good communicator and have problem-solving skills. ■

The Iowa Homeland Security and Emergency Management Division: While the threat of terrorism in Iowa is believed to be relatively low, floods, tornadoes, and plane crashes can and do happen in Iowa. The Iowa Homeland Security and Emergency Management Division was created to deal with these and other emergency situations, with an emphasis on building partnerships with state and local emergency management organizations, and a strong focus on customer service.

The Code of Iowa, Chapter 29C, establishes the Iowa Homeland Security and Emergency Management Division as a Division within the Department of Public Defense and provides for the appointment of an administrator. The Department consists of two divisions: Homeland Security and Emergency Management, and the Military; and is headed by the adjutant general of Iowa. While the daily activities of the Military Division and Homeland Security and Emergency Management Division differ, there are many common issues that lend themselves to cooperative efforts. For example, in emergency/disaster response and recovery issues, training and exercises, and services to individual citizens and public and private entities, the Iowa Homeland Security and Emergency Management Division and the Military Division continue to seek opportunities to jointly implement activities.

The Iowa Homeland Security and Emergency Management Division has the responsibility to support local entities as they plan and implement mitigation, preparedness, response, and recovery strategies. The Division provides technical assistance, training, exercise facilitation, communications, and other support necessary for establishing and maintaining local capabilities. The Iowa Homeland Security and Emergency Management Division is the link and coordinating entity that ensures consistency and compliance with various federal and state requirements and regulations.

The Division has the responsibility to work with all state agencies in Iowa, in support of their emergency management needs, and to better coordinate their services to citizens and public and private entities. Technical assistance, planning, exercise facilitation, and multi-agency collaborative efforts are part of the Division's role with state agencies. In addition, the Division assists the Iowa Emergency Response Commission to improve community preparedness for chemical emergencies. Code of Iowa, Chapter 30, sets forth the Division's duties in relation to the Iowa Emergency Response Commission.

The Division's responsibilities extend beyond state boundaries as well. The Division works effectively in cooperative efforts with other states to provide a mutual benefit through the multi-state Emergency Management Assistance Compact (EMAC). Since Iowa became a member of the Emergency Management Assistance Compact in 1997, it has deployed twenty-six state employees to other states. In addition, the Division coordinates, implements, and administers federal emergency management initiatives in a joint endeavor with the Federal Emergency Management Agency and other federal agencies, to ensure consistency within the state. The Division also relies on the National Emergency Management Association, the association of state emergency management directors. The National Emergency Management Association provides expertise in comprehensive emergency management and is a source of vital information and assistance for the Iowa Homeland Security and Emergency Management Division and other members.

Civil Defense Battalions

Some law enforcement agencies are establishing civil defense battalions of citizen volunteers to assist the agencies in cases of natural disasters and terrorist acts. A typical battalion is that formed by the Austin, Texas, Police Department.

Austin Civil Defense Battalion

Mission Statement: To be in readiness as well-trained civil defense volunteers to support the work of the Austin Police Department.

Executive Summary: The Austin Police Department (APD) is well positioned and well trained to respond to critical incidents as defined by events prior to September 11, 2001. The terrorist attacks on the United States on September 11 necessitated a fresh look at our ability to respond to a catastrophic event of heretofore unimagined proportions. An assessment of strengths and needs underscored our confidence in many areas of training and staffing. However, the identified areas needing additional resources led to the creation of a Major Event Team (MET) equipped and trained to handle terrorist attacks and/or civil unrest or panic resulting from such attacks. A natural part and extension of the MET is the creation of a Police Civil Defense Battalion, consisting of a well-trained corps of volunteers prepared to respond quickly to supplement the work of APD officers. These volunteers would begin working within APD immediately to become familiar with departmental procedures and to work in areas needing assistance at this time. The Police Civil Defense Battalion would consist of four companies, each trained to handle specially identified tasks with the goal of freeing officers to handle assignments requiring highly trained police officers. The Office of Community Liaison (OCL) has responsibility for recruitment, coordination and scheduling for training, and placement of volunteers.

Training in all areas will be offered and some immediate assignments will be given. Ongoing training will be offered to maintain readiness. Volunteers working outside of the police facilities will work in pairs only.

Structure: The four companies would be designed to work in clearly defined areas.

Company "A" (Aviation Detail)—Assigned to the Aviation Police, assignments would include:

- Information dissemination to airport visitors through the Airport Ambassadors program.
- Assist in getting housing and/or transportation for stranded passengers in the event of a crisis or closure of the airport.

Company "B" (Homeland Security Supplemental Services)—Assigned to the MET for immediate assignments in various areas within the department to ensure continued services and provide for newly identified needs:

- Daylight perimeter patrol of city facilities.
- Parking control and building access control for police and other city facilities.
- Work special events (e.g., New Year's Eve—work the barricades with officers providing information to citizens and reporting disturbances).
- Daylight patrol in areas where multiple offenses of similar types have been reported.

Company "C" (Headquarters Detail)—Immediate assignments to assist officers in critical areas:

- Work in the control booth at the main police station greeting visitors, providing information, and escorting visitors through the building.
- Abandoned Vehicle Volunteer Program—increase the number of volunteers tagging abandoned/junked vehicles on public property (opening up neighborhood streets for easier access by emergency vehicles).
- Assist in answering phones and providing information in all police facilities.
- Make copies and distribute information as needed.

Company "D" (Homeland Security)—Activated should a critical incident occur, assigned to the MET to provide centralized services:

- Former police officers may receive special assignments.
- Activate phone tree to call in volunteers and provide information to the community.
- Supplement 3-1-1 call-takers to handle callers seeking information only.
- Daylight incident perimeter control—maintaining police lines.
- Traffic control—freeing officers to work inside incident perimeters.
- Supplement Red Cross efforts by providing food and water for officers and victims—recruit restaurants to provide these provisions in the event of need; arrange for portable toilets and dumpsters at incident sites.
- Maintain list of volunteers who speak various languages.

- Maintain a "message board" for missing persons.
- Call the families of officers and other emergency workers at an incident scene with reassurance and information.
- Call neighborhood groups to enlist assistance as needed and contact congregational groups who have agreed to open facilities as shelters in each area command.
- Chaplains would respond to the scene and provide services as outlined in their volunteer protocol.
- Should dispatch fail, volunteers to go to each fire station to take calls and relay messages to officers.

How Do You Apply? You must be at least 18 years old and live or work in the Austin area. The Civil Defense Battalion requires its personnel to meet the following physical demands:

- Vision and hearing corrected to normal range.
- Ability to stand for two or more hours at a time.
- Ability to lift at least twenty pounds.
- Each applicant must complete the Civil Defense Battalion Application and the Personal History Form. Once these forms are completed, please deliver them in person so your thumbprint can be taken for a Criminal Background Check. The address is 1009 E. 11th St., Austin, TX 78701.

BOMB THREATS

Police frequently deal with bomb threats and most of the time they are not associated with "terrorist activity" but with the activities of a single disturbed person. Regardless of the reason for the threat, the officer needs to treat each threat as if it were credible. Anything that looks or resembles explosive material is extremely dangerous and should be handled only by experts. As a patrol officer on the scene, your primary concern is the safety of the public.

Frequently, bomb threats are false reports designed to create excitement or disruption. The attention caused by the arrival of emergency vehicles may stimulate repeated bomb threats. To offset this, many law enforcement agencies, when responding to a bomb threat, require that the approach of emergency vehicles be as unobtrusive as possible.

The *New York Manual for Police* (2005, 3-10-1) recommends the following steps when you receive a bomb threat:

- Obtain as much information as possible.
  - Where is the bomb located?
  - When will it go off?
  - What does it look like?
  - What kind of explosive is involved?
  - Why was it placed?
- Note the time of the call and the exact words used.
- Note whether the caller was male or female; adult or child; and approximate age.

- Describe the speech characteristics of the caller to include whether the caller was slow, rapid, or normal; loud; disguised; broken; accented; sounded sincere or insincere.
- Note presence or absence of background noise.
- Notify the appropriate superior.
- Record all pertinent information.

The first officer on the scene of a bomb threat in most cases should attempt to evacuate the area. Do not use elevators during an evacuation. (**Note:** The final decision to evacuate is generally the sole responsibility of the person in charge of the establishment.) If appropriate, a thorough search should be made of the area. Care should be taken in the use of police radios because the radio transmissions may detonate the bomb. Open all doors and windows in the building being searched to minimize damage, if the device detonates. If possible, use telephones for communication purposes. If an actual or suspected device is located, secure the area and request expert assistance. Do not take any action to move or disarm the device—leave that to the experts. If a device is located, do not terminate the search; there may be more than one device on the scene.

HOSTAGES

Hostage negotiation is one of the most publicized actions of law enforcement agencies and also one of the most misunderstood actions that police officers undertake. The FBI divides hostage situations into four broad categories: the terrorist situation, the prison situation, the criminal situation, and the mentally disturbed situation.

Training for hostage negotiators is complex and requires significant communications skills. Except in unusual situations, an officer should wait for trained negotiators before attempting to negotiate with any hostage taker.

The patrol officer should attempt to obtain as much information as possible on the hostage takers to pass on to the negotiator. There are primary information goals that are needed for a successful negotiation. The officer must attempt to obtain specific information about the incident so that the negotiator can negotiate with the suspect realistically. In doing this, the officer should attempt to determine the motivation and intent of the hostage takers and whether or not they are mentally disturbed. The officer must listen to what the hostage taker is saying for clues as to the mental condition or motivation of the hostage taker.

The patrol officer's duties in a hostage situation include:

- Approach the scene with caution—there may be sniper fire.
- Do not use the siren when approaching the scene.
- If necessary, evacuate persons from the area.
- Protect witnesses in a safe area for later debriefing.
- Keep the desk officer or your supervisor informed of the severity of the situation and any unusual difficulties.
- When the Hostage Negotiation Team arrives and you are relieved, report to the senior officer on the scene for debriefing.

Source: Manual for Police of New York State, 2005, 03-35-3.

Manual for Police of New York State 03-35-1 (2005)

When a person is held hostage; the situation must be carefully surveyed and evaluated. The safety of the police and hostage(s) is the most important consideration in any hostage situation. Experience demonstrates that the most desirable approach to such a situation is through the use of trained hostage negotiators. Reckless and imprudent action must be avoided.

Several police agencies throughout New York State have hostage negotiation teams. The state police maintain a team in each of their troops. The most important element of a hostage negotiation situation is time. Time is a tool used to de-escalate these tense situations. The more time that is gained through negotiations, the more likely it is that the situation will be concluded without violence.

SUMMARY

- A patrol officer's response to a natural disaster or terrorist act can be learned.

- The preparation for handling any disaster begins in your head. Patrol officers should think about what disasters they could encounter and how they would respond to each.

- Whether it's an act of terrorism or a natural disaster, it is likely that a patrol officer will be the first responder. The primary responsibilities of first responders when they arrive at the scene are to protect life, maintain order, conduct traffic control, protect property from further damage, help establish communications, and assist in the coordination of the response of other emergency personnel.

- One of the officer's first responsibilities as a first responder at the scene of an emergency is to assess the situation and communicate an assessment to supervisors. Traditional crime is characterized by spontaneity, lack of planning, and pecuniary or personal motives. In contrast, terrorism generally involves persons or groups motivated by political or social goals, ideological justification, and considerable forethought and planning.

- Threat assessment is a systematic effort to identify and evaluate existing or potential terrorist threats to a jurisdiction and its target assets. Due to the difficulty in accurately assessing terrorist capabilities, intentions, and tactics, threat assessments may yield only general information about potential risks.

- Vulnerability assessment is the identification of weaknesses in physical structures, personnel protection systems, processes, or other areas that may be exploited by terrorists. The vulnerability assessment also may suggest options to eliminate or mitigate those weaknesses.

- Risk assessment combines the assessments of criticality, threat, and vulnerability to determine the risk to an asset or group of assets.

- The Department of Homeland Security (DHS) has the primary goal of providing a unifying core for the national network of organizations and institutions involved in efforts to secure the nation. In the event of a terrorist attack, natural disaster, or other large-scale emergency, the DHS is expected to assume primary responsibility for ensuring that emergency response professionals are prepared for any situation.

- The FBI provides awareness information to reduce the vulnerability of U.S. persons, corporations, and institutions to intelligence and terrorist activities.

- Since September 11, 2001, most states have established a state homeland security agency.

- Some law enforcement agencies are establishing civil defense battalions of citizen volunteers to assist the agencies in cases of natural disasters and terrorist acts.

- Police frequently deal with bomb threats and most of the time they are not associated with "terrorist activity" but with the activities of a single disturbed person. Regardless of the reason for the threat, the officer needs to treat each threat as if it were credible. Anything that looks or resembles explosive material is extremely dangerous and should be handled only by experts. As a patrol officer on the scene, your primary concern is the safety of the public.

■ Hostage negotiation is one of the most publicized actions of law enforcement agencies and also one of the most misunderstood actions that police officers undertake.

Classroom Discussion Questions and Activities

1. Perform a terrorist risk assessment for your hometown or city.

2. List the types of natural disasters that may occur in your home county or parish and explain what actions should be taken in the event of a natural disaster.

3. Can we win the war on terrorism? Justify your opinion.

4. Explain the responsibilities of a first responder.

5. How does a terrorist act differ from an ordinary criminal act?

References

Assessing and managing the terrorism threat. (2005, September). NCJ Report 210680.

Griffith, D. (2006, September). Get real, America, *Police Magazine*, p. 12.

Ham, M. S. (2005, September). *Crimes committed by terrorist groups: Theory, research and prevention.* NCJRS Research Report 211203.

Hill, M. (2005, July 8). N.Y. boosts security, urges public vigilance. *Philadelphia Inquirer*, A-17.

Manual for Police of New York State. (2005). N. Denny (Ed.), Flushing, NY: Looseleaf Law Publications.

Perrotta, T. (2003, January 30). Court debates rules on police surveillance. *New York Law Journal*, 229, 1.

Richardson, L. (2006). *What terrorists want.* New York: Random House.

Smith, B. L., Damphousse, K. R., & Roberts, P. (2006, May). *Pre-incident indicators of terrorist incidents: The identification of behavioral, geographic, and temporal patterns of preparatory conduct.* Washington, DC: NCJRS, U.S. Department of Justice.

Wright, L. (2006). *The looming tower.* New York: Knopf.

Chapter 15

Ethics and Police Operations

CHAPTER OUTLINE

After completion of this chapter, you will be able to do the following:

- Explain what constitutes the study of ethics.
- Define key ethical terms.
- Explain what constitutes ethical behavior.
- Understand the three different types of police misconduct.
- Define what constitutes lying.
- Discuss ethical issues involved in lying and deception.
- Define and discuss values and the role they play in shaping our conduct.
- Explain why law enforcement agencies have codes of conduct.
- List the ethical issues involved in the off-duty employment by law enforcement officers.
- Explain how ethics acts as a restriction on human behavior.
- Define and explain Kantian ethics.
- List the sources of ethical problems.
- Discuss the concepts involved in moral development theory.
- Explain the functions of an internal affairs unit.

I N T R O D U C T I O N

In this chapter, the ethical concerns usually encountered by police during daily operations are examined. Students often use the term "dead Greeks" when studying ethics. This refers to the fact that the theoretical concepts of ethics are based largely on the writings of Plato and Socrates (dead Greeks). For example, many theoretical ethical discussions are based on Socrates' famous credo that "a life unexamined is not worth living" (Souryall, 2003, p. 4).

The goal of this chapter is to introduce the readers to the issues involving ethics and to provide a basic framework to help the reader understand ethical issues and choose courses of action based on those principles. Except for a brief discussion of what constitutes ethics, Socrates' credo is not the focus of this chapter. Instead, we will examine such questions as whether it is wrong for an officer to take a free cup of coffee or embellish the facts needed to support the stop of a vehicle carrying illegal drugs.

According to Larry Sherman (1974) police misconduct is considered as an impropriety of office. It is wrongdoing, the appearance of wrongdoing, or puzzling behavior that violates standards usually set down in departmental policies and procedures, for good reasons, that the employee may or may not be cognizant of. Misconduct is bad because it leaves the public free to speculate and draw sweeping generalizations about the profession of policing as a whole. The different types of misconduct are often classified as malfeasance, misfeasance, and nonfeasance, and will be defined later in the chapter.

Durham, North Carolina, Police Department
Law Enforcement Code of Ethics

The following Law Enforcement Code of Ethics is adopted as policy by the Durham Police Department. All Durham Police Personnel will conduct their assigned duties according to this Code:

As a law enforcement officer, my fundamental duty is to serve mankind; to safeguard lives and property; to protect the innocent against deception, the weak against oppression or intimidation, and the peaceful against violence and disorder; and to respect the constitutional rights of all persons to liberty, equality, and justice.

I will keep my private life unsullied as an example to all; maintain courage in the face of danger, scorn, or ridicule; develop self-restraint; and be constantly mindful of the welfare of others. Honest in thought and deed in both my personal and official life, I will be exemplary in obeying the laws of the land and the regulations of my department. What I see or hear of a confidential nature, or that which is confided in me in my official capacity will be kept ever secret unless revelation is necessary in the performance of my duty.

I will never act officiously or permit personal feelings, prejudices, animosities, or friendships to influence my decisions. With no compromise for criminals, and with relentless prosecution of criminals, I will enforce the law courageously and appropriately without fear or favor, malice or ill will, never employing unnecessary force or violence, and never accepting gratuities.

I recognize the badge of my office as a symbol of public faith, and I accept it as a public trust to be held so long as I am true to the ethics of police service. I will constantly strive to achieve those objectives and ideals, dedicating myself to my chosen profession—law enforcement.

WHAT IS ETHICS?

"Ethics deals with values, with good and bad, with right and wrong. We cannot avoid involvement in ethics, for what we do—and what we don't do—is always a possible subject of ethical evaluation. Anyone who thinks about what he or she ought to do is, consciously or unconsciously, involved in ethics."

—Peter Singer, 1991, p. v

ethics / A philosophy that examines the principles of right and wrong, good and bad. Ethics has also been defined as standards of fair and honest conduct.

"It is necessary only for the good man to do nothing for evil to triumph."
—Edmund Burke, 1729–1797 (Quoted in Somerset, 1957, p. 4)

Ethics examines issues involving right and wrong, good and bad, virtue and vice. Ethics has also been defined as standards of fair and honest conduct. To many, the word *ethics* suggests a set of standards by which a particular group or community decides to regulate its behavior to distinguish what is legitimate or acceptable in pursuit of their aims from what is not (Flew, 1999, p. 23). For example, the American Bar Association has ethical standards for attorneys.

The terms *morality* and *ethics* are frequently used interchangeably. According to Muraskin and Muraskin, ethics is a philosophy that examines the principles of right and wrong, good and bad. Morality, on the other hand, is a practice of these principles on a regular basis, culminating in a moral life. Accordingly, morality is conduct that is related to integrity. Under this definition, a person may be viewed as ethical by virtue of knowing the principles of right and wrong, but only those who internalize the principles and faith and fully apply them in their relationships with others should be considered moral (Muraskin & Muraskin, 2001). Based on the foregoing, consider the following questions: Can a law enforcement officer be ethical and immoral? Can a law enforcement officer be moral without understanding the ethical issues involved? In this latter situation, would the officer be considered unethical and moral?

Although many writers, like Muraskin and Muraskin, make a distinction between ethics and morality, the two terms are used interchangeably in common practice and are treated as equivalent in this chapter.

There are two basic questions involving ethics: What should I do? How should I be? Under this approach, ethics involves the evaluation of actions and lives, choices and characters. This orientation is a rational argument toward the production of reasons to support one's choices of action (Ryan, 2001, pp. 7–8). The use of the rational argument approach indicates that individuals should develop their own moral reasons to guide their conduct rather than merely parroting the views of others. For example, why is stealing unethical or immoral? The rational argument approach would use rational arguments to support answers to this question. To state that stealing is unethical because it is a violation of the law would be to parrot the views of the lawmakers (Muraskin & Muraskin, 2001).

The problems of ethics are problems about human conduct at the individual level. Not unlike other members of our society, law enforcement officers have obligations that need to be considered in formulating choices of action. Some of these obligations are placed on the officer by being a member of society. Some are placed on the officer based on ethical decisions that the officer has made. In addition, many obligations are placed on the officer by the accepting of the position of law enforcement officer. When a person enters into a marriage arrangement, the person promises to perform certain obligations. The law enforcement officer promises to support and enforce the laws of the government when the officer accepts the position. These obligations place additional restrictions on our choices of ethical courses of action.

What are the consequences of our actions that should be considered in determining the ethical course of action? A central feature of ethics is that it should make us consider the results of our chosen course of action and the effects of that action on others. Accordingly, the welfare of others is critical in our ethical evaluations. The decision of law enforcement officers as to whether to fire their weapon at an escaping criminal should also consider whether innocent bystanders will be harmed by the discharge of the weapon. If it is likely that the weapon will hurt some innocent person, would it be ethical to ignore that risk and fire into the crowd?

Too often the problems that law enforcement personnel get involved in are not recognized as ethical issues until it is too late to consider the appropriate course of action. A streetwise police officer once remarked that the overriding ethical framework that a police officer should use is to ask the rhetorical question: "Would I be ashamed to explain my actions to my grandmother?"

Anatole France, in *Le Lys Rouge* (*The Red Lily*), stated that, "in law, in its majestic equality forbids both the poor man and the rich man to sleep under the bridge, to beg in the streets, and to steal bread" (France, 1927). What does France mean by that statement? Would it be immoral for a mother to steal bread to keep her children alive? Would it make any difference if the mother did or did not understand ethical principles?

WHAT CONSTITUTES ETHICAL BEHAVIOR?

John Stuart Mill contended that it was the business of ethics to tell us what our duties are, or by what test we may know them; but no system of ethics requires that the sole motive of all we do shall be a feeling of duty. On the contrary, ninety-nine hundredths of all our actions are done from other motives, and rightly so done, if the rule of duty does not condemn them (Mill, 1863, pp. 419–420). Everyone has an opinion as to what constitutes ethical conduct. As Aristotle stated centuries ago: "It is hard to be accounted an expert in ethics because every person seems to think he knows something about it. In fact, everyone does" (Souryall, 2003, p. 7).

Often ethics is erroneously considered the practice of telling or counseling people how to act. Ethics, however, is not designed to instruct people on how to act. Ethics is also not concerned with values-clarification. The real concern of ethics is not with what one *does* value, but with what one *should* value (Facione, Scherer, & Attig, 1978, p. 10). Ethics' immediate goal is knowledge, not forcing, causing, or encouraging people to act in certain ways (Facione, Scherer, & Attig, 1978, p. 10). Once people have the knowledge, then "the knowledge" can serve as a guide to help program their behavior.

The traditional approach to ethics is an individualistic one. Our notions of good and bad, moral and amoral, are based primarily on our considerations of a person as an individual. Accordingly, the morality of any profession, including policing, cannot be separated from the morality of the individuals who constitute that entity, and the entity and the individuals who make up that entity need to be studied together.

Kentucky State Police Code of Ethics

Kentucky State Police Vision Statement

The Kentucky State Police strive to maintain the highest standards of excellence, utilizing training and technology to create a safe environment for citizens and continuing as a national leader in law enforcement.

Kentucky State Police Mission Statement

The Kentucky State Police promote public safety through service, integrity, and professionalism, utilizing partnerships to:

- Prevent, reduce, and deter crime and the fear of crime
- Enhance highway safety through education and enforcement
- Safeguard property and protect individual rights

Kentucky State Police Goals and Objectives

GOAL 1: Human Resource Development—Provide a highly motivated and competent workforce to deliver police services to citizens of the Commonwealth.

GOAL 2: Highway Safety—Reduce the number of traffic crashes involving injury and death on Kentucky's highways.

GOAL 3: Reduce/Prevent Crime—Contribute to the creation of safe communities by initiating efforts to reduce and prevent crime in rural Kentucky.

GOAL 4: Information Technology—Utilize technology to deliver real-time information for the efficient delivery of police services.

ETHICS AS A RESTRICTION ON BEHAVIOR

It is often stated that ethical restrictions on behavior are unconscious; that is, when we alter our behavior for ethical reasons we often do not realize that it's our values and morals that guide our action. Does it matter that our values and moral guidelines are unconsciously held? According to one philosopher:

> Ethics, like metaphysics, is no more certain and no less dangerous because it is unconsciously held. There are few judges, psychoanalysts, or economists today who do not begin a consideration of their typical problems with some formula designed to cause all moral ideals to disappear and to produce an issue purified for the procedure of positive empirical science. But the ideals have generally retired to hats from which later wonders will magically arise. (Cohen, 1959, p. 3)

One of the important questions that should be examined in any study of ethics in the law enforcement context is: Is ethics a fundamental component of

Voices of Experience

Wellness

Excerpts from an interview between Cliff Roberson and former police officer, Bill Lally. Professor Lally is presently Chair of the Criminal Justice Department, ITT Technical Institute, Ft. Wayne, Indiana.

Q: *Explain to the readers the importance of wellness for police officers.*

A: Policing is a dynamic job. I have had days where nothing has happened for the first seven hours of a shift and then everything breaks loose. Your body's stress level often goes from low to high in a matter of seconds. The officers need to be aware that there are different aspects of a police officer's job that can cause wear and tear on the body.

With shift work, you are working hours that you are not normally awake, such as a second or third shift. You may have rotating days off, which means that your sleeping habits will be different on your off-days. Therefore, your sleeping habits will be interrupted and your sleeping habits are dictated by the job. For example, when I worked third shift I actually slept in two shifts. I would get home by 7:00 A.M., go to bed by 8:00 A.M., and get up before noon. Then I would get up and do the chores or take care of other matters. I would then go back to sleep at about 7:00 P.M. and get up at 9:00 P.M. and get ready to go to work. That has an adverse affect on my body. Not only was I

only getting at most six hours sleep combined, it was broken into two parts. In effect I was taking two long naps each day.

There is also eating problems. When you work second or third shift or when you have a busy day there is a tendency not to take time to eat three good meals each day. What ends up happening is that officers tend to eat a lot of fast food, especially on the third shift when fast food places are the only places open. I would suggest that you try to fix yourself something. Take time to prepare yourself a good meal. It is important that you eat three times a day. Don't skip the first meal in a hurry to get ready for work.

Sleeping and dieting are two important facets of your life to focus on. The third thing is to have a hobby that has nothing to do with law enforcement. Young officers tend to want to eat, sleep, and live police work. When they are on their off-time they are on the shooting range, reading police magazines, working on their weapons, etc. When you are doing nothing but policing, your stress levels never have an opportunity to come down from a high. This may be okay for a few years, but eventually it will wear your body down. ■

the decision making, or only a narrowly defined constraint on individual conduct?

Ethical egoism describes the view that human conduct should be based exclusively on self-interest. This concept is a normative statement regarding the best way to lead a life and what makes human conduct good or bad. Ethical egoism implies that the right thing to do is to always pursue self-interest. Can people ever act on motives other than those of self-interest? Can a police officer ever act on motives other than those of self-interest? The Greek philosopher, Epicurus (341–270 B.C.), taught that human beings come to exist simply as parts of nature and like other natural things seek their own self-interest (Facione, Scherer, & Attig, 1978, p. 39). According to Epicurus, self-interest is self-pleasure and is naturally desirable. He also taught that true pleasure was achieved with peace of mind and that other things such as wealth, political power, or fame do not guarantee pleasure.

Utilitarianism is another ethical theory that, among other things, attempts to answer the question: What makes an action good or bad? The classical utilitarian, Jeremy Bentham, attempted to provide an objective means for making value judgments. According to Bentham, two important questions face utilitarianism: (1) good or bad consequences for whom, and (2) how we calculate the value of the consequences. Two classical theories of utilitarianism have developed. The first, by Bentham, holds that pleasure is the only thing of intrinsic value to people and thus worthy of pursuit. The second, developed by John Stuart Mill, states that happiness is the only thing of intrinsic value and that happiness is not merely the sum total of our pleasures of whatever variety.

Under Bentham's concept, also referred to as *hedonistic utilitarianism*, actions and practices are right if they lead to pleasure or prevent pain. They are wrong if they lead to pain or prevent pleasure. The measure to use in calculating pleasure and pain depends on the intensity and duration. The present-day approach using Bentham's theory would be to use a cost–benefit analysis of proposed conduct.

According to Mill, the good which is happiness is not merely the sum total of pleasures because there are important qualitative as well as quantitative differences among pleasures. Accordingly, two lives of equal quantitative pleasures may have different values because one may include pleasures of a higher quality. Mill contended that higher pleasures, such as intellectual or spiritual pleasures, were preferable to the more sensual pleasures, such as eating and sex.

utilitarianism / A theory that attempts to answer what makes an action good by evaluating the sum total of the pleasures and pain that a course of action would bring.

KANTIAN ETHICS

One popular approach to solving ethical problems is by using the approach popularized by the eighteenth-century German philosopher, Immanuel Kant. This approach focuses on principles to define what is permissible and what is prohibited. To Kant, the essence of morality is strict respect for certain duties, and such respect supersedes any other goal. Kant contended that one's duty in a given situation could be deduced from fundamental *a priori* principles that were open to the careful inquirer, and such principles were independent of experience. According to Kant, duty is distinct from pleasure, moral virtue is the supreme good, and moral worth is measured neither by the consequences of persons' actions nor by their benevolence, but rather, by the persons' intentions to obey the moral laws. Accordingly, certain self-evident truths provide "the categorical imperative" for moral behavior (Walton, 1988). An examination of Nash's approach to solving ethical behavior (presented later in this chapter) indicates that her approach is a Kantian approach. A similar influence can be noted in the approaches recommended by Benson and Gilbert (also discussed later in this chapter).

> ## Sources of Ethical Problems
>
> - Personal gain involving activity of a dubious nature
> - Individual values in conflict with departmental goals
> - Competitive pressures
> - Cross-cultural considerations

Laura Nash (1981), in a widely read *Harvard Business Review* article, listed twelve questions that individuals should pose in examining the ethics of a decision. She contends that the guidelines are a practical approach to considering the ethical dimensions of a decision:

1. Have you defined the problem accurately? [Obtain a clear understanding of the problem. The more facts that are collected and the more precise the use of the facts, the less emotional your approach to the problem will be.]

2. How would you define the problem if you stood on the other side of the fence? [Look at the issue from the perspective of those who may question your conduct or those who are most likely adversely affected by your decision.]

3. How did the situation occur? [Look into the history of the situation and make certain that you are dealing with a problem, not a symptom.]

4. To whom and what do you give your loyalties as a person and a member of the organization? [Individuals and supervisors must ask to whom or what they owe the greater loyalty.]

5. What is your intention in making this decision? [Ask yourself, "Why am I really doing this?" If you are uncomfortable with the answer, don't make the decision.]

6. How does this intention compare with likely results? [Often, regardless of the intent, the results are likely to be harmful. Accordingly, it is important to think through the likely outcome.]

7. Whom could your decision injure? [Even though an action may have a legitimate use, what is the likelihood that it could cause harm to some?]

8. Can you discuss the problem with the affected persons before making a decision? [If your decision will harm others, can you discuss it with them first and obtain their views on it?]

9. Are you confident that your position will hold up in the long run? [Will today's decision be tomorrow's bad decision?]

10. Could you disclose without qualm your decision or action to your supervisor? [Would you be comfortable in seeing your action reported on television?]

11. What is the symbolic potential of your action if misunderstood? [How will others perceive your actions?]

12. Under what conditions would you allow exceptions to your stand? [What conflicting principles or circumstances provide a morally acceptable basis for making an exception to one's normal institutional codes?]

MORAL DEVELOPMENT

moral development / The theory that we develop morally similar to our physical development. The theory contends that because we are not born with the ability to understand and apply moral standards to our actions, we develop them similar to the manner in which we learn to do physical things, such as ride a bicycle.

An awareness of the patterns of **moral development** may help one understand what is involved in developing a moral position and how to formulate one's own moral positions.

According to Kohlberg, we develop morally similar to our physical development. Because we are not born with the ability to understand and apply moral standards to our actions, we develop them similar to the manner in which we learn to ride a bicycle or play baseball. Kohlberg, after years of research, devised a sequence of six stages in the development of a person's ability to reason regarding moral matters. (Kohlberg, 1986, pp. 36–51). He grouped the maturation of moral development into three levels, each with two stages. A summary of the six stages follows (Velasquez, 1982):

Level One: Preconventional Stages: These are the first stages and they are characterized by unquestioning obedience and the gratification of one's own needs.

Stage One: Punishment and Obedience Orientation: At this stage, the physical consequences of an act wholly determine the goodness or badness. The operative rule may be stated as: "Do the right thing and defer to the superior physical power of authorities in order to avoid punishment."

Stage Two: Instrument and Relativity Orientation: This is the stage whereby the child identifies right and wrong according to whatever satisfies the desires or needs that the child cares about. The operative rule may be stated as: "Respect the needs and desires of others in order to get the best for you."

Level Two: Conventional Stages: At the conventional stages, the individual recognizes that meeting expectations of others, such as family, peer groups, friends, or employees, is valuable in its own right.

Stage Three: Interpersonal Concordance Orientation: The right conduct at this stage is that conduct is viewed as what pleases and helps others and/or elicits social approval, such as, being the "good son or good daughter." This is the Charlie Brown of *Peanuts* approach (Barry, 1985, p. 15). The operative rule for this stage is: "Do the right thing to please others in order to be good in your own eyes."

Level Three: Postconventional Stages: These stages represent the higher level of values and are the autonomous or principle stages. At this level, there is a questioning of the existing social and legal system in the light of social utility and abstract principles, such as justice and human dignity. At this stage, we no longer accept the values and norms of our group, but attempt to view situations that impartially take into consideration everyone's interest.

Stage Four: Law and Order Orientation: The perceived conduct explained in stage three is broadened to include one's own nation. At this stage, the individual is still authority oriented but also recognizes a personal stake in the maintenance of law and order. The operative rule for stage four should be: "Be duty bound to society's norms and respect the law in order to maintain social harmony."

Stage Five: Social Contract Orientation: This stage is characterized by the recognition of social contract, an implicit agreement between the individual and society. According to Kohlberg, stage five is expressed in the U.S. Constitution and represents the "official morality" of the U.S. government. He believes that less than a majority of people reach this level.

Stage Six: Universal Ethical Principles Orientation: The final stage of Kohlberg's moral development includes the formulation of abstract moral principles. Right action is viewed in terms of universal ethical principles because of their logical comprehensiveness. At this stage, the individual acts in a certain way because the action is perceived as conforming to moral principles that the individual believes as the legitimate criteria for evaluating all other moral rules and arrangements. According to Kohlberg, few individuals reach this stage.

The six stages according to Kohlberg are sequential, in that people must pass through each of the earlier ones before advancing to the next higher level. According to Kohlberg, the majority of American people never advance beyond stages three and four.

VALUES

The term **value** is used in many different ways. Some of its meanings are subjective and some are objective. For example, in economics, values refer to the utility or usefulness of something or some person. Value also has subjective meanings in philosophy. Philosophical values are judgments about classes of objects or phenomena. Philosophers debate whether the value of truthfulness is absolute or situational; that is, it is good to be truthful, but are there situations where truth might do more harm than good? There is one common core to the various uses of the term *value*. Value refers to the "worth" of a system, object, and so on (Tracy, 1989). In this chapter, when we speak of values, we are referring to moral values.

values / Beliefs that guide a person's or organization's behavior.

Arnold Mitchell states that values, more than anything else, are what we believe, what we dream, and what we value (Mitchell, 1986, p. 33). Values are those concepts that we value. They act as filters, standards of behavior, and conflict resolvers. Values are also the forces that cause or motivate us to act. Values underpin our attitudes.

Our values are primarily derived from our early formative years. They do, however, change over time. Most people believe that our moral values are learned and that we generally acquire them from our parents, teachers, clergy, and peers. The learning process may be formal, as in school, or informal.

Conflict among values is inevitable. Our innate values often conflict with one another. In order to resolve value conflicts, we prioritize our competing values. For example, we may value life, but our values regarding our duties as a police officer may require us to place our life in danger in order to perform our duties. Accordingly, we must prioritize our conflicting values of continuing life and providing police protection to the public.

Paul Whisenand (1982) lists the following general propositions regarding human values:

- The actual number of values that we possess is relatively small when compared to our interests, attitudes, and motives.
- Human beings tend to have similar values.

- Values are organized into hierarchical "value systems."
- The origin of our values can be traced back to our formative years, our culture, institutions, and society.

The Validity of Values of Others

The focus should not be so much on how to change other people to conform to our standards and our values. Rather, we must learn how to accept and understand others in their own right, acknowledging the validity of their values, their behavior. American Indians believed that "to know another . . . you must walk a trail in his moccasins." This is a classic challenge for understanding others. If we can understand and respect other people and their values, then we can interact with them in a more effective manner (Massey, 1979, pp. 79–80).

LAW ENFORCEMENT VALUES

In discussing values and police officers, often the comment is made that the occupational experience of police officers affects their value judgments and that police in general have different values than other citizens. Milton Rokeach conducted a research project on the possible value gap between police and citizens. One hundred and fifty-three Midwestern police officers were asked to rank certain values. Their rankings were compared to those of a sample of adults with no connection to law enforcement. Four of his hypotheses follow:

- *Police have value systems that are distinctly different than those of other groups in American society.* Rokeach concluded that this hypothesis was false. With regard to the thirty-six values considered in this research, police officers are not distinctly different from other groups in American society.
- *Police value systems are highly similar to value systems of those with comparable backgrounds.* Rokeach concluded that this second hypothesis was true. Police have values similar to other adults with comparable backgrounds.
- *Police values are a function of personality predispositions.* Rokeach concluded that this hypothesis was true. Personality, rather than occupation, tends to account for the selection of guiding principles.
- *Police values are a function of occupational socialization.* Rokeach concluded that this hypothesis was false. Occupational experience did not change the way officers used values as guides (Rokeach, Miller, & Snyder, 1971, p. 150).

Departmental Values

Values are beliefs that guide a person's or organization's behavior. All organizations have values. The values are expressed through the actions of the organization. For example, actions or conduct that a police department considers as serious misconduct is a statement of what that department's values are in that area.

A police department's values can be ascertained by studying its administration and its policing style. For example, how does an administrator react to internal and external police ethical problems? A department that independently adopts an aggressive tactical orientation has a different set of values from the department that actively engages citizens in the crime prevention planning. Often, values are taken for granted until a public crisis focuses on a police department. The crisis may indicate that there is a disparity between publicly stated values and actual workplace values.

Management Tools

Organizational values can be important management tools in three circumstances:

- When management's values are incorporated into the administrative systems and culture of the organization and thereby become work ethics for the organization.
- When management values are suited to the challenges and tasks facing the organization and thereby lead to organizational success.
- When the management, through values, is superior to any other kind of management control (Wasserman & More, 1988).

Organizational Culture

Organizational culture in a police department represents a complex pattern of beliefs and expectations shared by its members. It is often defined as the shared philosophies, ideologies, values, beliefs, assumptions, expectations, attitudes, and norms (Hellriegel, Slocum, & Woodman, 1991, p. 302). The dimensions of an organizational culture include:

organizational culture /
Often defined as the shared philosophies, ideologies, values, beliefs, assumptions, expectations, attitudes, and norms of an organization.

- Behavioral regularities that are observable: commonly used language, rituals, and ceremonies
- Shared norms
- Dominant values
- Accepted rules of the game that newcomers must learn
- The feeling or climate conveyed by the physical manner in which the organization interacts with outsiders

Movies like the 1987 movie *The Big Easy*, and books like *The Cops are Robbers* and *Buddy Boys*, paint the picture of corrupt police officers who started ignoring little things until the distinction between right and wrong became blurred and the officers became robbers. These scenarios point out the need to stress individual values and ethics and "to thy ownself be true." According to Vane King, ethical issues and values are most certainly not a new concern in law enforcement; however, they have never been so publicized, nor have the stakes involved been so high (King, 1991, p. 94).

Personal Gratuities

"Our problem is not to find better values, but to be faithful to those we profess."

—John Gardner

A constant ethical problem faced by police officers involves the question of personal gratuities. According to some researchers, the fact that free coffee is being accepted by the police reveals only the surface problem. Many contend that police who become "dirty" got their start by accepting small gratuities and by the failure of police administrators to take a strong position against "acceptable" gratuities. For an excellent discussion on this problem, see Benson and Skinner.

Personal gratuities also create an unfavorable public perception of police. In the popular song, "Walk Like an Egyptian," the Bangles sang: "If you want to find all the cops, they're hangin' out in the doughnut shop." In a 1987 movie, *Raising Arizona*, a businessman's son was kidnapped. An outlaw contacts him and offers to find his son. The outlaw states he can do what the police cannot and that to find an outlaw, one should hire an outlaw. To find a doughnut, hire a cop. The two examples indicate that many people believe that officers spend most of their time in restaurants and doughnut shops drinking free coffee and eating free or less-than-full-price food.

Citizens who observe the police abuse their power for a free cup of coffee are likely also to believe that the same officers will be willing to take payoffs. Benson and Skinner (1980, p. 33) advocate that the solution to this problem is to first require that every supervisor demand completely and unequivocally that any personal gratuity is wrong, and second, that all officers must be educated in skills to avoid offered gratuities and the accompanying embarrassments.

Is It OK to Accept Free Coffee?

Is it OK to accept rewards for an act you are being paid to do, such as helping people?

Is it OK to take police department pens home?

Voices of Experience

Free Coffee

Excerpt from an interview between Cliff Roberson and former police officer, Ronald Wilson, currently Chair, Criminal Justice Department, Colorado Northwestern Community College, Rangeley, Colorado.

Q: *Assume that you are a police officer in uniform. You walk into a restaurant for a cup of coffee and a sandwich. When you attempt to pay for the coffee, the clerk indicates that the coffee is free to police officers. What should you do?*

A: These types of ethical situations are going to occur on a daily basis, I don't care whether the officer is in New York, L.A., or Rangeley, Colorado. We have a policy in Colorado that it is not ethically correct for police officers to accept gratuities. The same policy existed when I was in Michigan and South Carolina. Because it is impolite to reject a gift when offered, I advise the officers to determine the cost of the products and leave at least that amount as a tip. ■

Individual Guidance

There are some basic ethics tests that individual officers may use for guidance in questionable situations. The tests recommended by Benson and Skinner (1988) include:

- **Common sense test:** Does the questioned act make sense?
- **Publicity test:** Would you be embarrassed if the conduct was reported on the front page of your paper?
- **One's best self test:** Does the conduct fit your concept of your best self?
- **Most admired personality test:** What would your father or mother do in this situation?
- **Hurting someone else test:** Does your conduct cause "internal pain" to someone else?
- **Foresight test:** What are the long-term effects of your conduct?

If your proposed conduct fails any of the prior tests, then don't take the action. Some commonsense recommendations for avoiding offered gratuities include:

- Vary your habits and places. [If you are regularly observed in the same restaurant all the time, people will assume that you are receiving gratuities.]
- Develop a set response without fanfare to avoid the offer of free coffee or food. [Know the price of the food and on your way out, leave that amount with the cashier with a smile and a thank you.]
- Develop a set of responses to insist that the bill be paid. [Explain to the cashier that you appreciate her thoughts but you would feel better if you paid for the food.]
- Explain that accepting free meals or coffee is against departmental policy.

Steven Brenner and Earl Molander (1997) list the factors that contribute to unethical behavior in business. These same factors appear to be valid for police work and include:

- the behavior example set by superiors in the department
- the behavior of fellow employees
- the ethical climate of the profession
- society's moral climate
- organizational policy or lack thereof
- personal financial needs or desires

Leadership Roles

Most researchers contend that police supervisors set the moral tone of the department and that top management serves as a key reference point for all subordinates (King, 1991). If that is so, then supervisors are obligated to set an ethical example for other officers to follow. In addition, top administrators should be willing and able to discipline violators of ethical standards. Often inaction by those in key positions is considered as approval of the conduct in question. A key duty of police executives is to evaluate what the public expects of its police and then communicate clearly and inculcate values (fairness, honesty, reliability, and accountability to the others in the department). Police leaders have the responsibility to develop an ethical environment that eliminates public suspicion and lessens the temptations toward unethical conduct.

Edmonton, Canada, Police Rethinking Cussing Policy

According to an article published in the *Edmonton Journal* (August 19, 2006, p. 4), the Edmonton, Canada, Police Service is reviewing a policy that lets police cuss on the job. It was estimated that the Edmonton Police Commission receives an estimated three complaints a week that involve an officer using profanity. The police chief, Mike Boyd, said the force is reconsidering whether the boys in blue should be able to talk a blue streak. "I'm not sure there is a necessity to use profanity in policing," Boyd said. "There actually is a policy in place which permits it under certain circumstances. I'm working on that policy."

The commission noted that some members of the public see cursing by police officers as a loss of control on the officers' part. The current rules allow police officers to curse if they believe the situation necessitates it. An expert on police trash talk, however, says swearing only causes anger and a breakdown in communication.

Michael Quinn, a Minneapolis police officer who wrote *Walking With the Devil: The Police Code of Silence*, spoke about officer swearing while in Edmonton for the Canadian Association of Police Boards conference.

When Boyd, the police chief, arrived in Edmonton at the beginning of the year, he made professionalism a cornerstone priority. According to Boyd, the cussing policy exists to give officers more flexibility in dealing with certain members of the public.

The current policy is to allow swearing in certain situations—"perhaps in high-risk situations." According to Boyd, that may be the only language a certain offender understands. It's obviously different if it's an elderly woman caught jaywalking. He noted that officers' common sense should dictate when foul language is inappropriate and added that officers are expected to maintain professionalism when dealing with the public.

The Death of Socrates, 1787, from Met Museum. Many theoretical ethical discussions are based on Socrates' famous credo that "a life unexamined is not worth living."

LYING AND DECEPTION

"False words are not only evil in themselves, but they infect the soul."
                                                                    —Socrates

"A good man does not lie. It is this intuition which brings lying so naturally within the domain of things categorically wrong. Yet many lies do little if any harm, and some lies do real good. How are we to account for this stringent judgment on lying, particularly in face of the possible trivial, if not positively beneficial, consequences of lying?"
                                                        —Charles Fried, 1978, p. 54

Rank Order the Lies Listed Here with Number 1 Being the Most Unethical and Number 7 Being the Least Unethical

___ a.   A doctor telling a dying patient that he will get well.

___ b.   A police officer telling a defendant that the co-defendant has confessed and blamed the defendant for the murder.

___ c.   An officer telling a suspect that she has the evidence to establish the suspect's guilt to the crime in an attempt to get the suspect to confess.

___ d.   Informing a suspect that unless he confesses, his cousin, who is a police officer, will be fired from the police department.

___ e.   Falsely stating on the witness stand that the defendant made a right turn without giving the proper turn signal as a reason for stopping the car in which a young kidnapped victim was discovered in the trunk.

___ f.   Falsely stating your true age in an employment interview when answering a question that should not have been asked in the interview.

___ g.   You write a letter of recommendation for your best friend and include in the letter an exaggerated evaluation of your friend.

Sissela Bok distinguishes between two conceptual domains: the abstract question of truth and falsity, and the moral question of intended truthfulness or deception. She contends that veracity cannot be established by the truth or falsity of what one says, but on the basis of whether one intends to mislead (Souryall, 2003, p. 227). When Bok published her first edition of *Lying: Moral Choice in Public and Private Life* in 1978, she stated that there had been a relatively small number of studies on the concept of the issues of truthfulness and deceit. In her second edition in 1999, she noted that since her first edition the issues had received considerable debate (Bok, 1999, p. xiii).

Bok (1999, p. 14) describes a deceptive person as not one who is merely wrong or mistaken, but one who is intentionally deceitful or treacherous. She defines a liar as one who intentionally undertakes to deceive others by communicating messages that are intended to mislead them. She notes that a lie may be verbal, written, or conveyed via sign language. For example, the shaking of one's head may constitute a lie. According to Bok: "A lie is a statement, believed by the liar to be false, made to another person with the intention that the person be deceived by the statement" (Bok, 1999, p. 17). Note, her definition of what constitutes a "statement" is very broad. Under Bok's definition of a lie, intention is a key element. Accordingly, it appears that if my statement is in fact true, but I believe it to be false when I make it, I am telling a lie.

principle of veracity / Bok's principle that establishes a very strong moral presumption against lying.

Bok's **principle of veracity** is the principle that establishes a very strong moral presumption against lying. Under her principle there is a strong presumption that any lie is wrong. She asks the rhetorical question: What would it be like to live in a world in which truth-telling was not the common practice? She makes it clear that we benefit enormously by living in a world in which the practice of truth-telling is widespread. She also notes that the social practice of truth-telling has great value, both generally and personally. Her principle of veracity is a moral principle because it tells you not to lie even when you could get away with it. There are two steps to defending the principle: (1) the fact that each of us personally benefits from a system that we want others to do their part in maintaining, and (2) a principle of reciprocity that requires each of us to do our part in maintaining the system of truth-telling.

Are Some Lies Justified?

Samuel Johnson, a nineteenth-century English scholar, is reported to have made the following statement: "The general rule is that truth should never be violated; there must, however, be some exceptions. What if a murderer should ask you which way a man has gone?" (Bok, 1999, p. 40). Immanuel Kant would have disagreed. Kant saw the formal duty of an individual to everyone was to be truthful. He contended that truthfulness in a statement cannot be avoided, however great the disadvantage may be. According to Kant, the duty to be truthful is absolute. Kant stated: "By a lie a man throws away and, as it were, annihilates his dignity as a man" (Kant, 1797, p. 123).

As noted earlier, Bok's principle of veracity has a strong presumption against lying. Lying is usually wrong, but not always. The presumption can be overcome. The problem under Bok's principle is deciding when lying is morally justified. She offers a mechanical procedure for deciding this question under her scheme of applied publicity. Her scheme has an introspective and an active part.

Under the introspective part, you must ask the following questions:

- Are there truthful alternatives?
- What is the context of the lie; that is, the relationship between the liar and the person being lied to?
- What are the effects of the lie? The good? The bad?
- Considering the context of the lie and the relationship of the parties, what are the arguments for and against the lying?
- What are the effects on the practice of veracity itself?
- When you weigh the considerations and decide on a conclusion, how would your conclusion and the reasons you made it impress other reasonable persons?

Under the active part, you need to see how an actual audience responds to your reflections. Would they agree with your conclusions? Your aim is to arrive at a decision that would be acceptable to a reasonable public. Bok sees the active part as a check on the introspective part. She notes that the active part cannot actually be carried out most of the time. When it is impractical, you need to fall back on your judgment as to how an actual audience would respond to your conclusions.

Lying and the Courts

In *Bumper v. North Carolina*, 391 U.S. 543 (1968), the U.S. Supreme Court stated that consent to search a home was invalid because the grandmother who gave consent had been falsely informed that the officers had a search warrant. As noted in Chapter 5, the U.S. Supreme Court also ruled a confession involuntary where the defendant was falsely informed that his cousin, a policeman, would be in trouble if the defendant did not confess [*Spano v. New York*, 360 U.S. 315 (1959)]. However, the Court has sanctioned the use of trickery and deceit in interrogation [*Frazier v. Cupp*, 394 U.S. 731 (1969)]. The Court indicated that unlike promises, trickery and deceit do not present the risk of inducing false confessions. In *People v. Afieri*, 95 Cal. 3rd 533 (1982), however, a California court held that a confession obtained after a defendant was informed that his fingerprints were found on a flashlight used in the crime was inadmissible. Apparently, the general rule in U.S. jurisdictions is that officers may lie in interrogations as long as the lie is not likely to induce a false confession.

In obtaining consent to enter and search a home, the general rule is that officers may lie regarding their position or identity, but may not lie about the reason why they want to enter the home. For example, officers may deny that they are police officers in order to be invited into the home of a suspect. Thus, an officer may pose as a drug user and request permission to enter the apartment in order to buy drugs from the suspect. In this situation, the officer's identity was lied about but not the reason. The officer actually wanted to buy drugs from the suspect in order to catch the suspect in a drug deal.

There appears to be no reported cases where the courts have justified lying by police officers in a judicial proceeding. Judicial proceedings include documents submitted to a court. In one case there was a question as to whether officers had lied in an affidavit to obtain a search warrant. The U.S. Supreme Court, in *Franks v. Delaware*, 438 U.S. 154 (1978), stated that:

> When the Fourth Amendment demands a factual showing sufficient to comprise probable cause, the obvious assumption is that there will be a truthful showing. This does not mean "truthful" in the sense that every fact recited in the warrant affidavit is necessarily correct, for probable cause may be founded upon hearsay and upon information received from informants, as well as upon information within the affiant's own knowledge that sometimes must be garnered hastily. But surely it is to be "truthful" in the sense that the information put forth is believed or appropriately accepted by the affiant (officer) as true.

OFF-DUTY EMPLOYMENT

Off-duty employment often creates ethical problems. Are there some off-duty jobs that police should be restricted from? Should an officer be allowed to work as a bouncer for a night club that has a reputation as a trouble spot? Should police officers be allowed to wear their uniforms while performing off-duty employment? For example, a church in Houston, Texas, hires off-duty officers to direct Sunday morning traffic. The officers work in their official uniforms. An example of a state directive on off-duty employment of police officers is the following one from the state of Alabama.

Ethics and the Employment of Off-Duty Police Officers in the State of Alabama

[Ethics Commission decision as published by the Alabama League of Municipalities]

For many years, municipal officials have struggled with the issues surrounding the off-duty employment of police officers. Pursuant to the generally accepted wisdom, police officers are considered to be on the job twenty-four hours a day. In many cases, however, police officers must supplement their incomes by seeking secondary employment. Because of this, Alabama law implicitly recognizes the need for officers to accept off-duty employment. [See Sections 6-5-338 and 36-25-5(c), Code of Alabama, 1975.]

In addition to the financial benefits the officer receives from accepting off-duty employment, the benefits private employers receive by having a uniformed officer visible in their business is obvious. A less often understood aspect of off-duty employment, however, is that municipalities themselves also have an interest in allowing officers to accept off-duty work in some circumstances. The public can benefit greatly by having trained police officers available and visible.

For instance, having a uniformed officer seen working security by potential violators at school functions or in high-traffic areas like malls may prevent crimes from occurring. Even if the crime is not prevented, apprehending violators may be easier because the officer will be close at hand.

Despite the public benefits, however, off-duty employment of police officers raises many issues, such as liability concerns, that must be resolved. This is especially true where the officer will use the uniform, car, weapon, or other public equipment during off-duty employment. Again, the public has an interest in allowing the officer to use this equipment while off duty. Also, because officers are expected to be on duty twenty-four hours a day, they may be called upon to act in their official capacity at any time, making it important for them to have ready access to official equipment.

When off-duty officers are called upon to act in an official capacity, they become municipal representatives, and, generally speaking, the municipality becomes liable for any negligent action the officers take. The liability issues of off-duty employment have plagued Alabama municipalities for years, largely as the result of a $1.6 million judgment against an Alabama city for actions taken by an off-duty officer.

These aspects have been addressed many times before and will not be covered by this article, other than to point out a 1994 statute, Section 6-5-338, Code of Alabama, 1975, which extends tort immunity protection to police officers and requires private employers of police officers to obtain insurance to indemnify the officer against claims.

Instead, this decision is devoted to an examination of the ethical issues that surround a police officer's acceptance of off-duty employment and the use of public equipment in the course of that employment, specifically pursuant to Section 36-25-5(c) of the Code. Recently, a police chief and several of his officers were required by the Ethics Commission to repay money they had received from off-duty employment because of alleged ethical violations. This article is intended to address these issues in the hopes that other officers may avoid ethical problems in the future.

The Ethics Law: Generally speaking, the Alabama Ethics Law prohibits public officials and employees from using their official position or any public equipment to benefit themselves financially. However, Section 36-25-5(c), Code of Alabama, provides:

> (c) No public official or public employee shall use or cause to be used equipment, facilities, time, materials, human labor, or other public property under his or her discretion or control for the private benefit or business benefit of the public official, public employee, any other person, or principal campaign committee as defined in Section 17-22-2, which would materially affect his or her financial interest, except as otherwise provided by law or as provided pursuant to a lawful employment agreement regulated by agency policy.

Thus, Section 36-25-5(c) prohibits the use of public equipment or facilities unless another law provides otherwise, or unless an employment agreement or policy permits the use of the equipment. This means that the first step in allowing the off-duty use of public equipment by police officers is the enactment by the municipal governing body of a policy permitting that use. Without a specific policy in place, Section 36-25-5(c) seems to be an absolute prohibition against the use of public equipment during off-duty employment.

Although this section does not prohibit an officer from taking off-duty employment, officials should be aware that the municipality may have a policy in place that prohibits officers from taking off-duty jobs. This would be perfectly valid. This may be necessary because some courts have held municipalities liable for the acts of off-duty officers because the municipal policy heavily regulated the off-duty employment [*City of Birmingham v. Benson*, 631 So.2d 902 (Ala. 1993)]. This is a policy issue that the municipality must weigh before deciding to allow off-duty employment.

Even where the municipality decides that the positive effects of having officers work off-duty jobs outweigh the potential liability, the municipality must then decide whether to allow the use of public equipment and, if so, should retain some control over what municipal equipment may be used during the off-duty employment.

Although the municipality will want to address the issue of off-duty employment in more detail than can be done in this article, to allow officers to work off-duty jobs the policy should at a minimum state something similar to the following:

Police officers of the City/Town of _____ may accept off-duty employment subject to the restrictions and guidelines set out herein. Any officer seeking to accept outside employment must file with the chief of police a request for approval of outside employment. This request shall include the location and nature of the outside employment; the date and hours to be worked; the name of the outside employer; the duties of the outside employment; whether the job is a one-time event or is continuous; whether the job is to be worked in uniform; a list of any public equipment that may be used during the job; and any other information required by the chief of police. The chief of police shall approve or disapprove of any outside employment in writing. The chief of police may place conditions not inconsistent with this policy upon the acceptance of any outside employment. Public equipment may be used only as approved by the chief of police.

This policy should be adapted to meet local needs and requirements. For instance, an official other than the police chief may be assigned the duty of assigning off-duty jobs. To avoid ethical problems under Section 36-25-5(c), however, the policy must include a statement permitting the use of public equipment during the off-duty employment. The municipality may want to specifically list the types of equipment that an off-duty officer may use. The municipality should retain a written copy of the approval or disapproval of outside employment, which should include a list of equipment the officer is entitled to use on the off-duty job.

Additional issues to consider including in the policy are a definition of off-duty employment; requiring the private employer to sign a hold-harmless agreement; whether all officers will be allowed to work off-duty jobs (for instance, the municipality may want to restrict some supervisors from accepting off-duty jobs due to the hours they will be expected to be on duty); the type of employment that will be allowed; the number of off-duty hours an officer may work; whether the officer should file a statement following the employment as to the duties the officer performed; and how far outside the municipality the officer may work, among other issues.

Compensatory Time: One aspect of off-duty employment that seems blatantly obvious, but has created problems in the past, is that the outside employment must take place when the officer is not on duty. An officer may not draw pay from both a private employer and the municipality at the same time.

Closely related to this issue is the use of compensatory time. Comp time is time off from work that is granted either by federal or local law or ordinance in return for extra on-duty hours worked. Although the municipality may in its policies grant comp time for regular hours worked, generally comp time is given only for hours above the normal hours a person is required to work.

This operates in a manner similar to overtime pay. As an example, under the Fair Labor Standards Act (FLSA), police officers may be required to work up to forty-three hours in a week. Once an officer works more than forty-three hours (or other hours, based on the pay period), the municipal employer must either give the officer comp time or overtime pay. Under the FLSA, payment for overtime pay or comp time is at time-and-a-half.

Hours that are used to compute both the number of regular hours worked and comp time used are time spent on duty. That is, a municipality can only

(continued)

compensate an employee for time worked for the municipality. Outside employment time does not enter into the computation. Continuing to follow the previous example, if a police officer works forty-five hours in a week (assuming a pay period of one week), the officer would be entitled to three hours of comp time—that is, one-and-one-half-hours for every hour of overtime worked, or overtime pay at time-and-a-half. Depending on the municipal policy in place, comp time can be used similar to leave time. Officers are not on the clock when they use comp time. Because of this, if the municipal policy allows outside employment, the officer may use comp time to work outside employment. Bear in mind that the rule applies only to officers who are subject to the FLSA. If a municipality employs fewer than five law enforcement personnel, the municipality is excused from the overtime and comp time provisions of the FLSA as to those employees. Additionally, certain employees are exempt from these provisions of the FLSA because of the jobs they hold. This may include supervisory police officers. The FLSA includes tests to determine if an individual is an exempt employee and, if so, that employee is not entitled to any overtime pay or comp time.

Despite this, the municipality may decide that it wants to grant comp time to these employees. This action must be taken by the municipal governing body through the adoption of a policy allowing the use of overtime pay. This step is extremely important. While an employee who is exempt from the FLSA may be entitled to leave time, and may, if allowed by municipal policies, use this off-duty time to work a second job, these employees are not entitled to comp time unless the municipality adopts a policy providing for it. From the point of view of the Ethics Commission, a municipal policy establishing a written comp time program for employees who are not covered by the FLSA is mandatory before they can have time off from work (other than pursuant to regular leave time) to work an off-duty job.

Other Requirements: No municipal employees may use on-duty time for purposes related to off-duty employment. This rule extends, not only to the officer, but also to employees who are not being hired by the outside employer. For instance, a secretary may not use time at work to schedule off-duty work for police officers. Of course, the secretary may use work time for purposes that are related to on-duty work. For instance, it will probably be necessary to maintain a record of which officers are working off-duty jobs, where they are working, and the hours they are at the off-duty location. Additionally, supervisors should not receive pay or any other benefit for assigning or approving off-duty work for officers.

Conclusion: The municipal governing body has the power to decide whether municipal police officers may work off-duty jobs. If the council elects to allow this type of work, it must establish a written policy to this effect. The League encourages municipalities to work closely with the municipal attorney, police chief, and liability insurance carrier in the drafting and implementation of a policy on off-duty employment. If public equipment will be used on the off-duty job, this must be spelled out in the policy pursuant to Section 36-25-5(c).

In addition to a policy allowing off-duty employment, the council must pass a policy granting comp time to officers who are exempt from the FLSA, if these officers will be allowed to use comp time to work off duty. All off-duty work must be performed on the officer's own time. Finally, bear in mind that on-duty municipal employees may not use their time to help in any way with the off-duty employment, and supervisors should not accept payment for assigning officers.

Ethics Rulings: The Ethics Commission will address any questions regarding officers working off-duty jobs. The commission can be reached at (334) 242-2997. The commission has released the following opinions related to off-duty employment of police officers:

- A law enforcement officer may work for another law enforcement agency on his day off. (AO No. 95-105)
- A deputy sheriff may purchase and operate a wrecker service provided that all work done for the service is done on his own time, whether annual leave or after hours; that no public equipment, facilities, time, materials, labor, or other public property will be used to assist him with the wrecker services; that he doesn't use his public position to benefit him in his private business; and that no confidential information gained while on his public job is used in the operation of the wrecker service. (AO No. 98-06)

- A deputy may not serve civil papers for attorneys during off-duty hours because this is one of the deputy's functions as an employee of the sheriff's department. (AO No. 98-25)
- A municipal police detective may work part-time for an attorney investigating civil matters or matters outside the county in which his jurisdiction lies, provided that he does not involve himself in any matters concerning the county while performing this part-time work. The detective may serve civil papers, provided service of the papers is not the normal function of the police department for which he works. Outside employment must comply with any municipal policies or regulations. (AO No. 98-28)
- A municipal chief of police may not practice law during his off-duty hours because the chief is on duty twenty-four hours a day. (AO No. 98-32)
- A probation officer may practice law or serve as a municipal prosecutor in his free time, provided all provisions of the Ethics Law are complied with. His law practice must not involve individuals he supervises and he may not practice criminal law in the area in which he has jurisdiction as a probation officer. (AO No. 98-36)
- A police officer may perform security consulting work during his off-duty hours, provided that he doesn't use his public position to assist him in the private work, he does not use any public equipment, and that he performs the work on his own time. The work must comply with municipal guidelines and regulations. (AO No. 98-37)
- A municipal police dispatcher may not accept employment with a local bonding company because the opportunity arose because of her position as police dispatcher and because it would be difficult to separate her duties as a dispatcher from those as an agent for the bonding company. (AO No. 98-39)
- An off-duty state trooper may be paid to serve as an instructor at a police academy, provided that the provisions of the Ethics Law are complied with. (AO No. 99-01)
- A police officer may not also serve as coroner in the county in which he resides and is employed because it would be difficult to separate the duties of both positions and it would be difficult not to use the public equipment in one position in the performance of another. (AO No. 99-04)

Source: Reprinted by permission of Alabama League of Municipalities at www.alalm.org/Employment%20of% 20Off-Duty%20Police%20Officers.html. Accessed online August 28, 2006.

INTERNAL AFFAIRS UNIT

Most researchers agree that the effectiveness of any police department depends greatly on its internal integrity and external reputation in the community. Accordingly, it is important that any allegations of police misconduct be investigated quickly and efficiently. Failing to investigate citizens' complaints or requiring citizens to prove acts of misconduct before taking action can lead to a loss of public confidence in the department. In addition, the department has a duty to do more than just investigate citizens' complaints. When there is reason to believe that police misconduct has occurred, the department has the responsibility to initiate its own investigation. To establish and maintain public confidence, all investigations of police misconduct must be objective, thorough, and fair to all concerned. The different types of misconduct are **malfeasance**, **misfeasance**, and **nonfeasance**.

The standard unit for the internal investigation of police misconduct complaints is the internal affairs unit. In large departments, this may consist of several full-time officers. In a small department, it may consist of the part-time assignment of one officer. In most departments, to ensure that the chief is responsible for and kept current on matters involving internal discipline, the unit reports directly to the chief of police.

malfeasance / The intentional commission of a prohibited act or intentional unjust performance of some act of which the party had no right (e.g., gratuity, perjury, use of police resource for personal use).

misfeasance / The performance of a duty or act that one is obligated or permitted to do in a manner that is improper, sloppy, or negligent (e.g., report writing, unsafe operation of motor vehicle, aggressively "reprimanding" a citizen, improper searching of arrestees).

nonfeasance / The failure to perform an act that one is obligated to do, either by law or directive, due to omission or failure to recognize the obligation (e.g., failure to file a report).

The internal affairs unit should be concerned with serious violations on the part of police officers. It should not become involved in issues properly belonging to command. For example, it should not be concerned with issues that can be resolved by supervisors, such as reports of tardiness, improper dress, and absenteeism. The unit should conduct all investigations impartially, objectively, and with integrity. The activities of the unit should be well documented for the benefit of both the public and the officers.

Ideally, the department will have a clear, comprehensive written directive that delineates the processes and procedures to be used in investigating police misconduct. All complaints, even those determined to be unfounded, should be recorded. The recording also helps the police department refute any claims that complaints are being ignored. Each complaint, whether in person, by telephone, or in writing, should be taken courteously and recorded. Most departments retain their records of internal investigations for two to five years, purging the files if no subsequent complaints are filed within that period.

One difficult question in dealing with police misconduct investigations is how much of the information is to be released and to whom. On one hand is the person who filed the complaint with the desire to know how the complaint is being handled and on the other hand is the confidentiality rights of the officer being investigated. Records of internal investigations should not be retained with individual personnel records. The segregation of the files helps strengthen the confidentiality of the internal affairs records. The separation also makes the records more difficult to obtain in civil court actions, in that the party requesting the records in a court action has the duty to establish the necessity for their disclosure. [For an excellent discussion on the confidentiality of internal affairs records see *Frankenhauser v. Rizzo*, 59 R.F.D. 339 (E.D. Pa., 1973).]

CASE STUDY: Excerpts from *Frankenhauser v. Rizzo*
1973 U.S. Dist. LEXIS 14556 (E.D. Pa, 1973)

The plaintiffs (spouse and children of individual killed by the police department) sued the City of Philadelphia and its mayor (Rizzo) under 42 U.S.C.S. sec. 1983 to recover damages for the wrongful death of their husband and father who was shot and killed by Philadelphia police officers. After the shooting, the police conducted an exhaustive investigation. The spouse and children sought copies of the police investigation under Federal Rule of Civil Procedure 26(b)(1).

Court's Opinion: Paul Frankenhauser, was shot and killed by police in a dyeworks in the Kensington section of Philadelphia on the afternoon of September 1, 1970. Named as defendants were the police officers who allegedly fired the fatal shots and their superiors in command, the city, and the mayor. The complaint alleges that the decedent and his brother, Joseph, who was with him, were unarmed, that neither the decedent nor his brother had threatened the police during the course of the encounter and chase that resulted in the shooting, and that there was no provocation or justifiable cause for the police action. In their answers, the defendants have asserted that one of the Frankenhauser brothers was armed, that the police had heard shots and thus had reasonable cause to believe that one of the brothers was armed, that the Frankenhausers acted in such a fashion that the policemen involved believed that they were in danger of being seriously injured, that the officers acted in a reasonable manner, and that the shooting was justified. Before the court is a discovery motion (request for documents) which raises principally the question of whether plaintiffs have the right to inspect and copy witnesses' statements to police and the reports of the police investigations made in the aftermath of the episode, or whether these reports and statements are properly the subject of an executive privilege.

The police department investigation that followed the shooting was apparently extensive. Many statements and photographs were taken, all of the physical evidence was analyzed, and an autopsy was performed on the decedent. The defendants, represented by the City Solicitor of Philadelphia, have now agreed to make available to the plaintiffs their radio tapes of the incident, physical evidence regarding the killing, physical evidence taken from the home of the decedent following his death, the autopsy report on the decedent, photographs of the scene of the killing, a list of all known witnesses to the killing, and a list of previous or subsequent events involving Paul and Joseph Frankenhauser and decedent's wife, who is a plaintiff in the action. However, the defendants have refused to accede to the plaintiffs' requests for discovery of the following:

1. reports of the analysis of physical evidence made by the police department
2. the results of polygraph examinations conducted by the police
3. statements, signed or unsigned, from police or civilian witnesses to the killing
4. police investigation reports relating to the killing
5. police reports of previous incidents involving Paul or Joseph Frankenhauser
6. written communications, reports, references to, or accounts of all communications among members of the police department or between members of the police department and any other person or law enforcement agency regarding Paul or Joseph Frankenhauser.

The admissibility of polygraph examinations at trial has been the subject of a number of recent opinions. No record on the reliability of polygraph examinations has been developed in this proceeding. For the present at least, we are inclined to agree with those courts holding that the results of polygraph tests are inadmissible in a judicial proceeding. Moreover, whatever view one takes on the admissibility of polygraph examinations, at this point we fail to perceive how disclosure of the results of the polygraph tests would lead to the discovery of other admissible evidence, which is the general test for scope of discovery under rule 26 (b)(1). We note that the plaintiffs have not undertaken to show the Court just whose polygraph examinations are involved, what the examination results would tend to show, or how those results would lead to the discovery of other admissible evidence, if any.

The facts here do not support the privilege claim. Executive privilege is the government's privilege to prevent disclosure of certain information whose disclosure would be contrary to the public interest. The defendants (City and police) argue that police investigations such as the one here involved are made under a veil of confidentiality and that it would contravene the public interest and would impair the functioning of the police department if the results of such investigations were disclosed. They contend that destruction of the confidentiality of police investigative records would have a "chilling effect" upon the department and would impede candid and conscientious self-evaluation of actions of the department. Defendants further assert that parties to police operations would become reluctant to talk, that witnesses would hesitate to come forward, and that law enforcement officials' actions would be guided less by the call of duty than by a continual fear of lawsuits arising out of their official conduct.

First, we do not believe that rare instances of disclosure pursuant to a court order made after application of a balancing test comprising detailed standards such as those enumerated here would deter citizens from revealing information to the police. Neither do we perceive any impact of the disclosure of factual statements surrounding an investigation of a shooting upon persons who gave them. Police officers are, of course, willing to cooperate, and we believe that the average citizen is also willing to cooperate with law enforcement officials. Disclosure under the circumstances of this case would not reveal any details of police self-evaluation, because we will limit disclosure to factual data, as opposed to evaluative summaries and recommendations. Furthermore, over two years have elapsed since the completion of the investigation, and no criminal charges have been brought against anyone; it is unrealistic to believe that any will be brought, notwithstanding the fact that there is no statute of limitations on homicide. Neither does it appear that any intradepartmental disciplinary actions have been instituted as the result of the events in question, and it is equally unrealistic to believe that any will be at this late date. Furthermore, no party seeking discovery is actually or potentially a defendant in any criminal case arising out of the incidents in question.

While we intimate no view whatever as to the merits of the plaintiffs' cause of action, a reading of the complaint reveals that its allegations are substantial and that it was apparently brought in good faith. The plaintiffs' need for the facts contained in the police

(continued)

investigative files is manifest. The police investigation was conducted promptly after the incident occurred and certainly should be comprehensive and reliable. Most of the eyewitnesses to the shooting were police officers, and the widow and children had no means to duplicate the police investigation. Interviews or depositions at this late date could not do so.

There is no doubt that production of a statement should be ordered if a witness has a faulty memory and can no longer relate details of the event. . . . The mere lapse of time is in itself enough to justify production of material otherwise protected as work product . . . . The notion that memory fades with the passage of time needs no demonstration.

The statement of a witness taken immediately after the accident is a catalyst of unique value in the development of the truth through the judicial process. It should be available to both parties no matter which one obtained it. . . .

The foregoing application of the balancing test makes it clear that the plaintiffs are entitled to discovery of the signed statements of witnesses and those portions of the police reports containing factual data. No harm to the public interest can flow from such discovery. The same reasoning applies to the analysis of physical evidence made by the police department. Indeed, plaintiffs might be entitled to such information even in a criminal case. Notwithstanding the foregoing, we shall not require disclosure of the evaluative summary portion of the police investigative reports and will order those portions excised before delivery to the plaintiffs.

The final question in the case involves the request for "police reports of previous incidents involving Paul or Joseph Frankenhauser and written communications, reports, references to, or accounts of all communications among members of the police department or between members of the police department and any other person or law enforcement agency regarding Paul or Joseph Frankenhauser." According to representations made by the plaintiffs' counsel at oral argument, this data is material to the issue of whether the police had probable cause to believe that the Frankenhauser brothers were armed, dangerous, engaging in violations of the law, etc. While the request is reasonable under the circumstances, because of its unusual nature and our inability to foresee just what type of data is involved, we will inspect the sought material *in camera* prior to ruling on the discovery motion. We will apply the standards articulated in this opinion and will take special note of whether the reports consist of factual data or evaluation and opinion.

In accordance with the foregoing opinion, we enter the following Order.

1. Defendants shall produce to the plaintiffs for inspection and copying the following materials from the files containing the police investigation of the incident described in the plaintiffs' complaint:
    (a) reports of the analysis of physical evidence made by the police department
    (b) statements, signed or unsigned, by police or civilian witnesses to the killing and the events leading up to the killing
    (c) police investigation reports relating to the killing and the events leading up to the killing, except for such portions of those reports as constitute opinion and evaluative summary
2. The plaintiffs' motion to compel discovery of polygraph examination reports is denied as beyond the proper scope of discovery.
3. Copies of police reports of previous incidents involving Paul or Joseph Frankenhauser, and written communications among members of the police department or between members of the police department and any other person or law enforcement agency regarding Paul or Joseph Frankenhauser, shall be furnished by defendants to the Court for *in camera* inspection within twenty days, whereupon the Court shall in due course rule upon the amenability of the matters thus furnished to discovery in accordance with the standards enunciated in this Opinion.

The ideal internal affairs department carefully observes the rights of the principals involved. When an officer is being interviewed, the IACP recommends the following conditions:

- The interview will be conducted at a reasonable hour, and unless immediate action is required, while the officer is on duty.

- The officer should be informed prior to the interview of who will be present at the interview and the name of the officer in charge of the investigation.
- The officer should be informed of the nature of the investigation and the names of the complainants.
- The interview should be held during a reasonable period, allowing time for personal necessities and reasonable rest periods.
- The interview should be recorded and all persons participating in the interview should be aware of the recording.
- The officer should be afforded the assistance of counsel or other representative of the officer's choice, at all times during the interview (International Association of Chiefs of Police, Training Key 299: The Disciplinary Process-Internal Affairs R). [**Note:** In most states there are state statutes that provide protection for the officers similar to those previously noted.]

Whether or not the officer may be required or pressured to take a polygraph exam or ordered to appear in a lineup depends on state law. State law must also be considered in determining whether an officer may under threat of firing be required to take physical tests such as voice-print analyses or providing hair samples. In most states, officers may be ordered in administrative investigations to answer questions and incriminate themselves. Such forced statements, however, may not be used in criminal proceedings. Volunteered statements are generally admissible in criminal proceedings, if the requirements of the Miranda rule have been complied with. Generally, under federal law, police officers may not be forced into making statements to be used in criminal proceedings under threat of losing their jobs.

The citizen who made the complaint has a right to make the complaint anonymously. The citizen should receive acknowledgment that the complaint was received and that appropriate action will be taken. The citizen should also be advised of an officer who will be the contact person for more information regarding the complaint.

INTERNATIONAL ASSOCIATION OF ETHICS TRAINERS

More police careers are destroyed because of ethical issues than any other reason. As noted by many researchers, including Neil Trautman, founder of the International Association of Ethics Trainers, "Ethics training is the greatest need in law enforcement." As noted by Samuel Johnson in 1750, "Men more frequently require to be reminded than informed."

An excellent resource of information on ethics for police officers is the International Association of Ethics Trainers. The association was founded in 1991 to assist those interested in promoting high ethical standards. It provides information and resources to educators, trainers, administrators, and leaders primarily in, but not limited to, law enforcement. The address of the association is P.O. Box 388191, Chicago, IL 60638-8191.

How Willing Are Officers to Report Misconduct?

The following survey regarding reported misconduct by police officers was taken from NIJ Research Report "Enhancing Police Integrity" published December 2005. The complete report may be obtained from the NIJ at website www.ojp.usdoj.gov/nij.

The survey results suggest that, more than any other factor, concern for the welfare of their peers led officers to refrain from reporting the misconduct of other officers. Officers shielded a colleague willingly if the misconduct occurred for what they perceived to be good reasons, such as sleeping on duty because a sick spouse or child prevented an officer from getting enough sleep. On the other hand, officers reluctantly concealed misconduct they perceived to be irresponsible, chronic, or exploitative, such as sleeping on duty because of excessive partying or off-duty employment. Only when another officer's exploitation of their support became unbearable, chronic, or put their own position at risk, would officers alert a supervisor to the misconduct. Even then, they sought to conceal their identities.

Although this concern for colleagues can explain officers not reporting serious misconduct, this was not the case in the three agencies studied. The researchers believe that the relative success these agencies had in encouraging officers to come forward derived from four strategies used to weaken officers' tendency not to report misconduct:

- They made it explicit that they would discipline either an officer's failure to report a colleague's misconduct or a supervisor's failure to discipline an errant officer.

- They fired any officer caught lying during a misconduct investigation, no matter how minor the offense under investigation. This action was highly valued because of its dampening effect on officers' willingness to conceal a peer's misconduct.

- One agency rewarded officers who reported their colleagues' misconduct and, to avoid repercussions and possible antagonism from fellow officers, they allowed anonymous and confidential reporting.

- Because the loyalty and support that officers come to expect from one another can be a source of the failure to report misconduct, the agencies sought to prevent the bond among officers from becoming too strong. To do this, two agencies regularly rotated new supervisors between service areas, patrol districts, and patrol teams. One agency also introduced racial, ethnic, gender, educational, political, cultural, religious, and generational diversity into the department.

SUMMARY

- Ethics is the normative study of individual conduct. It is also defined as a set of rules that define right and wrong conduct. Ethics deals with fundamental human relationships. Ethical rules tell us when our behavior is acceptable and when it is disapproved and considered as wrong.

- Often ethics is erroneously considered the practice of telling or counseling people how to act. Ethics, however, is not designed to instruct people on how to act. Ethics is also not concerned with values clarification.

- The real concern of ethics is not what one *does* value, but what one *should* value. Ethics' immediate goal is knowledge, not forcing, causing, or encouraging people to act in certain ways. Once people have the knowledge then "the knowledge" can serve as a guide to help program their behavior.

- The traditional approach to ethics is an individualistic one. Our notions of good and bad, moral and amoral, are based primarily on our considerations of a person as an individual. It is often stated that ethical restrictions on behavior are unconscious; that is, when we alter our behavior for ethical reasons we often do not realize that it's our values and morals that guide our action.

- Ethical egoism describes the view that human conduct should be based exclusively on self-interest. This concept is a normative statement regarding the best way to lead a life and what makes human conduct good or bad. Ethical egoism implies that the right thing to do is to always pursue self-interest.

- Utilitarianism is an ethical theory that among other things attempts to answer the question: What makes an action good or bad? The classical utilitarian, Jeremy Bentham, attempted to provide an objective means for making value judgments. According to him, two important questions face utilitarianism: (1) good or bad consequences for whom, and (2) how do we calculate the value of the consequences.

- We develop morally similar to our physical development. Because we are not born with the ability to understand and apply moral standards to our action we develop it similar to the manner in which we learn to ride a bicycle or play baseball.

- The term *value* is used in many different ways. Some of its meanings are subjective and some are objective. For example, in economics, values refers to the utility or usefulness of some thing or person. Value also has subjective meanings in philosophy.

- Philosophical values are judgments about classes of objects or phenomena. Philosophers debate whether the value of truthfulness is absolute or situational; that is, it is good to be truthful, but are there situations where truth might do more harm than good?

- There is one common core to the various uses of the term *value*. Value refers to "worth" to a system, object, and so forth. All organizations have values. The values are expressed through the actions of the organization.

- A police department's values can be ascertained by studying its administration and discussing its policing style. For example, how should an administrator react to internal and external police ethical problems? A department that independently adopts an aggressive tactical orientation has a different set of values than the department that actively engages citizens in crime prevention planning. Often values are taken for granted until a public crisis focuses on a police department.

Classroom Discussion Questions and Activities

1. Your Personal Hall of Fame: Make a list of the ten persons that you admire most. Then make a list of qualities that you admire most regarding the persons listed. Examine the list. The items listed probably reflect character traits, abilities, and other qualities that you admire and therefore place a high value on.

2. Make a list of the ten things that you enjoy (value) most. Rank the list from 1 to 10 with 1 being your most valued activity. Next, place an "a" by those activities that you have done in the last two weeks; a "b" by those you have done within the last three months; a "c" by those that you have not done within the last year; and a "d" by those that you have not done within the past two years. Examine the list. How does the assigned letter compare with the assigned number? For example, do your 1s and 2s have an "a" designation? Are there any patterns in your list? Do you need to reassign your rankings? What does the list demonstrate regarding where your values lie?

3. Assume you have just graduated from the academy and you are assigned to a two-person patrol unit with a veteran police officer. The two of you take a lunch break at a local restaurant. When you ask for your check, the veteran asks, "Why are you doing that? The food is free to us, that is why we stopped at this place." What actions should you take at this point?

4. Officer West reported to internal affairs that Officer White, a ten-year veteran, had a habit of eating in the more expensive restaurants in the city and leaving without paying the check. What do you think of Officer West's conduct? Is he a snitch? Would you blow the whistle on Officer White?

5. Assume you are still assigned to the patrol unit mentioned in number 3. For no apparent reason, the veteran who is driving stops a car in front of him that is being driven by three young minorities. He orders the individuals out of the car and finds drugs in the car. You are assigned to write up the report of the arrest. He explains to you that all you need to do is to indicate that the car was weaving to justify the stop. What actions should you take at this point?

6. One night while on duty as a patrol officer, you walk into a bar. At the end of the counter are two fellow police officers. You know that the officers are on duty and that they are drinking beer and are in a good mood. They invite you to join them. What actions should you take at this point?

7. Discuss why departure from ethical conduct on the part of one police officer can affect all the officers in the department.

8. Is it ever permissible for a police officer to give false testimony in court to ensure that a dangerous criminal goes to jail?

9. Explain the differences between ethics and values.

10. Review Professor Nash's twelve questions. Which of them can be helpful in assessing the ethics of a law enforcement course of action?

References

Barry, V. (1985). *Applying ethics: A text with readings* (2nd ed.). Belmont, CA: Wodsworth, p. 15.

Benson, B. L., & Skinner, G. H. (1988, December). Doughnut shop ethics: There are answers. *The Police Chief.*

Bok, S. (1999). *Lying: Moral choice in public and private life* (2nd ed.). New York: Vintage Press.

Brenner, S., & Molander, E. (1977, January–February). Is the ethics of business changing? *Harvard Business Review.*

Cohen, F. S. (1959). *Ethical systems and legal ideals.* Ithaca, NY: Greenwood Press, p. 3.

Facione, P. A., Scherer, D., & Attig, T. (1978). *Values and society.* Englewood Cliffs, NJ: Prentice-Hall.

Flew, A. (1999). *A dictionary of philosophy* (2nd ed.). New York: Gramercy.

France, A. (1927). *Le Lys Rouge.* Paris: (unknown binding) (English translation 2005) *The Red Lily*, London: Kissinger Press.

Fried, C. (1978). *Right and wrong.* Cambridge, MA: Harvard University Press.

Hellriegel, D., Slocum, Jr, J. W., & Woodman, R. W. (1991). *Organizational behavior* (5th ed.). St. Paul: West, p. 302.

International Association of Chiefs of Police. (undated). *Training key 299: The disciplinary process-internal affairs role.*

Kant, I. (1797). *On a supposed right to lie from altrustic motives.* Reprinted in appendix to Bok, S. (1999). *Lying: Moral choice in public and private life* (2nd ed.). New York: Vintage Books.

King, V. R. (1991, January). Rededicating ourselves to leadership and ethics in law enforcement. *FBI Law Enforcement Bulletin*, p. 24.

Kohlberg, L. (1976). Moral stages and moralization: The cognitive-development approach. In T. Lickona (Ed.), *Moral development and behavior: Theory, research, and social issues.* New York: Rinehart & Winston, pp. 31–52.

Massey, M. (1979). *The people puzzle: Understanding yourself and others.* Reston, VA: Reston, pp. 79–80.

Mill, J. S. (1863). *Utilitarianism.* As republished in *The Utilitarians* (1961). New York: Dolphin Books, pp. 419–420.

Mitchell, A. (1986). *The nine American lifestyles.* New York: Macmillan, p. 33.

Muraskin, R., & Muraskin, M. (2001). *Morality and the law.* Upper Saddle River, NJ: Prentice-Hall.

Nash, L. L. (1981, November–December). Ethics without the sermon. *Harvard Business Review.*

Rokeach, M., Miller, M. G., & Snyder, J. A. (1971). The value gap between police and policed. *Journal of Social Issues*, *27*, 155–171.

Ryan, F. W. (2001). *Socrates' justice from Ancient Greece: How we evolve to nonviolence, brotherhood and lasting peace.* Lima, OH: Wyndham Hall Press.

Sherman, L. (1974). *Police corruption: A sociological perspective.* Garden City, NJ: Doubleday.

Singer, P. (1991). *A companion to ethics.* Oxford: Basil Blackwell.

Somerset, H. V. F. (ed.). (1957). *A notebook of Edmund Burke.* Cambridge: Cambridge University Press.

Souryall, S. S. (2003). *Ethics in criminal justice: In search of the truth* (3rd ed.). Cincinnati, OH: Anderson.

Tracy, L. (1989). *The living organization.* New York: Prager.

Velasquez, M. G. (1982). *Business ethics: Concepts and cases.* Englewood Cliffs, NJ: Prentice-Hall.

Walton, C. C. (1988). *The moral manager.* New York: Harper & Row.

Wasserman, R., & More, M. H. (1988, November). Values in policing. *Perspectives on policing.* U.S. Department of Justice, No. 8.

Whisenand, P. (1982). *The effective police manager.* Englewood Cliffs, NJ: Prentice Hall.

Glossary

18th Street   An Hispanic gang formed in the 1960s, composed of individuals with mixed racial backgrounds.

activity log   A log kept by police patrol officers during patrol shift. The log is a record of all activities performed by the officer during the patrol shift. For example, all dispatched calls, car stops, building checks, and other self-initiated activities are recorded. This includes the time the call or activity was initiated, the time the officer arrived at the scene, and the time the call was cleared.

admission   A statement provided by an accused of a fact or facts pertinent to the issue that helps establish the accused's guilt, but does not admit actual guilt.

AMBER Alert   The notification to the general public, by various media outlets, that a confirmed abduction of a child has happened. AMBER is an acronym for "America's Missing: Broadcast Emergency Response," and was named for nine-year-old Amber Hagerman, who was abducted and murdered in Arlington, Texas in 1996.

anthropometry   A personal identification method based on eleven body measurements.

anti-gang tactics   Tactics targeted to reduce gang problems; includes mediation, situational crime prevention, working with families, and other strategies.

associative evidence   Any evidence that can link a suspect to a crime.

authoritarian personality   A psychological construct of a personality type likely to be prejudiced and to use others as scapegoats.

beat   A geographical area of responsibility for a police patrol officer during a tour of duty. A beat is sometimes referred to as a response area or response zone.

bloodstain pattern analysis   The study of blood as it comes in contact with a surface.

bright-line rule   A rule that has been established by court decisions that provides clear guidance to police officers.

broken windows theory   Based on an article titled "Broken Windows" by James Q. Wilson and George L. Kelling, which appeared in the March 1982 edition of *The Atlantic Monthly*. This theory uses the analogy that if a few broken windows on a vacant residence are left unrepaired, the tendency is for vandals to break more windows. Eventually, they may even break into the building, and if it's unoccupied, take up residence in the building or light fires inside. Broken windows and other neighborhood decay give the impression that no one cares about the neighborhood, which then becomes breeding grounds for criminal activity. The idea is that small disorder problems should be promptly addressed by the police and the community or they may lead to more serious crime problems.

building blocks   Memory tools designed to ensure that the officer covers **who, what, when, where, why**, and **how** in each investigative report.

bureaucracy   A concept referring to the way that the administrative execution and enforcement of legal rules is socially organized. Most police departments are highly bureaucratic. A bureaucratic organization is characterized by standard operating procedures (rule following), formal division of authority, hierarchy, and impersonal relationships.

burglary   The unlawful entry into a structure to commit a felony or theft. For reporting purposes this definition includes: unlawful entry with intent to commit a larceny or felony, breaking and entering with intent to commit a larceny, housebreaking, safecracking, and all attempts to commit any of the aforementioned.

burnout   Job burnout is a form of stress that police officers may suffer to some degree at various times in their career. Burnout becomes critical when an officer is distressed and begins to feel fatigued and frustrated every day with no relief. In police culture, burnout is sometimes mistaken for an attitude problem.

CAD/RMS   Computer Assisted Dispatch/Records Management System that provides access to criminal justice database inquiries.

carjacking   A crime of motor vehicle theft from a person who is present. In many cases the carjacker is armed, and the driver of the car is forced out of the car at gunpoint.

chain of command   The line of authority and responsibility in a police agency along which orders are passed.

chain of custody   A chronological record of those individuals who have had custody of the evidence from its initial acquisition until its final disposition.

child abuse   The physical or psychological mistreatment of a child by his or her parents (including adoptive parents), guardians, or other adults. While this term emphasizes carrying out wrong acts, a related term is child neglect: not doing what is necessary, negligence. The combined problem area is often called child abuse and neglect.

class characteristics   Evidence that has characteristics, that are common to a group of similar objects. Examples of evidence with class characteristics include soil, glass, and paint.

coactive policing   An approach where the police, the community, and other public and private resources work together to solve crime and crime-related problems.

communication A transmission whose primary purpose is to transmit information.

community partnerships A strategy that entails the police and the public working together in partnerships to solve problems in the community.

Community Policing Era A currently evolving era of policing that promotes and supports organizational strategies to address the causes and reduce the fear of crime and social disorder through problem-solving tactics and police—community partnerships.

community policing A strategy of policing that focuses on the police working with the public to prevent and solve crime-related problems. Community policing is a strategy that entails organizational reengineering, problem solving, and partnerships; a philosophy in which the police are seen as members of the community, with police officers being part of where they live and work. Community policing often entails a three-pronged approach: (1) partnerships, (2) problem solving, and (3) organizational transformation. Police agencies that subscribe to this philosophy tend to do much more community work than traditional police departments.

CompStat A crime-control model based on computer-driven statistics. It has been described as "a comprehensive, continuous analysis of results for improvement and achievement of prescribed outcomes."

Computer Voice Stress Analyzer (CVSA) An instrument that tries to detect deception by analyzing the level of stress in a person's voice.

conditional offer of employment An employment offer extended to a police applicant contingent on the applicant successfully completing the latter stages of the selection process, such as psychological testing and medical and drug screening.

confession A direct acknowledgment of guilt on the part of the individual providing the statement.

conflict resolution Also referred to as dispute resolution. The process of resolving a dispute or a conflict by providing an equitable settlement to both side's needs and interests so that they are satisfied with the outcome. The objective of conflict resolution is to end conflicts before they start or before they escalate to physical fighting.

consent to search Authorization given to the police to search someone's home or other location by the person who has care, custody, and control of such place.

crime early warning system (CEWS) A computer program that maps crime forecasts by geographic area to provide a jurisdiction-wide scan for areas perhaps needing changes in tactical deployment of police.

Crime Prevention Through Environmental Design (CPTED) A multidisciplinary approach to deterring criminal behavior. CPTED strategies rely upon the ability to influence offender decisions that precede criminal acts. Most recent implementations of CPTED occur solely within the built environment.

crime prevention Actions taken by the police and the community to reduce crime risks and build individual and community safety.

crime scene A location where a criminal offense occurred and where evidence of the crime may be located. It is not necessarily the only location where the crime took place. Indeed, there are primary, secondary, and often tertiary crime scenes.

crime scene log A log that is kept at the crime scene, that documents persons present at the crime, what time they arrived, what time they left, and what action they took. This includes not only police personnel, but also medical and fire personnel. Provides permanent documentation of those present at the crime scene.

CrimeStat A spatial statistics program for the analysis of crime incident locations.

Crimewatch An Oakland, California Police Department website that allows individuals to map a selection of various crimes. The crimes may be displayed by police beat, district, or street address.

criminal geographic targeting (CGT) models Computer-generated models that help investigators determine where serial criminals most likely reside given the locations of their crimes. The CGT model adheres to the assumption that a distance relationship exists between the residences of serial offenders and where they choose to commit their crimes.

culture A system of shared beliefs, values, customs and behaviors that the members of different groups use to cope with their world and with one another, and that are transmitted from generation to generation.

curtilage The area outside the home itself, but so close to and intimately connected with the home and the activities that normally go on there that it can reasonably be considered part of the home.

cybercrime Criminal offenses carried out with the use of the computer. Child pornography, theft of a password or user identification, and releasing viruses are examples of cybercrime.

cynicism A modern cynic typically has a highly skeptical attitude toward social norms. In policing, officers may become cynical of the ritualistic purpose of police work and will tend to question the validity of a substantial proportion of beliefs, policies and procedures, and rules and regulations. Cynicism can affect the officer's productivity and impact the morale of other police officers.

departmental regulations Police department regulations govern the conditions of police service, annual leave, overtime, promotion, and have an influence on almost all daily police activities. Departmental regulations are usually broader and cover internal matters, such as dress and grooming standards, when compared with standard operating procedures which focus more on field procedures.

differential response   A system in which police calls are prioritized by the seriousness of the offense. For example, some calls for police services are time critical and some can be deferred. Some police responses must be made in person while others can be handled by a telephone report unit or other city departments.

digital evidence   Information stored or transmitted in binary form that may be relied on in court.

directed patrol   A strategy where police officers are assigned to patrol and give attention to specific problem areas that are identified through problem or crime analysis.

directive approach   Where the interviewer establishes the purpose of the interview and controls its pacing.

DNA   DNA is a long polymer of nucleotides (a polynucleotide) and encodes the sequence of the amino acid residues in proteins using the genetic code, a triplet code of nucleotides.

domestic violence   Violence that occurs within a family or an intimate relationship, including spouse beating and child abuse. Domestic violence is one of the most common forms of gender-based violence and is often characterized by long-term patterns of abusive behavior and control; violence between adult intimate partners. An abusive behavior used by one person in a relationship to control the other. Domestic violence typically involves an assault or battery upon a member of a household including a spouse, parent, child, blood-related family member, or others domiciling in the same place.

dumb terminals   Computer terminals that are limited to basic functions and do not allow officers direct access to criminal justice databases, automated field reporting, or the department's intranet and wireless network.

dying declaration   A statement by a person who is conscious and reasonably believes that death is imminent concerning what he or she believes to be the cause or circumstances of death that can be introduced into evidence during a trial in certain cases.

ebonics   Distinctive dialect with a complex language structure found among many African-Americans.

emergency operations mode   When a police car is traveling with red lights and siren in operation. This is sometimes referred to as "code three" driving.

emergency radio traffic   Usually given to officers who check out a potentially dangerous scene. This basically means that officers should keep minimal radio traffic (stay off the radio) unless absolutely necessary or until emergency traffic is released by officers on the dangerous scene.

Enterpol   A suite of computer applications designed primarily for small-to-medium size police departments, but which can also handle larger agencies. The suite assists in dispatching, information management, and facility records, from initial 911 call to booking and release or incarceration. Enterpol is an IBM Lotus Domino-based solution, based on the Domino platform.

ethics   A philosophy that examines the principles of right and wrong, good and bad. Ethics has also been defined as standards of fair and honest conduct.

ethnic group   A group set apart from others because of its national origin or distinctive cultural patterns.

evidence   Anything that assists in proving or disproving a fact. Any object that can establish that a crime has been committed, or any object that can link a suspect to a crime, or provide a link between the victim and a crime. The weapon used in a homicide is considered evidence that can assist in proving the crime of murder.

Exclusionary rule   A rule of evidence that excludes evidence from being admitted in a criminal trial on the question of the defendant's guilt or innocence that was obtained in violation of the defendant's constitutional rights.

field interview   A police practice of stopping a person and demanding an explanation of why that person is in a certain place at a particular time. This information is usually recorded on a field interview card and indexed for intelligence purposes; the stopping and interviewing of a person by a police officer when there is an absence of suspicious circumstances.

field notes   Notes made at the scene of a crime for the purpose of compiling facts in the order in which they presented themselves.

fingerprint evidence   Fingerprints collected at a crime scene or on items of evidence from a crime scene. Fingerprint evidence can assist in identifying the perpetrator of a crime.

first responder   Individuals or groups responding directly to the scene of an incident, such as firefighters, law enforcement, and emergency medical service.

foot patrol   A method where police officers patrol their assigned beat on foot. The objective is that police officers will become better acquainted with citizens and thus more knowledgeable about community concerns. Many police agencies have brought foot patrol back into their operations as a result of evolving community policing strategies.

forensic   An adjective relating to law courts or to public debate; based on a Latin word meaning "pertaining to law."

forensic science   The study and application of scientific facts and techniques to legal problems.

Franks hearing   A hearing that looks at the issue of police misconduct in production of the affidavit used to support the finding of probable cause.

frisk   Also referred to as a pat down search. A noninvasive precautionary frisk or pat-down search of the outer clothing of a suspect. The purpose of the frisk is to protect the officer. The justification for the frisk is discussed in the case of *Terry v. Ohio*, 392 U.S. 1, 88 S.Ct. 1868, 20 1.Ed.2d 889 (1968).

"Fruit of the Poison Tree" Doctrine   A rule of evidence, that holds that evidence obtained by exploiting an unreasonable search or seizure is subject to suppression at trial.

geographic information systems (GIS)   Computerized systems that consist of a constellation of hardware and software that integrate computer graphics with a relational database for purposes of managing and displaying data about geographic locations.

ghetto   An area within a city in which members of a particular cultural, ethnic, religious, or national group live in high concentration. The term *ghetto* is now commonly associated with notions of deprivation, unemployment, and social exclusion and is sometimes used interchangeably with the term *inner-city*.

graffiti   Illegal or unauthorized defacing of a building, wall, or other structure or object by painting, drawing, or otherwise marking it with words, pictures, or symbols. Graffiti is often painted on property by gang members who use it as a means to mark their territory and communicate with rival gang members.

hate crime   A crime where the offender chooses the victim based on the victim's race, ethnicity, or religion.

homelessness   A situation, where a person does not have a permanent place of residence. Often homeless persons live on the street or in abandoned buildings.

hot spots   Areas of concentrated crime.

individual characteristics   Evidence that has characteristics, that are unique to a given object and set it apart from similar objects. Examples of evidence with individual characteristics, including fingerprints, palm prints, and footprints.

information gathering interview   An interview generally conducted during the preliminary investigation of a crime with the purpose of gathering information.

interrogation   Controlled questioning calculated to discover and confirm the truth from the responses of an individual, in spite of his or her intentions and efforts to conceal the truth.

interview   A nonaccusatory questioning of an individual for the purposes of obtaining information.

investigative stop   The stopping and interviewing of a person where there is the possibility that criminal activity may be occurring or has occurred.

Kansas City preventive patrol experiment   This seminal experiment found that traditional routine patrol strategies in marked police cars do not appear to affect the level of crime, nor does it affect the public's feeling of security. The experiment demonstrated that urban police departments can successfully test patrol deployment strategies and that they can manipulate patrol resources without jeopardizing public safety.

labeling theory   A sociological approach introduced by Howard Becker that attempts to explain why certain people are viewed as deviants and others engaging in the same behavior are not.

Latin Kings   An Hispanic gang, also known as the Almighty Latin King Nation (ALKN), formed in Chicago in the mid-1960s.

Locard principle   A principle that holds that every contact leaves a trace.

magistrate   A judicial officer or judge with the authority to issue warrants.

major outlaw motorcycle gangs   The Hell's Angels, Bandidos, Outlaws, and Pagans. These gangs have been identified as being involved in murder, bombings, extortion, arson, and assault.

malfeasance   The intentional commission of a prohibited act or intentional unjust performance of some act of which the party had no right (e.g., gratuity, perjury, use of police resource for personal use).

manufactured fibers   Fibers that are either regenerated fibers or fibers made from substances created in a laboratory.

MDTs   Mobile data terminals located in a patrol vehicle.

melting pot   A place where immigrants of different ethnicity or cultures form an integrated and homogenous society.

microspectrophotometer   An instrument used to analyze the chemical identity of the fiber and any dyes used to color the fiber.

Miranda Myths   The concept that there are numerous misconceptions about what the *Miranda v. Arizona* decision means. Two of the most popular misconceptions are: (1) anything gained in violation of Miranda is inadmissible, and (2) the warning must be given on traffic stops.

misfeasance   The performance of a duty or act that one is obligated or permitted to do in a manner that is improper, sloppy, or negligent (e.g., report writing, unsafe operation of motor vehicle, aggressively "reprimanding" a citizen, improper searching of arrestees).

missing person   Someone who has disappeared for a long period of time, commonly with no known reason. Their photographs are often posted on bulletin boards, postcards, and websites.

modus operandi   Often abbreviated as "MO," this is a Latin phrase, translated as "mode of operation. It is used in police work to describe a criminal's characteristic patterns and style of work.

moral development   The theory that we develop morally similar to our physical development. The theory contends that because we are not born with the ability to understand and apply moral standards to our actions, we develop them similar to the manner in which we learn to do physical things, such as ride a bicycle.

MS-13   A primarily El Salvadoran street gang that originated in Los Angeles in the 1980s.

multiculturalism   A term used to describe many cultures learning to get along with one another with mutual respect.

narcotic offenses   Drug-related crimes that run the gamut from simple possession of marijuana to the sale of heroin.

National Crime Information Center (NCIC)   A computerized index of criminal justice information (i.e., criminal record history information, fugitives, stolen properties, missing persons). It is available to federal, state, and local law enforcement and other criminal justice agencies and is operational twenty-four hours a day, 365 days a year.

National Response Team (NRT)   A planning, policy, and coordinating body; providing national-level policy guidance prior to an incident and does not respond directly to an incident.

natural fibers   Fibers from animal fur, silkworms, or plants.

neighborhood watch   A citizens' organization devoted to crime prevention within their neighborhoods. Neighborhood watch members stay alert to unusual activity in their neighborhoods and contact the police.

nondirective approach   Where the interviewer allows the interviewee to determine the approach and scope of the interview.

nonfeasance   The failure to perform an act that one is obligated to do, either by law or directive, due to omission or failure to recognize the obligation (e.g., failure to file a report).

open fields   The portion of a premises that is outside the curtilage of the home or business. "Open fields" are not protected by the Fourth Amendment.

organizational change   Sometimes referred to as organizational reengineering. A process of reviewing and changing an organizational culture. Organizational change may include changes in policy and procedures, organizational values, organizational structure, management, and leadership. Organizational change is necessary for the successful implementation of community policing strategies.

organizational culture   Often defined as the shared philosophies, ideologies, values, beliefs, assumptions, expectations, attitudes, and norms of an organization.

per curiam decision   A court decision where all the justices agree and there is no principle author of the opinion.

phonetic alphabet   List of words used to identify letters in a message transmitted by radio or telephone.

place theories   Theories that explain why crime events occur at specific locations.

pluralism   The notion that various groups in a society have mutual respect for one another's culture, a respect that allows minorities to express their own culture without suffering prejudice or hostility.

police canine   A dog that is trained specifically to assist police officers and similar law-enforcement personnel with their work. They are also known as police K-9s.

police officer   A member of a police department who is sworn to make arrests and carries a firearm. A police officer performs general patrol and/or special law enforcement assignments in the protection of life and property; enforces city, county, and state laws and regulations; performs a variety of activities and operations associated with crime prevention, traffic enforcement, crime/accident investigation and reporting, and related law enforcement areas; and performs related duties and responsibilities as required.

police pursuit   A police pursuit is an active attempt by an officer operating a police vehicle to apprehend the driver or occupants of a motor vehicle when the driver is aware of those attempts and is resisting apprehension by fleeing in the motor vehicle.

Political Era   An era of American policing which spanned from the 1840s until around the 1930s. This era was the bedrock of early American policing. During the Political Era, policing was dominated by political control. During this era there were close ties between the police and politicians.

polygraph (lie detector)   An instrument that records physiological reactions of the person being examined to specific questions in an effort to detect deception.

positional asphyxia   Most simply defined as death that occurs because the position of a person's body interferes with respiration (breathing) and the person cannot get out of that position. Death occurs due to the person's inability to breathe anymore. Any body position that obstructs the airway or that interferes with the muscular or mechanical means of getting air into and out of the body will result in a positional asphyxia death if the person cannot get out of it.

prejudice   A negative attitude that rejects an entire group

preliminary investigation   The investigation of the crime scene usually performed by first responding police officers immediately after the crime has been detected and reported.

preliminary report   A report that details a crime incidence completed by the first responding police patrol officer. The preliminary report is used by detectives in the subsequent follow-up investigation.

principle of veracity   Bok's principle that establishes a very strong moral presumption against lying.

proactive policing   When police work with the community to prevent crime. Community policing and neighborhood watch programs are two examples of proactive policing.

probable cause   Exists where the facts and circumstances within the officer's knowledge and of which he or she has reasonably trustworthy information is sufficient to warrant a person of reasonable caution to believe that an offense has been or is being committed.

problem solving   A critical element of the community policing strategy. Problem solving is a tactic used to produce long-term solutions to problems of crime or decay in communities. Police, residents, and other agencies or organizations work together to identify and find the causes for neighborhood crime problems, then develop responses to the problems based on the problems' causes; the systematic identification of the actual and potential causes of crime and conflict within the community that can be analyzed with the results guiding development of measures that address the problems in the short, medium, and long-term. Problem solving also involves conflict resolution and other creative methods to address service delivery and police–community relations problems.

problem solving interview   An interview that is directed to determine who committed the crime.

proof beyond a reasonable doubt   The level of certainty a juror must have to find a defendant guilty of a crime. Proof beyond a reasonable doubt is proof of such a convincing character that you would be willing to rely and act upon it without hesitation. The burden of proof in a criminal trial before an individual may be found guilty.

questioned document   Generally considered as any signature, handwriting, typewriting, or other mark whose source or authenticity is in dispute or doubtful.

racial profiling   The practice of constructing a set of characteristics or behaviors based on race and using that set of characteristics to decide whether an individual might be guilty of some crime and therefore worthy of a stop, investigation, or arrest.

racism   A doctrine that one race is superior. Racism may be expressed individually and consciously, through explicit thoughts, feelings, or acts; or socially and unconsciously, through institutions that promote inequality between races.

radio spectrum   The complete range of frequencies from approximately 30 kHz up to more than 300 GHz that can be used for radio communications.

radio wave   The basic building block of radio communications. Like waves on a pond, a radio wave is a series of repeating peaks and valleys.

reactive policing   When police respond to crime calls after they have been committed.

Reform Era   An era of American policing that sought to correct the inherent problems created by the Political Era. The Reform Era emphasized an organization indoctrinated along traditional lines: highly centralized, bureaucratic, and designed on the premise of divisions of labor and unity of control.

repeat victimization theories   Theories that pertain to questions of why the same victims are targeted repeatedly.

restraint asphyxia   Restraining an offender in a manner to physically restrict the body's movement. The factor that distinguishes a restraint asphyxia death from a positional asphyxia death is that some form of restraint is the reason the victim could not escape the asphyxiating position.

RICO predicate act   A basic criminal act; can include any substantive criminal act such as illegal drug distribution, fraud, theft, or illegal gambling.

riot   A public disturbance by three or more persons acting in an unruly and disorderly manner, and resulting in the potential risk of injury to persons, damage to property, and disruption of the public peace.

risk assessment   Assessment that combines criticality, threat, and vulnerability assessments to complete the portrait of risk to an asset or group of assets.

road rage   The deliberate dangerous and/or violent behavior under the influence of heightened, violent emotion such as anger and frustration, with regard to the use of automobiles. Road rage is violence exhibited by drivers in traffic.

robbery   The crime of seizing property through the use of force or the threat of the use of force. Because violence is an ingredient of most robberies, this sometimes results in the serious injury or murder of the victims.

SARA   A problem-solving model that stands for (S) scanning, (A) analysis, (R), response, (A) assessment.

scapegoating   When a person or group is blamed irrationally for another person's or group's problems or difficulties.

School COP Program   A computer program that does mapping with bitmap images. Incidents (crimes) are geocoded when you pick the location where they occurred. After the data is entered, you can map all incidents or any subset of incidents.

search warrant   An official order signed by a judge or magistrate authorizing a search of someone's home or other location. The controlling principles governing search warrants are generally provided by the U.S. Constitution's Fourth Amendment.

search   A government intrusion into an area or interest where a person has a reasonable expectation of privacy.

selection type interview   An interview that is used in law enforcement to screen out or weed out individuals.

self-fulfilling prophecy   The tendency of individuals to respond to and act on the basis of stereotypes, a predisposition that can lead to the validation of false definitions.

standard operating procedure   A written and codified manual of a police organization. The *Standard Operating Procedure Manual* is a roadmap that assists police officers in the field as a guide.

standing Based on the rule that defendants generally must assert their own legal rights and interests, and cannot rest their claim to relief on the legal rights or interests of another person.

stereotyping Unreliable generalizations about all members of a group that do not take into account individual differences within the group.

street theories Theories that deal with crimes that occur at a slightly higher level than specific places; that is, over small, stretched areas such as streets or blocks.

Sur 13 Southern gangs that are closely associated with the Mexican Mafia and often use the number 13 in their gangs and tagging, as M is the thirteenth letter of the alphabet.

terrorism The unlawful use of force or violence against persons or property to intimidate or coerce a government, the civilian population, or any segment thereof, in furtherance of political or social objectives; Criminal acts caused by persons or groups motivated by political or social goals, ideological justification, and considerable forethought and planning.

Terry stop A temporary stop with reasonable suspicion based on articulable facts that criminal activity is involved.

threat assessment A technique used by law enforcement authorities for the purpose of evaluating and describing the nature and degree of a threat. Involves efforts to identify, assess, and manage individuals and groups who may pose threats of targeted violence.

testimonial evidence Evidence that may be presented by witnesses at a trial or other type of hearing. Generally, testimonial evidence is given by a witness to the crime or by an expert.

tracing evidence Evidence that results from the transfer of small quantities of materials. Tracing evidence is usually in the form of small particles and includes such items as hair, paint, glass, and fibers.

Uniform Crime Report The Uniform Crime Reports are crime indexes, published annually by the Federal Bureau of Investigation, which summarize the incidence and rate of certain reported crimes within the United States.

utilitarianism A theory that attempts to answer what makes an action good by evaluating the sum total of the pleasures and pain that a course of action would bring.

values Beliefs that guide a person's or organization's behavior.

verbal communications Language that is either written or oral.

vulnerability assessment The identification of weaknesses in physical structures, personnel protection systems, processes, or other areas that may be exploited by terrorists.

warrant A writ or judicial order issued by a court of law directing a law enforcing officer to arrest or seize a specifically named person, or to search a specific known location for fruits or instrumentalities of a crime.

writing A method of recording and communicating ideas by means of a system of visual marks.

zero tolerance A police tactic where officers engage in aggressive patrolling, including stopping persons for minor violations. Zero tolerance tactics are usually carried out in areas that have a high incidence of crime.

Index

Bold page numbers indicate marginal definitions, italic page numbers indicate figures.